Trial Practice Series

DETERMINING ECONOMIC LOSS IN INJURY AND DEATH CASES

Wm. Gary Baker, Ph.D.
Professor of Finance
and Assistant Dean
School of Business
Washburn University of
Topeka

Michael K. Seck, J.D., M.B.A.
Partner: Fisher, Patterson,
Sayler & Smith
Topeka, Kansas
Member of the Kansas Bar

SHEPARD'S/McGRAW-HILL, INC.
P.O. Box 1235
Colorado Springs, Colorado 80901

McGRAW-HILL BOOK COMPANY
New York ● St. Louis ● San Francisco ● Auckland ● Bogotá
Caracas ● Colorado Springs ● Hamburg ● Lisbon ● London
Madrid ● Mexico ● Milan ● Montreal ● New Delhi ● Oklahoma City
Panama ● Paris ● San Juan ● São Paulo ● Singapore ● Sydney
Tokyo ● Toronto

Shepard's Trial Practice Series

2345678910 SHCU 89654321098

Library of Congress Cataloging-in-Publication Data
Baker, Wm. Gary.
  Determining economic loss in injury and death cases / Wm. Gary Baker, Michael Seck.
      p.   cm.—(Shepard's trial practice series)
  Includes index.
  ISBN 0-07-172000-6
  1. Damages—United States.   2. Lost earnings damages—United States.   3. Personal injuries—United States.   4. Death by wrongful act—United States.   5. Forensic economics—United States. I. Seck, Michael. II. Title. III. Series: Trial practice series.
KF1250.B35 1987
346.7303'23'0269—dc19
[347.3063230269]   87-25647
                                                                                      CIP

ISBN 0-07-172000-6

To My Best Friend, Pat

Gary Baker

The author gratefully dedicates this book to Professors Malcolm R. Burns and David Shulenburger of the University of Kansas Schools of Economics and Business, respectively, for their firm committment to excellence in education, as well as their patience and guidance.

Michael K. Seck

Preface

This book, *Determining Economic Loss in Injury and Death Cases*, is designed to assist the practicing attorney in his or her understanding of the present value of a future income stream. The book is intended to be a practical guide to assist in the understanding of the methods employed by economists when they calculate present value of future streams of money.

As with any major undertaking, the final product is the result of the efforts of more than one individual. This is the case with this undertaking.

I would like to thank several groups of people for their support in this undertaking. First, I would like to thank the attorneys, both plaintiff and defense, who asked me to be involved in economic evaluations.

The second group to be acknowledged is the administration of Washburn University. These men encouraged me and one of my colleagues, Jim Eck, were encouraged to present seminars addressing the question of present value. These seminars, coordinated by Shirley Byrnes, were presented through out the United States. This was also a very learning experience. It is the preperation for the seminars and the presentation of the seminars which lead to the writting of the book.

Two collegues have also been instrumental in the developement of the seminars and the book, Dr. James Eck and Reed Davis. Thank you.

A third group deserving recognition is the support staff of Washburn University's School of Business.

And finally, thanks to my wife, Pat, and the gang, Bill, Matt, Jeff, and Anne, without whose encouragement and understanding this would not have been completed.

Gary Baker

Contents

Detailed

2 The Base Dollars

3 Modifications to the Base Dollar Amount
Due to Disability

4 Historic Loss

7   Combining Growth and Discount

8   The Age Earnings Profile

9   Worklife Expectancy

13 Household Services

14 Federal Income Taxes

17 Selecting an Economist

18 Case Studies

19   Worksheet for Estimating Present Value

20   Evaluating Structured Settlements

Tables

Index

1 The Economist's Role and Overview

1

§1.01   The Role of an Economist

More and more economists and actuaries are being asked by attorneys to assist in the economic evaluation of loss resulting from an injury. Economists and actuaries are being retained by the plaintiff's attorney to assist in the calculation of (1) historic losses, (2) future income, and (3) future expenses. Defense attorneys are retaining economists to review the plaintiff's economist's report and to assist the defense attorney in his or her preparation for trial cross-examination of plaintiff's economist.

§1.02   Plaintiff's Economist's Role

The plaintiff's economist performs three different functions. First, the economist calculates the loss suffered by the plaintiff as a result of an injury caused by the actions of the defendant. Second, if the case goes to trial, the economist must educate the jury on what *present value* is and how it is calculated. Finally, after explaining what present value is, the economist must give his or her opinion on past and future loss.

§1.03   —Types of Losses Economists Can Estimate

Economists calculate dollar losses, in-kind dollar losses, and increases in expenses. The economic analysis involves dollar losses from wages, fringe benefits, retirement programs, dividend income, rental income, royalty income, lost income from having put a spouse through school and then divorcing, increase in asset values during a marriage, and lost profits from a business. *In-kind dollar losses* are the result of someone receiving a benefit for which dollars were not actually paid. Examples of in-kind benefits would include the lost output from a garden, or the value of household services provided by a husband, a wife, or a child.

The other calculation the economist can make is the estimate of future expenses that may be incurred as a result of an injury. These expenses may be nursing home care, therapy, additional personal equipment such as vehicle modification for the handicapped, modifications to the home, drugs, future surgery, and the like.

§1.04   —Calculating Plaintiff's Loss

Plaintiff's loss may consist of lost income as a result of the injury or additional expenses resulting from the injury. The economist is to make the estimate of historic losses and future losses.

Typically, the *historic loss* is from the time of the injury until the assumed date of the trial. The *future loss* is from the date of the trial forward. The future loss of wages may run to age 65, or some other assumed termination date, while additional expenses may run throughout the injured party's life.

In the calculation of the present value of future income and future medical expenses, the economist must determine the basis for the dollar forecast, an appropriate growth rate for future income and expenses, and, finally, an appropriate discount rate, or interest rate.

§1.05 —Types of Losses Economists Cannot Estimate

Economists cannot estimate losses which do not have a dollar value attached. Economists do not estimate the value of pain and suffering, or the joy of having a child. The economic loss is a loss which can have a dollar amount assigned to it. In **§1.03,** the in-kind value of a garden was mentioned. The economist could estimate the dollar value of the produce from the garden but not the satisfaction of having a garden and raising one's own vegetables.

§1.06 Defendant's Economist's Role

The primary role of the defendant's economist is to review the written report of the plaintiff's economist and assist the defense attorney in preparation for trial. Typically, a defense attorney who retains an economist does not list the economist as a witness, since an economist testifying for the defense would establish the minimum loss. On summation, plaintiff's attorney would argue the loss is between the dollar amount estimated by the plaintiff's economist and the dollar amount estimated by the defendant's economist.

§1.07 Overview of the Book

In estimating the present value of future income and the present value of future expenses, the following basic formula is used:

$$\text{Present Value} = \sum_{t=0}^{n} \$ \, (1+g)^t / (1+d)^t$$

Where:

"$\$$" represents the beginning earnings or expenses

"g" represents the annual growth rate of the dollars

"d" represents the annual interest rate, or discount rate, used to reduce the future dollar stream to present value

"t" represents the number of years into the future the analysis occurs

This formula can be modified to take into account partial disability of an injured party, adjustments for mortality, adjustments for participating in the labor force, adjustments for seeking employment, consumption, household services, and taxes. When these other variables are entered into the analysis, the formula is expanded and referred to as an extended analysis. The formula used in the extended analysis is:

$$\text{Present Value} = \sum_{t=0}^{n} \$ * M * [(1+g)^t / (1+d)^t] * PL * PS * PF * C * HS * TX$$

Where:

"$"   represents the beginning earnings or expenses

"M"   represents the modification to lost income due to a disability

"g"   represents the annual growth rate of the dollars

"d"   represents the annual interest rate, or discount rate, used to reduce the future dollar stream to present value

"t"   represents the number of years into the future the analysis occurs

"PL"   represents the probability an individual will live each successive year (mortality adjustment)

"PS"   represents the probability an individual will seek employment

"PF"   represents the probability an individual will find employment

"C"   represents individual consumption

"HS"   represents household services

"TX"   represents personal income taxes

The extended formula will appear at the beginning of each of the chapters which addresses one of the variables. The variable being addressed will be underlined. How each of the variables affects the size of the present value figure will be explained in the chapter.

A brief overview of each chapter appears below. The overview will indicate what variable is being examined and how that variable affects the present value. That is, does the variable, when included in the analysis, cause the present value to become larger, or does the variable cause the present value to become smaller? The basic formula, or basic analysis, uses the four variables—dollars, growth rate, discount rate, and the number of years—to calculate the present value of a future income stream or the present value of a future stream of expenses. The extended analysis uses all 11 variables to calculate the present value of the income or expense stream.

There are only two approaches which should properly be considered. Either the analysis uses 4 variables, or it uses all 11. One should not pick and choose which variables should be included.

§1.08   —Chapter 2: The Base Dollars

$$\text{Present Value} = \sum_{t=0}^{n} \underline{\$} * M * (1+g)^t / (1+d)^t * PL * PS * PF * C * HS * TX$$

Chapter 2 is concerned with the base dollar amount, "$", used in the present value calculation. The economist can address three types of calculations.

The first type of calculation is designed to estimate the present value of the future income stream. The income stream in a broad sense can include wages or salary, overtime compensation, rental income, dividend income, medical expenses, nursing home care, domestic services, fringe benefits, health insurance costs, and retirement benefits.

The second type of calculation is designed to estimate the present value of future in-kind benefits. An example of in-kind services is household services. A death or injury can result in the loss of these services. Although there is no actual cash involved in the providing of the services, there can be a cash loss if the services must be hired to replace the loss.

The third type of calculation is designed to estimate the present value of future medical expenses. The medical expenses include doctors' fees, hospital charges, prescription drugs, therapy, and any expenses connected with environmental modification.

Determining the base dollar amount used in the calculation of the present value is the purpose of Chapter 2. The higher the base dollar amount, the larger the present value will be.

§1.09   —Chapter 3: Modifications to the Base Dollar Amount Due to Disability

$$\text{Present Value} = \sum_{t=0}^{n} \$ * \underline{M} * (1+g)^t / (1+d)^t * PL * PS * PF * C * HS * TX$$

The basic formula for calculating the present value of future income can be modified to reflect disability. If a person is disabled, the ability to earn may be reduced but not eliminated. "M" represents the degree to which an individual's earning capacity has been diminished or modified. The larger the reduction in earning capacity, the larger the present value figure will be.

§1.10   —Chapter 4: Historic Loss

Historic loss is the loss of income and household services, plus incurred expenses, from the date of the injury to an arbitrarily assumed date. Typically, the assumed date is the expected date of the trial. The present value of future income, household services, and future expenses begins on the day the historic loss ends and continues until retirement or death.

If there is a considerable time between the time of the injury and the date of the trial, inflation adjustments may be made to estimate the lost income.

Typically, historic losses are the summation of verifiable expenses, forgone income resulting from the injury, plus the loss of household services.

The historic loss is usually a small portion of the total loss which the economist estimates. Usually, the most speculative portion of the historic loss is the loss of household services. The size of the historic loss does not affect the size of the present value of future losses.

§1.11 —Chapter 5: Determination of Growth Rates

$$\text{Present Value} = \sum_{t=0}^{n} \$ * M * \underline{(1+g)^t}/(1+d)^t * PL * PS * PF * C * HS * TX$$

The growth rate applied to earnings and to current expenses is critical to the calculation of the present value. Different growth rates may be applicable to different losses. For example, the growth rate used to calculate the present value of a future income stream may be different from the growth rate used to calculate the present value of future medical expenses.

Chapter 5 discusses the concept of growth rates, how growth rates may be calculated from existing data, and how the growth rates are applied in the present value analysis. The impact of various growth assumptions is also demonstrated. The higher the growth rate, the larger the present value of the future income and future expenses will be.

§1.12 —Chapter 6: Discount Rates—The Present Value Calculation

$$\text{Present Value} = \sum_{t=0}^{n} \$ * M * (1+g)^t/\underline{(1+d)^t} * PL * PS * PF * C * HS * TX$$

The *discount rate* is synonymous with the term *interest rate*. The terms refer to the rate at which funds invested in an asset earn a return. Chapter 6 addresses what discounting to present value means, how different discount rates are calculated, and how the size of the discount rate affects the present value calculation. The larger the discount rate, the lower the present value will be.

§1.13 —Chapter 7: Combining Growth and Discount

$$\text{Present Value} = \sum_{t=0}^{n} \$ * M * \underline{(1+g)^t/(1+d)^t} * PL * PS * PF * C * HS * TX$$

Chapter 7 combines the concept of a growth rate with the concept of a discount rate. The two methods of calculating the present value of a future income stream are presented. A worksheet is developed that permits the calculation of the present value of future income streams given assumed growth and discount rates.

§1.14   —Chapter 8: The Age Earnings Profile

The age earnings profile is cross-sectional economic data showing that highest earnings accrue to those in their mid-fifties. Many attorneys improperly use the earnings profile to argue that an individual's earnings will peak prior to retirement. The argument is that, after some age, earnings will decline for the full-time workers. Chapter 8 addresses this issue.

§1.15   —Chapter 9: Work Life Expectancy

Work life expectancy tables are government publications showing how long a person of a certain age is likely to work. Work life tables for men and women are presented. The work life table is incorporated into the extended formula by using the mortality tables and the probability of seeking and the probability of finding employment. Work life tables would lower the present value of the future income stream.

§1.16   —Chapter 10: Mortality Adjustment

$$\text{Present Value} = \sum_{t=0}^{n} \$ * M * (1+g)^t/(1+d)^t * \underline{PL} * PS * PF * C * HS * TX$$

Mortality tables are presented for men and women by race. The adjustment for mortality is made by adjusting each year's present value calculation for the probability of living. Chapter 10 shows how the annual adjustments are made. Mortality adjustments lower the present value of the future income stream.

§1.17   —Chapter 11: The Probability of Seeking and the Probability of Finding Employment

$$\text{Present Value} = \sum_{t=0}^{n} \$ * M * (1+g)^t/(1+d)^t * PL * \underline{PS * PF} * C * HS * TX$$

The probability of seeking employment shows how likely it is an individual will seek or try to find employment. This figure is combined with the probability of finding employment. The two should be used together and combined with the probability of living when calculating the present value of the income stream. The adjustment for seeking and finding employment reduces the present value of the income stream.

§1.18   —Chapter 12: Individual Consumption

$$\text{Present Value} = \sum_{t=0}^{n} \$ * M * (1+g)^t/(1+d)^t * PL * PS * PF * \underline{C} * HS * TX$$

Personal consumption refers to the portion of one's income that is used to benefit the individual directly. Usually, the question of personal consumption arises only in a wrongful death action, since consumption would continue if the individual were disabled. Adjustments for personal consumption would cause the present value of the income stream to be diminished.

§1.19 —Chapter 13: Household Services

$$\text{Present Value} = \sum_{t=0}^{n} \$ * M * (1+g)^t)/(1+d) * PL * PS * PF * C * \underline{HS} * TX$$

The valuing of household services is included in a somewhat misleading manner. Actually, household services are a dollar loss and can be included in Chapter 2 as a dollar loss. Household services are included in the extended analysis because of the unique problems presented by these services. Household services refer to such things as washing the dishes, mowing the yard, and painting the house. While such services may be taken as part of the individual's responsibility to the family, the value of such services may be difficult to estimate. In addition to estimation errors, it must be noted that replacing household services must be done with after-tax dollars. If mowing the yard cost $10, the economist must be in a position to estimate the before-tax cost of the expense.

§1.20   —Chapter 14: Federal Income Taxes

$$\text{Present Value} = \sum_{t=0}^{n} \$ * M * (1+g)^t/(1+d)^t * PL * PS * PF * C * HS * \underline{TX}$$

If federal income taxes are to be included, then the economist must estimate the tax rates for each of the future years for which the analysis is being done. Additionally, the economist must estimate the tax deductible items for the individual for each future year in order to estimate the appropriate marginal tax rate to apply to the estimate. Studies indicate that inclusion of the individual tax rate causes the present value of the future stream of money to increase.

§1.21   —Chapter 15: A Quick Method for Estimating the Present Value of Future Income

Chapter 15 demonstrates the Alaska Plan. This method permits the growth rate employed by the economist to be exactly equal to the discount rate employed. An example of the method is presented.

§1.22   —Chapter 16: Judging the Economist's Estimate of Present Value

A short model is presented in Chapter 16 showing how to evaluate the present value of the future income stream. This model is much easier to use when the economist has employed the basic present value model rather than the extended model.

§1.23   —Chapter 17: Selecting an Economist

Basic criteria for the selection of an economist are presented in Chapter 17. Recognizing there are not right economists for any case, the critical characteristics are integrity and the ability to communicate a difficult area clearly to the jury.

§1.24   —Chapter 18: Case Studies

Chapter 18 demonstrates how the present value of an economic loss would be calculated for a college professor, college student, an individual with a work history, and an individual without a work history.

§1.25   —Chapter 19: Worksheets for Estimating Present Value

Chapter 19 presents worksheets to permit the attorney to estimate the present value of future income or future expenses. In addition to making present value calculations, the worksheets can be used to estimate the present value of settlement offers. Examples are also worked out.

§1.26   —Chapter 20: Evaluating Structured Settlements

The tax considerations affecting structured settlements are discussed in Chapter 20. Additionally, the structured settlement is explained and examined from the plaintiff's point of view and from the defendant's point of view.

§1.27   —Chapter 21: Sample Testimony

Chapter 21 presents sample testimony, or questions, which can be used to qualify the expert witness. Questions are presented to assist in the cross-examination of the expert as well.

2 The Base Dollars

$$\text{Present Value} = \sum_{t=0}^{n} \underline{\$} * M * (1+g)^t/(1+d)^t * PL * PS * PF * C * HS * TX$$

§2.01   Introduction

The base dollar amount in the present value equation is "$" and represents the current dollar amount of what is being forecast. When estimating a present value figure, the economist will be forecasting the present value of a future cash inflow, like income, or the present value of a future cash outflow, like medical expenses, or both.

This chapter explains where the economist may obtain the data used as the basis for the economic forecast and how the economist uses the data. The critical point is that *base dollars* are the current dollars. The base dollars may be historic data which has been obtained and "moved" to current dollars. "Moving to current dollars" means taking an historic value and increasing or projecting it to today's value. The higher the base dollars used in the present value equation, the greater will be the present value of the cash inflow or outflow.

§2.02   What Economists Estimate

Economists attempt to estimate two different types of dollar flows. The first type is the *income flow.* The second type is the *expense flow.*

In the cash *inflow* analysis, the economist estimates the present value of a future stream of dollars that the plaintiff will not receive as a result of an injury. In the cash *outflow* analysis, the economist estimates the present value of future expenses. These additional expenses are directly attributable to the injury.

§2.03   —Types of Income Losses

Income losses experienced by the plaintiff may be cash losses or in-kind losses. Cash losses are the result of reduced earning capacity and are reflected in lower wages or salaries. Since fringe benefits are usually a percentage of wages or salaries, lower wages and salaries will result in lower fringe benefits. Other cash losses the plaintiff may experience include reduced rental income, reduced interest income, reduced dividend income, reduced capital gains, and reduced business or farm income.

In addition to the loss of cash income, the economist may calculate the in-kind loss. An in-kind income is a nonmonetary income.[1] The most common example of in-kind income is the value to a family of household services. If an accident leaves a family member unable to perform housework, then the rest of the family experiences a loss of in-kind services.

---

[1] C. McConnell, Economics: Principles, Problems and Policies 744 (McGraw-Hill, Inc. 10th ed 1987).

§2.04 —Types of Medical Expenses

The most common types of expenses that economists estimate include ongoing medical expenses and expenses incurred as a result of an injury. Medical expenses would include doctors' fees, hospital care, surgery, therapy, prescription drugs, and nursing care. It is not uncommon to have the present value of future medical expenses exceed the present value of the future income stream. This is particularly true when the injured party requires full-time institutional care. Expenses incurred as the result of an injury could include transportation for medical treatment.

The base dollar amount, "$", used in the present value formula is the current cost of the expense being estimated. The larger the current expenses, the greater will be the present value of the expenses.

§2.05 Sources for Determining the Base Dollar Amount of Wages and Salaries When Calculating the Present Value of Future Wages

The base dollar amount used to calculate the present value of the plaintiff's future income stream may be obtained from different sources. The particular source utilized by the economist will depend on what information can be made available to the economist.

Sources of information which can be utilized by the economist to establish the base dollar income include the plaintiff's spouse, federal income tax form, W-2 form, employer records, the Standard Industrial Classification Tables, the Statistical Abstracts of the United States, Bureau of Census data published for each state, and various professional publications that establish income levels. Which source is used depends on what is available.

§2.06 —The Plaintiff or Spouse

While information provided by the plaintiff or spouse may be very helpful, it must be considered suspect. Usually, the plaintiff or spouse can provide accurate information regarding income from employment, and this information can be further verified. But often in a death case the value of the deceased increases in the eyes of the spouse.

Consider the letter written by a widow plaintiff. The plaintiff was separated from her husband. She lived in Florida, and he lived in Arizona. He was killed while riding in his girlfriend's car in Arizona. The plaintiff anticipated that she and her husband would reconcile and wrote:

> He maintained various capabilities, and skills such as tuning and maintenance on his own vehicles, electrical, plumbing, repair work on the home, yardwork, and also the painting of the exterior of the home. He could fix just about everything in the home such as the furnace and

maintenance on appliances around the home. He was a jack-of-all-trades. He would babysit for his children, fix their bicycles and put together toys for them.

It seemed that anything that needed to be done, he was capable of doing.

The attorney and the economist must take care to not put too much weight on some of a spouse's statements.

§2.07 —Plaintiff's Income Tax Return

The plaintiff's 1040 federal income tax return may be used as a basis for determining his or her level of income. The tax return contains information concerning income from wages, salaries, tips, interest, dividends, and capital gains. Business, partnership, and farm incomes are included on the tax returns, as well as income from rents, royalties, trusts, and estates.

When the 1040 tax form is used to determine the level of plaintiff's income, care must be used to distinguish between income that would be affected as a result of an injury and income that would not be affected. For example, wages may cease as a result of an injury, but dividend income may continue. Therefore, it would not be proper to include the dividend income as part of the lost income.

Wages, Salaries, and Tips

Wages, salaries, and tips generally constitute the largest portion of income for most working families. The line item on the 1040 form represents the sum of the wages, salaries, and tips of both the husband and wife if a joint tax return is being filed. The distribution of income between husband and wife must be determined by examining the employees' copies of the W-2 forms attached to the tax return.

The W-2 form will state the name of the employee, the name of the employer, the tax year, the employee's social security number, the name of the state to which state income tax was sent, the total number of dollars paid to the employee, and the total amount of the taxes withheld by the employer.

The W-2 form does not indicate the hourly rate of compensation or the number of hours worked per year. Suppose a plaintiff's W-2 form indicated an annual income of $18,000. There are several questions that would need to be answered before an economic analysis could proceed. How many hours did the plaintiff work during the year? Was part of the $18,000 overtime pay? If so, what is the rate of overtime pay, and how many overtime hours did the plaintiff work? Would overtime hours have continued in the future? If so, how many hours per year and for how many years into the future?

Interest and Dividend Income

Interest is the payment for the use of capital. Dividends are payments to the owners of a corporation from the earnings of the corporation. Interest is paid to debt holders; dividends are paid to owners, or equity holders.

The return to debt and equity is not usually affected by the actions of an owner of the securities. The level of interest and dividend income would not be affected as a result of an injury to the owner and, therefore, should not be included in the base dollar amount used to estimate the present value of the future income stream.

The level of interest and dividend income to a family may be reduced as the result of an injury to an individual if the injured party is the manager of the funds. In this case, the loss of income would not be total; what needs to be estimated is the difference in income, if any, before and after the injury.

Interest and dividend income may stop, or decline, if the injured party owns a business in which he or she is a major factor in its success. Suppose the president of a small construction company had loaned the corporation money. Interest would be paid to the debt holder (president) periodically. If the president were injured, and the company's success was dependent on the president, then the interest income may cease. The interest income would properly be an amount that should be included in the present value calculation. The same line of reasoning could also be applied to dividends.

Income from Capital Gains

Capital gains occur when an asset is sold for more than the purchase price.[2] The capital gains typically reported on the individual 1040 form are from the purchase and sale of bonds and common stocks, although gains from the sale of other types of assets, such as art, may be reported here.

The loss a family could experience is the loss of management expertise provided by the injured or deceased party. However, the principle would not be lost.

For example, an insurance company's portfolio manager borrowed $25,000 in 1979 to make personal investments. At the time of his death in 1985, the portfolio had grown to $395,000. In addition to the portfolio, he had repaid the $25,000 loan and retired a $77,000 mortgage on his home. Of the total portfolio, $50,000 was divided among his three minor children. The children ranged in age from 2 to 14. Following his death a wrongful death suit was filed. The family recognized the principle of the portfolio would remain in tact, but argued the loss of expertise in portfolio management was the loss to the family. His personal records, and the records at the brokerage houses where he did business, indicated his portfolio appreciated more than 50 per cent per year for the six years he managed the funds.

The loss of capital gains is a loss the economist can estimate. The economist estimates the increase in principle rather than a level of income.

---

[2] The definition of capital gains does not apply in the case of an individual purchasing and subsequently selling zero coupon bonds and low coupon bonds.

Income from Businesses, Partnerships, and Farms

The income reported from a business, partnership, or farm which appears on the 1040 form is an accounting figure properly designed to minimize an individual's personal tax liability. To determine the economic value of the business to an individual, or his or her family, requires the examination of more detailed records.

In the most basic evaluation, the economist estimates the cash flow from the business rather than the reported income from the business. The cash flow is the earnings from the business plus the noncash expenses. The most common type of noncash expenses is depreciation. Thus, the cash flow would equal earnings after taxes plus depreciation. The cash flow would be used as the base dollar amount in the calculation of the present value of the future income stream.

A more detailed analysis may reveal the benefits of the business or partnership far exceed the level indicated by the tax return. The business may provide an automobile and its maintenance, travel funds, life and health insurance policies, and retirement plans. In the case of a farm, maintenance to the home may be written off as a business expense. Personal vehicles may also use "farm gas." All these considerations would fall into the category of business valuation.

Some businesses have buy-out agreements. These agreements establish how the ownership of the business will be transferred at the time of an owner's withdrawal. The amount of money may be stipulated in the buy-out agreement, or a formula may be stated. In either case, the plaintiff, or the plaintiff's heirs, may suffer a loss of income and may also suffer a loss of principle. The loss of income is used as a base dollar amount in the calculation of the present value of the future income. The loss of principle is a one-time loss.

Income from Rents, Royalties, Trusts, and Estates

Income from rent may be much like income from stocks and bonds. The income may continue regardless of the health of the owner of the property. If injury has caused the owner of the property to hire maintenance or management, then the economist may use these added expenses as the base dollar amount used to calculate the present value of the future expenses. The increase in expenses represents a decrease in income from the rental properties.

Royalty is an income from a copyright, patent, or other such property. Royalty income may or may not continue, depending on the source of the income. If the royalty is from ownership of a song or book or something that does not have to be updated, then the royalty will continue regardless of the health of the owner. In this case the income would not be included as a base dollar loss.

What might be included as a base dollar loss is the royalty from a book which needs to be updated to be marketable. For example, a college text book on income tax needs to be updated as the tax laws change. If injury prevents the author from being able to update the book, then it would become outdated, resulting in a loss of income.

Income from estates and trusts is not usually dependent on the health of the recipient. There is, however, the potential loss where the proceeds from an estimate or trust would go to a different family member after the death of an individual. Likewise, if the full value of the estate had not been received, there could be a loss to heirs. In these cases survivors may experience a loss that should be included in the economic analysis.

§2.08   —Employer Records

Employer records can be the basis for estimating the present value of a future income stream. The records will usually state the name of the employee, the date of initial employment, the hourly rate of compensation or salary paid at the time of the initial hiring, and any subsequent increases in compensation. All this information is valuable to the economist.

Consider the situation where the deceased had gone to work for a firm producing medical instruments and supplies. His initial employment date was January 2, 1971. The employer records indicate the deceased received wage increases on the anniversary of his employment (*see* Table 2-1). Employment was terminated January 2, 1985, the date of the employee's death.

Table 2-1 Employer Records

January 1 of Each Year	Hourly Wage Rate
1971	$3.46
1972	3.75
1973	3.96
1974	4.27
1975	4.55
1976	4.80
1977	5.05
1978	5.38
1979	6.05
1980	6.70
1981	7.23
1982	7.75
1983	8.35
1984	8.99
Employment Terminated January 2, 1985	
1985	9.65
1986	10.10

The wages that appear in Table 2-1 in boldface are hourly wages the deceased never actually earned. The wages represent what the employer states the deceased would have earned had employment continued. The base dollar amount that the economist will employ is the $10.10 per hour. The annual dollar loss appearing in the formula will be $21,008, which is 2,080 hours per year times the hourly wage of $10.10.

However, the defense attorney will, on cross-examination, point out that the deceased never did earn $10.10 per hour. The most he ever earned was $8.99 per hour. Thus, the annual salary that should have been used was $18,699 (2,080 hours times $8.99 per hour).

The economist should be able to tie the $8.99 per hour, appearing on the employer's records, to the W-2 form filed with the employee's 1984 federal tax return. If the income shown on the W-2 form is in excess of $18,699, it would be reasonable to assume overtime.

The question of overtime compensation should be resolved by the economist before the economic analysis proceeds. Suppose the W-2 form indicates an income in 1984 of $18,699. This would appear to be straight-time of $8.99 per hour for 2,080 hours. But is is also possible that the deceased worked 26 weeks for 60 hours per week at double-time for hours in excess of 40 hours per week. This raises the questions for the defense of how long the overtime would have continued. What happens if no overtime was assumed and employment was just half of the year? Clearly, the annual income would be $9.350.

§2.09   —Total Private Nonagricultural Sector Wages

In some cases there is no earnings history available, and the economist must turn to other sources to establish a base dollar amount. One such source is the government publication showing the average hourly wages paid in the private nonagricultural sector of the economy (*see* Table 2-2).

Table 2-2 Total Private Nonagricultural Hourly Wages

Year	Hourly Wage Rate
1980	$6.66
1981	7.25
1982	7.68
1983	8.02
1984	8.33
1985	8.58
1986	8.76

Source: Economic Report of the President 292, Table B41 (1987).

The 1986 wage rate of $8.76 is the most recent data available. The annual income would be $18,221 (2,080 hours per year times $8.76 per hour). This would be the base dollar amount used in the formula to make the present value analysis.

§2.10 —The Standard Industrial Classification Tables

The Standard Industrial Classification[3] (SIC) system was developed by the United States government to facilitate collection and analysis of economic data on economic establishments. The goal is to make sure the data is comparable. An establishment is defined as an economic unit generally at a single physical location where business is conducted or where services or industrial operations are performed. All establishments are assigned a three- or four-digit code based on broad economic divisions. The code may be obtained from the SIC Manual or from other business handbooks or directories. The directories include Standard and Poor's *Register of Corporations* or the *Million Dollar Directory.* [4] The economic categories are as follows:

Division A 01-09 Agricultural, Forestry, Fishing, Hunting and Trapping
Division B 10-14 Mining
Division C 15-17 Construction
Division D 20-39 Manufacturing
Division E 40-49 Transportation, Communications, Electric, Gas and Sanitary Services
Division F 50-51 Wholesale Trade
Division G 52-59 Retail Trade
Division H 60-67 Finance, Insurance, Real Estate
Division I 70-89 Services
Division J 91-97 Public Administration
Division K 90   Nonclassification establishments

The SIC tables state the average number of hours worked per week by the production workers, the average weekly overtime hours, and the average hourly rate of pay. A specific SIC table may be used to estimate the base dollar amount used in the present value equation.

Example: SIC Code #384 is Medical Instruments and Supplies. Table 2-3 shows the average hourly wage paid for the years 1978 to 1983.

Table 2-3 Calculating the Present Value of Future Wages Medical Instruments and Supplies Hourly Wages SIC Code 384

Year	Hourly Wage Rate
1978	$4.93
1979	5.30

[3] US Government Printing Office, Standard Industrial Classification Tables Manual (Washington, DC).

[4] R. Vukas, Description of SIC Codes (Washburn Univ. 1987) (unpublished manuscript); Standard & Poor's Register of Corporations (McGraw-Hill, Inc 1987); Dun's Marketing Service, Million Dollar Directory (1987).

Year	Hourly Wage Rate
1980	5.80
1981	6.43
1982	7.00
1983	7.38

This information can be used to calculate the base dollar amount in the present value equation. The average hourly rate of compensation of $7.38 times 2,080 hours per year yields the base dollar amount of $15,350. Since the most recent data is 1983, the economist would move the hourly rate forward to reflect a more current rate of compensation. *See* **§4.05.** The current rate of compensation would be used as the basis for calculating the present value.

§2.11 —Median Income as Reported in the Statistical Abstracts of the United States

Another source of information available to the economist when there is no history of earnings available is the Statistical Abstracts of the United States,[5] which provides income data based on the sex and educational attainment of the individual. Table 2-4 presents median income data for men.

Table 2-4 Median Money Income of Persons with Income by Sex and Educational Attainment 1970 to 1978 (In Thousands of Dollars)

	Male			
	1970	1974	1976	1978
Median Income	$7,900	$9,000	$10,100	$11,700
Elementary School				
Less than 8 years	3,600	4,500	5,000	5,600
8 years	5,400	6,400	6,800	7,500
High School				
1-3 years	7,300	7,600	7,800	8,600
4 years	8,800	9,900	10,700	12,300
College				
1-3 years	9,900	9,800	10,600	12,500
4 years	12,100	13,400	15,400	17,400
5 or more years	13,400	16,200	18,000	21,000

The most recent data, 1978, is used as the basis for the income calculation. The dollar amount is then inflated to reflect current dollars. The current dollars are the base dollar amount used to make the present value calculation.

---

[5] US Dept of Commerce, Bureau of Census, Statistical Abstracts of the United States.

§2.12 —State Data Published by the Bureau of Census

The United States Department of Commerce, Bureau of Census, publishes income data by state. The income data is based on sex, age, education attainment, and race. The income data can also be obtained for rural or urban residents. Table 2-5 shows 1980 census data for the state of Colorado.

Table 2-5 Income Based on 1980 Census Data State of Colorado

	Male		
		Education	
	8th Grade	High School Graduate	College Graduate
35 to 44 years old			
Mean Annual Income	$13,338	$17,406	$27,813
Mean Annual Earnings	13,011	16,503	26,333
Mean Weekly Earnings	383	339	542

If the injured party was a 40-year-old male with a high school education, then the mean annual earnings in 1980 was $16,503. This figure would be used as the base for calculating a current level of income. The current level of income would be used as the base dollar amount in the present value calculation.

The economist must be careful to use earnings rather than income, since income is a broader term than earnings. *Earnings* refers to wages, while *income* includes wages, interest, dividends, and other sources of money.

§2.13 —The Federal Minimum Wage

In the absence of an earnings history, the minimum wage can serve as the base dollar amount. The minimum wage is $3.35 per hour. Full-time employment would result in an annual income of $6,968. The $6,968 would be the base dollar amount used to calculate the present value of a future income stream.

§2.14 —Professional Publications

There are professional organizations that publish income data. One such organization is the American Assembly of Collegiate Schools of Business.[6]

---

[6] The American Assembly of Collegiate Schools of Business (AACSB) is a nonprofit corporation comprised of member organizations and institutions devoted to the promotion and improvement of higher education for business administration and management. It is the sole accrediting agency for baccalaureate and masters degree programs in business administration and accounting.

The AACSB publishes a variety of literature; including the *AACSB Membership Directory*,

Table 2-6 presents the 1985-1986 median salaries of faculty members of schools of business.

Table 2-6 Median Salaries School of Business Faculty By Rank

Rank	1985-86
Professor	$47,500
Associate Professor	39,500
Assistant Professor	35,500
Instructor	23,500

These earnings figures can be used by the economist as the base dollar amount used to calculate the present value of the future income stream.

Similar income data can be obtained for attorneys, accountants, nurses, and most professional occupations. Starting salaries for most occupations requiring a college education can be obtained from the placement offices of most colleges and universities.

§2.15 Sources for Determining the Base Dollar Amount of Medical Expenses When Calculating the Present Value of Future Medical Expenses

As with wages, the present value of the future medical expenses is dependent upon the base dollar amount used in the present value formula. The base dollar amount is the current cost. The current dollar costs of medical expenses are usually obtained from local sources. That is, the doctor will testify how often he or she will need to see the patient and how much he or she will charge for office visits. The number of visits times the cost per visit is the current base dollar amount the economist will use to calculate the present value of the future doctor bills.

In a similar fashion, the economist will rely on medical experts to determine how often surgery may be required and what the current cost of the surgery is. The economist will make the forecast of the present value of the future surgeries. The forecast for drugs, nursing care, therapy, environmental modification for the handicapped, or any other medical expense depends on medical information. The economist relies on some input on the current cost, and then makes the calculation of the present value of the future expenses.

---

its *Articles of Incorporation and Bylaws*, the *Accreditation Council Policies and Procedures*, a brochure describing the full range of programs and activities undertaken in addition to accreditation, and the *AACSB Salary Survey* compiled by the AACSB Statistical Service.

§2.16   Sources for Determining the Base Dollar Amount When Calculating the Present Value of Household Services

The value of household services is usually thought of as an economic contribution of a wife. In this vein there have been several articles written which estimate the value of a housewife. One expert has estimated the types of jobs the housewife performs, the number of hours worked by a housewife, and then suggested the value is found by multiplying the hours by the local wage rate.[7] Another estimated that a 27-year-old white housewife with a 4-year-old child works 57 hours per week,[8] while a third estimated the value of a 35-year-old white housewife and mother of children ages 14, 13, and 10 to be $670 per week.[9]

However, the two most widely quoted sources for estimating the value of household services are the Gauger and Walker study, The Dollar Value of Household Work,[10] and the Jefferson Standard Company estimate of the economic value of a housewife. The Jefferson Standard study cited in Sylvia Porter's *New Money Book for the 80's.* [11]

The Gauger-Walker study established the dollar value, in 1979 dollars, for household work performed by the wife, husband, and teenage children. The dollar value of the household services is a function of the number of children in the household, the age of the youngest child, and whether the wife is employed outside the home. Table 2-7 presents the 1979 dollar value of household services.

Table 2-7 Gauger-Walker Value of Household Services 1979 Dollars

# of Children		Employed-Wife Households			Nonemployed Wife Households		
		Wife	Husband	Teen	Wife	Husband	Teen
0	Under 25	$4,700	$1,800		$7,000	$1,100	
	25-39	5,000	1,900		8,000	1,600	
	40-54	5,900	1,100		8,400	2,100	
	55 plus	6,000	1,500		7,400	2,700	
	Age of Youngest Child	Wife	Husband	Teen	Wife	Husband	Teen
1	12-17	$6,700	$2,400	$1,400	$9,600	$2,700	$1,200
	6-11	8,000	1,500	-	9,400	2,000	-

---

[7] Kirby, *The Economic Expert*, 31, No 3 J Mo 201 (Apr-May 1975).

[8] Kiker, *Evaluating Household Services*, Trial, Feb 1980, at 34-35.

[9] Durham, *The Valuation of the Production of a Deceased Housewife*, 4, No 5 J Kan Trial Law Assn, 18-23 (1980-81).

[10] Gauger & Walker, *The Dollar Value of Household Work*, 60 Info Bull (New York State College of Human Ecology 1980).

[11] S. Porter, *New Money Book For The 80's* 621 (1980).

# of Children	Age of Youngest Child	Employed-Wife Households			Nonemployed Wife Households		
		Wife	Husband	Teen	Wife	Husband	Teen
	2-5	6,200	2,000	-	9,100	2,400	-
	1	8,300	600	-	9,900	2,300	-
	Under 1	*	*	-	10,900	2,100	-
2	12-17	6,300	2,100	1,000	10,000	2,200	1,100
	6-11	7,200	2,000	1,100	9,900	2,100	1,100
	2-5	8,300	2,400	1,500	1,100	2,200	900
	1	8,400	5,000	*	11,700	2,200	*
	Under 1	10,200	2,100	*	12,600	2,000	*
3	12-17	5,000	2,100	1,100	9,000	1,400	1,000
	6-11	8,600	2,000	1,700	9,900	2,200	1,600
	2-5	10,200	2,800	*	10,700	1,900	1,000
	1	11,500	3,200	*	11,600	2,200	1,400
	Under 1	8,700	2,800	*	13,300	2,000	
4	12-17	8,700	1,900	1,700	8,400	1,400	1,000
	6-11	7,200	1,400	1,100	10,700	1,900	1,100
	2-5	*	*	*	12,000	2,000	1,100
	1	*	*	*	11,800	2,600	800
	Under 1	*	*	*	13,700	2,600	
5-6	12-17	*	*	*	-	-	-
	6-11	*	*	*	11,500	2,000	1,700
	2-5	*	*	*	12,000	2,100	900
	1	*	*	*	9,900	700	
	Under 1	*	*	*	13,600	2,600	1,000
7-9	6-11	-	-	-	*	*	*
	2-5	*	*	*	11,900	2,900	1,400
	1	-	-	-	*	*	*
	Under 1	-	-	-	15,200	2,600	*

- No cases reported
* Averages not calculated because fewer than four cases.

The 1979 dollars are increased to current values, and the current values serve as the base dollar amount used by the economist to calculate the present value of the household services.

In 1979, the Jefferson Standard Company estimated the annual value of household services to be $18,862.48. The value was estimated by determining 12 job categories performed by a housewife. The categories include nursemaid, housekeeper, cook, dishwasher, laundress, food buyer, chauffer, gardner, maintaince man, seamstress, dietitian, and practical nurse. The number of hours spent each week in each of the categories ranged from 44.6 as nursemaid to .6 hours as a practical nurse. The number of hours were multiplied by an appropriate wage rate to estimate the annual value of the housewife.

§2.17   Determining the Base Dollar Amount When Calculating the Present Value of Retirement Benefits.

Most retirement benefits are a defined benefit plan, a money purchase plan, or a profit-sharing plan. A *defined-benefit plan* is one in which the benefit an employee receives upon retirement can be determined from a formula defined in the plan. Annual contributions to the plan are in the amount needed to provide for the benefit.

A *money purchase plan* provides for a stipulated annual contribution by the employee. No specific benefit is formulated in advance. Each employee will receive whatever benefit the total contributions made during employment will purchase at the time of the employee's retirement.

A *profit-sharing plan* has a defined annual contribution by the employer. The contribution is usually from the employer's current or accumulated profits. At retirement the employee's benefit is a portion of the contributions the employer has made.

Under the defined benefit plan the economist will calculate the present value of the retirement benefit by using the specified formula. Usually the formula will specify benefits as a per cent of the last five years' earnings times a factor. The factor may represent the number of months or years the employee has been with the firm. The plaintiff's last five years of earnings have been calculated by the economist when the present value analysis was done.

Under the money purchase plan the economist will have to make judgments about how much money will be available to purchase the retirement benefits, and what the money will be able to purchase. If this occurrence is very far in the future, the economist will be reluctant to make a very definite statement about what retirement benefits can be purchased.

§2.18   Cross-Examining the Economist

The primary purpose of cross-examination about the base dollar amount is to show that the figure does not represent what the plaintiff earned and, therefore, the present value of the loss has been overstated. For example, if a person were injured two years ago and, at the time of trial, the economist used a base dollar amount which represented an increased wage from the time of the injury to what the individual would have earned today had the injury not occurred, counsel should attempt to point out that the plaintiff *never* earned the amount of money the economist has used as the base dollar amount in the present value calculation. It can also be argued that the use of the increased base dollar amount also resulted in a higher fringe benefit being lost. Had the economist used the actual earnings plaintiff received, the present value of the loss would have been less.

§2.19 Summary

The economist is retained to calculate the present value of a cash inflow and/or the present value of a cash outflow. The cash inflows represents lost wages, fringe benefits, dividend income, rental income, in-kind income, and other income that will be diminished or interrupted as a result of the plaintiff's injury. In addition to the cash inflow, the economist estimates the present value of the cash outflows. These outflows are doctor's fees, nursing care, surgical fees, hospital fees, environmental modification, and any other expenses that are incurred as a result of the injury.

The base dollar amount used will depend on what information is made available to the economist. If the employee's records or employer's records are available, they will serve as the basis for the economic analysis. In the absence of this type of information, the economist will turn to other published sources as a basis for calculating the current dollar amount of the loss or expense.

3

Modifications to the Base Dollar Amount Due to Disability

$$\text{Present Value} = \sum_{t=0}^{n} \$ * \underline{M} * (1+g)^t/(1+d)^t * PL * PS * PF * C * HS * TX$$

§3.01   Introduction

Chapter 2 established the base dollar amount used to calculate the present value of the future income stream. The basis for the dollar amount was that the plaintiff would be unable to return to work. The modifications to base dollar amounts represent adjustments for disability, since the future income may not be totally eliminated when the plaintiff is injured. The nature of the injury may render the plaintiff only partially disabled, reducing the earning capacity of the plaintiff but not totally eliminating the plaintiff's ability to earn.

This chapter distinguishes between total disability and partial disability. Degrees of disability are usually in medical terms and must be translated to economic terms. The chapter explores the methods for translating degrees of medical disability to degrees of economic disability.

§3.02   The Degrees of Disability

Disability may be either total or partial, temporary or permanent. If the injury has left the plaintiff totally disabled, then the plaintiff will be unable to obtain any type of gainful employment. In an economic sense the analysis can proceed as if the case were a wrongful death case. In other words, the "M" appearing in the formula is 100 per cent. The loss of future income is total. If the disability is temporary, then the analysis continues until the time the disability will cease.

If the disability is not total, it is necessary to establish the degree to which the earning capacity has been reduced. This is difficult to do and is beyond the expertise of most economists. One expert who evaluates the earning capacity of the disabled is the clinical psychologist. The data provided by the clinical psychologist becomes the input data, the value "M," for the economist estimating the present value of the future income.

§3.03   Is There a Loss?

It is possible that an injury does not alter the capacity of the individual to earn an income. For instance, after injury, the plaintiff may be forced to retrain and, as a result, the income after retaining increases. In this case there would be no economic loss. Consider another situation where the plaintiff, a 22-year-old high school graduate, is paralyzed from the waist down as a the result of an accident. The disability is judged to be permanent, and the plaintiff is unable to return to work in the construction industry. As a result, the injured party returns to college and graduates with a degree in accounting. It is very possible there is no loss in the present value of future income resulting from the injury.

There may be ongoing medical expenses, pain and suffering, and reduced income while the plaintiff attends school, but the present value of the lost income may be negative. Negative present value of lost income means the present value of the future income stream after the injury, and after retraining as an accountant, is higher than the present value of the future income stream as a construction worker.

§3.04   Using a Clinical Psychologist

A clinical psychologist may be used to determine the reduced work capacity of the plaintiff. This is done by determining the occupational skill levels of the plaintiff before the injury and comparing them to the occupational skill levels after the injury. The result may be expressed in terms of the number of Standard Industrial Classification occupations that the party could handle before the injury as compared to the number that can be handled after the injury.

Using the information provided by the clinical psychologist, the economist then determines the wage levels that existed for the types of jobs the plaintiff could hold before the injury and compares them to the wage levels that existed for the types of jobs the plaintiff can hold after the injury. The difference in the wage rates represents the loss to the plaintiff and is the basis for the economist's forecast.

The nature of the jobs that can be held by the plaintiff is determined by the psychologist.

§3.05   Translating Injury to a Part of the Body to the Body as a Whole

When an injury occurs to one part of an individual's body, the medical profession may translate the injury to the body as a whole. For example, if a person loses the right arm, the translation may be that this is a 25 per cent disability to the body as a whole. Two publications that assist physicians in making the translation are *Guides to the Evaluation of Permanent Impairment*, published by the American Medical Association, and the *Manual for Orthopedic Surgeons*, published by the American Academy of Orthopedic Surgeons.[1]

These publications are of no value in making the economic evaluation of the lost income. Consider the example of an individual who loses the little finger on the left hand. This may translate to a 10 per cent disability to the body as a whole. To the college professor, accountant, or lawyer, there may be no reduction of income. Thus, no economic loss exists. However, to the concert pianist the economic loss is 100 per cent, since the result is an inability to perform.

§3.06   Using Minimum Wage as the Alternative Income

After an injury occurs, the economist may use the minimum wage as the alternative source of income. The present value of the future loss can be handled one of two ways: as a reduction of earning capacity of a stated per cent, or as the difference between the two income figures.

For example, a plaintiff earned $8 an hour as a construction worker before a back injury. The testimony indicates the injury is permanent and such that the plaintiff should not return to the construction field. The injury will not permit heavy work, but the plaintiff is permitted to return to work. The economist, in the absence of alternative information, may assume an alternative income at the minimum wage of $3.35 per hour. The calculation of the present value of future income may be done in one of two ways. First, the $3.35 per hour represents 41.89 per cent of earnings before the injury. The loss of income is 58.11 per cent of the preinjury level (100% − 41.89%). The present value calculation would enter $8 per hour as the income level and enter 58.11 per cent as the value "M" for modification, or reduction in income. The resulting present value represents the loss to the plaintiff.

The second method is to enter the dollar loss as $4.65 per hour. This is the $8 per hour earned before the accident less the $3.35 earned after the accident. In this case, there would be no entry for modifications to income for disability since the modification is reflected in the dollar amount used to calculate the

---

[1] American Medical Assn, Committee of Rating of Mental & Physical Impairment, Guide to the Evaluation of Permanent Impairment, Manual for Orthopedic Surgeons for the Evaluation of Permanent Physical Impairment (2d ed 1977).

loss of income. Both methods of evaluation would result in the same present value of future loss.

§3.07   Using Time and Motion Studies to Estimate Loss

In order to establish the degree of disability sustained by an individual, a time and motion specialist may be called. The specialist would take movies of the plaintiff performing certain types of jobs. The time to complete a job after the injury would be compared to the time required to perform the same task by a person who is not injured. The additional time reflects the degree of disability.

An example would be to film and evaluate the time it takes an injured person to get out a box of cereal, pour the cereal in a bowl, add milk and sugar, eat, and clean up. This amount of time would be compared to the time required for an uninjured person. The difference represents the degree of disability.

The degree of disability established by the time and motion specialist can be translated to an economic value by the specialist. The economist then incorporates the economic value into the analysis of the lost income.

§3.08   Incorporating Government Statistics into the Economic Analysis

In the absence of specific information regarding the economic loss due to disability, the economist may turn to government publications in order to establish the loss. The reduction in income due to disability is categorized by race and by sex. The data appears in the *Disability Survey 72*, Health and Human Services, Social Security Administration, April 1981. Tables 3-1 through 3-4 present the effect of disability on earnings.

Table 3-1 Effect of Disability on Earnings

Percentage decline in earnings by degree of disability and amount of work undertaken by those who worked as compared to a nondisabled individual working full-time (50-52 Weeks)

White Men	Severely Disabled	Occupationally Disabled	Secondary Disability
Full-Time			
(50-52 Weeks)	15.59%	20.30%	16.22%
(26-49 Weeks)	46.66%	42.34%	34.89%
Part-Time			
(26 Weeks +)	77.48%	71.98%	67.20%
Intermittent	78.60%	54.96%	48.15%
AVERAGE	52.42%	32.37%	26.95%
Percentage Who Worked	41.90%	91.60%	91.40%

Severely Disabled means unable to work or unable to work regularly.

Occupationally Disabled means able to work regularly, but unable to do the same work as before the onset of disability, or unable to work full-time.

Secondary Work Limitations means able to work full-time, regularly, doing the same work as before onset, but with some limitation to the kind or amount of work.

Table 3-2 Effect of Disability on Earnings

Percentage decline in earnings by degree of disability and amount of work undertaken by those who worked as compared to a nondisabled individual working full-time (50-52 Weeks)

Black Men	Severely Disabled	Occupationally Disabled	Secondary Disability
Full-Time			
(50-52 Weeks)	*	23.56%	2.47%
(26-49 Weeks)	*	59.40%	*
Part-Time			
(26 weeks +)	*	*	*
Intermittent	86.12%	*	86.01%
AVERAGE	72.26%	50.36%	28.75%
Percentage Who Worked	60.10%	29.70%	79.80%

Severely Disabled means unable to work or unable to work regularly.

Occupationally Disabled means able to work regularly, but unable to do the same work as before the onset of disability, or unable to work full-time.

Secondary Work Limitations means able to work full-time, regularly, doing the same work as before onset, but with some limitation to the kind or amount of work.

* Means the number in the cell was less than 50,000 people.

Table 3-3 Effect of Disability on Earnings

Percentage decline in earnings by degree of disability and amount of work undertaken by those who worked as compared to a nondisabled individual working full-time (50-52 Weeks)

White Women	Severely Disabled	Occupationally Disabled	Secondary Disability
Full-Time			
(50-52 Weeks)	19.78%	16.04%	5.84%
(26-49 Weeks)	43.62%	39.50%	36.89%
Part-Time			
(26 weeks +)	71.89%	72.01%	63.17%
Intermittent	78.62%	86.58%	70.56%
AVERAGE	63.84%	55.15%	29.72%
Percentage Who Worked	18.00%	53.40%	54.40%

Severely Disabled means unable to work or unable to work regularly.

Occupationally Disabled means able to work regularly, but unable to do the same work as before the onset of disability, or unable to work full-time.

Secondary Work Limitations means able to work full-time, regularly, doing the same work as before onset, but with some limitation to the kind or amount of work.

Table 3-4 Effect of Disability on Earnings

Percentage decline in earnings by degree of disability and amount of work undertaken by those who worked as compared to a nondisabled individual working full-time (50-52 Weeks)

Black Women	Severely Disabled	Occupationally Disabled	Secondary Disability
Full-Time			
(50-52 Weeks)	*	*	34.85%
(26-49 Weeks)	*	*	17.10%
Part-Time			
(26 weeks +)	83.58%		*
Intermittent	93.78%	85.01%	*
AVERAGE	84.13%	79.03%	37.81%
Percentage Who Worked	25.10%	71.70%	79.90%

Severely Disabled means unable to work or unable to work regularly.

Occupationally Disabled means able to work regularly, but unable to do the same work as before the onset of disability, or unable to work full-time.

Secondary Work Limitations means able to work full-time, regularly, doing the same work as before onset, but with some limitation to the kind or amount of work.

* Means the number in the cell was less than 50,000 people.

The economist uses the percentage decline in earnings as "M" in the present value formula. The economist will want someone else to determine the degree of disability. That is, the economist will say: "If the plaintiff is occupationally disabled, then the loss of income is __." The economist will not want to say: "In my opinion the plaintiff is occupationally disabled."

§3.09   Summary

The economist estimates the loss of the present value in the future income stream resulting from disability. The degree of disability will be left to someone else. The economist initially calculates the present value of the future income stream as though the loss were for a permanently and totally disabled person.

The economist then multiplies the loss by a per cent representing the degree of disability experienced by the plaintiff. The economist typically will not make the decision on the degree of economic disability.

4

Historic Loss

§4.01 Introduction

This chapter will explain what *historic loss* is, what values are included in historic loss, and how historic loss is calculated. Some economists include, whether by design or by accident, prejudgment interest in the calculation of the historic loss. **Section 4.07** demonstrates how prejudgment interest may be included in the calculation of the historic loss.

§4.02 What Is Meant by Historic Loss

Historic loss is the economic loss that occurs between the date of the injury and some arbitrarily assumed date. The assumed date utilized by the economist is usually the plaintiff's birthday or the date of trial. The date of the trial will be the assumed end of the historic loss. The historic losses may consist of as many as three types: lost income, lost household services, and incurred medical expenses.

Lost income occurs when an injury leaves the plaintiff in a position where he or she is unable to continue to work or continues to work at a reduced level. In either case, the plaintiff has a lower income than before the injury. The difference of income before and after the accident is the basis for determining lost income.

Lost household services represents the plaintiff's inability to perform household chores after the injury. Again, the loss does not mean the plaintiff is unable to perform any household services, only that he or she is unable to perform them at the same level as before the accident.

There are cases where an injury may leave the plaintiff without employment but some of the damages are mitigated because the value of household services increases after the accident. Suppose a female grade school teacher and mother of two grade school children suffers an injury to the larynx, rendering her unable to continue in the classroom. The loss to the family may be the income the woman is unable to earn since she cannot continue in the classroom, but some of the loss may be mitigated since the value of her household services may increase if she is unable to find alternative employment outside the home.

The historical medical expenses are the sum of what has been spent on medical care from the date of the injury to the date of the trial. The term *medical care* takes on the broadest of terms when the historic expenses are being calculated. The expenses include hospital care, physician's fees, prescription and nonprescription drugs, therapy of all types, transportation expenses to and from medical facilities, possibly dental care, and whatever other costs may be attributed to the injury.

§4.03 Comparing Disability to Death

Economically, the size of the historic lost income and lost household services is the same for the totally, permanently disabled person as it is for the person who has died. In both cases the ability to replace income or household services is absent. However, in the cases where the plaintiff is partially disabled, the reduced ability to earn or provide household services must be considered. The historic loss experienced by a partially disabled plaintiff depends on the degree of disability suffered.

§4.04 Calculating the Historic Wage Loss When Specific Wage Increases are Known

Assume the plaintiff was injured three years ago today, on the tenth anniversary of his employment. At the time of the injury the annual earnings were $10,400, based on a wage of $5 per hour. Since the injury, the plaintiff has been unable to return to work. The historic loss from wages is what the plaintiff could have earned had the injury not occurred.

The basis for estimating the historic lost income is dependent on the information available to the economist. If employer records indicate that wage increases occurred on the employment anniversary, then the date of wage increases is established. How much the wage increased may be determined by looking at a similar employee's record, or may be supplied by the employer.

If the employer testifies that the wage scale of $5 per hour went into effect on the day of the injury and the employer further testified that the injured party would have received $5.50 and $6 per hour on the successive two anniversaries of employment, the historic loss is calculated based on this record. The first year following the injury the plaintiff would have earned $10,400, ($5 per hour times 2,080 hours per year); the second year following the injury the annual income would have been $11,440 ($5.50 per hour times 2,080 hours per year); the third year following the injury the annual income would have been $12,480, ($6 per hour times 2,080 hours per year). The total historic loss would be the sum of these three amounts, $34,320.

In this case the basis for estimating the historic loss of income is the testimony of the employer. Had the employer been unable or unwilling to testify, the economist would have to turn to other sources to estimate historic wage increases.

§4.05 Calculating the Historic Wage Loss When Specific Wage Increases Are Not Known

When the wage increases are unavailable from the employer, the economist must turn to other sources to establish how the wage "probably" increased. Sources used to increase historic wages include the wages reported in the Standard Industrial Classification Tables, wages reported for the total private nonagricultural sector of the economy, the Consumer Price Index, and the Industrial Production Index.

When using the Consumer Price Index as a measure of how historic wages increased, the economist is no longer estimating historic lost income, but rather is estimating lost purchasing power. Here the economist is estimating how much money it would have taken to maintain plaintiff's purchasing power had the injury not occurred.

§4.06   —Using the Rate of Growth in Wages Paid in the Total Private Nonagricultural Sector

There are two problems faced by the economist. First, the employer was unable or unwilling to provide information concerning wage rates that would have prevailed since the accident. Second, the data available through government statistics is not current enough. That is, there is no estimate for the current year's wage rate.

Table 4-1 Total Private Nonagricultural Hourly Wages 1980 - 1986

Year	Hourly Wage Rate
1980	$6.66
1981	7.25
1982	7.68
1983	8.02
1984	8.33
1985	8.58
1986	8.76

Source: Economic Report of the President, 292, Table B41 (1987).

Table 4-1 shows the total private nonagricultural hourly wages for the period 1980 through 1986. The economist may use this type of data to estimate how wages grew in the private nonagricultural sector of the economy. In 1985 the hourly rate was $8.58, an increase of 3 per cent from the 1984 hourly wage of $8.33. The 1986 wage of $8.76 is 2.1 per cent more than the 1985 wage of $8.58. The concept of growth rates and how growth rates are calculated is examined in Chapter 5.

Working under the assumption that the injury occurred in 1984 when the plaintiff was earning $5 per hour, the economist would permit the 1984 wage to increase by 3 per cent, as indicated by the growth rate of the private nonagricultural sector of the economy, to $5.15 per hour. The $5.15 per hour represents the plaintiff's wage in 1985. Multiplying the hourly wage by 2,080 hours of work per year, the economist estimates the 1985 lost income to be $10,712.

The 1986 hourly wage is estimated by multiplying the 1985 hourly rate of $5.15 by the growth rate of wages for 1986. The increase was 2.1 per cent. The 1986 hourly wage is $5.26 and estimate of the annual income is $10,941.

Recall that the plaintiff was earning $5 per hour at the time of the injury. The wage increased by 3 per cent the following year to $5.15 per hour. Had there no basis for increasing the loss for the third year following the injury, the economist may use the $5.15 hourly wage rate as the basis for the third year's lost income. The historic losses are presented in Table 4-2.

Table 4-2 Historic Lost Income Using Rate of Change of Wages in the Private Nonagricultural Sector as the Basis for Wage Increases

Year	Hourly Rate	Total Hours Worked	Total Annual Wages
1984	$5.00	2,080	$10,400
1985	5.15	2,080	10,712
1986	5.26	2,080	10,941
	Total Historic Lost Income		$32,053

Using this approach, the economist has established an historic loss of $32,053.

§4.07   —Using the Consumer Price Index

Table 4-3 presents the historic rates of inflation from 1980 through 1986. The rate of inflation would indicate how the wage should have increased if the purchasing power of the individual was to be maintained.

Table 4-3 Consumer Price Index 1980 - 1986

Year	Index	Percentage Change
1980	246.8	13.52
1981	272.4	10.37
1982	289.1	6.13
1983	298.4	3.22
1984	311.1	4.26
1985	322.2	3.57
1986	328.4	1.92

Source: Economic Report of the President 307, Table B55 (1987).

At the time of the injury in 1984, the plaintiff was earning $5 per hour. If the wage increased at the same rate as inflation, then the wage in 1985 would have been $5.18 per hour, which is 3.57 per cent more than the 1984 wage. The 1986 hourly wage would have been $5.28, or 1.92 per cent higher than the 1985 wage. Table 4-4 shows the historic loss of income if the Consumer Price Index had been used to increase the past wages.

Table 4-4 Historic Lost Income Using The Consumer Price Index as the Wage Inflator

Year	Hourly Rate	Total Hours Worked	Total Annual Wages
1984	$5.00	2,080	$10,400

Year	Hourly Rate	Total Hours Worked	Total Annual Wages
1985	5.18	2,080	10,774
1986	5.28	2,080	10,982
	Total Historic Lost Income		$32,156

Using the Consumer Price Index to estimate the historic loss of purchasing power, the economist established an historic loss of $32,156.

§4.08 —Using the Industrial Production Index

As Table 4-5 shows, the Industrial Production Index registered a slight increases for 1985 and 1986.

Table 4-5 Industrial Production Index 1980 - 1985

Year	Index	Percentage Change
1980	108.60	−1.90
1981	111.00	2.21
1982	103.10	−7.12
1983	109.20	5.92
1984	121.80	11.54
1985	123.80	1.06
1986	125.10	1.05

Source: Economic Report of the President 296, Table 45 (1987).

If the economist were to use the Industrial Production Index as a basis for calculating the historic lost wages, then the $5 per hour wage in 1984 would be estimated to increase to $5.05 hour. This is the hourly wage that would also be used to estimate the 1986 hourly wage. The 1986 hourly rate would be $5.10.

Table 4-6 Historic Lost Income Using Rate of Change Indicated by the Change in the Industrial Production Index as the Basis for Wage Increases

Year	Hourly Rate	Total Hours Worked	Total Annual Wages
1984	$5.00	2,080	$10,400
1985	5.05	2,080	10,504
1986	5.10	2,080	10.608
	Total Historic Lost Income		$31,612

Using the Industrial Production Index as the basis of the historic wage changes, the historic loss of income is $31,612. This is lower than either of the other two estimates of lost income.

§4.09 Calculating the Historic Medical Expense

Historic medical expenses represent bills already incurred. The inclusion of historic medical expenses in an economist's report should only be done for convenience or clarity. There should be no need for analysis other than possibly summing the total of the already incurred expenses.

§4.10 Calculating the Historic Value of Lost Household Services

Calculating the value of lost household services requires establishing the amount of time the plaintiff spent in performing this type of service. In the absence of specific information, the value of household services may be estimated from the Gauger and Walker study[1] or the Sylvia Porter book,[2] discussed in §2.16, other studies estimating the value of household services.[3] As with wages, the economist will increase the value of household services from the date of the accident to the date of the trial to reflect the increased value of services caused by inflation.

Suppose an injury occurred January 2, 1984, leaving a 30-year-old housewife and mother of two children totally disabled. The case goes to trial January 2, 1987. The economist is to testify regarding the value of the household services. The Gauger and Walker study establishes the value of household services for a wife not employed outside the home. The 1979 value of household services appears in Table 4-7.

Table 4-7 Gauger-Walker Value of Household Services 1979 Dollars

# of Children		Employed-Wife Households			Nonemployed Wife Households		
		Wife	Husband	Teen	Wife	Husband	Teen
0	Under 25	$4,700	$1,800		$7,000	$1,100	
	25-39	5,000	1,900		8,000	1,600	
	40-54	5,900	1,100		8,400	2,100	
	55 plus	6,000	1,500		7,400	2,700	

---

[1] Gauger & Walker, *The Dollar Value of Household Work*, 60 Info Bull (New York State College of Human Ecology 1980).

[2] S. Porter, *New Money Book For The 80's*, 621 (1980).

[3] Other studies include: Kiker, *Evaluating Household Services*, Trial, Feb 1980, at 34-36; Hurt & Kiker, *Evaluation of Household Services, Methodology and Estimation*, 46 No 4 J Risk & Ins 697; Durham, *The Valuation of the Production of a Deceased Housewife*, 4 No 5 Kan Trial L Assn 18.

# of Children	Youngest Child	Employed-Wife Households			Nonemployed Wife Households		
		Wife	Husband	Teen	Wife	Husband	Teen
1	12-17	$6,700	$2,400	$1,400	$9,600	$2,700	$1,200
	6-11	8,000	1,500	-	9,400	2,000	-
	2-5	6,200	2,000	-	9,100	2,400	-
	1	8,300	600	-	9,900	2,300	-
	Under 1	*	*	-	10,900	2,100	-
2	12-17	6,300	2,100	1,000	10,000	2,200	1,100
	6-11	7,200	2,000	1,100	9,900	2,100	1,100
	2-5	8,300	2,400	1,500	1,100	2,200	900
	1	8,400	5,000	*	11,700	2,200	*
	Under 1	10,200	2,100	*	12,600	2,000	*
3	12-17	5,000	2,100	1,100	9,000	1,400	1,000
	6-11	8,600	2,000	1,700	9,900	2,200	1,600
	2-5	10,200	2,800	*	10,700	1,900	1,000
	1	11,500	3,200	*	11,600	2,200	1,400
	Under 1	8,700	2,800	*	13,300	2,000	
4	12-17	8,700	1,900	1,700	8,400	1,400	1,000
	6-11	7,200	1,400	1,100	10,700	1,900	1,100
	2-5	*	*	*	12,000	2,000	1,100
	1	*	*	*	11,800	2,600	800
	Under 1	*	*	*	13,700	2,600	
5 - 6	12-17	*	*	*	-	-	-
	6-11	*	*	*	11,500	2,000	1,700
	2-5	*	*	*	12,000	2,100	900
	1	*	*	*	9,900	700	
	Under 1	*	*	*	13,600	2,600	1,000
7 - 9	6-11	-	-	-	*	*	*
	2-5	*	*	*	11,900	2,900	1,400
	1	-	-	-	*	*	*
	Under 1	-	-	-	15,200	2,600	*

- No cases reported

* Averages not calculated because there were fewer than 4 cases.

To establish the value of household services, the economist must know the age of the youngest child. Assume the youngest child is six years old. The 1979 value of household services is $9,900.

In order to determine the inflated value of the household services, the economist will increase the value from the 1979 values to the inflation-adjusted values that would reflect the economic loss each year. Table 4-3 in §4.07 shows the historic rates of inflation which are used to "move" the historic values to inflation-adjusted values.

The 1979 value of household services was $9,900. The rate of inflation in 1980 was 13.52 per cent. The value of household services in 1980 would have been $11,238, or 13.52 per cent more than in 1979. In a similar fashion, the 1980 value is inflated to the 1981 value. Table 4-8 shows how the 1979 value is "brought forward" to inflation-adjusted values.

Table 4-8 Value of Household Services Inflation Adjusted

Year	Base Dollars	Rate of Inflation	Increased Value of Services	Value of Services
1979	$ 9,900	-	-	-
1980	-	13.52%	$1,338	$11,238
1981	11,238	10.37	1,165	12,403
1982	12,403	6.13	760	13,163
1983	13,163	3.22	424	13,587
1984	13,587	4.26	579	14,166
1985	14,166	3.57	506	14,672
1986	14,672	1.92	282	14,954

This approach gives a value for household services for the three years 1984, 1985, and 1986. The historic value of the lost household services would be the sum of the values for those three years, or $43,792, ($14,166 + $14,672 + $14,954).

Had the Sylvia Porter information been used as the basis for estimating the value of the household services, the procedure would have been the same. However, the value of the lost services would have been $83,441. This is the $18,862 dollar value of household services established in 1979 inflated to the 1984, 1985, and 1986 values.

§4.11 Incorporating Prejudgment Interest into the Analysis

Some states permit the inclusion of prejudgment interest as part of the historic loss.[4] Prejudgment interest is the interest that could have been earned on the wage or household services had the plaintiff been compensated for the loss at the time the loss occurred. The lost interest would be calculated by establishing a fair rate of return and calculating the interest that could have been earned had the money been received and invested.

Using the Gauger and Walker value of household services developed in §4.10, the interest is calculated on an average annual figure. Table 4-8 shows the value of household services in 1984 to be $14,166. The figure assumes the value is paid in a lump sum to the plaintiff. The forgone interest to be calculated requires knowledge of when the payment was to be made. If the full amount of the annual service is paid on January 2, 1984, the date of the injury, then interest would accrue on the entire principal. If the principal was paid at the

---

[4] Annotation, *Validity and Construction of State Statute or Rule Allowing Changing Rate of Prejudgement Interest in Tort Actions*, 40 ALR4th 147 (1985).

end of the year, then no interest would accrue through 1984. A third alternative is to permit the principal to be paid in 12 equal payments, meaning the value of the service is provided on a monthly basis. Under this last approach, interest would be paid on one-half the principal.

Allowing an acceptable interest rate to be 8 per cent per year throughout the historic loss. The three different methods of "paying" the services result in three different prejudgment interest calculations.

§4.12   —Calculating Prejudgment Interest When Payment for Services Occurs at the Beginning of the Year

The first year, 1984, the value of the household services was $14,166. Since the money is paid at the beginning of the year, interest is paid on the full principal at the annual rate of 8 per cent. Interest during the first year would total $1,133 ($14,166 × 8%).

When interest is added to the principal, the sum at the end of the first year would equal $15,299. This is the beginning principal for the second year. To the $15,299 the value of the second year's household services are added ($14,672). This increases the principal at the beginning of 1985 to $29,971. During the second year, interest at 8 per cent would be earned on the full $29,971. Interest would equal $2,398 ($29,971 × 8%), and the ending principal would be $32,369.

The same occurs in the third year. The value of the third year's household services, $14,954, raises the principal to $47,323. During the third year, interest at 8 per cent earns an additional $3,786. Thus, on January 2, 1987, at the time of the trial, the historic loss totals $51,109. This figure includes the value of household services plus the interest that could have been earned on the money. The value of the household services was $43,792, and the interest income totaled $7,317.

Table 4-9 presents the calculation of the interest payments when payment for services occurs at the beginning of the year.

Table 4-9 Interest Calculations When Payment Occurs at the Beginning of the Year

Year	Value of Household Services	Beginning Principal	Interest Earned (8%)	Ending Principal
1984	$14,166	$14,166	$1,133	$15,299
1985	14,672	29,971	2,398	32,369
1986	14,954	47,323	3,786	51,109

§4.13 —Calculating Prejudgment Interest When Payment for Services Occurs at the End of the Year

Table 4-10 shows that the ending principal when payment of services occurs at the end of the year is $46,494, or $4,615 less than when the payments are made at the beginning of the year. The difference in the amount in principal at the end of 1986 is due solely to different interest income, a result of the timing of the payments for services.

Table 4-10 Interest Calculations When Payment Occurs at the End of the Year

Year	Beginning Principal	Interest Earned (8%)	Value of Household Services	Ending Principal
1984	$ 0	$ 0	$14,166	$14,166
1985	14,166	1,133	$14,166	29,465
1986	29,465	2,357	14,672	46,494

§4.14 —Calculating Prejudgment Interest When Payment for Services Occurs at the End of Each Month

When payment for household services occurs monthly rather than annually, the ending principal plus interest will be more than when payments occur at the end of the year and be less than when payments occur at the beginning of the year. Annual payments represent the two extreme values for principal plus interest.

To calculate the principal plus interest for monthly payments, it is assumed that one-half the annual principal is at interest throughout the entire year. Table 4-11 shows the calculation of the principal plus interest.

Table 4-11 Interest Calculations When Payment Occurs Monthly

Year	Value of Household Services	Average Principal	Interest Earned (8%)	Ending Principal
1984	$14,166	7,083	$ 567	$14,733
1985	14,762	22,068	1,765	31,261
1986	14,954	38,738	3,099	49,314

§4.15 Moving Historic Losses to Current Dollars

Some economists will not apply forgone interest calculations to the historic loss. Rather, the economist will argue that historic losses should be stated in terms of current dollars. This means that the economic loss occurring in 1984 of $14,166, discussed in §4.10, must be converted to current dollars in order to maintain the lost purchasing power. This is accomplished by increasing the historic value of household services to reflect increases in the Consumer Price Index. This permits the plaintiff to recover the same purchasing power that was lost as a result of the injury. Table 4-12 shows the historic loss increased to current dollars. The value of the household services in 1984 was $14,166. The rate of inflation reported in 1985 was 3.57 per cent. In order to maintain the purchasing power of the 1984 dollars the plaintiff would need 3.57 per cent more dollars in 1985, or $14,671. The $14,671 in 1985 dollars would provide the same purchasing power as the $14,166 in 1984.

Table 4-12 Value of Household Services Current Dollars

Year	Value of Household Services	Annual Inflation Rate	Value of Household Services in Current Dollars
1984	$14,166	3.57% in 1985	$14,672
1985	14,672	1.92% in 1986	14,954
1986	14,954		14,671

A more rigorous example would be the situation where the housewife was killed January 2, 1980, and the case goes to trial January 2, 1987. The goal of the economist is to present the historic loss of household services to the jury. Assuming the same fact situation as in §4.10, the present value of the inflation-adjusted household services would be the sum of the last column in Table 4-13. The value of the household services totals $94,183.

Table 4-13 Value of Household Services Inflation Adjusted

Year	Base Dollars	Rate of Inflation	Increased Value of Services	Value of Household Services
1979	$ 9,900			
1980		13.52%	$1,338	$11,238
1981	11,238	10.37	1,165	12,403
1982	12,403	6.13	760	13,163
1983	13,163	3.22	424	13,587
1984	13,587	4.26	579	14,166
1985	14,166	3.57	506	14,672
1986	14,672	1.92	282	14,954
			Total	$94,183

§4.16   A Question on Using Current Dollars When Prejudgment Interest Is Not Permitted

When household services were adjusted for inflation (Table 4-13), the present value of the loss was $94,183.

There is the argument that if the state does not permit the inclusion of prejudgment interest, then it should not permit the adjustment to current purchasing power. The line of reasoning is that part of the inflation rate is interest. That is, the nominal rate of interest includes a real return plus an inflation premium. Thus, to permit the increase of the historic loss to current dollars permits the inclusion of historic interest.

§4.17   Including Both Prejudgment Interest and Adjustment to Current Purchasing Power

If both prejudgment interest and adjustment to current purchasing power are included, the analysis requires knowledge of the base wage, the historic rate of inflation, and the appropriate interest rate earned on investments. The analysis must be done year by year.

Care must be taken not to doublecount inflation. Interest rates are composed of two parts: the real rate of interest plus the inflation premium.[5] If interest has been computed after values have been inflated, a doublecounting of inflation has occurred.

§4.18   Summary

Historic loss refers to the loss of income, the value of the household services which the plaintiff was unable to perform as a result of an injury, and the accumulated medical expenses. The historic loss includes a time period from the date of the injury to the date of the trial.

If a significant period of time has elapsed between the time of the injury and the date of the trial, the economist will permit annual increases in historic wages and the value of the household services. Historic medical expenses should be a summation of past bills.

Wage increases may be determined from employer records or, if those are not available, from government statistics. Household services may also be increased to reflect the increased value of the services. The increase in value is usually accomplished by permitting growth in the value of services to occur at the annual rate of change in the Consumer Price Index.

If prejudgment interest is included in the analysis, the economist will calculate the amount of interest that would have been earned had the dollar value of the wages, services, or medical expenses been invested at the time the loss occurred.

---

[5] P. Rose & D. Fraser, Financial Institutions (2d ed 1985).

If the economist converts the historic loss of wages, services, and medical expenses to current dollars, then he or she is repaying past dollars without a loss of purchasing power.

§4.19   Direct Examination of the Economist

The plaintiff's attorney wants the jury to understand what the historic loss is. The time frame must be clearly identified as from the date of the injury to the date of trial.

Having established that, it is necessary to establish what losses the plaintiff experienced. Is the analysis of historical loss going to include lost wages, lost household services, or both?

The plaintiff's attorney also wants to point out to the jury how conservative the economist was in the analysis. In examining the economist on wages, the attorney may wish to focus on the point that the plaintiff never "advanced" in position. That is, throughout the entire analysis the economist was attempting to determine the wages that would have been earned at the same job, not at a "better" job.

Likewise, with household services the plaintiff's attorney wishes to point out how conservative the analysis was. For example, if the economist employed the more conservative Gauger and Walker study for household services rather than the Jefferson Standard study, this should be brought to the attention of the jury.

§4.20   Cross-Examination of the Economist

The goal of cross-examination of the economist is to call into question the assumption he or she made in arriving at the value of the plaintiff's historic loss. By showing that the assumptions are arbitrary, it can be argued that the historic loss is overstated. If the historic loss is overstated, there is no reason to believe the estimates of the present value of future income are any more accurate.

Questions that may be asked of the economist include:

Q. Isn't it true that the plaintiff was injured in 1984?

Q. Isn't it true that you forecast a wage for 1986 which the plaintiff did not earn?

Q. Isn't it true that your calculation of the historic loss includes wages which plaintiff never earned?

Q. Isn't it true that you let the value of household services increase at the historical rate of inflation?

Q. Isn't it true that you have no evidence that this would be an appropriate rate?

Q. Did you base your analysis on the Gauger and Walker Study?

Q. Isn't it true that you did not determine whether the value of household services in that study was appropriate for this part of the country?

Q. Isn't it true that you did not determine whether the plaintiff would
have worked about the house as specified in that study?

There are many questions which can be asked the economist which will elicit
a negative response, or "I did not consider that." By showing the factors that
the economist did not consider or the information he or she did not obtain
prior to rendering an opinion, it can be shown that there is no basis for the
economist's assumptions and, therefore, the value of the historic loss is
overstated.

5

Determination of Growth Rates

$$\text{Present Value} = \sum_{t=0}^{n} \$ * M * \underline{(1 + g)^t} / (1+d)^t * PL * PS * PF * C * HS * TX$$

§5.01   Introduction

The understanding of the concepts of growth and growth rates is critical to understanding the calculation of the present value of an income stream. There are two important items to consider when evaluating growth rates: (1) how the growth rate is established, i.e., the methodology, and (2) how the growth rate is applied in the analysis.

The major purposes of this chapter are to demonstrate what growth rates are, how growth rates are established, from what sources growth rates may be estimated, how the growth rates are used to forecast future values, and how the different methods used to estimate growth rates lead to different conclusions. In addition, this chapter will distinguish between real growth rates and nominal growth rates.

§5.02   The Concept of Growth

Growth, or rate of growth, refers to how quickly something increases in size. This growth rate may refer to how the market value of one's home or the value of a common stock investment has increased over time.

If a person purchased a house for $12,000 and sold the house 33 years later for $60,000, the value of the house has increased, or grown. The question which might be asked is: what is the annual rate of growth of the investment on the house? Did the value of the house grow at an annual rate of 3 per cent, or at some other rate of growth?

In cases of wrongful death or disability, the same concept can be applied to the injured party's income or wages. For example, suppose the injured party went to work for a construction firm nine years ago at $2.50 per hour. Last year the individual was injured. At the time of the injury the individual was earning $9 per hour. Over the course of employment, the annual rate of increase in the individual's hourly wage can be calculated. This growth rate can be used as the estimate of the future growth of wages.

In a similar manner, if an injury results in ongoing medical expenses, it is necessary to estimate the rate of growth associated with the future recurring medical expenses. This may be done by using the historic rate of growth of medical costs as a guide to the future rate of growth of medical costs.

§5.03   Methods Used to Calculate Growth Rates

The concept of growth is not difficult to grasp nor is growth difficult to calculate. There are different methods which can be employed to calculate growth rates. The rate of growth may be calculated by using the exponential growth formula, the average percentage change formula, or the linear regression formula. The two most common methods employed, and the ones that will be discussed here, are the exponential growth formula and the average percentage change formula.

§5.04   Calculating Growth Rates Using Exponential Growth

If $1,000 of principal was deposited in an interest-bearing account for one year, how much would be in the account at the end of the year? The answer, of course, depends on what interest rate is being paid on the account. The interest rate in this case represents the growth rate. If the interest rate paid is 6 per cent, then the account would earn $60 during the year. The ending amount in the account would be $1,000 in principal plus the $60 earned in interest, or $1,060.

$$\$1,060 = \$1,000 + \$60$$

The $1,060, the amount in the account at the end of one year, is called the ending value, or future value. The $1,000 deposited in the account at the beginning of the year is called the beginning value, or present value. The difference between the two will reflect the growth rate or interest earned on the funds. The relationship can be written in the following form:

Present Value * (1 + Growth Rate) = Future Value
or
Beginning Value * (1 + Growth Rate) = Ending Value

The expresion (1 + Growth Rate) shows how large the future value, or ending value, of the invested principal will be in one year. Since the growth rate is 6 per cent, the expression becomes (1 + .06), or 1.06. This means that in one year the future value, or ending value, will be 1.06 times the present value.

Suppose the $1,000, known as the principal, present value, or beginning value, was to be invested for two years earning 6 per cent each year, and the interest was to be compounded. *Compounded* means that interest during the second year will be paid on the $60 interest earned in the first year.

The $1,060 in the account at the end of the first year would be invested for another year, earning another 6 per cent. At the end of the second year, the account would be worth $1,123.60.

Present Value * (1 + Growth Rate) = Future Value
$1,060 * (1 + .06) = $1,123.60

During the second year interest amounted to $63.60 (the ending amount of $1,123.60 less the beginning amount of $1,060). The effect of compounding can be seen when the amount of interest earned in the first year is compared to the amount of interest earned in the second year. During the first year $60 was earned in interest. During the second year $63.60 was earned in interest. The $3.60 more in interest in the second year is the result of the first year's interest of $60 earning 6 per cent in year two.

The future value, or ending value, of the $1,000 invested for two years at 6 per cent per year can be calculated in the following manner:

$$\text{Future Value} = \$1,000 * (1 + \text{Growth Rate}) * (1 + \text{Growth Rate})$$
or
$$\text{Future Value} = \$1,000 \quad (1 + .06) * (1 + .06)$$
$$\text{Future Value} = \$1,123.60$$

The expression $(1 + .06)$ represents the annual rate of growth of the principal. There will be one such expression for every year the funds are invested. If the funds were invested for three years, then the expression $(1 + .06)$ would appear three times. If the funds were invested for nine years, it would appear nine times.

Instead of writing out the expression $(1 + \text{Growth Rate})$ for each year being considered, an exponent is used to state the number of years being considered, or the number of times the expression should be written. The formula was:

$$\text{Future Value} = \$1,000 * (1 + .06) * (1 + .06)$$

and now becomes:

$$\text{Future Value} = \$1,000 * (1 + .06)^2$$

where 2, the exponent, represents the number of years the funds will be invested. One-might note in passing that this is the source of the term *exponential growth.*

If the funds were to be invested for nine years, then the exponent would be 9 and the formula would be:

$$\text{Future Value} = \$1,000 * (1 + .06)^9$$

Using the exponential growth formula, the general expression for calculating the future value of a sum of money is:

$$\text{Future Value} = \text{Present Value} * (1 + \text{Growth Rate})^t$$

Where:

A "g" represents the growth rate
A "t" represents the number of periods compounding occurs.
"Present Value" represents the investment made today.

A table can be constructed to facilitate the calculation of the future value of an investment. The table is used to establish what is called a *growth factor.* A growth factor determines the future value of $1 and is calculated by using the following formula:

$$(1 + g)^t$$

Consider an investment earning 6 per cent per year for one year. To find the growth factor, use Table 5-1 and find the value where the row for one period intersects with the column headed 6 per cent. The value, or growth factor, is 1.06. The growth factor is then multiplied by the present value to determine the future value.

$$\text{Future Value} = \text{Present Value} * (1 + \text{Growth Rate})^t$$
$$\text{Future Value} = \text{Present Value} * (\text{Growth Factor})$$
$$\text{Future Value} = \text{Present Value} * 1.06$$

Thus, the future value of $1 received one year from now earning 6 per cent annually would be $1 times the growth factor of 1.06 per cent, or $1.06. Had the present value been $100, then the future value would have been $100 times the growth factor of 1.06, or $106.

Had $900 (Present Value) been invested for seven years at 8 per cent per year, the growth factor would be 1.714 (see Table 5-1). Stated differently, the investment would become 1.714 times larger.

$$\text{Future Value} = \text{Present Value} * (1 + \text{Growth Rate})^t$$
$$\text{Future Value} = \$900 * (1 + .08)^7$$
$$\text{Future Value} = \$900 * 1.714$$
$$\text{Future Value} = \$1,542.60$$

Table 5-1 Growth Table

Period	.020	.040	.060	.080
0	1.000	1.000	1.000	1.000
1	1.020	1.040	1.060	1.080
2	1.040	1.082	1.124	1.166
3	1.061	1.125	1.191	1.260
4	1.082	1.170	1.262	1.360
5	1.104	1.217	1.338	1.469
6	1.126	1.265	1.419	1.587
7	1.149	1.316	1.504	1.714
8	1.172	1.369	1.594	1.851
9	1.195	1.423	1.689	1.999

A more complete growth table is presented in Appendix A.

Example One. What is the future value of $500 invested for eight years at 8 per cent? From Table 5-1, the growth factor is found by reading down the column headed eight percent until it intersects with the row corresponding to year eight. The growth factor of 1.851 is multiplied by $500 to arrive at the future value of $925.50.

Example Two. What is the future value of $4 invested at 2 per cent for three years? The growth factor is 1.061 and, when multiplied by the present value of $4, yields a future value of $4.244.

Many of the calculators in use today have the key y^x, called a power function key. It is read, "Raise the value of y to the xth power." Using the previous example of investing $900 for seven years at 8 per cent, the expression would be: "Raise the value of 1.08 to the 7th power." This would be accomplished by entering 1.08 into the calculator, pressing the "y to the x key," 7 equals. The resulting display should be 1.714, the same factor as appears in Table 5-1.

To determine the future value, the factor displayed on the calculator is multiplied by the present value to determine the future value.

Step One: Enter 1 plus the growth rate (1 + .08)
Step Two: Press the key "y to the x"
Step Three: Enter the number of periods growth that will occur (7)
Step Four: Press "=" (The growth factor 1.714 should be displayed)
Step Five: To calculate future value, press "times" and enter the present value of $900
Step Six: Press "=". The result should be the future value of $1,542.60.

§5.05 Solving for Growth Using Exponential Growth Rates

To this point, the growth rate has been known and the future value had to be calculated. In some cases what is unknown is the growth rate. By using Table 5-1, or a calculator, the growth rate may be calculated.

Recall there are four variables involved in the growth calculation. Three variables are known and the fourth is to be calculated. Up to this point, what is known is the present value, the growth rate, and the number of periods growth is to occur. What is being calculated is the future value.

When calculating a growth rate, what is known is the present value, the future value, and the number of periods growth occurs; that is, the number of periods between the future value and the present value. What is not known is the growth rate earned by the investment.

Returning to the question posed in **§5.02,** if a house was purchased for $12,000 and sold 33 years later for $60,000, what was the rate of growth of the investment? The answer to this question can be determined by using the exponential growth formula. What is known is the present value of the house, the future value of the house, and the number of years (growth periods) the house was owned.

$$\text{Future Value} = \text{Present Value} * (1 + \text{Growth Rate})^t$$

The ending value, or future value, is $60,000. The beginning value or present value is $12,000. This means the initial investment of $12,000 has grown at some rate, g, to become $60,000. Since growth has occurred over a 33-year period, t equals 33. What must be calculated is the growth rate.

$$\text{Future Value} = \text{Present Value} * (1 + \text{Growth Rate})^t$$
$$\$60,000 = \$12,000 * (1 + \text{Growth Rate})^{33}$$

This formula can be rearranged as follows:

$$\$60,000 = (1 + \text{Growth Rate})^{33}$$
$$\overline{\phantom{\$60,000 = (1 + \text{Growth Rate})^{33}}}$$
$$\$12,000$$
$$5 = (1 + \text{Growth Rate})^{33}$$
$$5 = (1 + \text{Growth Rate})$$

By referring to the growth table in Appendix A, the growth rate can be determined. The relevant portion of that table is presented in Table 5-2. Since "t," the number of periods of growth occurring, is known to be 33, and since the growth factor is known to be 5, look across row 33 until the growth factor of 5 is found. Read up the column to find the rate of growth. As it turns out, the annual rate of growth of the investment in the house is 5 per cent annually. Or, $12,000 invested at 5 per cent for 33 years will grow to $60,000.

Table 5-2 Growth Table

Year	0.000	.010	.020	.030	.040	.050
25	1.000	1.282	1.641	2.094	2.666	3.386
26	1.000	1.295	1.673	2.157	2.772	3.556
27	1.000	1.308	1.707	2.221	2.883	3.733
28	1.000	1.321	1.741	2.288	2.999	3.920
29	1.000	1.335	1.776	2.357	3.119	4.116
30	1.000	1.348	1.811	2.427	3.243	4.322
31	1.000	1.361	1.848	2.500	3.373	4.538
32	1.000	1.375	1.885	2.575	3.508	4.765
33	1.000	1.389	1.922	2.652	3.648	5.000
34	1.000	1.403	1.961	2.732	3.794	5.253
35	1.000	1.417	2.000	2.814	3.946	5.516

Rather than referring to a table to find the annual growth rate, the calculator can be used. If the calculator has the "y to the x" key, then the growth rate can be determined exactly. Returning to the above example, recall:

$$5 = (1 + \text{Growth Rate})^{33}$$

This can be rewritten as:

$$\sqrt[33]{5} = (1 + \text{Growth Rate})$$

This is read as the 33rd root of 5 is equal to 1 plus the growth rate. Using the calculator with the "y to the x" key:

Step One: Enter "5," the growth factor
Step Two: Press the "y to the x" key
Step Three: Enter the number of periods that growth occured, "33"
Step Four: Press the key "1/X," call the reciprocal
Step Five: Press "=." The factor 1.049979 should appear on the display
Step Six: Press minus 1, (-1), =. The display should show a value of

.049979, which is the annual growth rate using exponential growth

§5.06   Calculating Growth Rates Using Average Percentage Change

When a growth rate is calculated using the method of average percentage change, the economist is striking the average of a series of one-year exponential growth rates. Consider the following values for a $100 investment:

Table 5-3

Year	Investment
1980	$100.00
1981	104.30
1982	107.74
1983	114.45
1984	127.00
1985	138.01

To find the annual rate of increase in the investment from one year to the next, the difference between the two values is divided by the earlier value. In this case, the difference between the 1980 and 1981 values is divided by the 1980 value. The annual rate of increase in the investment is:

$$\frac{1981\ \text{Investment minus 1980 Investment}}{1980\ \text{Investment}}$$

$$\frac{104.30 - 100.00}{100.00}$$

$$\frac{4.30}{100.00}$$

4.30 per cent

In a like manner, the annual rate of return on the investment is computed for each year. The results are presented in Table 5-4.

Table 5-4

Year	Investment	Percentage Return on the Investment
1980	100.00	
1981	104.30	4.30
1982	107.74	3.30
1983	114.45	6.23
1984	127.00	10.97
1985	138.01	8.67
	Sum	33.47
	Average	6.69

The average percentage change is calculated by adding up the column "Percentage Return on the Investment" and dividing by the number of observations, in this case five. The sum of the column is 33.47 and the average percentage change, or growth rate, is 6.69 per cent annually. Again, the rate of growth is estimated to be 6.69 per cent annually. The calculation of the average percentage change requires the calculation of the percentage change from year to year and then determination of the average of the annual changes.

§5.07 —Strengths and Weaknesses of the Methods

Two methods used to calculate growth rates have been examined: the exponential growth and the average percentage change. There are certain characteristics each method possesses that need to be explored.

The exponential growth rate, while easy to calculate, ignores all values between the beginning number and the ending number. Consider the purchase of a share of stock in XYZ Corporation on January 2, 1980. If the stock is sold on January 2, 1986, the rate of growth in the investment is determined by comparing the beginning and ending value of the stock. That is to say, all values between the beginning and ending value are ignored. Suppose two stocks, XYZ and ABC, were both purchased January 2, 1980. Table 5-5 shows the price of each stock on January 2 of the following years.

Table 5-5

Year	XYZ	ABC
1980	$20.00	$20.00
1981	20.00	35.00
1982	20.00	45.00
1983	20.00	55.00
1984	20.00	65.00
1985	20.00	100.00
1986	42.00	42.00

Both stocks opened in 1980 at a price of $20 per share and closed the year 1986 at $42 per share. Using the exponential growth rate, both would have the same growth rate. The $20 invested at the beginning of 1980 has grown at some rate and reached $42 by the end of 1986. The growth rate is 13.16 per cent. But the exponential growth process ignores all the price activity that occurred between the beginning and ending period. Note the difference in the price behavior of the two stocks. The shortcoming is that all activity between the first and last years is ignored. This can result in a biased growth rate being used in the analysis.

The shortcomings of the average percentage change should also be examined. Average percentage change takes into consideration each year's change in values. Consider the following example of changes in salary:

Table 5-6

Year	Salary	Percentage Change
1985	$10,000	
1986	20,000	+ 100%
1987	10,000	- 50%
	Sum	+ 50%

There are two years where the average percentage change was calculated. From 1985 to 1986 the salary increased from $10,000 to $20,000, for an increase of 100 per cent. From 1986 to 1987 the salary decreased from $20,000 to $10,000, for a 50 per cent decrease in salary. On the average the salary had an average increase of 25 per cent [(100% - 50%)/2], yet the beginning and ending salary are the same.

§5.08 The Effect of Growth Rates on Future Earnings

The larger the growth rate employed by the economist, the larger will be the present value of the future earnings. Typically, the plaintiff's attorney will argue for a higher growth rate, and the defendant's attorney will argue for a lower growth rate. The plaintiff's attorney usually argues for a higher growth rate by asking the economist whether the growth rate employed was conservative. The defendant's attorney in turn will ask the economist: "Isn't it true that if a lower growth rate had been employed, then the present value of the future earnings would have been lower?"

The answer to both questions is yes.

§5.09 The Effect of Mathematical Rounding on the Calculated Value of Future Earnings

When examining the growth rate employed to estimate future values, do not ignore the effect mathematical rounding can have on the future values. For example, assume the following annual wages have been gathered from an employer's records:

Table 5-7

Year	Salary
1980	$10,000
1981	11,000
1982	12,300
1983	13,900

Year	Salary
1984	15,200
1985	16,700
1986	19,400

By using the exponential growth method to calculate the historic rate of growth of wages, an annual growth rate of 11.677 per cent is established. This growth rate may be rounded to 12 per cent. If the future wage is to be projected over a long period of time, the roundings may lead to significant differences in the future wage. The further into the future the forecast is being made, the more significant the rounding becomes.

Suppose the $19,400 is the basis for the forecast and a 30-year projection is being made. The growth formula to determine the wages 30 years from today is:

$$\text{Future Value} = \$19,400 * (1 + \text{Growth Rate})^{30}$$

The growth rate may take on the value of 11.677 per cent or be rounded to 12 per cent. The future value using 11.677 per cent is calculated to be $532,983. Using a growth rate of 12 per cent, the future salary is calculated to be $581,222, or 9 per cent higher. This difference is due strictly to rounding 11.677 per cent to 12 per cent.

Had the forecast been only for five years, then the projected salary at the 11.677 per cent annual growth rate is $33.699. An annual growth rate of 12 per cent projects earnings in five years to be $34,189, only 1.5 per cent more than the unrounded value.

§5.10   Sources of Growth Information

In order to determine a growth rate of monies to be received in the future, the economist must establish a basis for the growth rate. Often this is done by examining historic data. The historic growth rate established is then used as the growth rate for future wage or cost projections. The following sections, §§5.09-5.18, present sources of information from which the growth rate may be calculated. Each section shows what the growth rate is, using exponential growth rates and, when possible, the average percentage change. A summary of the data is in §5.19. Sections 5.09 through 5.18 may be omitted without loss of continuity.

§5.11   —Client or Spouse Information

The client and spouse are often the least reliable sources of information available. Usually, the client can give information regarding the income level or how "helpful" an individual was about the home. The client cannot usually provide adequate information on which to base decisions concerning rates of growth of wages. One of the losses considered in a wrongful death or disability case can be that of household services. Often, after the death of a spouse, the deceased partner's worth is substantially altered in the eyes of the survivor.

§5.12 —Employer Records

The following table presents the employer's records and shows the individual's hourly wages. Both the average annual percentage change in wages and the exponential growth rate in the wages are calculated. The growth rate in wages using average percentage change averages 7.42 per cent annually, while growth was 7.40 per cent using exponential change.

Table 5-8

January 1 of each Year	Hourly Wage Rate	Annual Percentage Change
1971	$3.46	
1972	3.75	8.38
1973	3.96	5.60
1974	4.27	7.83
1975	4.55	6.56
1976	4.80	5.49
1977	5.05	5.21
1978	5.38	6.53
1979	6.05	12.45
1980	6.70	10.74
1981	7.23	7.91
1982	7.75	7.19
1983	8.35	7.74
1984	8.99	7.66
1985	9.65	7.34
1986	10.10	4.66
Average Percentage Change		7.42%
Exponential Growth Rate		7.40%

§5.13 —Individual Tax Returns

When using the tax returns as a source of information, the economist must be careful to take the amount listed as wages and salaries. If the spouse of the injured party works, then care must be exercised to deduct that portion which was earned by the spouse. Likewise, care must be taken not to include income which would continue. For example, rental income could continue regardless of the condition of the plaintiff or injured party. This could also be true of dividend income, interest income, and perhaps royalty income.

For the growth rate of wages to be determined, at least two tax returns, or preferably W-2 forms would be necessary. If the 1978 and 1985 W-2 forms were the only two forms available, the exponential growth formula could be used to show the growth rate of wages. For example, if the 1978 wage shown on the W-2 form is $11,190 and the 1985 wage is shown as $20,072, then the growth rate would be 8.71 per cent compounded annually.

§5.14 —Total Private Nonagricultural Hourly Wages

The average hourly wage paid in the total private nonagricultural sector of the United States economy is presented in Table 5-9. The wages were $1.52 per hour in 1952 and have increased steadily each year to the 1986 wage of $8.76 per hour. The average annual percentage increase in wages from 1952 through 1986 inclusive was 5.31 percent, while the exponential rate of growth of wages for the same period of time was 5.29 per cent.

Table 5-9 Total Private Nonagricultural Hourly Wages

Year	Hourly Wage Rate	Annual Percentage Change
1952	$1.52	
1953	1.61	5.92
1954	1.65	2.48
1955	1.71	3.64
1956	1.80	5.26
1957	1.89	5.00
1958	1.95	3.17
1959	2.02	3.59
1960	2.09	3.47
1961	2.14	2.39
1962	2.22	3.74
1963	2.28	2.70
1964	2.36	3.51
1965	2.46	4.24
1966	2.56	4.07
1967	2.68	4.69
1968	2.85	6.34
1969	3.04	6.67
1970	3.23	6.25
1971	3.45	6.81
1972	3.70	7.25
1973	3.94	6.49
1974	4.24	7.61
1975	4.53	6.84
1976	4.86	7.28
1977	5.25	8.02

Year	Hourly Wage Rate	Annual Percentage Change
1978	5.69	8.38
1979	6.16	8.26
1980	6.66	8.12
1981	7.25	8.86
1982	7.68	5.93
1983	8.02	4.43
1984	8.33	3.87
1985	8.57	2.88
1986	8.76	2.22
	Average Percentage Change	5.31%
	Exponential Growth Rate	5.29%

Table 5-9 shows the private nonagricultural wage and the average percentage from one year to the next. Table 5-10 shows the average percentage change from the beginning year (the top row) to any year up to 1986. For example, the wage paid in the private nonagricultural sector in the economy in 1959 was $2.02 per hour (*see* Table 5-9). By 1980 the wage had grown to $6.66 per hour. Table 5-10 shows the average percentage increase in wages from 1959 to 1980 to be 5.86 per cent. If the economist is using a time frame of 1975 to 1986, then Table 5-10 indicates the average growth in wages for that period of time is 6.2 per cent.

Table 5-10 Private Nonagricultural Wage Average Percentage Change

Table 5-10A

From / To	1952	1953	1954	1955	1956	1957	1958	1959
1952								
1953	5.92							
1954	4.20	2.48						
1955	4.01	3.06	3.64					
1956	4.33	3.79	4.45	5.26				
1957	4.46	4.10	4.63	5.13	5.00			
1958	4.25	3.91	4.27	4.48	4.09	3.17		
1959	4.15	3.86	4.13	4.26	3.92	3.38	3.59	
1960	4.07	3.80	4.02	4.10	3.81	3.41	3.53	3.47
1961	3.88	3.63	3.79	3.81	3.52	3.16	3.15	2.93
1962	3.87	3.64	3.78	3.80	3.56	3.27	3.30	3.20
1963	3.76	3.54	3.66	3.67	3.44	3.18	3.18	3.07
1964	3.74	3.54	3.65	3.65	3.45	3.22	3.23	3.16
1965	3.78	3.60	3.70	3.71	3.53	3.35	3.38	3.34
1966	3.80	3.64	3.73	3.74	3.59	3.43	3.46	3.44
1967	3.86	3.71	3.80	3.82	3.69	3.56	3.60	3.60

From To	1952	1953	1954	1955	1956	1957	1958	1959
1968	4.01	3.89	3.99	4.01	3.91	3.81	3.87	3.90
1969	4.17	4.06	4.16	4.20	4.12	4.05	4.13	4.18
1970	4.28	4.19	4.30	4.34	4.27	4.22	4.30	4.37
1971	4.42	4.33	4.44	4.49	4.44	4.40	4.50	4.57
1972	4.56	4.49	4.60	4.66	4.62	4.59	4.69	4.78
1973	4.65	4.59	4.70	4.76	4.73	4.71	4.81	4.90
1974	4.79	4.73	4.84	4.91	4.89	4.88	4.99	5.08
1975	4.87	4.83	4.94	5.00	4.99	4.99	5.10	5.19
1976	4.98	4.93	5.05	5.11	5.11	5.11	5.22	5.31
1977	5.10	5.06	5.18	5.25	5.24	5.26	5.37	5.46
1978	5.22	5.20	5.31	5.38	5.39	5.41	5.52	5.62
1979	5.34	5.31	5.43	5.50	5.51	5.53	5.65	5.75
1980	5.44	5.42	5.53	5.61	5.62	5.65	5.76	5.86
1981	5.55	5.54	5.65	5.73	5.75	5.78	5.89	6.00
1982	5.57	5.55	5.66	5.74	5.76	5.79	5.90	6.00
1983	5.53	5.52	5.62	5.69	5.71	5.73	5.84	5.93
1984	5.48	5.46	5.56	5.63	5.64	5.67	5.76	5.85
1985	5.40	5.38	5.48	5.54	5.55	5.57	5.65	5.73
1986	5.31	5.29	5.37	5.43	5.44	5.45	5.53	5.60

Table 5-10B

From To	1960	1961	1962	1963	1964	1965	1966	1967
1961	2.39							
1962	3.07	3.74						
1963	2.94	3.22	2.70					
1964	3.09	3.32	3.11	3.51				
1965	3.32	3.55	3.48	3.87	4.24			
1966	3.44	3.65	3.63	3.94	4.15	4.07		
1967	3.62	3.82	3.84	4.12	4.33	4.38	4.69	
1968	3.96	4.18	4.26	4.57	4.83	5.03	5.52	6.34
1969	4.26	4.49	4.60	4.92	5.20	5.44	5.90	6.50
1970	4.46	4.69	4.81	5.11	5.37	5.60	5.99	6.42
1971	4.67	4.90	5.03	5.32	5.58	5.80	6.15	6.52
1972	4.89	5.11	5.25	5.54	5.79	6.01	6.33	6.66
1973	5.01	5.23	5.36	5.63	5.87	6.07	6.36	6.63
1974	5.20	5.41	5.55	5.81	6.04	6.24	6.51	6.77
1975	5.31	5.51	5.65	5.90	6.11	6.30	6.55	6.78
1976	5.43	5.63	5.77	6.00	6.21	6.39	6.62	6.84
1977	5.58	5.78	5.92	6.15	6.35	6.53	6.75	6.96
1978	5.74	5.93	6.07	6.30	6.50	6.67	6.89	7.09
1979	5.87	6.06	6.20	6.42	6.61	6.78	6.99	7.18

From To	1960	1961	1962	1963	1964	1965	1966	1967
1980	5.98	6.17	6.31	6.52	6.71	6.87	7.07	7.26
1981	6.12	6.31	6.44	6.65	6.83	7.00	7.19	7.37
1982	6.11	6.29	6.42	6.61	6.78	6.93	7.11	7.27
1983	6.04	6.20	6.32	6.50	6.66	6.79	6.95	7.10
1984	5.95	6.10	6.21	6.38	6.52	6.64	6.78	6.91
1985	5.82	5.97	6.06	6.22	6.35	6.45	6.58	6.68
1986	5.69	5.82	5.90	6.04	6.16	6.25	6.36	6.45

Table 5-10C

From To	1968	1969	1970	1971	1972	1973	1974	1975
1969	6.67							
1970	6.46	6.25						
1971	6.58	6.53	6.81					
1972	6.74	6.77	7.03	7.25				
1973	6.69	6.70	6.85	6.87	6.49			
1974	6.85	6.88	7.04	7.12	7.05	7.61		
1975	6.84	6.87	7.00	7.05	6.98	7.23	6.84	
1976	6.90	6.93	7.05	7.09	7.06	7.25	7.06	7.28
1977	7.02	7.07	7.19	7.25	7.25	7.44	7.38	7.65
1978	7.16	7.22	7.34	7.41	7.44	7.63	7.63	7.90
1979	7.26	7.32	7.44	7.52	7.56	7.73	7.76	7.99
1980	7.33	7.39	7.51	7.58	7.63	7.79	7.82	8.01
1981	7.45	7.51	7.63	7.71	7.76	7.92	7.97	8.15
1982	7.34	7.39	7.49	7.55	7.58	7.70	7.71	7.84
1983	7.15	7.18	7.25	7.29	7.29	7.37	7.35	7.41
1984	6.94	6.96	7.01	7.03	7.01	7.05	7.00	7.02
1985	6.70	6.70	6.74	6.73	6.69	6.71	6.62	6.60
1986	6.45	6.44	6.45	6.43	6.37	6.36	6.26	6.20

Table 5-10D

From To	1976	1977	1978	1979	1980	1981	1982	1983
1977	8.02							
1978	8.20	8.38						
1979	8.22	8.32	8.26					
1980	8.20	8.25	8.19	8.12				
1981	8.33	8.40	8.41	8.49	8.86			
1982	7.93	7.91	7.79	7.64	7.39	5.93		
1983	7.43	7.33	7.12	6.83	6.41	5.18	4.43	
1984	6.98	6.83	6.58	6.24	5.77	4.74	4.15	3.87
1985	6.53	6.34	6.05	5.68	5.19	4.28	3.72	3.37
1986	6.10	5.88	5.57	5.19	4.70	3.86	3.35	2.99

Table 5-10E

From	1984	1985
To		
1985	2.88	
1986	2.55	2.22

Source: Economic Report of the President 292 (1987).

§5.15 —Standard Industrial Classification Tables

When the individual has no earnings history, or a very limited earnings history, the economist will turn to other sources in order to establish a growth rate for wages. Usually the sources used will be government publications. One such publication is the Standard Industrial Classification Tables. As was stated in §2.07, the Standard Industrial Classification Tables are used to facilitate the collection and analysis of economic data. Since the SIC Tables are present hourly wages, the data may be used to establish growth rates for annual wages.

The average hourly wage paid in the Medical Instruments and Supplies Sector of the economy is presented in Table 5-11. The wages of $1.54 per hour in 1952 had increased steadily each year to the 1983 wage of $7.38 per hour. The average annual percentage increase in wages from 1952 through 1983 inclusive was 5.21 per cent, while the exponential rate of growth of wages for the same period of time was 5.18 per cent.

Table 5-11 Medical Instruments and Supplies Hourly Wages SIC Code 384

Year	Hourly Wage Rate	Annual Percentage Change
1952	$1.54	
1953	1.59	3.25
1954	1.64	3.14
1955	1.67	1.83
1956	1.74	4.19
1957	1.82	4.60
1958	1.90	4.40
1959	1.96	3.16
1960	2.00	2.04
1961	2.03	1.50
1962	2.09	2.96
1963	2.13	1.91
1964	2.20	3.29
1965	2.26	2.73
1966	2.35	3.98
1967	2.48	5.53
1968	2.61	5.24

Year	Hourly Wage Rate	Annual Percentage Change
1969	2.75	5.36
1970	2.91	5.82
1971	3.04	4.47
1972	3.17	4.28
1973	3.36	5.99
1974	3.65	8.63
1975	4.02	10.14
1976	4.31	7.21
1977	4.58	6.26
1978	4.93	7.64
1979	5.30	7.51
1980	5.80	9.43
1981	6.43	10.86
1982	7.00	8.86
1983	7.38	5.43

Average Percentage Change 5.21%

Exponential Growth Rate 5.18%

Source: Standard Industrial Classification Tables Manual, U.S. Government Printing Office, Washington, D.C. 143.

§5.16   —Statistical Abstracts of the United States

Tables 5-12 and 5-13 show the median money income for men and women, respectively. These sources of information permit the economist to estimate historic growth rates for the employee based on the number of years of education completed by the individual. When using this source, the growth rate must be calculated using the exponential growth method since not all years are presented. The tables indicate that the median income for men who are high school graduates increased from $8,800 in 1970 to $12,300 in 1978. This is an increase of 6.71 per cent per year. During the same period of time, the income of women in the same category have increased 4.94 per cent annually, from $3,400 to $5,000.

Table 5-12 Median Money Income of Persons with Income by Sex and Educational Attainment 1970 to 1978 (In Thousands of Dollars)

Male

	1970	1974	1976	1978	Growth Rate
Median Income	$7,900	$9,000	$10,100	$11,700	5.03%
Elementary School					
Less than 8 years	3,600	4,500	5,000	5,600	5.68%
8 years	5,400	6,400	6,800	7,500	4.19%

Male

	1970	1974	1976	1978	Growth Rate
High School					
1-3 years	7,300	7,600	7,800	8,600	2.07%
4 years	8,800	9,900	10,700	12,300	4.27%
College					
1-3 years	9,900	9,800	10,600	12,500	2.96%
4 years	12,100	13,400	15,400	17,400	4.65%
5 or more years	13,400	16,200	18,000	21,000	5.77%

Source: US Bureau of Census, Population Report Series P= 60, at 18-500 to -501.

Table 5-13 Median Money Income of Persons with Income by Sex and Educational Attainment 1970 to 1978 (In Thousands of Dollars)

Female

	1970	1974	1976	1978	Growth Rate
Median Income	$2,600	$3,300	$3,900	$4,400	6.80%
Elementary School					
Less than 8 years	1,400	2,100	2,400	2,700	8.56%
8 years	1,800	2,400	2,800	3,100	7.03%
High School					
1-3 years	2,400	2,800	3,100	3,300	4.06%
4 years	3,400	3,800	4,600	5,000	4.94%
College					
1-3 years	3,700	3,800	4,400	5,200	4.35%
4 years	5,400	6,200	7,100	7,800	4.70%
5 or more years	7,900	10,100	10,200	11,100	4.34%

Source: US Bureau of Census, Population Report Series P-60, at 18-500 to -501.

§5.17 —Consumer Price Index

The Consumer Price Index (CPI), published each month by the Bureau of Labor Statistics, is a measure of changes in prices of a fixed "market basket" of goods and services purchased as a normal part of daily life. The CPI considers sales tax but considers neither income tax nor money withheld for Social Security. Price information is collected in 85 areas from nearly 32,400 business enterprises, 24,000 tenants, and 18,000 housing units. "The CPI is

the most representative measure of prices paid by the 'average' American."[1]
It is sometimes referred to as the *cost of living index.*[2]

The historical increase in the CPI can be used as an estimate for the future
growth rate of wages. The rationale is that increases in future wages are an
attempt to maintain purchasing power. Or stated another way, in calculating
the present value of the future income stream, the economist is attempting to
leave the injured party no worse off than had the injury not occurred, by
maintaining the purchasing power of the salary to be received in future periods.

Using the average percentage change, the CPI has increased 4.31 per cent
annually from 1952 to 1986 inclusively, while the exponential growth rate
indicates an average increase of 4.26 per cent annually.

Table 5-14 Consumer Price Index 1952 to 1986

Year	Index	Percentage Change
1952	79.5	
1953	80.1	.75
1954	80.5	.50
1955	80.2	-.37
1956	81.4	1.50
1957	84.3	3.56
1958	86.6	2.73
1959	87.3	.81
1960	88.7	1.60
1961	89.6	1.01
1962	90.6	1.12
1963	91.7	1.21
1964	92.9	1.31
1965	94.5	1.72
1966	97.2	2.86
1967	100.0	2.88
1968	104.2	4.20
1969	109.8	5.37
1970	116.3	5.92
1971	121.3	4.30
1972	125.3	3.30
1973	133.1	6.23
1974	147.7	10.97
1975	161.2	9.14

[1] Chapman, *The Consumer Price Index: A History and Source List,* Reference Serv Rev 47-51 (Winter, 1985).

[2] "When the CPI was first instituted in 1917, it was called the Cost-of-Living Index for the United States, and was used by the Shipbuilding Labor Adjustment Board to crease a fair wage scale for workers in shipbuilding yards."

Year	Index	Percentage Change
1976	170.5	5.77
1977	181.5	6.45
1978	195.4	7.66
1979	217.4	11.26
1980	246.8	13.52
1981	272.4	10.37
1982	289.1	6.13
1983	298.4	3.22
1984	311.1	4.26
1985	322.2	3.57
1986	328.4	1.92

Average Percentage Change 4.31% Exponential Growth Rate 4.26%

Table 5-15 shows the rate of inflation from any year to any year. For example, the average rate of inflation for the period 1975 to 1980 was 8.93 per cent. By reading across the bottom line, 1986, the highest average rate of inflation ending in 1986 was 7.25 per cent. This is the average rate of inflation for the period 1973 to 1986 inclusive.

Table 5-15 Consumer Price Index Average Percentage Change

Table 5-15A

From To	1952	1953	1954	1955	1956	1957	1958	1959
1953	.75							
1954	.63	.50						
1955	.29	.06	−.37					
1956	.59	.54	.56	1.50				
1957	1.19	1.30	1.56	2.53	3.56			
1958	1.44	1.58	1.85	2.60	3.15	2.73		
1959	1.35	1.45	1.64	2.15	2.37	1.77	.81	
1960	1.39	1.48	1.64	2.04	2.18	1.71	1.21	1.60
1961	1.34	1.42	1.55	1.87	1.94	1.54	1.14	1.31
1962	1.32	1.38	1.49	1.76	1.81	1.45	1.14	1.24
1963	1.31	1.37	1.46	1.69	1.72	1.41	1.15	1.24
1964	1.31	1.36	1.45	1.65	1.67	1.40	1.18	1.25
1965	1.34	1.39	1.47	1.66	1.68	1.44	1.26	1.33
1966	1.45	1.50	1.59	1.77	1.79	1.60	1.46	1.55
1967	1.55	1.60	1.69	1.86	1.89	1.73	1.61	1.71
1968	1.71	1.78	1.87	2.04	2.08	1.95	1.87	1.99
1969	1.93	2.00	2.10	2.28	2.34	2.24	2.19	2.33
1970	2.15	2.23	2.34	2.52	2.59	2.52	2.50	2.66
1971	2.26	2.35	2.45	2.63	2.71	2.65	2.64	2.79
1972	2.31	2.40	2.50	2.67	2.74	2.69	2.69	2.83

From	1952	1953	1954	1955	1956	1957	1958	1959
To								
1973	2.50	2.59	2.70	2.87	2.95	2.91	2.92	3.07
1974	2.89	2.99	3.11	3.29	3.39	3.38	3.43	3.60
1975	3.16	3.27	3.40	3.59	3.70	3.70	3.76	3.95
1976	3.27	3.38	3.51	3.69	3.80	3.81	3.87	4.05
1977	3.39	3.50	3.63	3.82	3.93	3.95	4.01	4.19
1978	3.56	3.67	3.80	3.98	4.10	4.12	4.19	4.37
1979	3.84	3.96	4.10	4.29	4.41	4.45	4.53	4.71
1980	4.19	4.32	4.46	4.66	4.79	4.84	4.94	5.13
1981	4.40	4.53	4.68	4.88	5.01	5.07	5.17	5.37
1982	4.46	4.59	4.73	4.92	5.05	5.11	5.21	5.40
1983	4.42	4.54	4.68	4.86	4.99	5.04	5.13	5.31
1984	4.41	4.53	4.67	4.84	4.96	5.01	5.10	5.27
1985	4.39	4.50	4.63	4.80	4.91	4.96	5.04	5.21
1986	4.32	4.42	4.55	4.71	4.81	4.86	4.93	5.08

Table 5-15B

From	1960	1961	1962	1963	1964	1965	1966	1967
To								
1961	1.01							
1962	1.07	1.12						
1963	1.11	1.17	1.21					
1964	1.16	1.21	1.26	1.31				
1965	1.28	1.34	1.42	1.52	1.72			
1966	1.54	1.64	1.78	1.96	2.29	2.86		
1967	1.73	1.85	2.00	2.19	2.49	2.87	2.88	
1968	2.04	2.19	2.36	2.59	2.92	3.31	3.54	4.20
1969	2.41	2.58	2.79	3.06	3.41	3.83	4.15	4.79
1970	2.76	2.95	3.18	3.47	3.83	4.25	4.59	5.16
1971	2.90	3.09	3.31	3.57	3.89	4.26	4.53	4.95
1972	2.93	3.11	3.31	3.54	3.82	4.12	4.33	4.62
1973	3.19	3.37	3.57	3.81	4.09	4.38	4.60	4.89
1974	3.74	3.95	4.19	4.46	4.77	5.11	5.40	5.76
1975	4.10	4.32	4.57	4.85	5.17	5.52	5.81	6.18
1976	4.21	4.42	4.66	4.92	5.22	5.54	5.81	6.13
1977	4.34	4.55	4.78	5.03	5.32	5.62	5.87	6.16
1978	4.52	4.73	4.96	5.20	5.48	5.77	6.02	6.30
1979	4.88	5.09	5.33	5.58	5.87	6.16	6.42	6.71
1980	5.31	5.54	5.78	6.05	6.35	6.65	6.93	7.24
1981	5.55	5.78	6.02	6.29	6.58	6.89	7.16	7.46
1982	5.58	5.79	6.03	6.28	6.56	6.84	7.09	7.37
1983	5.47	5.68	5.89	6.13	6.38	6.64	6.86	7.11
1984	5.42	5.62	5.82	6.04	6.28	6.52	6.72	6.94
1985	5.35	5.53	5.72	5.93	6.15	6.37	6.55	6.76
1986	5.22	5.39	5.56	5.75	5.96	6.16	6.32	6.50

Table 5-15C

From\To	1968	1969	1970	1971	1972	1973	1974	1975
1969	5.37							
1970	5.65	5.92						
1971	5.20	5.11	4.30					
1972	4.72	4.51	3.80	3.30				
1973	5.02	4.94	4.61	4.76	6.23			
1974	6.01	6.14	6.20	6.83	8.60	10.97		
1975	6.46	6.64	6.79	7.41	8.78	10.05	9.14	
1976	6.37	6.52	6.62	7.08	8.03	8.63	7.45	5.77
1977	6.38	6.51	6.59	6.98	7.71	8.08	7.12	6.11
1978	6.51	6.64	6.73	7.07	7.70	8.00	7.25	6.63
1979	6.94	7.10	7.23	7.60	8.21	8.54	8.06	7.78
1980	7.49	7.68	7.86	8.25	8.87	9.25	8.97	8.93
1981	7.71	7.91	8.09	8.47	9.04	9.39	9.17	9.17
1982	7.60	7.77	7.92	8.25	8.75	9.03	8.79	8.74
1983	7.31	7.45	7.56	7.83	8.25	8.45	8.17	8.05
1984	7.12	7.23	7.33	7.56	7.91	8.07	7.78	7.63
1985	6.91	7.00	7.08	7.27	7.58	7.69	7.40	7.22
1986	6.63	6.70	6.75	6.92	7.18	7.25	6.94	6.74

Table 5-15D

From\To	1976	1977	1978	1979	1980	1981	1982	1983
1977	6.45							
1978	7.06	7.66						
1979	8.46	9.46	11.26					
1980	9.72	10.81	12.39	13.52				
1981	9.85	10.70	11.72	11.95	10.37			
1982	9.23	9.79	10.32	10.01	8.25	6.13		
1983	8.37	8.69	8.90	8.31	6.57	4.67	3.22	
1984	7.86	8.06	8.13	7.50	5.99	4.53	3.74	4.26
1985	7.38	7.50	7.48	6.84	5.51	4.29	3.68	3.91
1986	6.84	6.88	6.78	6.14	4.91	3.82	3.24	3.25

Table 5-15E

From\To	1984	1985
1985	3.57	
1986	2.75	1.92

Source: Economic Report of the President, 307, Table B55 (1987).

§5.18 —Industrial Production Index

If the Industrial Production Index is used to calculate the rate of growth of wages, then the growth rates are 3.82 per cent and 3.63 per cent when using the average percentage change or the exponential growth rate, respectively.

Table 5-16 Industrial Production Index 1952 to 1986

Year	Index	Percentage Change
1952	37.2	—
1953	40.4	8.60
1954	36.2	−10.40
1955	43.0	18.78
1956	44.9	4.42
1957	45.5	1.34
1958	42.6	−6.37
1959	47.7	11.97
1960	48.8	2.31
1961	49.1	.61
1962	53.2	8.35
1963	56.3	5.83
1964	60.1	6.75
1965	66.1	9.98
1966	72.0	8.93
1967	73.5	2.08
1968	77.6	5.58
1969	81.2	4.64
1970	78.5	−3.33
1971	79.6	1.40
1972	87.3	9.67
1973	94.4	8.13
1974	93.0	−1.48
1975	84.8	−8.82
1976	92.6	9.20
1977	100.0	7.99
1978	106.5	6.50
1979	110.7	3.94
1980	108.6	−1.90
1981	111.0	2.21
1982	103.1	−7.12
1983	109.2	5.92
1984	121.8	11.54
1985	123.8	1.98
1986	125.1	1.05

Average Percentage Change   3.82%
Exponential Growth Rate   3.63%

Like the other tables, Table 5-17 can be used to show the average rate of growth in the Industrial Production Index for any time period between 1952 and 1986 inclusive.

Table 5-17 Industrial Production Index Average Percentage Change

Table 5-17A

From To	1952	1953	1954	1955	1956	1957	1958	1959
1952								
1953	8.60							
1954	−.90	−10.40						
1955	5.66	4.19	18.78					
1956	5.35	4.27	11.60	4.42				
1957	4.55	3.54	8.18	2.88	1.34			
1958	2.73	1.55	4.54	−.21	−2.52	−6.37		
1959	4.05	3.29	6.03	2.84	2.31	2.80	11.97	
1960	3.83	3.15	5.41	2.73	2.31	2.63	7.14	2.31
1961	3.47	2.83	4.72	2.38	1.97	2.13	4.96	1.46
1962	3.96	3.45	5.18	3.23	3.03	3.37	5.81	3.76
1963	4.13	3.68	5.25	3.56	3.43	3.78	5.81	4.27
1964	4.35	3.96	5.40	3.91	3.85	4.21	5.97	4.77
1965	4.78	4.46	5.82	4.52	4.53	4.93	6.54	5.64
1966	5.08	4.81	6.07	4.92	4.97	5.37	6.84	6.11
1967	4.88	4.61	5.77	4.68	4.71	5.04	6.31	5.61
1968	4.92	4.68	5.75	4.75	4.78	5.09	6.24	5.60
1969	4.91	4.67	5.68	4.74	4.77	5.05	6.09	5.51
1970	4.45	4.20	5.12	4.21	4.19	4.41	5.31	4.70
1971	4.29	4.05	4.90	4.03	4.00	4.20	5.01	4.43
1972	4.56	4.34	5.16	4.36	4.36	4.56	5.34	4.83
1973	4.73	4.53	5.32	4.57	4.58	4.78	5.53	5.07
1974	4.45	4.25	4.98	4.25	4.24	4.42	5.09	4.63
1975	3.87	3.65	4.32	3.60	3.56	3.68	4.27	3.79
1976	4.09	3.89	4.54	3.87	3.84	3.97	4.54	4.11
1977	4.25	4.07	4.69	4.05	4.04	4.17	4.73	4.32
1978	4.33	4.16	4.77	4.16	4.15	4.28	4.82	4.44
1979	4.32	4.15	4.74	4.15	4.14	4.27	4.77	4.41
1980	4.10	3.93	4.48	3.91	3.89	4.00	4.47	4.11
1981	4.03	3.87	4.40	3.84	3.82	3.92	4.37	4.03
1982	3.66	3.49	3.99	3.44	3.40	3.48	3.89	3.54
1983	3.73	3.57	4.05	3.53	3.49	3.58	3.97	3.64
1984	3.97	3.82	4.29	3.79	3.77	3.86	4.25	3.94
1985	3.91	3.76	4.22	3.73	3.71	3.79	4.17	3.87
1986	3.82	3.68	4.12	3.64	3.62	3.70	4.06	3.76

Table 5-17B

From To	1960	1961	1962	1963	1964	1965	1966	1967
1961	.61							
1962	4.48	8.35						
1963	4.93	7.09	5.83					
1964	5.39	6.98	6.29	6.75				
1965	6.31	7.73	7.52	8.37	9.98			
1966	6.74	7.97	7.87	8.55	9.45	8.93		
1967	6.08	6.99	6.71	6.94	7.00	5.50	2.08	
1968	6.01	6.79	6.52	6.66	6.64	5.53	3.83	5.58
1969	5.86	6.52	6.26	6.33	6.24	5.31	4.10	5.11
1970	4.94	5.42	5.06	4.05	3.58	2.24	2.30	
1971	4.62	5.02	4.65	4.50	4.18	3.22	2.08	2.07
1972	5.04	5.44	5.15	5.08	4.87	4.14	3.34	3.59
1973	5.28	5.67	5.42	5.38	5.23	4.64	4.03	4.35
1974	4.80	5.12	4.85	4.76	4.56	3.96	3.34	3.52
1975	3.89	4.12	3.80	3.63	3.34	2.68	1.99	1.97
1976	4.22	4.46	4.18	4.06	3.83	3.27	2.71	2.78
1977	4.44	4.68	4.44	4.34	4.15	3.67	3.19	3.30
1978	4.56	4.79	4.57	4.48	4.32	3.88	3.46	3.59
1979	4.52	4.74	4.53	4.45	4.30	3.89	3.50	3.62
1980	4.20	4.39	4.17	4.08	3.91	3.50	3.12	3.20
1981	4.11	4.28	4.07	3.97	3.81	3.42	3.06	3.12
1982	3.60	3.74	3.51	3.39	3.20	2.80	2.42	2.44
1983	3.70	3.84	3.62	3.51	3.34	2.98	2.63	2.66
1984	4.01	4.16	3.97	3.88	3.74	3.41	3.10	3.16
1985	3.93	4.07	3.88	3.79	3.65	3.34	3.04	3.09
1986	3.82	3.95	3.76	3.67	3.53	3.23	2.94	2.99

Table 5-17C

From To	1968	1969	1970	1971	1972	1973	1974	1975
1969	4.64							
1970	.66	−3.33						
1971	.91	−.96	1.40					
1972	3.10	2.58	5.54	9.67				
1973	4.10	3.97	6.40	8.90	8.13			
1974	3.17	2.88	4.43	5.44	3.32	−1.48		
1975	1.46	.93	1.78	1.88	−.72	−5.15	−8.82	
1976	2.43	2.11	3.02	3.34	1.76	−.37	.19	9.20
1977	3.05	2.85	3.73	4.12	3.00	1.72	2.79	8.59
1978	3.39	3.25	4.07	4.46	3.59	2.68	3.72	7.90
1979	3.44	3.32	4.06	4.39	3.64	2.89	3.76	6.91
1980	3.00	2.85	3.46	3.69	2.95	2.21	2.82	5.15
1981	2.94	2.79	3.35	3.55	2.86	2.21	2.73	4.66

From	1968	1969	1970	1971	1972	1973	1974	1975
To								
1982	2.22	2.03	2.48	2.58	1.87	1.17	1.50	2.98
1983	2.46	2.31	2.74	2.85	2.23	1.64	1.99	3.34
1984	3.01	2.90	3.34	3.49	2.98	2.51	2.91	4.21
1985	2.95	2.84	3.25	3.39	2.90	2.47	2.83	3.99
1986	2.84	2.74	3.12	3.23	2.77	2.36	2.68	3.72

Table 5-17D

From	1976	1977	1978	1979	1980	1981	1982	1983
To								
1977	7.99							
1978	7.25	6.50						
1979	6.15	5.22	3.94					
1980	4.13	2.85	1.02	−1.90				
1981	3.75	2.69	1.42	.16	2.21			
1982	1.94	.73	−.72	−2.27	−2.45	−7.12		
1983	2.51	1.59	.61	−.22	.34	−.60	5.92	
1984	3.59	2.96	2.37	2.06	3.05	3.32	8.54	11.17
1985	3.41	2.84	2.32	2.04	2.83	2.99	6.36	6.57
1986	3.17	2.64	2.16	1.90	2.53	2.60	5.03	4.73

Table 5-17E

From	1984	1985
To		
1985	1.98	
1986	1.51	1.05

Source: Economic Report of the President, 296 (1987)

§5.19   —Census Data

The United States Department of Commerce, Bureau of Census, publishes population and income data by state. As an example, Table 5-18 presents income data for the state of Colorado by education and age of worker. If the economist can obtain the 1970 census data, then the rate of growth of wages could be calculated using the exponential growth formula.

Table 5-18 Income Based on 1980 Census Data State of Colorado

35 to 44 years old

	8th Grade	Education High School Graduate	College Graduate
Mean Annual Income	$13,338	$17,406	$27,813
Mean Annual Earnings	13,011	16,503	26,333
Mean Weekly Earnings	383	339	542

The census data for the state of Colorado breaks the income data down into rural Colorado, the Colorado Springs Standard Metropolitan Statistical Area, and the Denver-Boulder Standard Metropolitan Statistical Area. The income data is also presented by sex and race. The category of race includes white, black, Asian and Pacific Islander, and Spanish origin. Incomes in each of these categories are presented by age category: 18-24, 25-34, 35-44, 45-54, 55-64, 60-64, and over 65.

§5.20 —Professional Publications

Many professional organizations publish salary data. If the data can be obtained, the growth rates may be estimated.

For example, the American Assembly of Collegiate Schools of Business Statistical Service publishes annual salary data for university faculty members employed by schools of business. Table 5-19 shows the salaries for the 1981-1982 academic year and the 1985-1986 academic year. Also shown on the table are the growth rates of salaries between those two points in time as calculated by the exponential growth rate.

Table 5-19 Median Salaries School of Business Faculty by Rank

Rank	1981-82	1985-86	Growth Rate
Professor	$36,500	$47,500	6.81%
Associate Professor	29,500	39,500	7.57
Assistant Professor	25,500	35,500	8.62
Instructor	18,500	23,500	6.16

Other professional publications which would contain income levels would be the American Institute of Certified Public Accountants, trade magazines, and union publications. The *Occupational Outlook Handbook,* published by the United States Department of Labor, Bureau of Labor Statistics, describes various jobs and gives salary ranges.

§5.21 —Medical Price Index

When medical expenses are being estimated, the Medical Price Index may be used to establish the appropriate growth rate. Table 5-20 shows the Medical Price Index from 1952 through 1986 inclusive. As the table indicates, the average percentage increase in the index is 6.07 per cent, while the exponential growth rate is 6.10 per cent.

Table 5-20 Medical Price Index 1952 to 1985

Year	Index	Percentage Change
1952	59.3	—
1953	61.4	3.54
1954	63.4	3.26
1955	64.8	2.21
1956	67.2	3.70
1957	69.9	4.02
1958	73.2	4.72
1959	76.4	4.37
1960	79.1	3.53
1961	81.4	2.91
1962	83.5	2.58
1963	85.6	2.51
1964	87.3	1.99
1965	89.5	2.52
1966	93.4	4.36
1967	100.0	7.07
1968	106.1	6.10
1969	113.4	6.88
1970	120.6	6.35
1971	128.4	6.47
1972	132.5	3.19
1973	137.7	3.92
1974	150.5	9.30
1975	168.6	12.03
1976	184.7	9.55
1977	202.4	9.58
1978	219.4	8.40
1979	239.7	9.25
1980	265.9	10.93
1981	294.5	10.76
1982	328.7	11.61
1983	357.3	8.70
1984	379.2	6.13
1985	403.1	6.30
1986	433.5	7.54

Average Percentage Change 6.07%
Exponential Growth Rate 6.10%

Table 5.21 presents the annual average rate of increase in the Medical Price Index for the years 1952 through 1986 inclusive.

Table 5-21 Medical Price Index Average Percentage Change

Table 5-21A

From / To	1952	1953	1954	1955	1956	1957	1958	1959
1952								
1953	3.54							
1954	3.40	3.26						
1955	3.00	2.73	2.21					
1956	3.18	3.06	2.96	3.70				
1957	3.35	3.30	3.31	3.86	4.02			
1958	3.57	3.58	3.66	4.15	4.37	4.72		
1959	3.69	3.71	3.80	4.20	4.37	4.55	4.37	
1960	3.67	3.69	3.76	4.07	4.16	4.21	3.95	3.53
1961	3.58	3.59	3.64	3.88	3.91	3.88	3.60	3.22
1962	3.48	3.48	3.51	3.69	3.69	3.62	3.35	3.01
1963	3.40	3.38	3.40	3.54	3.52	3.44	3.18	2.88
1964	3.28	3.25	3.25	3.37	3.33	3.23	2.98	2.70
1965	3.22	3.19	3.19	3.29	3.24	3.14	2.92	2.67
1966	3.30	3.28	3.29	3.38	3.35	3.28	3.10	2.91
1967	3.55	3.55	3.58	3.69	3.69	3.66	3.54	3.43
1968	3.71	3.72	3.76	3.88	3.89	3.88	3.79	3.73
1969	3.90	3.92	3.96	4.09	4.12	4.13	4.07	4.04
1970	4.03	4.06	4.11	4.24	4.28	4.30	4.26	4.25
1971	4.16	4.20	4.25	4.38	4.42	4.45	4.43	4.44
1972	4.11	4.14	4.19	4.31	4.35	4.37	4.34	4.34
1973	4.10	4.13	4.18	4.29	4.32	4.34	4.32	4.31
1974	4.34	4.38	4.43	4.55	4.60	4.63	4.63	4.65
1975	4.67	4.73	4.80	4.93	4.99	5.04	5.06	5.11
1976	4.88	4.94	5.01	5.15	5.22	5.28	5.31	5.37
1977	5.07	5.13	5.21	5.35	5.43	5.50	5.54	5.60
1978	5.19	5.26	5.34	5.48	5.56	5.63	5.68	5.75
1979	5.34	5.41	5.50	5.64	5.72	5.80	5.85	5.92
1980	5.54	5.62	5.71	5.85	5.94	6.02	6.08	6.16
1981	5.72	5.80	5.90	6.04	6.13	6.22	6.28	6.37
1982	5.92	6.00	6.10	6.24	6.34	6.44	6.51	6.60
1983	6.01	6.09	6.19	6.33	6.43	6.52	6.59	6.69
1984	6.01	6.09	6.19	6.33	6.42	6.51	6.58	6.66
1985	6.02	6.10	6.19	6.32	6.41	6.50	6.57	6.65
1986	6.07	6.14	6.23	6.36	6.45	6.54	6.60	6.68

Table 5-21B

From / To	1960	1961	1962	1963	1964	1965	1966	1967
1961	2.91							

From To	1960	1961	1962	1963	1964	1965	1966	1967
1962	2.74	2.58						
1963	2.67	2.55	2.51					
1964	2.50	2.36	2.25	1.99				
1965	2.50	2.40	2.34	2.25	2.52			
1966	2.81	2.79	2.84	2.95	3.44	4.36		
1967	3.42	3.50	3.69	3.98	4.65	5.71	7.07	
1968	3.75	3.87	4.09	4.41	5.01	5.84	6.58	6.10
1969	4.10	4.25	4.49	4.82	5.38	6.10	6.68	6.49
1970	4.33	4.48	4.72	5.04	5.55	6.15	6.60	6.44
1971	4.52	4.68	4.92	5.22	5.68	6.20	6.57	6.45
1972	4.41	4.55	4.74	4.99	5.37	5.77	6.01	5.80
1973	4.37	4.49	4.67	4.88	5.21	5.54	5.71	5.49
1974	4.72	4.86	5.05	5.29	5.62	5.96	6.16	6.03
1975	5.21	5.38	5.59	5.85	6.20	6.57	6.81	6.78
1976	5.48	5.65	5.87	6.13	6.48	6.84	7.09	7.09
1977	5.72	5.90	6.12	6.38	6.72	7.07	7.31	7.34
1978	5.87	6.05	6.26	6.51	6.84	7.17	7.40	7.43
1979	6.05	6.22	6.44	6.68	7.00	7.32	7.55	7.59
1980	6.29	6.47	6.69	6.93	7.24	7.56	7.79	7.84
1981	6.51	6.69	6.90	7.15	7.45	7.76	7.98	8.05
1982	6.74	6.92	7.14	7.38	7.68	7.98	8.21	8.29
1983	6.82	7.00	7.21	7.45	7.74	8.02	8.24	8.31
1984	6.80	6.96	7.16	7.38	7.65	7.92	8.12	8.19
1985	6.78	6.94	7.13	7.34	7.59	7.84	8.03	8.08
1986	6.80	6.96	7.14	7.34	7.59	7.83	8.00	8.05

Table 5.21C

From To	1968	1969	1970	1971	1972	1973	1974	1975
1969	6.88							
1970	6.61	6.35						
1971	6.57	6.41	6.47					
1972	5.72	5.34	4.83	3.19				
1973	5.36	4.98	4.53	3.56	3.92			
1974	6.02	5.85	5.72	5.47	6.61	9.30		
1975	6.88	6.88	6.98	7.11	8.42	10.66	12.03	
1976	7.21	7.26	7.41	7.60	8.70	10.29	10.79	9.55
1977	7.47	7.55	7.72	7.93	8.88	10.11	10.39	9.57
1978	7.57	7.64	7.80	8.00	8.80	9.77	9.89	9.18
1979	7.72	7.80	7.97	8.15	8.86	9.68	9.76	9.20
1980	7.99	8.09	8.26	8.46	9.12	9.86	9.96	9.54
1981	8.20	8.31	8.49	8.69	9.30	9.97	10.07	9.75
1982	8.44	8.56	8.75	8.96	9.53	10.16	10.26	10.01
1983	8.46	8.57	8.75	8.94	9.46	10.01	10.09	9.85

From	1968	1969	1970	1971	1972	1973	1974	1975
To								
1984	8.32	8.41	8.56	8.72	9.18	9.66	9.69	9.43
1985	8.20	8.28	8.41	8.55	8.96	9.38	9.39	9.12
1986	8.16	8.24	8.35	8.48	8.86	9.24	9.23	8.98

Table 5-21D

From	1976	1977	1978	1979	1980	1981	1982	1983
To								
1977	9.58							
1978	8.99	8.40						
1979	9.08	8.83	9.25					
1980	9.54	9.53	10.09	10.93				
1981	9.78	9.83	10.31	10.84	10.76			
1982	10.09	10.19	10.64	11.10	11.18	11.61		
1983	9.89	9.94	10.25	10.50	10.36	10.16	8.70	
1984	9.42	9.40	9.56	9.63	9.30	8.81	7.42	6.13
1985	9.07	9.01	9.10	9.07	8.70	8.19	7.04	6.22
1986	8.92	8.85	8.90	8.85	8.51	8.06	7.17	6.66

Table 5-21E

From	1984	1985
To		
1985	6.30	
1986	6.92	7.54

Source: Economic Report of the President, 307, Table B55 (1987).

§5.22 Comparing the Growth Rates

The present value of the future income stream is directly affected by the size of the growth factor. Table 5-22 shows the impact of changing the growth rates.

In the following example, the current salary is $20,000. The present value is being calculated for this year and 29 future years. The only variable is the growth rate. The table also shows the annual salary 29 years in the future. The assumed discount rate, or interest rate, is zero.

Table 5-22 Present Value of Future Wages

	Growth Rate	Salary In 28 Years	Present Value
Employer Records			
Average Percentage Change	7.42%	$159,404	$2,038,164
Exponential Growth Rate	7.40%	158,356	2,030,783
Standard Industrial Classification			
Total Private Nonagricultural			
Average Percentage Change	5.31%	89,670	1,401,729
Exponential Growth Rate	5.29%	89,178	1,396,886

	Growth Rate	Salary In 28 Years	Present Value
Standard Industrial Classification			
Medical Instruments and Supplies			
Average Percentage Change	5.21%	87,234	1,377,704
Exponential Growth Rate	5.18%	86,515	1,370,590
Consumer Price Index			
Average Percentage Change	4.31%	67,996	1,181,589
Exponential Growth Rate	4.26%	67,057	1,171,681
Industrial Production Index			
Average Percentage Change	3.82%	59,317	1,088,560
Exponential Growth Rate	3.63%	56,248	1,054,824

The current salary is $20,000. Depending on the growth rate employed, the salary 29 years in the future will range from a low of $56,248 to a high of $159,404. In the same fashion, the growth rate is also the only variable affecting the size of the present value of future wages. The range is from a low of $1,054,824 to a high of $2,038,164. These highs and lows may be seen in Tables 5-23 and 5-24.

Table 5-23 Future Annual Wage Earnings Growth Based on Earnings Changes Indicated by Employer's Records

Period	Future Salary 7.42% Annual Growth	Total Income	Future Salary 7.40% Annual Growth	Total Income
0	$20,000	$20,000	$20,000	$20,000
1	21,484	41,484	21,480	41,480
2	23,078	64,562	23,070	64,550
3	24,791	89,353	24,777	89,326
4	26,630	115,983	26,610	115,936
5	28,606	144,588	28,579	144,516
6	30,728	175,317	30,694	175,210
7	33,009	208,325	32,966	208,175
8	35,458	243,783	35,405	243,580
9	38,089	281,872	38,025	281,605
10	40,915	322,787	40,839	322,444
11	43,951	366,738	43,861	366,305
12	47,212	413,950	47,107	413,411
13	50,715	464,665	50,592	464,004
14	54,478	519,143	54,336	518,340
15	58,520	577,663	58,357	576,697
16	62,863	640,526	62,676	639,373
17	67,527	708,053	67,314	706,686

Period	Future Salary 7.42% Annual Growth	Total Income	Future Salary 7.40% Annual Growth	Total Income
18	72,538	780,590	72,295	778,981
19	77,920	858,510	77,645	856,626
20	83,701	942,211	83,390	940,016
21	89,912	1,032,124	89,561	1,029,577
22	96,584	1,128,707	96,189	1,125,766
23	103,750	1,232,457	103,307	1,229,073
24	111,448	1,343,906	110,951	1,340,024
25	119,718	1,463,623	119,162	1,459,186
26	128,601	1,592,224	127,980	1,587,166
27	138,143	1,730,367	137,450	1,724,616
28	148,393	1,878,760	147,622	1,872,238
29	159,404	2,038,164	158,546	2,030,783

Table 5-24 Future Annual Wage And Total Life Time Income Earnings Growth Based on Changes in the Industrial Production Index

Period	Future Salary 3.82% Annual Growth	Total Income	Future Salary 3.63% Annual Growth	Total Income
0	$20,000	$20,000	$20,000	$20,000
1	20,764	40,764	20,726	40,726
2	21,557	62,321	21,478	62,204
3	22,381	84,702	22,258	84,462
4	23,236	107,937	23,066	107,528
5	24,123	132,061	23,903	131,432
6	25,045	157,105	24,771	156,203
7	26,001	183,107	25,670	181,873
8	26,995	210,102	26,602	208,475
9	28,026	238,127	27,568	236,042
10	29,096	267,224	28,568	264,611
11	30,208	297,432	29,605	294,216
12	31,362	328,794	30,680	324,896
13	32,560	361,354	31,794	356,690
14	33,804	395,157	32,948	389,638
15	35,095	430,252	34,144	423,782
16	36,436	466,688	35,383	459,165
17	37,827	504,515	36,668	495,832
18	39,272	543,788	37,999	533,831

Period	Future Salary 3.82% Annual Growth	Total Income	Future Salary 3.63% Annual Growth	Total Income
19	40,773	584,561	39,378	573,209
20	42,330	626,891	40,807	614,017
21	43,947	670,838	42,289	656,306
22	45,626	716,464	43,824	700,129
23	47,369	763,833	45,415	745,544
24	49,178	813,011	47,063	792,607
25	51,057	864,068	48,772	841,379
26	53,007	917,076	50,542	891,921
27	55,032	972,108	52,377	944,298
28	57,135	1,029,243	54,278	998,576
29	59,317	1,088,560	56,248	1,054,824

The attorney should make sure the proper growth rate is employed by the economist. For example, it would be improper for the economist to use the rate of growth indicated by the Medical Price Index when calculating the present value of a future wage stream. Likewise, growth rates based on wages would be inappropriate when calculating future medical expenses.

§5.23 Summary

Growth rates are critical to the present value calculation. The higher the growth rate, the greater the present value of the future income stream. Growth rates are typically calculated using the average percentage change method or the exponential rate of growth. Care should be taken to insure that the growth rate employed by the economist is a relevant growth rate. Finally, the attorney should make sure that mathematical rounding has not added an unusually large amount of money to the economist's figures.

§5.24 Direct Examination

The purpose of the direct examination is to educate the jury in the economic principles needed to establish the economic loss. The economist, while in the courtroom, is primarily an educator. The economist is to explain what the present value concept is, how it is done mathematically, and how it is relevant in this case. Since a growth rate is employed, it is necessary for the economist to explain why growth is important, how it is incorporated into the analysis, and why the particular growth rate was chosen.

§5.25 Cross-Examination

The cross-examination is to establish two things. First, it is essential that the cross-examination establish the figures used as the growth rate are historically accurate. This means that the source and the numbers should be examined for accuracy. The second thing the defense attorney wishes to do is introduce the thought to the jury that the economist has used a growth rate that purposefully increases the size of the economic loss.

For example, if the economist has relied upon data published by the Bureau of Labor Statistics, United States Department of Labor, check to make sure that data available for the specific city or region might not result in a lower growth rate than that for the nation as a whole. The national statistics may tend to ignore geographic differences in certain job categories.

The tables showing the growth rates over the different time periods can also be used to show that the economist could have picked a different time frame and thus used a different growth rate, i.e., a lower growth rate.

6 Discount Rates: The Present Value Calculation

$$\text{Present Value} = \sum_{t=0}^{n} \$ * M * (1+G)^t/(1+D)^t * PL * PS * PF * C * HS * TX$$

§6.01   Introduction

This chapter will explain what present value is and how present value is calculated. Since the present value is determined by the rate of earnings on invested funds, returns on alternative investments will be explored, and the impact that alternative investments have on present value will be evaluated.

This chapter also contains the return each year for several types of investments. The average annual return by year from 1952 through 1986 is presented for investments in three-month Treasury Bills, six-month Treasury Bills, one-year Treasury Bills, long term government securities with 10-year maturities, Moody's Aaa Bonds, Moody's Baa Bonds, and high grade municipal Bonds.

§6.02   What Is Meant by Discounting and Present Value

When the economist calculates the present value of a future stream of dollars, be it income, medical expenses, household services, or dividends, it is necessary to reduce future dollars to present dollars called *present value*. The reducing of future dollars to present dollars is *discounting*. Stated another way, discounting determines the present value of future dollars.

Although discussed in the context of the Employer's Liability Act of April 22, 1908,[1] as amended by the Act of April 5, 1910,[2] the United States Supreme Court in *Chesapeake & Ohio Railroad v Kelly*[3] mandated that awards for future damages be discounted to present value at some appropriate discount rate. The appropriate rate of interest was recognized as that which would be earned on "the best and safest investments."[4] As a result, both state and federal courts have developed varying approaches.[5]

An example of discounting occurs when a family plans to pay $5,000 college tuition for a child five years from today. It is not necessary to place $5,000 in an investment account today. Money invested will earn a return each year. What must be placed in the account today is an amount of money which, when combined with the interest earned, will be equal to $5,000 in five years. The amount of money placed in the account today is the present value of $5,000. How much should be placed in the account depends on the interest rate, or earnings rate. The amount of money earned in interest will depend on what type of investment is made.

---

[1] Ch 149, 35 Stat 65.

[2] Ch 143, 36 Stat 291.

[3] 241 US 485 (1916).

[4] *Id.* 491.

[5] Baulieu v Elliot, 434 P2d 665 (Alaska 1967); Kuczkowski v Bolubasz, 491 Pa 561, 421 A2d 1027 (1980).

§6.03   The Present Value Formula for One Future Payment

In order to determine the present value of one dollar received in the future, the following formula is employed:

$$\text{Present Value} = 1/(1+i)^t$$

Where   "i" is the interest or discount rate
         "t" is the number of periods until the dollar is received

If the interest or discount rate is assumed to be 6 per cent and "t" is assumed to be 12 years, then the expression asks: "What is the present value of $1 received in 12 years if the investment earns 6 per cent per year?"

Table 6-1 can be used to determine the present value of one dollar received some time in the future. A more complete table is presented in Appendix B.

Table 6-1   Present Value of $1 Payment Received in "t" Periods

	Discount Rate in Per Cent				
Period	2%	4%	6%	8%	10%
1	.980	.962	.943	.926	.909
2	.961	.925	.890	.857	.826
3	.942	.889	.840	.794	.751
4	.924	.855	.792	.735	.683
5	.906	.822	.747	.681	.621
6	.888	.790	.705	.630	.564
7	.871	.760	.665	.583	.513
8	.853	.731	.627	.540	.467
9	.837	.703	.592	.500	.424
10	.820	.676	.558	.463	.386
11	.804	.650	.527	.429	.350
12	.788	.625	.497	.397	.319
13	.773	.601	.469	.368	.290
14	.758	.577	.442	.340	.263
15	.743	.555	.417	.315	.239

To find the present value of $1 received in 12 years earning 6 per cent per period, read across the row labeled "12" until it intersects with the column headed "6%." Where they intersect the factor is .497. The present value of $1 received in 12 periods earning at 6 per cent is 49.7 cents. The .497 is also called the *present value factor.*

In order to find the present value of more than one dollar, the present value factor is multiplied by the number of dollars to be received in the future.

Returning to the earlier question of the tuition payment of $5,000 in five years, the amount of money that must be set aside now depends on the amount of interest the investment can earn. Suppose current investments earn 10 per cent. The discount factor from Table 6-1 would be .621. The discount factor is found where the row headed "5" intersects with the column headed "10%." This means that for every one dollar needed in five years, 62.1 cents must be invested now. The present value of the tuition payment is $3,105, or $5,000 times the factor of .621.

§6.04   The Present Value Formula When Payments Occur in More Than One Future Period

Many times the payments made, or income received, occurs more than once. Such is the case with mortgage payments, car payments, and tuition payments. Likewise, income is not received once in a lifetime but rather each month of employment.

Suppose $5,000 in annual tuition were to be paid each year for four years with the first payment starting one year from today. What is the present value of the tuition payments? The present value will depend on the interest which can be earned on the investment. Assume the current earnings on passbook savings is 6 per cent per year.

The present value of the four tuition payments would be calculated by multiplying the annual payment of $5,000 by the discount factor found in Table 6-1.

Table 6-2 The Present Value of Tuition Payments

Year	Tuition	Factor		
1	$5,000	× .943	=	$ 4,715
2	5,000	× .890	=	4,450
3	5,000	× .840	=	4,200
4	5,000	× .792	=	3,960
	Present Value			$17,325

The present value of the tuition payment for each year is shown in Table 6-2. The present value of the payment due in one year is $4,715, for year two the present value is $4,450, and so on. The present value of all the tuition payments is $17,325.

Since all future payments are the same, the present value factors could have been summed and multiplied by the future value $5,000. The sum of the factors is 3.465 and, when multiplied by $5,000, yields the same present value of $17,325.

The following formula can be used to determine the present value factor, or present value of $1, when there are "t" future payments.

$$\text{Present Value} = \frac{1[1/(1+i)^t]}{i}$$

Where   "i" is the interest or discount rate
"t" is the number of periods payments are received

The formula may be used to calculate the present value of a stream of future payments. For example, what is the present value of $1 received each year for the next 5 years if the investment earns 6 per cent per year. Table 6-3 presents the present value factors.

All Table 6-3 does is add. Any factor on the table is the summation from Table 6-1. In the tuition example, the sum of discount factors from Table 6-1 was 3.465. This factor can be found in Table 6-3 where the row "4" intersects with the column headed "6%."

Table 6-1 is used when one future payment occurs; Table 6-3 is used when more than one future payment occurs. When using Table 6-3 the payments must be equal.

Table 6-3 Present Value of $1 Payment Received Each Period for "t" Periods

Discount Rate in Per Cent

Period	2%	4%	6%	8%	10%
1	.980	.962	.943	.926	.909
2	1.942	1.886	1.833	1.783	1.736
3	2.884	2.775	2.673	2.577	2.487
4	3.808	3.630	3.465	3.312	3.170
5	4.713	4.452	4.212	3.993	3.791
6	5.601	5.242	4.917	4.623	4.355
7	6.472	6.002	5.582	5.206	4.868
8	7.325	6.733	6.210	5.747	5.335
9	8.162	7.435	6.802	6.247	5.759
10	8.983	8.111	7.360	6.710	6.145
11	9.787	8.760	7.887	7.139	6.495
12	10.575	9.385	8.384	7.536	6.814
13	11.348	9.986	8.853	7.904	7.103
14	12.106	10.563	9.295	8.244	7.367
15	12.849	11.118	9.712	8.559	7.606

§6.05 —Calculating Present Value When Payments Do Not Start Immediately

Tuition payments for a younger child may not start for six years. When the tuition payments do start they will be $6,000 each year for four years. The present value of the payments will depend on the interest which can be earned on the investment. Assume an 8 per cent yield on the investment.

There are two methods for calculating the present value of the future tuition payments. The first method is to treat each payment separately using Table 6-1. The other method is to treat them as identical future payments and use Table 6-3. In either case the answers should be the same.

Using Table 6-1 the future value of $6,000 is multiplied by the appropriate discount factor in order to determine the present value of each individual payment. The entire present value is then determined by summing the present value of the individual payments.

Table 6-4 Present Value of Tuition Payments

Period	Tuition Payment		Discount Factor		Present Value
6	$6,000	×	.630	=	$ 3,780
7	6,000	×	.583	=	3,498
8	6,000	×	.540	=	3,240
9	6,000	×	.500	=	3,000

Total Present Value $13,518

The present value of the future tuition payments is $13,518. The same results can be achieved using Table 6-3. A stream of tuition payments starting in one year ending nine years from today has a present value factor of 6.247. But the first five years are not to be paid, thus they may be deducted. The present value factor for the first five years is 3.993. The difference between 6.247 and 3.993 is 2.254, which is the present value factor of $1 received in years six through nine. The present value of the tuition payments is $6,000 times the factor 2.254 which equals $13,524. The differences in the two answers is due to rounding in the tables.

§6.06 —Calculating Present Value When Payments Are Not the Same Size

If the future payments are not the same size, then Tables 6-1 and 6-3 are combined to find the present value. Suppose an individual were to receive from a trust fund the following payments: $10,000 in five years, $12,000 in six years, and $12,000 in ten years, and $3,000 each year for ten years with payments starting in three years.

Again, it is necessary to make an interest assumption. Suppose the funds can be invested to earn 10 per cent annually. Once the interest rate is known, the present value can be determined. The present value of the three payments of $10,000, $12,000, and $15,000 can be calculated using Table 6-1. The annual payment of $3,000 for ten years can be calculated from either table, but it is faster to use Table 6-3.

From Table 6-1:

Year	Amount to Be Received	Discount Factor	Present Value
5	$ 5,000	.621	$ 3,105
6	10,000	.564	5,640
10	12,000	.386	4,632
	Present Value		$13,377

From Table 6-3:
Discount factor for 12 years at 10% =   6.814

Discount factor for   2 years at 10% = $\underline{1.736}$

The difference   5.078

The annual payment of $3,000 times the factor of 5.078 gives a present value of the annuity of $15,234. This added to the present value of the lump sum payments gives a total present value of $28,611.

§6.07   A Primer on Evaluating Structured Settlements

The process presented in §§6.03-6.06 can be used in evaluating basic structured settlement offers.[6] The defendant or the defendant's insurance carrier makes an offer to the plaintiff or plaintiff's attorney. The offer may appear in the following form:

> The plaintiff will be paid $5,000 on the fifth, tenth and fifteenth anniversaries of the settlement. In addition, the plaintiff will receive $12,000 per year for 15 years, the first payment to be on the first anniversary of the settlement.

In order to estimate the present value of the offer, it would be necessary to determine the interest being assumed by the defendant or the defendant's insurance carrier. If the interest rate can be determined, the present value can be calculated using Tables 6-1 and 6-3.

If the interest rate is 8 per cent, the $5,000 payments received the fifth, tenth, and fifteenth anniversaries have a present value of $3,405, $2,315, and $1,575, respectively. The 15-year annuity is $12,000 times the present value factor 8.559 (from Table 6-3). The present value of the annuity is $102,708. The offer is $110,003, which is the sum of the present value of the 15-year annuity and the three payments of $5,000 each.

§6.08   How the Discount or Interest Rate Affects Present Value

It is extremely important to choose an appropriate discount rate. The higher the interest rate, the smaller will be the present value of the future stream of dollars. For example, suppose the present value of $10,000 received each year for the next 15 years is to be calculated. If the appropriate interest rate is 2 per cent annually, then the discount factor is 12.849 (from Table 6-3) and the present value is $128,490. However, if the appropriate discount rate is 10 per cent annually, then the discount factor declines to 7.606 and the present value of the stream of income is only $76,060. The difference between the two figures, $52,430, is due strictly to the difference in the interest rate assumed.

The defendant's attorney will argue that the economist's discount rate is too

---

[6] N. Jacob & R. Pettit, Investments 504 (1984).

low, while the plaintiff's attorney will argue that the economist has been very conservative by using such a high interest assumption.

§6.09   Types of Investments

There is much debate over what is an appropriate type of investment to consider when discounting to present value. **Sections 6.11 through 6.18** will present different types of investments and calculate the yields on the various investments. These sections may be skipped without loss of continuity. The investments which will be considered are: three-month Treasury Bills; six-month Treasury Bills; one-year Treasury Bills; long-term government bonds; corporate bonds; municipal bonds; common stock; and finally, combinations of the various investments.

§6.10   Returns

The following sections show the historical returns which could have been earned on alternative investments. The tables show what the average annual return on the investments starting in any year from 1952 and running through 1986. These tables may be used as a quick reference to determine the approximate yield from various investments. These sections can be skipped without loss of continuity.

§6.11   —Three-Month Treasury Bills

A Treasury Bill (T-Bill) is a short-term obligation of the United States government. The bills mature in 13, 26, or 52 weeks. The 13-week and 26-week bills are auctioned each week by the Treasury Department and the 52-week bills are auctioned once a month.[7] T-Bills are sold in increments of $5,000, starting at $10,000. The bills pay no interest; rather, they are sold at discount. This means that, if the purchase of a $10,000 T-Bill maturing in one year is made today, the purchase price will be less than $10,000. The difference between the purchase price and the $10,000 maturity value is the return, or interest, paid on the investment. As Table 6-5 shows, an investment in three-month Treasury Bills has averaged a return of 5.39 per cent since 1952.

---

[7] There are other types of bonds, such as the low-coupon bond and the zero-rate bond. In the case of the low-coupon bond, the semiannual interest payments are less than the market would dictate. Consequently, the bonds' selling price is below par value. This means that some of the return to the investor is being returned through a capital gain. Zero rate bonds pay no interest. The return is the difference between the current price and the maturity value.

Table 6-5 Return on Three-Month Treasury Bills

Year	Yield in Per Cent
1952	1.76
1953	1.93
1954	.95
1955	1.753
1956	2.66
1957	3.27
1958	1.84
1959	3.41
1960	2.93
1961	2.38
1962	2.78
1963	3.16
1964	3.55
1965	3.95
1966	4.88
1967	4.32
1968	5.34
1969	6.68
1970	6.46
1971	4.35
1972	4.07
1973	7.04
1974	7.89
1975	5.38
1976	4.99
1977	5.27
1978	7.22
1979	10.04
1980	11.51
1981	14.08
1982	10.69
1983	8.63
1984	9.58
1985	7.49
1986	5.98
Average Return	5.39%

Table 6-6 Return on Three-Month Treasury Bills (Average)

Table 6-6A

From / To	1952	1953	1954	1955	1956	1957	1958	1959
1952	1.77							
1953	1.85	1.93						
1954	1.55	1.44	.95					
1955	1.60	1.54	1.35	1.75				
1956	1.81	1.82	1.79	2.21	2.66			
1957	2.05	2.11	2.16	2.56	2.96	3.27		
1958	2.02	2.07	2.09	2.38	2.59	2.56	1.84	
1959	2.20	2.26	2.31	2.59	2.79	2.84	2.62	3.41
1960	2.28	2.34	2.40	2.64	2.82	2.86	2.73	3.17
1961	2.29	2.35	2.40	2.61	2.75	2.77	2.64	2.91
1962	2.33	2.39	2.44	2.63	2.75	2.77	2.67	2.88
1963	2.40	2.46	2.51	2.69	2.80	2.82	2.75	2.93
1964	2.49	2.55	2.61	2.77	2.89	2.92	2.86	3.04
1965	2.59	2.66	2.72	2.88	2.99	3.03	3.00	3.17
1966	2.75	2.82	2.89	3.05	3.16	3.21	3.21	3.38
1967	2.85	2.92	2.99	3.14	3.26	3.32	3.32	3.48
1968	2.99	3.07	3.14	3.30	3.42	3.48	3.50	3.67
1969	3.20	3.28	3.37	3.53	3.65	3.73	3.77	3.94
1970	3.37	3.46	3.55	3.71	3.84	3.92	3.98	4.15
1971	3.42	3.50	3.59	3.75	3.87	3.95	4.00	4.17
1972	3.45	3.53	3.62	3.77	3.88	3.96	4.01	4.16
1973	3.61	3.70	3.79	3.94	4.06	4.14	4.20	4.35
1974	3.80	3.89	3.98	4.14	4.26	4.35	4.41	4.57
1975	3.88	3.98	4.07	4.22	4.34	4.43	4.49	4.65
1976	3.93	4.02	4.11	4.25	4.37	4.46	4.52	4.67
1977	3.98	4.07	4.16	4.30	4.41	4.50	4.56	4.70
1978	4.10	4.19	4.28	4.42	4.53	4.62	4.68	4.83
1979	4.31	4.41	4.50	4.64	4.76	4.85	4.93	5.07
1980	4.56	4.66	4.76	4.91	5.03	5.13	5.21	5.37
1981	4.88	4.98	5.09	5.24	5.38	5.49	5.58	5.74
1982	5.07	5.18	5.29	5.45	5.58	5.70	5.79	5.96
1983	5.18	5.29	5.40	5.56	5.69	5.80	5.90	6.06
1984	5.31	5.42	5.54	5.69	5.83	5.94	6.04	6.20
1985	5.38	5.49	5.60	5.75	5.88	5.99	6.09	6.25
1986	5.39	5.50	5.61	5.75	5.88	5.99	6.09	6.24

Table 6-6B

From / To	1960	1961	1962	1963	1964	1965	1966	1967
1960	2.93							
1961	2.66	2.38						

From To	1960	1961	1962	1963	1964	1965	1966	1967
1962	2.70	2.58	2.78					
1963	2.81	2.77	2.97	3.16				
1964	2.96	2.97	3.16	3.35	3.55			
1965	3.12	3.16	3.36	3.55	3.75	3.95		
1966	3.38	3.45	3.66	3.88	4.13	4.42	4.88	
1967	3.49	3.57	3.77	3.97	4.17	4.38	4.60	4.32
1968	3.70	3.79	4.00	4.20	4.41	4.62	4.85	4.83
1969	4.00	4.12	4.33	4.55	4.79	5.03	5.30	5.45
1970	4.22	4.35	4.57	4.79	5.03	5.27	5.54	5.70
1971	4.23	4.35	4.55	4.74	4.94	5.14	5.34	5.43
1972	4.22	4.33	4.50	4.68	4.84	5.01	5.16	5.20
1973	4.42	4.54	4.71	4.89	5.06	5.23	5.39	5.47
1974	4.65	4.78	4.96	5.14	5.32	5.50	5.67	5.77
1975	4.73	4.85	5.02	5.19	5.36	5.53	5.69	5.78
1976	4.74	4.85	5.02	5.18	5.34	5.48	5.62	5.70
1977	4.77	4.88	5.04	5.19	5.33	5.47	5.59	5.66
1978	4.90	5.01	5.16	5.31	5.46	5.59	5.72	5.79
1979	5.16	5.27	5.43	5.59	5.74	5.89	6.03	6.12
1980	5.46	5.59	5.75	5.92	6.08	6.24	6.39	6.50
1981	5.85	5.99	6.17	6.35	6.52	6.70	6.87	7.00
1982	6.07	6.21	6.39	6.57	6.75	6.93	7.11	7.25
1983	6.17	6.32	6.49	6.67	6.85	7.02	7.19	7.33
1984	6.31	6.45	6.63	6.80	6.98	7.15	7.32	7.45
1985	6.36	6.49	6.66	6.83	7.00	7.16	7.32	7.45
1986	6.34	6.47	6.64	6.80	6.96	7.11	7.26	7.38

Table 6-6C

From To	1968	1969	1970	1971	1972	1973	1974	1975
1968	5.34							
1969	6.01	6.68						
1970	6.16	6.57	6.46					
1971	5.71	5.83	5.40	4.35				
1972	5.38	5.39	4.96	4.21	4.07			
1973	5.66	5.72	5.48	5.15	5.55	7.04		
1974	5.98	6.08	5.96	5.84	6.33	7.46	7.89	
1975	5.96	6.05	5.94	5.84	6.21	6.92	6.87	5.84
1976	5.85	5.92	5.81	5.70	5.97	6.44	6.24	5.42
1977	5.79	5.84	5.74	5.64	5.85	6.21	6.00	5.37
1978	5.92	5.98	5.90	5.83	6.05	6.38	6.24	5.83
1979	6.27	6.35	6.32	6.30	6.54	6.90	6.88	6.67
1980	6.67	6.78	6.79	6.82	7.10	7.47	7.54	7.48
1981	7.19	7.34	7.39	7.48	7.79	8.20	8.35	8.41
1982	7.44	7.59	7.66	7.76	8.07	8.47	8.63	8.72

From To	1968	1969	1970	1971	1972	1973	1974	1975
1983	7.51	7.66	7.73	7.83	8.12	8.48	8.63	8.71
1984	7.64	7.78	7.85	7.95	8.23	8.58	8.72	8.80
1985	7.63	7.76	7.83	7.92	8.18	8.49	8.61	8.68
1986	7.54	7.66	7.72	7.80	8.03	8.31	8.41	8.45

Table 6-6D

From To	1976	1977	1978	1979	1980	1981	1982	1983
1976	4.99							
1977	5.13	5.27						
1978	5.83	6.24	7.22					
1979	6.88	7.51	8.63	10.04				
1980	7.81	8.51	9.59	10.77	11.51			
1981	8.84	9.61	10.70	11.86	12.77	14.03		
1982	9.13	9.82	10.73	11.61	12.14	12.45	10.87	
1983	9.07	9.65	10.38	11.02	11.26	11.18	9.75	8.63
1984	9.13	9.64	10.27	10.78	10.92	10.78	9.69	9.11
1985	8.96	9.40	9.92	10.31	10.35	10.12	9.14	8.56
1986	8.69	9.06	9.48	9.77	9.73	9.43	8.51	7.92

Table 6-6E

From To	1984	1985	1986
1984	9.58		
1985	8.53	7.48	
1986	7.68	6.73	5.98

Source: Economic Report of the President, 324, Table B68 (1987).

§6.12   Six-Month Treasury Bills

As indicated by Table 6-7, the six-month, or 26-week, Treasury Bill was first issued in 1960. Since that time, the average annual yield has been 6.515 per cent.

Table 6-7 Return on Six-Month Treasury Bills

Year	Yield in Per cent
1960	3.247
1961	2.605
1962	2.908
1963	3.253
1964	3.686
1965	4.055
1966	5.082

Year	Yield in Per cent
1967	4.630
1968	5.470
1969	6.853
1970	6.562
1971	4.511
1972	4.466
1973	7.178
1974	7.926
1975	6.122
1976	5.266
1977	5.510
1978	7.572
1979	10.017
1980	11.374
1981	13.811
1982	11.084
1983	8.750
1984	9.800
1985	7.660
1986	6.030
Average Return	6.400%

Table 6-8 Return on Six-Month Treasury Bill (Average)

Table 6-8A

From To	1959	1960	1961	1962	1963	1964	1965	1966
1959	3.83							
1960	3.54	3.25						
1961	3.23	2.93	2.60					
1962	3.15	2.92	2.76	2.91				
1963	3.17	3.00	2.92	3.08	3.25			
1964	3.26	3.14	3.11	3.28	3.47	3.69		
1965	3.37	3.29	3.30	3.48	3.66	3.87	4.05	
1966	3.58	3.55	3.60	3.80	4.02	4.27	4.57	3.58
1967	3.70	3.68	3.75	3.94	4.14	4.36	4.59	3.70
1968	3.88	3.88	3.96	4.15	4.36	4.58	4.81	3.88
1969	4.15	4.18	4.28	4.49	4.72	4.96	5.22	4.15
1970	4.35	4.40	4.51	4.72	4.95	5.19	5.44	4.35
1971	4.36	4.41	4.51	4.70	4.90	5.11	5.31	4.36
1972	4.37	4.41	4.51	4.68	4.86	5.04	5.20	4.37
1973	4.56	4.61	4.71	4.89	5.07	5.25	5.42	4.56
1974	4.77	4.83	4.94	5.12	5.31	5.49	5.67	4.77
1975	4.85	4.91	5.02	5.19	5.37	5.55	5.71	4.85
1976	4.87	4.93	5.04	5.20	5.36	5.52	5.68	4.87

From To	1959	1960	1961	1962	1963	1964	1965	1966
1977	4.90	4.96	5.06	5.22	5.37	5.52	5.66	4.90
1978	5.04	5.10	5.20	5.36	5.51	5.66	5.80	5.04
1979	5.27	5.35	5.46	5.61	5.77	5.93	6.08	5.27
1980	5.55	5.63	5.75	5.92	6.09	6.25	6.41	5.55
1981	5.91	6.00	6.13	6.31	6.49	6.67	6.85	5.91
1982	6.12	6.22	6.36	6.54	6.72	6.90	7.08	6.12
1983	6.23	6.33	6.46	6.64	6.82	6.99	7.17	6.23
1984	6.37	6.47	6.60	6.78	6.95	7.13	7.30	6.37
1985	6.41	6.51	6.64	6.81	6.98	7.15	7.32	6.41
1986	6.40	6.50	6.62	6.78	6.94	7.10	7.26	6.40

Table 6-8B

From To	1967	1968	1969	1970	1971	1972	1973	1974
1967	3.68							
1968	3.88	3.96						
1969	4.18	4.28	4.49					
1970	4.40	4.51	4.72	4.95				
1971	4.41	4.51	4.70	4.90	5.11			
1972	4.41	4.51	4.68	4.86	5.04	5.20		
1973	4.61	4.71	4.89	5.07	5.25	5.42	5.59	
1974	4.83	4.94	5.12	5.31	5.49	5.67	5.85	5.95
1975	4.91	5.02	5.19	5.37	5.55	5.71	5.88	5.97
1976	4.93	5.04	5.20	5.36	5.52	5.68	5.82	5.90
1977	4.96	5.06	5.22	5.37	5.52	5.66	5.80	5.86
1978	5.10	5.20	5.36	5.51	5.66	5.80	5.93	6.01
1979	5.35	5.46	5.61	5.77	5.93	6.08	6.23	6.31
1980	5.63	5.75	5.92	6.09	6.25	6.41	6.57	6.68
1981	6.00	6.13	6.31	6.49	6.67	6.85	7.02	7.15
1982	6.22	6.36	6.54	6.72	6.90	7.08	7.26	7.39
1983	6.33	6.46	6.64	6.82	6.99	7.17	7.34	7.47
1984	6.47	6.60	6.78	6.95	7.13	7.30	7.47	7.60
1985	6.51	6.64	6.81	6.98	7.15	7.32	7.48	7.61
1986	6.50	6.62	6.78	6.94	7.10	7.26	7.41	7.53

Table 6-8C

From To	1975	1976	1977	1978	1979	1980	1981	1982
1975	6.14							
1976	6.04	6.11						
1977	5.99	6.04	5.94					
1978	6.13	6.20	6.12	6.07				
1979	6.45	6.54	6.51	6.51	6.76			
1980	6.83	6.95	6.95	6.99	7.27	7.62		

From To	1975	1976	1977	1978	1979	1980	1981	1982
1981	7.33	7.47	7.52	7.61	7.92	8.30	8.45	
1982	7.58	7.73	7.80	7.90	8.21	8.58	8.74	8.84
1983	7.65	7.80	7.87	7.97	8.25	8.60	8.74	8.83
1984	7.78	7.92	7.99	8.10	8.37	8.70	8.84	8.93
1985	7.77	7.91	7.97	8.07	8.32	8.62	8.74	8.81
1986	7.68	7.80	7.86	7.94	8.17	8.43	8.53	8.58

Table 6-8D

From To	1983	1984	1985	1986
1983	9.17			
1984	9.24	9.74		
1985	9.08	9.50	10.00	
1986	8.80	9.16	9.56	9.81

Source: Economic Report of the President, 324, Table B68 (1987).

§6.13   —One-Year Treasury Bills

The annual return on the one-year Treasury Bill has averaged 6.01 per cent for the period of time 1952 to 1986 inclusive. This can be seen on Table 6-9.

Table 6-9 Return on One-Year Treasury Bills

Year	Yield in Per Cent
1952	1.84
1953	2.11
1954	.93
1955	1.93
1956	2.91
1957	3.66
1958	2.13
1959	4.29
1960	3.66
1961	2.89
1962	3.10
1963	3.41
1964	3.89
1965	4.23
1966	5.34
1967	4.94
1968	5.76
1969	7.28
1970	6.94
1971	4.90

Year	Yield in Per Cent
1972	5.01
1973	7.54
1974	8.35
1975	6.72
1976	5.84
1977	6.06
1978	8.39
1979	10.80
1980	12.22
1981	15.13
1982	12.45
1983	9.65
1984	11.01
1985	8.55
1986	6.47
Average Return	6.01%

Table 6-10 One-Year Treasury Bills (Average)

Table 6-10A

From To	1952	1953	1954	1955	1956	1957	1958	1959
1952	1.84							
1953	1.98	2.11						
1954	1.63	1.52	.93					
1955	1.70	1.66	1.43	1.93				
1956	1.94	1.97	1.92	2.42	2.91			
1957	2.23	2.31	2.36	2.83	3.29	3.66		
1958	2.22	2.28	2.31	2.66	2.90	2.90	2.13	
1959	2.48	2.57	2.64	2.98	3.25	3.36	3.21	4.29
1960	2.61	2.70	2.79	3.10	3.33	3.44	3.36	3.98
1961	2.64	2.72	2.80	3.07	3.26	3.33	3.24	3.61
1962	2.68	2.76	2.83	3.07	3.23	3.29	3.21	3.49
1963	2.74	2.82	2.89	3.11	3.26	3.31	3.25	3.47
1964	2.83	2.91	2.98	3.19	3.33	3.38	3.34	3.54
1965	2.93	3.01	3.09	3.28	3.42	3.47	3.45	3.64
1966	3.09	3.18	3.26	3.45	3.59	3.66	3.66	3.85
1967	3.20	3.29	3.38	3.57	3.70	3.78	3.79	3.97
1968	3.35	3.45	3.54	3.72	3.86	3.94	3.97	4.15
1969	3.57	3.67	3.77	3.96	4.11	4.20	4.24	4.44
1970	3.75	3.86	3.96	4.15	4.30	4.39	4.45	4.64
1971	3.81	3.91	4.01	4.19	4.33	4.43	4.48	4.66
1972	3.86	3.97	4.06	4.24	4.37	4.46	4.52	4.69
1973	4.03	4.14	4.24	4.41	4.55	4.65	4.71	4.88
1974	4.22	4.33	4.43	4.61	4.75	4.85	4.92	5.10

From To	1952	1953	1954	1955	1956	1957	1958	1959
1975	4.32	4.43	4.54	4.71	4.85	4.95	5.02	5.19
1976	4.38	4.49	4.59	4.76	4.89	4.99	5.06	5.23
1977	4.45	4.55	4.65	4.82	4.95	5.04	5.11	5.27
1978	4.59	4.70	4.80	4.97	5.10	5.20	5.27	5.43
1979	4.82	4.93	5.03	5.20	5.33	5.44	5.52	5.68
1980	5.07	5.19	5.30	5.47	5.61	5.72	5.81	5.98
1981	5.41	5.53	5.65	5.83	5.98	6.10	6.20	6.38
1982	5.63	5.76	5.89	6.06	6.22	6.34	6.45	6.63
1983	5.76	5.89	6.01	6.19	6.34	6.47	6.57	6.75
1984	5.92	6.05	6.17	6.35	6.50	6.63	6.74	6.92
1985	5.99	6.12	6.24	6.42	6.57	6.69	6.80	6.97
1986	6.01	6.13	6.25	6.42	6.56	6.68	6.79	6.96

Table 6-10B

From To	1960	1961	1962	1963	1964	1965	1966	1967
1960	3.66							
1961	3.28	2.89						
1962	3.22	3.00	3.10					
1963	3.27	3.13	3.25	3.41				
1964	3.39	3.32	3.47	3.65	3.89			
1965	3.53	3.50	3.66	3.84	4.06	4.23		
1966	3.79	3.81	3.99	4.22	4.49	4.79	5.34	
1967	3.93	3.97	4.15	4.36	4.60	4.84	5.14	4.94
1968	4.14	4.20	4.38	4.59	4.83	5.07	5.35	5.35
1969	4.45	4.54	4.74	4.98	5.24	5.51	5.83	5.99
1970	4.68	4.78	4.99	5.22	5.48	5.75	6.05	6.23
1971	4.70	4.79	4.98	5.19	5.41	5.63	5.86	5.96
1972	4.72	4.81	4.98	5.17	5.37	5.55	5.74	5.80
1973	4.92	5.02	5.20	5.39	5.58	5.77	5.96	6.05
1974	5.15	5.26	5.44	5.63	5.83	6.03	6.23	6.34
1975	5.25	5.35	5.53	5.72	5.91	6.09	6.28	6.38
1976	5.28	5.38	5.55	5.72	5.90	6.07	6.24	6.33
1977	5.33	5.42	5.58	5.75	5.91	6.07	6.22	6.30
1978	5.49	5.59	5.75	5.91	6.08	6.24	6.39	6.48
1979	5.75	5.86	6.03	6.20	6.37	6.54	6.71	6.81
1980	6.06	6.18	6.35	6.53	6.72	6.90	7.07	7.20
1981	6.47	6.61	6.79	6.99	7.19	7.38	7.58	7.73
1982	6.73	6.87	7.06	7.26	7.46	7.66	7.86	8.02
1983	6.85	6.99	7.18	7.37	7.57	7.77	7.96	8.12
1984	7.02	7.16	7.35	7.54	7.74	7.93	8.12	8.28
1985	7.08	7.21	7.39	7.58	7.77	7.95	8.14	8.29
1986	7.05	7.18	7.36	7.53	7.71	7.89	8.06	8.20

Table 6-10C

From To	1968	1969	1970	1971	1972	1973	1974	1975
1968	5.76							
1969	6.52	7.28						
1970	6.66	7.11	6.94					
1971	6.22	6.37	5.92	4.90				
1972	5.98	6.03	5.62	4.96	5.01			
1973	6.24	6.33	6.10	5.82	6.28	7.54		
1974	6.54	6.67	6.55	6.45	6.97	7.95	8.35	
1975	6.56	6.68	6.58	6.50	6.90	7.54	7.54	6.72
1976	6.48	6.57	6.47	6.39	6.69	7.11	6.97	6.28
1977	6.44	6.52	6.42	6.35	6.59	6.90	6.74	6.21
1978	6.62	6.70	6.64	6.60	6.84	7.15	7.07	6.75
1979	6.97	7.08	7.05	7.07	7.34	7.67	7.69	7.56
1980	7.37	7.50	7.52	7.58	7.88	8.24	8.34	8.34
1981	7.92	8.09	8.16	8.27	8.61	9.01	9.19	9.31
1982	8.23	8.40	8.49	8.62	8.96	9.35	9.55	9.70
1983	8.31	8.49	8.57	8.70	9.01	9.38	9.56	9.70
1984	8.47	8.64	8.73	8.86	9.17	9.51	9.69	9.83
1985	8.47	8.63	8.72	8.84	9.12	9.43	9.59	9.70
1986	8.37	8.51	8.59	8.69	8.94	9.22	9.35	9.43

Table 6-10D

From To	1976	1977	1978	1979	1980	1981	1982	1983
1976	5.84							
1977	5.95	6.06						
1978	6.76	7.22	8.39					
1979	7.77	8.42	9.60	10.80				
1980	8.66	9.37	10.47	11.51	12.22			
1981	9.74	10.52	11.64	12.72	13.68	15.13		
1982	10.13	10.84	11.80	12.65	13.27	13.79	12.45	
1983	10.07	10.67	11.44	12.05	12.36	12.41	11.05	9.65
1984	10.17	10.71	11.38	11.88	12.09	12.06	11.04	10.33
1985	10.00	10.46	11.02	11.39	11.49	11.34	10.39	9.71
1986	9.68	10.06	10.51	10.78	10.77	10.53	9.61	8.90

Table 6-10E

From To	1984	1985	1986
1984	11.01		
1985	9.74	8.47	
1986	8.65	7.47	6.47

Source: The Federal Reserve Bulletin, 1985-1986 inclusive.

§6.14 —Long-Term Government Securities

Long-term government securities are securities which do not mature for at least 10 years. Table 6-11 shows the 1952-1986 returns for long-term government securities with over a 10-year composite maturity. The average return was 6.49 per cent.

Table 6-11 Return on Long-Term Government Securities Composite of Over Ten-Year Maturities

Year	Yield in Per Cent
1952	2.68
1953	2.93
1954	2.53
1955	2.84
1956	3.08
1957	3.47
1958	3.43
1959	4.07
1960	4.01
1961	3.90
1962	3.95
1963	4.00
1964	4.15
1965	4.21
1966	4.66
1967	4.85
1968	5.25
1969	6.10
1970	6.59
1971	5.74
1972	5.63
1973	6.30
1974	6.99
1975	6.98
1976	6.78
1977	7.06
1978	7.89
1979	8.74
1980	10.81
1981	12.87
1982	12.23
1983	10.84

Year	Yield in Per Cent
1984	11.99
1985	10.75
1986	7.68
Average Return	6.49%

Table 6-12 Long-Term Government Securities
Composite of Over Ten-Year Maturities
(Average)

Table 6-12A

From To	1952	1953	1954	1955	1956	1957	1958	1959
1952	2.60							
1953	2.73	2.85						
1954	2.62	2.62	2.40					
1955	2.67	2.69	2.61	2.82				
1956	2.77	2.81	2.80	3.00	3.18			
1957	2.92	2.98	3.01	3.22	3.42	3.65		
1958	2.97	3.04	3.07	3.24	3.38	3.48	3.32	
1959	3.14	3.22	3.28	3.46	3.62	3.77	3.83	4.33
1960	3.25	3.33	3.40	3.57	3.72	3.85	3.92	4.22
1961	3.31	3.39	3.46	3.61	3.75	3.86	3.91	4.11
1962	3.37	3.45	3.52	3.66	3.78	3.88	3.92	4.07
1963	3.42	3.50	3.56	3.69	3.80	3.89	3.93	4.06
1964	3.48	3.56	3.62	3.74	3.85	3.93	3.97	4.08
1965	3.54	3.61	3.68	3.79	3.89	3.97	4.01	4.11
1966	3.63	3.71	3.77	3.89	3.98	4.06	4.11	4.21
1967	3.72	3.80	3.87	3.98	4.07	4.16	4.21	4.30
1968	3.84	3.91	3.98	4.10	4.20	4.28	4.34	4.44
1969	3.99	4.08	4.15	4.27	4.37	4.46	4.53	4.64
1970	4.17	4.26	4.34	4.46	4.57	4.67	4.75	4.87
1971	4.27	4.36	4.44	4.56	4.67	4.77	4.85	4.97
1972	4.36	4.45	4.53	4.65	4.76	4.86	4.94	5.06
1973	4.47	4.56	4.65	4.77	4.88	4.98	5.06	5.17
1974	4.61	4.70	4.79	4.91	5.02	5.12	5.21	5.32
1975	4.75	4.84	4.93	5.05	5.17	5.27	5.36	5.48
1976	4.86	4.96	5.05	5.17	5.28	5.39	5.48	5.60
1977	4.96	5.06	5.15	5.27	5.38	5.48	5.58	5.69
1978	5.09	5.19	5.28	5.40	5.51	5.62	5.71	5.83
1979	5.25	5.34	5.44	5.56	5.67	5.78	5.88	6.00
1980	5.46	5.56	5.66	5.79	5.91	6.02	6.12	6.25
1981	5.74	5.85	5.96	6.09	6.21	6.34	6.45	6.58
1982	5.98	6.09	6.20	6.34	6.47	6.59	6.71	6.85
1983	6.14	6.25	6.36	6.50	6.63	6.76	6.88	7.02
1984	6.33	6.44	6.56	6.70	6.83	6.96	7.08	7.23

From To	1952	1953	1954	1955	1956	1957	1958	1959
1985	6.45	6.57	6.69	6.82	6.96	7.09	7.21	7.35
1986	6.49	6.60	6.72	6.85	6.98	7.11	7.23	7.37

Table 6-12B

From To	1960	1961	1962	1963	1964	1965	1966	1967
1960	4.12							
1961	4.00	3.88						
1962	3.98	3.92	3.95					
1963	3.99	3.94	3.98	4.00				
1964	4.03	4.00	4.05	4.10	4.19			
1965	4.07	4.06	4.11	4.16	4.24	4.28		
1966	4.19	4.20	4.27	4.35	4.46	4.60	4.92	
1967	4.30	4.33	4.40	4.49	4.62	4.76	5.00	5.07
1968	4.45	4.49	4.58	4.69	4.82	4.98	5.21	5.36
1969	4.67	4.73	4.84	4.97	5.13	5.32	5.58	5.80
1970	4.92	5.00	5.12	5.27	5.45	5.66	5.93	6.19
1971	5.02	5.10	5.22	5.37	5.54	5.73	5.97	6.18
1972	5.11	5.19	5.31	5.45	5.61	5.79	6.00	6.19
1973	5.24	5.32	5.44	5.58	5.73	5.91	6.11	6.28
1974	5.39	5.48	5.60	5.74	5.90	6.07	6.27	6.44
1975	5.55	5.65	5.77	5.91	6.07	6.25	6.44	6.61
1976	5.67	5.77	5.90	6.04	6.19	6.36	6.55	6.71
1977	5.77	5.87	5.99	6.13	6.28	6.44	6.62	6.78
1978	5.91	6.01	6.13	6.27	6.42	6.58	6.76	6.91
1979	6.09	6.19	6.32	6.46	6.61	6.77	6.95	7.11
1980	6.34	6.45	6.59	6.74	6.90	7.07	7.25	7.42
1981	6.69	6.81	6.95	7.11	7.29	7.47	7.67	7.85
1982	6.96	7.09	7.24	7.41	7.59	7.78	7.98	8.17
1983	7.13	7.26	7.42	7.58	7.76	7.95	8.15	8.34
1984	7.35	7.48	7.64	7.80	7.98	8.17	8.38	8.57
1985	7.47	7.61	7.76	7.93	8.10	8.29	8.49	8.68
1986	7.48	7.61	7.76	7.92	8.09	8.26	8.45	8.63

Table 6-12C

From To	1968	1969	1970	1971	1972	1973	1974	1975
1968	5.65							
1969	6.16	6.67						
1970	6.56	7.01	7.35					
1971	6.46	6.73	6.75	6.16				
1972	6.41	6.60	6.57	6.19	6.21			
1973	6.48	6.65	6.64	6.40	6.53	6.84		
1974	6.63	6.80	6.82	6.69	6.87	7.20	7.56	

From / To	1968	1969	1970	1971	1972	1973	1974	1975
1975	6.80	6.97	7.02	6.95	7.15	7.46	7.78	7.99
1976	6.89	7.05	7.10	7.06	7.24	7.50	7.72	7.80
1977	6.95	7.09	7.14	7.11	7.27	7.48	7.64	7.67
1978	7.08	7.22	7.28	7.28	7.43	7.64	7.80	7.86
1979	7.28	7.42	7.50	7.52	7.68	7.90	8.07	8.17
1980	7.60	7.76	7.86	7.91	8.10	8.34	8.56	8.72
1981	8.05	8.23	8.36	8.46	8.69	8.96	9.22	9.46
1982	8.38	8.57	8.72	8.83	9.08	9.36	9.64	9.90
1983	8.55	8.74	8.89	9.01	9.25	9.52	9.79	10.04
1984	8.78	8.97	9.13	9.25	9.49	9.77	10.03	10.28
1985	8.88	9.07	9.22	9.34	9.57	9.83	10.08	10.31
1986	8.82	8.99	9.13	9.24	9.45	9.68	9.90	10.09

Table 6-12D

From / To	1976	1977	1978	1979	1980	1981	1982	1983
1976	7.61							
1977	7.52	7.42						
1978	7.81	7.92	8.41					
1979	8.22	8.42	8.93	9.44				
1980	8.87	9.18	9.77	10.45	11.46			
1981	9.71	10.13	10.80	11.60	12.69	13.91		
1982	10.18	10.61	11.24	11.95	12.79	13.46	13.00	
1983	10.29	10.68	11.22	11.78	12.37	12.67	12.05	11.10
1984	10.53	10.90	11.39	11.89	12.38	12.61	12.18	11.77
1985	10.54	10.87	11.30	11.71	12.09	12.21	11.79	11.39
1986	10.28	10.55	10.90	11.21	11.46	11.46	10.97	10.46

Table 6-12E

From / To	1984	1985	1986
1984	12.44		
1985	11.53	10.62	
1986	10.25	9.15	7.68

Source: Economic Report of the President, 324, Table B68 (1987).

§6.15   —Moody's Aaa Corporate Bonds

Corporate bonds are debt instruments issued by United States corporations. Bonds made two promises to the purchaser of the bond: (1) to pay interest semiannually, and (2) to repay the amount borrowed, or principal, at some future date.[8] Bond rating services have developed categories to assist the

---

[8] Standard & Poor's Corp, Bond Guide 10 (Mar 1985).

investor in evaluating the bond's ability to pay interest to repay principal. Two such rating services are Moody's and Standard and Poor's.

The ratings, running from the highest and most secure bond, to the lowest, or least secure bond, are "AAA" to "DDD-D" for Standard and Poor's and "Aaa" to "C" for Moody's.

Bonds rated "Aaa" "have an extremely strong capacity to pay interest and repay principal."[9] Table 6-13 shows the return on Moody's Aaa rated corporate bonds averaged 7 per cent. from 1952 to 1986 inclusive.

Table 6-13 Moody's Aaa Corporate Bond Yields

Year	Yield in Per Cent
1952	2.96
1953	3.20
1954	2.90
1955	3.06
1956	3.36
1957	3.89
1958	3.79
1959	4.38
1960	4.41
1961	4.35
1962	4.33
1963	4.26
1964	4.40
1965	4.49
1966	5.13
1967	5.51
1968	6.18
1969	7.03
1970	8.04
1971	7.39
1972	7.21
1973	7.44
1974	8.57
1975	8.83
1976	8.43
1977	8.02
1978	8.73
1979	9.63
1980	11.94
1981	14.17

[9] *Id.*

Year	Yield in Per Cent
1982	13.79
1983	12.04
1984	12.71
1985	11.37
1986	9.02
Average Return	7.00%

Table 6-14 Corporate Bonds (Moody's Aaa)

Table 6-14A

From / To	1952	1953	1954	1955	1956	1957	1958	1959
1952	2.96							
1953	3.08	3.20						
1954	3.02	3.05	2.90					
1955	3.03	3.05	2.98	3.06				
1956	3.10	3.13	3.11	3.21	3.36			
1957	3.23	3.28	3.30	3.44	3.62	3.89		
1958	3.31	3.37	3.40	3.52	3.68	3.84	3.79	
1959	3.44	3.51	3.56	3.70	3.85	4.02	4.08	4.38
1960	3.55	3.62	3.68	3.81	3.97	4.12	4.19	4.39
1961	3.63	3.70	3.77	3.89	4.03	4.16	4.23	4.38
1962	3.69	3.77	3.83	3.95	4.07	4.19	4.25	4.37
1963	3.74	3.81	3.87	3.98	4.10	4.20	4.25	4.35
1964	3.79	3.86	3.92	4.02	4.13	4.23	4.27	4.36
1965	3.84	3.91	3.97	4.07	4.17	4.26	4.30	4.37
1966	3.93	4.00	4.06	4.15	4.25	4.34	4.39	4.47
1967	4.03	4.10	4.16	4.26	4.36	4.45	4.50	4.58
1968	4.15	4.23	4.30	4.40	4.50	4.59	4.66	4.74
1969	4.31	4.39	4.47	4.57	4.68	4.78	4.86	4.95
1970	4.51	4.59	4.68	4.79	4.90	5.01	5.10	5.21
1971	4.65	4.74	4.83	4.94	5.06	5.17	5.26	5.38
1972	4.77	4.87	4.95	5.07	5.19	5.30	5.39	5.51
1973	4.90	4.99	5.08	5.19	5.31	5.43	5.52	5.64
1974	5.06	5.15	5.24	5.36	5.48	5.60	5.70	5.82
1975	5.21	5.31	5.41	5.53	5.65	5.77	5.87	6.00
1976	5.34	5.44	5.54	5.66	5.78	5.90	6.01	6.13
1977	5.44	5.54	5.64	5.76	5.88	6.00	6.11	6.23
1978	5.57	5.67	5.77	5.88	6.01	6.13	6.23	6.36
1979	5.71	5.81	5.91	6.03	6.16	6.28	6.39	6.51
1980	5.93	6.03	6.14	6.26	6.39	6.52	6.63	6.76
1981	6.20	6.31	6.42	6.55	6.69	6.82	6.94	7.08
1982	6.45	6.56	6.68	6.81	6.95	7.09	7.22	7.36
1983	6.62	6.74	6.86	6.99	7.13	7.27	7.40	7.55
1984	6.81	6.93	7.05	7.18	7.33	7.47	7.60	7.75

From	1952	1953	1954	1955	1956	1957	1958	1959
To								
1985	6.94	7.06	7.18	7.32	7.46	7.60	7.73	7.88
1986	7.00	7.12	7.24	7.37	7.51	7.65	7.78	7.92

Table 6-14B

From	1960	1961	1962	1963	1964	1965	1966	1967
To								
1960	4.41							
1961	4.38	4.35						
1962	4.36	4.34	4.33					
1963	4.34	4.31	4.29	4.26				
1964	4.35	4.33	4.33	4.33	4.40			
1965	4.37	4.37	4.37	4.38	4.45	4.49		
1966	4.48	4.49	4.52	4.57	4.67	4.81	5.13	
1967	4.61	4.64	4.69	4.76	4.88	5.04	5.32	5.51
1968	4.78	4.83	4.90	5.00	5.14	5.33	5.61	5.84
1969	5.01	5.08	5.17	5.29	5.46	5.67	5.96	6.24
1970	5.28	5.37	5.49	5.63	5.83	6.06	6.38	6.69
1971	5.46	5.56	5.68	5.83	6.02	6.25	6.55	6.83
1972	5.59	5.69	5.82	5.96	6.15	6.37	6.64	6.89
1973	5.73	5.83	5.95	6.10	6.28	6.49	6.74	6.97
1974	5.92	6.02	6.15	6.30	6.49	6.70	6.94	7.17
1975	6.10	6.21	6.34	6.50	6.68	6.89	7.13	7.36
1976	6.24	6.35	6.48	6.64	6.82	7.02	7.25	7.46
1977	6.33	6.45	6.58	6.73	6.91	7.10	7.31	7.51
1978	6.46	6.57	6.71	6.85	7.03	7.21	7.42	7.62
1979	6.62	6.74	6.87	7.02	7.19	7.38	7.58	7.77
1980	6.87	7.00	7.13	7.29	7.47	7.66	7.87	8.07
1981	7.20	7.34	7.49	7.65	7.84	8.04	8.27	8.47
1982	7.49	7.63	7.79	7.96	8.15	8.36	8.59	8.81
1983	7.68	7.82	7.98	8.15	8.35	8.56	8.78	9.00
1984	7.88	8.03	8.19	8.36	8.56	8.76	8.99	9.20
1985	8.02	8.16	8.32	8.49	8.68	8.89	9.11	9.32
1986	8.05	8.19	8.35	8.51	8.70	8.89	9.10	9.30

Table 6-14C

From	1968	1969	1970	1971	1972	1973	1974	1975
To								
1968	6.18							
1969	6.61	7.03						
1970	7.08	7.54	8.04					
1971	7.16	7.49	7.71	7.39				
1972	7.17	7.42	7.55	7.30	7.21			
1973	7.21	7.42	7.52	7.35	7.33	7.44		
1974	7.41	7.61	7.73	7.65	7.74	8.01	8.57	

From	1968	1969	1970	1971	1972	1973	1974	1975
To								
1975	7.59	7.79	7.91	7.89	8.01	8.28	8.70	8.83
1976	7.68	7.87	7.99	7.98	8.10	8.32	8.61	8.63
1977	7.71	7.88	7.99	7.98	8.08	8.26	8.46	8.43
1978	7.81	7.97	8.07	8.08	8.18	8.34	8.52	8.50
1979	7.96	8.12	8.23	8.25	8.36	8.52	8.70	8.73
1980	8.26	8.44	8.57	8.62	8.76	8.95	9.16	9.26
1981	8.69	8.88	9.03	9.12	9.30	9.53	9.79	9.96
1982	9.03	9.23	9.40	9.51	9.71	9.96	10.23	10.44
1983	9.21	9.42	9.59	9.71	9.90	10.14	10.41	10.62
1984	9.42	9.62	9.80	9.92	10.12	10.36	10.62	10.83
1985	9.53	9.73	9.89	10.02	10.21	10.44	10.69	10.88
1986	9.50	9.69	9.84	9.96	10.13	10.33	10.56	10.72

Table 6-14D

From	1976	1977	1978	1979	1980	1981	1982	1983
To								
1976	8.43							
1977	8.22	8.02						
1978	8.39	8.38	8.73					
1979	8.70	8.79	9.18	9.63				
1980	9.35	9.58	10.10	10.79	11.94			
1981	10.15	10.50	11.12	11.91	13.05	14.17		
1982	10.67	11.05	11.65	12.38	13.30	13.98	13.79	
1983	10.84	11.19	11.72	12.31	12.98	13.33	12.91	12.04
1984	11.05	11.38	11.86	12.38	12.93	13.18	12.85	12.38
1985	11.08	11.38	11.80	12.24	12.67	12.82	12.48	12.04
1986	10.90	11.14	11.49	11.83	12.15	12.18	11.79	11.29

Table 6-14E

From	1984	1985	1986
To			
1984	12.71		
1985	12.04	11.37	
1986	11.03	10.20	9.02

Source: Economic Report of the President, 324, Table B68 (1987).

§6.16 —Moody's Baa Corporate Bonds

Bonds rated "Baa" are considered more risky than bonds rated "Aaa." Corporations with debt rated "Baa" is considered as having earnings adequate to pay interest and repay principal.[10] Table 6-15 shows the average annual

---

[10] R. Kolb, Investments 44 (1986).

return on "Baa" bonds for the period 1952 through 1986 inclusive. Returns on bonds rated "Baa" averaged 7.97 per cent.

Table 6-15 Moody's Baa Corporate Bond Yields

Year	Yield in Percent
1952	3.52
1953	3.74
1954	3.51
1955	3.53
1956	3.88
1957	4.71
1958	4.73
1959	5.05
1960	5.19
1961	5.08
1962	5.02
1963	4.86
1964	4.83
1965	4.87
1966	5.67
1967	6.23
1968	6.94
1969	7.81
1970	9.11
1971	8.56
1972	8.16
1973	8.24
1974	9.50
1975	10.61
1976	9.75
1977	8.97
1978	9.49
1979	10.69
1980	13.67
1981	16.04
1982	16.11
1983	13.55
1984	14.19
1985	12.72
1986	10.39
Average Return	7.97%

Table 6-16 Corporate Bonds (Moody's Baa)

Table 6-16A

From To	1952	1953	1954	1955	1956	1957	1958	1959
1952	3.52							
1953	3.63	3.74						
1954	3.59	3.62	3.51					
1955	3.58	3.59	3.52	3.53				
1956	3.64	3.67	3.64	3.71	3.88			
1957	3.81	3.87	3.91	4.04	4.29	4.71		
1958	3.95	4.02	4.07	4.21	4.44	4.72	4.73	
1959	4.08	4.16	4.24	4.38	4.59	4.83	4.89	5.05
1960	4.21	4.29	4.37	4.51	4.71	4.92	4.99	5.12
1961	4.29	4.38	4.46	4.60	4.77	4.95	5.01	5.11
1962	4.36	4.44	4.52	4.65	4.81	4.96	5.01	5.08
1963	4.40	4.48	4.56	4.67	4.82	4.95	4.99	5.04
1964	4.43	4.51	4.58	4.69	4.82	4.93	4.97	5.00
1965	4.47	4.54	4.61	4.70	4.82	4.93	4.95	4.99
1966	4.55	4.62	4.69	4.79	4.90	5.00	5.03	5.07
1967	4.65	4.73	4.80	4.90	5.01	5.11	5.15	5.20
1968	4.79	4.87	4.94	5.04	5.16	5.27	5.32	5.37
1969	4.95	5.04	5.12	5.23	5.35	5.46	5.52	5.60
1970	5.17	5.26	5.35	5.47	5.60	5.72	5.80	5.89
1971	5.34	5.44	5.53	5.65	5.78	5.91	6.00	6.09
1972	5.48	5.57	5.67	5.79	5.92	6.05	6.14	6.24
1973	5.60	5.70	5.80	5.92	6.05	6.18	6.27	6.37
1974	5.77	5.87	5.98	6.10	6.23	6.36	6.46	6.57
1975	5.97	6.08	6.19	6.31	6.45	6.59	6.69	6.81
1976	6.12	6.23	6.34	6.47	6.61	6.75	6.85	6.97
1977	6.23	6.34	6.45	6.58	6.72	6.85	6.96	7.08
1978	6.35	6.46	6.57	6.70	6.84	6.97	7.08	7.20
1979	6.51	6.62	6.73	6.86	7.00	7.13	7.24	7.36
1980	6.76	6.87	6.99	7.12	7.26	7.41	7.52	7.65
1981	7.07	7.19	7.31	7.45	7.60	7.75	7.88	8.01
1982	7.36	7.49	7.61	7.76	7.92	8.07	8.21	8.35
1983	7.55	7.68	7.81	7.96	8.12	8.28	8.41	8.56
1984	7.75	7.88	8.02	8.17	8.33	8.49	8.63	8.78
1985	7.90	8.03	8.16	8.31	8.47	8.63	8.77	8.92
1986	7.97	8.10	8.23	8.38	8.54	8.69	8.83	8.97

Table 6-16B

From To	1960	1961	1962	1963	1964	1965	1966	1967
1960	5.19							
1961	5.13	5.08						

From / To	1960	1961	1962	1963	1964	1965	1966	1967
1962	5.10	5.05	5.02					
1963	5.04	4.99	4.94	4.86				
1964	5.00	4.95	4.90	4.85	4.83			
1965	4.97	4.93	4.89	4.85	4.85	4.87		
1966	5.07	5.05	5.05	5.06	5.12	5.27	5.67	
1967	5.22	5.22	5.25	5.29	5.40	5.59	5.95	6.23
1968	5.41	5.44	5.49	5.57	5.71	5.93	6.28	6.59
1969	5.65	5.70	5.78	5.89	6.06	6.30	6.66	6.99
1970	5.96	6.04	6.15	6.29	6.49	6.77	7.15	7.52
1971	6.18	6.27	6.39	6.54	6.75	7.03	7.39	7.73
1972	6.33	6.43	6.55	6.70	6.91	7.17	7.50	7.80
1973	6.47	6.57	6.69	6.84	7.04	7.29	7.59	7.86
1974	6.67	6.78	6.91	7.07	7.27	7.51	7.80	8.07
1975	6.92	7.03	7.17	7.34	7.54	7.79	8.08	8.35
1976	7.08	7.20	7.34	7.51	7.71	7.95	8.23	8.49
1977	7.19	7.31	7.45	7.61	7.80	8.03	8.30	8.53
1978	7.31	7.43	7.57	7.72	7.92	8.14	8.39	8.61
1979	7.48	7.60	7.74	7.90	8.09	8.31	8.55	8.77
1980	7.77	7.90	8.05	8.22	8.42	8.64	8.89	9.12
1981	8.15	8.29	8.45	8.63	8.84	9.08	9.34	9.58
1982	8.50	8.65	8.82	9.01	9.22	9.47	9.74	9.99
1983	8.71	8.86	9.03	9.22	9.44	9.68	9.95	10.20
1984	8.93	9.08	9.26	9.45	9.67	9.91	10.17	10.42
1985	9.07	9.23	9.40	9.59	9.80	10.04	10.30	10.54
1986	9.12	9.27	9.44	9.62	9.83	10.06	10.30	10.54

Table 6-16C

From / To	1968	1969	1970	1971	1972	1973	1974	1975
1968	6.94							
1969	7.38	7.81						
1970	7.95	8.46	9.11					
1971	8.11	8.49	8.84	8.56				
1972	8.12	8.41	8.61	8.36	8.16			
1973	8.14	8.38	8.52	8.32	8.20	8.24		
1974	8.33	8.56	8.71	8.62	8.63	8.87	9.50	
1975	8.62	8.86	9.03	9.01	9.13	9.45	10.05	10.61
1976	8.74	8.97	9.13	9.14	9.25	9.53	9.95	10.18
1977	8.77	8.97	9.11	9.11	9.21	9.41	9.71	9.78
1978	8.83	9.02	9.15	9.16	9.25	9.43	9.66	9.71
1979	8.99	9.17	9.31	9.33	9.43	9.61	9.84	9.90
1980	9.35	9.55	9.70	9.76	9.90	10.12	10.38	10.53
1981	9.82	10.05	10.23	10.33	10.51	10.77	11.09	11.32
1982	10.24	10.48	10.68	10.82	11.02	11.31	11.65	11.92

From	1968	1969	1970	1971	1972	1973	1974	1975
To								
1983	10.45	10.68	10.89	11.03	11.23	11.51	11.84	12.10
1984	10.67	10.90	11.11	11.25	11.46	11.73	12.05	12.31
1985	10.78	11.01	11.21	11.35	11.55	11.81	12.11	12.34
1986	10.76	10.98	11.16	11.29	11.47	11.71	11.98	12.18

Table 6-16D

From	1976	1977	1978	1979	1980	1981	1982	1983
To								
1976	9.75							
1977	9.36	8.97						
1978	9.40	9.23	9.49					
1979	9.72	9.72	10.09	10.69				
1980	10.51	10.71	11.28	12.18	13.67			
1981	11.44	11.77	12.47	13.47	14.86	16.04		
1982	12.10	12.49	13.20	14.13	15.27	16.07	16.11	
1983	12.28	12.65	13.26	14.01	14.84	15.23	14.83	13.55
1984	12.50	12.84	13.39	14.04	14.71	14.97	14.62	13.87
1985	12.52	12.83	13.31	13.85	14.38	14.52	14.14	13.49
1986	12.32	12.58	12.98	13.42	13.81	13.83	13.39	12.71

Table 6-16E

From	1984	1985	1986
To			
1984	14.19		
1985	13.46	12.72	
1986	12.43	11.55	10.39

Source: Economic Report of the President, 324, Table B68 (1987).

§6.17 —Standard and Poor's High-Grade Municipal Bonds

Municipal bonds are debt instruments issued by governmental or quais-govermental agencies. These agencies are not associated with the federal government.[11] The unique thing about municipal bonds is that they are free of federal income tax. Table 6-17 shows the returns to municipal bonds over the period 1952 to 1986 inclusive. As the table indicates, the return to municipal bonds averaged 5.42 per cent.

The problem with using the municipal bond yield is that one must know the individual's marginal tax rate. For example, suppose an individual paid no federal income tax. Then there would be no reason for the individual to purchase bonds free of federal taxation. Thus, corporate bonds would be the

[11] R. Ibbotson, R. Sinquefield, Stocks, Bonds, Bills and Inflation: The Past and the Future 7 (The Fin Analyst Research Found, Univ of Va 1987); Harris, *Selecting Income Growth and Discount Rates in Wrongful Death and Injury Cases: Comment,* 44, No 1 J Risk & Ins 117-32 (Mar 1977).

best investment. As the individual's tax rate increases, the tax-free bonds become more and more attractive.

After-tax returns on taxable corporate bonds must be compared to returns on tax-free municipal bonds. The following equation shows how to calculate the before-tax equivalent yield for municipal bonds:

Before-Tax Yield—Tax-Free Yield / (1 - Marginal Tax Rate)

If a municipal bond was paying 8 per cent tax free and the individual has a marginal tax rate of 40 per cent, then the taxable equivalent yield would be:

Before Tax Yield = .08/(1- .4)
Before Tax Yield = .08 / .6
Before Tax Yield = .133 or 13.3%

The desirability of holding a municipal bond is dependent on the individual's tax position. Thus, there is no way to determine the before-tax equivalent for a municipal bond since it is different for each individual. However, as Table 6-17 indicates the average annual yield on high-grade municipal bonds has averaged 5.42 per cent for the period 1952 to 1986 inclusive.

Table 6-17 High-Grade Municipal Bond Yields Standard and Poor's

Year	Yield in Per cent
1952	2.19
1953	2.72
1954	2.37
1955	2.53
1956	2.93
1957	3.60
1958	3.56
1959	3.95
1960	3.73
1961	3.46
1962	3.18
1963	3.23
1964	3.22
1965	3.27
1966	3.82
1967	3.98
1968	4.51
1969	5.81
1970	6.51
1971	5.70
1972	5.27
1973	5.18

Year	Yield in Per cent
1974	6.09
1975	6.89
1976	6.49
1977	5.56
1978	5.90
1979	6.39
1980	8.51
1981	11.23
1982	11.27
1983	9.47
1984	10.15
1985	9.18
1986	7.38
Average Return	5.42%

Table 6-18 High-Grade Municipal Bonds (Standard and Poor's)

Table 6-18A

From / To	1952	1953	1954	1955	1956	1957	1958	1959
1952	2.19							
1953	2.46	2.72						
1954	2.43	2.54	2.37					
1955	2.45	2.54	2.45	2.53				
1956	2.55	2.64	2.61	2.73	2.93			
1957	2.72	2.83	2.86	3.02	3.27	3.60		
1958	2.84	2.95	3.00	3.16	3.36	3.58	3.56	
1959	2.98	3.09	3.16	3.31	3.51	3.70	3.75	3.95
1960	3.06	3.17	3.24	3.38	3.55	3.66	3.67	3.71
1961	3.10	3.21	3.27	3.39	3.54	3.66	3.58	3.58
1962	3.11	3.20	3.26	3.37	3.49	3.58	3.58	3.58
1963	3.12	3.21	3.25	3.35	3.46	3.53	3.52	3.51
1964	3.13	3.21	3.25	3.34	3.43	3.49	3.48	3.46
1965	3.14	3.21	3.25	3.33	3.41	3.47	3.45	3.43
1966	3.18	3.25	3.30	3.37	3.45	3.50	3.49	3.48
1967	3.23	3.30	3.35	3.42	3.49	3.55	3.54	3.54
1968	3.31	3.38	3.42	3.50	3.57	3.63	3.63	3.63
1969	3.45	3.52	3.57	3.65	3.73	3.79	3.81	3.83
1970	3.61	3.69	3.74	3.83	3.92	3.99	4.02	4.06
1971	3.71	3.79	3.85	3.94	4.03	4.10	4.14	4.18
1972	3.79	3.87	3.93	4.01	4.10	4.17	4.21	4.26
1973	3.85	3.93	3.99	4.08	4.16	4.23	4.27	4.32
1974	3.95	4.03	4.09	4.18	4.26	4.34	4.38	4.43
1975	4.07	4.15	4.22	4.31	4.39	4.47	4.52	4.58

From / To	1952	1953	1954	1955	1956	1957	1958	1959
1976	4.17	4.25	4.32	4.41	4.49	4.57	4.62	4.68
1977	4.22	4.30	4.37	4.46	4.54	4.62	4.67	4.73
1978	4.28	4.36	4.43	4.52	4.60	4.68	4.73	4.79
1979	4.36	4.44	4.50	4.59	4.68	4.75	4.80	4.86
1980	4.50	4.58	4.65	4.74	4.83	4.91	4.97	5.03
1981	4.73	4.81	4.89	4.98	5.08	5.16	5.23	5.30
1982	4.95	5.04	5.12	5.22	5.32	5.41	5.48	5.56
1983	5.09	5.18	5.26	5.36	5.46	5.56	5.63	5.72
1984	5.24	5.34	5.42	5.52	5.63	5.72	5.80	5.89
1985	5.36	5.45	5.54	5.64	5.74	5.84	5.92	6.01
1986	5.42	5.51	5.59	5.70	5.80	5.89	5.97	6.06

Table 6-18B

From / To	1960	1961	1962	1963	1964	1965	1966	1967
1960	3.73							
1961	3.59	3.46						
1962	3.46	3.32	3.18					
1963	3.40	3.29	3.21	3.23				
1964	3.36	3.27	3.21	3.23	3.22			
1965	3.35	3.27	3.23	3.24	3.25	3.27		
1966	3.42	3.36	3.34	3.38	3.44	3.54	3.82	
1967	3.49	3.45	3.45	3.50	3.57	3.69	3.90	3.98
1968	3.60	3.58	3.60	3.67	3.76	3.90	4.10	4.25
1969	3.82	3.83	3.88	3.98	4.10	4.28	4.53	4.77
1970	4.07	4.10	4.17	4.29	4.45	4.65	4.93	5.20
1971	4.20	4.24	4.32	4.45	4.60	4.80	5.05	5.30
1972	4.28	4.33	4.41	4.53	4.68	4.86	5.09	5.30
1973	4.35	4.40	4.47	4.59	4.73	4.89	5.10	5.28
1974	4.46	4.52	4.60	4.72	4.85	5.01	5.21	5.38
1975	4.62	4.67	4.76	4.88	5.02	5.18	5.38	5.55
1976	4.73	4.79	4.88	5.00	5.13	5.29	5.48	5.64
1977	4.77	4.83	4.92	5.04	5.16	5.31	5.48	5.64
1978	4.83	4.89	4.98	5.09	5.21	5.36	5.52	5.66
1979	4.91	4.97	5.06	5.17	5.29	5.42	5.58	5.71
1980	5.08	5.15	5.24	5.35	5.48	5.62	5.77	5.91
1981	5.36	5.44	5.54	5.66	5.80	5.95	6.12	6.27
1982	5.63	5.72	5.82	5.96	6.10	6.26	6.44	6.60
1983	5.79	5.88	5.99	6.12	6.27	6.43	6.60	6.77
1984	5.96	6.06	6.17	6.31	6.45	6.62	6.79	6.96
1985	6.09	6.18	6.30	6.43	6.58	6.74	6.91	7.07
1986	6.14	6.23	6.34	6.47	6.61	6.77	6.93	7.09

Table 6-18C

From To	1968	1969	1970	1971	1972	1973	1974	1975
1968	4.51							
1969	5.16	5.81						
1970	5.61	6.16	6.51					
1971	5.63	6.01	6.11	5.70				
1972	5.56	5.82	5.83	5.48	5.27			
1973	5.50	5.69	5.67	5.38	5.22	5.18		
1974	5.58	5.76	5.75	5.56	5.51	5.63	6.09	
1975	5.75	5.92	5.94	5.83	5.86	6.05	6.49	6.89
1976	5.83	5.99	6.02	5.94	5.98	6.16	6.49	6.69
1977	5.80	5.94	5.96	5.88	5.91	6.04	6.26	6.31
1978	5.81	5.94	5.95	5.88	5.91	6.02	6.19	6.21
1979	5.86	5.98	6.00	5.94	5.97	6.07	6.22	6.25
1980	6.06	6.19	6.23	6.20	6.25	6.38	6.55	6.62
1981	6.43	6.58	6.64	6.66	6.75	6.92	7.13	7.28
1982	6.77	6.94	7.02	7.06	7.19	7.38	7.63	7.82
1983	6.94	7.10	7.20	7.25	7.38	7.57	7.81	8.00
1984	7.13	7.29	7.39	7.46	7.59	7.79	8.02	8.22
1985	7.25	7.41	7.51	7.57	7.71	7.89	8.12	8.30
1986	7.25	7.40	7.50	7.56	7.68	7.86	8.06	8.23

Table 6-18D

From To	1976	1977	1978	1979	1980	1981	1982	1983
1976	6.49							
1977	6.03	5.56						
1978	5.98	5.73	5.90					
1979	6.08	5.95	6.14	6.39				
1980	6.57	6.59	6.93	7.45	8.51			
1981	7.35	7.52	8.01	8.71	9.87	11.23		
1982	7.95	8.19	8.72	9.43	10.44	11.40	11.57	
1983	8.14	8.38	8.85	9.43	10.20	10.76	10.52	9.47
1984	8.36	8.60	9.03	9.55	10.19	10.61	10.40	9.81
1985	8.45	8.66	9.05	9.50	10.02	10.32	10.09	9.60
1986	8.35	8.53	8.86	9.23	9.64	9.83	9.55	9.04

Table 6-18E

From To	1984	1985	1986
1984	10.15		
1985	9.66	9.18	
1986	8.90	8.28	7.38

Source: Economic Report of the President, 324, Table B68 (1987).

§6.18   —Common Stock

Common stock represents fractional ownership in a corporation. The corporation may be large or small. For the common stock of a company to be traded on the New York Stock Exchange, certain conditions must have been met by the company. Of importance is that the corporate stock is widely held and there is a ready market for the stock. This means if the individual wishes to buy or sell a security on the exchange it can be done almost immediately.

Returns to common stock may be in one of two forms. The return may be in the form of dividends or in the form of capital gains or both. Capital gains occur when the investment is sold for more than the original purchase price.

Table 6-19 shows the return on common stock. The common stock total return index is based upon the Standard and Poor's Composite Index. The return was calculated by adding the dividends received to the change in price and dividing this sum by the beginning price.

Table 6-19 Returns on Common Stock

Year	Per Cent
1952	18.4
1953	-1.0
1954	52.6
1955	31.6
1956	6.6
1957	-10.8
1958	43.4
1959	12.0
1960	.5
1961	26.9
1962	-8.7
1963	22.8
1964	16.5
1965	12.5
1966	-10.1
1967	24.0
1968	11.1
1969	-8.5
1970	4.0
1971	14.3
1972	19.0
1973	-14.7
1974	-26.5
1975	37.2
1976	23.8
1977	-7.2
1978	6.6
1979	18.4

Year	Per Cent
1980	32.4
1981	-4.9
Average Return	11.4%

Source: R. Ibbotson & R. Sinquefield, Stocks, Bonds, Bills and Inflation: The Past and The Future, 133 exhibit B-32 (The Financial Analysts Research Foundation, University of Virginia 1982).

§6.19 —Combinations of Investments

Some economists argue the present value should be discounted at a combination of various returns. For example, an economist may argue that the appropriate investment would be one-third of the money invested in one-year Treasury Bills and the balance in long-term government bonds. Using the average historic returns on long-term government bonds, 6.49 per cent, and the average historic return on Treasury Bills, 6.01 per cent, the weighted average of these returns can be calculated. The weighted average would be 6.32 per cent, and this would be the discount rate used to calculate present value.

Table 6-20 Weighted Return to a Portfolio

Investment	Return	Weight	Weighted Average Return
Treasury Bill	6.01%	33.3%	2.00%
Long-term Government Bond	6.49%	66.6%	4.32%
		Portfolio return	=6.32%

§6.20   Evaluating Returns

The above tables show the historical returns that have been achieved through alternative investments. The lowest 1952-1986 average return was from the three-month Treasury Bills, which averaged 5.39 per cent annually. The largest return was from investments in common stocks, which averaged 11.4 per cent for the same period of time.

What is of importance is that as the return on the investment increases so does the risk associated with earning the return. That is to say, the return on common stock is more risky than the return on three-month Treasury Bills.

Table 6-21 shows the present value of a future income stream using the various discount rates established by various investment vehicles. The present value is based on a annual income of $20,000 starting today and being earned this year and each year for an additional 29 years. It is assumed the annual growth rate of the future income is zero, and only the discount rate changes.

Table 6-21 Present Value of The Future Income Stream Using Different Discount Rates

Investment	Present Value of the Salary Paid in 29 Years	Present Value of Total Future Wages
3-Month Treasury Bill		
Average Yield 5.39%	$4,364	$310,100
6-Month Treasury Bill		
Average Yield 6.40%	$3,309	$280,794
1-Year Treasury Bill		
Average Yield 6.01%	$3,681	$291,530
Long-Term Government Bonds		
Average Yield 6.49%	$3,229	$278,412
Moody's Aaa Bonds		
Average Yield 7.00%	$2,811	$265,553
Moody's Baa Bonds		
Average Yield 7.97%	$2,164	$243,790
Municipal Bonds		
Average Yield 5.42%	$4,328	$309,156
Weighted Portfolio		
Average Yield 6.32%	$3,382	$282,940

The present value of the salary paid in the twenty-ninth year ranges from a low of $2,164 to a high of $4,364. Likewise, the present value of the income stream varies from a low of $243,790 to a high of $310,100. The only variable which can account for this difference is the discount rate, or the rate earned on invested funds.

§6.21 Summary

The investment chosen by the economist as the appropriate one will have a significant impact on the size of the present value estimate. The higher the return, the lower will be the present value estimate.

The range of investment returns can be determined from the tables in Chapter 6. The range of investment returns is from the low of 5.39 per cent, when funds are invested in a three-month Treasury Bills, to 7.97 per cent, when funds are invested in Moody's Baa Bonds.

7 Combining Growth and Discount

$$\text{Present Value} = \sum_{t=0}^{n} \$ * M * (1+g)^t/(1+d)^t * PL * PS * PF * C * HS * TX$$

§7.01 Introduction

The calculation of the present value of an income stream requires establishing values for four variables. The variables are the dollars to be used as the beginning value, "$" in the formula, the growth rate of the dollars, the discount rate, and the number of years into the future the estimate is made. Chapter 2, "The Base Dollars," showed various sources on which the current dollar value could be based. Chapter 5, "Determination of Growth Rates," examined various methods to calculate growth rates of earnings or expenses and presented sources from which growth rates could be estimated. Chapter 6, "Discount Rates: The Present Value Calculation," showed how discounting to the present value is accomplished and presented source material for establishing the appropriate discount rate.

It is the purpose of this chapter to demonstrate how the present value is determined when a growth rate and a discount rate are used simultaneously. This method of calculating the present value is known as the *simultaneous method*.

121

A second method will also be examined. The second method calculates an average future income figure and discounts the average to present value.

Finally, a worksheet will be developed so anyone can calculate the present value of a future stream of dollars using the simultaneous method. Note that the simultaneous method is the appropriate method to use when calculating the present value of an income stream. The calculation requires deciding what values to use for dollars, "$"; growth, "g"; discount, "d"; and time, "t."

§7.02 Reviewing the Growth Factor

The growth formula has been used to calculate the future value of one dollar. The formula for growth is:

$$\text{Future Value} = (1 + g)^t$$

Where:

> "g" is the rate of growth per year
> "t" is the number of years growth will occur

The growth factor can be determined by using a calculator or by looking up the growth factor in Appendix A. A portion of Appendix A appears in Table 7-1.

Table 7-1 Growth Table

Year	.01	.02	.03	.04	.05
1	1.010	1.020	1.030	1.040	1.050
2	1.020	1.040	1.061	1.082	1.103
3	1.030	1.061	1.093	1.125	1.158
4	1.041	1.082	1.126	1.170	1.216
5	1.051	1.104	1.159	1.217	1.276
6	1.062	1.126	1.194	1.265	1.340
7	1.072	1.149	1.230	1.316	1.407
8	1.083	1.172	1.267	1.369	1.477
9	1.094	1.195	1.309	1.423	1.551
10	1.105	1.219	1.344	1.480	1.629
11	1.116	1.243	1.384	1.539	1.710
12	1.127	1.268	1.426	1.601	1.796
13	1.138	1.294	1.469	1.665	1.886
14	1.149	1.319	1.513	1.732	1.980
15	1.161	1.346	1.558	1.801	2.079
16	1.173	1.373	1.605	1.873	2.183
17	1.184	1.400	1.653	1.948	2.292
18	1.196	1.428	1.702	2.026	2.407
19	1.208	1.457	1.754	2.107	2.527

Growth Rate in Per Cent

Growth Rate in Per Cent

Year	.01	.02	.03	.04	.05
20	1.220	1.486	1.806	2.191	2.653
21	1.232	1.516	1.860	2.279	2.786
22	1.245	1.546	1.916	2.370	2.925
23	1.257	1.577	1.974	2.465	3.072
24	1.270	1.608	2.033	2.563	3.225
25	1.282	1.641	2.094	2.666	3.386

If $1,000 were to be received in 12 years and the investment were growing at 4 per cent annually, the future value would be $1,601. This is the present value of $1,000 times the future value factor of 1.601.

§7.03 Reviewing the Discount Factor

The discount formula is used to calculate the present value of a dollar to be received in the future. The present value formula is:

$$\text{Present Value} = \frac{1}{(1+i)^t}$$

Where:

"i" is the interest or discount
"t" is the number of years until money is to be received

The discount factor can be determined by using a calculator or by looking up the present value factor in Appendix B. A portion of Appendix B is presented in Table 7-2.

Table 7-2 Discount Table

Year		Discount Rate			
	.02	.04	.06	.08	.10
1	.980	.962	.943	.926	.909
2	.961	.925	.890	.857	.826
3	.942	.889	.840	.794	.751
4	.924	.855	.792	.735	.683
5	.906	.822	.747	.681	.621
6	.888	.790	.705	.630	.564
7	.871	.760	.665	.583	.513
8	.853	.731	.627	.540	.467
9	.837	.703	.592	.500	.424
10	.820	.676	.558	.463	.386
11	.804	.650	.527	.429	.350
12	.788	.625	.497	.397	.319
13	.773	.601	.469	.368	.290
14	.758	.577	.442	.340	.263

Year	Discount Rate				
	.02	.04	.06	.08	.10
15	.743	.555	.417	.315	.239
16	.728	.534	.394	.292	.218
17	.714	.513	.371	.270	.198
18	.700	.494	.350	.250	.180
19	.686	.475	.331	.232	.164
20	.673	.456	.312	.215	.149
21	.660	.439	.294	.199	.135
22	.647	.422	.278	.184	.123
23	.634	.406	.262	.170	.112
24	.622	.390	.247	.158	.102
25	.610	.375	.233	.146	.092

To determine the present value of $1,000 to be received in 15 years when the money is invested at 8 per cent, the future value, $1,000, is multiplied by the present value factor from Table 7-2. The present value factor is .315. The present value of the $1,000 is $315.

§7.04   Combining Growth and Discount

When the present value of a future stream of money is being estimated, the calculation for growth and the calculation for discount must be made. When both calculations are being made, the equation can be written as follows:

$$\text{Present Value} = (1 + g)^t / (1 + d)^t$$

Where:

"g" is the annual rate of growth
"d" is the annual rate of discount
"t" is the number of years being considered

This formula gives the present value factor of $1. There is a factor for each year and for each growth and discount rate combination. Table 7-3 shows the present value factors for various growth and discount combinations when "t" equals 25 years. A more complete table appears in Appendix C.

Table 7-3 Present Value Year 25

Discount Rate	Growth Rate				
	0.00	.02	.04	.06	.08	.10
.00	25.00	32.67	43.31	58.16	78.95	108.18
.02	19.52	25.00	32.50	42.82	57.14	77.06
.04	15.62	19.61	25.00	32.33	42.36	56.18
.06	12.78	15.75	19.70	25.00	32.17	41.92
.08	10.67	12.93	15.88	19.79	25.00	32.01

Discount Rate	Growth Rate					
	0.00	.02	.04	.06	.08	.10
.10	9.08	10.82	13.07	16.00	19.87	25.00
.12	7.84	9.22	10.96	13.21	16.12	19.95
.14	6.87	7.97	9.35	11.10	13.34	16.24
.16	6.10	6.99	8.10	9.49	11.24	13.47
.18	5.47	6.21	7.11	8.23	9.62	11.37

Table 7-3 can be used to determine the present value of a stream of money to be received or expended for the next 26 years. The first payment would occur today, followed by 25 additional payments.

Suppose an individual will receive 26 annual payments. The first payment is today for $2,000 and will be followed by 25 more annual payments each growing at 4 per cent annually. This can be viewed as an annuity growing at 4 per cent annually. The present value of such an annuity depends on the current interest rate. If the current interest is 8 per cent, then the present value factor would be found where the row headed ".08" intersects the column headed ".04." The present value factor is 15.88. Multiplying the present value factor by the annual income of $2,000 gives the present value of $31,760. To this amount the first payment of $2,000 must be added. The present value totals $33.760.

Likewise, if an individual were to receive $1,000 per year starting immediately and continuing for an additional 25 years, with a growth rate of 2 per cent and a discount rate of 10 per cent, the present value factor would be 10.82. The present value of the stream on future payments would be $10,820. The total present value would be $12,820.

§7.05 Constructing a Worksheet to Calculate the Present Value of Future Income

When a stream of income is to start immediately, the following worksheet can be used to determine the present value of that stream.

Worksheet #1
Present Value of Annual Income

1. The monthly payment of _____
    times 12 equals an annual payment of   _____.

    The annual payments will be made
    this year plus _____ more years.
    (Year number from Appendix C.)

    The annual payments will grow
    at _____ per year. (Column Number)

    The interest rate, or discount
    rate, is _____. (Row Number)

2. The present value factor is on
    year number _____ of Appendix C where
    column _____ and row _____
    intersect. The factor is _____.

3. Multiply the annual payment which
    is _____ by the factor of _____.

    The present value of the future payments is   _____.

4. The present value of the future income
    plus the income paid in year 1 is
    (the sum of line 1 and line 3)   _____.

Example 1. Suppose the income stream to be evaluated is $1,000 per month
for 26 years with the monthly payment growing at 2 per cent annually. The
appropriate interest rate is 6 per cent. The first payment is paid immediately,
and there are 25 years of future payments. Worksheet #2 is used to calculate
the present value of the stream. The worksheet converts the monthly payments
to annual payments for the purpose of calculating present value.

Worksheet #1
Present Value of Annual Income
2% Annual Growth of Wages
8% Annual Interest Rate

1. The monthly payment of $1,000
    times 12 equals an annual payment of $12,000.

    The annual payments will be made
    this year plus 25 more years.
    (Year #25 from Appendix C.)

    The annual payments will grow
    at 2% per year. (Column headed 2%)

    The interest rate, or discount
    rate, is 8%. (Row for 8%)

2. The present value factor is on
    year number 25 of Appendix C where
    column 2% and row 8%
    intersect. The factor is 12.93.

3. Multiply the annual payment which
    is $12,000 by the factor of 12.93.

    The present value of the future payments is $155,160.

4. The present value of the future income
    plus the income paid in year 1 is
    (the sum of line 1 and line 3) $167,160.

Example 2. Suppose a 35-year-old plaintiff was earning $800 per month at the
time of the injury. The economist has forecast an annual salary increase of 4

per cent and assumed an interest rate, or discount rate, of 6 per cent annually. The plaintiff is expected to have worked to age 65, or for 30 more years. Worksheet #1 can be used to determine the present value of the income stream.

Worksheet #1
Present Value of Annual Income

1. The monthly payment of $800
    times 12 equals an annual payment of $ 9,600.

    The annual payments will be made
    for this year plus 29 more years.
    (Year number from Appendix C.)

    The annual payments will grow
    at 4% per year. (Column Number)

    The interest rate, or discount
    rate, is 6%. (Row Number)

2. The present value factor is on
    year number 29 of Appendix C where
    column 4% and row 6%
    intersect. The factor is 22.07.

3. Multiply the annual payment which
    is $9,600 by the factor of 22.07.
    The present value of the future payments is $211,872.

4. The present value of the future income
    plus the income paid in year 1 is
    (the sum of line 1 and line 3) $221,472.

§7.06   Using the Worksheet to Cross-Examine the Economist about Growth Rates

On cross-examination the defense attorney may wish to question the size of the growth rate of wages assumed by plaintiff's economist. The lower the growth rate the lower will be the present value. The defense attorney will want the economist to assume that the plaintiff's income would experience no growth at all. Then the present value would be lower. Worksheet #1 can be used to recalculate the present value of the income stream in Example 1. The growth rate is zero, the discount rate remains at 8 per cent annually, and the monthly income is $1,000 per month.

Worksheet #1
Present Value of Annual Income
0% Annual Growth of Wages
8% Annual Interest Rate

1. The monthly payment of $1,000
    times 12 equals an annual payment of $ 12,000.

The annual payments will be made
for this year plus 25 more years.
(Year number from Appendix C.)

The annual payments will grow
at 0% per year. (Column Number)

The interest rate, or discount
rate, is 8%. (Row Number)

2. The present value factor is on
    year number 25 of Appendix C where
    column 0% and row 8%
    intersect. The factor is 10.675.

3. Multiply the annual payment which
    is $12,000 by the factor of 10.675.

    The present value of the future income is $128,100.

4. The present value of the future income
    plus the income paid in year 1 is
    (the sum of line 1 and line 3) $140,100.

The reduction on the present value from $167,160 to $140,100 is due to the decrease in the growth rate of wages. An additional reduction on the present value can be achieved if the interest rate is assumed to be larger than the economist's stated rate of 8 per cent annually.

The tables from §§5.14-5.18 can be used to provide different growth rates. For example, if the growth rate employed is CPI for 1957 to 1984, then Table 5-15 shows the growth rate to be 5.01 per cent, rounded to 5 per cent. This can be "plugged" into the worksheet. The present value becomes $224,428.

§7.07 Using the Worksheet to Cross-Examine the Economist about Discount Rates

On cross-examination the defense attorney may wish to question the size of the interest rate assumption made by plaintiff's economist. The higher the discount rate, the lower will be the present value. Using the same example as in §7.06, the defense attorney may wish to pursue the present value question using a different discount rate. Assume the fact situation is the same except the discount rate, at the defense attorney's suggestion, is now 10 per cent.

Worksheet #1
Present Value of Annual Income
0% Annual Growth of Wages
10% Annual Interest Rate

1. The monthly payment of $1,000
    times 12 equals an annual payment of $ 12,000.

    The annual payments will be made
for this year plus 25 more years.
(Year number from Appendix C.)

    The annual payments will grow
at 0% per year. (Column Number)

    The interest rate, or discount
rate, is 10%. (Row Number)

2. The present value factor is on
year number 25 of Appendix C where
column 0% and row 10%
intersect. The factor is 9.077.

3. Multiply the annual payment which
is $12,000 by the factor of 9.077.
The present value of the future income is $108,924.

5. The present value of the future income
plus the income paid in year 1 is
(the sum of line 1 and line 3) $120,924.

The present value of the future income stream was $167,160 when the economist used the growth rate of 2 per cent annually and a discount rate of 8 per cent. When the growth rate was permitted to be 0 per cent and the discount rate was increased to 10 per cent annually, the present value of the future income stream declined to $120,924. The decline in present value of $46,236 is because of the decline in the annual growth rate and the increase in the annual discount rate.

Chapter 6 allows for the choice of various discount rates from different time periods and different investment vehicles.

§7.08 Summary

The present value of a future stream of income can be calculated when the base wage, the annual growth rate, the annual interest rate, and the number of years the payments are to be made are known. The worksheet developed calculates the present value when the monthly or annual payments start immediately. There is an error introduced into the analysis when the monthly payments are converted to annual payments.

The use of this worksheet permits the attorney to estimate the present value of the future income stream, given various assumptions regarding the growth rate and the discount rate of the stream of money. The same worksheet can be used if the calculation is for the present value of future medical expenses.

8

The Age Earnings Profile

§8.01   Introduction

The age earnings profile is used by some economists when estimating the present value of a future income stream. This chapter will explain what the age earnings profile is, how it is constructed, how it is interpreted, and how it is combined with the present value formula to make the calculation of the present value of future wages. The last part of the chapter will be devoted to demonstrating what the age earnings profile does not show and why the age earnings profile is inappropriate and should not be used when making the present value calculations.

§8.02 The Age Earnings Profile

"At any given point in time, earnings of individuals in virtually all careers are a mathematical function of the age of the individual worker."[1] The age earnings profile is constructed from cross-sectional data and shows the income of different individuals at different ages for a given year. Cross-sectional data means that the data is gathered at a specific point or moment in time. For example, an age earnings profile could be constructed for earnings on a given day, or for average earnings during a given month, or, as is more common, average earnings during a given year. Since the age earnings profile is constructed at a point in time, the earnings at each age represent earnings of different individuals.

§8.03 Calculating Median Income

The following example is used to show how the age earnings profile is constructed. In the table below there are 24 different workers identified as worker *A* through worker *X*. Each worker is referred to as an *observation*. Each of these workers, or observations, is between the ages of 25 and 64 inclusively. Finally, the income level of each observation is given.

Table 8-1 Raw Data

Worker	Age	Income
A	42	$ 8,942
B	37	14,311
C	28	8,943
D	63	9,071
E	51	10,261
F	52	9,882
G	48	9,980
H	54	8,146
I	32	5,000
J	29	9,126
K	46	9,871
L	48	9,871
M	39	10,546
N	36	9,954
O	40	10,258
P	61	9,001
Q	54	9,990
R	53	14,333
S	58	10,100
T	32	11,346

---

[1] L. Bassett, The Use of Economists In Personal Injury Actions (Vol 1984, No 2).

Worker	Age	Income
U	26	12,469
V	59	100,000
W	64	9,070
X	57	9,071

In order to make the data more understandable, the data could be reclassified in various statistical ways. One way is to construct a frequency distribution that would indicate the median income by age groups. Permit the age groupings to be by 10 year intervals, starting with age 25. In this case the class interval is 10 years. One would construct four class intervals, each with a 10-year spread or interval. Within each class interval the median income can be calculated.[2]

In the age group 25-34 there are five observations, or workers. They are workers C, I, J, T, and U. When ranked from the lowest to the highest salary, the ranking appears as follows:

Table 8-2 Median Income Age Group 25-34

Worker	Age	Income
I	32	$ 5,000
C	28	8,943
J	29	9,126
T	32	11,346
U	26	12,469

By definition, the median number of a group is the number that divides the group into two equal parts. In this case the median income would be $9,126. There are two observations with incomes less than $9,126, and two observations with incomes greater than $9,126. Again, the median income for the age group 25-34 is $9,126.

In the age group 35-44 there are five observations. They are workers A, B, M, N, and O. When ranked by salary the order appears as follows:

Table 8-3 Median Income Age group 35-44

Worker	Age	Income
A	42	$ 8,942
N	36	9,954
O	40	10,258
M	39	10,546
B	37	14,311

The 40 year-old worker O, with an income of $10,258, represents the median income. There are two workers with an income less than $10,258 and two workers with incomes above $10,258.

---

[2] T. Yamane, Statistics, an Introductory Analysis 368 (1964).

The age group 45-54 is a little different from the previous two groups. The previous group had an odd number of observations. This meant the middle observation was the median income. In the age group 45-54 there is an even number of observations. The eight workers are ranked by salary:

Table 8-4 Median Income Age Group 45-54

Worker	Age	Income
H	54	$ 8,146
K	46	9,871
L	48	9,871
F	52	9,882
G	48	9,980
Q	54	9,990
E	51	10,261
R	53	14,333

Since there is an even number of observations, the median income will be found between the fourth and fifth observations in the class interval. The income for worker F is $9,882 and the income for worker G is $9,980. The median income for this age group would be half-way between these two observations. In this case the median income for the age group 45-54 is $9,931 = (($9,882 + $9,980)/2).

Finally, the median income for the age group 55-64 is calculated in exactly the same manner. That is, the six observations in this category are ranked by salary as follows:

Table 8-5 Median Income Age Group 55-64

Worker	Age	Income
P	61	$ 9,001
W	64	9,070
D	63	9,071
X	57	9,071
S	58	10,100
V	59	100,000

Since there is an even number of observations in the class interval 55-64, the average of the middle two observations is used to determine the class median. However, in this case the third and fourth observations, when ranked by salary, have the same value; thus, the median income would be this value, or $9,071. The thing to note in this class interval is the $100,000 income does not affect the median income of the class interval. The median income of the age categories is used to estimate the age earnings profile.

§8.04   The Source of the Data

The following table presents the 1970, 1975, and 1980 median money income for year-round full-time male workers with income[3] and is an age earnings profile. This type of data may be found in the *Statistical Abstracts of the United States* and the "Monthly Labor Review."

Table 8-6 Age Earnings Profile

Age	1970 Wages	1975 Wages	1980 Wages
14-19	$ 3,950	$ 5,657	$ 7,753
20-24	6,655	8,251	12,109
25-34	9,126	12,727	17,724
35-44	10,258	14,730	21,777
45-54	9,931	14,808	22,323
55-64	9,071	13,518	21,053
65+	6,754	11,485	17,307

There are several things to notice concerning the table. First, and this is of great significance, the data are cross-sectional in nature. This means that in 1970, 1975, and 1980 each full-time, year-round male worker was categorized by age. Once the workers were categorized by age, the median income for each age group was calculated. Thus, the age earnings profile is for a specific moment in time.

Second, the class intervals are of different sizes, i.e., the age categories do not contain the same number of years. The age group 14-19 includes six years, while the age group 20-24 contains only five years. Each of the categories 25-34, 35-44, 45-54, and 55-64 contain 10 years while the last category, 65 plus, is open-ended.

A third thing to note is that earnings peak prior to retirement. The 1970 data show that wages peaked somewhere between the ages of 35 and 44, and in 1975 and 1980 wages peaked in the age category 45-54. The data presented by these age earnings profiles suggest that earnings peak but do not show at what age, only what age category.

§8.05   The Equation for Calculating the Age Earnings Profile

The age categories and median incomes are restated in the following table:

---

[3] US Dept of Commerce, Bureau of the Census, Statistical Abstracts of the United States 469 (104th ed, 1984).

Table 8-7 Age Earnings Profile

| | 1970 | 1975 | 1980 |
| | Wages | Wages | Wages |
Age			
25-34	9,126	12,727	17,724
35-44	10,258	14,730	21,777
45-54	9,931	14,808	22,323
55-64	9,071	13,518	21,053

The equation used to construct the age earnings profile is called a second degree polynomial.[4] The equation is:

Income = C(0) + C(2)*A+C(2)*A

Where:

"A" represents the age of the individual.

"C" represents the coefficient.

It is beyond our scope to demonstrate how the coefficients in the above equations are determined from the age earnings profile. Let it be sufficient to say the coefficients are as follows:

Table 8-8 Age Earnings Coefficients

	1980	1975	1970
C(0)	-8,565.67128	-1,787.84005	-13.3074985
C(1)	1,289.69736	727.346228	-7.88476788
C(2)	-13.3074985	-7.88476788	4.98000129

Using the above equation and inserting the 1980 coefficients into the equation, the income for a 25-year-old is calculated to be:

Income = -8,565.67128+1,289.69736 * (25)

-13.3074985 * $(25)^2$

= $ 15,360

At age 63 the equation yields an income of $19,868:

Income = -8,565.671289+1,289.69736 * (63)

-13.3074985 * $(63)^2$

= $ 19,868

---

[4] Nagy, Harry, Ph.D., Chairman of the Physics and Astronomy Dept of Washburn Univ, wrote the program used to calculate the coefficients in the equations in this chapter.

§8.06   Using the Equation to Construct the Age Earnings Profile

By letting age be the variable (A) and using the coefficients estimated in §8.05, the following age earnings profiles are determined for the years 1980, 1975, and 1970:

Table 8-9 Age Earnings Profile

Age	1980 Age Earnings Profile	1975 Age Earnings Profile	1970 Age Earnings Profile
22	13,367	10,398	7,808
23	14,058	10,770	8,022
24	14,722	11,127	8,226
25	15,360	11,468	8,420
26	15,971	11,793	8,605
27	16,555	12,103	8,779
28	17,113	12,396	8,943
29	17,644	12,674	9,098
30	18,149	12,936	9,242
31	18,626	13,183	9,377
32	19,078	13,413	9,501
33	19,502	13,628	9,616
34	19,901	13,827	9,721
35	20,272	14,010	9,815
36	20,617	14,178	9,900
37	20,935	14,330	9,975
38	21,227	14,466	10,040
39	21,492	14,586	10,094
40	21,730	14,690	10,139
41	21,942	14,779	10,174
42	22,127	14,852	10,199
43	22,286	14,909	10,214
44	22,418	14,950	10,219
45	22,523	14,976	10,214
46	22,602	14,986	10,199
47	22,654	14,980	10,175
48	22,679	14,958	10,140
49	22,678	14,921	10,095
50	22,650	14,868	10,040
51	22,596	14,799	9,976
52	22,515	14,714	9,901
53	22,408	14,613	9,816
54	22,273	14,497	9,722
55	22,113	14,365	9,617
56	21,925	14,217	9,503

Age	1980 Age Earnings Profile	1975 Age Earnings Profile	1970 Age Earnings Profile
57	21,711	14,053	9,378
58	21,470	13,874	9,244
59	21,203	13,679	9,100
60	20,909	13,468	8,945
61	20,589	13,241	8,781
62	20,242	12,999	8,607
63	19,868	12,740	8,423
64	19,467	12,466	8,228

Note the median income of the age groups does not appear in the above table. This is true because the median income corresponds to the midpoints of the class intervals. The midpoint of the first class, 25-34, is 29.5 years of age. The corresponding income would be the median income in 1980 of $17,897. Similarly, the midpoints of the other class intervals would be 39.5, 49.5, and 59.5, respectively.

Both the profiles show that individual's wages peak. Using the 1970 data, wages peak at age 44, at $10,219, while the 1975 data suggest that wages peak at age 46, with earnings equal to $14,986. In 1980 wages peaked at age 48 when earnings were $22,679. The increasing and decreasing of the wages at various ages is known as the age earnings effect. This is sometimes stated as the effect that age has on the individual earnings.

§8.07   The Age Earnings Effect

The age earnings effect is calculated by dividing each successive earnings by the previous year's (age) earnings. Thus, in 1980 the age earnings effect for a 23-year-old is that the earnings are 5.20 per cent higher than those of a 22-year-old. A 24-year-old's income is 4.76 per cent higher than a 23-year-old's. It is the percentage changes that are important when the economist uses the age earnings profile in the calculation of economic loss. The following table shows how, in 1980, each successive year's income is related to the previous year's income:

Table 8-10 Age Earnings Effect (1980)

Age	1980 Age Earnings Profile	Age Earnings Effect (Percentage)
22	$ 13,367	
23	14,058	5.17
24	14,722	4.72
25	15,360	4.33
26	15,971	3.98

Age	1980 Age Earnings Profile	Age Earnings Effect (Percentage)
27	16,555	3.66
28	17,113	3.37
29	17,644	3.10
30	18,149	2.86
31	18,626	2.63
32	19,078	2.43
33	19,502	2.22
34	19,901	2.05
35	20,272	1.86
36	20,617	1.70
37	20,935	1.54
38	21,227	1.39
39	21,492	1.25
40	21,730	1.11
41	21,942	.98
42	22,127	.84
43	22,286	.72
44	22,418	.59
45	22,523	.47
46	22,602	.35
47	22,654	.23
48	22,679	.11
49	22,678	0
50	22,650	-.11
51	22,596	-.23
52	22,515	-.35
53	22,408	-.47
54	22,273	-.59
55	22,113	-.71
56	21,925	-.84
57	21,711	-.97
58	21,470	-1.10
59	21,203	-1.23
60	20,909	-1.38
61	20,589	-1.52
62	20,242	-1.68
63	19,868	-1.84
64	19,467	-2.01

§8.08   Making the Data Current

Since the most recent data are the 1980 age earnings profile, it is necessary to *move* the data to 1986 data. This is done by applying a growth rate which would represent the growth rate of wages from 1980 to 1986. Let us assume that wages have grown at the rate of 3 per cent per year for the five-year period. This would mean that each wage would grow by 15.92 per cent. This is calculated by using the growth formula $[(1+g)^5$ The value of the expression equals 1.1592 when "g" equals 3 per cent and means that the 1986 wages are 1.1592 per cent higher than the 1980 wages. In this manner the economist has *moved* the 1980 wages to a 1986 wage level. It is the 1986 earnings that are used to estimate the future earnings if the individual has no earnings history. The following are the 1986 wage levels:

Table 8-11 Current Income

Age	1980 Age Earnings Profile	1986 Earnings Profile
22	13,367	15,495
23	14,058	16,296
24	14,722	17,066
25	15,360	17,805
26	15,971	18,514
27	16,555	19,191
28	17,113	19,837
29	17,644	20,453
30	18,149	21,038
31	18,626	21,591
32	19,078	22,115
33	19,502	22,607
34	19,901	23,069
35	20,272	23,499
36	20,617	23,899
37	20,935	24,268
38	21,227	24,606
39	21,492	24,914
40	21,730	25,189
41	21,942	25,435
42	22,127	25,650
43	22,286	25,834
44	22,418	25,987
45	22,523	26,109
46	22,602	26,200
47	22,654	26,261

[5] R. Brealey & S. Myers, Principles of Corporate Finance 31 (McGraw-Hill, Inc 1981).

Age	1980 Age Earnings Profile	1986 Earnings Profile
48	22,679	26,289
49	22,678	26,288
50	22,650	26,256
51	22,596	26,193
52	22,515	26,099
53	22,408	25,975
54	22,273	25,819
55	22,113	25,633
56	21,925	25,415
57	21,711	25,167
58	21,470	24,888
59	21,203	24,579
60	20,909	24,238
61	20,589	23,867
62	20,242	23,465
63	19,868	23,031
64	19,467	22,566

As expected, the 1980 data and the *current* 1986 data show the same trend. That is, both income levels peak at age 48. It is 1986 data that is used in making the economic forecast of present value. The economist uses the appropriate growth and discount rates to establish the present value of the income stream.

§8.09   Two Ways to Go

When the economist is estimating present value of future income, the plaintiff will either have an earnings history or the plaintiff will not have an earnings history. **Section 8.10** demonstrates how the present value of the future income is determined if the individual has no earnings history. **Section 8.11** demonstrates how the present value of the future income is determined if the individual has an earnings history.

§8.10   —Calculating the Present Value of Future Income When the Individual Has No Earnings History

In the absence of an earnings history, the current data, as calculated in **§8.08,** are used as the basis for making the economic forecast. If the plaintiff is a 39-year-old high school graduate with no earnings history, then the economist would state that the age earnings profile indicates the salary, or base wage, would be $24,914, as shown on the previous table.

Using the age earnings effect, an age earnings profile for the plaintiff is constructed. The age earnings effect indicates that a 40-year-old high school graduate will earn 1.11 per cent more than a 39-year-old worker. Accordingly, the $24,914 is increased by 1.11 per cent to become earnings of $25,191 at age 40. In like manner, the earnings of a 41-year-old worker are .76 per cent larger than a 40-year-old worker. The earnings of $25,356 are increased by .76 per cent to become earnings of $25,550 for the 41-year-old worker. It is the last column in Table 8-12 below, Age Earnings Profile for a 39-year-old, that is considered the 1986 earnings of the individual. The numbers in this column are used in calculating the present value of the future income.

Table 8-12 Earnings Profile No Previous Earnings History

Age	1986 Base Earnings	Age Earnings Effect (Per Cent)	Age Earnings Profile for a 39-Year-Old
39	$24,914		$24,914
40		1.11	25,191
41		.98	25,438
42		.84	25,652
43		.72	25,837
44		.59	25,989
45		.47	26,111
46		.35	26,202
47		.23	26,262
48		.11	26,291
49		0	26,291
50		-.11	26,262
51		-.23	26,202
52		-.35	26,110
53		-.47	25,987
54		-.59	25,834
55		-.71	25,651
56		-.84	25,436
57		-.97	25,189
58		-1.10	24,912
59		-1.23	24,606
60		-1.38	24,266
61		-1.52	23,897
62		-1.68	23,496
63		-1.84	23,064
64		-2.01	22,600

The formula[5] used to calculate the present value is:

$$\text{Present Value} = \sum_{t=0}^{n} \left[\$ \left[1+g \right]^t / \left[1 + d \right]^t \right]$$

Where $ is the annual wage.
       g   is the growth rate of wages.
       d   is the interest or discount rate.
       t   is the number of years to be calculated
       n   is the last year

Assume the annual growth rate of wages is 3 per cent (g), and the annual discount rate is 4 per cent (d). The annual salary ($) is the salary shown in Table 8-12 in the column Age Earnings Profile for a 39-Year-Old. For the first year the present value of the future wage would be $25,102. The calculations are as follows:

Present Value
  Year
    1 = $25,346 [1 + .03]^1 [1 + .04]^1 = $25,102
    2 =   25,539 [1 + .03]^2 [1 + .04]^2 =   25,050
    3 =   25,695 [1 + .03]^3 [1 + .04]^3 =   24,961

The calculations would continue until the plaintiff reaches age 64. There would be one calculation for each year being estimated. The sum of the calculations for each year is the present value of the future income stream.

The following table shows the age of the plaintiff, the year, the period, the base wage calculated from the age earnings profile, the future wage after the growth rate has been applied, the present value of each year's wage, and, finally, the sum of the present value. The sum of the present value of each of the future wages, $583,877, represents the loss estimated by the economist.

Table 8-13 Present Value of Future Income No Previous Earnings History

Age	Period	1980 Age Earnings Profile	1986 Earnings	3% Growth Rate Annually	4% Interest Rate Annually
39	0	$ 21,492	$ 24,914	$ 24,914	$ 24,914
40	1	21,730	25,189	25,945	24,947
41	2	21,942	25,435	26,984	24,948
42	3	22,127	25,650	28,028	24,917
43	4	22,286	25,834	29,076	24,854
44	5	22,418	25,987	30,126	24,761
45	6	22,523	26,109	31,176	24,639
46	7	22,602	26,200	32,223	24,487
47	8	22,654	26,261	33,267	24,308
48	9	22,679	26,289	34,301	24,099
49	10	22,678	26,288	35,329	23,867
50	11	22,650	26,256	36,344	23,608
51	12	22,596	26,193	37,345	23,326
52	13	22,515	26,099	38,327	23,018

Age	Period	1980 Age Earnings Profile	1986 Earnings	3% Growth Rate Annually	4% Interest Rate Annually
53	14	22,408	25,975	39,290	22,689
54	15	22,273	25,819	40,225	22,336
55	16	22,113	25,633	41,133	21,961
56	17	21,925	25,415	42,007	21,565
57	18	21,711	25,167	42,845	21,149
58	19	21,470	24,888	43,641	20,714
59	20	21,203	24,579	44,392	20,260
60	21	20,909	24,238	45,090	19,787
61	22	20,589	23,867	45,732	19,297
62	23	20,242	23,465	46,310	18,789
63	24	19,868	23,031	46,817	18,264
64	25	19,467	22,566	47,248	17,724
	Total	567,070	657,347	968,115	585,228

§8.11 —Calculating the Present Value of Future Income When the Individual Has An Earnings History

When the analysis is for a person with an earnings history, the current wages are substituted in the age earnings profile at the individual's current age. The current wage becomes the base wage in the earnings profile. The percentage changes calculated in the profile are used to increase or decrease the future income based on the starting wage. Consider the 39-year-old high school graduate earning $30,000 at the time of the accident. The following age earnings profile would be established.

Table 8-14 Earnings Profile Previous Earnings History

Age	1986 Base Earnings	Age Earnings Effect (Per Cent)	Age Earnings Profile for a 39-Year-Old
39	$30,000		$30,000
40		1.11	30,333
41		.98	30,630
42		.84	30,887
43		.72	31,109
44		.59	31,293
45		.47	31,440
46		.35	31,550
47		.23	31,623
48		.11	31,658

Age	1986 Base Earnings	Age Earnings Effect (Per Cent)	Age Earnings Profile for a 39-Year-Old
49		0	31,658
50		—.11	31,623
51		—.35	31,550
52		—.35	31,440
53		—.47	31,292
54		—.59	31,107
55		—.71	30,886
56		—.97	30,627
57		—.97	30,330
58		—1.10	29,996
59		—1.23	29,627
60		—1.38	29,218
61		—1.68	28,774
62		—1.68	28,291
63		—1.84	27,770
64		—2.01	27,212

As before, the age earnings profile is used to calculate the present value of the future wage. The following table shows the age of the plaintiff, the year, the base wage calculated from the age earnings profile, the future wage after the growth rate has been applied, the present value of each year's wage, and, finally, the sum of the present value. The sum of the present value of each of the future wages, $697,525, represents the loss estimated by the economist.

Table 8-15 Present Value of Future Income Previous Earnings History

Age	Period	Year	Base Wage	Future Wage (3% Annual Growth)	Present Value (4% Discount)
39	0	1986	$ 30,000	$ 30,000	$ 30,000
40	1	1987	30,279	31,187	29,988
41	2	1988	30,509	32,367	29,925
42	3	1989	30,695	33,541	29,818
43	4	1990	30,836	34,706	29,667
44	5	1991	30,938	35,866	29,479
45	6	1992	31,003	37,019	29,257
46	7	1993	31,031	38.164	29,002
47	8	1994	31,031	39,309	28,723
48	9	1995	31,065	40,533	28,478
49	10	1996	31,003	41,665	28,147
50	11	1997	30,916	42,795	27,799
51	12	1998	30,805	43,921	27,433
52	13	1999	30,673	45,044	27,052

Age	Period	Year	Base Wage	Future Wage (3% Annual Growth)	Present Value (4% Discount)
53	14	2000	30,520	46,164	26,659
54	15	2001	30,349	47,283	26,255
55	16	2002	30,164	48,404	25,843
56	17	2003	29,968	49,533	25,429
57	18	2004	29,761	50,666	25,010
58	19	2005	29,547	51,811	24,592
59	20	2006	29,328	52,970	24,175
60	21	2007	29,105	54,144	23,760
61	22	2008	28,881	55,339	23,351
62	23	2009	28,662	56,567	22,951
63	24	2010	28,444	57,821	22,557
64	25	2011	28,234	59,116	22,175
		Totals	$783,747	$1,155,935	$697,525

§8.12   Shortcomings of Using the Age Earnings Profile

Recall that the age earnings profile is constructed from cross-sectional data. The profiles presented in the table below show that, in 1970, wages peaked when the worker was 44 years of age and earning $10,219. In 1975, wages peaked at age 46 when earnings were $14,986 and, in 1980, wages peaked at age 48 when earnings reached $22,679.

Some economists will argue that all three age earnings profiles indicate that the income of the worker will decline after age 46. This is wrong. What the three profiles do indicate is that a worker over age 46 will earn less than a younger worker. The profile does not say that earnings will decline.

Intuitively one can see that claiming an individual's income will decline after age 46 does not make sense. We, as members of the labor force, do not expect a decrease in salary because we get older. By the same token, it is not unreasonable to say that a person age 55 will earn less than a person age 50. This is what the profile is demonstrating.

Approaching the age earnings profile in a different fashion, we could examine the earnings in 1970 of any worker in the labor force. For example the 42-year-old worker's earnings were $10,199 in 1970. According to the economist using the profile, earnings should decline after age 46. However, in 1975, when the worker is 47 years of age, the earnings have grown to $14,976, and by 1980, when the worker is 52 years of age, earnings have grown to $22,515. The table does not suggest that earnings fall as a person gets older, but rather suggests that earnings of younger workers may exceed earnings of older workers.

Table 8-16 Age Earnings Profiles

Age	1970 Age Earnings Profile	1975 Age Earnings Profile	1980 Age Earnings Profile
22	$7,808	$10,398	$13,367
23	8,022	10,770	14,058
24	8,226	11,127	14,722
25	8,420	11,468	15,360
26	8,605	11,793	15,971
27	8,779	12,103	16,555
28	8,943	12,396	17,113
29	9,098	12,674	17,644
30	9,242	12,936	18,149
31	9,377	13,183	18,626
32	9,501	13,413	19,078
33	9,616	13,628	19,502
34	9,721	13,827	19,901
35	9,815	14,010	20,272
36	9,900	14,178	20,617
37	9,975	14,330	20,935
38	10,040	14,466	21,227
39	10,094	14,586	21,492
40	10,139	14,690	21,730
41	10,174	14,779	21,942
42	10,199	14,852	22,127
43	10,214	14,909	22,286
44	10,219	14,950	22,418
45	10,214	14,976	22,523
46	10,199	14,986	22,602
47	10,175	14,980	22,654
48	10,140	14,958	22,679
49	10,095	14,921	22,678
50	10,040	14,868	22,650
51	9,976	14,799	22,596
52	9,901	14,714	22,515
53	9,816	14,613	22,408
54	9,722	14,497	22,273
55	9,617	14,365	22,113
56	9,503	14,217	21,925
57	9,378	14,053	21,711
58	9,244	13,874	21,470
59	9,100	13,679	21,203
60	8,945	13,468	20,909
61	8,781	13,241	20,589

Age	1970 Age Earnings Profile	1975 Age Earnings Profile	1980 Age Earnings Profile
62	8,607	12,999	20,242
63	8,423	12,740	19,868
64	8,228	12,466	19,467

If the profiles were graphed, each year's profile would peak but the 1975 profile would indicate higher earnings at each age level than would the 1970 profile. In the same fashion, the 1980 profile would peak but earnings at each age would be higher than that indicated by the 1975 profile.

Chart 8.1 Age Earnings Profiles

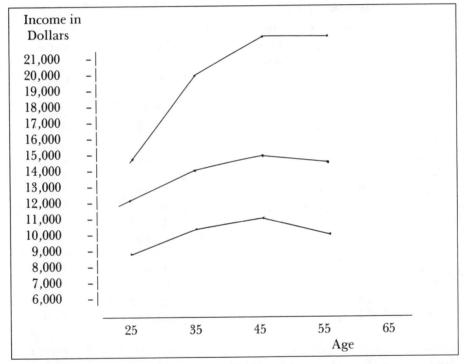

When estimating the present value of a future income stream, the economist is dealing in time series analysis. Time series analysis refers to analyzing data, or making estimates, from different points in time, or for different points in time. The error the economist has made when using the age earnings profile is using cross-sectional data to estimate a time series phenomenon.

§8.13 Proper Use of the Age Earnings Profile

If the economist plans to use the age earnings profile as the basis for making the economic forecast, the economist would be analyzing a case where the plaintiff has no earnings history. The economist would be concerned only with the wage indicated by the age earnings profile as a median income for that age person. For example, suppose the plaintiff were a 24-year-old male military veteran recently separated from the service but not yet in the labor force. The economist might suggest the 1986 age earnings profile, see Table 8-11, for a 24-year-old full-time male worker indicates earnings of $17,066 per year. This would become the base wage which would be permitted to grow and be discounted to present value. Table 8-17 shows the growth and discount of the $17,066. The growth rate is assumed to be 3 per cent and the discount rate is assumed to be 4 per cent.

Table 8-17 Present Value of Future Income No Previous Earnings History Proper Use of Age Earnings Profile

Age	Period	1986 Base Income	Future Wage (3% Annual Growth)	Present Value (4% Annual Interest)
24	0	17,066	$ 17,066	$ 17,066
25	1		17,578	16,902
26	2		18,105	16,739
27	3		18,648	16,578
28	4		19,208	16,419
29	5		19,784	16,261
30	6		20,378	16,105
31	7		20,989	15,950
32	8		21,619	15,797
33	9		22,267	15,644
34	10		22,935	15,494
35	11		23,623	15,345
36	12		24,332	15,198
37	13		25,062	15,052
38	14		25,814	14,907
39	15		26,588	14,763
40	16		27,386	14,622
41	17		28,207	14,481
42	18		29,054	14,342
43	19		29,925	14,204
44	20		30,823	14,067
45	21		31,748	13,932
46	22		32,700	13,798
47	23		33,681	13,665
48	24		34,692	13,534
49	25		35,732	13,404
50	26		36,804	13,275
51	27		37,909	13,147

Age	White		Black and Other Women	
	Life Expectancy	Active Years in Labor Force	Life Expectancy	Active Years in Labor Force
32	48.0	19.6	44.5	19.0
33	47.0	19.0	43.5	18.3
34	46.0	18.3	42.6	17.7
35	45.1	17.7	41.7	17.0
36	44.1	17.0	40.7	16.3
37	43.1	16.4	39.8	15.7
38	42.2	15.8	38.9	15.0
39	41.2	15.1	38.0	14.4
40	40.3	14.4	37.1	13.8
41	39.3	13.8	36.2	13.1
42	38.4	13.1	35.3	12.5
43	37.5	12.4	34.5	11.9
44	36.5	11.8	33.6	11.3
45	35.6	11.1	32.7	10.8
46	34.7	10.5	31.9	10.2
47	33.8	9.9	31.1	9.6
48	32.9	9.2	30.2	9.0
49	32.0	8.6	29.4	8.5
50	31.1	8.0	28.6	7.9
51	30.2	7.4	27.8	7.4
52	29.3	6.9	27.0	6.8
53	28.4	6.3	26.2	6.3
54	27.6	5.8	25.5	5.7
55	26.7	5.3	24.7	5.2
56	25.9	4.7	23.9	4.7
57	25.0	4.3	23.2	4.2
58	24.2	3.8	22.4	3.8
59	23.4	3.4	21.7	3.4
60	22.6	3.0	21.0	3.0
61	21.8	2.6	20.3	2.6
62	21.0	2.3	19.6	2.3
63	20.2	2.0	19.0	2.0
64	19.4	1.8	18.3	1.7
65	18.7	1.5	17.7	1.5
66	17.9	1.4	17.0	1.3
67	17.2	1.2	16.4	1.1
68	16.4	1.0	15.7	.9
69	15.7	.9	15.1	.8
70	15.0	.8	14.5	.7
71	14.3	.7	13.9	.6
72	13.6	.6	13.4	.5
73	13.0	.5	12.9	.5

Age	White		Black and Other Women	
	Life Expectancy	Active Years in Labor Force	Life Expectancy	Active Years in Labor Force
74	12.3	.4	12.3	.4
75	11.7	.3	11.8	.4

Source: US Dept of Labor, Bureau of Labor Statistics, Worklife Estimates: Effects of Race and Education Bulletin 2254 (Feb 1986).

§9.02   How Worklife Expectancy Is Used in the Present Value Calculation: Cross-Examination

Table 9-3 presents the present value of a future income stream. The analysis starts with a 25-year-old male who was earning $20,000 at the time of the injury. The growth rate employed is 4 per cent, and the discount rate employed is 6 per cent. As the table shows, the present value of the future income stream, assuming the individual worked uninterrupted to age 65, is $565,228.

Table 9-3 Present Value of Future Income

Age	Period	Present Value of Future Income	Total Income
25	0	$20,000	$ 20,000
26	1	19,623	39,623
27	2	19,252	58,875
28	3	18,889	77,764
29	4	18,533	96,297
30	5	18,183	114,480
31	6	17,840	132,320
32	7	17,503	149,823
33	8	17,173	166,997
34	9	16,849	183,846
35	10	16,531	200,377
36	11	16,219	216,596
37	12	15,913	232,509
38	13	15,613	248,123
39	14	15,318	263,441
40	15	15,029	278,470
41	16	14,746	293,216
42	17	14,468	307,684
43	18	14,195	321,878
44	19	13,927	335,805
45	20	13,664	349,469
46	21	13,406	362,876
47	22	13,153	376,029
48	23	12,905	388,934

Age	Period	Present Value of Future Income	Total Income
49	24	12,662	401,596
50	25	12,423	414,018
51	26	12,188	426,207
52	27	11,958	438,165
53	28	11,733	449,898
54	29	11,511	461,409
55	30	11,294	472,703
56	31	11,081	483,784
57	32	10,872	494,656
58	33	10,667	505,323
59	34	10,466	515,789
60	35	10,268	526,057
61	36	10,074	536,131
62	37	9,884	546,016
63	38	9,698	555,713
64	39	9,515	565,228

The defense attorney will want to ask the plaintiff's economist whether the figure of $565,228 takes into account the worklife expectancy calculation. It does not.

The economist will be asked to examine the worklife expectancy table (Table 9-1). The table shows that a 25-year-old white male has a worklife expectancy of 33.8 years. This means the individual would exit the labor force at age 58.8 years. From Table 9-3, the present value of the income stream to age 58.8 is $513,696. This figure is 80 percent times $10,466 (the difference between $515,789 and $505,323) plus $505,323 ($8373 + $505,323 = $513,696).

Using the worklife expectancy table has decreased the present value of the future income stream from $565,228 to $513,696. This is a decline in the present value of the future income stream of $51,532.

Had the plaintiff been a 25-year-old black male, the worklife would be 28.6 years. This would reduce the present value of future income to $456,805. This is a reduction of $108,423.

In a similar fashion, the worklife expectancy of women can be employed to reduce the present value of the future income stream. For example, the worklife expectancy for a 25-year-old white female is 24.1 years, and for a 25-year-old black female the worklife expectancy is 23.5 years. The reduction in the present value of the future income stream for a 25-year-old white female is from $565,228 to $402,835, and for the black female the present value of the future income is reduced to $395,265.

§9.03   Reconsidering the Worklife Table

Care must be taken not to put too much meaning on the worklife tables. The worklife tables state how many years will be spent in the labor force, not which years will be spent in the labor force.

The worklife expectancy table indicates that a 25-year-old white female will spend 24.1 years in the labor force. As illustrated in **§9.02,** this caused the present value of the future income to decrease from $565,228 to $402,835. But the illustration assumes the woman was in the labor force for the next 24.1 years. Suppose the woman exited the labor force at age 25 to have a family and returned to the labor force at age 40. If the woman worked uninterrupted to age 65, she would have "fullfilled" the worklife expectancy of 24.1 years.

Under the latter approach the present value of the future income stream would be $301,787. This is the present value of the income stream if the woman works uninterrupted from age 25 to age 65 less the present value of the income stream from age 25 to age 40. The worklife is 25 years, and is between ages 40 and 65, after the child-bearing years.

This example points out the problem with the worklife expectancy table. The table indicates how many years the individual is expected to be an active participant in the labor force but not which years the participation in the labor force will occur. The timing of the participation will affect the present value of the income stream.

The worklife table measures movement into and out of the labor force. It does not mean the person is employed, only that they are actively seeking employment.[3] This means that worklife years can include a person who is unemployed but seeking employment.

During the course of discovery, the defense counsel should have determined the method by which the economist calculated the plaintiff's work life expectancy. It is generally agreed that the United States Department of Labor publishes the most authoritative study on worklife.[4] Other methods arbitrarily select the age at which a worker is eligible for social security benefits or a mandatory retirement age. The inherent weakness in these methods is that they tend to ignore a worker's withdrawal from the labor force, such as for marriage, child-rearing, or sickness, as well as the possibility of death. By failing to take this into account, the present value of a lost stream of earnings may be overstated.

§9.04 Summary

The worklife tables show how many years an individual is expected to be active in the labor force. The tables do not distinguish between employment and unemployment, nor do they indicate which years an individual will be economically active.

---

[3] US Dept of Labor, Bureau of Labor Statistics, Worklife Estimates: Effects of Race and Education, Bulletin 2254, at 33 (Feb 1986).

[4] US Dept of Labor, Bureau of Labor Statistics, Special Labor Force Report, Length of Working Life for Men and Women 187 (rev ed 1976).

10

Mortality Adjustment

$$\text{Present Value} = \sum_{t=0}^{n} \$(1+g)^t/(1+d)^t * PL * PS * PF * C * TX * H$$

§10.01   Introduction

Mortality expectations are sometimes introduced with the expectation that the present value of the future income stream can be reduced. This may or may not be the case. However, when the calculation of the present value of future medical expenses is made, the use of mortality expectation to determine present value is essential.

This chapter will look at what a mortality table is, what types of mortality tables there are, how mortality tables are constructed, and how mortality tables may be used in the present value calculation.

§10.02   Mortality Tables

Mortality tables reflect the number of persons per thousand for ages 0 to age 100 who will die during a particular year.[1] They do not reflect which persons will die, but how many persons will die. In addition to the probability of dying,

---

[1] G. Reynolds, The Mortality Merchants 46 (1978).

most mortality tables will also state the life expectancy. Mortality tables can be constructed for the entire population or for a part of the population. Mortality tables are constructed for the different sexes and for the different races.

Table 10-1 is a mortality table for the entire population of the United States.[2] The first column shows the age of the individual. The second column shows the life expectancy of an individual of that age. The third column states the probability a person of that age will die. For example, a four-year-old has a life expectancy of 71.6 years, and the probability of death occurring at the age of four is .41 per cent, less than one-half a per cent. The mortality table shows the life expectancy at each age and the probability of dying at each of the ages.

Table 10-1 Mortality Table and Life Expectancy for the Total Population

Age	Life Expectancy	Probability of Death per Thousand
0	74.6	1.55
1	74.4	.78
2	73.5	.61
3	72.5	.49
4	71.6	.41
5	70.6	.35
6	69.6	.32
7	68.6	.28
8	67.7	.25
9	66.7	.22
10	65.7	.19
11	64.7	.19
12	63.7	.23
13	62.7	.33
14	61.7	.47
15	60.8	.63
16	59.8	.78
17	58.9	.90
18	57.9	.98
19	57.0	1.03
20	56.0	1.08
21	55.1	1.13
22	54.1	1.16
23	53.2	1.18
24	52.3	1.18

[2] US Dept of Commerce, Bureau of the Census, Statistical Abstracts of the United States 469 (104th ed 1984).

Age	Life Expectancy	Probability of Death per Thousand
25	51.3	1.18
26	50.4	1.18
27	49.5	1.18
28	48.5	1.19
29	47.6	1.22
30	46.6	1.25
31	45.7	1.28
32	44.7	1.32
33	43.8	1.38
34	42.9	1.41
35	41.9	1.47
36	41.0	1.55
37	40.0	1.65
38	39.1	1.78
39	38.2	1.98
40	37.2	2.10
41	36.3	2.30
42	35.4	2.58
43	34.5	2.79
44	33.6	3.08
45	32.7	3.41
46	31.8	3.76
47	30.9	4.15
48	30.1	4.59
49	29.2	5.07
50	28.3	5.58
51	27.5	6.14
52	26.7	6.73
53	25.8	7.35
54	25.0	8.00
55	24.2	8.70
56	23.4	9.47
57	22.6	10.30
58	21.9	11.20
59	21.1	12.19
60	20.4	13.25
61	19.6	14.38
62	18.9	15.62
63	18.2	16.99
64	17.5	18.49
65	16.8	20.10
70	13.7	29.62
75	10.8	43.72

Age	Life Expectancy	Probability of Death per Thousand
80	8.3	65.40
85+	6.3	1000.00

Source: US Dept of Commerce, Bureau of Census, Life Expectancy Statistical Abstracts of the United States 69, Table 106 (106th ed 1986).

There are different mortality tables constructed for each race and for each sex. Thus, there are four tables which are subsets of the mortality table of the total population. The four tables are white-male, white-female, black-male, and black-female. These tables appear in Table 10-2 and Appendix F.

Table 10-2 Life Expectancy and Probability of Dying By Race and Sex

	Life Expectancy				Probability of Dying			
	White		Black		White		Black	
Age	Male	Female	Male	Female	Male	Female	Male	Female
0	71.5	78.8	64.9	73.5	11.26	8.88	21.59	17.71
1	71.3	78.5	65.4	73.8	.82	.63	1.18	.97
2	70.4	77.5	64.4	72.9	.61	.50	.97	.81
3	69.4	76.5	63.5	71.9	.48	.40	.81	.67
4	68.4	75.6	62.6	71.0	.40	.33	.69	.55
5	67.5	74.6	61.6	70.0	.36	.28	.59	.46
6	66.5	73.6	60.6	69.1	.34	.24	.51	.38
7	65.5	72.6	59.7	68.1	.32	.21	.45	.32
8	64.5	71.7	58.7	67.1	.28	.19	.40	.28
9	63.6	70.7	57.7	66.1	.24	.17	.35	.25
10	62.6	69.7	56.7	65.1	.20	.16	.32	.23
11	61.6	68.7	55.8	64.2	.19	.16	.32	.23
12	60.6	67.7	54.8	63.2	.26	.19	.38	.24
13	59.6	66.7	53.8	62.2	.42	.23	.49	.27
14	58.6	65.7	52.8	61.2	.64	.29	.65	.31
15	57.7	64.7	51.9	60.2	.89	.37	.83	.36
16	56.7	63.8	50.9	59.2	1.12	.43	1.02	.42
17	55.8	62.8	50.0	58.3	1.31	.90	1.22	.48
18	54.9	61.8	49.0	57.3	1.44	.51	1.44	.54
19	53.9	60.9	48.1	56.3	1.51	.52	1.66	.60
20	53.0	59.9	47.2	55.4	1.58	.52	1.89	.66
21	52.1	58.9	46.2	54.4	1.64	.52	2.13	.72
22	51.2	58.0	45.3	53.4	1.68	.53	2.35	.79
23	50.3	57.0	44.5	52.5	1.68	.53	2.53	.86
24	49.4	56.0	43.6	51.5	1.66	.53	2.69	.93
25	48.4	55.0	42.7	50.6	1.62	.54	2.84	1.00
26	47.5	54.1	41.8	49.6	1.56	.54	3.00	1.08
27	46.6	53.1	40.9	48.7	1.55	.55	3.17	1.16
28	45.7	52.1	40.1	47.7	1.54	.56	3.34	1.23

| | Life Expectancy | | | | Probability of Dying | | | |
| | White | | Black | | White | | Black | |
Age	Male	Female	Male	Female	Male	Female	Male	Female
29	44.7	51.2	39.2	46.8	1.54	.58	3.53	1.30
30	43.8	50.2	38.3	45.8	1.56	.61	3.73	1.38
31	42.9	49.2	37.5	44.9	1.58	.64	3.93	1.46
32	41.9	48.2	36.6	44.0	1.60	.67	4.12	1.56
33	41.0	47.3	35.8	43.0	1.63	.71	4.30	1.67
34	40.1	46.3	34.9	42.1	1.68	.76	4.48	1.80
35	39.1	45.3	34.1	41.2	1.74	.82	4.69	1.94
36	38.2	44.4	33.2	40.3	1.82	.89	4.92	2.09
37	37.3	43.4	32.4	39.3	1.92	.97	5.17	2.26
38	36.3	42.5	31.6	38.4	2.05	1.07	5.45	2.45
39	35.4	41.5	30.7	37.5	2.21	1.18	5.76	2.66
40	34.5	40.6	29.9	36.6	2.40	1.31	6.09	2.89
41	33.6	39.6	29.1	35.7	2.63	1.46	6.49	3.15
42	32.7	38.7	28.3	34.8	2.89	1.61	6.98	3.44
43	31.8	37.7	27.5	34.0	3.19	1.79	7.59	3.77
44	30.9	36.8	26.7	33.1	3.53	1.98	8.32	4.12
45	30.0	35.9	25.9	32.2	3.91	2.19	9.11	4.51
46	29.1	34.9	25.1	31.4	4.34	2.42	9.95	4.93
47	28.2	34.0	24.4	30.5	4.83	2.67	10.84	5.39
48	27.3	33.1	23.6	29.7	5.38	2.95	11.79	5.92
49	26.5	32.2	22.9	28.9	6.01	3.25	12.79	6.50
50	25.6	31.3	22.2	28.0	6.69	3.58	13.86	7.13
51	24.8	30.4	21.5	27.2	7.42	3.94	14.99	7.80
52	24.0	29.6	20.8	26.5	8.20	4.33	16.17	8.47
53	23.2	28.7	20.2	25.7	9.02	4.74	17.40	9.14
54	22.4	27.8	19.5	24.9	9.89	5.17	18.69	9.83
55	21.6	27.0	18.9	24.1	10.83	5.65	20.03	10.53
56	20.8	26.1	18.2	23.4	11.84	6.17	21.45	11.29
57	20.1	25.3	17.6	22.7	12.95	6.74	22.96	12.16
58	19.3	24.4	17.0	21.9	14.16	7.35	24.61	13.18
59	18.6	23.6	16.5	21.2	15.47	8.02	26.36	14.31
60	17.9	22.8	15.9	20.5	16.85	8.74	28.22	15.54
61	17.2	22.0	15.3	19.8	18.35	9.52	30.14	16.79
62	16.5	21.2	14.8	19.2	20.04	10.39	32.14	18.01
63	15.8	20.4	14.3	18.5	21.95	11.34	34.21	19.14
64	15.2	19.6	13.8	17.9	24.07	12.39	36.34	20.22
65	14.5	18.9	13.3	17.2	26.37	13.53	38.56	21.32
70	11.6	15.3	10.9	14.1	39.77	20.64	51.42	29.32
75	9.1	12.0	8.8	11.3	59.43	32.44	65.36	40.20
80	7.0	9.0	6.7	8.6	88.01	52.55	85.43	58.70
85	5.3	6.7	4.8	6.5	1000	1000	1000	1000

Source: US Dept of Commerce, Bureau of Census, Statistical Abstracts of the United States (106th ed 1986).

As Table 10-2 indicates, females have a greater life expectancy than males, and whites have a greater life expectancy than blacks.

§10.03   Types of Mortality Tables

Mortality tables may be select tables, ultimate tables, or aggregrate tables. *Select mortality tables* are based on the mortality experience of persons recently insured. *Ultimate mortality tables* exclude those insured in the early years of the insurance contract. *Aggregrate mortality tables* include all insured.[3]

Select mortality tables reflect the life expectancy based on the experience of the persons insured in the most recent years. This group has a low mortality expectation relative to others in the same age group, since to become insured they must be in good health. This select period may run from five years to as long as fifteen years.[4]

The ultimate table is the mortality table covering the period after the select period. This means the benefits of "healthy selection" have worn off.[5]

The aggregrate table includes the mortality data of both tables.[6]

The mortality tables used by an insurance company have a healthy bias. The insurance company requires the insured to pass a medical examination prior to being insured; thus, the unhealthy are not insured. In addition to this bias, the insurance company makes two other adjustments. The first is *gradation*, and the second is *margin*.[7]

Gradation is used to modify mortality results that do not appear to be supported by the population. The objective of gradation is to provide for smooth changes in life expectancy and in the probability of dying. If, for some unexplained reason, there were no deaths among all the 38-year-old persons insured, gradation would be used to smooth the results.

Margin is used to provide a cushion. The death rates are increased over what was actually experienced in order to provide a cushion of safety.

Mortality tables are calculated by assuming that no person lives beyond age 100. If a person reaches age 100, the insurance company will pay the face value of the life insurance policy as if the person had died. When this occurs, the person is said "to have outlived the mortality table."

§10.04   Annuities

An *annuity* is a series of payments made at various designated times in the future.[8] The payments may be weekly, monthly, semiannually, or whatever is

---

[3] K. Black Jr., & H. Skipper, Jr., Insurance 317 (11th ed 1987).

[4] *Id* 55.

[5] *Id.*

[6] *Id.*

[7] *Id.* 318.

[8] J. Viscione & G. Roberts, Contemporary Financial Management 65 (1987).

agreed. The annuity may start immediately or it may be deferred. If the annuity is deferred, then the date on which the first payment will be made by the insurance company is stated in the contract.

Annuities may be *ordinary annuities* or *annuities due*. An ordinary annuity is paid at the beginning of the payment period. An annuity due is paid at the end of the payment period.

For example, consider an annual annuity for $10,000. The annuity is to start in one year. If the annuity is an ordinary annuity, the first payment will be made one year from today. If the annuity is an annuity due, then the first payment will be made in two years.

§10.05   Annuity Mortality Tables

Mortality tables used for life insurance purposes are different from the mortality tables used for annuity purposes. Persons who purchase annuities are usually in better health than the general population. In order for the insurance company to charge a proper annuity premium, the mortality expectation for the annuity table is lower than the life insurance mortality table.

To be more explicit, the life insurance contract pays off when the insured dies. In order to assure enough money to pay all the claims, the mortality table will be "padded." That is, the probability of dying will be increased, causing the premium to be higher. Likewise, for the annuity contract the "padding" is done by reducing the probability of dying. The annuity contract pays if the individual is alive. To lower the probability of dying increases the premiums for the annuity.

§10.06   Calculating the Probability of Living

The probability of living can be calculated from the mortality tables appearing in Table 10-2. To calculate the probability of living, the probability of dying must be known for each age.

It is critical to recognize that there is one mortality table for each and every age. There is a mortality table for a one-year-old, mortality table for a ten-year-old, and so on for each age. For the person age 1 there is the probability of living to age 2, and to age 3, and to age 98, and to age 99. The probability of a person living from age 1 to age 99 is different from the probability of a person age 2 living to age 99. The person age 2 has already survived to age 2; the person age 1 has not.

The construction of the probability of living requires knowing the individual's race and age. Suppose the probability of living is being constructed for a 40-year-old black male. The probability of living can be constructed from the data presented in Table 10-2.

The table states the life expectancy of a 40-year-old black male is 29.9 years and the probability of dying is 6.09 per thousand. The probability of a 40-year-old black male living to age 41 is 99.391 per cent. The formula for this calculation is:

Probability of Living = 1-[6.09/1000]

The 40-year-old individual has a 99.391 per cent chance of living to age 41. The 41-year-old black male has a life expectancy of 29.1 years, and the probability of dying is 6.49 per thousand. As expected, as the individual ages the life expectancy decreases and the probability of death increases. The probability of a 41-year-old black male living to age 42 is 99.351% = (1-[6.49/1,000]). The question, though, is what is the probability that a 40-year-old black male will live to age 42. The probability of living from age 40 to age 41 is 99.391 per cent. The probability of living from age 41 to age 42 is 99.351 per cent. The probability of living from age 40 to age 42 is the multiplication of the two values, or 98.746 per cent.

Table 10-3 presents several probabilities. The second column is the probability of dying during that year. Out of 1,000 40-year-old black males, 6.09 will die. This does not mean that a fraction of a person will die, but rather that 609 men out of 100,000 will die. The third column is the probability of living. It is 1 minus the probability of dying. The fourth column is the probability of living from age 40 to any successive age through age 70. It is the fourth column that is used when the present value of a future income stream or medical payment stream is calculated.

Table 10-3 Probability of Living 40-Year-Old Black Male

Age	Probability of Dying per Thousand	Probability of Living	of Living to Age
40	6.09	.99391	.99391
41	6.49	.99351	.98746
42	6.98	.99302	.98057
43	7.59	.99241	.97312
44	8.32	.99168	.96503
45	9.11	.99089	.95624
46	9.95	.99005	.94672
47	10.84	.98916	.93646
48	11.79	.98821	.92542
49	12.79	.98721	.91358
50	13.86	.98614	.90092
51	14.99	.98501	.88742
52	16.17	.98383	.87307
53	17.40	.98260	.85787
54	18.69	.98131	.84184
55	20.03	.97997	.82498
56	21.45	.97855	.80728
57	22.96	.97704	.78875

Age	Probability of Dying per Thousand	of Living	of Living to Age
58	24.61	.97539	.76934
59	26.36	.97364	.74906
60	28.22	.97178	.72792
61	30.14	.96986	.70598
62	32.14	.96786	.68329
63	34.21	.96579	.65991
64	36.34	.96366	.63593
65	38.56	.96144	.61141
66	40.84	.95916	.58644
67	43.26	.95674	.56107
68	45.83	.95417	.53536
69	48.54	.95146	.50937
70	51.42	.94858	.48318

§10.07   Two Approaches to Mortality-Adjusted Medical Payments

The purpose of adjusting a stream of medical payments for mortality is to recognize the probability that a person may die any year. Even economists recognize that individuals may die before age 100. The mortality adjustment to future payments is done using one of two methods: (1) by calculating the present value to life expectancy, or (2) by making the annual adjustment for the probability of living each year to age 100.

Consider a situation where a 40-year-old black male is injured. The annual medical expense is $20,000. The appropriate growth rate is 4 per cent annually, and the appropriate discount rate is 6 per cent annually. Table 10-4 shows the present value calculations with annual mortality adjustments.

Table 10-4 Present Value

Period	Age	Present Value Annual Income	Total Income	Probability of Living	Adjusted Annual Income	Total Income
0	40	$20,000	$20,000	.99391	$19,878	$19,878
1	41	19,623	39,623	.98746	19,377	39,255
2	42	19,252	58,875	.98057	18,878	58,133
3	43	18,889	77,764	.97312	18,381	76,515
4	44	18,533	96,297	.96503	17,885	94,399
5	45	18,183	114,480	.95624	17,387	111,786
6	46	17,840	132,320	.94672	16,890	128,676
7	47	17,503	149,823	.93646	16,391	145,067
8	48	17,173	166,997	.92542	15,892	160,960
9	49	16,849	183,846	.91358	15,393	176,353

Period	Age	Present Value		Probability of	Adjusted	
		Annual Income	Total Income	Living	Annual Income	Total Income
10	50	16,531	200,377	.90092	14,893	191,246
11	51	16,219	216,596	.88742	14,393	205,639
12	52	15,913	232,509	.87307	13,893	219,533
13	53	15,613	248,123	.85787	13,394	232,927
14	54	15,318	263,441	.84184	12,896	245,822
15	55	15,029	278,470	.82498	12,399	258,221
16	56	14,746	293,216	.80728	11,904	270,125
17	57	14,468	307,684	.78875	11,411	281,537
18	58	14,195	321,878	.76934	10,920	292,457
19	59	13,927	335,805	.74906	10,432	302,889
20	60	13,664	349,469	.72792	9,946	312,835
21	61	13,406	362,876	.70598	9,465	322,300
22	62	13,153	376,029	.68329	8,988	331,287
23	63	12,905	388,934	.65991	8,516	339,804
24	64	12,662	401,596	.63593	8,052	347,856
25	65	12,423	414,018	.61141	7,595	355,451
26	66	12,188	426,207	.58644	7,148	362,599
27	67	11,958	438,165	.56107	6,709	369,308
28	68	11,733	449,898	.53536	6,281	375,589
29	69	11,511	461,409	.50937	5,864	381,453
30	70	11,294	472,703	.48318	5,457	386,910
31	71	11,081	483,784	.45711	5,065	391,975
32	72	10,872	494,656	.43124	4,688	396,664
33	73	10,667	505,323	.40563	4,327	400,991
34	74	10,466	515,789	.38036	3,981	404,971
35	75	10,268	526,057	.35550	3,650	408,622
36	76	10,074	536,131	.33099	3,334	411,956
37	77	9,884	546,016	.30691	3,034	414,990
38	78	9,698	555,713	.28335	2,748	417,738
39	79	9,515	565,228	.26041	2,478	420,215
40	80	9,335	574,564	.23816	2,223	422,439
41	81	9,159	583,723	.21500	1,969	424,408
42	82	8,986	592,709	.19121	1,718	426,126
43	83	8,817	601,526	.16712	1,473	427,600
44	84	8,650	610,176	.14315	1,238	428,838
45	85	8,487	618,664	.11979	1,017	429,855
46	86	8,327	626,991	.09753	812	430,667
47	87	8,170	635,161	.07691	628	431,295
48	88	8,016	643,177	.05840	468	431,763
49	89	7,865	651,041	.04240	333	432,097
50	90	7,716	658,757	.02918	225	432,322

Period	Age	Present Value		Probability of	Adjusted	
		Annual Income	Total Income	Living	Annual Income	Total Income
51	91	7,571	666,328	.01882	142	432,464
52	92	7,428	673,756	.01122	83	432,548
53	93	7,288	681,043	.00606	44	432,592
54	94	7,150	688,194	.00289	21	432,613
55	95	7,015	695,209	.00117	8	432,621
56	96	6,883	702,092	.00038	3	432,623
57	97	6,753	708,845	.00009	1	432,624
58	98	6,626	715,470	.00001	0	432,624
59	99	6,501	721,971	0.00000	0	432,624

The life expectancy of a 40-year-old black male is 29.9 years, rounded to 30 years. From the fourth column the present value of the $20,000 per year of medical expenses to life expectancy of age 70 is found to be $472,703. If the entire life to age 100 is considered, the present value of the future medical expenses, mortality adjusted, is $432,624.

§10.08   Comparing Mortality Results

Consider again the fact situation outlined in §10.07. The present value of $20,000 per year for 25 years, growing at 9 per cent annually and being discounted at 6 per cent annually, was calculated to be $401,596. When mortality adjustments are made, the present value of the income stream changes.

Table 10-5 presents the present value of an income stream beginning at age 40: (1) with mortality adjusted to life expectancy and (2) to age 99.

The life expectancy of a 40-year-old white male is 35 years. The present value of the income stream from 40 to 65, growing at 4 per cent and discounted at 6 per cent, is $401,596. With mortality adjusted to life expentancy, age 75, the present value is $526,057. The present value of the income stream, mortality adjusted to age 99, is $486,462. Table 10-5 shows the present values of income streams, mortality adjusted, for race and sex. The present value of the income stream is calculated to life expectance and to age 99.

The next to the last column is the present value to life expectancy, with certainty.

Table 10-5 Present Value of $20,000 per Year Annual Growth Rate = 4% Annual Discount Rate = 6%

Present value beginning at age 40

   To age 65 with no mortality adjustment $401,596

		Present Value To	
Mortality Table		Life Expectancy	Age 99
(U.S. Tables)	Age	Dollars	
White Male	35	$526,057	$486,462
Black Male	30	461,409	432,624
White Female	41	574,654	548,545
Black Female	37	536,131	502,483

§10.09   Conclusion

The mortality adjustment is needed when the present value of future medical expenses is being calculated. Economists either calculate the present value annually, adjusting for mortality, or calculate the present value with certainty to life expectancy.

The choice of mortality tables will have an effect on the size of the present value figure. Government life expectancy tables are based on the total population, while insurance company mortality tables are based on only that part of the population which is healthy enough to be insured. However, insurance company mortality tables are "padded" in order to provide for a margin of error.

11

The Probability of Seeking and the Probability of Finding Employment

$$\text{Present Value} = \sum_{t=0}^{n} \$ * (1+g)^t/(1+d)^t * PL * \underline{PS * PF} * C * TX * H$$

§11.01   Introduction

When the uncertainties of life are introduced into the computation of the present value of a future income stream, then the probability of a person seeking a job and the probability of finding a job enter the calculation. This chapter will present data on the probability of seeking employment, data on the probability of finding employment, explain what the data mean, and demonstrate one way to use the data in the present value calculation.

§11.02   The Probability of Seeking Employment

The probability that an individual will seek employment is referred to by government statistics as *participation rates.* A person may seek employment but not find employment; he or she is, however, participating in the labor force, i.e., the unemployed portion of the labor force.

Participation rates represent the proportion of the population in the labor

169

force.[1] The labor force participation rate is the ratio of the labor force to the noninstitutional population.[2] The labor force includes all resident armed forces. The civilian labor force ratio excludes the armed forces and is defined as the ratio of the civilian labor force to the civilian noninstitutional population.

The participation rates are calculated based on race and sex of the individual. Tables 11-1 through 11-4 present the participation rates for white males, white females, black males, and black females, respectively. The most recent data are from 1983. Data on black males and females only go back to 1972.

Table 11-1 Participation Rates White Males 1954 - 1983

Year	Age							
	16-17	18-19	20-24	25-34	35-44	45-54	55-64	65+
1983	46.9	71.3	86.1	95.2	96.0	91.9	70.0	17.1
1982	49.3	70.5	86.3	95.6	96.0	92.2	71.0	17.9
1981	51.5	73.5	87.0	95.8	96.1	92.4	71.5	18.5
1980	53.6	74.1	87.2	95.9	96.2	92.1	73.1	19.1
1979	55.3	74.5	87.6	96.1	96.4	92.2	73.6	20.1
1978	55.3	75.3	87.2	96.0	96.3	92.1	73.9	20.4
1977	53.8	74.9	86.8	96.0	96.2	92.2	74.7	20.2
1976	51.8	73.5	86.2	95.9	96.0	92.5	75.4	20.3
1975	51.8	72.8	85.5	95.8	96.4	92.9	76.5	21.8
1974	53.3	73.6	86.5	96.3	96.7	93.0	78.1	22.5
1973	52.7	72.3	85.8	96.3	96.8	93.5	79.0	22.5
1972	50.2	71.0	84.3	96.0	97.0	94.0	81.2	24.4
1971	49.2	67.8	83.2	96.3	97.0	94.7	82.6	25.6
1970	48.9	67.4	83.3	96.7	97.3	94.9	83.3	26.7
1969	48.8	66.3	82.6	97.0	97.4	95.1	83.9	27.3
1968	47.7	65.7	82.4	97.2	97.6	95.4	84.7	27.3
1967	47.9	66.1	84.0	97.5	97.7	95.6	84.9	27.1
1966	47.1	65.4	84.4	97.5	97.6	95.8	84.9	27.2
1965	44.6	65.8	85.3	97.4	97.7	95.9	85.2	27.9
1964	43.5	66.6	85.7	97.5	97.6	96.1	86.1	27.9
1963	42.4	67.8	85.8	97.4	97.8	96.2	86.6	28.4
1962	42.9	66.4	86.5	97.4	97.9	96.0	86.7	30.6
1961	44.3	66.2	87.6	97.7	97.9	95.9	87.8	31.9
1960	46.0	69.0	87.6	97.7	97.9	96.1	87.2	33.3
1959	45.4	70.3	87.3	97.5	98.0	96.3	87.9	34.3
1958	46.8	69.4	86.7	97.2	98.0	96.6	88.2	35.7
1957	49.6	71.6	86.7	97.2	98.0	96.6	88.0	37.7
1956	51.3	71.9	87.6	97.4	98.1	96.8	88.9	40.0

---

[1] US Dept of Labor, Technical Notes, Current Population Survey (Household Survey), Handbook of Labor Statistics, Bulletin 2217, at 1-3 (June 1985).

[2] Id 2.

Year				Age				
	16-17	18-19	20-24	25-34	35-44	45-54	55-64	65+
1955	48.0	71.7	85.6	97.8	98.3	96.7	88.4	39.5
1954	47.1	70.4	86.4	97.5	98.2	96.8	89.2	40.4
Average	48.9	70.1	85.8	96.8	97.2	94.6	81.8	27.1

Source: US Dept of Labor, Bureau of Labor Statistics, Handbook of Labor Statistics 20 (June 1985).

Table 11-2 Participation Rate White Females 1954 – 1983

Year				Age				
	16-17	18-19	20-24	25-34	35-44	45-54	55-64	65+
1983	43.9	64.1	72.1	68.7	68.2	68.2	41.1	7.8
1982	44.6	64.6	71.8	67.8	67.5	67.5	41.5	7.8
1982	46.1	64.2	71.5	66.4	66.4	66.4	40.9	7.9
1980	47.2	65.1	70.6	64.8	65.0	65.0	40.9	7.9
1979	49.0	65.7	70.5	63.1	63.0	63.0	41.5	8.1
1978	48.8	64.6	69.3	61.2	60.7	60.7	41.1	8.1
1977	45.8	63.3	67.8	58.5	58.9	58.9	40.7	7.9
1976	43.8	61.7	66.3	56.0	57.1	57.1	40.7	7.9
1975	42.7	60.4	65.5	53.8	54.9	54.9	40.6	8.0
1974	43.3	60.4	63.9	51.3	53.6	53.6	40.4	8.0
1973	41.7	58.8	61.7	48.7	52.2	53.4	40.7	8.7
1972	39.3	57.4	59.4	46.0	50.7	53.4	41.9	0.0
1971	36.3	55.0	58.0	43.7	50.2	53.6	42.5	9.3
1970	36.6	55.0	57.7	43.2	49.9	53.7	42.6	9.5
1969	35.2	54.6	56.4	41.7	48.6	53.0	42.6	9.7
1968	33.0	53.3	54.0	40.6	47.5	51.5	42.0	9.4
1967	32.3	52.7	53.1	39.7	46.4	50.9	41.9	9.3
1966	31.8	53.1	50.0	37.7	45.0	50.6	41.1	9.4
1965	28.7	50.6	49.2	36.3	44.4	49.9	40.3	9.7
1964	28.4	49.6	48.8	35.0	43.3	50.2	39.4	9.9
1963	27.8	51.3	47.3	34.8	43.1	49.5	38.9	9.4
1962	27.9	51.6	47.1	34.1	42.2	48.9	38.0	9.8
1961	29.4	51.9	46.9	34.3	41.8	48.9	37.2	10.5
1960	30.0	51.9	45.7	34.1	41.5	48.6	36.2	10.6
1959	29.9	50.8	44.5	33.4	41.4	47.8	35.7	10.0
1958	28.8	52.3	46.0	33.6	41.4	46.5	34.5	10.1
1957	32.1	52.6	45.8	33.6	41.5	45.4	33.7	10.2
1956	33.5	53.0	46.5	33.2	41.5	44.4	34.0	10.6
1955	29.9	52.0	45.8	32.8	40.0	42.7	31.8	10.5
1954	29.3	52.1	44.4	32.5	39.3	39.8	29.1	9.1
Average	36.6	56.5	56.6	45.4	50.2	53.3	39.1	8.8

Source: US Dept of Labor, Bureau of Labor Statistics, Handbook of Labor Statistics 20 (June 1985).

Table 11-3 Participation Rate Black Males 1972 - 1983

Year				Age				
	16-17	18-19	20-24	25-34	35-44	45-54	55-64	65+
1983	24.7	55.0	79.4	89.0	89.7	84.5	62.6	14.0
1982	24.6	55.3	78.7	89.2	89.8	82.2	61.9	15.9
1981	29.2	55.0	79.2	88.9	89.3	82.7	62.1	16.0
1980	31.0	56.7	79.8	90.8	89.1	83.1	61.7	16.3
1979	30.8	57.9	80.6	90.7	90.4	84.6	64.8	19.4
1978	32.1	59.6	78.8	90.8	90.6	83.3	67.9	21.0
1977	30.4	57.9	79.3	90.7	90.9	82.0	65.5	19.9
1976	29.0	55.0	79.1	90.9	89.9	82.4	65.1	19.7
1975	29.7	57.4	78.8	91.5	89.3	83.5	67.6	20.5
1974	34.1	61.7	83.5	92.7	90.3	84.1	68.9	21.5
1973	32.5	61.1	83.7	91.8	91.0	87.5	69.5	22.4
1972	34.3	60.0	82.6	92.6	91.0	85.6	72.5	24.3
Average	30.2	57.7	80.3	90.8	90.1	83.8	65.8	19.2

Source: US Dept of Labor, Bureau of Labor Statistics, Handbook of Labor Statistics 72 (June 1985).

Table 11-4 Participation Rates Black Females 1972 - 1983

Year				Age				
	16-17	18-19	20-24	25-34	35-44	45-54	55-64	65+
1983	20.8	44.4	59.1	72.3	72.6	62.3	44.8	8.2
1982	23.3	43.3	60.1	70.2	71.7	62.4	44.8	8.5
1981	23.9	44.0	61.1	70.0	69.8	62.0	45.4	9.3
1980	24.6	45.0	60.2	70.5	68.1	61.4	44.8	10.2
1979	27.5	45.9	61.5	70.1	68.0	59.6	44.0	10.9
1978	26.4	48.3	62.7	70.6	67.2	59.4	43.8	11.1
1977	21.5	44.3	59.3	68.5	64.1	57.9	43.7	10.5
1976	23.2	42.6	56.9	66.7	63.0	56.8	43.7	11.3
1975	25.0	43.8	55.9	62.8	62.0	56.6	43.1	10.7
1974	22.7	44.6	58.8	62.4	62.2	56.4	42.8	10.4
1973	23.9	45.1	58.0	62.7	61.7	56.1	44.7	11.4
1972	21.0	44.3	57.0	60.8	61.4	57.2	44.0	12.6
Ave	23.6	44.6	59.2	67.3	66.0	59.0	44.1	10.4

Source: US Dept of Labor, Bureau of Labor Statistics, Handbook of Labor Statistics 21 (June 1985).

   The average participation rate is calculated for each of the age groups. As the tables indicate, there is a chance that men and women will be participating in the labor force at age 16. Likewise, there is a chance each will be participating in the labor force after age 65. Since the age category 65+ is open-ended, there is a statistical chance of participating in the labor force each year after an individual reaches age 65.

Note the significant change in the participation rate of women in the labor force. In 1954, white women between the ages of 25 and 54 had a probability of participating in the labor force ranging between 32 per cent and 39 per cent. By 1983 the probability of participating in the labor force had increased to 68 per cent.

§11.03   The Probability of Finding Employment

The probability of finding employment is the employment rate. It is one (1) minus the unemployment rate. To determine the employment rate, the labor force must be estimated.

The civilian labor force is the total of all employed and unemployed persons. The labor force, as distinguished from the civilian labor force, includes the members of the armed forces serving in the United States.[3] The full-time labor force includes all civilians working full-time schedules. This definition would include persons with full-time schedules but temporarily employed part-time due to economic reasons. Also included in the definition of full-time labor force are unemployed persons seeking full-time work.[4] The employment rate is one (1) minus the ratio of the number of workers unemployed to the labor force.

Table 11-5 Employment Rates White Males 1954 - 1983

Year	Age							
	16-17	18-19	20-24	25-34	35-44	45-54	55-64	65+
1983	77.4	81.3	86.2	91.0	93.6	94.3	94.4	96.8
1982	75.8	80.0	85.7	91.1	93.8	94.7	94.9	96.8
1981	80.1	83.6	88.4	93.9	96.0	96.4	96.6	97.6
1980	81.5	85.5	88.9	94.1	96.4	96.7	96.9	97.5
1979	83.9	87.7	92.6	96.4	97.5	97.5	97.5	96.9
1978	83.1	89.2	92.4	96.3	97.5	97.5	97.4	96.1
1977	82.4	87.0	90.7	95.0	96.9	97.0	96.7	95.1
1976	80.3	84.5	89.1	94.4	96.3	96.3	96.0	95.2
1975	80.3	82.8	86.8	93.7	95.5	95.6	95.9	95.0
1974	83.8	88.5	92.2	96.5	97.6	97.8	97.5	97.0
1973	84.9	90.0	93.5	97.0	98.2	98.0	97.6	97.1
1972	83.6	87.6	91.5	96.6	97.5	97.5	97.0	96.7
1971	82.9	86.5	90.6	96.0	97.1	97.2	96.8	96.6
1970	84.3	88.0	92.2	96.9	97.7	97.7	97.3	96.8
1969	87.5	92.1	95.4	98.3	98.6	98.6	98.3	97.9
1968	87.7	91.8	95.4	98.3	98.6	98.5	98.3	97.6
1967	87.3	91.0	95.8	98.1	98.4	98.2	97.8	97.2
1966	87.5	91.1	95.9	97.9	98.3	98.3	97.5	96.3

---

[3] US Dept of Labor, Technical Notes, Current Population Survey (Household Survey), Handbook of Labor Statistics, Bulletin 2217, at 2. (June 1985).

[4] *Id.*

Year	Age							
	16-17	18-19	20-24	25-34	35-44	45-54	55-64	65+
1965	85.3	88.6	94.1	97.4	97.7	97.7	96.9	97.0
1964	83.8	86.6	92.6	97.0	97.5	97.1	96.5	96.4
1963	82.2	85.8	92.2	96.1	97.1	96.7	96.0	95.9
1962	84.9	87.3	92.0	96.2	96.9	96.5	95.9	95.9
1961	83.5	84.9	90.0	95.1	96.0	95.6	94.7	94.8
1960	85.4	86.5	91.7	95.9	96.7	96.4	95.9	96.0
1959	85.0	87.0	92.5	96.2	96.8	96.3	95.8	95.5
1958	85.1	83.5	88.3	94.4	95.6	95.2	94.8	95.0
1957	88.1	88.9	92.9	97.3	97.5	97.0	96.6	91.8
1956	88.8	90.3	93.9	97.2	97.8	97.2	96.9	96.6
1955	87.8	89.6	93.0	97.3	97.4	97.1	96.1	96.2
1954	86.0	87.0	90.2	95.8	96.4	96.2	95.7	95.8
Average	84.0	87.1	91.6	95.9	97.0	96.9	96.5	96.2

Source: US Dept of Labor, Bureau of Labor Statistics, Handbook of Labor Statistics 71 (June 1985).

Table 11-6 Employment Rate White Females 1954 - 1983

Year	Age							
	16-17	18-19	20-24	25-34	35-44	45-54	55-64	65+
1983	79.6	83.6	89.7	92.4	93.8	94.5	95.3	96.9
1982	78.8	82.4	89.1	92.0	93.6	94.5	95.0	96.9
1981	81.6	84.7	90.9	93.4	94.9	95.8	96.3	96.6
1980	82.7	86.9	91.5	93.7	95.1	95.7	96.9	97.0
1979	84.1	87.5	92.2	94.4	95.8	96.3	97.0	96.9
1978	82.9	87.6	91.7	94.2	95.5	96.2	97.0	96.3
1977	81.8	85.8	90.7	93.3	94.7	95.0	95.6	95.1
1976	81.8	84.9	89.6	92.4	94.2	95.0	95.2	94.7
1975	80.8	83.9	88.8	91.5	93.4	94.2	94.9	94.7
1974	83.6	87.0	91.8	94.3	95.7	96.4	96.7	96.1
1973	84.3	89.1	93.0	94.9	96.3	96.9	97.2	97.2
1972	83.0	87.7	91.8	94.5	95.5	96.5	96.7	96.3
1971	83.4	85.9	91.5	93.7	95.1	96.1	96.7	96.4
1970	84.7	88.1	93.1	94.7	95.7	96.6	97.4	96.8
1969	86.2	90.0	94.5	95.8	96.8	97.6	97.9	97.6
1968	86.1	89.0	94.1	96.1	96.9	97.7	97.9	97.3
1967	87.1	89.4	94.0	95.3	96.3	97.1	97.7	97.4
1966	85.5	89.3	94.7	96.3	96.7	97.3	97.8	97.3
1965	85.0	86.6	93.6	52.0	95.9	97.0	97.3	97.3
1964	82.9	86.8	92.9	94.8	95.5	96.4	96.5	96.6
1963	81.9	86.8	92.6	94.2	95.4	96.1	96.5	97.0
1962	84.4	88.7	92.3	94.6	95.5	96.3	96.6	96.0
1961	83.0	86.4	91.6	93.4	94.4	95.2	95.7	96.3
1960	85.5	88.5	92.8	94.3	95.8	96.0	96.7	97.2

Year	**Age**							
	16-17	18-19	20-24	25-34	35-44	45-54	55-64	65+
1959	86.7	88.9	93.3	95.0	95.3	96.0	96.0	96.6
1958	84.4	89.0	92.6	93.4	94.4	95.1	95.7	96.5
1957	88.1	92.1	94.9	95.3	96.3	97.0	97.0	96.5
1956	87.9	91.7	94.9	96.0	96.5	96.7	96.5	97.7
1955	88.4	92.3	94.9	95.7	96.2	96.6	96.4	97.8
1954	88.0	90.6	93.6	94.3	95.1	95.6	95.5	97.2
Average	84.1	87.7	92.4	92.9	95.4	96.1	96.5	96.7

Source: US Dept of Labor, Bureau of Labor Statistics, Handbook of Labor Statistics 21 (June 1985).

Table 11-7 Employment Rates Black Males 1972 - 1983

Year	**Age**							
	16-17	18-19	20-24	25-34	35-44	45-54	55-64	65+
1983	47.3	52.7	68.6	80.6	86.5	88.6	89.0	88.2
1982	47.3	52.9	68.5	79.9	86.6	91.0	89.7	90.7
1981	56.8	60.8	73.6	85.6	90.7	92.2	93.9	92.5
1980	60.3	63.8	76.3	86.6	91.8	92.8	93.8	91.3
1979	62.1	67.8	81.3	90.4	93.7	94.8	94.9	93.6
1978	57.0	67.1	79.0	90.2	94.9	95.1	95.6	93.4
1977	59.0	61.8	77.0	88.2	93.8	95.1	94.0	92.2
1976	59.2	64.0	77.4	88.0	92.5	92.7	93.7	91.3
1975	58.1	64.1	75.3	87.3	91.3	90.7	93.7	91.3
1974	60.1	71.7	83.8	91.9	95.7	95.8	96.4	94.7
1973	64.3	77.0	86.8	93.8	96.1	96.8	96.8	96.7
1972	63.3	71.6	85.1	92.8	95.2	96.2	95.6	94.6
Average	57.9	64.6	77.7	87.9	92.4	93.5	93.9	92.5

Source: US Dept of Labor, Bureau of Labor Statistics, Handbook of Labor Statistics 72 (June 1985).

Table 11-8 Employment Rate Black Females 1972 - 1983

Year	**Age**							
	16-17	18-19	20-24	25-34	35-44	45-54	55-64	65+
1983	51.4	52.0	68.2	81.4	88.6	90.1	92.7	93.7
1982	55.8	51.4	70.4	82.2	89.3	91.5	93.9	95.5
1981	53.5	60.2	73.6	85.1	90.2	93.1	95.3	94.0
1980	57.1	61.8	76.5	86.8	91.8	93.6	95.5	95.0
1979	57.3	63.1	77.4	87.9	92.8	94.8	95.3	96.0
1978	55.0	61.3	77.3	88.1	92.2	94.4	94.8	95.2
1977	50.5	59.6	74.5	86.4	91.3	94.2	95.2	96.5
1976	51.6	62.4	77.2	86.4	91.5	94.1	94.6	96.6
1975	58.8	59.4	75.7	86.6	91.0	93.0	94.7	96.3
1974	59.8	64.0	81.0	91.0	93.4	95.6	96.4	98.0

Year				Age				
	16-17	18-19	20-24	25-34	35-44	45-54	55-64	65+
1973	61.4	65.8	81.6	89.7	94.4	96.1	96.7	96.2
1972	58.0	59.9	82.1	89.5	92.4	95.4	96.3	97.4
Average	55.9	60.1	76.3	86.8	91.6	93.8	95.1	95.9

Source: US Dept of Labor, Bureau of Labor Statistics, Handbook of Labor Statistics 72-73 (June 1985).

§11.04   Incorporating the Probability of Seeking Employment and the Probability of Finding Employment into the Present Value Analysis

Since the probability of seeking employment and the probability of finding employment are measures of uncertainty, it seems reasonable to include these probabilities in the present value calculation when mortality adjustments are made. Stated differently, if the uncertainty of living is included in the present value analysis, then the uncertainty of seeking employment and the uncertainty of finding employment should also be included in the analysis.

The government statistics indicate that there is a probability of seeking employment after age 65. Likewise, there is a probability of finding employment after age 65.

The seeking and finding employment figures are incorporated into the analysis by using the averages. That is, each of the Tables 11-1 through 11-8 calculates the average probability of seeking and finding employment. These averages are employed in the present value analysis.

§11.05   An Example of Using the Probability of Seeking and the Probability Finding Employment in the Present Value Analysis

Consider the fact situation where a 40-year-old white male was killed. At the time of his death he was earning $25,000. The present value calculation employs a growth rate of wages of 2 per cent and a discount, or interest rate, of 4 per cent. Table 11-9 shows the present value of the future income if the deceased were to work uninterrupted to age 65.

Table 11-9 Present Value Working Uninterrupted to Age 65

Period	Age	Future Value	Present Value	Total
0	40	25,000	25,000	25,000
1	41	25,500	24,519	49,519
2	42	26,010	24,048	73,567
3	43	26,530	23,585	97,152

Period	Age	Future Value	Present Value	Total
4	44	27,061	23,132	120,284
5	45	27,602	22,687	142,971
6	46	28,154	22,251	165,221
7	47	28,717	21,823	187,044
8	48	29,291	21,403	208,447
9	49	29,877	20,991	229,438
10	50	30,475	20,588	250,026
11	51	31,084	20,192	270,218
12	52	31,706	19,804	290,021
13	53	32,340	19,423	309,444
14	54	32,987	19,049	328,493
15	55	33,647	18,683	347,176
16	56	34,320	18,324	365,500
17	57	35,006	17,971	383,471
18	58	35,706	17,626	401,096
19	59	36,420	17,287	418,383
20	60	37,149	16,954	435,337
21	61	37,892	16,628	451,965
22	62	38,649	16,308	468,274
23	63	39,422	15,995	484,268
24	64	40,211	15,687	499,955
25	65	41,015	15,385	515,341
26	66	41,835	15,090	530,431
27	67	42,672	14,799	545,230
28	68	43,526	14,515	559,745
29	69	44,396	14,236	573,980
30	70	45,284	13,962	587,942
31	71	46,190	13,693	601,636
32	72	47,114	13,430	615,066
33	73	48,056	13,172	628,238
34	74	49,017	12,919	641,156
35	75	49,997	12,670	653,826
36	76	50,997	12,426	666,253
37	77	52,017	12,187	678,440
38	78	53,057	11,953	690,393
39	79	54,119	11,723	702,116
40	80	55,201	11,498	713,614
41	81	56,305	11,277	724,891
42	82	57,431	11,060	735,951
43	83	58,580	10,847	746,798
44	84	59,751	10,639	757,436
45	85	60,946	10,434	767,870
46	86	62,165	10,233	778,103
47	87	63,409	10,036	788,140

Period	Age	Future Value	Present Value	Total
48	88	64,677	9,843	797,983
49	89	65,970	9,654	807,637
50	90	67,290	9,469	817,106
51	91	68,635	9,286	826,392
52	92	70,008	9,108	835,500
53	93	71,408	8,933	844,433
54	94	72,837	8,761	853,194
55	95	74,293	8,592	861,786
56	96	75,779	8,427	870,213
57	97	77,295	8,265	878,479
58	98	78,841	8,106	886,585
59	99	80,417	7,950	894,535

Table 11-9 shows the present value of working uninterrupted to each age through age 99. But the present value of the income stream reported by the economist is $499,995. This is the present value of the income stream working uninterrupted to age 65. If the probability of living and the probabilities of seeking and finding employment are included in the analysis, then the present value figure should be calculated through age 99. This calculation is presented in Table 11-10.

Table 11-10 Present Value of Future Income The Probability of Living and the Probabilities of Seeking and Finding Employment Are Included

Period	Age	Present Value	Living	Probabilities of Seeking Employment	Probabilities of Finding Employment	Adjusted Present Value	Adjusted Total
0	40	$25,000	.99760	.972	.970	$23,514	$ 23,514
1	41	24,519	.99498	.972	.970	23,002	46,516
2	42	24,048	.99210	.972	.970	22,494	69,010
3	43	23,585	.98894	.972	.970	21,991	91,001
4	44	23,132	.98545	.972	.970	21,492	112,493
5	45	22,687	.98159	.946	.969	20,414	132,907
6	46	22,251	.97733	.946	.969	19,934	152,841
7	47	21,823	.97261	.946	.969	19,456	172,297
8	48	21,403	.96738	.946	.969	18,980	191,277
9	49	20,991	.96156	.946	.969	18,503	209,780
10	50	20,588	.95513	.946	.969	18,025	227,805
11	51	20,192	.94804	.946	.969	17,548	245,353
12	52	19,804	.94027	.946	.969	17,069	262,422
13	53	19,423	.93179	.946	.969	16,590	279,012
14	54	19,049	.92257	.946	.969	16,110	295,121
15	55	18,683	.91258	.818	.965	13,458	308,580
16	56	18,324	.90178	.818	.965	13,043	321,623
17	57	17,971	.89010	.818	.965	12,627	334,250
18	58	17,626	.87750	.818	.965	12,209	346,459

Present Period Age			Living	Probabilities of Seeking Employment	Finding Employment	Adjusted Present Value	Adjusted Total
19	59	17,287	.86392	.818	.965	11,789	358,247
20	60	16,954	.84936	.818	.965	11,367	369,615
21	61	16,628	.83378	.818	.965	10,944	380,559
22	62	16,308	.81707	.818	.965	10,518	391,077
23	63	15,995	.79913	.818	.965	10,090	401,167
24	64	15,687	.77990	.818	.965	9,657	410,824
25	65	15,385	.75933	.271	.962	3,046	413,870
26	66	15,090	.73759	.271	.962	2,902	416,771
27	67	14,799	.71467	.271	.962	2,757	419,529
28	68	14,515	.69056	.271	.962	2,613	422,142
29	69	14,236	.66526	.271	.962	2,469	424,611
30	70	13,962	.63880	.271	.962	2,325	426,936
31	71	13,693	.61128	.271	.962	2,182	429,118
32	72	13,430	.58273	.271	.962	2,040	431,159
33	73	13,172	.55324	.271	.962	1,900	433,058
34	74	12,919	.52291	.271	.962	1,761	434,819
35	75	12,670	.49183	.271	.962	1,625	436,444
36	76	12,426	.46022	.271	.962	1,491	37,935
37	77	12,187	.42822	.271	.962	1,361	439,296
38	78	11,953	.39602	.271	.962	1,234	440,530
39	79	11,723	.36381	.271	.962	1,112	441,642
40	80	11,498	.33179	.271	.962	995	442,636
41	81	11,277	.29861	.271	.962	878	443,514
42	82	11,060	.26467	.271	.962	763	444,277
43	83	10,847	.23049	.271	.962	652	444,929
44	84	10,639	.19666	.271	.962	545	445,474
45	85	10,434	.16385	.271	.962	446	445,920
46	86	10,233	.13280	.271	.962	354	446,274
47	87	10,036	.10419	.271	.962	273	446,547
48	88	9,843	.07869	.271	.962	202	446,749
49	89	9,654	.05680	.271	.962	143	446,892
50	90	9,469	.03885	.271	.962	96	446,988
51	91	9,286	.02489	.271	.962	60	447,048
52	92	9,100	.01473	.271	.962	35	447,083
53	93	8,933	.00790	.271	.962	18	447,101
54	94	8,761	.00373	.271	.962	9	447,110
55	95	8,592	.00150	.271	.962	3	447,113
56	96	8,427	.00048	.271	.962	1	447,114
57	97	8,265	.00011	.271	.962	0	447,114
58	98	8,106	.00001	.271	.962	0	447,115
59	99	7,950	0.00000	.271	.962	0	447,115

The probabilities of living, seeking, and finding employment reduce the present value of the future income stream from $499,995 (*see* Table 11-9) to $447,115.

The impact of including the probabilities of living, seeking, and finding employment vary with race and sex. The actual calculations are not present here, but Table 11-11 shows the present value of an income stream using the current fact situation but altering the race and sex. Note that, if the person works uninterrupted to age 65, the present value of the future income stream will be $499,995 and the race and sex of the individual will have no impact on the present value.

Table 11-11 Present Value by Race and Sex

	Male	Female
White	$447,115	$232,035
Black	$322,518	$280,820

The present value of a future income stream adjusted for the probabilities of seeking and finding employment for women are biased downward. The present value calculation uses the average seeking employment rate and the average finding employment rate. This means that the early years keep the average much lower than would be indicated by the more recent patterns.

§11.06 Summary

The adjustment to present value of future income for the probabilities of seeking and finding employment reduce the dollar loss. The adjustments should be done with the mortality adjustment, and the analysis should run through age 99. The reductions to present value are more significant for women than for men. This is due in part to the changing activity of women in the labor force.

12 Individual Consumption

$$\text{Present Value} = \sum_{t=0}^{n} \$ * (1+g)^t/(1+d)^t * PL * PS * PF * \underline{C} * TX * H$$

§12.01 Introduction

The purpose of this chapter is to define consumption and discuss the impact consumption has on the present value of a future income stream. To this end, different sources addressing the question of individual consumption are examined. Finally, the short-coming of the consumption data is examined.

§12.02 Definitions

An economist defines consumption as the total demand for all consumer goods and services.[1] However, this is not the appropriate definition for the forensic economist. The forensic economist is concerned with what portion of income goes solely to the support of an individual. For example: suppose a house payment is $700 per month. If it is a two-member household, it may be

---

[1] W. Baumol & A. Blinder, Economics 114 (3d ed 1985).

viewed that half of that house payment is for each of the individuals. However, if one of the individuals is deceased, the house payment does not fall by half. Consequently, in a wrongful death case, what is being examined is not what portion of the house payment would be attributed to the deceased, but what sorts of expenditures on the deceased will in fact cease with his or her death. Examples of expenditures which cease would be a clothing expenditure, a portion of the food budget, life insurance and disability insurance premiums. Examples of expenditures which would not cease would be home-owner's insurance, house payments, and automobile insurance.

§12.03   When Consumption Matters

The economist is employed to estimate the present value of an income stream. The methodology for calculating the present value of the income stream is the same whether the plaintiff was injured or killed. However, how consumption alters the present value of the income stream depends on whether the plaintiff was disabled or killed.[2] If the plaintiff was disabled, there may be no reason to reduce the present value of the future income stream. In some cases consumption may increase as a result of the disability. The injury may result in increased needs for medication, home or transportation modification, and other medical expenses. These factors affecting the present value should be treated individually rather than simply indicating that consumption increases. That is, rather than saying consumption will be higher, an estimate should be made for the present value of future medication or the present value of future home or transportation modifications which are a result of the disability.

§12.04   Sources of Consumption Information

The major sources of consumption information used by economists today are *Injury and Recovery in the Course of Employment* by Earl F. Cheit,[3] and the United States Department of Labor.[4] Cheit reports that consumption of head of household ranges from 18 per cent of income when there are two adults and four minor children, to 30 per cent of income when there are two adults and no minor children. The consumption of the head of household is dependant on the number of minor children present. Table 12-1 presents the relationship

---

[2] Franz, *Should Income Taxes Be Included When Calculating Lost Earnings*, Trial, Oct 1982, at 53-57.

[3] E. Cheit, Injury and Recovery in the Course of Employment (1961).

[4] U.S. Dept of Labor, Revised Equivalency Scale for Urban Families of Different Size, Age and Composition, Derived from the Bureau of Labor Statistics of Consumer Expenditures (1960-61).

[5] Cheit *supra* note 3, at 78.

between consumption of head of household and number of minor children at home.

Table 12-1 Consumption by Head of Household with Dependant Children

Number of Dependant Children	Per Cent of Income Consumed by Head of Household
0	30%
1	26%
2	22%
3	20%
4	18%

Table 12-1 indicates that, if the household consists of two adults and two minor dependent children, the head of household consumes 22 per cent of the family income. As the children grow and eventually leave home, the head of the household consumes more of the family income. With only one minor dependent child at home the head of the household consumes 26 per cent of the income. With no dependent children the consumption increases to 30 per cent of the family income.

Table 12-2 Revised Equivalency Scale for Urban Families of Different Sizes, Ages and Composition

(A 4-person family—husband, age 35 to 54; wife; 2 children, older child 6 to 15 years of age, equals 100%)

Size and type of family	Age of Head			
	Under 35	35-54	55-64	65+
One person	35	36	32	28
Two persons: average	47	59	59	52
Husband, wife	49	60	59	51
One parent, one child	40	57	60	58
Three persons: average	62	81	86	77
Husband, wife (child under 6)	62	69	—	—
Husband, wife, one child, (child 6-15)	62	82	88	81
Husband, wife, one child, (child 16-17)	—	91	88	77
Husband, wife, one child, (child over 18)	—	82	85	77
One parent, 2 children	67	76	82	75
Four persons: average	74	99	109	91

Size and type of family	Age of Head			
	Under 35	35-54	55-64	65+
Husband, wife (children under 6)	72	80	—	—
Husband, wife, two children, (older child 6-15)	77	100	105	95
Husband, wife, two children, (older child 16-17)	—	113	125	—
Husband, wife, two children, (older child over 18)	-	96	110	89
One parent, three children	88	96	—	—
Five persons: average	94	118	124	—
Husband, wife (children under 6)	87	97	—	—
Husband, wife, three children (older child 6-15)	96	116	120	—
Husband, wife, three children (older child 16-17)	—	128	138	—
Husband, wife, three children (older child over 18)	—	119	124	—
One parent, four children	108	117	—	—
Six persons: average	111	138	143	—
Husband, wife (children under 6)	101	—	—	—
Husband, wife, four children, (older child 6-15)	110	132	140	—
Husband, wife, four children, (older child 16-17)	—	146	—	—
Husband, wife, four children, (older child over 18)	—	149	—	—
One parent, five children	125	137	—	—

Source: Derived from the US Dept of Labor, Bureau of Labor Statistics, Survey of Consumer Expenditures (1960-61).

Table 12-2 presents the consumption for the head of household based on the age of head of household and the number of family members. The impact of children on the head of household's consumption is determined by the age of the oldest child.

The Revised Equivalency Scale, from which Table 12-2 is derived, is an index. The "typical" family had two parents present and two minor children. The oldest child was between ages 6 and 15, and the head of the household was between ages 35 and 54. The Revised Equivalency Scale sets the consumption of the family at 100 per cent. That is, to maintain an assumed standard of living takes 100 per cent of their income. All other family structures are relative to this family.

If the family structure is the same as the "typical" family, except there is only one child present and the child is between ages 6 and 15, then the index number in Table 12-2 is 82. This means the family of three needs 82 per cent of what the family of four needs in order to maintain the same standard of living.

If the family consists of two parents and four children, with the oldest child between ages 6 and 15 and the head of household between ages 35 and 54, then the index number is 132. This means the family of six needs 132 per cent of the income the "typical" family of four needs in order to maintain the same standard of living.

By comparing positions on the table, the head of household's consumption can be estimated. Suppose the head of the household of the "typical" family is killed. The family structure changes from two adults, head of household between age 35 and 54, with two children, oldest between ages 6 and 15, to a family of one adult, two children. The index value is 76. This means the family of three needs 76 per cent of what the family of four needed to maintain the same standard of living. The head of household consumed 24 per cent of the family income.

Both the Cheit report and the Revised Equivalency Scale suggest consumption is a function of family size; however, the Revised Equivalency Scale adds age of head of household as a factor affecting consumption. Since the family size and age of head of household affect consumption, the economist must know the birth dates of the deceased, the deceased's spouse, and each of the minor children in order to reduce the income for consumption.

§12.05 Fact Situation

A white male earning $20,000 a year was born 35 years ago today. The two children were born eight years and ten years ago today. The assumption of having all the same birth dates allows for the avoidance of calculation of fractions of years. The growth and discount rates to be applied when calculating the present value of future income are 4 and 6 per cent, respectively. Table 12-3 shows the present value calculation of future income if the deceased had worked uninterrupted to age 65. No modifications have been made for mortality or the probability of seeking and finding employment. As Table 12-3 indicates, present value of future income is $461,409.

The present value of the future income may be altered to reflect the loss to the survivors by reducing the present value figure for the amount of the income that would have been consumed by the deceased. How much income is reduced will depend on which of the consumption schedules is employed.

Table 12-3 Present Value of Future Income

Period	Age	Present Value by Year	Total Present Value
0	35	$20,000	$ 20,000
1	36	19,623	39,623
2	37	19,252	58,875

Period	Age	Present Value by Year	Total Present Value
3	38	18,889	77,764
4	39	18,533	96,297
5	40	18,183	114,480
6	41	17,840	132,320
7	42	17,503	149,823
8	43	17,173	166,997
9	44	16,849	183,846
10	45	16,531	200,377
11	46	16,219	216,596
12	47	15,913	232,509
13	48	15,613	248,123
14	49	15,318	263,441
15	50	15,029	278,470
16	51	14,746	293,216
17	52	14,468	307,684
18	53	14,195	321,878
19	54	13,927	335,805
20	55	13,664	349,469
21	56	13,406	362,876
22	57	13,153	376,029
23	58	12,905	388,934
24	59	12,662	401,596
25	60	12,423	414,018
26	61	12,188	426,207
27	62	11,958	438,165
28	63	11,733	449,898
29	64	11,511	461,409

§12.06   Consumption Using the Cheit Report

The $461,409 present value of future income is reduced by the amount the deceased would have consumed. According to the figures from the Cheit book, the consumption of the head of household would have been 22 per cent with two dependent children. The reduction of 22 per cent per year would continue until the oldest child leaves home. This is assumed to occur at age 18.

Table 12-4 presents the present value adjusted for consumption. Since the head of household consumes 22 per cent of the income, the adjusted present value is 78 per cent of the unadjusted amount. When the oldest child leaves home, the head of household's consumption increases to 26 per cent of the family income. The loss of income to the wife and remaining child is 74 per cent of the total income. The reduction of the income stream is from $461,409 to $345,223. The difference of $116,186 is the present value of the consumption of the head of household using the figures presented in the Cheit report.

Table 12-4 Present Value of Future Income Adjusted for Consumption

Period	Head	Ages of Child #1	Ages of Child #2	Present Value Year	Present Value Total	Consumption	Adjusted Present Value Year	Adjusted Value Total
0	35	10	8	$20,000	$20,000	.22	$15,600	$15,600
1	36	11	9	19,623	39,623	.22	15,306	31,200
2	37	12	10	19,252	58,875	.22	15,017	46,506
3	38	13	11	18,889	77,764	.22	14,734	61,523
4	39	14	12	18,533	96,297	.22	14,456	76,256
5	40	15	13	18,183	114,480	.22	14,183	90,712
6	41	16	14	17,840	132,320	.22	13,915	104,894
7	42	17	15	17,503	149,823	.22	13,653	118,810
8	43	18	16	17,173	166,997	.22	13,395	132,462
9	44		17	16,849	183,846	.26	12,468	145,857
10	45		18	16,531	200,377	.26	12,233	158,326
11	46			16,219	216,596	.30	11,354	170,559
12	47			15,913	232,509	.30	11,139	181,912
13	48			15,613	248,123	.30	10,929	193,052
14	49			15,318	263,441	.30	10,723	203,981
15	50			15,029	278,470	.30	10,521	214,704
16	51			14,746	293,216	.30	10,322	225,224
17	52			14,468	307,684	.30	10,127	235,546
18	53			14,195	321,878	.30	9,936	245,674
19	54			13,927	335,805	.30	9,749	255,610
20	55			13,664	349,469	.30	9,565	265,359
21	56			13,406	362,876	.30	9,384	274,923
22	57			13,153	376,029	.30	9,207	284,308
23	58			12,905	388,934	.30	9,034	293,515
24	59			12,662	401,596	.30	8,863	302,549
25	60			12,423	414,018	.30	8,696	311,412
26	61			12,188	426,207	.30	8,532	320,108
27	62			11,958	438,165	.30	8,371	328,640
28	63			11,733	449,898	.30	8,213	337,010
29	64			11,511	461,409	.30	8,058	345,223

§12.07 Consumption Using the Revised Equivalency Scale

The Revised Equivalency Scale indicates the family of four needs 100 per cent of the income to maintain a given standard of living. With the death of the head of household the family structure changes to three members (one adult). The scale indicates that this family structure requires only 76 per cent of the income level the family of four needed in order to maintain the same standard of living. The head of the household consumed 24 per cent of the family income.

When the oldest child reaches age 18, the family structure will be two adults, one child. The family requires 91 per cent of what the typical family needs. When the family structure changes to one adult and one child, the family needs only 57 per cent of what the typical family needs. This implies that the head of the household consumed 34 per cent of the family income (91% − 57%).

When the youngest child leaves home, the consumption of the head of household will be 24 per cent of the income. The family needs would drop from 60 per cent of the typical family to 36 per cent of the typical family. Finally, when the head of household reaches age 55, the percentage of income consumed by the head of household is 27 per cent.

Table 12-5 shows the present value of the future income stream reduced for consumption using the Revised Equivalency Scale. The reduction in income is $111,048 and is the present value of the consumption of the deceased.

Table 12-5 shows the reduction for consumption starting with a family of four: two adults, two children, head of household, 35 years old. If the family structure changes to one adult and two children, then only 76 per cent of the income is needed to provide the same standard of living. Thus the consumption relation is 24 per cent. The 24 per cent consumption is used until the eldest child reaches age 18.

Were the head of household still living, the family structure would be one child age 16 and two adults, head of household between age 35 and 54. To maintain the standard of living a family of this structure requires 91 per cent of the income of a family of four. The head of household is decreased resulting in a single parent and single child age 16. This family structure requires 57 per cent of the *bare income*. The head of household consumes 34 per cent of the income. Two years later, the youngest child reaches age 18 and the family structure changes to one adult. But the comparison is to two adults, no children, head of household between age 35 and 54. Two adults require 60 per cent of the bare income, one adult requires 36 per cent. The consumption for head of household is 24 per cent.

In the same fashion, when the head of household is 55, two people require 59 per cent of the bare income while one person requires 32 per cent. The head of household consumed 27 per cent of income.

Table 12-5 Present Value of Future Income Adjusted for Consumption

Period	Head	Ages of Child #1	Ages of Child #2	Present Value Year	Present Value Total	Consumption	Adjusted Present Year	Adjusted Value Total
0	35	10	8	$20,000	$20,000	.24	$15,200	$15,200
1	36	11	9	19,623	39,623	.24	14,913	30,400
2	37	12	10	19,252	58,875	.24	14,632	45,313
3	38	13	11	18,889	77,764	.24	14,356	59,945
4	39	14	12	18,533	96,297	.24	14,085	74,301
5	40	15	13	18,183	114,480	.24	13,819	88,386
6	41	16	14	17,840	132,320	.24	13,558	102,205
7	42	17	15	17,503	149,823	.24	13,303	115,763
8	43	18	16	17,173	166,997	.24	13,052	129,066
9	44		17	16,849	183,846	.34	11,120	142,117
10	45		18	16,531	200,377	.34	10,911	153,238
11	46			16,219	216,596	.24	12,327	164,148
12	47			15,913	232,509	.24	12,094	176,475
13	48			15,613	248,123	.24	11,866	188,569
14	49			15,318	263,441	.24	11,642	200,435

Period	Head	Ages of Child #1	Child #2	Present Value Year	Total	Consumption	Adjusted Present Year	Value Total
15	50			15,029	278,470	.24	11,422	212,077
16	51			14,746	293,216	.24	11,207	223,499
17	52			14,468	307,684	.24	10,995	234,706
18	53			14,195	321,878	.24	10,788	245,702
19	54			13,927	335,805	.24	10,584	256,490
20	55			13,664	349,469	.27	9,975	267,074
21	56			13,406	362,876	.27	9,787	277,049
22	57			13,153	376,029	.27	9,602	286,835
23	58			12,905	388,934	.27	9,421	296,437
24	59			12,662	401,596	.27	9,243	305,858
25	60			12,423	414,018	.27	9,069	315,101
26	61			12,188	426,207	.27	8,897	324,170
27	62			11,958	438,165	.27	8,730	333,067
28	63			11,733	449,898	.27	8,565	341,797
29	64			11,511	461,409	.27	8,403	350,361

§12.08 Problems with Two Incomes

The Cheit study indicates that, if the family consists of two adults, the head of the household consumes 30 per cent of the income. The Revised Equivalency Scale suggests the consumption of the head of household between ages 35 and 54 would be 27 per cent.

If an individual were earning $20,000 a year at the time of death, the $20,000 income would be reduced by 30 per cent for consumption, leaving a loss of $14,000 per year. Suppose both parties worked, each earning $20,000 per year. Total income is $40,000. Of this figure, 30 per cent is consumption, or $12,000 is consumed by each adult. The $12,000 consumed subtracted from the $20,000 income leaves an annual loss of $8,000. Neither consumption report clearly addresses the impact of dual incomes on the consumption of a household member.

§12.09 Problems Interpreting the Consumption Table

There are certain relationships presented on the Revised Equivalency Table that imply a head of household has negative consumption. If the family were husband, wife, and three children under six years of age, and the head of the household is under 35, then the family would need 87 per cent of what the typical family of four would need to maintain a lifestyle. If the husband died, then the family of four, with one parent, would need 88 per cent of what the typical family needed in order to maintain that lifestyle. This implies that the husband had negative consumption.

Another problem is with interpretation of the numbers on the table. Consider a family of two adults with the head of household between ages 55 and 64. The two adults need 59 per cent of the income of the family of four.

If the head of household dies, then the single adult needs 32 per cent of what the family of four would need. This implies that the head of household consumed 27 per cent of the income.

There is an improper way to interpret the table. Some argue that 32 per cent of the income needed to support one adult is 54 per cent of the 59 per cent needed to support both adults (54% = 32% / 59%). Thus, the consumption of the head of household is 46 per cent of the total income (100% − 54% = 46%).

§12.10 Cross-Examining the Economist

During the pretrial discovery defense counsel will have had the opportunity to determine what information the economist obtained regarding personal consumption of the decedent. More likely than not, the economist did not obtain such information for the simple reason that the actual figures on an individual's personal consumption are extremely difficult to determine. During cross-examination defense counsel will want to obtain an admission from the economist that the individual's personal consumption figures were not taken into account. An argument might be made that the opinion of the economist is not supported by factual information regarding the decedent.[6]

§12.11 Summary

Current work being done in the area of consumption supports the basic conclusions of the Cheit report and the Revised Equivalency Scale.[7] Consumption of an adult seems to be approximately 30 per cent of the total family income. There are no studies addressing how the impact of dual incomes affect the consumption level of the individual.

---

[6] Higgins v Kinnebrew Motors, Inc, 547 F2d 1223, 1225-26 (5th Cir 1977).

[7] The effect of consumption on the present value of a stream of income may be governed by a statute which specifies the types of damages recoverable for wrongful death.

13 Household Services

$$\text{Present Value} = \sum_{t=0}^{n} [\$ * (1+g)^t/(1+d)^t] * PL * PS * PF * C * \underline{HS} * TX$$

§13.01 Introduction

Household services refer to the economic value provided to the household by either spouse or by minor children. These services are provided on a noncash basis. The most common testimony is to the value of household services provided by a mother/housewife not employed outside the home. This chapter will review some of the sources that can be used to estimate the value of household services and how the estimates of household services are made.

§13.02 Sylvia Porter Study

The Sylvia Porter Study[1] estimates the value of a housewife's services. Table

---

[1] S. Porter, New Money Book For The 80's 621 (1980); Stewart & Greenhalgh, *Work History Patterns and the Occupational Attainment of Women*, 94 Econ J 498-519 (Sept 1984).

13-1 shows the types of jobs a housewife performs, the number of hours spent on each job, and the economic value of the jobs.[2] As the table indicates, the housewife spends 99.6 hours per week in domestic work. The 1979 dollar estimate of household services is $18,862.48.[3] This is the economic value of the housewife not employed outside the home. The value would be the dollars in the present value equation.

The problem with the study's household service figure is that it does not identify the size of the family and the number or age of the children. Consequently, the housewife is expected to contribute equally each year regardless of family size or age of the family members.

Table 13-1 Hours Spent by a Housewife in Domestic Work

	Hours per week
Nursemaid	44.5
Housekeeper	17.5
Cook	13.1
Dishwasher	6.2
Laundress	5.9
Food Buyer	3.3
Chauffer	2.0
Gardner	2.3
Maintenance	1.7
Seamstress	1.3
Dietian	1.2
Practical Nurse	.6
Total	99.6

§13.03 Gauger-Walker Study

The Gauger-Walker study[4] estimates the economic value of household services of the husband, wife, and teenage children. Based on whether or not the wife is employed outside the home, the economic values of the husband, wife, and teenage children are estimated. The economic values are a function of the number of children in the family, the age of the youngest child in the family, and the age of the head of household. The economic values are presented in Table 13-2.

---

[2] Porter, *supra* note 1.

[3] *Id.*

[4] Gauger, & Walker, *The Dollar Value of Household Work*, 60 Info Bull (New York State College of Human Ecology 1980).

Table 13-2 Dollar Value of Household Services
Gauger-Walker Study 1979 Dollars

# of Children	Age of Wife	Employed-Wife Households			Nonemployed Wife Households		
		Wife	Husband	Teen	Wife	Husband	
0	Under 25	$4,700	$1,800		$7,000	$1,100	
	25-39	5,000	1,900		8,000	1,600	
	40-54	5,900	1,100		8,400	2,100	
	55 plus	6,000	1,500		7,400	2,700	
	Age of Youngest Child	Wife	Husband		Wife	Husband	Teen
1	12-17	$6,700	$2,400	$1,400	$9,600	$2,700	$1,200
	6-11	8,000	1,500	†	9,400	2,000	†
	2-5	6,200	2,000	†	9,100	2,400	†
	1	8,300	600	†	9,900	2,300	†
	Under 1	*	*	†	10,900	2,100	†
2	12-17	$6,300	$2,100	$1,000	$10,000	$2,200	$1,100
	6-11	7,200	2,000	1,100	9,900	2,100	1,100
	2-5	8,300	2,400	1,500	1,100	2,200	900
	1	8,400	5,000	*	11,700	2,200	*
	Under 1	10,200	2,100	*	12,600	2,000	*
3	12-17	$5,000	$2,100	$1,100	$9,000	$1,400	$1,000
	6-11	8,600	2,000	1,700	9,900	2,200	1,600
	2-5	10,200	2,800	*	10,700	1,900	1,000
	1	11,500	3,200	*	11,600	2,200	1,400
	Under 1	8,700	2,800	*	13,300	2,000	*
4	12-17	$8,700	$1,900	$1,700	$8,400	$1,400	$1,000
	6-11	7,200	1,400	1,100	10,700	1,900	1,100
	2-5	*	*	*	12,000	2,000	1,100
	1	*	*	*	11,800	2,600	800
	Under 1	*	*	*	13,700	2,600	*
5 - 6	12-17	*	*	*	†	†	†
	6-11	*	*	*	$11,500	$2,000	$1,700
	2-5	*	*	*	12,200	2,100	900
	1	*	*	*	9,900	700	*
	Under 1	*	*	*	13,600	2,600	1,000
7 - 9	6-11	†	†	†	*	*	*
	2-5	*	*	*	$11,900	$2,900	$1,400
	1	†	†	†	*	*	*
	Under 1	†	†	†	15,200	2,600	*

As the family structure changes, the economic contributions of each member

---

† No cases.

* Averages not calculated because there were fewer than 4 cases.

of the household changes. In order to calculate the present value of household services, the economist must know the birth dates of the husband, wife, and each of the children.

§13.04 Fact Situation

A Caucasian couple, both celebrating their thirty-eighth birthday today, have two children. The children, ages ten and eight, are also celebrating their birthdays today. The wife is not employed outside the home. The present value of the household services of the wife is calculated in §13.05 using the Jefferson Standard information. **Section 13.06** calculates the present value of the household services of the wife using the Gauger-Walker information. **Section 13.07** calculates the present value of the household services of the husband.

The value of household services will grow at 4 per cent per year and will be discounted to present value at 6 per cent per year. The purpose is to show the present value of household services for the wife and husband using the data available.

§13.05 Calculating the Present Value of the Household Services of the Wife Using the Sylvia Porter Information

Since the Jefferson Standard information is 1979 data, the economist may "move" the dollar value forward. That is, the 1979 value of household services will be inflated to represent 1986 values. If the figures are inflated using the Consumer Price Index, the 1986 value of a housewife's services would be $28,502. It is this amount that would be used as the dollar value when calculating the present value of the lost services (Table 13-3). The present value of the household services is calculated to age 65 and is $607,387. This assumes household services are provided annually to age 65 and then cease.

Table 13-3 Present Value of Household Services of the Wife Using the Sylvia Porter Figures

Period	Age	Present Value Annual Income	Total Present Value
0	38	$28,502	$28,502
1	39	27,964	56,466
2	40	27,437	83,903
3	41	26,919	110,822
4	42	26,411	137,233
5	43	25,913	163,145
6	44	25,424	188,569
7	45	24,944	213,513
8	46	24,473	237,987
9	47	24,012	261,998

Period	Age	Present Value Annual Income	Total Present Value
10	48	23,559	285,557
11	49	23,114	308,671
12	50	22,678	331,349
13	51	22,250	353,599
14	52	21,830	375,430
15	53	21,418	396,848
16	54	21,014	417,862
17	55	20,618	438,480
18	56	20,229	458,709
19	57	19,847	478,556
20	58	19,473	498,029
21	59	19,105	517,134
22	60	18,745	535,879
23	61	18,391	554,270
24	62	18,044	572,314
25	63	17,704	590,018
26	64	17,370	607,387

It may be more appropriate to calculate the present value of household services through the life expectancy of the spouse. That is, the present value of the household services of the wife are mortality-adjusted, using the probability the husband will live each year. The husband's mortality expectation is used since he has the shorter life expectancy. This calculation is presented in Table 13-4.

Table 13-4 The Present Value of a Wife's Household Services Mortality-Adjusted by the Husband's Life Expectancy

Period	Age	Present Value	Total	Chance of Husband Living	Adjusted Present Value	Total
0	38	$28,502	$28,502	.99795	$28,444	$28,444
1	39	27,964	56,466	.99574	27,845	56,289
2	40	27,437	83,903	.99335	27,254	83,543
3	41	26,919	110,822	.99074	26,670	110,213
4	42	26,411	137,233	.98788	26,091	136,304
5	43	25,913	163,145	.98473	25,517	161,821
6	44	25,424	188,569	.98125	24,947	186,768
7	45	24,944	213,513	.97741	24,381	211,148
8	46	24,473	237,987	.97317	23,817	234,965
9	47	24,012	261,998	.96847	23,255	258,220
10	48	23,559	285,557	.96326	22,693	280,913
11	49	23,114	308,671	.95747	22,131	303,044

Period	Age	Present Value	Total	Chance of Husband Living	Adjusted Present Value	Total
12	50	22,678	331,349	.95107	21,568	324,613
13	51	22,250	353,599	.94401	21,004	345,617
14	52	21,830	375,430	.93627	20,439	366,056
15	53	21,418	396,848	.92782	19,873	385,929
16	54	21,014	417,862	.91865	19,305	405,233
17	55	20,618	438,480	.90870	18,735	423,969
18	56	20,229	458,709	.89794	18,164	442,133
19	57	19,847	478,556	.88631	17,591	459,724
20	58	19,473	498,029	.87376	17,014	476,738
21	59	19,105	517,134	.86024	16,435	493,173
22	60	18,745	535,879	.84575	15,853	509,027
23	61	18,391	554,270	.83023	15,269	524,296
24	62	18,044	572,314	.81359	14,681	538,976
25	63	17,704	590,018	.79573	14,087	553,063
26	64	17,370	607,387	.77658	13,489	566,552
27	65	17,042	624,429	.75610	12,885	579,438
28	66	16,720	641,149	.73445	12,280	591,718
29	67	16,405	657,554	.71163	11,674	603,392
30	68	16,095	673,649	.68762	11,067	614,460
31	69	15,792	689,441	.66243	10,461	624,920
32	70	15,494	704,935	.63609	9,855	634,776
33	71	15,201	720,136	.60868	9,253	644,028
34	72	14,915	735,051	.58025	8,654	652,683
35	73	14,633	749,684	.55089	8,061	660,744
36	74	14,357	764,041	.52069	7,475	668,219
37	75	14,086	778,127	.48974	6,899	675,118
38	76	13,820	791,947	.45826	6,333	681,451
39	77	13,560	805,507	.42640	5,782	687,233
40	78	13,304	818,811	.39434	5,246	692,479
41	79	13,053	831,863	.36227	4,729	697,208
42	80	12,806	844,670	.33038	4,231	701,439
43	81	12,565	857,235	.29734	3,736	705,175
44	82	12,328	869,562	.26355	3,249	708,424
45	83	12,095	881,658	.22951	2,776	711,200
46	84	11,867	893,525	.19582	2,324	713,523
47	85	11,643	905,168	.16316	1,900	715,423
48	86	11,423	916,591	.13223	1,511	716,934
49	87	11,208	927,799	.10375	1,163	718,096
50	88	10,996	938,795	.07835	862	718,958
51	89	10,789	949,584	.05656	610	719,568
52	90	10,585	960,169	.03868	409	719,978
53	91	10,386	970,555	.02479	257	720,235

Period	Age	Present Value	Total	Chance of Husband Living	Adjusted Present Value	Total
54	92	10,190	980,745	.01467	149	720,385
55	93	9,997	990,742	.00786	79	720,463
56	94	9,809	1,000,551	.00372	36	720,500
57	95	9,624	1,010,174	.00149	14	720,514
58	96	9,442	1,019,617	.00048	4	720,518
59	97	9,264	1,028,880	.00011	1	720,519
60	98	9,089	1,037,970	.00001	0	720,520
61	99	8,918	1,046,887	.00000	0	720,520

Adjusting the present value of the wife's household services for the probability of the husband living increases the present value of the future stream from $607,387 to $720,520.

It might be argued that the value of household services should be mortality-adjusted using the probability of the husband living and the probability of the wife living since both have a statistical probability of dying each year. Table 13-5 presents the present value of the same income stream with the mortality adjustment for both the husband and the wife.

Table 13-5 Present Value of Household Services Adjusted by the Probability of the Husband and the Wife Both Living

Period	Age	Present Value	Probability of Living Husband	Probability of Living Wife	Adjusted Present Value	Total Present Value
0	38	$28,502	.99795	.99893	$28,413	$28,413
1	39	27,964	.99574	.99775	27,783	56,196
2	40	27,437	.99335	.99644	27,157	83,353
3	41	26,919	.99074	.99499	26,536	109,889
4	42	26,411	.98788	.99339	25,918	135,808
5	43	25,913	.98473	.99161	25,303	161,110
6	44	25,424	.98125	.98965	24,689	185,799
7	45	24,944	.97741	.98748	24,075	209,875
8	46	24,473	.97317	.98509	23,462	233,336
9	47	24,012	.96847	.98246	22,847	256,183
10	48	23,559	.96326	.97956	22,229	278,412
11	49	23,114	.95747	.97638	21,608	300,021
12	50	22,678	.95107	.97288	20,983	321,004
13	51	22,250	.94401	.96905	20,354	341,358
14	52	21,830	.93627	.96485	19,721	361,079
15	53	21,418	.92782	.96028	19,083	380,162
16	54	21,014	.91865	.95531	18,442	398,604
17	55	20,618	.90870	.94992	17,797	416,401

Period	Age	Present Value	Probability of Living		Adjusted Present Value	Total Present Value
			Husband	Wife		
18	56	20,229	.89794	.94406	17,148	433,550
19	57	19,847	.88631	.93769	16,495	450,044
20	58	19,473	.87376	.93080	15,837	465,881
21	59	19,105	.86024	.92317	15,172	481,054
22	60	18,745	.84575	.91510	14,507	495,561
23	61	18,391	.83023	.90639	13,839	509,401
24	62	18,044	.81359	.89697	13,168	522,569
25	63	17,704	.79573	.88680	12,493	535,061
26	64	17,370	.77658	.87581	11,814	546,875
27	65	17,042	.75610	.86396	11,132	558,007
28	66	16,720	.73445	.85124	10,454	568,461
29	67	16,405	.71163	.83761	9,778	578,239
30	68	16,095	.68762	.82301	9,109	587,348
31	69	15,792	.66243	.80740	8,446	595,794
32	70	15,494	.63609	.79073	7,793	603,587
33	71	15,201	.60868	.77287	7,151	610,738
34	72	14,915	.58025	.75376	6,523	617,261
35	73	14,633	.55089	.73335	5,912	623,173
36	74	14,357	.52069	.71162	5,320	628,493
37	75	14,086	.48974	.68854	4,750	633,243
38	76	13,820	.45826	.66394	4,205	637,447
39	77	13,560	.42640	.63782	3,688	641,135
40	78	13,304	.39434	.61019	3,201	644,336
41	79	13,053	.36227	.58109	2,748	647,084
42	80	12,806	.33038	.55055	2,329	649,414
43	81	12,565	.29734	.51677	1,931	651,344
44	82	12,328	.26355	.47974	1,559	652,903
45	83	12,095	.22951	.43960	1,220	654,123
46	84	11,867	.19582	.39665	922	655,045
47	85	11,643	.16316	.35140	668	655,712
48	86	11,423	.13223	.30459	460	656,172
49	87	11,208	.10375	.25721	299	656,472
50	88	10,996	.07835	.21049	181	656,653
51	89	10,789	.05656	.16584	101	656,754
52	90	10,585	.03868	.12477	51	656,805
53	91	10,386	.02479	.08868	23	656,828
54	92	10,190	.01467	.05873	9	656,837
55	93	9,997	.00786	.03557	3	656,840
56	94	9,809	.00372	.01919	1	656,840
57	95	9,624	.00149	.00887	0	656,840
58	96	9,442	.00048	.00330	0	656,840
59	97	9,264	.00011	.00088	0	656,840

Period	Age	Present Value	Probability of Living Husband	Probability of Living Wife	Adjusted Present Value	Total Present Value
60	98	9,089	.00001	.00013	0	656,840
61	99	8,918	0.00000	0.00000	0	656,840

The present value of the housewife's services are $656,840 when the income is adjusted for the probability of both the wife and husband living.

§13.06 Calculating the Present Value of the Household Services of the Wife Using the Gauger-Walker Study

The Gauger-Walker study estimates the number of hours spent by each member of the family performing household services. The time spent in household services is based on their 1967-1968 survey of 1,378 families.[5]

The categories of activities included kitchen helper, cleaning person, housekeeper, laundry worker, yard worker, child-care worker, homemaker, and dressmaker. The number of hours the family members spent in each category was estimated. The dollar value of the household service was estimated by multiplying the local wage rate by the number of hours spent in each activity. The wage rates were obtained from the United States Bureau of Labor Statistics "Job Bank" for May 1979.[6]

The most recent Gauger-Walker study was done in 1979. In order to make a more current estimate, the 1979 dollar value of household services found in Table 13-2 was increased to current values. This was done by increasing the 1979 values to 1986 values by the rate of change in the Consumer Price Index. Table 13-6 presents the 1986 value of household services.

Table 13-6 Dollar Value of Household Services Gauger-Walker Study 1986 Dollars

# of Children	Employed-Wife Households Wife	Wife	Husband	Teen	Nonemployed Wife Households Wife	Husband
0	Under 25	$7,102	$2,720		$10,577	$1,662
	25-39	7,555	2,871		12,088	2,418
	40-54	8,915	1,662		12,692	3,173
	55 plus	9,066	2,267		11,181	4,080

[5] Gauger & Walker, *The Dollar Value of Household Work*, 60 Info Bull 5 (New York State College of Human Ecology, 1980).

[6] *Id* 7.

# of Children	Employed-Wife Households Youngest Child	Wife	Husband	Teen	Nonemployed Wife Households Wife	Husband	Teen
1	12-17	$10,124	$3,626	$2,115	$14,506	$4,080	$1,813
	2-5	9,368	3,022	†	13,750	3,626	
	1	12,541	907	†	14,959	3,475	
	Under 1				16,470	3,173	
2	12-17	$9,519	$3,173	$1,511	$15,110	$3,324	$1,662
	6-11	10,879	3,022	1,662	14,959	3,173	1,662
	2-5	12,541	3,626	2,267	15,662	3,324	1,360
	1	12,692	7,555	*	17,679	3,324	*
	Under 1	15,412	3,173	*	19,039	3,022	*
3	12-17	$ 7,555	$3,173	$1,662	$13,599	$2,115	$1,511
	6-11	12,994	3,022	2,568	14,959	3,324	2,418
	2-5	15,412	4,230	*	16,168	2,871	1,511
	1	17,377	4,835	*	17,528	3,324	2,115
	Under 1	13,146	4,230	*	20,096	3,022	*
4	12-17	$13,146	$2,871	$2,568	$12,692	$2,115	$1,511
	6-11	10,879	2,115	1,662	16,168	2,871	1,662
	2-5	*	*	*	18,132	3,022	1,662
	1	*	*	*	17,830	3,929	1,209
	Under 1	*	*	*	20,700	3,929	*
5 - 6	12-17	*	*	*	†	†	†
	6-11	*	*	*	$17,377	$3,022	$2,568
	2-5	*	*	*	18,434	3,173	1,360
	1	*	*	*	14,959	1,058	
	Under 1	*	*	*	20,550	3,929	1,511
7 - 9	6-11	†	†	†	*	*	*
	2-5	*	*	*	17,980	4,381	2,115
	1	†	†	†	*	*	*
	Under 1	†	†	†	22,967	3,929	*

The analysis for determining the present value of household services using the economic value of the housewife based on the Walker-Gauger study is a bit different. In this case the age of the children and the age of the wife affect the economic value of the services. Table 13-6 shows that in 1986 the annual value of a housewife not employed outside the home and having two children ages 8 and 10 is $14,959. When the oldest child reaches age 12, the value of the housewife's services increases to $15,110. When the oldest child leaves home at age 18, the family structure changes to one child age 16. The 1986 dollar value of the housewife not employed outside the home and having a 16-year-old child is $14,506.

---

* Averages not calculated because there were fewer than 4 cases.

When the second child leaves home, the value of the household service is based on the age of the head of the household. Since the youngest child left home at age 18, it would be 10 years after the analysis began. Currently the youngest child is age 8. This means the head of household is 10 years older. The 1986 dollar value of the household services of a housewife not employed outside the home when the head of household is 48 years old is $12,692. This remains the annual dollar value of the household services until the head of household reaches age 55. At age 55 the dollar value of the services decreases to $11,181 and remains at this level.

It is these 1986 values that are used to determine the present value of the household services. Table 13-7 presents the 1986 dollar value of the household services. The reason for the dollar changes is the changing structure of the family.

Table 13-7 1986 Dollar Value of a Housewife's Services

Age of Head	Members of the Family Child #1	Child #2	Dollar Value of Housewife's Services
38	10	8	$14,959
39	11	9	14,959
40	12	10	15,110
41	13	11	15,110
42	14	12	15,110
43	15	13	15,110
45	16	14	15,110
46	17	15	15,110
47		16	14,506
48		17	14,506
49			12,692
50			12,692
51			12,692
52			12,692
53			12,692
54			12,692
55			11,181
56			11,181
57			11,181
58			11,181
59			11,181
.			.
.			.
.			.

It is the dollar values listed in Table 13-7 that are used to calculate the dollar value of the household services. The future value of each of these figures must be calculated in order to make the proper present value forecast. The dollar value $15,110 is the 1986 dollar value of the housewife's services expected in two years. The $15,110 must be inflated, or permitted to grow, for the two-year period before the discounting can occur. The annual growth rate of household services was 4 per cent (**§13.04**).

Table 13-8 shows the present value of household services. The present value of the services to age 65 is $281,324. The present value figure has taken into account the changing structure of the family.

Table 13-8 Future Value and Present Value of Household Services of a Housewife
Growth Rate = 4%
Discount Rate = 6%

Period	Head	Ages Child #1	Child #2	1986 Value	Future Value	Present Value	Total Value
	38	10	8	$14,959	$14,959	$14,959	$14,959
1	39	11	9	14,959	15,557	14,677	29,636
2	40	12	10	15,110	16,343	14,545	44,181
3	41	13	11	15,110	16,997	14,271	58,452
4	42	14	12	15,110	17,677	14,001	72,453
5	43	15	13	15,110	18,384	13,737	86,191
6	44	16	14	15,110	19,119	13,478	99,669
7	45	17	15	15,110	19,884	13,224	112,892
8	46		16	14,506	19,852	12,456	125,348
9	47		17	14,506	20,647	12,221	137,569
10	48			12,692	18,787	10,491	148,059
11	49			12,692	19,539	10,293	158,352
12	50			12,692	20,320	10,099	168,451
13	51			12,692	21,133	9,908	178,359
14	52			12,692	21,978	9,721	188,080
15	53			12,692	22,858	9,538	197,618
16	54			12,692	23,772	9,358	206,975
17	55			11,181	21,779	8,088	215,063
18	56			11,181	22,651	7,936	222,999
19	57			11,181	23,557	7,786	230,785
20	58			11,181	24,499	7,639	238,424
21	59			11,181	25,479	7,495	245,918
22	60			11,181	26,498	7,353	253,272
23	61			11,181	27,558	7,215	260,486
24	62			11,181	28,660	7,078	267,565
25	63			11,181	29,807	6,945	274,510
26	64			11,181	30,999	6,814	281,324
27	65			11,181	32,239	6,685	288,009
28	66			11,181	33,529	6,559	294,568
29	67			11,181	34,870	6,435	301,004
30	68			11,181	36,264	6,314	307,318
31	69			11,181	37,715	6,195	313,512

Period	Head	Ages Child #1	Child #2	1986 Value	Future Value	Present Value	Total Value
32	70			11,181	39,224	6,078	319,590
33	71			11,181	40,793	5,963	325,554
34	72			11,181	42,424	5,851	331,405
35	73			11,181	44,121	5,740	337,145

How far the value of the household services are extended into the future is a value judgment. Should the calculation stop at age 65, should it continue until the husband's life expectancy, or should the calculation be mortality-adjusted for the probability of each of the adults living? If the analysis extends to the husband's life expectancy, then the figure can be read from Table 13-8. Appendix F states that the life expectancy of a 38-year-old Caucasian male is 36.3 years. The analysis would extend until the husband reaches age 72.3 years. The present value of the household services would be between $331,405 and $337,145.

If the analysis is adjusted by the probability that both the husband and wife will live, then the present value of the future household services would be extended to age 99, since both have a probability of living to that age. The column in Table 13-8 headed "Present Value" would be multiplied by the probability that the husband would live each successive year and the probability that the wife would live each successive year that the sum is computed. The present value of the mortality-adjusted household services of the housewife is $299,257. This calculation is presented in Table 13-9.

Table 13-9 Mortality-Adjusted Value of Household Services of the Wife

Period	Age	Present Value	Probability of Living Male	Female	Adjusted Present Values Annual	Total
0	38	$14,959	.99795	.99893	$14,912	$14,912
1	39	14,677	.99574	.99775	14,581	29,494
2	40	14,545	.99335	.99644	14,397	43,891
3	41	14,271	.99074	.99499	14,068	57,959
4	42	14,001	.98788	.99339	13,740	71,699
5	43	13,737	.98473	.99161	13,414	85,113
6	44	13,478	.98125	.98965	13,088	98,202
7	45	13,224	.97741	.98748	12,763	110,965
8	46	12,456	.97317	.98509	11,941	122,906
9	47	12,221	.96847	.98246	11,628	134,533
10	48	10,491	.96326	.97956	9,899	144,432
11	49	10,293	.95747	.97638	9,622	154,054
12	50	10,099	.95107	.97288	9,344	163,398
13	51	9,908	.94401	.96905	9,064	172,462
14	52	9,721	.93627	.96485	8,782	181,244

Period	Age	Present Value	Probability of Living Male	Probability of Living Female	Adjusted Present Values Annual	Adjusted Present Values Total
15	53	9,538	.92782	.96028	8,498	189,742
16	54	9,358	.91865	.95531	8,212	197,954
17	55	8,088	.90870	.94992	6,982	204,935
18	56	7,936	.89794	.94406	6,727	211,662
19	57	7,786	.88631	.93769	6,471	218,133
20	58	7,639	.87376	.93080	6,213	224,346
21	59	7,495	.86024	.92317	5,952	230,298
22	60	7,353	.84575	.91510	5,691	235,989
23	61	7,215	.83023	.90639	5,429	241,418
24	62	7,078	.81359	.89697	5,166	246,584
25	63	6,945	.79573	.88680	4,901	251,484
26	64	6,814	.77658	.87581	4,634	256,119
27	65	6,685	.75610	.86396	4,367	260,486
28	66	6,559	.73445	.85124	4,101	264,587
29	67	6,435	.71163	.83761	3,836	268,423
30	68	6,314	.68762	.82301	3,573	271,996
31	69	6,195	.66243	.80740	3,313	275,309
32	70	6,078	.63609	.79073	3,057	278,366
33	71	5,963	.60868	.77287	2,805	281,171
34	72	5,851	.58025	.75376	2,559	283,730
35	73	5,740	.55089	.73335	2,319	286,049
36	74	5,632	.52069	.71162	2,087	288,136
37	75	5,526	.48974	.68854	1,863	290,000
38	76	5,422	.45826	.66394	1,650	291,649
39	77	5,319	.42640	.63782	1,447	293,096
40	78	5,219	.39434	.61019	1,256	294,352
41	79	5,120	.36227	.58109	1,078	295,430
42	80	5,024	.33038	.55055	914	296,343
43	81	4,929	.29734	.51677	757	297,101
44	82	4,836	.26355	.47974	611	297,712
45	83	4,745	.22951	.43960	479	298,191
46	84	4,655	.19582	.39665	362	298,552
47	85	4,567	.16316	.35140	262	298,814
48	86	4,481	.13223	.30459	180	298,995
49	87	4,397	.10375	.25721	117	299,112
50	88	4,314	.07835	.21049	71	299,183
51	89	4,232	.05656	.16584	40	299,223
52	90	4,152	.03868	.12477	20	299,243
53	91	4,074	.02479	.08868	9	299,252
54	92	3,997	.01467	.05873	3	299,255
55	93	3,922	.00786	.03557	1	299,257
56	94	3,848	.00372	.01919	0	299,257

Period	Age	Present Value	Probability of Living Male	Female	Adjusted Present Values Annual	Total
57	95	3,775	.00149	.00887	0	299,257
58	96	3,704	.00048	.00330	0	299,257
59	97	3,634	.00011	.00088	0	299,257
60	98	3,566	.00001	.00013	0	299,257
61	99	3,498	0.00000	0.00000	0	299,257

§13.07   Calculating the Present Value of the Household Services of the Husband

Had the fact situation in **§13.04** been such that the husband had been killed or permanently disabled, then the analysis would proceed in exactly the same way, except the value of the household services of the husband would have been used. This information is in Table 13-6.

Table 13-10 1986 Dollar Value of A Husband's Services

Ages of Members of the Family Head	Child #1	Child #2	Dollar Value of Husband's Services
38	10	8	$ 3,173
39	11	9	3,173
40	12	10	3,324
41	13	11	3,324
42	14	12	3,324
43	15	13	3,324
45	16	14	3,324
46	17	15	3,324
47		16	4,080
48		17	4,080
49			3,173
50			3,173
51			3,173
52			3,173
53			3,173
54			3,173
55			4,080
56			4,080
57			4,080
58			4,080
59			4,080
.			.
.			.

The values appearing in the last column of Table 13-10 are the 1986 dollar values of household services of the husband. They are used to calculate the present value of the household services. The present value calculation of the services appears in Table 13-11. The present value of the husband's household services calculated to age 65 is $75,473. The present value of the household services to life expectancy is between $93,747 and $95,842. The present value of the household services adjusted by the probability that both the husband and wife will live is $83,089.

Table 13-11 Mortality-Adjusted Value of Household Services of the Husband

Period	Age	Present Value	Total Income	Probability of Living Male	Probability of Living Female	Adjusted Present Values Annual	Adjusted Present Values Total
0	38	$3,173	$ 3,173	.99795	.99893	$3,163	$3,163
1	39	3,113	6,286	.99574	.99775	3,093	6,256
2	40	3,103	9,390	.99335	.99644	3,072	9,328
3	41	3,045	12,435	.99074	.99499	3,002	12,330
4	42	2,987	15,422	.98788	.99339	2,932	15,261
5	43	2,931	18,353	.98473	.99161	2,862	18,123
6	44	2,876	21,229	.98125	.98965	2,793	20,916
7	45	2,822	24,050	.97741	.98748	2,723	23,639
8	46	3,503	27,554	.97317	.98509	3,359	26,998
9	47	3,437	30,991	.96847	.98246	3,270	30,268
10	48	2,623	33,614	.96326	.97956	2,475	32,743
11	49	2,573	36,187	.95747	.97638	2,406	35,149
12	50	2,525	38,712	.95107	.97288	2,336	37,485
13	51	2,477	41,189	.94401	.96905	2,266	39,751
14	52	2,430	43,619	.93627	.96485	2,195	41,946
15	53	2,384	46,003	.92782	.96028	2,124	44,070
16	54	2,339	48,343	.91865	.95531	2,053	46,123
17	55	2,951	51,294	.90870	.94992	2,548	48,671
18	56	2,896	54,190	.89794	.94406	2,455	51,126
19	57	2,841	57,031	.88631	.93769	2,361	53,487
20	58	2,787	59,818	.87376	.93080	2,267	55,754
21	59	2,735	62,553	.86024	.92317	2,172	57,926
22	60	2,683	65,236	.84575	.91510	2,077	60,003
23	61	2,633	67,869	.83023	.90639	1,981	61,984
24	62	2,583	70,452	.81359	.89697	1,885	63,869
25	63	2,534	72,986	.79573	.88680	1,788	65,657
26	64	2,486	75,473	.77658	.87581	1,691	67,348
27	65	2,440	77,912	.75610	.86396	1,594	68,942
28	66	2,393	80,306	.73445	.85124	1,496	70,438
29	67	2,348	82,654	.71163	.83761	1,400	71,838
30	68	2,304	84,958	.68762	.82301	1,304	73,142
31	69	2,261	87,219	.66243	.80740	1,209	74,351

Period	Age	Present Value	Total Income	Probability of Living Male	Female	Adjusted Present Values Annual	Total
32	70	2,218	89,436	.63609	.79073	1,116	75,466
33	71	2,176	91,613	.60868	.77287	1,024	76,490
34	72	2,135	93,747	.58025	.75376	934	77,424
35	73	2,095	95,842	.55089	.73335	846	78,270
36	74	2,055	97,897	.52069	.71162	762	79,031
37	75	2,016	99,914	.48974	.68854	680	79,711
38	76	1,978	101,892	.45826	.66394	602	80,313
39	77	1,941	103,833	.42640	.63782	528	80,841
40	78	1,904	105,738	.39434	.61019	458	81,299
41	79	1,868	107,606	.36227	.58109	393	81,693
42	80	1,833	109,439	.33038	.55055	333	82,026
43	81	1,799	111,238	.29734	.51677	276	82,303
44	82	1,765	113,003	.26355	.47974	223	82,526
45	83	1,731	114,734	.22951	.43960	175	82,700
46	84	1,699	116,433	.19582	.39665	132	82,832
47	85	1,667	118,099	.16316	.35140	96	82,928
48	86	1,635	119,735	.13223	.30459	66	82,994
49	87	1,604	121,339	.10375	.25721	43	83,037
50	88	1,574	122,913	.07835	.21049	26	83,063
51	89	1,544	124,457	.05656	.16584	14	83,077
52	90	1,515	125,973	.03868	.12477	7	83,084
53	91	1,487	127,459	.02479	.08868	3	83,088
54	92	1,459	128,918	.01467	.05873	1	83,089
55	93	1,431	130,349	.00786	.03557		83,089
56	94	1,404	131,753	.00372	.01919		83,089
57	95	1,378	133,131	.00149	.00887		83,089
58	96	1,352	134,482	.00048	.00330		83,089
59	97	1,326	135,809	.00011	.00088		83,089
60	98	1,301	137,110	.00001	.00013		83,089
61	99	1,277	138,386	0.00000	0.00000		83,089

§13.08 Other Sources of Information

There are several other sources which address the dollar value of household services. One expert estimates that a 27-year-old female with a 4-year-old child, not employed outside the home, spends 57 hours per week providing household services.[7]

Another article discusses the methodology to employ in the calculation of

---

[7] Kiker, *Evaluating Household Services*, Trial, Feb 1980, at 34-35; Bradshaw, *The Scope of 'Pecuniary Loss' Since Wentling v. M.A.S.*, 9, No 2 J Kan Trial Law Assn 7-11 (1985-86); Hunt & Kiker, *Valuation of Household Services: Methodology and Estimation*, 46, No 4 J Risk & Ins 697, 697-706 (1980).

the present value of household services.[8] It suggests the hours spent in various types of employment should be multiplied by the local wage rates in order to get a current value. Once the current dollar value of household services is determined, the values should be increased by an appropriate growth rate and then discounted to present value at an appropriate discount rate.

A third source suggests the 35-year-old mother of three children, not employed outside the home, spends 90 hours per week performing household services.[9] It suggests the dollar value of the services is $670 per week.

§13.09   Taxes and Household Services

Household services are noncash services. To replace the services requires purchasing the services in the open market. This requires replacing services with after-tax dollars. To estimate the present value of household services in before-tax dollars, the present value is divided by one minus the marginal tax rate. If the family is in the 28 per cent tax bracket, then to replace $100 of household services requires the family to have $139 ($139 less 28 per cent for taxes leaves the $100 necessary to purchase the household services in the open market). The calculation of the present value of the household services requires valuing the household services at the before-tax equivalent.

§13.10   Summary

Household services are provided by husbands, wives, and children. The most typical case of valuing household services is for the deceased, or disabled, housewife not employed outside the home.

When household services are valued, the economist must decide what time frame the analysis will cover and what methodology will be employed. Should the analysis cover the time period until the person providing the service reaches age 65, or should the analysis run until the person receiving the services reaches age 65? Or should the analysis run, with certainty, until the person providing the service reaches life expectancy, or until the person receiving the service reaches life expectancy? Should the analysis run, mortality-adjusted, to age 100? If so, should the mortality adjustment be made according to the person receiving or providing the service? Should the analysis be done using the joint probability of mortality?

The impact of mortality on the present value of the analysis can be affected by the selection of the mortality table. Recall from Chapter 10 that the government mortality tables do not contain the same bias that insurance company tables do. This means that using the government mortality tables would result in a lower present value than would using a life insurance mortality table.

Regardless of how the analysis is performed, the household services are an after-tax service. The value should be recalculated on a before-tax basis since the services are paid for after state and federal taxes are paid.

---

[8] Kirby, *The Economic Expert*, 31, No 3 J Mo B 201 (Apr-May 1975).

[9] Durham, *The Valuation of the Production of a Deceased Housewife*, 4, No 5 Kan Trial Law Assn, 18, 18-23 (1980-81).

14   Federal Income Taxes

$$\text{Present Value} = \sum_{t=0}^{n} \$ * (1+g)^t/(1+d)^t * PL * PS * PF * C * HS * \underline{TX}$$

§14.01   Introduction

Initially it would appear that taxes would reduce the size of the present value award. This chapter will address that question and review the major problems arising from including taxes in the present value calculation.[1]

---

[1] In Norfolk & Western Ry v Liepelt, 444 US 490, *rehg denied*, 445 US 972 (1980), the Supreme Court of the United States addressed the issue of whether a state court could prohibit admission of evidence concerning the effect of income taxation on future earnings in the context of an action under the Federal Employer's Liability Act (FELA), 45 USC §51 *et seq*. The Court held that the recovery of damages in FELA actions was a matter of federal law, rejecting the argument that the effect of future income taxes was too speculative. However, a majority of jurisdictions still hold that the jury should not be instructed regarding the effects of income taxation on the amount of any damages received in a wrongful death action. *See generally*, Annot, *Propriety of Taking Income Tax into Consideration in Fixing Damages in Personal Injury or Death Action*, 16 ALR4th 589 (1983); Annot, *Propriety of Considering Future Income Taxes in Awarding Damages Under Federal Tort Claims Act*, 47 ALR Fed 735 (1980).

§14.02   The Federal Income Tax

Since taxes are a fact of life today, any discussion of loss and compensation for that loss is incomplete without discussion of the effect of taxes on the present value of future income. Taxes may be paid at the point of a sale, i.e., sales tax, or taxes may be withheld by an employer, i.e., state and federal income tax and social security tax. Taxes are paid on investment income, although they may not be withheld. Regardless of how the taxes are paid, they represent a reduction in the discretionary income available to the plaintiff or the plaintiff's survivors. This chapter will limit the discussion to federal income taxes.

The 1988 Individual Federal Income Tax rates are presented in Tables 14-1, 14-2, and 14-3. As the tables indicate, there are two categories of taxpayers, married and single. There are two categories of single taxpayers, single and single with dependent children.

Tax rates are defined in two ways. The average tax rate is the tax liability divided by the taxable income. The marginal tax rate is the proportion of the last dollar of income that is paid in taxes. The marginal tax rates for both single and married taxpayers are 15, 28, and 33 per cent. Which marginal tax rate is in effect depends on the filing status and the income level of the taxpayer.

Table 14-1 states that for the single taxpayer having a taxable income of less than $17,850 per year the tax due is 15 per cent. If the taxable income is above $17,850 and below $43,150, then the tax liability is $2,678 plus 28 per cent of the income above $17,850. In a like fashion, if the taxable income is between $43,150 and $89,560, then the tax due is $9,762 plus 33 per cent of the earnings above $43,150. When taxable income exceeds $89,560, the tax liability is $25,077 plus 28 per cent of the income above $89,560.

Table 14-1 1988 Tax Rates for Single Taxpayers

Taxable Income		Tax		Percent on Excess		
0		0		15%		
0 to $17,850	=	15%				
$17,850 to $43,150	=	$2,678	+	28%	>	$17,850
$43,150 to $89,560	=	$9,762	+	33%	>	$43,150
$89,560+		$25,077	+	28%	>	$89,560

Table 14-2 1988 Tax Rates for Single Taxpayers Head of Household

Taxable Income	Tax		Head of Household Percent on Excess	
0	0		15%	
0 to $23,900	15%			
$23,900 to $61,650	$3,585	+	28% >	$23,900

			Head of Household Percent
Taxable Income	Tax		on Excess
$61,650 to $123,790	$14,155	+	33% > $61,650
$123,790+	$34,661	+	28% > $123,790

Table 14-3 1988 Tax Rates for Married Taxpayers

			Percent
Taxable Income	Tax		on Excess
0	0		15%
0 to $29,750	15%		
$24,975 to $71,900	$4,463		28% > $24,975
$71,900 to $149,250	$16,265	+	33% > $71,900
$149,250+	$41,750	+	28% >

Consider a taxable income of $25,000. If the taxpayer is single, the tax liability is $4,680. For this taxpayer the average tax rate is 18.72 per cent, and the marginal tax rate is 28 per cent. If the taxpayer is a single head of household, the tax liability is $3,893. The average tax rate is 15.57 per cent, and the marginal tax rate is 28 per cent. For the married taxpayers the tax liability is $3,750. The average tax rate is 15 per cent and the marginal tax rate is 15 per cent.

§14.03 Reducing Future Income for Federal Income Taxes

Based on the data in Table 14-1, the present value of a future income stream, reduced for federal income taxes, will decline by an amount either 15, 28, or 33 per cent, something in between, depending on the taxable income. The present value will be reduced by 15 per cent when the future income to be earned never exceeds $17,850 for a single person, $23,900 for single head of household, or $29,750 for a couple. If the income always exceeds these amounts, then the reduction in present value will require knowing what the taxable income is each future year and applying the appropriate reduction.

If the current income level is $25,000 and is being forecast for the next 20 years, with an annual growth of wages of 4 per cent and an annual discount rate of 6 per cent, then the present value of the future income stream is $501,995. To reduce future income for taxes, the income for each future year must be made. The forecasted value for each future year is presented in Table 14-4.

Table 14-4 Present Value of Future Income Streams
Single Taxpayer

Period	Age	Without Taxes		With Taxes	
		Future Income	Present Value	Future Income	Present Value
0	40	25,000	25,000	20,320	20,320
1	41	26,000	24,528	21,040	19,849
2	42	27,040	24,066	21,789	19,392
3	43	28,122	23,611	22,568	18,948
4	44	29,246	23,166	23,377	18,517
5	45	30,416	22,729	24,220	18,098
6	46	31,633	22,300	25,096	17,692
7	47	32,898	21,879	26,007	17,296
8	48	34,214	21,466	26,954	16,911
9	49	35,583	21,061	27,940	16,537
10	50	37,006	20,664	28,964	16,174
11	51	38,486	20,274	30,030	15,820
12	52	40,026	19,892	31,139	15,475
13	53	41,627	19,516	32,291	15,139
14	54	43,292	19,148	33,483	14,810
15	55	45,024	18,787	34,643	14,455
16	56	46,825	18,432	35,850	14,112
17	57	48,698	18,085	37,105	13,779
18	58	50,645	17,743	38,410	13,457
19	59	52,671	17,409	39,767	13,144
20	60	54,778	17,080	41,179	12,840
21	61	56,969	16,758	42,647	12,545
22	62	59,248	16,442	44,174	12,258
23	63	61,618	16,131	45,761	11,980
24	64	64,083	15,827	47,413	11,710
			$501,995		$391,259

How much of an income reduction occurs for taxes depends on the filing status of the taxpayers. Table 14-4 also presents the after-tax dollars available each year to the single taxpayer. The table also shows the present value of the after-tax income. In order to make the after-tax calculation, the economist assumes that the filing status of the taxpayer will not change and that the tax structure will not change. The reduction for taxes causes the present value of the future income stream to decrease to $391,259.

Table 14-5 makes exactly the same calculations for a married couple. If income taxes are ignored, the present value of the future income stream remains $501,995, while inclusion of income taxes reduces the present value of the income stream to $412,217.

Table 14-5 Present Value of Future Income Streams
Married Taxpayer

Period	Age	Without Taxes		With Taxes	
		Future Income	Present Value	Future Income	Present Value
0	40	$25,000	$25,000	$21,250	$21,250
1	41	26,000	24,528	22,100	20,849
2	42	27,040	24,066	22,984	20,456
3	43	28,122	23,611	23,903	20,070
4	44	29,246	23,166	24,859	19,691
5	45	30,416	22,729	25,767	19,254
6	46	31,633	22,300	26,643	18,782
7	47	32,898	21,879	27,554	18,325
8	48	34,214	21,466	28,501	17,882
9	49	35,583	21,061	29,487	17,453
10	50	37,006	20,664	30,511	17,037
11	51	38,486	20,274	31,577	16,634
12	52	40,026	19,892	32,686	16,244
13	53	41,627	19,516	33,838	15,865
14	54	43,292	19,148	35,037	15,497
15	55	45,024	18,787	36,284	15,140
16	56	46,825	18,432	37,581	14,793
17	57	48,698	18,085	38,929	14,457
18	58	50,645	17,743	40,332	14,130
19	59	52,671	17,409	41,790	13,812
20	60	54,778	17,080	43,307	13,503
21	61	56,969	16,758	44,885	13,203
22	62	59,248	16,442	46,526	12,911
23	63	61,618	16,131	48,232	12,627
24	64	64,083	15,827	50,006	12,351
			501,995		412,217

§14.04 Evaluating the Reduction for Taxes

If the present value analysis is done properly, and the growth and interest assumptions are correct, there should be no remaining principal when the plaintiff reaches age 65. Table 14-6 shows that, if the assumptions are made, the principal will be exhausted when the plaintiff reaches age 61. In fact, there is a shortage of over $175,000.

Tables 14-5 and 14-6 work together to show the shortfall in the award when the award is reduced for income tax. The present value of future wages of $412,217 is the after-tax award. The first year's after-tax income of $21,250 is deducted from the award. The remaining principal is invested to earn 6 per cent annual interest. The interest income for the first year is $23,458. The interest income is a taxable income. The tax on the interest income is $6,033. The tax is deducted from the interest income leaving $17,428 for the increase in principal. The principal increases to $408,392. From the principle of $408,392 the second year's after-tax income is deducted. As Table 14-6 indicates, the principal will be inadequate. That is, there is insufficient money in the fund to provide the future income to retirement at age 65.

The reason for the shortfall is two-fold. The award to plaintiff is not a taxable income but the interest income is taxable. The present value of the award is computed using after-tax dollars, but the after-tax dollars earn taxable income. Second, the status of the taxpayer changed from married with a joint return to single, thus the effective tax rates changed.

Table 14-6 Impact of Taxes on the Award

Age	Beginning Principal	Annual Income	Principal at Interest	Interest Income	Tax on Interest	Added To Principal	Ending Principal
40	$412,217	$21,250	$390,967	$23,458	$6,033	17,425	408,392
41	408,392	22,100	386,292	23,178	5,955	17,223	403,515
42	403,515	22,984	380,531	22,832	5,858	16,974	397,504
43	397,504	23,903	373,601	22,416	5,741	16,675	390,276
44	390,276	24,859	365,416	21,925	5,604	16,321	381,737
45	381,737	25,767	355,970	21,358	5,445	15,913	371,883
46	371,883	26,643	345,241	20,714	5,265	15,449	360,690
47	360,690	27,554	333,136	19,988	5,062	14,926	348,063
48	348,063	28,501	319,561	19,174	4,834	14,340	333,902
49	333,902	29,487	304,415	18,265	4,579	13,686	318,101
50	318,101	30,511	287,589	17,255	2,588	14,667	302,256
51	302,256	31,577	270,679	16,241	2,436	13,805	284,484
52	284,484	32,686	251,798	15,108	2,266	12,842	264,640
53	264,640	33,838	230,802	13,848	2,077	11,771	242,572
54	242,572	35,037	207,535	12,452	1,868	10,584	218,120
55	218,120	36,284	181,836	10,910	1,637	9,274	191,109
56	191,109	37,581	153,529	9,212	1,382	7,830	161,358
57	161,358	38,929	122,429	7,346	1,102	6,244	128,673
58	128,673	40,332	88,341	5,300	795	4,505	92,847
59	92,847	41,790	51,057	3,063	460	2,604	53,660
60	53,660	43,307	10,353	621	93	528	10,881
61	10,881	44,885	(34,004)				
62		46,526	(80,530)				
63		48,232	(128,762)				
64		50,006	(178,768)				

It is worth noting that, if the tax status of the receivers of the award does not change, the award will still be insufficient, but the shortfall will not occur as quickly.

§14.05 Problems Associated with Reducing the Present Value of a Future Income Stream for Taxes

In order to reduce the future income stream for income taxes, the economist must make accurate forecasts concerning the future income, family structure, expenditures by type and size, and the level of household services. **Sections 14.06** through **14.10** briefly address the difficulty of forecasting each of these items.

§14.06 —Income Forecasting

Income is received from wages and salaries, investment income, rents, royalties, and farm income. In order to reduce future income levels for income tax, the exact dollar amount of income must be known and the source of the income must be known.

For example, an individual has income from investments, dividends, and capital gains totaling $20,000 annually, plus a taxable salary of $20,000. Total taxable income for the individual is $40,000. The tax liability for a married couple would be $7,333. If the couple had no investment income, the tax liability would be only $3,000. Is the difference of $4,333 in the tax liability due to the salary or to the investment income?

If the present value of the future income stream is calculated ignoring income tax, the present value is $401,596. Reduced for income tax, the award would be $335,269. The award would be insufficient, and the principal would be exhausted when plaintiff reaches age 62. Had the award been reduced at the higher tax rate, the principal would be exhausted sooner.

This same problem exists when there are two incomes in the family. Suppose each party earned $20,000 each. Is the injured party's income to be reduced for income tax at the higher or lower of the two rates? In either case, the reduction for taxes will cause the principal to be exhausted before fully compensating the plaintiff.

§14.07 —Family Structure

When income streams are being reduced for income taxes, the age of each of the dependents must be known since the personal exemptions reduce the taxable income. Since the family can claim each child as a dependent under certain conditions through college, a decision must be made regarding the likelihood that the child will attend college.

In a similar manner the mortality of each of the family members must be considered since, if premature death occurs, the number of dependents will change. As the number of dependents changes, the taxable income changes.

Since alimony is a deductible expense when calculating taxable income, the analysis must consider the likelihood of the marriage surviving.

§14.08   —Expenditure Forecasting

Just as the family structure must be forecast, so must the level of expenditures be forecast. Income taxes are based on taxable income. Taxable income is total income less certain expenses. Deductible expenses include medical expenses after a deductible is met, state and local taxes, interest on the home mortgage, and, for a while yet, a portion of interest on credit cards and automobile loans.

To properly forecast the level of taxes, the medical expenses must be forecast by year. What illnesses will each family member have? Will the illnesses require medical care, and if so will the expenses be covered by the health insurance policy? If the policy does not cover the illnesses, will the expenses be large enough to qualify for a deduction of medical expenses? How many years will the illnesses continue? This type of analysis of medical expenses requires the economist to forecast the exact nature of illness and the coverage provided by the health insurance carrier and to perform the analysis on an annual basis.

The same problems arise with interest deductions. To properly estimate the tax liability, the annual mortgage interest must be known. This requires knowing the amortization schedule for the mortgage and determining if the home will ever be refinanced or paid off at an accelerated rate. If refinancing or acceleration occurs, the economist must determine at what rate these occur.

Automobile interest and credit card interest require forecasting the frequency with which families purchase cars, the amount borrowed, the annual interest rate, and the life of the loan. Credit cards require the economist to make similar estimates. All estimates must be made on an annual basis.

§14.09   —Tax Schedules

To reduce the income stream for taxes, the economist must forecast the tax schedule for each year the analysis is being performed. Typically, the economist would assume the current tax structure would remain unchanged throughout the period the analysis occurs. To do otherwise would require the economist to predict how the Congress will alter the tax structure. This analysis would also have to be done year by year.

If there are state and local income taxes to be considered, the same forecast would have to be made. The economist must determine, by year, how the state and local governments will act. Since state and local taxes are deductible when calculating federal income tax liability, the economist, to be accurate in the analysis, must also calculate, by year, all local levies, school taxes, and other assessments.

§14.10   —Household Services

If taxes are to be included in the present value analysis, the household services must be calculated on a before-tax basis. To do this requires forecasting the annual value of the household services and the tax rate that will be applicable in each of those years.

Let the value of household services be estimated at $8,000 per year. If the family income is less than $29,750, the marginal tax rate is 15 per cent. The replacement value of the household services is $9,412. This is $8,000 divided by one minus the marginal tax rate, or $8,000 / (1−.15). Since the value of household services is expected to increase annually, the marginal tax rate may change. Table 14-7 shows the after-tax and before-tax value of household services calculated for a 25-year period. The marginal tax rate is based on the assumption that no additional family income is being earned. Household services are assumed to grow in value at 4 per cent annually.

Table 14-7 Value of Household Services

Period	Future Value Tax	Before Tax	Present Value After Tax
0	$8,000	$9,412	$9,412
1	8,320	9,788	9,234
2	8,653	10,180	9,060
3	8,999	10,587	8,889
4	9,359	11,010	8,721
5	9,733	11,451	8,557
6	10,123	11,909	8,395
7	10,527	12,385	8,237
8	10,949	12,881	8,081
9	11,386	13,396	7,929
10	11,842	13,932	7,779
11	12,316	14,489	7,633
12	12,808	15,069	7,489
13	13,321	15,671	7,347
14	13,853	16,298	7,209
15	14,408	16,950	7,073
16	14,984	17,628	6,939
17	15,583	18,333	6,808
18	16,207	19,067	6,680
19	16,855	19,829	6,554
20	17,529	20,622	6,430
21	18,230	21,447	6,309
22	18,959	22,305	6,190
23	19,718	23,197	6,073
24	20,506	24,125	5,958
		Present Value	$188,986

The inclusion of taxes in the value of household services will cause the present value of the service to increase from $160,638 to $188,986. This value would be much higher if the analysis also included lost income. The other factor causing the value to be low is that the interest income from the award is taxable.

§14.11   Summary

The inclusion of taxes considerably complicates the present value calculation. The economist is required to make annual forecasts of income, types of income, expenditures, tax rates, and value of household services. There is evidence that the inclusion of income taxes in the present value analysis will cause the present value of an award to be increased.

15

A Quick Method for Estimating the Present Value of Future Income

$$\text{Present Value} = \sum_{t=0}^{n} \$ * M * \overline{(1 + g)^t / (1 + d)^t} * PL * PS * PF * C * HS * TX$$

§15.01 Introduction

When the economist is estimating the present value of a future income stream, it is necessary to estimate the growth rate of wages and the discount rate, or interest rate, that should be used to obtain the present value. If all variables are constant except the growth rate, the larger the growth rate employed by the economist the larger the present value of the future income stream. Likewise, if all variables are constant except the discount rate, the larger the discount rate employed by the economist the smaller the present value of the future income stream.

A debate between economists, and one that spills over into the courtroom, is over the appropriate growth and discount rates. Some states have attempted to resolve this issue by requiring the growth and discount rates to be equal. Two states which have done this are Alaska and Pennsylvania.[1]

§15.02   The Alaska Plan: A Quick Estimate of the Present Value of the Future Income Stream

The Alaska plan states the growth rate and discount rate employed by the economist must be equal. When this occurs, the formula for present value reduces to a multiplication of the dollar loss times the number of years the loss is to be experienced. The present value formula is:[2]

$$\text{Present Value} = \$ * N$$

The "$" amount is the base dollar amount and "N" is the number of years the loss occurs.

The term *Alaska plan* has come to mean that the growth and discount rates are equal. The Alaska plan does provide a quick method for estimating the present value of a future income stream. While not technically accurate, the equating of the growth and discount rates, thus making the present value calculation a quick multiplication, does provide the attorney with a good "ball park" figure which should not be far off what the economist will conclude.

However, the Alaska plan has two problems. First, the plan is not based on economic fact. This means that either the growth rate or discount rate employed by the economist will be too high or too low. Second, if the income stream does not have a growth rate, then the use of different growth and discount rates can lead to different present value figures. This can best be seen when calculating the present value of a retirement program.

§15.03   An Example of Estimating the Present Value of Lost Income Using the Alaska Plan

Mr. Smith was injured and is unable to pursue gainful employment. At the time he was injured he was earning $20,000 per year. Today is Mr. Smith's thirty-fifth birthday. The present value of the future income until Mr. Smith retires at age 65, using the Alaska plan, is $600,000.

$$\text{Present Value} = \$ * N$$
$$\text{Present Value} = \$20,000 * 30$$
$$\text{Present Value} = \$ \, 600,000$$

---

[1] Beaulieu v Elliott, 434 P2d 665 (Ala 1967); Kuczkowski v Bolubasz, 491 Pa 561, 421 A2d 1027 (1980).

[2] Franz, *Simplified Calculation of Future Lost Earnings*, Trial, Aug 1977, at 34-37.

Suppose the economist is estimating the present value of the future income using a 6 per cent growth rate and a 6 per cent discount rate. Table 15-1 shows the present value calculation by year. The last column, Total Loss, represents the present value of the future income stream and indicates the present value of the total loss of income to age 65 is $600,000.

Table 15-1 Present Value of Future Income With 6 Per Cent Growth and Discount Rates

Year	Age	Wage	Growth Rate	Discount Rate	Present Value Annual Wage	Total Loss
1987	35	$20,000	(1+.06) / (1+.06)		$20,000	$20,000
1988	36	20,000	(1+.06) / (1+.06)		20,000	40,000
1989	37	20,000	(1+.06) / (1+.06)		20,000	60,000
1990	38	20,000	(1+.06) / (1+.06)		20,000	80,000
1991	39	20,000	(1+.06) / (1+.06)		20,000	100,000
1992	40	20,000	(1+.06) / (1+.06)		20,000	120,000
1993	41	20,000	(1+.06) / (1+.06)		20,000	140,000
1994	42	20,000	(1+.06) / (1+.06)		20,000	160,000
1995	43	20,000	(1+.06) / (1+.06)		20,000	180,000
1996	44	20,000	(1+.06) / (1+.06)		20,000	200,000
1997	45	20,000	(1+.06) / (1+.06)		20,000	220,000
1998	46	20,000	(1+.06) / (1+.06)		20,000	240,000
1999	47	20,000	(1+.06) / (1+.06)		20,000	260,000
2000	48	20,000	(1+.06) / (1+.06)		20,000	280,000
2001	49	20,000	(1+.06) / (1+.06)		20,000	300,000
2002	50	20,000	(1+.06) / (1+.06)		20,000	320,000
2003	51	20,000	(1+.06) / (1+.06)		20,000	340,000
2004	52	20,000	(1+.06) / (1+.06)		20,000	360,000
2005	53	20,000	(1+.06) / (1+.06)		20,000	380,000
2006	54	20,000	(1+.06) / (1+.06)		20,000	400,000
2007	55	20,000	(1+.06) / (1+.06)		20,000	420,000
2008	56	20,000	(1+.06) / (1+.06)		20,000	440,000
2009	57	20,000	(1+.06) / (1+.06)		20,000	460,000
2010	58	20,000	(1+.06) / (1+.06)		20,000	480,000
2011	59	20,000	(1+.06) / (1+.06)		20,000	500,000
2012	60	20,000	(1+.06) / (1+.06)		20,000	520,000
2013	61	20,000	(1+.06) / (1+.06)		20,000	540,000
2014	62	20,000	(1+.06) / (1+.06)		20,000	560,000
2015	63	20,000	(1+.06) / (1+.06)		20,000	580,000
2016	64	20,000	(1+.06) / (1+.06)		20,000	600,000

Table 15-2 shows exactly the same calculations, but the growth and discount rates have been increased to 10 per cent. annually. The present value of the future income stream does not change; it remains at $600,000.

Table 15-2 Present Value of Future Income With 10 Per Cent Growth and Discount Rates

Year	Age	Wage	Growth Rate	Discount Rate	Present Value Annual Wage	Present Value Total Loss
1987	35	$20,000	(1+.10) / (1+.10)		$20,000	$20,000
1988	36	20,000	(1+.10) / (1+.10)		20,000	40,000
1989	37	20,000	(1+.10) / (1+.10)		20,000	60,000
1990	38	20,000	(1+.10) / (1+.10)		20,000	80,000
1991	39	20,000	(1+.10) / (1+.10)		20,000	100,000
1992	40	20,000	(1+.10) / (1+.10)		20,000	120,000
1993	41	20,000	(1+.10) / (1+.10)		20,000	140,000
1994	42	20,000	(1+.10) / (1+.10)		20,000	160,000
1995	43	20,000	(1+.10) / (1+.10)		20,000	180,000
1996	44	20,000	(1+.10) / (1+.10)		20,000	200,000
1997	45	20,000	(1+.10) / (1+.10)		20,000	220,000
1998	46	20,000	(1+.10) / (1+.10)		20,000	240,000
1999	47	20,000	(1+.10) / (1+.10)		20,000	260,000
2000	48	20,000	(1+.10) / (1+.10)		20,000	280,000
2001	49	20,000	(1+.10) / (1+.10)		20,000	300,000
2002	50	20,000	(1+.10) / (1+.10)		20,000	320,000
2003	51	20,000	(1+.10) / (1+.10)		20,000	340,000
2004	52	20,000	(1+.10) / (1+.10)		20,000	360,000
2005	53	20,000	(1+.10) / (1+.10)		20,000	380,000
2006	54	20,000	(1+.10) / (1+.10)		20,000	400,000
2007	55	20,000	(1+.10) / (1+.10)		20,000	420,000
2008	56	20,000	(1+.10) / (1+.10)		20,000	440,000
2009	57	20,000	(1+.10) / (1+.10)		20,000	460,000
2010	58	20,000	(1+.10) / (1+.10)		20,000	480,000
2011	59	20,000	(1+.10) / (1+.10)		20,000	500,000
2012	60	20,000	(1+.10) / (1+.10)		20,000	520,000
2013	61	20,000	(1+.10) / (1+.10)		20,000	540,000
2014	62	20,000	(1+.10) / (1+.10)		20,000	560,000
2015	63	20,000	(1+.10) / (1+.10)		20,000	580,000
2016	64	20,000	(1+.10) / (1+.10)		20,000	600,000

No matter what growth or discount rates are used, as long as the two values are equal, the calculation reduces to the multiplication of the current income level times the number of years being forecasted.

This can further be seen by looking at each page in Appendix C. Appendix C combines the growth and discount rates and presents the present value factor by year. Table 15-3 presents the present value factors of one dollar received each year for 30 years.

Table 15-3 Present Value Factors Year 30

Discount Rate	Growth Rates					
	0%	2%	4%	6%	8%	10%
0%	30.000	41.379	58.328	83.802	122.346	180.943
2%	22.396	30.000	41.110	57.527	81.995	118.708
4%	17.292	22.518	30.000	40.854	56.768	80.300
6%	13.765	17.458	22.635	30.000	40.609	56.048
8%	11.258	13.940	17.620	22.749	30.000	40.374
10%	9.427	11.426	14.112	17.777	22.859	30.000
12%	8.055	9.583	11.593	14.280	17.931	22.967
14%	7.003	8.198	9.738	11.756	14.445	18.082
16%	6.177	7.132	8.339	9.891	11.918	14.607
18%	5.517	6.294	7.261	8.479	10.042	12.077

Note that on the diagonal, where the growth rate and discount rates are the same, the present value factor is 30.00. Again this demonstrates that, when the growth rate and the discount rate are the same, the present value factor is equal to the number of years for which the loss is being calculated.

The use of the Alaska plan does provide a good indicator of the present value of an income stream that is expected to grow. However, when calculating the present value of a the retirement benefit that is not expected to grow, the growth and discount rates assumed prior to retirement do matter. **Section 15.04** examines the present value of a defined contribution plan, and **§15.05** examines the present value of a defined benefit plan.

§15.04 An Example of Estimating the Present Value of Retirement Benefits Using a Defined Contribution Plan

A defined contribution plan specifies, or defines, the monies contributed by the employee and employer to the retirement plan. For example, the plan may specify that 8 per cent of the employee's salary will be contributed to the retirement plan. The size of the retirement annuity is determined when the individual retires. The retirement annuity purchased depends on the amount of money available.

Table 15-4 shows the income earned each year with differing growth assumptions. In each case the current, or beginning, salary is $20,000. The annual growth of income ranges from 2 to 10 per cent. The defined contribution is 8 per cent of the annual income. In each case the present value of the future income stream is $600,000 if the discount rate used is the same as the growth rate.

Table 15-4 Future Value of $20,000 Annual Income Growing at Different Rates

Year	Age	Annual Growth Rate				
		.02	.04	.06	.08	.10
1987	35	$20,000	$20,000	$20,000	$20,000	$20,000
1988	36	20,400	20,800	21,200	21,600	22,000
1989	37	20,808	21,632	22,472	23,328	24,200
1990	38	21,224	22,497	23,820	25,194	26,620
1991	39	21,649	23,397	25,250	27,210	29.282
1992	40	22,082	24,333	26,765	29,387	32,210
1993	41	22,523	25,306	28,370	31,737	35,431
1994	42	22,974	26,319	30,073	34,276	38,974
1995	43	23,433	27,371	31,877	37,019	42,872
1996	44	23,902	28,466	33,790	39,980	47,159
1997	45	24,380	29,605	35,817	43,178	51,875
1998	46	24,867	30,789	37,966	46,633	57,062
1999	47	25,365	32,021	40,244	50,363	62,769
2000	48	25,872	33,301	42,659	54,392	69,045
2001	49	26,390	34,634	45,218	58,744	75,950
2002	50	26,917	36,019	47,931	63,443	83,545
2003	51	27,456	37,460	50,807	68,519	91,899
2004	52	28,005	38,958	53,855	74,000	101,089
2005	53	28,565	40,516	57,087	79,920	111,198
2006	54	29,136	42,137	60,512	86,314	122,318
2007	55	29,719	43,822	64,143	93,219	134,550
2008	56	30,313	45,575	67,991	100,677	148,005
2009	57	30,920	47,398	72,071	108,731	162,805
2010	58	31,538	49,294	76,395	117,429	179,086
2011	59	32,169	51,266	80,979	126,824	196,995
2012	60	32,812	53,317	85,837	136,970	216,694
2013	61	33,468	55,449	90,988	147,927	238,364
2014	62	34,138	57,667	96,447	159,761	262,200
2015	63	34,820	59,974	102,234	172,542	288,420
2016	64	35,517	62,373	108,368	186,345	317,262
Average of last 5 years		$34,151	$57,756	$96,775	$160,709	$264,588

Table 15-5 represents 8 per cent of the employee's annual income. This would represent the amount of money contributed to the retirement program. The contributions are different since the annual growth rate of wages ranges from 2 to 10 per cent.

Table 15-5 The Contribution of the Employer Plus the Employee Assuming 4 Per Cent by Both

Year	Age	Annual Growth Rate				
		2%	4%	6%	8%	10%
1987	35	$ 1,200	$ 1,200	$ 1,200	$ 1,200	$ 1,200
1988	36	1,224	1,248	1,272	1,296	1,320
1989	37	1,248	1,298	1,348	1,400	1,452
1990	38	1,273	1,350	1,429	1,512	1,597
1991	39	1,299	1,404	1,515	1,633	1,757
1992	40	1,325	1,460	1,606	1,763	1,933
1993	41	1,351	1,518	1,702	1,904	2,126
1994	42	1,378	1,579	1,804	2,057	2,338
1995	43	1,406	1,642	1,913	2,221	2,572
1996	44	1,434	1,708	2,027	2,399	2,820
1997	45	1,463	1,776	2,149	2,591	3,112
1998	46	1,492	1,847	2,278	2,798	3,424
1999	47	1,522	1,921	2,415	3,022	3,766
2000	48	1,552	1,998	2,560	3,264	4,143
2001	49	1,583	2,078	2,713	3,525	4,557
2002	50	1,615	2,161	2,876	3,807	5,013
2003	51	1,647	2,248	3,048	4,111	5,514
2004	52	1,680	2,337	3,231	4,440	6,065
2005	53	1,714	2,431	3,425	4,795	6,672
2006	54	1,748	2,528	3,631	5,179	7,339
2007	55	1,783	2,629	3,849	5,593	8,073
2008	56	1,819	2,735	4,079	6,041	8,880
2009	57	1,855	2,844	4,324	6,524	9,768
2010	58	1,892	2,958	4,854	7,046	10,745
2011	59	1,930	3,076	4,859	7,609	11,820
2012	60	1,969	3,199	5,150	8,218	13,002
2013	61	2,008	3,327	5,459	8,876	14,302
2014	62	2,048	3,460	5,787	9,586	15,732
2015	63	2,089	3,598	6,134	10,353	17,305
2016	64	2,131	3,742	6,502	11,181	19,036
Sum of the Contribution		$48,682	$67,302	$94,870	$135,940	$197,393
Present Value		$26,876	$20,750	$16,518	$ 13,509	$ 11,312

Table 15-5 also shows the total contributions made by the employee and employer to the retirement fund. When the wages are assumed to grow at 2 per cent annually, the total contribution made by both the employee and employer is $48,682. When the growth rate of wages increases to 10 per cent annually, the total contribution increases to $197,393. In both cases contributions to the retirement program are 8 per cent of wages.

It is this amount of money, ranging from $48,682 to $197,393, which is used to purchase the retirement annuity. These figures represent the future value of the pension plan. The size of the annuity will depend on the market conditions which prevail and the terms included in the annuity.

The question facing the economist is: "What is the present value of the defined contribution plan?" The appropriate discount factor to employ under the Alaska plan is the same as the growth factor. Therefore, the present value of the $48,682 must be discounted for 30 years in order to determine the present value.

Table 15-5 shows the present value of the defined contribution plan of 8 per cent of the wage using a discount rate equal to the assumed growth rate. The present value of the defined contribution plan, using a 2 per cent growth and discount rate is $26,876. If the annual growth and discount rate is 10 per cent, then the present value of the defined contribution plan is $11,312.

§15.05   An Example of Estimating the Present Value of Retirement Benefits Using a Defined Benefit Plan

A defined benefit plan states a formula which will be used to calculate the employee's retirement benefit. For example, a defined retirement benefit might be 10 per cent of the average annual income earned the last five years of employment. The growth assumption will change the amount of income earned the last years, thus changing the annual retirement income.

If the present value of the retirement benefit is to be estimated, the economist will use 10 per cent of the average income earned the last five years as the annual retirement income. Using the example in Table 15-5, the annual retirement would range from $3,415, when the growth rate and discount rate were assumed to be 2 per cent, to $26,459, when the growth and discount rates were assumed to be 10 per cent. Recall that Table 15-1 and Table 15-2 show the present value of the future income to be $600,000 regardless of the growth and interest assumptions. The difference is the retirement benefit and the cost of the retirement benefit.

Table 15-6 shows the annual retirement income for the 16-year period from age 65 to age 80. The economist must discount the income to present value. In other words, the economist will state the dollars needed today in order to fund a 16-year annuity starting in 30 years when Mr. Smith reaches age 65. What is different about this annuity is that it does not grow, i.e., the annual retirement benefit is level.

Table 15-6 Annual Retirement Benefits Defined Benefit Plan

Age	2%	4%	6%	8%	10%
65	$3,415	$5,776	$9,677	$16,071	$26,459
66	3,415	5,776	9,677	16,071	26,459
67	3,415	5,776	9,677	16,071	26,459
68	3,415	5,776	9,677	16,071	26,459
69	3,415	5,776	9,677	16,071	26,459
70	3,415	5,776	9,677	16,071	26,459
71	3,415	5,776	9,677	16,071	26,459
72	3,415	5,776	9,677	16,071	26,459
73	3,415	5,776	9,677	16,071	26,459
74	3,415	5,776	9,677	16,071	26,459
75	3,415	5,776	9,677	16,071	26,459
76	3,415	5,776	9,677	16,071	26,459
77	3,415	5,776	9,677	16,071	26,459
78	3,415	5,776	9,677	16,071	26,459
79	3,415	5,776	9,677	16,071	26,459
80	3,415	5,776	9,677	16,071	26,459

Determining the present value of the retirement benefit is a two-step process. First, the cost of the 16-year annuity, which starts at age 65, must be determined; and second, the present value of a 16-year annuity which starts paying in 30 years must be determined.

Table 15-7 shows the cost of the retirement annuity which is to be purchased when Mr. Smith reaches age 65. The price of a 16-year annuity, paying $3,415 annually and earning interest at 2 per cent per year is $47,295. The price of an annuity paying $26,459 annually and earning 10 per cent year is $227,706. However, these annuities do not start for another 30 years, when Mr. Smith reaches age 65. Therefore, the present value calculation requires discounting the cost of the annuity another 30 years. This last step is determining the present value of the cost of the annuity which is to begin in 30 years. Stated differently, how much money does it take today to provide $47,295 in 30 years? The $47,295 would be used to purchase a 16-year annuity paying $3,415 annually.

For the larger annuity the same question would be asked, that is, how much money does it take today to provide $227,706 in 30 years? The $227,706 would be used to purchase a 16-year annuity paying $26,459 annually.

What is the appropriate interest rate to use when discounting the money needed in 30 years? The answer is provided in the Alaska plan. The discount rate is the same rate as the growth rate. If the growth and discount rate of wages were 2 per cent when the present value of the future income was calculated, the appropriate discount rate is 2 per cent. If the growth and discount rate used was 10 per cent, then the appropriate discount rate is 10 per cent.

Table 15-7 Retirement Benefits at Age 65

	Discount Rate				
	2%	**4%**	**6%**	**8%**	**10%**
Annual Retirement Income	$3,415	$5,776	$9,677	$16,071	$26,459
Age					
65	$3,415	$5,776	$9,677	$16,071	$26,459
66	3,348	5,554	9,129	14,881	24,054
67	3,282	5,340	8,612	13,778	21,867
68	3,218	5,135	8,125	12,758	19,879
69	3,155	4,937	7,665	11,813	18,072
70	3,093	4,747	7,231	10,938	16,429
71	3,032	4,565	6,822	10,127	14,935
72	2,973	4,389	6,436	9,377	13,578
73	2,915	4,220	6,071	8,683	12,343
74	2,858	4,058	5,728	8,040	11,221
75	2,801	3,902	5,404	7,444	10,201
76	2,747	3,752	5,098	6,893	9,274
77	2,693	3,608	4,809	6,382	8,431
78	2,640	3,469	4,537	5,909	7,664
79	2,588	3,335	4,280	5,472	6,967
80	2,537	3,207	4,038	5,066	6,334
Cost of age 65	$47,295	$69,996	$103,662	$153,630	$227,706
Present Value at age 35	$26,111	$21,580	$18,050	$15,267	$13,050

The present value of $47,295 to be received in 30 years, and discounted at 2 per cent per year, is $26,111. Had the rate of growth of the wage been 6 per cent annually, the discount rate would have to be 6 per cent. In this case the annual retirement income, starting at age 65, would be $9,677. The present value of the retirement annuity would be $18,050. Likewise, the present value of the retirement benefit with a 10 per cent annual growth and discount rate would be $13,050.

The Alaska plan requires that the growth and discount rates be equal. This results in the present value of the future stream of income being the same regardless of the growth and discount assumption. When the present value of the retirement benefit is being estimated, the higher the assumed growth and discount rate, the lower the present value of the benefit.

§15.06   An Example of Estimating the Present Value of Medical Expenses

Suppose an injured party is 30 years old and expected to need medical attention every fifth year. Further assume the cost of such attention costs $10,000 today. The economist is attempting to forecast the present value of the medical expenses, with certainty, to age 65. The first medical attention will be required five years from today. Table 15-8 shows the age of the individual when the medical attention is required and the cost in today's dollars, i.e., $10,000.

Table 15-8 Medical Expense Every Five Years

Age	Cost in Current Dollars
30	$10,000
35	10,000
40	10,000
45	10,000
50	10,000
55	10,000
60	10,000
65	10,000

It is the goal of the economist to forecast the present value of the future medical expenses. The sum of the total expenses is $80,000. Since medical expenses are expected to grow annually, the economist's job is to forecast an appropriate growth and discount rate. Under the Alaska plan the growth and discount rate must be the same. Table 15-9 shows the present value of each future medical expense given different growth and discount assumptions.

Table 15-9 Present Value of Future Medical Expenses

Age	Year in Future	Growth Rate and Discount Rate 2%	4%	6%	8%	10%
30	0	$10,000	$10,000	$10,000	$10,000	$10,000
35	5	$10,000	10,000	10,000	10,000	10,000
40	10	$10,000	10,000	10,000	10,000	10,000
45	15	$10,000	10,000	10,000	10,000	10,000
50	20	$10,000	10,000	10,000	10,000	10,000
55	25	$10,000	10,000	10,000	10,000	10,000
60	30	$10,000	10,000	10,000	10,000	10,000
65	35	$10,000	10,000	10,000	10,000	10,000
		$80,000	$80,000	$80,000	$80,000	$80,000

Regardless of the growth and discount rate assumptions, the present value of the future medical expenses does not change. The implied assumption made under the Alaska plan is that the rate of growth of wages is the same as the rate of growth of medical expenses.

§15.07 Summary

When calculating the present value of a future stream of money using the Alaska plan, the growth rate used in the calculation must equal the discount rate. This permits the quick calculation of the present value of the future stream of money. The present value of the future stream is the current dollar amount times the number of years the money is to be received.

When the present value of periodic payments is to be estimated, the same assumption of growth rate equal to discount rate is made. Again, the present value is equal to the current payment times the number of future payments to be made.

A shortcoming of the method is the assumption that all growth rates are the same and equal to all discount rates. There is justification for the assumption of a constant discount rate. Regardless of what the future expenses are, the same investment can be made, therefore the same discount rate. But the assumption that the growth rate of wages and the growth rate of medical expenses will be the same over time does not have economic justification.

Finally, when the present value of a retirement plan is being calculated, the assumption of the growth rate does have an impact on the present value of the benefit. This is true because the retirement income does not grow.

The larger the growth rate used under the Alaska plan, the larger will be the income used to calculate the retirement benefit. The larger the growth rate and discount rate assumed, the larger the retirement benefit and the smaller the present value of the benefit.

16 Judging the Economist's Estimate of Present Value

$$\text{Present Value} = \sum_{t=0}^{n} \$ * (1+g)^t/(1+d)^t$$

§16.01   Introduction

After the economist has rendered a report, it is necessary to determine the accuracy of the work. The purpose is to see whether the economist's assumptions give the result intended by the economist.

Using the basic formula, shown above, the economist must determine a value for each of the four variables, "$," "t," "g," and "d." The variables are the current dollar amount, the number of years over which the estimate is being made, the annual growth rate of dollars, and the appropriate discount rate.

§16.02   Fact Situation

The plaintiff is the widow of a 45-year-old white male killed one year ago today. At the time of the accident the deceased was earning $25,000 per year. The economist has assumed the deceased would have worked uninterrupted to age 65. The growth and discount rates assumed by the economist are 5 and 6 per cent, respectively.

§16.03   Present Value Calculation

Table 16-1 shows the present value calculation of future income using the formula stated above and the assumptions stated in §16.02.

Table 16-1 Present Value of Future Income
Growth Rate = 5%
Discount Rate = 6%

Age	Year	Period	Future Income	Present Value	Total
45	1987	0	$25,000	$25,000	$25,000
46	1988	1	26,250	24,764	49,764
47	1989	2	27,562	24,531	74,295
48	1990	3	28,941	24,299	98,594
49	1991	4	30,388	24,070	122,664
50	1992	5	31,907	23,843	146,506
51	1993	6	33,502	23,618	170,124
52	1994	7	35,178	23,395	193,519
53	1995	8	36,936	23,174	216,694
54	1996	9	38,783	22,956	239,649
55	1997	10	40,722	22,739	262,389
56	1998	11	42,758	22,525	284,913
57	1999	12	44,896	22,312	307,225
58	2000	13	47,141	22,102	329,327
59	2001	14	49,498	21,893	351,220
60	2002	15	51,973	21,687	372,907
61	2003	16	54,572	21,482	394,389
62	2004	17	57,300	21,279	415,668
63	2005	18	60,165	21,079	436,747
64	2006	19	63,174	20,880	457,626

The economist's testimony is that the present value of the future income is $457,626. This assumes that the first payment of future income is $25,000 and occurs today. Future income grows at 5 per cent annually, while interest is 6 per cent annually. If the calculations are done properly and the economist's assumptions are followed, then when the final payment is made 19 years from today, there should be no money left in the fund.

§16.04   How to Test the Economist's Estimate

Table 16-2 shows how to test the economist's estimate. The economist has determined that $457,626 is the present value of the future income stream. At the beginning of the first year the economist deducts $25,000 from the principal to make the first year's salary payment. The remaining principal of $432,626 is invested at 6 per cent. The annual interest income of $25,958 is added to the principal, resulting in the ending principal of $458,584.

At the beginning of the second year the annual salary of $25,000 has grown at 5 per cent annually and became $26,250. This is in accordance with the assumption of an annual 5 per cent growth in wages. The salary for the second year is deducted from the balance of $458,584, leaving a balance of $432,334 to earn annual interest of 6 per cent. Table 16-2 shows the annual interest income and salary paid.

If the economist's analysis has been done properly, there should be no money left in the fund when the person would have reached age 65. This is the case shown in Table 16-2.

Table 16-2 Judging the Present Value of Loss

Year	Age	Beginning Principal	Annual Income	Principal at Interest	Annual Income	Ending Principal
1987	45	$457,626	$25,000	$432,626	$25,958	$458,584
1988	46	458,584	26,250	432,334	25,940	458,274
1989	47	458,274	27,562	430,711	25,843	456,554
1990	48	456,554	28,941	427,613	25,657	453,270
1991	49	453,270	30,388	422,882	25,373	448,255
1992	50	448,255	31,907	416,348	24,981	441,329
1993	51	441,329	33,502	407,827	24,470	432,296
1994	52	432,296	35,178	397,119	23,827	420,946
1995	53	420,946	36,936	384,009	23,041	407,050
1996	54	407,050	38,783	368,267	22,096	390,363
1997	55	390,363	40,722	349,640	20,978	370,619
1998	56	370,619	42,758	327,860	19,672	347,532
1999	57	347,532	44,896	302,636	18,158	320,794
2000	58	320,794	47,141	273,653	16,419	290,072
2001	59	290,072	49,498	240,573	14,434	255,008
2002	60	255,008	51,973	203,035	12,182	215,217
2003	61	215,217	54,572	160,645	9,639	170,283
2004	62	170,283	57,300	112,983	6,779	119,762
2005	63	119,762	60,165	59,597	3,576	63,172
2006	64	63,172	63,174*	0	0	0

*due to rounding

When the economist testifies that a growth rate and the discount rate are not equal but to simplify the calculation the two have been set equal, the economist is making improper economic judgments. The economist usually argues that the assumption of growth being equal to the discount rate will simplify the present value calculation but have no significant impact on the dollar amount estimated to be the present value of the future stream of income.

When the economist sets the growth and discount rates equal, one of two possible conditions exists. The growth rate is less than the discount rate but the two are set equal to each other, or the growth rate is greater than the discount rate but the two are set equal to each other.

Section 16.05 shows the present value calculation when the growth and discount rates are equal. If the two are equal and that has justification, then there would be no money left in the fund at the end of the annuity period.

Section 16.07 shows the present value calculation when the growth rate of wages exceeds the discount rate but they are assumed to be equal.

§16.05   Calculating the Present Value When the Growth Rate Equals the Discount Rate

The economist has testified that the growth rate for wages has an historical average which is equal to the historical average for the discount rate. Tables 16-3 and 16-4 show the present value of the two possible assumptions. That is, Table 16-3 shows the present value of the income stream if the annual growth and discount rates are equal at 4.5 per cent.

Table 16-3 Present Value of Future Income
Growth Rate = 4.5%
Discount Rate = 4.5%

Age	Year	Period	Future Income	Present Value	Total
45	1987	0	$25,000	$25,000	$25,000
46	1988	1	26,125	25,000	50,000
47	1989	2	27,301	25,000	75,000
48	1990	3	28,529	25,000	100,000
49	1991	4	29,813	25,000	125,000
50	1992	5	31,155	25,000	150,000
51	1993	6	32,557	25,000	175,000
52	1994	7	34,022	25,000	200,000
53	1995	8	35,553	25,000	225,000
54	1996	9	37,152	25,000	250,000
55	1997	10	38,824	25,000	275,000
56	1998	11	40,571	25,000	300,000
57	1999	12	42,397	25,000	325,000
58	2000	13	44,305	25,000	350,000
59	2001	14	46,299	25,000	375,000
60	2002	15	48,382	25,000	400,000
61	2003	16	50,559	25,000	425,000
62	2004	17	52,834	25,000	450,000
63	2005	18	55,212	25,000	475,000
64	2006	19	57,697	25,000	500,000

Table 16-4 shows exactly the same present value even though the growth and discount rates have increased to 6 per cent annually. Whenever the growth and discount rates are assumed to be the same, the present value will be the same, regardless of what rate is used.

Table 16-4 Present Value of Future Income
Growth Rate = 6%
Discount Rate = 6%

Age	Year	Period	Future Income	Present Value	Total
45	1987	0	$25,000	$25,000	$25,000
46	1988	1	26,125	25,000	50,000
47	1989	2	27,301	25,000	75,000
48	1990	3	28,529	25,000	100,000
49	1991	4	29,813	25,000	125,000
50	1992	5	31,155	25,000	150,000
51	1993	6	32,557	25,000	175,000
52	1994	7	34,022	25,000	200,000
53	1995	8	35,553	25,000	225,000
54	1996	9	37,152	25,000	250,000
55	1997	10	38,824	25,000	275,000
56	1998	11	40,571	25,000	300,000
57	1999	12	42,397	25,000	325,000
58	2000	13	44,305	25,000	350,000
59	2001	14	46,299	25,000	375,000
60	2002	15	48,382	25,000	400,000
61	2003	16	50,559	25,000	425,000
62	2004	17	52,834	25,000	450,000
63	2005	18	55,212	25,000	475,000
64	2006	19	57,697	25,000	500,000

Tables 16-5 and 16-6 show how the 20-year annuity will be paid out under the different growth and interest assumptions. As indicated on both tables, there would be no money left in the fund at the end of the 20-year period.

Table 16-5 Judging the Present Value of Future Income
Growth Rate = 4.5%
Discount Rate = 4.5%

Year	Age	Beginning Principal	Annual Income	Principal at Interest	Annual Income	Ending Principal
1987	45	$500,000	$25,000	$475,000	$28,500	$503,500
1988	46	503,500	26,500	477,000	28,620	505,620
1989	47	505,620	28,090	477,530	28,652	506,182
1990	48	506,182	29,775	476,406	28,584	504,991
1991	49	504,991	31,562	473,429	28,406	501,835
1992	50	501,835	33,456	468,379	28,103	496,482
1993	51	496,482	35,463	461,019	27,661	488,680
1994	52	488,680	37,591	451,089	27,065	478,154
1995	53	478,154	39,846	438,308	26,298	464,607

Year	Age	Beginning Principal	Annual Income	Principal at Interest	Annual Income	Ending Principal
1996	54	464,607	42,237	422,370	25,342	447,712
1997	55	447,712	44,771	402,941	24,176	427,117
1998	56	427,117	47,457	379,660	22,780	402,439
1999	57	402,439	50,305	352,134	21,128	373,262
2000	58	373,262	53,323	319,939	19,196	339,136
2001	59	339,136	56,523	282,613	16,957	299,570
2002	60	299,570	59,914	239,656	14,379	254,035
2003	61	254,035	63,509	190,526	11,432	201,958
2004	62	201,958	67,319	134,639	8,078	142,717
2005	63	142,717	71,358	71,358	4,282	75,640
2006	64	75,640	75,640	0	0	0

Table 16-6 Judging the Present Value of Future Income
       Growth Rate = 6%
       Discount Rate = 6%

Year	Age	Beginning Principal	Annual Income	Principal at Interest	Annual Income	Ending Principal
1987	45	500,000	25,000	475,000	28,500	503,500
1988	46	503,500	26,500	477,000	28,620	505,620
1989	47	505,620	28,090	477,530	28,652	506,182
1990	48	506,182	29,775	476,406	28,584	504,991
1991	49	504,991	31,562	473,429	28,406	501,835
1992	50	501,835	33,456	468,379	28,103	496,482
1993	51	496,482	35,463	461,019	27,661	488,680
1994	52	488,680	37,591	451,089	27,065	478,154
1995	53	478,154	39,846	438,308	26,298	464,607
1996	54	464,607	42,237	422,370	25,342	447,712
1997	55	447,712	44,771	402,941	24,176	427,117
1998	56	427,117	47,457	379,660	22,780	402,439
1999	57	402,439	50,305	352,134	21,128	373,262
2000	58	373,262	53,323	319,939	19,196	339,136
2001	59	339,136	56,523	282,613	16,957	299,570
2002	60	299,570	59,914	239,656	14,379	254,035
2003	61	254,035	63,509	190,526	11,432	201,958
2004	62	201,958	67,319	134,639	8,078	142,717
2005	63	142,717	71,358	71,358	4,282	75,640
2006	64	75,640	75,640	0	0	0

§16.06   Testing the Assumption of Equivalence: The Growth Rate Is Less than the Discount Rate

The economist may testify that the appropriate growth rate to use in the analysis is 4.5 per cent and the appropriate discount rate is 6 per cent. But in order to simplify the analysis the growth and discount rate have been set equal to each other. Since the two are equal, the present value is the multiplication of the current income level, $25,000, times the number of years being forecast, 20 years. The present value is $500,000.

In reality the growth rate was less than the discount rate. Thus the assumption that the growth and discount rates should be equal does not have a basis in economic fact. Table 16-7 shows what happens to the principal of $500,000 when a growth rate of 4.5 per cent and a discount rate of 6 per cent are used.

Table 16-7 Judging the Present Value of Future Income
Growth Rate = 4.5%
Discount Rate = 6%

Year	Age	Beginning Principal	Annual Income	Principal at Interest	Annual Income	Ending Principal
1987	45	$500,000	$25,000	$475,000	$28,500	$503,500
1988	46	503,500	26,125	477,375	28,642	506,018
1989	47	506,018	27,301	478,717	28,723	507,440
1990	48	507,440	28,529	478,911	28,735	507,645
1991	49	507,645	29,813	477,832	28,670	506,502
1992	50	506,502	31,155	475,348	28,521	503,869
1993	51	503,869	32,557	471,312	28,279	499,591
1994	52	499,591	34,022	465,569	27,934	493,504
1995	53	493,504	35,553	457,951	27,477	485,428
1996	54	485,428	37,152	448,276	26,897	475,172
1997	55	475,172	38,824	436,348	26,181	462,529
1998	56	462,529	40,571	421,958	25,317	447,275
1999	57	447,275	42,397	404,878	24,293	429,171
2000	58	429,171	44,305	384,866	23,092	407,958
2001	59	407,958	46,299	361,659	21,700	383,359
2002	60	383,359	48,382	334,977	20,099	355.075
2003	61	355,075	50,559	304,516	18,271	322,787
2004	62	322,787	52,834	269,952	16,197	286,150
2005	63	286,150	55,212	230,938	13,856	244,794
2006	64	244,794	57,697	187,097	11,226	198,323

Table 16-7 shows that, when the individual reaches age 64, the money has not been used up. In fact, when a growth rate of 4.5 per cent and a discount rate of 6 per cent are employed, as the economist testified and were the true rates, there is an excess of $198,323. In fact, the larger the spread, i.e., the more the discount rate exceeds the growth rate, the greater will be the excess in the fund.

§16.07   Testing the Assumption of Equivalence: The Growth Rate Exceeds the Discount Rate

If the growth rate is larger than the discount rate, the fund will have an insufficient amount of money to properly compensate the plaintiff. The economist may testify that the appropriate growth rate to use in the analysis is 7 per cent and the appropriate discount rate is 6 per cent. In order to simplify the analysis, the economist has set the growth and discount rates equal to each other at 6 per cent. The present value of the income stream would be $500,000.

Table 16-8 Judging the Present Value of Future Income
Growth Rate = 7%
Discount Rate = 6%

Year	Age	Beginning Principal	Annual Income	Principal at Interest	Annual Income	Ending Principal
1987	45	$500,000	$25,000	$475,000	$28,500	$503,500
1988	46	503,500	26,750	476,750	28,605	505,355
1989	47	505,355	28,622	476,732	28,604	505,336
1990	48	505,336	30,626	474,710	28,483	503,193
1991	49	503,193	32,770	470,423	28,225	498,648
1992	50	498,648	35,064	463,585	27,815	491,400
1993	51	491,400	37,518	453,882	27,233	481,114
1994	52	481,114	40,145	440,970	26,458	467,428
1995	53	467,428	42,955	424,473	25,468	449,942
1996	54	449,942	45,961	403,980	24,239	428,219
1997	55	428,219	49,179	379,040	22,742	401,783
1998	56	401,783	52,621	349,161	20,950	370,111
1999	57	370,111	56,305	313,806	18,828	332,635
2000	58	332,635	60,246	272,389	16,343	288,732
2001	59	288,732	64,463	224,269	13,456	237,725
2002	60	237,725	68,976	168,749	10,125	178,874
2003	61	178,874	73,804	105,070	6,304	111,374
2004	62	111,374	78,970	32,404	1,944	34,348
2005	63	34,348	84,498	(50,151)	(3,009)	(53,160)
2006	64	(53,160)	90,413	(143,573)	(8,614)	(152,187)

Table 16-8 shows that there is insufficient money in the fund to allow for the expected 7 per cent growth of wages. The fund is exhausted when the individual would have reached age 63.

The more the growth rate exceeds the discount rate the greater will be the inadequacy of the fund. Stated differently, the more the growth rate exceeds the discount rate, the sooner the fund will be exhausted.

§16.08   Summary

When an economist calculates the present value of a future income stream, it is necessary to state the growth rate and the discount rate. If the economist arbitrarily alters the growth or discount rate, the present value will be improperly altered.

If the "true" growth rate is less than the "true" discount rate but the economist sets the two values equal, the present value will be overstated. This would over-compensate the plaintiff. If the "true" growth rate is greater than the "true" discount rate but the economist sets the two values equal, the present value will be understated. This would under-compensate the plaintiff.

17

Selecting an Economist

§17.01   The Plaintiff's Economist

It is not necessary to search far and wide for an expert economist. They can be found at local junior colleges, colleges, and universities. The academic affiliation will usually give credibility to an economist's testimony.

The plaintiff's economist should have all the characteristics of "a good witness"—one head, neatly dressed, articulate, confident but not argumentative. Often what the economist says is not as important as how well he or she says it.

Experience as an expert witness is helpful, but every economist has to have a first case. If the individual understands present value and comes across as a sincere and caring person, in all likelihood the jury will listen to what he or she has to say.

Whatever has not been included in the analysis—probability of seeking employment, probability of being employed, the worklife expectancy table, the higher returns on long-term government bonds—will not bother the jury if the economist appears sincere and confident. The points of contention on cross-examination will provide a learning experience for the novice economist-witness, but will not generally harm the credibility.

§17.02   The Defense Economist

The number of heads the defense economist has is not important since he or she is only needed to help prepare for the cross-examination of the plaintiff's economist. Competent economists can be found in all types of businesses, banks, brokerage firms, insurance companies, federal and state government, and the local junior colleges and universities.

Since the defense economist's job is to help prepare the defense attorney for the cross-examination of the plaintiff's economist, there is no such thing as "proper credentials." The economist needs only to understand the present value concept and be aware of areas of disagreement. The defense economist is truly the case of an economist who is heard but not seen. The defense economist does not usually testify since his or her testimony would permit the plaintiff's attorney to establish a floor for the economic loss.

18

Case Studies

§18.01 Introduction

Economists submit reports to attorneys all the time. In order to evaluate the economist's report properly, the attorney, or the attorney's economist, should try to review several different reports prepared by the same economist. When examining different reports, the goal is to find where the economist is consistent from report to report and where he or she is inconsistent.

If any of the variables in the analyses change, the defense attorney should attempt to determine whether the economist had sufficient reason for the changes. In some cases the variables will change. For example, in two cases involving a wrongful death, there is no expectation that both decedents would have exactly the same income. However, both might be the same age. If the analysis by plaintiff's economist took place in the same year, the growth rates for wages may be the same. If this is not the case, why?

This chapter presents four different reports submitted by the same economist in four different cases. The reports cover six years. There are different types of losses. From reading the reports of the economist, the nature of the loss estimated should be evident. If the report is not clear, then it is necessary to get additional information, either through interrogatories or deposition.[1]

Sections 18.02, 18.04, 18.06, and 18.08 present the fact situations addressed by the economist. Sections 18.03, 18.05, 18.07, and 18.09 present the economist's reports in their entirety. There is some duplication in the reports presented. The purpose is to compare and contrast the reports.

§18.02 Example 1: Wrongful Death of a Housewife and Mother Not Employed outside the Home, A 1980 Report—Background

Mrs. Roberta Smith was a white female, 23 years old at the time of her death in a plane crash. She was born May 25, 1953, and died January 6, 1977. She was married to Robert Smith, her high school sweetheart. This was the only marriage for both. Son Smith was born in August 1972, and daughter Smith was born in September 1976. At the time of her death Mrs. Smith was a housewife. She was planning on returning to the labor force to supplement the family income. Prior to the birth of her children she had worked part-time at a local discount store. She worked five days a week from July 1974 through June 1975 at minimum wage.

The present value of lost household services and the present value of future wages are to be calculated.

§18.03 —The Economist's Report in Example 1

Economist's Name
Home Address
City, State 00000
September 28, 1980

Attorney, Attorney, and Attorney
Attn: Senior Attorney
Street Address
City, State 00000

RE: Roberta Smith

---

[1] Fed R Civ P 26(b)(4)(A)i.

Dear Attorney:

Enclosed please find the calculations you requested in the Roberta Smith case.

Table I shows the present value of Mrs. Smith's services as a mother from October 1, 1980, until the youngest child graduates from high school in May 1994.

Table II shows the present value of Mrs. Smith's services as mother from October 1, 1980, until the youngest child graduates from college in May 1998.

The two values of a mother's services are calculated using the American Council of Life Insurance figures published in *The Sylvia Porter New Money Book For the 80's.*

Table III shows the present value of Mrs. Smith's future income. She would return to the labor force following the youngest child's graduation from high school or college.

If I may be of further assistance, please do not hesitate to contact me.

Sincerely,

Economist's Name

Table I Present Value of Services of Roberta Smith as Mother from October 1, 1980, until Youngest Child Graduates from High School in May 1994

	Funds Invested		
	Savings & Loans	Long-Term Government	Earnings Equal Inflation
Sylvia Porter	$322,748	$289,287	$291,299
American Council of Life Insurance	334,370	299,703	301,789

Table II Present Value of Services of Roberta Smith as Mother from October 1, 1980, until Youngest Child Graduates from College in May 1998

	Funds Invested		
	Savings & Loans	Long-Term Government	Earnings Equal Inflation
Sylvia Porter	$431,614	$373,226	$376,558
American Council of Life Insurance	447,156	386,666	390,117

Table III Present Value of Future Earnings (Mrs. Smith Returns to Labor Force after Youngest Child Graduates from High School or College and Works at Minimum Wage until Retirement at Age 65 in May 2018)

	Savings & Loans	Funds Invested Long-Term Government	Earnings Equal Inflation
Following High School Graduation 6/1/94 to 5/31/18	$284,296	$143,109	$148,000
Following College Graduation 6/1/98 to 5/31/18	$260,845	$118,518	$124,000

In determining the present value of the lost household services and the present value of future wages, the following assumptions were made:

1. The economic value of a mother's household services is based on the American Council of Life Insurance's 1978 estimate of $17,351.88

2. Mrs. Smith would work full-time outside the home after the youngest child's graduation from high school. She would be paid the current minimum wage of $3.10 throughout her employment

3. Mrs. Smith's life expectancy is based on "Expectation of Life and Mortality Rates," published by the U.S. National Center for Health Statistics, Vital Statistics of the United States

4. To calculate the present value of future losses, funds are invested at the historic real returns earned on passbook savings, long-term government securities and earnings growth is equal to inflation. The source of the information is the Federal Reserve Bulletin

§18.04 Example 2: Lost Income and Medical Expenses of a Permanently Disabled Minor, A 1982 Report—Background

Jennifer Jones is a 10-year-old Caucasian female born September 15, 1972. She was permanently and totally disabled in June 1982.

The present value of the lost income and future medical care is to be calculated. Medical expenses currently run $1,200 per month.

§18.05 —The Economist's Report in Example 2

Economist's Name
University Address
City, State 00000
November 29, 1982

Attorney, Attorney, and Attorney
Attn: Attorney
Street Address
City, State 00000

RE: Jennifer Jones

Dear Attorney:

Enclosed please find the calculations you requested in the Jennifer Jones case.

The total loss is the sum of the present value of the future medical expenses plus the present value of the future income stream. The income stream employed depends on the assumptions concerning Jennifer Jones's future education.

If you have any questions, please do not hesitate to contact me.

Sincerely,
Economist's Name

Economic Analysis
Jennifer Jones

PART I.   Background Statistics
Sex: Female
Race: Caucasian
Born: September 15, 1972
Date of Accident: May 15, 1982
Injury: Total Permanent Disability
Earnings History: None
Retirement Date: May 15, 2037
Age at Retirement: 65
Date of Analysis: November 22, 1982
Date of Present Value: September 15, 1982

PART II. Present Value

Present Value of Future Medical Expenses
Calculated to Life Expectancy
Jennifer Jones

Present Value of Future Medical Expenses $ 1,017,387

**Present Value of Future Wages
Jennifer Jones**

High School Graduate	College Graduate	Minimum Wage 1982
$266,120*	$386,135*	$290,313
$297,218**	$434,252**	

* From the 1981 Statistical Abstracts of the United States, increased to 1982 income using the historical growth rate of wages.

** From the 1981 Statistical Abstracts of the United States, increased to 1982 income using the historical growth rate of the Consumer Price Index.

Jennifer Jones does not enter the labor force until either the completion of high school or the completion of college.

The present value of future streams of income and medical expenses are calculated using the following formula:

$$\text{Present Value} = \sum_{t=0}^{n} \$ \, [(1 + g)^t / (1 + d)^t]$$

Where the variables are:

$ = median income for women

g = the rate of growth of wages

d = the rate of earnings on invested funds

   When calculating the present value of wages, the growth rate and discount rate (rate of earnings on invested funds) are calculated on the historic spread between the Consumer Price Index and the return in one-year Treasury Bills, 1952-1981 inclusive.

   When calculating the present value of medical expenses, the growth rate and discount rate (rate of earnings on invested funds) are calculated on the historic spread between the Medical Price Index and the return in one-year Treasury Bills, 1952-1981 inclusive.

t = the number of years covered in the analysis

   When the loss of wage is calculated, it is from September 15, 1982, until retirement at age 65. "t" equals 55. Employment does not occur until age 18 or 22 depending on the assumption concerning education.

   When the present value of medical expenses is being calculated, "t" equals 68.9, the life expectancy of Jennifer Jones.

§18.06   Example 3: Permanant and Total Disability of an Employed Mother, A 1986 Report—Background

On January 1, 1986, Mrs. Zipper was permanently and totally disabled in an automobile accident. The nature of her injuries are such that she requires institutional care currently costing $135 per day. It does not appear her life expectancy is altered.

Mrs. Zipper, a Caucasian, was born August 1, 1959. She is married and the mother of two minor children. At the time of the accident she was employed as a grade school principal, earning $23,500 annually. Her employment contract was a 12-month contract.

§18.07 —The Economist's Report in Example 3

Economic Consultants, Inc.
Address
City, State 00000
July 7, 1986

Attorney, Attorney, and Attorney
Attn: Senior Attorney
Street Address
City, State 00000

RE: Mrs. Zipper

Dear Attorney:

The case involving Mrs. Zipper has been evaluated. The present value of the loss is $3,210,910. This amount is the sum of the historic loss plus the present value of the future loss.

The historic loss represents the lost income from the date of the injury, January 1, 1986, to August 1, 1986. This loss is $11,750.

The present value of the future loss consists of two parts: (1) the present value of the lost income beginning August 1, 1986, and continuing to age 65, and (2) the present value of the future medical expenses, beginning August 1, 1986, and continuing, mortality adjusted, throughout her expected life. The present value of the future loss is $3,185,881.

This loss is the economic loss sustained by Mrs. Zipper's family and does not include loss of services, attention, marital care, advice, or protection to Mr. Zipper or any of the minor children. The figure is exclusive of the value of household services and is not reduced for personal consumption.

The economic evaluation is based on information received from your office as detailed in Part I of this report. The methodology and other sources of information employed in preparing this report appear in Parts II and III.

If there is an error in the information contained in Part I, please contact me immediately so that I may provide you with a corrected copy.

Sincerely,
Economist

Summary of Loss to
Mrs. Zipper

Historic Loss
From January 1, 1986, to August 1, 1986
    Wages .... $ 11,750

Present Value of Future Loss
Beginning August 1, 1986

Wages to age 65	$ 685,541
Medical expenses	2,500,340
Total Loss	**$3,197,631**

Economic Analysis
Mrs. Zipper

PART I

Date of Birth:	August 1, 1959
Current Age:	27
Race:	Caucasian
Sex:	Female
Date of Accident:	January 1, 1986
Injury:	Permanent and total disability
Life Expectancy (absent the accident):	53.1 years
Education:	College Graduate

Earnings History:

Year	Elementary Principal
1986	$23,500
1985	22,000
1984	20,500*
1983	16,500
1982	13,900

* Mrs. Zipper became a principal

Retirement Age:	65
Marital Status:	Married
Dependents:	2 minor children
Date of Analysis:	July 7, 1986
Date of Present Value:	August 1, 1986

PART II. Calculation of Economic Loss

The present value of the loss is calculated by using the following formula:

$$\text{Present Value of Future Income} = \sum_{t=0}^{n} \$ \left[(1 + g)^t / (1 + d)^t \right]$$

The four variables in this formula are $, t, g, and d.

$ - Represents the basis for calculating the economic loss resulting from the injury. The wage calculation is based on annual earnings of $23,500 as an elementary school principal. The medical costs are based on institutional care costing $135 per day.

t - Represents time and starts on the present value date, August 1, 1986, and runs until period "t." When calculating the present value of the future wage period, "t" is when Mrs. Zipper reaches age 64. This means retirement occurs at age 65. When the present value of medical expenses is calculated, "t" is 99, but medical expenses are mortality adjusted.

g - Represents the growth rate for wages or medical expenses. The growth rate of wages is 4.39 per cent annually. This is the 1952-1985 historic rate of change in the Consumer Price Index. The growth rate of medical expenses is 6.02 per cent, the 1952-1985 historic rate of change in the Medical Price Index.

d - Represents the discount rate or rate at which dollars received will earn interest. The discount rate is 5.99 per cent annually. This is the 1952-1985 historic yield on one-year Treasury Bills. There are many types of investments which can be made today, ranging from passbook savings to speculating in futures markets. While there is no such thing as a risk-free investment, the one-year Treasury Bill is used as a surrogate. For example, if we are receiving $1,000 one year from today, we might be willing to receive some amount less than $1,000 today. This is true because we could invest the money for one year and earn interest. The rate of earnings is the interest rate, or discount rate.

PART III. Bibliography

Probability of Living: Life Expectancy Tables, U.S. National Center for Health Statistics, Vital Statistics of U.S. 1982, as cited in Statistical Abstracts of the United States, 1986

Job Participation Rate: Civilian Labor Force Participation Rate By Sex, Race and Age, Handbook of Labor Statistics, U.S. Department of Labor, Bureau of Labor Statistics, December 1980, Bulletin 2070

Probability of Employment: Unemployment Rates by Sex, Race and Age, Handbook of Labor Statistics, U.S. Department of Labor, Bureau of Labor Statistics, December 1980, Bulletin 2070

Consumption: Revised Equivalence Scale for Urban Families of Different Size, Age and Composition, Derived from the U.S. Department of Labor, Bureau of Labor Statistics of Consumer Expenditures, 1960-1961

Value of Household Services: The Dollar Value of Household Work, William H. Gauger and Kathryn E. Walker, New York State College of Human Ecology, Cornell University, Ithaca, New York

Present Value
of Future Wages
as of August 1, 1986

Prepared: July 7, 1986
Name: Mrs. Zipper
Birthdate: August 1, 1959
Age: 27

Life Expectancy at 27 is 53.1 years
U.S. Life Tables (1982) - White Females
The adjusted sum was computed using participation and employment rates (1978-1982) - White Females

Annual Income   = $ 23,500.00
Annual Growth Rate   =   4.39%
Annual Discount Rate =   5.99%

Age	Period	Present Value	Sum	Probability of Living	Probability of Seeking	Probability of Finding	Adjusted Income	Adjusted Sum
27	0	23,500	23,500	.99945	.454	.929	9,906	9906.05
28	1	23,145	46,645	.99889	.454	.929	9,751	19657.10
29	2	22,796	69,441	.99831	.454	.929	9,598	29255.37
30	3	22,452	91,893	.99770	.454	.929	9,448	38702.99
31	4	22,113	114,006	.99706	.454	.929	9,299	48002.03
32	5	21,779	135,785	.99640	.454	.929	9,153	57154.56
33	6	21,450	157,235	.99569	.454	.929	9,008	66162.53
34	7	21,126	178,361	.99493	.454	.929	8,865	75027.77
35	8	20,808	199,169	.99412	.454	.954	8,959	83986.80
36	9	20,493	219,662	.99323	.454	.954	8,816	92802.73
37	10	20,184	239,846	.99227	.454	.954	8,674	101477.16
38	11	19,879	259,726	.99121	.454	.954	8,534	110011.50
39	12	19,579	279,305	.99004	.454	.954	8,396	118407.08
40	13	19,284	298,588	.98874	.454	.954	8,258	126665.10
41	14	18,993	317,581	.98730	.454	.954	8,121	134786.58
42	15	18,706	336,287	.98571	.454	.954	7,986	142772.59
43	16	18,423	354,710	.98394	.454	.954	7,851	150623.96
44	17	18,145	372,856	.98199	.454	.954	7,718	158341.49
45	18	17,871	390,727	.97984	.533	.961	8,969	167310.96
46	19	17,602	408,329	.97747	.533	.961	8,813	176123.66
47	20	17,336	425,665	.97486	.533	.961	8,656	184780.14
48	21	17,074	442,739	.97199	.533	.961	8,501	193280.80
49	22	16,817	459,556	.96883	.533	.961	8,345	201625.92
50	23	16,563	476,118	.96536	.533	.961	8,190	209815.64
51	24	16,313	492,431	.96155	.533	.961	8,034	217849.95
52	25	16,066	508,497	.95739	.533	.961	7,879	225728.72

Age	Period	Present Value	Sum	Probability of Living	Probability of Seeking	Probability of Finding	Adjusted Income	Adjusted Sum
53	26	15,824	524,321	.95285	.533	.961	7,723	233451.76
54	27	15,585	539,906	.94793	.533	.961	7,567	241018.90
55	28	15,350	555,256	.94257	.391	.965	5,459	246477.96
56	29	15,118	570,374	.93676	.391	.965	5,343	251821.45
57	30	14,890	585,264	.93044	.391	.965	5,227	257048.79
58	31	14,665	599,929	.92360	.391	.965	5,111	262159.39
59	32	14,444	614,372	.91620	.391	.965	4,993	267152.47
60	33	14,226	628,598	.90819	.391	.965	4,875	272027.19
61	34	14,011	642,609	.89954	.391	.965	4,755	276782.62
62	35	13,799	656,408	.89020	.391	.965	4,635	281417.60
63	36	13,591	669,999	.88010	.391	.965	4,513	285930.84
64	37	13,386	683,385	.86920	.391	.965	4,390	290320.88
65	38	13,184	696,569	.85744	.391	.967	4,274	294594.99
66	39	12,985	709,553	.84462	.391	.967	4,147	298741.64
67	40	12,789	722,342	.83079	.391	.967	4,017	302758.84
68	41	12,596	734,938	.81600	.391	.967	3,886	306644.97
69	42	12,406	747,343	.80032	.391	.967	3,754	310398.87
70	43	12,218	759,562	.78380	.391	.967	3,621	314019.79
71	44	12,034	771,596	.76577	.391	.967	3,484	317504.03
72	45	11,852	783,448	.74635	.391	.967	3,345	320848.64
73	46	11,673	795,121	.72566	.391	.967	3,203	324051.45
74	47	11,497	806,618	.70384	.391	.967	3,060	327111.03
75	48	11,323	817,941	.68100	.391	.967	2,916	33026.67
76	49	11,153	829,094	.65617	.391	.967	2,767	332793.59
77	50	10,984	840,078	.62961	.391	.967	2,615	335408.43
78	51	10,818	850,897	.60159	.391	.967	2,461	337869.17

Age	Period	Present Value	Sum	Probability of Living	Probability of Seeking	Probability of Finding	Adjusted Income	Adjusted Sum
79	52	10,655	861,552	.57239	.391	.967	2,306	340175.14
80	53	10,494	872,046	.54231	.391	.967	2,152	342326.95
81	54	10,336	882,382	.48813	.391	.967	1,908	344234.52
82	55	10,180	892,561	.41623	.391	.967	1,602	345836.57
83	56	10,026	902,588	.33520	.391	.967	1,271	347107.27
84	57	9,875	912,462	.25407	.391	.967	949	348055.87
85	58	9,726	922,188	.18054	.391	.967	664	348719.76
86	59	9,579	931,767	.11974	.391	.967	434	349153.41
87	60	9,434	941,201	.07374	.391	.967	263	349416.45
88	61	9,292	950,493	.04192	.391	.967	147	349563.72
89	62	9,152	959,645	.02184	.391	.967	76	349639.30
90	63	9,013	968,658	.01035	.391	.967	35	349674.57
91	64	8,877	977,535	.00441	.391	.967	15	349689.37
92	65	8,743	986,279	.00167	.391	.967	6	349694.90
93	66	8,611	994,890	.00055	.391	.967	2	349696.71
94	67	8,481	1,003,371	.00016	.391	.967	1	349697.21
95	68	8,353	1,011,725	.00004	.391	.967	0	349697.33
96	69	8,227	1,019,952	.00001	.391	.967	0	349697.35
97	70	8,103	1,028,055	.00000	.391	.967	0	349697.36
98	71	7,981	1,036,036	.00000	.391	.967	0	349697.36
99	72	7,860	1,043,896	0.00000	.391	.967	0	349697.36

Present Value
of Future Medical Expenses
as of August 1, 1986

Prepared: July 7, 1986
Name: Mrs. Zipper
Birthdate: August 1, 1959
Age: 27
Life Expectancy at 27 is 53.1 years
U.S. Life Tables (1982) - White Females
The adjusted sum was computed using U.S. Life
Tables (1982) - White Females
Annual Medical Expenses   = $49,275
Annual Growth Rate   =   6.02%
Annual Discount Rate   =   5.97%

Age	Period	Present Value	Total	Probability of Living	Adjusted Total
27	0	$49,275	$ 49,275	.99945	$ 49,248
28	1	49,298	98,573	.99889	98,491
29	2	49,322	147,895	.99831	147,730
30	3	49,345	197,240	.99770	196,961
31	4	49,368	246,608	.99706	246,184
32	5	49,391	295,999	.99640	295,397
33	6	49,415	345,414	.99569	344,599
34	7	49,438	394,852	.99493	393,786
35	8	49,461	444,313	.99412	442,957
36	9	49,485	493,798	.99323	492,106
37	10	49,508	543,306	.99227	541,231
38	11	49,531	592,837	.99121	590,327
39	12	49,555	642,392	.99004	639,388
40	13	49,578	691,970	.98874	688,408
41	14	49,601	741,571	.98730	737,379
42	15	49,625	791,196	.98571	786,295
43	16	49,648	840,844	.98394	835,146
44	17	49,672	890,516	.98199	883,923
45	18	49,695	940,211	.97984	932,617
46	19	49,719	989,930	.97747	981,215
47	20	49,742	1,039,672	.97486	1,029,707
48	21	49,766	1,089,438	.97199	1,078,078
49	22	49,789	1,139,227	.96883	1,126,315
50	23	49,813	1,189,039	.96536	1,174,402
51	24	49,836	1,238,875	.96155	1,222,322
52	25	49,860	1,288,735	.95739	1,270,057

Age	Period	Present Value	Total	Probability of Living	Adjusted Total
53	26	49,883	1,338,618	.95285	1,317,589
54	27	49,907	1,388,524	.94793	1,364,896
55	28	49,930	1,438,455	.94257	1,411,959
56	29	49,954	1,488,408	.93676	1,458,753
57	30	49,977	1,538,385	.93044	1,505,254
58	31	50,001	1,588,386	.92360	1,551,435
59	32	50,024	1,638,411	.91620	1,597,268
60	33	50,048	1,688,459	.90819	1,642,721
61	34	50,072	1,738,531	.89954	1,687,762
62	35	50,095	1,788,626	.89020	1,732,357
63	36	50,119	1,838,745	.88010	1,776,467
64	37	50,143	1,888,887	.86920	1,820,050
65	38	50,166	1,939,054	.85744	1,863,065
66	39	50,190	1,989,243	.84462	1,905,456
67	40	50,214	2,039,457	.83079	1,947,173
68	41	50,237	2,089,694	.81600	1,988,167
69	42	50,261	2,139,955	.80032	2,028,392
70	43	50,285	2,190,240	.78380	2,067,805
71	44	50,308	2,240,548	.76577	2,106,330
72	45	50,332	2,290,881	.74635	2,143,895
73	46	50,356	2,341,237	.72566	2,180,437
74	47	50,380	2,391,616	.70384	2,215,896
75	48	50,403	2,442,020	.68100	2,250,221
76	49	50,427	2,492,447	.65617	2,283,310
77	50	50,451	2,542,898	.62961	2,315,075
78	51	50,475	2,593,373	.60159	2,345,440
79	52	50,499	2,643,871	.57239	2,374,345
80	53	50,522	2,694,394	.54231	2,401,744
81	54	50,546	2,744,940	.48813	2,426,417
82	55	50,570	2,795,510	.41623	2,447,466
83	56	50,594	2,846,104	.33520	2,464,425
84	57	50,618	2,896,722	.25407	2,477,285
85	58	50,642	2,947,364	.18054	2,486,428
86	59	50,666	2,998,030	.11974	2,492,495
87	60	50,690	3,048,719	.07374	2,496,233
88	61	50,713	3,099,433	.04192	2,498,358
89	62	50,737	3,150,170	.02184	2,499,467
90	63	50,761	3,200,931	.01035	2,499,992
91	64	50,785	3,251,717	.00441	2,500,216
92	65	50,809	3,302,526	.00167	2,500,301
93	66	50,833	3,353,359	.00055	2,500,329
94	67	50,857	3,404,216	.00016	2,500,337

Age	Period	Present Value	Total	Probability of Living	Adjusted Total
95	68	50,881	3,455,098	.00004	2,500,339
96	69	50,905	3,506,003	.00001	2,500,340
97	70	50,929	3,556,932	.00000	2,500,340
98	71	50,953	3,607,885	.00000	2,500,340
99	72	50,977	3,658,863	0.00000	2,500,340

Participation Rate
White Females
Ages

Year	16-17	18-19	20-24	25-34	35-44	45-54	55-64	65+
1954	29.3	52.1	44.4	32.5	39.4	39.8	29.1	9.1
1955	29.9	52.0	45.8	32.8	39.9	42.7	31.8	10.5
1956	33.5	53.0	46.5	33.2	41.5	44.4	34.0	10.6
1957	32.1	52.6	45.8	33.6	41.5	45.4	33.7	10.2
1958	28.8	52.3	46.1	33.6	41.4	46.5	34.5	10.1
1959	29.9	50.8	44.5	33.4	41.4	47.8	35.7	10.2
1960	30.0	51.9	45.7	34.1	41.5	48.6	36.2	10.6
1961	29.4	51.9	46.9	34.3	41.8	48.9	37.2	10.5
1962	27.9	51.6	47.1	34.1	42.2	48.9	38.0	9.8
1963	27.9	51.3	47.3	34.8	43.1	49.5	38.9	9.4
1964	28.5	49.6	48.8	35.0	43.3	50.2	39.4	9.9
1965	28.7	50.6	49.2	36.3	44.3	49.9	40.3	9.7
1966	31.8	53.1	51.0	37.7	45.0	50.6	41.1	9.4
1967	32.3	52.7	53.1	39.7	46.4	50.9	41.9	9.2
1968	33.0	53.3	54.0	40.6	47.5	51.5	42.0	9.4
1969	35.2	54.6	56.4	41.7	48.6	53.0	42.6	9.7
1970	36.6	55.0	57.7	43.2	49.9	53.7	42.6	9.5
1971	36.4	55.0	57.9	43.6	50.2	53.7	42.5	9.3
1972	39.3	57.4	59.4	45.8	50.7	53.4	42.0	9.0
1973	41.7	58.9	61.6	48.5	52.2	53.4	40.8	8.7
1974	43.3	60.4	63.8	51.1	53.7	54.3	40.4	8.0
1975	42.7	60.4	65.4	53.5	54.9	54.3	40.7	8.0
1976	43.8	61.8	66.2	55.8	57.1	54.7	40.8	8.0
1977	45.8	63.3	67.7	58.3	58.9	55.4	40.8	8.0
1978	48.9	64.6	69.3	61.0	60.7	56.7	41.2	8.1
1979	49.1	65.8	70.5	62.9	63.0	58.1	41.6	8.1
1980	47.2	65.1	70.6	64.8	65.0	59.6	40.9	7.9
1981	46.1	64.2	71.5	66.4	66.4	60.9	40.9	7.9
1982	44.6	64.6	71.8	67.8	67.5	61.4	41.5	7.8
Averages								
52-82	36.3	56.2	56.1	44.5	49.6	51.7	39.1	9.19
78-82	47.2	64.9	70.7	64.6	64.5	59.3	41.2	7.96

Employment Rate
White Females
Ages

Year	16-17	18-19	20-24	25-34	35-44	45-54	55-64	65+
1954	88.0	90.6	93.6	94.3	95.1	95.6	95.5	97.2
1955	88.4	92.3	94.9	95.7	96.2	96.6	96.4	97.8
1956	87.9	91.7	94.9	96.0	96.5	96.7	96.5	97.7
1957	88.1	92.1	94.9	95.3	96.3	97.0	97.0	96.5
1958	84.4	89.0	92.6	93.4	94.4	95.1	95.7	96.5
1959	86.7	88.9	93.3	95.0	95.3	96.0	96.0	96.6
1960	85.5	88.5	92.8	94.3	95.8	96.0	96.7	97.2
1961	83.0	86.4	91.6	93.4	94.4	95.2	95.7	96.3
1962	84.4	88.7	92.3	94.6	95.5	96.3	96.6	96.0
1963	81.9	86.8	92.6	94.2	95.4	96.1	96.5	97.0
1964	82.9	86.8	92.9	94.8	95.5	96.4	96.5	96.6
1965	85.0	86.6	93.6	52.0	95.9	97.0	97.3	97.3
1966	85.5	89.3	94.7	96.3	96.7	97.3	97.8	97.3
1967	87.1	89.4	94.0	95.3	96.3	97.1	97.7	97.4
1968	86.1	89.0	94.1	96.1	96.9	97.7	97.9	97.3
1969	86.2	90.0	94.5	95.8	96.8	97.6	97.9	97.6
1970	84.7	88.1	93.1	94.7	95.7	96.6	97.4	96.8
1971	83.4	85.9	91.5	93.7	95.1	96.1	96.7	96.4
1972	83.0	87.7	91.8	94.5	95.5	96.5	96.7	96.3
1973	84.3	89.1	93.0	94.9	96.3	96.9	97.2	97.2
1974	83.6	87.0	91.8	94.3	95.7	96.4	96.7	96.1
1975	80.8	83.9	88.8	91.5	93.4	94.2	94.9	94.7
1976	81.8	84.9	89.6	92.4	94.2	95.0	95.2	94.7
1977	81.8	85.8	90.7	93.3	94.7	95.0	95.6	95.1
1978	82.9	87.6	91.7	94.2	95.5	96.2	97.0	96.3
1979	84.1	87.5	92.2	94.4	95.8	96.3	97.0	96.9
1980	82.7	86.9	91.5	93.7	95.1	95.7	96.9	97.0
1981	81.6	84.7	90.9	93.4	94.9	95.8	96.3	96.6
1982	78.8	82.4	89.1	92.0	93.6	94.5	95.0	96.9

Averages

54-82	84.3	87.9	92.5	92.9	95.5	96.2	96.6	96.6
78-82	82.0	85.8	91.1	93.5	95.0	95.7	96.4	96.7

Dollar Value of Household Services
William H. Gauger and Kathryn E. Walker
1979 Dollars

Number of Children	Age of Wife	Employed-Wife Households			Nonemployed Wife Households	
		Wife	Husband	Teen	Wife	Husband
0	Under 25	$4,700	$1,800		$7,000	$1,100
	25-39	5,000	1,900		8,000	1,600
	40-54	5,900	1,100		8,400	2,100
	55 plus	6,000	1,500		7,400	2,700

Number of Children	Age of Youngest Child	Employed-Wife Households			Nonemployed Wife Households		
		Wife	Husband	Teen	Wife	Husband	Teen
1							
	12-17	$6,700	$2,400	$1,400	$9,600	$2,700	1,200
	6-11	8,000	1,500	†	9,400	2,000	†
	2-5	6,200	2,000	†	9,100	2,400	†
	1	8,300	600	†	9,900	2,300	†
	Under 1	*	*	†	10,900	2,100	†
2	Age of Youngest Child						
	12-17	$6,300	$2,100	$1,000	$10,000	$2,200	$1,100
	6-11	7,200	2,000	1,100	9,900	2,100	1,100
	2-5	8,300	2,400	1,500	1,100	2,200	900
	1	8,400	5,000		11,700	2,200	*
	Under 1	10,200	2,100		12,600	2,000	*
3	Age of Youngest Child						
	12-17	$5,000	$2,100	$1,100	$9,000	$1,400	$1,000
	6-11	8,600	2,000	1,700	9,900	2,200	1,600
	2-5	10,200	2,800	*	10,700	1,900	1,000
	1	11,500	3,200	*	11,600	2,200	1,400
	Under 1	8,700	2,800	*	13,300	2,000	*
4	Age of Youngest Child						
	12-17	$8,700	$1,900	$1,700	$8,400	$1,400	$1,000
	6-11	7,200	1,400	1,100	10,700	1,900	1,100
	2-5	*	*	*	12,000	2,000	1,100
	1	*	*	*	11,800	2,600	800
	Under 1	*	*	*	13,700	2,600	*
5-6	Age of Youngest Child						
	12-17	*	*	*	†	†	†
	6-11	*	*	*	$11,500	$2,000	$1,700
	2-5	*	*	*	12,200	2,100	900
	1	*	*	*	9,900	700	
	Under 1	*	*	*	13,600	2,600	1,000
7-9	Age of Youngest Child						
	6-11	†	†	†	*	*	*
	2-5	*	*	*	$11,900	$2,900	$1,400
	1	†	†	†	*	*	*
	Under 1	†	†	†	15,200	2,600	*

* Averages not calculated because there were fewer than 4 cases.
† No cases.

Dollar Value of Household Services
William H. Gauger and Kathryn E. Walker
1985 Dollars

Number of Children	Age of Wife	Employed Wife Households			Nonemployed Wife Households		
		Wife	Husband	Teen	Wife	Husband	
0	Under 25	$6,961	$2,666		$10,367	$1,629	
	25-39	7,405	2,814		11,848	2,370	
	40-54	8,738	1,629		12,441	3,110	
	55 plus	8,886	2,222		10,960	3,999	
	Age of Youngest Child	Wife	Husband		Wife	Husband	Teen
1	12-17	$9,923	$3,555	$2,073	$14,218	$3,999	1,777
	6-11	11,848	2,222	†	13,922	2,962	†
	2-5	9,183	2,962	†	13,478	3,555	†
	1	12,293	889	†	14,662	3,406	†
	Under 1	*	*	†	16,144	3,110	†
2	**Age of Youngest Child**						
	12-17	$9,331	$3,110	$1,481	$14,811	$3,258	1,629
	6-11	10,664	2,962	1,629	14,662	3,110	1,629
	2-5	12,293	3,555	2,222	1,629	3,258	1,333
	1	12,441	7,405	*	17,328	3,258	*
	Under 1	15,107	3,110	*	18,661	2,962	*
3	**Age of Youngest Child**						
	12-17	$7,405	$3,110	$1,629	$13,330	$2,073	1,481
	6-11	12,737	2,962	2,518	14,662	3,258	2,370
	2-5	15,107	4,147	*	15,847	2,814	1,481
	1	17,032	4,739	*	17,180	3,258	2,073
	Under 1	12,885	4,147	*	19,698	2,962	*
4	**Age of Youngest Child**						
	12-17	$12,885	$2,814	$2,518	$12,441	$2,073	1,481
	6-11	10,664	2,073	1,629	15,847	2,814	1,629
	2-5	*	*	*	17,773	2,962	1,629
	1	*	*	*	17,477	3,851	1,185
	Under 1	*	*	*	20,291	3,851	*
5-6	**Age of Youngest Child**						
	12-17	*	*	*	†	†	†
	6-11	*	*	*	$17,032	$2,962	2,518
	2-5	*	*	*	1,777	3,111	1,333
	1	*	*	*	14,662	1,037	
	Under 1	*	*	*	20,142	3,851	1,481

* Averages not calculated because there were fewer than 4 cases.
† No cases.

Number of Children 7-9	Employed Wife Households Age of Youngest Child	Wife	Husband	Teen	Nonemployed Wife Households Wife	Husband	Teen
	6-11	†	†	†	*	*	*
	2-5	*	*	*	$17,625	$4,295	2,073
	1	†	†	†	*	*	*
	Under 1	†	†	†	22,512	3,851	*

* Averages not calculated because there were fewer than 4 cases.
† No cases.

Consumer Price Index
Average Percentage Change

From To	1952	1953	1954	1955	1956	1957	1958	1959
1952								
1953	.75							
1954	.63	.50						
1955	.29	.06	-.37					
1956	.59	.54	.56	1.50				
1957	1.19	1.30	1.56	2.53	3.56			
1958	1.44	1.58	1.85	2.60	3.15	2.73		
1959	1.35	1.45	1.64	2.15	2.37	1.77	.81	
1960	1.39	1.48	1.64	2.04	2.18	1.71	1.21	1.60
1961	1.34	1.42	1.55	1.87	1.94	1.54	1.14	1.31
1962	1.32	1.38	1.49	1.76	1.81	1.45	1.14	1.24
1963	1.31	1.37	1.46	1.69	1.72	1.41	1.15	1.24
1964	1.31	1.36	1.45	1.65	1.67	1.40	1.18	1.25
1965	1.34	1.39	1.47	1.66	1.68	1.44	1.26	1.33
1966	1.45	1.50	1.59	1.77	1.79	1.60	1.46	1.55
1967	1.55	1.60	1.69	1.86	1.89	1.73	1.61	1.71
1968	1.71	1.78	1.87	2.04	2.08	1.95	1.87	1.99
1969	1.93	2.00	2.10	2.28	2.34	2.24	2.19	2.33
1970	2.15	2.23	2.34	2.52	2.59	2.52	2.50	2.66
1971	2.26	2.35	2.45	2.63	2.71	2.65	2.64	2.79
1972	2.31	2.40	2.50	2.67	2.74	2.69	2.69	2.83
1973	2.50	2.59	2.70	2.87	2.95	2.91	2.92	3.07
1974	2.89	2.99	3.11	3.29	3.39	3.38	3.43	3.60
1975	3.16	3.27	3.40	3.59	3.70	3.70	3.76	3.95
1976	3.27	3.38	3.51	3.69	3.80	3.81	3.87	4.05
1977	3.39	3.50	3.63	3.82	3.93	3.95	4.01	4.19
1978	3.56	3.67	3.80	3.98	4.10	4.12	4.19	4.37
1979	3.84	3.96	4.10	4.29	4.41	4.45	4.53	4.71
1980	4.19	4.32	4.46	4.66	4.79	4.84	4.94	5.13
1981	4.40	4.53	4.68	4.88	5.01	5.07	5.17	5.37
1982	4.46	4.59	4.73	4.92	5.05	5.11	5.21	5.40
1983	4.42	4.54	4.68	4.86	4.99	5.04	5.13	5.31

From	1952	1953	1954	1955	1956	1957	1958	1959
To								
1984	4.41	4.53	4.67	4.84	4.96	5.01	5.10	5.27
1985	4.39	4.50	4.63	4.80	4.91	4.96	5.04	5.21

From	1960	1961	1962	1963	1964	1965	1966	1967
To								
1961	1.01							
1962	1.07	1.12						
1963	1.11	1.17	1.21					
1964	1.16	1.21	1.26	1.31				
1965	1.28	1.34	1.42	1.52	1.72			
1966	1.54	1.64	1.78	1.96	2.29	2.86		
1967	1.73	1.85	2.00	2.19	2.49	2.87	2.88	
1968	2.04	2.19	2.36	2.59	2.92	3.31	3.54	4.20
1969	2.41	2.58	2.79	3.06	3.41	3.83	4.15	4.79
1970	2.76	2.95	3.18	3.47	3.83	4.25	4.59	5.16
1971	2.90	3.09	3.31	3.57	3.89	4.26	4.53	4.95
1972	2.93	3.11	3.31	3.54	3.82	4.12	4.33	4.62
1973	3.19	3.37	3.57	3.81	4.09	4.38	4.60	4.89
1974	3.74	3.95	4.19	4.46	4.77	5.11	5.40	5.76
1975	4.10	4.32	4.57	4.85	5.17	5.52	5.81	6.18
1976	4.21	4.42	4.66	4.92	5.22	5.54	5.81	6.13
1977	4.34	4.55	4.78	5.03	5.32	5.62	5.87	6.16
1978	4.52	4.73	4.96	5.20	5.48	5.77	6.02	6.30
1979	4.88	5.09	5.33	5.58	5.87	6.16	6.42	6.71
1980	5.31	5.54	5.78	6.05	6.35	6.65	6.93	7.24
1981	5.55	5.78	6.02	6.29	6.58	6.89	7.16	7.46
1982	5.58	5.79	6.03	6.28	6.56	6.84	7.09	7.37
1983	5.47	5.68	5.89	6.13	6.38	6.64	6.86	7.11
1984	5.42	5.62	5.82	6.04	6.28	6.52	6.72	6.94
1985	5.35	5.53	5.72	5.93	6.15	6.37	6.55	6.76

From	1968	1969	1970	1971	1972	1973	1974	1975
To								
1969	5.37							
1970	5.65	5.92						
1971	5.20	5.11	4.30					
1972	4.72	4.51	3.80	3.30				
1973	5.02	4.94	4.61	4.76	6.23			
1974	6.01	6.14	6.20	6.83	8.60	10.97		
1975	6.46	6.64	6.79	7.41	8.78	10.05	9.14	
1976	6.37	6.52	6.62	7.08	8.03	8.63	7.45	5.77
1977	6.38	6.51	6.59	6.98	7.71	8.08	7.12	6.11
1978	6.51	6.64	6.73	7.07	7.70	8.00	7.25	6.63
1979	6.94	7.10	7.23	7.60	8.21	8.54	8.06	7.78

From	1968	1969	1970	1971	1972	1973	1974	1975
To								
1980	7.49	7.68	7.86	8.25	8.87	9.25	8.97	8.93
1981	7.71	7.91	8.09	8.47	9.04	9.39	9.17	9.17
1982	7.60	7.77	7.92	8.25	8.75	9.03	8.79	8.74
1983	7.31	7.45	7.56	7.83	8.25	8.45	8.17	8.05
1984	7.12	7.23	7.33	7.56	7.91	8.07	7.78	7.63
1985	6.91	7.00	7.08	7.27	7.58	7.69	7.40	7.22

From	1976	1977	1978	1979	1980	1981	1982	1983
To								
1977	6.45							
1978	7.06	7.66						
1979	8.46	9.46	11.26					
1980	9.72	10.81	12.39	13.52				
1981	9.85	10.70	11.72	11.95	10.37			
1982	9.23	9.79	10.32	10.01	8.25	6.13		
1983	8.37	8.69	8.90	8.31	6.57	4.67	3.22	
1984	7.86	8.06	8.13	7.50	5.99	4.53	3.74	4.26
1985	7.38	7.50	7.48	6.84	5.51	4.29	3.68	3.91

From	1984	1985
To		
1985	3.57	

Average Return 1-Year Treasury Bills

From	1952	1953	1954	1955	1956	1957	1958	1959
1952	1.84							
1953	1.98	2.11						
1954	1.63	1.52	.93					
1955	1.70	1.66	1.43	1.93				
1956	1.94	1.97	1.92	2.42	2.91			
1957	2.23	2.31	2.36	2.83	3.29	3.66		
1958	2.22	2.28	2.31	2.66	2.90	2.90	2.13	
1959	2.48	2.57	2.64	2.98	3.25	3.36	3.21	4.29
1960	2.61	2.70	2.79	3.10	3.33	3.44	3.36	3.98
1961	2.64	2.72	2.80	3.07	3.26	3.33	3.24	3.61
1962	2.68	2.76	2.83	3.07	3.23	3.29	3.21	3.49
1963	2.74	2.82	2.89	3.11	3.26	3.31	3.25	3.47
1964	2.83	2.91	2.98	3.19	3.33	3.38	3.34	3.54
1965	2.93	3.01	3.09	3.28	3.42	3.47	3.45	3.64
1966	3.09	3.18	3.26	3.45	3.59	3.66	3.66	3.85
1967	3.20	3.29	3.38	3.57	3.70	3.78	3.79	3.97
1968	3.35	3.45	3.54	3.72	3.86	3.94	3.97	4.15
1969	3.57	3.67	3.77	3.96	4.11	4.20	4.24	4.44
1970	3.75	3.86	3.96	4.15	4.30	4.39	4.45	4.64

From	1952	1953	1954	1955	1956	1957	1958	1959
1971	3.81	3.91	4.01	4.19	4.33	4.43	4.48	4.66
1972	3.86	3.97	4.06	4.24	4.37	4.46	4.52	4.69
1973	4.03	4.14	4.24	4.41	4.55	4.65	4.71	4.88
1974	4.22	4.33	4.43	4.61	4.75	4.85	4.92	5.10
1975	4.32	4.43	4.54	4.71	4.85	4.95	5.02	5.19
1976	4.38	4.49	4.59	4.76	4.89	4.99	5.06	5.23
1977	4.45	4.55	4.65	4.82	4.95	5.04	5.11	5.27
1978	4.59	4.70	4.80	4.97	5.10	5.20	5.27	5.43
1979	4.82	4.93	5.03	5.20	5.33	5.44	5.52	5.68
1980	5.07	5.19	5.30	5.47	5.61	5.72	5.81	5.98
1981	5.41	5.53	5.65	5.83	5.98	6.10	6.20	6.38
1982	5.63	5.76	5.89	6.06	6.22	6.34	6.45	6.63
1983	5.76	5.89	6.01	6.19	6.34	6.47	6.57	6.75
1984	5.92	6.05	6.17	6.35	6.50	6.63	6.74	6.92
1985	5.97	6.10	6.22	6.39	6.54	6.67	6.78	6.95

From To	1960	1961	1962	1963	1964	1965	1966	1967
1960	3.66							
1961	3.28	2.89						
1962	3.22	3.00	3.10					
1963	3.27	3.13	3.25	3.41				
1964	3.39	3.32	3.47	3.65	3.89			
1965	3.53	3.50	3.66	3.84	4.06	4.23		
1966	3.79	3.81	3.99	4.22	4.49	4.79	5.34	
1967	3.93	3.97	4.15	4.36	4.60	4.84	5.14	4.94
1968	4.14	4.20	4.38	4.59	4.83	5.07	5.35	5.35
1969	4.45	4.54	4.74	4.98	5.24	5.51	5.83	5.99
1970	4.68	4.78	4.99	5.22	5.48	5.75	6.05	6.23
1971	4.70	4.79	4.98	5.19	5.41	5.63	5.86	5.96
1972	4.72	4.81	4.98	5.17	5.37	5.55	5.74	5.80
1973	4.92	5.02	5.20	5.39	5.58	5.77	5.96	6.05
1974	5.15	5.26	5.44	5.63	5.83	6.03	6.23	6.34
1975	5.25	5.35	5.53	5.72	5.91	6.09	6.28	6.38
1976	5.28	5.38	5.55	5.72	5.90	6.07	6.24	6.33
1977	5.33	5.42	5.58	5.75	5.91	6.07	6.22	6.30
1978	5.49	5.59	5.75	5.91	6.08	6.24	6.39	6.48
1979	5.75	5.86	6.03	6.20	6.37	6.54	6.71	6.81
1980	6.06	6.18	6.35	6.53	6.72	6.90	7.07	7.20
1981	6.47	6.61	6.79	6.99	7.19	7.38	7.58	7.73
1982	6.73	6.87	7.06	7.26	7.46	7.66	7.86	8.02
1983	6.85	6.99	7.18	7.37	7.57	7.77	7.96	8.12
1984	7.02	7.16	7.35	7.54	7.74	7.93	8.12	8.28
1985	7.05	7.19	7.37	7.55	7.74	7.92	8.11	8.25

From To	1968	1969	1970	1971	1972	1973	1974	1975
1968	5.76							
1969	6.52	7.28						
1970	6.66	7.11	6.94					
1971	6.22	6.37	5.92	4.90				
1972	5.98	6.03	5.62	4.96	5.01			
1973	6.24	6.33	6.10	5.82	6.28	7.54		
1974	6.54	6.67	6.55	6.45	6.97	7.95	8.35	
1975	6.56	6.68	6.58	6.50	6.90	7.54	7.54	6.72
1976	6.48	6.57	6.47	6.39	6.69	7.11	6.97	6.28
1977	6.44	6.52	6.42	6.35	6.59	6.90	6.74	6.21
1978	6.62	6.70	6.64	6.60	6.84	7.15	7.07	6.75
1979	6.97	7.08	7.05	7.07	7.34	7.67	7.69	7.56
1980	7.37	7.50	7.52	7.58	7.88	8.24	8.34	8.34
1981	7.92	8.09	8.16	8.27	8.61	9.01	9.19	9.31
1982	8.23	8.40	8.49	8.62	8.96	9.35	9.55	9.70
1983	8.31	8.49	8.57	8.70	9.01	9.38	9.56	9.70
1984	8.47	8.64	8.73	8.86	9.17	9.51	9.69	9.83
1985	8.44	8.59	8.68	8.79	9.07	9.38	9.54	9.64

From To	1976	1977	1978	1979	1980	1981	1982	1983
1976	5.84							
1977	5.95	6.06						
1978	6.76	7.22	8.39					
1979	7.77	8.42	9.60	10.80				
1980	8.66	9.37	10.47	11.51	12.22			
1981	9.74	10.52	11.64	12.72	13.68	15.13		
1982	10.13	10.84	11.80	12.65	13.27	13.79	12.45	
1983	10.07	10.67	11.44	12.05	12.36	12.41	11.05	9.65
1984	10.17	10.71	11.38	11.88	12.09	12.06	11.04	10.33
1985	9.94	10.39	10.93	11.30	11.38	11.21	10.23	9.49

From To	1984	1985
1984	11.01	
1985	9.41	7.81

Medical Price Index

From To	1952	1953	1954	1955	1956	1957	1958	1959
1953	3.54							
1954	3.40	3.26						
1955	3.00	2.73	2.21					
1956	3.18	3.06	2.96	3.70				

From	1952	1953	1954	1955	1956	1957	1958	1959
To								
1957	3.35	3.30	3.31	3.86	4.02			
1958	3.57	3.58	3.66	4.15	4.37	4.72		
1959	3.69	3.71	3.80	4.20	4.37	4.55	4.37	
1960	3.67	3.69	3.76	4.07	4.16	4.21	3.95	3.53
1961	3.58	3.59	3.64	3.88	3.91	3.88	3.60	3.22
1962	3.48	3.48	3.51	3.69	3.69	3.62	3.35	3.01
1963	3.40	3.38	3.40	3.54	3.52	3.44	3.18	2.88
1964	3.28	3.25	3.25	3.37	3.33	3.23	2.98	2.70
1965	3.22	3.19	3.19	3.29	3.24	3.14	2.92	2.67
1966	3.30	3.28	3.29	3.38	3.35	3.28	3.10	2.91
1967	3.55	3.55	3.58	3.69	3.69	3.66	3.54	3.43
1968	3.71	3.72	3.76	3.88	3.89	3.88	3.79	3.73
1969	3.90	3.92	3.96	4.09	4.12	4.13	4.07	4.04
1970	4.03	4.06	4.11	4.24	4.28	4.30	4.26	4.25
1971	4.16	4.20	4.25	4.38	4.42	4.45	4.43	4.44
1972	4.11	4.14	4.19	4.31	4.35	4.37	4.34	4.34
1973	4.10	4.13	4.18	4.29	4.32	4.34	4.32	4.31
1974	4.34	4.38	4.43	4.55	4.60	4.63	4.63	4.65
1975	4.67	4.73	4.80	4.93	4.99	5.04	5.06	5.11
1976	4.88	4.94	5.01	5.15	5.22	5.28	5.31	5.37
1977	5.07	5.13	5.21	5.35	5.43	5.50	5.54	5.60
1978	5.19	5.26	5.34	5.48	5.56	5.63	5.68	5.75
1979	5.34	5.41	5.50	5.64	5.72	5.80	5.85	5.92
1980	5.54	5.62	5.71	5.85	5.94	6.02	6.08	6.16
1981	5.72	5.80	5.90	6.04	6.13	6.22	6.28	6.37
1982	5.92	6.00	6.10	6.24	6.34	6.44	6.51	6.60
1983	6.01	6.09	6.19	6.33	6.43	6.52	6.59	6.69
1984	6.01	6.09	6.19	6.33	6.42	6.51	6.58	6.66
1985	6.02	6.10	6.19	6.32	6.41	6.50	6.57	6.65

From	1960	1961	1962	1963	1964	1965	1966	1967
To								
1961	2.91							
1962	2.74	2.58						
1963	2.67	2.55	2.51					
1964	2.50	2.36	2.25	1.99				
1965	2.50	2.40	2.34	2.25	2.52			
1966	2.81	2.79	2.84	2.95	3.44	4.36		
1967	3.42	3.50	3.69	3.98	4.65	5.71	7.07	
1968	3.75	3.87	4.09	4.41	5.01	5.84	6.58	6.10
1969	4.10	4.25	4.49	4.82	5.38	6.10	6.68	6.49
1970	4.33	4.48	4.72	5.04	5.55	6.15	6.60	6.44
1971	4.52	4.68	4.92	5.22	5.68	6.20	6.57	6.45
1972	4.41	4.55	4.74	4.99	5.37	5.77	6.01	5.80

From	1960	1961	1962	1963	1964	1965	1966	1967
To								
1973	4.37	4.49	4.67	4.88	5.21	5.54	5.71	5.49
1974	4.72	4.86	5.05	5.29	5.62	5.96	6.16	6.03
1975	5.21	5.38	5.59	5.85	6.20	6.57	6.81	6.78
1976	5.48	5.65	5.87	6.13	6.48	6.84	7.09	7.09
1977	5.72	5.90	6.12	6.38	6.72	7.07	7.31	7.34
1978	5.87	6.05	6.26	6.51	6.84	7.17	7.40	7.43
1979	6.05	6.22	6.44	6.68	7.00	7.32	7.55	7.59
1980	6.29	6.47	6.69	6.93	7.24	7.56	7.79	7.84
1981	6.51	6.69	6.90	7.15	7.45	7.76	7.98	8.05
1982	6.74	6.92	7.14	7.38	7.68	7.98	8.21	8.29
1983	6.82	7.00	7.21	7.45	7.74	8.02	8.24	8.31
1984	6.80	6.96	7.16	7.38	7.65	7.92	8.12	8.19
1985	6.78	6.94	7.13	7.34	7.59	7.84	8.03	8.08

From	1968	1969	1970	1971	1972	1973	1974	1975
To								
1969	6.88							
1970	6.61	6.35						
1971	6.57	6.41	6.47					
1972	5.72	5.34	4.83	3.19				
1973	5.36	4.98	4.53	3.56	3.92			
1974	6.02	5.85	5.72	5.47	6.61	9.30		
1975	6.88	6.88	6.98	7.11	8.42	10.66	12.03	
1976	7.21	7.26	7.41	7.60	8.70	10.29	10.79	9.55
1977	7.47	7.55	7.72	7.93	8.88	10.11	10.39	9.57
1978	7.57	7.64	7.80	8.00	8.80	9.77	9.89	9.18
1979	7.72	7.80	7.97	8.15	8.86	9.68	9.76	9.20
1980	7.99	8.09	8.26	8.46	9.12	9.86	9.96	9.54
1981	8.20	8.31	8.49	8.69	9.30	9.97	10.07	9.75
1982	8.44	8.56	8.75	8.96	9.53	10.16	10.26	10.01
1983	8.46	8.57	8.75	8.94	9.46	10.01	10.09	9.85
1984	8.32	8.41	8.56	8.72	9.18	9.66	9.69	9.43
1985	8.20	8.28	8.41	8.55	8.96	9.38	9.39	9.12

From	1976	1977	1978	1979	1980	1981	1982	1983
To								
1977	9.58							
1978	8.99	8.40						
1979	9.08	8.83	9.25					
1980	9.54	9.53	10.09	10.93				
1981	9.78	9.83	10.31	10.84	10.76			
1982	10.09	10.19	10.64	11.10	11.18	11.61		
1983	9.89	9.94	10.25	10.50	10.36	10.16	8.70	
1984	9.42	9.40	9.56	9.63	9.30	8.81	7.42	6.13

From	1976	1977	1978	1979	1980	1981	1982	1983
To								
1985	9.07	9.01	9.10	9.07	8.70	8.19	7.04	6.22

From	1984	1985
To		
1985	8.08	

Revised Equivalency Scale for Urban Families of Different Sizes, Ages, and Composition

(A 4-person family: husband, age 35-54; wife; 2 children, older child 6-15 years of age equals 100%)

Age of Head Size and Type of Family	Under 35	35-54	55-64	65+
One Person	35	36	32	28
Two Persons: Average	47	59	59	52
Husband, wife	49	60	59	51
One parent, one child	40	57	60	58
Three Persons: Average	62	81	86	77
Husband, wife (child under 6)	62	69	—	—
Husband, wife (child 6-15)	62	82	88	81
Husband, wife (child 16-17)	—	91	88	77
Husband, wife (child over 18)	—	82	85	77
One parent, 2 children	67	76	82	75
Four Persons: Average	74	99	109	91
Husband, wife (child under 6)	72	80	—	—
Husband, wife (older child 6-15)	77	100	105	95
Husband, wife (older child 16-17)	—	113	125	—
Husband, wife (older child over 18)	—	96	110	89
One parent, three children	88	96	—	—
Five Persons: Average	94	118	124	—
Husband, wife (child under 6)	87	97	—	—

Age of Head Size and Type of Family	Under 35	35-54	55-64	65+
Husband, wife (older child 6-15)	96	116	120	—
Husband, wife (older child 16-17)	—	128	138	—
Husband, wife (older child over 18)	—	119	124	—
One parent, four children	108	117	—	—
Six Persons: Average	111	138	143	—
Husband, wife (child under 6)	101	—	—	—
Husband, wife (older child 6-15)	110	132	140	—
Husband, wife (older child 16-17)	—	146	—	—
Husband, wife (older child over 18)	—	149	—	—
One parent, five children	125	137	—	—

§18.08   Example 4: Wrongful Death of a Caucasian Male, A 1986 Report—Background

On May 17, 1984, Mr. John Brown was killed. He was a Caucasian male born August 19, 1957. At the time of his death he was married and the father of three minor children. He had been employed by a municipality for the past six years, earning $21,540 per year from the municipality and $4,641 per year as an independent contractor.

§18.09   —The Economist's Report in Example 4

Economic Consultants, Inc.
Address
City, State 00000

December 31, 1986

Attorney, Attorney, and Attorney
Attn: Senior Attorney
Street Address
City, State

RE: Mr. John Brown

Dear Attorney:
The case involving Mr. John Brown has been evaluated. The present value of

the loss is $792,333. This amount is the sum of the historic loss plus the present value of the future loss.

The historic loss represents the lost income from the date of the injury, May 17, 1984, to the date of the trial, January 5, 1987. This loss is $67,068. The present value of the future loss, beginning January 5, 1987, and continuing to age 65, is $726,265. This loss is the economic loss sustained by Mr. Brown's family and does not include loss of services, attention, marital care, advice, or protection to Mrs. Brown or any of the minor children. This figure is exclusive of the value of household services and is not reduced for personal consumption.

The economic evaluation is based on information received from your office as detailed in Part I of this report. The methodology and other sources of information employed in preparing this report appear in Parts II and III.

If there is an error in the information contained in Part I, please contact me immediately so that I may provide you a corrected copy.

Sincerely,

The Economist, Ph.D.

Summary of Losses to
Mr. John Brown
Historic Loss
From May 17, 1984, to January 5, 1987
Wages . . . . $ 67,068
Present Value of Future Loss
Beginning January 5, 1987
Wages to age 65 . . . $725,884
Total Loss $792,952

Economic Analysis
Mr. John Brown
PART I.

Date of Birth:	August 29, 1957
Current Age:	29
Race:	Caucasian
Sex:	Male
Date of Accident:	May 17, 1984
Injury	Death
Life Expectancy (absent the accident):	44.7 years
Education:	High School Graduate

Earnings History:

Year	City	Contractor
1984	$10,092	$1,742
1983	18,255	3,403
1982	16,008	1,178
1981	12,781	1,882
1980	24,472	16,650

Age at Retirement: 65
Marital Status: Married
Dependents: 3 children
Date of Analysis: December 31, 1986
Date of Present Value: January 5, 1987

PART II. Calculation of Economic Loss

The present value of the loss is calculated by using the following formula:

$$\text{Present Value of Future Income} \ = \ \sum_{t=0}^{n} \$ \ [(1 + g)^t / (1 + d)^t]$$

The four variables in this formula are $, t, g, and d.

$ - Represents the basis for calculating the economic loss resulting from the injury. The wage calculation is based on annual earnings. The earnings are $21,540 as a municipal employee and $4,461 as an independent contractor. The municipal income is based on employer records, and the contracting income is based on individual tax records.

t - Represents time and starts on the present value date, January 5, 1987, and runs until period "n." Period "n" is when Mr. Brown reaches age 64. This means retirement occurs at age 65.

g - Represents the growth rate for wages. The growth rate is 4.39 per cent annually. This is the 1952-1985 historic rate of change in the Consumer Price Index.

d - Represents the discount rate or rate at which dollars received will earn interest. The discount rate is 5.99 per cent annually. This is the 1952-1985 historic yield on one-year Treasury Bills. There are many types of investments which can be made today, ranging from passbook savings to speculating in futures markets. While there is no such thing as a risk-free investment, the one-year Treasury Bill is used as a surrogate.

For example, if we are receiving $1,000 one year from today, we might be willing to receive some amount less than $1,000 today. This is true because we could invest the money for one year and earn interest. The rate of earnings is the interest rate, or discount rate.

PART III. Bibliography

Probability of Living: Life Expectancy Tables, U.S. National Center for Health Statistics, Vital Statistics of U.S., 1982, as cited in Statistical Abstracts of the United States, 1986

Job Participation Rate: Civilian Labor Force Participation Rate By Sex, Race and Age, Handbook of Labor Statistics, U.S. Department of Labor, Bureau of Labor Statistics, December 1980, Bulletin 2070

Probability of Employment: Unemployment Rates by Sex, Race and Age, Handbook of Labor Statistics, U.S. Department of Labor, Bureau of Labor Statistics, December 1980, Bulletin 2070

Consumption: Revised Equivalence Scale for Urban Families of Different Size, Age and Composition, derived from the Bureau of Labor Statistics of Consumer Expenditures - 1960-1961

Value of Household Services: The Dollar Value of Household Work, William H. Gauger and Kathryn E. Walker, New York State College of Human Ecology, Cornell University, Ithaca, New York

Present Value
of Future Income
as of January 5, 1987

Prepared: December 31, 1986
Name: John Brown
Birthdate: August 29, 1957
Age: 29

Life Expectancy at 29 is 44.7 years
U.S. Life Tables (1982) - White Males
The adjusted sum was computed using participation and employment rates (1978-1982) - White Males
Annual Income = $21,540
Annual Growth Rate = 4.39%
Annual Discount Rate = 5.99%

Age	Period	Present Value	Total	Probability of Living	Participation Rate	Employment Rate	Adjusted Total
29	0	$21,540	$21,540	.99846	.9588	.9436	$ 19,458
30	1	21,215	42,755	.99690	.9588	.9436	38,592
31	2	20,895	63,649	.99533	.9588	.9436	57,407
32	3	20,579	84,229	.99373	.9588	.9436	75,909
33	4	20,269	104,497	.99211	.9588	.9436	94,102
34	5	19,963	124,460	.99045	.9588	.9436	111,990
35	6	19,661	144,121	.98872	.9620	.9624	129,988
36	7	19,364	163,485	.98693	.9620	.9624	147,681
37	8	19,072	182,557	.98503	.9620	.9624	165,075
38	9	18,784	201,341	.98301	.9620	.9624	182,170
39	10	18,501	219,842	.98084	.9620	.9624	198,970
40	11	18,221	238,063	.97848	.9620	.9624	215,477
41	12	17,946	256,010	.97591	.9620	.9624	231,692
42	13	17,675	273,685	.97309	.9620	.9624	247,616
43	14	17,409	291,093	.96999	.9620	.9624	263,250
44	15	17,146	308,239	.96656	.9620	.9624	278,593
45	16	16,887	325,126	.96278	.9220	.9656	293,067
46	17	16,632	341,758	.95860	.9220	.9656	307,262
47	18	16,381	358,139	.95397	.9220	.9656	321,174
48	19	16,134	374,273	.94884	.9220	.9656	334,803
49	20	15,890	390,163	.94314	.9220	.9656	348,145
50	21	15,650	405,813	.93683	.9220	.9656	361,198
51	22	15,414	421,227	.92988	.9220	.9656	373,958
52	23	15,181	436,408	.92225	.9220	.9656	386,423
53	24	14,952	451,360	.91394	.9220	.9656	398,589
54	25	14,726	466,086	.90490	.9220	.9656	410,453
55	26	14,504	480,591	.89510	.7262	.9666	419,566
56	27	14,285	494,876	.88450	.7262	.9666	428,435

Age	Period	Present Value	Total	Probability of Living	Participation Rate	Employment Rate	Adjusted Total
57	28	14,069	508,945	.87304	.7262	.9666	437,057
58	29	13,857	522,802	.86068	.7262	.9666	445,429
59	30	13,648	536,450	.84737	.7262	.9666	453,547
60	31	13,442	549,892	.83309	.7262	.9666	461,408
61	32	13,239	563,131	.81780	.7262	.9666	469,007
62	33	13,039	576,170	.80141	.7262	.9666	476,343
63	34	12,842	589,012	.78382	.7262	.9666	483,408
64	35	12,648	601,661	.76496	.7262	.9666	490,200
65	36	12,457	614,118	.74478	.1920	.9698	491,928
66	37	12,269	626,388	.72346	.1920	.9698	493,580
67	38	12,084	638,472	.70098	.1920	.9698	495,158
68	39	11,902	650,374	.67732	.1920	.9698	496,659
69	40	11,722	662,096	.65251	.1920	.9698	498,083
70	41	11,545	673,641	.62656	.1920	.9698	499,430
71	42	11,371	685,012	.59956	.1920	.9698	500,699
72	43	11,199	696,211	.57157	.1920	.9698	501,891
73	44	11,030	707,241	.54264	.1920	.9698	503,006
74	45	10,864	718,105	.51289	.1920	.9698	504,043
75	46	10,700	728,804	.48241	.1920	.9698	505,004
76	47	10,538	739,343	.45140	.1920	.9698	505,890
77	48	10,379	749,722	.42002	.1920	.9698	506,702
78	49	10,222	759,944	.38843	.1920	.9698	507,441
79	50	10,068	770,012	.35684	.1920	.9698	508,110
80	51	9,916	779,928	.32544	.1920	.9698	508,711
81	52	9,766	789,695	.29289	.1920	.9698	509,244
82	53	9,619	799,314	.25960	.1920	.9698	509,709
83	54	9,474	808,787	.22607	.1920	.9698	510,107
84	55	9,331	818,118	.19289	.1920	.9698	510,443
85	56	9,190	827,308	.16071	.1920	.9698	510,718
86	57	9,051	836,359	.13025	.1920	.9698	510,937
87	58	8,915	845,274	.10219	.1920	.9698	511,107
88	59	8,780	854,054	.07718	.1920	.9698	511,233
89	60	8,647	862,701	.05571	.1920	.9698	511,323
90	61	8,517	871,218	.03810	.1920	.9698	511,383
91	62	8,388	879,606	.02441	.1920	.9698	511,421
92	63	8,262	887,868	.01445	.1920	.9698	511,443
93	64	8,137	896,005	.00775	.1920	.9698	511,455
94	65	8,014	904,019	.00366	.1920	.9698	511,461
95	66	7,893	911,912	.00147	.1920	.9698	511,463
96	67	7,774	919,686	.00047	.1920	.9698	511,463
97	68	7,657	927,343	.00011	.1920	.9698	511,464
98	69	7,541	934,884	.00001	.1920	.9698	511,464
99	70	7,427	942,311	.00000	.1920	.9698	511,464

Employment Rates
White Male
1954 - 1982
Inclusive

Year				Ages				
	16-17	18-19	20-24	25-34	35-44	45-54	55-64	65+
54	86.00	87.00	90.20	95.80	96.40	96.20	95.70	95.80
55	87.80	89.60	93.00	97.30	97.40	97.10	96.10	96.20
56	88.80	90.30	93.90	97.20	97.80	97.20	96.90	96.60
57	88.10	88.80	92.90	97.30	97.50	97.00	96.60	91.80
58	85.10	83.50	88.30	94.40	95.60	95.20	94.80	95.00
59	85.00	87.00	92.50	96.20	96.80	96.30	95.80	95.50
60	85.40	86.50	91.70	95.90	96.70	96.40	95.90	96.00
61	83.50	84.90	90.00	95.10	96.00	95.60	94.70	94.80
62	84.90	87.30	92.00	96.20	96.90	96.50	95.90	95.90
63	82.20	85.80	92.20	96.10	97.10	96.70	96.00	95.90
64	83.80	86.60	92.60	97.00	97.50	97.10	96.50	96.40
65	85.30	88.60	94.10	97.40	97.70	97.70	96.90	97.00
66	87.50	91.10	95.90	97.90	98.30	98.30	97.50	96.30
67	87.30	91.00	95.80	98.10	98.40	98.20	97.80	97.20
68	87.70	91.80	95.40	98.30	98.60	98.50	98.30	97.60
69	87.50	92.10	95.40	98.30	98.60	98.60	98.30	97.90
70	84.30	88.00	92.20	96.90	97.70	97.70	97.30	96.80
71	82.90	86.50	90.60	96.00	97.10	97.20	96.80	96.60
72	83.60	87.60	91.50	96.60	97.50	97.50	97.00	96.70
73	84.90	90.00	93.50	97.00	98.20	98.00	97.60	97.10
74	83.80	88.50	92.20	96.50	97.60	97.80	97.50	97.00
75	80.30	82.80	86.80	93.70	95.50	95.60	95.90	95.00
76	80.30	84.50	89.10	94.40	96.30	96.30	96.00	95.20
77	82.40	87.00	90.70	95.00	96.90	97.00	96.70	95.10
78	83.10	89.20	92.40	96.30	97.50	97.50	97.40	96.10
79	83.90	87.70	92.60	96.40	97.50	97.50	97.50	96.90
80	81.50	85.50	88.90	94.10	96.40	96.70	96.90	97.50
81	80.10	83.60	88.40	93.90	96.00	96.40	96.60	97.60
82	75.80	80.00	85.70	91.10	93.80	94.70	94.90	96.80
54-82 Ave	84.23	87.34	91.74	96.08	97.08	96.98	96.61	96.22
78-82 Ave	80.88	85.20	89.60	94.36	96.24	96.56	96.66	96.98

Participation Rates for
White Males
1954 - 1982
Inclusive

Year				Ages				
	16-17	18-19	20-24	25-34	35-44	45-54	55-64	65+
54	47.10	70.40	86.40	97.50	98.20	96.80	89.20	40.40
55	48.00	71.70	85.60	97.80	98.30	96.70	88.40	39.50
56	51.30	71.90	87.60	97.40	98.10	96.80	88.90	40.00
57	49.60	71.60	86.70	97.20	98.00	96.60	88.00	37.70
58	46.80	69.40	86.70	97.20	98.00	96.60	88.20	35.70
59	45.40	70.30	87.30	97.50	98.00	96.30	87.90	34.30
60	46.00	69.00	87.60	97.70	97.90	96.10	87.20	33.30
61	44.30	66.20	87.60	97.70	97.90	95.90	87.80	31.90
62	42.90	66.40	86.50	97.40	97.90	96.00	86.70	30.60
63	42.40	67.80	85.80	97.40	97.80	96.20	86.60	28.40
64	43.50	66.60	85.70	97.50	97.60	96.10	86.10	27.90
65	44.60	65.80	85.30	97.40	97.70	95.90	85.20	27.90
66	47.10	65.40	84.40	97.50	97.60	95.80	84.90	27.20
67	47.90	66.10	84.00	97.50	97.70	95.60	84.90	27.10
68	47.70	65.70	82.40	97.20	97.60	95.40	84.70	27.30
69	48.80	66.30	82.60	97.00	97.40	95.10	83.90	27.30
70	48.90	67.40	83.30	96.70	97.30	94.90	83.30	26.70
71	49.20	67.80	83.20	96.30	97.00	94.70	82.60	25.60
72	50.20	71.10	84.30	96.00	97.00	94.00	81.20	24.40
73	52.70	72.30	85.80	96.30	96.80	93.50	79.00	22.50
74	53.30	73.60	86.50	96.30	96.70	93.00	78.10	22.50
75	51.80	72.80	85.50	95.80	96.40	92.90	76.50	21.80
76	51.80	73.50	86.20	95.90	96.00	92.50	75.40	20.30
77	53.80	74.90	86.80	96.00	96.20	92.20	74.70	20.20
78	55.30	75.30	87.20	96.00	96.30	92.10	73.90	20.40
79	55.30	74.50	87.60	96.10	96.40	92.20	73.60	20.10
80	53.60	74.10	87.20	95.90	96.20	92.10	73.10	19.10
81	51.50	73.50	87.00	95.80	96.10	92.40	71.50	18.50
82	49.30	70.50	86.30	95.60	96.00	92.20	71.00	17.90
54-82 Ave								
	48.97	70.07	85.83	96.81	97.24	94.71	82.16	27.47
78-82 Ave								
	53.00	73.58	87.06	95.88	96.20	92.20	72.62	19.20

Dollar Value of Household Services
William H. Gauger and Kathryn E. Walker
1979 Dollars

0 Children

Age of Wife	Employed Wife Households Wife	Husband	Teen	Nonemployed Wife Households Wife	Husband
Under 25	$4,700	$1,800		$7,000	$1,100
25-39	5,000	1,900		8,000	1,600
40-54	5,900	1,100		8,400	2,100
55 plus	6,000	1,500		7,400	2,700

1 Child

Age of Youngest Child	Wife	Husband	Teen	Wife	Husband	Teen
12-17	$6,700	$2,400	$1,400	$9,600	$2,700	1,200
6-11	8,000	1,500	†	9,400	2,000	†
2-5	6,200	2,000	†	9,100	2,400	†
1	8,300	600	†	9,900	2,300	†
Under 1	*	*	†	10,900	2,100	†

2 Children

Age of Youngest Child	Wife	Husband	Teen	Wife	Husband	Teen
12-17	$6,300	$2,100	$1,000	$10,000	$2,200	$1,100
6-11	7,200	2,000	1,100	9,900	2,100	1,100
2-5	8,300	2,400	1,500	1,100	2,200	900
1	8,400	5,000	*	11,700	2,200	*
Under 1	10,200	2,100	*	12,600	2,000	*

3 Children

Age of Youngest Child	Wife	Husband	Teen	Wife	Husband	Teen
12-17	$5,000	$2,100	$1,100	$9,000	$1,400	$1,000
6-11	8,600	2,000	1,700	9,900	2,200	1,600
2-5	10,200	2,800	*	10,700	1,900	1,000
1	11,500	3,200	*	11,600	2,200	1,400
Under 1	8,700	2,800	*	13,300	2,000	*

4 Children

Age of Youngest Child	Wife	Husband	Teen	Wife	Husband	Teen
12-17	$8,700	$1,900	$1,700	$8,400	$1,400	$1,000
6-11	7,200	1,400	1,100	10,700	1,900	1,100
2-5	*	*	*	12,000	2,000	1,100
1	*	*	*	11,800	2,600	800
Under 1	*	*	*	13,700	2,600	*

5 - 6 Children

Age of Youngest Child	Wife	Husband	Teen	Wife	Husband	Teen
12-17	*	*	*	†	†	†
6-11	*	*	*	$11,500	$2,000	$1,700

* Averages not calculated because there were fewer than 4 cases.

† No cases.

5 - 6 Children Employed Wife Households	Wife	Husband	Teen	Nonemployed Wife Households Wife	Husband	Teen
Age of Youngest Child						
2-5	*	*	*	12,200	2,100	900
1	*	*	*	9,900	700	*
Under 1	*	*	*	13,600	2,600	1,000
7 - 9 Children Age of Youngest Child						
6-11	†	†	†	*	*	*
2-5	*	*	*	$11,900	$2,900	$1,400
1	†	†	†	*	*	*
Under 1	†	†	†	15,200	2,600	*

* Averages not calculated because there were fewer than 4 cases.
† No cases.

Dollar Value of Household Services
William H. Gauger and Kathryn E. Walker
1985 Dollars

0 Children Employed Wife Households	Wife	Husband	Teen	Nonemployed Wife Households Wife	Husband
Age of Wife					
Under 25	$6,961	$2,666		$10,367	$1,629
25-39	7,405	2,814		11,848	2,370
40-54	8,738	1,629		12,441	3,110
55 plus	8,886	2,222		10,960	3,999

1 Child Age of Youngest Child	Wife	Husband	Teen	Wife	Husband	Teen
12-17	$9,923	$3,555	$2,073	$14,218	$3,999	1,777
6-11	11,848	2,222	†	13,922	2,962	†
2-5	9,183	2,962	†	13,478	3,555	†
1	12,293	889	†	14,662	3,406	†
Under 1	*	*	†	16,144	3,110	†

2 Children Age of Youngest Child	Wife	Husband	Teen	Wife	Husband	Teen
12-17	$9,331	$3,110	$1,481	$14,811	$3,258	1,629
6-11	10,664	2,962	1,629	14,662	3,110	1,629
2-5	12,293	3,555	2,222	1,629	3,258	1,333
1	12,441	7,405	*	17,328	3,258	*
Under 1	15,107	3,110	*	18,661	2,962	*

* Averages not calculated because there were fewer than 4 cases.
† No cases.

Employed Wife Households 3 Children Age of Youngest Child	Wife	Husband	Teen	Nonemployed Wife Households Wife	Husband	Teen
12-17	$7,405	$3,110	$1,629	$13,330	$2,073	1,481
6-11	12,737	2,962	2,518	14,662	3,258	2,370
2-5	15,107	4,147	*	15,847	2,814	1,481

3 Children Age of Youngest Child	Wife	Husband	Teen	Wife	Husband	Teen
1	17,032	4,739	*	17,180	3,258	2,073
Under 1	12,885	4,147	*	19,698	2,962	*

4 Children Age of Youngest Child						
12-17	$12,885	$2,814	$2,518	$12,441	$2,073	1,481
6-11	10,664	2,073	1,629	15,847	2,814	1,629
2-5	*	*	*	17,773	2,962	1,629
1	*	*	*	17,477	3,851	1,185
Under 1	*	*	*	20,291	3,851	*

5 - 6 Children Age of Youngest Child						
12-17	*	*	*	†	†	†
6-11	*	*	*	$17,032	$2,962	2,518
2-5	*	*	*	1,777	3,111	1,333
1	*	*	*	14,662	1,037	*
Under 1	*	*	*	20,142	3,851	1,481

7 - 9 Children Age of Youngest Child						
6-11	†	†	†	*	*	*
2-5	*	*	*	$17,625	$4,295	2,073
1	†	†	†	*	*	*
Under 1	†	†	†	22,512	3,851	*

* Average not calculated because there are fewer than 4 cases.

† No cases.

Consumer Price Index
Average Percentage Change

From To	1952	1953	1954	1955	1956	1957	1958	1959
1952								
1953	.75							
1954	.63	.50						
1955	.29	.06	-.37					

From / To	1952	1953	1954	1955	1956	1957	1958	1959
1956	.59	.54	.56	1.50				
1957	1.19	1.30	1.56	2.53	3.56			
1958	1.44	1.58	1.85	2.60	3.15	2.73		
1959	1.35	1.45	1.64	2.15	2.37	1.77	.81	
1960	1.39	1.48	1.64	2.04	2.18	1.71	1.21	1.60
1961	1.34	1.42	1.55	1.87	1.94	1.54	1.14	1.31
1962	1.32	1.38	1.49	1.76	1.81	1.45	1.14	1.24
1963	1.31	1.37	1.46	1.69	1.72	1.41	1.15	1.24
1964	1.31	1.36	1.45	1.65	1.67	1.40	1.18	1.25
1965	1.34	1.39	1.47	1.66	1.68	1.44	1.26	1.33
1966	1.45	1.50	1.59	1.77	1.79	1.60	1.46	1.55
1967	1.55	1.60	1.69	1.86	1.89	1.73	1.61	1.71
1968	1.71	1.78	1.87	2.04	2.08	1.95	1.87	1.99
1969	1.93	2.00	2.10	2.28	2.34	2.24	2.19	2.33
1970	2.15	2.23	2.34	2.52	2.59	2.52	2.50	2.66
1971	2.26	2.35	2.45	2.63	2.71	2.65	2.64	2.79
1972	2.31	2.40	2.50	2.67	2.74	2.69	2.69	2.83
1973	2.50	2.59	2.70	2.87	2.95	2.91	2.92	3.07
1974	2.89	2.99	3.11	3.29	3.39	3.38	3.43	3.60
1975	3.16	3.27	3.40	3.59	3.70	3.70	3.76	3.95
1976	3.27	3.38	3.51	3.69	3.80	3.81	3.87	4.05
1977	3.39	3.50	3.63	3.82	3.93	3.95	4.01	4.19
1978	3.56	3.67	3.80	3.98	4.10	4.12	4.19	4.37
1979	3.84	3.96	4.10	4.29	4.41	4.45	4.53	4.71
1980	4.19	4.32	4.46	4.66	4.79	4.84	4.94	5.13
1981	4.40	4.53	4.68	4.88	5.01	5.07	5.17	5.37
1982	4.46	4.59	4.73	4.92	5.05	5.11	5.21	5.40
1983	4.42	4.54	4.68	4.86	4.99	5.04	5.13	5.31
1984	4.41	4.53	4.67	4.84	4.96	5.01	5.10	5.27
1985	4.39	4.50	4.63	4.80	4.91	4.96	5.04	5.21

From / To	1960	1961	1962	1963	1964	1965	1966	1967
1961	1.01							
1962	1.07	1.12						
1963	1.11	1.17	1.21					
1964	1.16	1.21	1.26	1.31				
1965	1.28	1.34	1.42	1.52	1.72			
1966	1.54	1.64	1.78	1.96	2.29	2.86		
1967	1.73	1.85	2.00	2.19	2.49	2.87	2.88	
1968	2.04	2.19	2.36	2.59	2.92	3.31	3.54	4.20
1969	2.41	2.58	2.79	3.06	3.41	3.83	4.15	4.79
1970	2.76	2.95	3.18	3.47	3.83	4.25	4.59	5.16

From / To	1960	1961	1962	1963	1964	1965	1966	1967
1971	2.90	3.09	3.31	3.57	3.89	4.26	4.53	4.95
1972	2.93	3.11	3.31	3.54	3.82	4.12	4.33	4.62
1973	3.19	3.37	3.57	3.81	4.09	4.38	4.60	4.89
1974	3.74	3.95	4.19	4.46	4.77	5.11	5.40	5.76
1975	4.10	4.32	4.57	4.85	5.17	5.52	5.81	6.18
1976	4.21	4.42	4.66	4.92	5.22	5.54	5.81	6.13
1977	4.34	4.55	4.78	5.03	5.32	5.62	5.87	6.16
1978	4.52	4.73	4.96	5.20	5.48	5.77	6.02	6.30
1979	4.88	5.09	5.33	5.58	5.87	6.16	6.42	6.71
1980	5.31	5.54	5.78	6.05	6.35	6.65	6.93	7.24
1981	5.55	5.78	6.02	6.29	6.58	6.89	7.16	7.46
1982	5.58	5.79	6.03	6.28	6.56	6.84	7.09	7.37
1983	5.47	5.68	5.89	6.13	6.38	6.64	6.86	7.11
1984	5.42	5.62	5.82	6.04	6.28	6.52	6.72	6.94
1985	5.35	5.53	5.72	5.93	6.15	6.37	6.55	6.76

From / To	1968	1969	1970	1971	1972	1973	1974	1975
1969	5.37							
1970	5.65	5.92						
1971	5.20	5.11	4.30					
1972	4.72	4.51	3.80	3.30				
1973	5.02	4.94	4.61	4.76	6.23			
1974	6.01	6.14	6.20	6.83	8.60	10.97		
1975	6.46	6.64	6.79	7.41	8.78	10.05	9.14	
1976	6.37	6.52	6.62	7.08	8.03	8.63	7.45	5.77
1977	6.38	6.51	6.59	6.98	7.71	8.08	7.12	6.11
1978	6.51	6.64	6.73	7.07	7.70	8.00	7.25	6.63
1979	6.94	7.10	7.23	7.60	8.21	8.54	8.06	7.78
1980	7.49	7.68	7.86	8.25	8.87	9.25	8.97	8.93
1981	7.71	7.91	8.09	8.47	9.04	9.39	9.17	9.17
1982	7.60	7.77	7.92	8.25	8.75	9.03	8.79	8.74
1983	7.31	7.45	7.56	7.83	8.25	8.45	8.17	8.05
1984	7.12	7.23	7.33	7.56	7.91	8.07	7.78	7.63
1985	6.91	7.00	7.08	7.27	7.58	7.69	7.40	7.22

From / To	1976	1977	1978	1979	1980	1981	1982	1983
1977	6.45							
1978	7.06	7.66						
1979	8.46	9.46	11.26					
1980	9.72	10.81	12.39	13.52				
1981	9.85	10.70	11.72	11.95	10.37			
1982	9.23	9.79	10.32	10.01	8.25	6.13		

From	1976	1977	1978	1979	1980	1981	1982	1983
To								
1983	8.37	8.69	8.90	8.31	6.57	4.67	3.22	
1984	7.86	8.06	8.13	7.50	5.99	4.53	3.74	4.26
1985	7.38	7.50	7.48	6.84	5.51	4.29	3.68	3.91

From	1984	1985
To		
1985	3.57	

Average Return One-Year Treasury Bills

From	1952	1953	1954	1955	1956	1957	1958	1959
1952	1.84							
1953	1.98	2.11						
1954	1.63	1.52	.93					
1955	1.70	1.66	1.43	1.93				
1956	1.94	1.97	1.92	2.42	2.91			
1957	2.23	2.31	2.36	2.83	3.29	3.66		
1958	2.22	2.28	2.31	2.66	2.90	2.90	2.13	
1959	2.48	2.57	2.64	2.98	3.25	3.36	3.21	4.29
1960	2.61	2.70	2.79	3.10	3.33	3.44	3.36	3.98
1961	2.64	2.72	2.80	3.07	3.26	3.33	3.24	3.61
1962	2.68	2.76	2.83	3.07	3.23	3.29	3.21	3.49
1963	2.74	2.82	2.89	3.11	3.26	3.31	3.25	3.47
1964	2.83	2.91	2.98	3.19	3.33	3.38	3.34	3.54
1965	2.93	3.01	3.09	3.28	3.42	3.47	3.45	3.64
1966	3.09	3.18	3.26	3.45	3.59	3.66	3.66	3.85
1967	3.20	3.29	3.38	3.57	3.70	3.78	3.79	3.97
1968	3.35	3.45	3.54	3.72	3.86	3.94	3.97	4.15
1969	3.57	3.67	3.77	3.96	4.11	4.20	4.24	4.44
1970	3.75	3.86	3.96	4.15	4.30	4.39	4.45	4.64
1971	3.81	3.91	4.01	4.19	4.33	4.43	4.48	4.66
1972	3.86	3.97	4.06	4.24	4.37	4.46	4.52	4.69
1973	4.03	4.14	4.24	4.41	4.55	4.65	4.71	4.88
1974	4.22	4.33	4.43	4.61	4.75	4.85	4.92	5.10
1975	4.32	4.43	4.54	4.71	4.85	4.95	5.02	5.19
1976	4.38	4.49	4.59	4.76	4.89	4.99	5.06	5.23
1977	4.45	4.55	4.65	4.82	4.95	5.04	5.11	5.27
1978	4.59	4.70	4.80	4.97	5.10	5.20	5.27	5.43
1979	4.82	4.93	5.03	5.20	5.33	5.44	5.52	5.68
1980	5.07	5.19	5.30	5.47	5.61	5.72	5.81	5.98
1981	5.41	5.53	5.65	5.83	5.98	6.10	6.20	6.38
1982	5.63	5.76	5.89	6.06	6.22	6.34	6.45	6.63
1983	5.76	5.89	6.01	6.19	6.34	6.47	6.57	6.75
1984	5.92	6.05	6.17	6.35	6.50	6.63	6.74	6.92
1985	5.97	6.10	6.22	6.39	6.54	6.67	6.78	6.95

From / To	1960	1961	1962	1963	1964	1965	1966	1967
1960	3.66							
1961	3.28	2.89						
1962	3.22	3.00	3.10					
1963	3.27	3.13	3.25	3.41				
1964	3.39	3.32	3.47	3.65	3.89			
1965	3.53	3.50	3.66	3.84	4.06	4.23		
1966	3.79	3.81	3.99	4.22	4.49	4.79	5.34	
1967	3.93	3.97	4.15	4.36	4.60	4.84	5.14	4.94
1968	4.14	4.20	4.38	4.59	4.83	5.07	5.35	5.35
1969	4.45	4.54	4.74	4.98	5.24	5.51	5.83	5.99
1970	4.68	4.78	4.99	5.22	5.48	5.75	6.05	6.23
1971	4.70	4.79	4.98	5.19	5.41	5.63	5.86	5.96
1972	4.72	4.81	4.98	5.17	5.37	5.55	5.74	5.80
1973	4.92	5.02	5.20	5.39	5.58	5.77	5.96	6.05
1974	5.15	5.26	5.44	5.63	5.83	6.03	6.23	6.34
1975	5.25	5.35	5.53	5.72	5.91	6.09	6.28	6.38
1976	5.28	5.38	5.55	5.72	5.90	6.07	6.24	6.33
1977	5.33	5.42	5.58	5.75	5.91	6.07	6.22	6.30
1978	5.49	5.59	5.75	5.91	6.08	6.24	6.39	6.48
1979	5.75	5.86	6.03	6.20	6.37	6.54	6.71	6.81
1980	6.06	6.18	6.35	6.53	6.72	6.90	7.07	7.20
1981	6.47	6.61	6.79	6.99	7.19	7.38	7.58	7.73
1982	6.73	6.87	7.06	7.26	7.46	7.66	7.86	8.02
1983	6.85	6.99	7.18	7.37	7.57	7.77	7.96	8.12
1984	7.02	7.16	7.35	7.54	7.74	7.93	8.12	8.28
1985	7.05	7.19	7.37	7.55	7.74	7.92	8.11	8.25

From / To	1968	1969	1970	1971	1972	1973	1974	1975
1968	5.76							
1969	6.52	7.28						
1970	6.66	7.11	6.94					
1971	6.22	6.37	5.92	4.90				
1972	5.98	6.03	5.62	4.96	5.01			
1973	6.24	6.33	6.10	5.82	6.28	7.54		
1974	6.54	6.67	6.55	6.45	6.97	7.95	8.35	
1975	6.56	6.68	6.58	6.50	6.90	7.54	7.54	6.72
1976	6.48	6.57	6.47	6.39	6.69	7.11	6.97	6.28
1977	6.44	6.52	6.42	6.35	6.59	6.90	6.74	6.21
1978	6.62	6.70	6.64	6.60	6.84	7.15	7.07	6.75
1979	6.97	7.08	7.05	7.07	7.34	7.67	7.69	7.56
1980	7.37	7.50	7.52	7.58	7.88	8.24	8.34	8.34
1981	7.92	8.09	8.16	8.27	8.61	9.01	9.19	9.31
1982	8.23	8.40	8.49	8.62	8.96	9.35	9.55	9.70

From To	1968	1969	1970	1971	1972	1973	1974	1975
1983	8.31	8.49	8.57	8.70	9.01	9.38	9.56	9.70
1984	8.47	8.64	8.73	8.86	9.17	9.51	9.69	9.83
1985	8.44	8.59	8.68	8.79	9.07	9.38	9.54	9.64

From To	1976	1977	1978	1979	1980	1981	1982	1983
1976	5.84							
1977	5.95	6.06						
1978	6.76	7.22	8.39					
1979	7.77	8.42	9.60	10.80				
1980	8.66	9.37	10.47	11.51	12.22			
1981	9.74	10.52	11.64	12.72	13.68	15.13		
1982	10.13	10.84	11.80	12.65	13.27	13.79	12.45	
1983	10.07	10.67	11.44	12.05	12.36	12.41	11.05	9.65
1984	10.17	10.71	11.38	11.88	12.09	12.06	11.04	10.33
1985	9.94	10.39	10.93	11.30	11.38	11.21	10.23	9.49

From To	1984	1985
1984	11.01	
1985	9.41	7.81

Revised Equivalency Scale for Urban Families of Different Sizes, Ages, and Composition

(A 4-person family: husband, age 35-54; wife; 2 children, older child 6-15 years of age equals 100%)

Age of Head Size and Type of Family	Under 35	35-54	55-64	65+
One Person	35	36	32	28
Two Persons: Average	47	59	59	52
Husband, wife	49	60	59	51
One parent, one child	40	57	60	58
Three Persons: Average	62	81	86	77
Husband, wife (child under 6)	62	69	—	—
Husband, wife (child 6-15)	62	82	88	81
Husband, wife (child 16-17)	—	91	88	77
Husband, wife (child over 18)	—	82	85	77
One parent, 2 children	67	76	82	75

Age of Head Size and Type of Family	Under 35	35-54	55-64	65+
Four Persons: Average	74	99	109	91
Husband, wife (child under 6)	72	80	—	—
Husband, wife (older child 6-15)	77	100	105	95
Husband, wife (older child 16-17)	—	113	125	—
Husband, wife (older child over 18)	—	96	110	89
One parent, three children	88	96	—	—
Five Persons: Average	94	118	124	—
Husband, wife (child under 6)	87	97	—	—
Husband, wife (older child 6-15)	96	116	120	—
Husband, wife (older child 16-17)	—	128	138	—
Husband, wife (older child over 18)	—	119	124	—
One parent, four children	108	117	—	—
Six Persons: Average	111	138	143	—
Husband, wife (child under 6)	101	—	—	—
Husband, wife (older child 6-15)	110	132	140	—
Husband, wife (older child 16-17)	—	146	—	—
Husband, wife (older child over 18)	—	149	—	—
One parent, five children	125	137	—	—

§18.10   Cross-Examination

The purpose of examining the four reports is to determine how the methodology of the economist may have changed over time. The reason for the changes should be determined.

The report in Example 1 (§18.03) is signed by an economist. The letterhead is the economist's home address, and the signature does not indicate whether the economist has a Ph.D.

The present value of household services and the present value of the wage is calculated using the historic real return earned on passbook savings, long-term government securities and when earnings equal inflation. There is no discussion of how the income figures grow in the future, if at all. Likewise, there is no discussion of other factors which could affect the present value of the income stream.

The second example report (§18.05) is signed by the economist, but a university is shown as the return address. Apparently the economist is employed by the university. It is probably worthwhile to determine if the employment is on a full-time or part-time basis. Often a university address implies an objectivity that is not well founded.

The present value formula employed by the economist is stated in the report. The growth rate of wages and medical expenses are mentioned. The growth rates and discount rates are treated as spreads, which is the same methodology used in Example 1. However, only one investment vehicle is used in Example 2. There is no discussion of the investment in passbook savings or long-term government securities.

Wages are calculated to age 65, with no allowance for unemployment or early retirement. Medical expenses are calculated to life expectancy.

The return address in Example 3 (§18.07) indicates an active consulting business. There is no way to tell if the economist has continued his or her association with the university. However, the economist has completed a Ph.D.

The report does state the present value formula, and a bibliography is included in the report. One investment vehicle is employed, the short-term government security. The present value of wages are calculated to age 65. The economist assumes no interruption in labor force activities.

Medical expenses are no longer calculated to life expectancy. The medical expense is calculated each year and adjusted each year for the probability of living. The economist has purchased, or at least has access to, a computer. Printouts are now included in the reports.

Tables have been included to enhance the report. The tables on the Consumer Price Index, the Medical Price Index, and the average return on the one-year Treasury Bill permit the determination of alternative growth and discount rates.

Included, but not used in the report, are tables on participation rates, employment rates, consumption, and household services.

The report in Example 4 (§18.09) is essentially the same as Example 3. The wage has been changed, and male participation and employment rates are used instead of female participation and employment rates.

It appears the economist has experience with evaluation processes. The cross-examination should focus on (1) why a lower growth rate for wages and medical expenses and higher interest rate were not used; (2) why a worklife expectancy table which would indicate retirement prior to age 65 was not considered; (3) why the present value figures did not allow for personal consumption; (4) why the evaluation did not consider state and federal income taxes; and (5) whether any consideration was given to the economic benefit of possible remarriage in the wrongful death cases. Finally, it can be pointed out that these are purely statistical analyses. Each of the analyses would be equally applicable to any person described in the background sections of the reports.

19

Worksheet for Estimating Present Value

§19.01 Introduction

The purpose of this chapter is to develop a worksheet to permit the attorney to calculate the present value of the economic loss. There is a worksheet for calculating the loss using the basic analysis and a worksheet for calculating the loss using the extended analysis.

The formula for calculating of economic loss using the basic analysis is:

$$\text{Present Value} = \$ * \sum_{t=0}^{n} [(1+g)^t/(1+d)^t]$$

The formula for the extended analysis is:

$$\text{Present Value} = \sum_{t=0}^{n} \$ * M * [(1+g)^t/(1+d)^t] * PL * PS * PF * C * TX * HHS$$

Where:

"$" represents the beginning earnings or expenses

"M" represents the modification to lost income due to a disability

"g" represents the annual growth rate of the dollars

"d" represents the annual interest rate, or discount rate, used to reduce the future dollar stream to present value

"t" represents the number of years into the future the analysis occurs

"PL" represents the probability an individual will live each successive year. This is the mortality adjustment

"PS" represents the probability an individual will seek employment

"PF" represents the probability an individual will find employment

"C" represents individual consumption

"HS" represents household services

"TX" represents personal income taxes

§19.02   Fact Situation

Mr. Jones, a Caucasian male, was totally disabled on his thirty-sixth birthday. Today is his thirty-seventh birthday. The birthdays are assumed in order to avoid the calculation of partial years. Had Mr. Jones not been injured, he would be currently earning $9 per hour plus $1 per hour in fringe benefits.

Mr. Jones performed the "normal" household services for a man who is married. The Jones' have no children.

The growth rate of wages in the future is 4 per cent annually, and the discount rate is assumed to be 6 per cent annually. The goal of the rest of the chapter is to demonstrate how the present value is calculated and not to argue whether the assumed growth rates, discount rates, salary, and fringe benefits are correct.

§19.03 Calculating Present Value of Future Income Using the Basic Analysis

The formula for calculating the present value of future loss using the basic analysis is:

$$\text{Present Value} = \$ * \sum_{t=0}^{n} [(1+g)^t/(1+d)^t]$$

Substituting the information in **§19.02** into the formula gives:

$$\text{Present Value} = \sum_{t=0}^{n} \$18.720 * [(1 + .04)^t/ (1 + .06)^t]$$

The formula states a payment, or salary, is received today, period 0, and there are 27 future payments. The first payment is $18,720. The future payments are to grow at 4 per cent annually and to be discounted at 6 per cent annually.

Recall from Chapter 7 that the expression below is a present value factor and can be found in Appendix C.

$$\sum_{t=0}^{n} [(1 + .04)^t/(1 + .06)^t]$$

Turn to the part in Appendix C headed YEAR 27. Read down the column headed "4% growth rate" until it intersects with the row "6% discount rate." Where the two intersect is the appropriate present value factor. In this case the factor is 20.91. Thus, the present value of the future wage is $18,720 for the first year plus $18,720 times 20.91 or $391,435. The present value of the total income, $410,155, is the sum of the current, or first year's, income, $18,720, plus the present value of the future income, $391,435.

§19.04 Worksheet for Calculating Present Value of Future Income Using the Basic Analysis

The following worksheet can be used to compute the present value of future income.

Basic Worksheet 19-1
Basic Analysis
Present Value of Income

I. Current Income
    A. Current annual income is   _____
    B. 65 minus the client's
        age equals _____.
        (This number is the year
        number in Appendix C.)

II.   Growth and Discount
    A.   The expected rate of
       growth of wages is _____.
       (This is the column number
       in Appendix C.)
    B.   The expected discount
       rate is _____.
       (This is the row number
       in Appendix C.)

III.   Present Value of Future Income
    A.   The present value factor is
       found in Appendix C. It is
       on the year number stated in
       I-B. _____.
    B.   The factor is where the
       column stated in II-A
       and the row stated
       in II-B intersect. The
       present value factor
       is _____.
    C.   The present value of future
       income is the current income,
       stated in I-A, times the present
       value factor, stated in III-B.
       The present value of the
       future income is
       _____ times _____
       equals   ========

IV.   Total Present Value
    The total present value of income
    is the sum of the two values
    (I-A plus III-C).   _____

§19.05   —Filling in the Worksheet to Calculate Present Value of Future Income Using the Basic Analysis

The following worksheet is filled in using the information provided in §19.02.

Basic Worksheet 19-2
Basic Analysis
Present Value of Income

I.   Current Income
    A.   Current annual income is $18,720

B. 65 minus the client's
age equals 27.
(This number is the year
number in Appendix C.)

II. Growth and Discount
A. The expected rate of
growth of wages is 4%.
(This is the column number
in Appendix C.)
B. The expected discount
rate is 6%.
(This is the row number
in Appendix C.)

III. Present Value of Future Income
A. The present value factor is
found in Appendix C. It is
on the year number stated in
I-B. 27.
B. The factor is where the
column stated in II-A
and the row stated
in II-B intersect. The
present value factor
is 20.91.
C. The present value of future
income is the current income,
stated in I-A, times the present
value factor, stated in III-B.
The present value of the
future income is
$18,720 times 20.91 equals $391,435

IV. Total Present Value
The total present value of income
is the sum of the two values $410,155
(I-A plus III-C).

§19.06 —A Second Example for Calculating Present Value of Future Income Using the Basic Analysis

The client is a 25-year-old black male earning $20,000 per year. The appropriate growth and discount rates are determined to be 2 and 4 per cent, respectively. The completed worksheet appears as follows:

Basic Worksheet 19-3
Basic Analysis
Present Value Future Income

I. Current Income
    A. Current annual income is $20,000
    B. 65 minus the client's
        age equals 40.
        (This number is the year
        number in Appendix C.)
II. Growth and Discount
    A. The expected rate of
        growth of wages is 2%.
        (This is the column number
        in Appendix C.)
    B. The expected discount
        rate is 4%.
        (This is the row number
        in Appendix C.)
III. Present Value of Future Income
    A. The present value factor is
        found in Appendix C. It is
        on the year number stated in
        I-B. 40.
    B. The factor is where the
        column stated in II-A
        and the row stated
        in II-B intersect. The
        present value factor
        is 27.54.
    C. The present value of future
        income is the current income,
        stated in I-A, times the present
        value factor, stated in III-B.
        The present value of the
        future income is
        $20,000 times 27.54 equals $550,800

IV. Total Present Value
    The total present value of income
    is the sum of the two values $570,800
    (I-A plus III-C).

§19.07 Calculating Present Value of Fringe Benefits Using the Basic Analysis

Using the example from §19.02, the fringe benefit was $1 per hour, or $2,080 per year. The worksheet would be filled out in the following manner:

Basic Worksheet 19-4
Basic Analysis
Present Value of Fringe Benefits

I.   Fringe Benefits
       A.   Annual fringe benefits are $2,080
       B.   65 minus the client's
            age equals 27.
            (This number is the year
            number in Appendix C.)

II.   Growth and Discount
       A.   The expected rate of
            growth of benefits is 4%.
            (This is the column number
            in Appendix C.)
       B.   The expected discount
            rate is 6%.
            (This is the row number
            in Appendix C.)

III.   Present Value of Future Benefits
       A.   The present value factor is
            found in Appendix C. It is
            on the year number stated in
            I-B. 27.
       B.   The factor is where the
            column stated in II-A
            and the row stated
            in II-B intersect. The
            present value factor
            is 20.91.
       C.   The present value of future
            benefits is the current benefits,
            stated in I-A, times the present
            value factor, stated in III-B.
            The present value of the
            future benefits is
            $2,080 times 20.91 equals $43,493

IV.   Total Present Value
       The total present value of benefits
       is the sum of the two values $45,573
       (I-A plus III-C).

Another approach is to consider the fringe benefits as a percentage of the hourly wage rate. In this case the fringe benefits package is 11.11 per cent of the hourly wage ($1.00/$9.00). The present value of the fringe benefits is 11.11 per cent of the present value of the income stream, or $45,568. The difference between the $45,568 and the $45,573 found in the worksheet is due to mathematical rounding differences.

§19.08   Calculating Present Value of Future Income Using the Extended Analysis

The extended analysis is time consuming. It is not difficult to calculate but, due to the quantity of numbers in the calculation of the present value, there is a good chance of error.

All the blanks on the worksheet must either be filled in or calculated. The columns headed "Age," "Period," "Income," "Growth Rate," "Discount Rate," "Probability of Living," "Probability of Seeking Employment," and "Probability of Finding Employment" are all columns that are filled in. The columns headed "Future Income," "Present Value," and "Adjusted Sum" must be calculated.

The worksheet will be developed using the fact situation in §19.02. Extended Worksheets 19-1A and 19-1B go together and are the worksheets used to calculate the present value of the future income.

The column "Age" will begin with the current age of the client, 37, and continue one year at a time until age 99 is reached. This means the column titled "Period," which starts at period 0, will continue until period 62. The column "Current Income" has, as the first entry, the client's annual income, which is $18,720. The value "g" in the column "Growth Rate" represents the annual rate of growth of wages, or 4 per cent annually. The value is entered as a decimal (.04). The column "Discount" is the interest assumption. In this case the discount rate is 6 per cent, and is also entered in decimal form (.06).

Extended Worksheet 19-1A
Extended Analysis
Present Value of Income

Age	Period	Current Income	Growth Rate	Future Income	Discount Rate	Present Value
Age	0	$Income	$(1+ g)^0$	$Value	$1/(1+ d)^0$	$Value
Age	1	$Income	$(1+ g)^1$	$Value	$1/(1+ d)^1$	$Value
Age	2	$Income	$(1+ g)^2$	$Value	$1/(1+ d)^2$	$Value
Age	3	$Income	$(1+ g)^3$	$Value	$1/(1+ d)^3$	$Value
Age	4	$Income	$(1+ g)^4$	$Value	$1/(1+ d)^4$	$Value
Age	5	$Income	$(1+ g)^5$	$Value	$1/(1+ d)^5$	$Value
.	.	.	.	.	.	.
.	.	.	.	.	.	.
.	.	.	.	.	.	.
.	.	.	.	.	.	.
Age	62	$Income	$(1+ g)^t$	$Value	$1/(1+ d)^t$	$Value

Extended Worksheet 19-1B
Extended Analysis
Present Value of Income

Age	Period	Present Value	Probability of Living	Participation Rate	Employment Rate	Adjusted Sum	Adjusted Total
Age	Per	$Income	Prob L	Part R	EmpRa	Adj Sum	Total
Age	Per	$Income	Prob L	Part R	EmpRa	Adj Sum	Total
Age	Per	$Income	Prob L	Part R	EmpRa	Adj Sum	Total
Age	Per	$Income	Prob L	Part R	EmpRa	Adj Sum	Total
Age	Per	$Income	Prob L	Part R	EmpRa	Adj Sum	Total
Age	Per	$Income	Prob L	Part R	EmpRa	Adj Sum	Total
Age	Per	$Income	Prob L	Part R	EmpRa	Adj Sum	Total
.	.	.	.	.	.	.	.
.	.	.	.	.	.	.	.
.	.	.	.	.	.	.	.
.	.	.	.	.	.	.	.
Age	Per	$Income	Prob L	Part R	EmpRa	Adj Sum	Total

The first three columns in Extended Worksheet 19-1B are found in Extended Worksheet 19-1A. The columns for probability of living, participation rate, and employment rate are found in Appendixes E and F.

The probability that Mr. Jones will live to any given age depends on his current age, 37, and which mortality table is employed. The table employed here is the United States White Male (Appendix F). The probabilities of living to each successive age are found in the table headed "Probability of Surviving through Age 'X' Starting from Age 37." Under the column headed "White Male" the probability 99.603 appears across from age 38. This is the probability of a 37-year-old white male living to age 38. It is read 99.603 per cent.

With respect to the worksheet, the probability that Mr. Jones will reach 37 is 1. He is 37. Therefore, under the heading "Probability of Living," and on the row where the age is 37, the probability of 1 is entered. From Appendix F the probability of 99.603 per cent is entered on the row for age 38. The entry will appear .99603. In a similar fashion, the rest of the worksheet is completed.

The figures presented by the fact situation in §19.02 have been filled in on Worksheets 19-2A and 19-2B. No calculations have been performed in the worksheets.

Extended Worksheet 19-2A
Extended Analysis
Present Value of Income

Age	Period	Current Income	Growth Rate	Future Income	Discount Rate	Present Value
37	0	$18,720	$(1+.04)^0$	$Value	$1/(1+.06)^0$	$Value
38	1	$18,720	$(1+.04)^1$	$Value	$1/(1+.06)^1$	$Value
39	2	$18,720	$(1+.04)^2$	$Value	$1/(1+.06)^2$	$Value
40	3	$18,720	$(1+.04)^3$	$Value	$1/(1+.06)^3$	$Value

Age	Period	Current Income	Growth Rate	Future Income	Discount Rate	Present Value
41	4	$18,720	$(1+.04)^4$	$Value	$1/(1+.06)^4$	$Value
42	5	$18,720	$(1+.04)^5$	$Value	$1/(1+.06)^5$	$Value
43	6	$18,720	$(1+.04)^6$	$Value	$1/(1+.06)^6$	$Value
44	7	$18,720	$(1+.04)^7$	$Value	$1/(1+.06)^7$	$Value
45	8	$18,720	$(1+.04)^8$	$Value	$1/(1+.06)^8$	$Value
46	9	$18,720	$(1+.04)^9$	$Value	$1/(1+.06)^9$	$Value
.	.	.	.	.	.	.
.	.	.	.	.	.	.
.	.	.	.	.	.	.
99	62	$18,720	$(1+.04)^{62}$	$Value	$1/(1+.06)^{62}$	$Value

Extended Worksheet 19-2B
Extended Analysis
Present Value of Income

Age	Period	Present Value	Probability of Living	Participation Rate	Employment Rate	Adjusted Sum	Adjusted Total
37	0	$Income	1.0000	1.0	1.0	Adj Sum	Total
38	1	Income	.99603	.9720	.970	Adj Sum	Total
39	2	Income	.99383	.9720	.970	Adj Sum	Total
40	3	Income	.99145	.9720	.970	Adj Sum	Total
41	4	Income	.98884	.9720	.970	Adj Sum	Total
42	5	Income	.98598	.9720	.970	Adj Sum	Total
43	6	Income	.98284	.9720	.970	Adj Sum	Total
44	7	Income	.97937	.9720	.970	Adj Sum	Total
45	8	Income	.97554	.9460	.969	Adj Sum	Total
46	9	Income	.97130	.9460	.969	Adj Sum	Total
.	.	.	.	.	.	.	.
.	.	.	.	.	.	.	.
.	.	.	.	.	.	.	.
99	62	Income	.00010	.2710	.9622	Adj Sum	Total

As the worksheets show, there are only three calculations necessary. First, the future income must be calculated in Worksheet 19-2A. The column "Future Income" shows to what level the annual income will grow. The future income is the current income growing at the stated growth rate. The growth is compounded annually. This calculation can be done with a hand-held calculator if the calculator has a *power function key*. The power function key is:

$$Y^x$$

The following procedure may be followed to calculate the future income:

Step 1.   Enter 1.04.

Step   2.   Press Yˣ key.
Step   3.   Press the number in the column headed "Period" (0).
Step   4.   Press =. (The value displayed is 1.00.)
Step   5.   Press × (multiplication key).
Step   6.   Enter $18,720.
Step   7.   Press =.

The value displayed is $18,720, which is the same as the current income. This will always occur when the exponent is "0." The exponent "0" means today. Following the same steps when the period is "1" gives the following results:

Step   1.   Enter 1.04.
Step   2.   Press Yˣ key.
Step   3.   Press the period number (1).
Step   4.   Press =. (The value displayed is 1.04.)
Step   5.   Press × (multiplication key).
Step   6.   Enter $18,720.
Step   7.   Press =.

The value displayed is $19,469. This is the income Mr. Jones can expect to be earning in one year. Following the same procedure for year 3, when the period or exponent value is 3, gives the following results:

Step   1.   Enter 1.04.
Step   2.   Press Yˣ key.
Step   3.   Press the period number (3).
Step   4.   Press =. (The value displayed is 1.125.)
Step   5.   Press × (multiplication key).
Step   6.   Enter $18,720.
Step   7.   Press =.

The value displayed is $21,057. This number is entered in the worksheet under the heading "Future Value" on the row for Period 3 (see Extended Worksheet 19-3A). Just to make sure the process is correct, the calculation will be done for when Mr. Jones is 99, or for period 62.

Step   1.   Enter 1.04.
Step   2.   Press Yˣ key.
Step   3.   Press the period number (62).
Step   4.   Press =. (The value displayed is 11.378.)
Step   5.   Press "×" (multiplication)
Step   6.   Enter $18,720
Step   7.   Press "="

The value displayed is $212,997. This is the future value of $18,720 if it grows at 4 per cent per year for 62 years.

Extended Worksheet 19-3A
Extended Analysis
Present Value of Income

Age	Period	Current Income	Growth Rate	Future Income	Discount Rate	Present Value
37	0	$18,720	$(1+.04)^0$	$18.720	$1/(1+.06)^0$	$Value
38	1	$18,720	$(1+.04)^1$	19,469	$1/(1+.06)^1$	$Value
39	2	$18,720	$(1+.04)^2$	20,248	$1/(1+.06)^2$	$Value
40	3	$18,720	$(1+.04)^3$	21,057	$1/(1+.06)^3$	$Value
41	4	$18,720	$(1+.04)^4$	21,900	$1/(1+.06)^4$	$Value
42	5	$18,720	$(1+.04)^5$	22,776	$1/(1+.06)^5$	$Value
43	6	$18,720	$(1+.04)^6$	23,687	$1/(1+.06)^6$	$Value
44	7	$18,720	$(1+.04)^7$	24,634	$1/(1+.06)^7$	$Value
45	8	$18,720	$(1+.04)^8$	25,620	$1/(1+.06)^8$	$Value
46	9	$18,720	$(1+.04)^9$	26,644	$1/(1+.06)^9$	$Value
.	.	.	.	.	.	.
.	.	.	.	.	.	.
.	.	.	.	.	.	.
.	.	.	.	.	.	.
99	62	$18,720	$(1+.04)^{62}$	212,997	$1/(1+.06)^{62}$	$Value

Extended Worksheet 19-3B
Extended Analysis
Present Value of Income

Age	Period	Present Value	Probability of Living	Participation Rate	Employment Rate	Adjusted Sum	Adjusted Total
37	0	$Income	1.0000	1.0	1.0	Adj Sum	Total
38	1	Income	.99603	.9720	.970	Adj Sum	Total
39	2	Income	.99383	.9720	.970	Adj Sum	Total
40	3	Income	.99145	.9720	.970	Adj Sum	Total
41	4	Income	.98884	1.0	.970	Adj Sum	Total
42	5	Income	.98598	.9720	.970	Adj Sum	Total
43	6	Income	.98284	.9720	.970	Adj Sum	Total
44	7	Income	.97937	.9720	.970	Adj Sum	Total
45	8	Income	.97554	.9460	.9690	Adj Sum	Total
46	9	Income	.97130	.9460	.9690	Adj Sum	Total

Age	Period	Present Value	Probability of Living	Participation Rate	Employment Rate	Adjusted Sum	Adjusted Total
.	.	.	.	.	.	.	.
.	.	.	.	.	.	.	.
.	.	.	.	.	.	.	.
99	62	Income	.00010	.2710	.9620	Adj Sum	Total

The next step is to calculate the present value of the future income. This, too, can be accomplished by using the power function key. As before, when the exponent is "0," the value of the expression becomes "1." Therefore, the present value of the income in period "0" is $18,720.

The following steps can be followed in calculating the present value of the future income. Recall the discount rate is 6 per cent:

Step 1. Enter 1.06.
Step 2. Press Y^x key.
Step 3. Press the period number (1).
Step 4. Press =. (The value displayed is 1.06.)
Step 5. Press the key 1/X.
Step 6. Press =. (The value displayed is .9434.)
Step 7. Press × (multiplication key).
Step 8. Enter $19,469 (the future value in period 1).
Step 9. Press =.

The value displayed is $18,367. This is the present value of the income received in Period 1.

If the period being examined is Period 4, then the results are:

Step 1. Enter 1.06.
Step 2. Press Y^x key.
Step 3. Press the period number (4).
Step 4. Press =. (The value displayed is 1.262.)
Step 5. Press the key 1/×.
Step 6. Press =. (The value displayed is .7921.)
Step 7. Press × (multiplication key).
Step 8. Enter $21,900, the future value in Period 4.
Step 9. Press =.

The value displayed is $17,347. This is the present value of the income received in four years. Worksheet 19-4A shows the calculation of the present values of the future incomes. The same process is followed when the exponent is 62. The present value of $212,997 received in 62 years and discounted at 6 per cent annually is $5,747.

Extended Worksheet 19-4A
Extended Analysis
Present Value of Income

Age	Period	Current Income	Growth Rate	Future Income	Discount Rate	Present Value
37	0	$18,720	$(1+.04)^0$	$18,720	$1/(1+.06)^0$	$18,720
38	1	$18,720	$(1+.04)^1$	19,469	$1/(1+.06)^1$	18,367
39	2	$18,720	$(1+.04)^2$	20,248	$1/(1+.06)^2$	18,020
40	3	$18,720	$(1+.04)^3$	21,057	$1/(1+.06)^3$	17,680
41	4	$18,720	$(1+.04)^4$	21,900	$1/(1+.06)^4$	17,347
42	5	$18,720	$(1+.04)^5$	22,776	$1/(1+.06)^5$	17,019

Age	Period	Current Income	Growth Rate	Future Income	Discount Rate	Present Value
43	6	$18,720	$(1+.04)^6$	23,687	$1/(1+.06)^6$	16,698
44	7	$18,720	$(1+.04)^7$	24,634	$1/(1+.06)^7$	16,383
45	8	$18,720	$(1+.04)^8$	25,620	$1/(1+.06)^8$	16,074
46	9	$18,720	$(1+.04)^9$	26,644	$1/(1+.06)^9$	15,774
.	.	.	.	.	.	.
.	.	.	.	.	.	.
.	.	.	.	.	.	.
99	62	$18,720	$(1+.04)^{62}$	212,997	$1/(1+.06)^{62}$	5,747

Extended Worksheet 19-4B
Extended Analysis
Present Value of Income

Age	Period	Present Value	Probability of Living	Participation Rate	Employment Rate	Adjusted Sum	Adjusted Total
37	0	$18,720	1.0000	1.00	1.00	Adj Sum	Total
38	1	18,367	.99603	.9720	.970	Adj Sum	Total
39	2	18,020	.99383	.9720	.970	Adj Sum	Total
40	3	17,680	.99145	.9720	.970	Adj Sum	Total
41	4	17,347	.98884	.9720	.970	Adj Sum	Total
42	5	17,019	.98598	.9720	.970	Adj Sum	Total
43	6	16,698	.98284	.9720	.970	Adj Sum	Total
44	7	16,383	.97937	.9720	.970	Adj Sum	Total
45	8	16,074	.97554	.9460	.969	Adj Sum	Total
46	9	15,774	.97130	.9460	.969	Adj Sum	Total
.	.	.	.	.	.	.	.
.	.	.	.	.	.	.	.
.	.	.	.	.	.	.	.
99	62	5,747	.00010	.2710	.9620	Adj Sum	Total

The final steps are to multiply across the rows and sum the results. The row for age 37 would result in the adjusted sum being equal to $18,720. The row for age 38 has an adjusted sum of $17,303. The column headed "Adjusted Total" is the running sum of the column "Adjusted Sum." During the ages of 37 and 38 Mr. Jones would have earned a total of $36,023. In the same manner the adjusted sum for age 39 is $16,898. The adjusted total for age 39 equals $52,921. The entire worksheet is completed in Worksheets 19-5A and 19-5B.

Extended Worksheet 19-5A
Extended Analysis
Present Value of Income

Age	Period	Current Income	Growth Rate	Future Income	Discount Rate	Present Value
37	0	$18,720	$(1+.04)^0$	$ 18,720	$1/(1+.06)^0$	$ 18,720
38	1	$18,720	$(1+.04)^1$	19,469	$1/(1+.06)^1$	18,367

Age	Period	Current Income	Growth Rate	Future Income	Discount Rate	Present Value
39	2	$18,720	$(1+.04)^2$	20,248	$1/(1+.06)^2$	18,020
40	3	$18,720	$(1+.04)^3$	21,057	$1/(1+.06)^3$	17,680
41	4	$18,720	$(1+.04)^4$	21,900	$1/(1+.06)^4$	17,347
42	5	$18,720	$(1+.04)^5$	22,776	$1/(1+.06)^5$	17,019
43	6	$18,720	$(1+.04)^6$	23,687	$1/(1+.06)^6$	16,698
44	7	$18,720	$(1+.04)^7$	24,634	$1/(1+.06)^7$	16,383
45	8	$18,720	$(1+.04)^8$	25,620	$1/(1+.06)^8$	16,074
46	9	$18,720	$(1+.04)^9$	26,644	$1/(1+.06)^9$	15,774
47	10	$18,720	$(1+.04)^{10}$	27,710	$1/(1+.06)^{10}$	18,720
48	11	$18,720	$(1+.04)^{11}$	19,469	$1/(1+.06)^{11}$	18,367
49	12	$18,720	$(1+.04)^{12}$	20,248	$1/(1+.06)^{12}$	18,020
50	13	$18,720	$(1+.04)^{13}$	21,057	$1/(1+.06)^{13}$	17,680
51	14	$18,720	$(1+.04)^{14}$	21,900	$1/(1+.06)^{14}$	17,347
52	15	$18,720	$(1+.04)^{15}$	22,776	$1/(1+.06)^{15}$	17,019
53	16	$18,720	$(1+.04)^{16}$	23,687	$1/(1+.06)^{16}$	16,698
54	17	$18,720	$(1+.04)^{17}$	24,634	$1/(1+.06)^{17}$	16,383
55	18	$18,720	$(1+.04)^{18}$	25,620	$1/(1+.06)^{18}$	16,074
56	19	$18,720	$(1+.04)^{19}$	26,644	$1/(1+.06)^{19}$	15,774
.	.	.	.	.	.	.
.	.	.	.	.	.	.
.	.	.	.	.	.	.
99	62	$18,720	$(1+.04)^{62}$	212,997	$1/(1+.06)^{62}$	5,747

Extended Worksheet 19-5B
Extended Analysis
Present Value of Income

Age	Period	Present Value	Probability of Living	Participation Rate	Employment Rate	Adjusted Sum	Adjusted Total
37	0	18,720	1.0000	1.000	1.000	18,720	18,720
38	1	18,367	.9960	.972	.970	17,248	35,968
39	2	18,020	.9938	.972	.970	16,885	52,854
40	3	17,680	.9914	.972	.970	16,527	69,381
41	4	17,347	.9888	.972	.970	16,173	85,553
42	5	17,019	.9859	.972	.970	15,822	101,375
43	6	16,698	.9828	.972	.970	15,473	116,848
44	7	16,383	.9793	.972	.970	15,128	131,976
45	8	16,074	.9755	.946	.969	14,374	146,350
46	9	15,771	.9713	.946	.969	14,042	160,392
47	10	15,473	.9666	.946	.969	13,710	174,102
48	11	15,181	.9614	.946	.969	13,379	187,482
49	12	14,895	.9556	.946	.969	13,048	200,529
50	13	14,614	.9492	.946	.969	12,716	213,246
51	14	14,338	.9421	.946	.969	12,384	225,629

Age	Period	Present Value	Probability of Living	Participation Rate	Employment Rate	Adjusted Sum	Adjusted Total
52	15	14,068	.9344	.946	.969	12,050	237,679
53	16	13,802	.9260	.946	.969	11,716	249,396
54	17	13,542	.9168	.946	.969	11,382	260,777
55	18	13,286	.9069	.818	.965	9,512	270,289
56	19	13,036	.8962	.818	.965	9,222	279,511
57	20	12,790	.8846	.818	.965	8,931	288,442
58	21	12,548	.8720	.818	.965	8,638	297,080
59	22	12,311	.8585	.818	.965	8,344	305,424
60	23	12,079	.8441	.818	.965	8,049	313,472
61	24	11,851	.8286	.818	.965	7,752	321,224
62	25	11,628	.8120	.818	.965	7,453	328,678
63	26	11,408	.7942	.818	.965	7,152	335,830
64	27	11,193	.7750	.818	.965	6,848	342,678
65	28	10,982	.7546	.271	.962	2,161	344,838
66	29	10,775	.7330	.271	.962	2,059	346,898
67	30	10,571	.7102	.271	.962	1,957	348,855
68	31	10,372	.6862	.271	.962	1,856	350,711
69	32	10,176	.6611	.271	.962	1,754	352,465
70	33	9,984	.6348	.271	.962	1,652	354,117
71	34	9,796	.6075	.271	.962	1,551	355,669
72	35	9,611	.5791	.271	.962	1,451	357,120
73	36	9,430	.5498	.271	.962	1,352	358,471
74	37	9,252	.5196	.271	.962	1,253	359,725
75	38	9,077	.4888	.271	.962	1,157	360,882
76	39	8,906	.4573	.271	.962	1,062	361,943
77	40	8,738	.4255	.271	.962	969	362,913
78	41	8,573	.3935	.271	.962	880	363,793
79	42	8,411	.3615	.271	.962	793	364,585
80	43	8,253	.3297	.271	.962	709	365,295
81	44	8,097	.2967	.271	.962	626	365,921
82	45	7,944	.2630	.271	.962	545	366,466
83	46	7,794	.2290	.271	.962	465	366,932
84	47	7,647	.1954	.271	.962	390	367,321
85	48	7,503	.1628	.271	.962	319	367,640
86	49	7,361	.1319	.271	.962	253	367,893
87	50	7,222	.1035	.271	.962	195	368,088
88	51	7,086	.0782	.271	.962	144	368,232
89	52	6,952	.0564	.271	.962	102	368,335
90	53	6,821	.0386	.271	.962	69	368,403
91	54	6,693	.0247	.271	.962	43	368,447
92	55	6,566	.0146	.271	.962	25	368,472
93	56	6,442	.0078	.271	.962	13	368,485
94	57	6,321	.0037	.271	.962	6	368,491
95	58	6,202	.0014	.271	.962	2	368,493
96	59	6,085	.0004	.271	.962	1	368,494
97	60	5,970	.0001	.271	.962	0	368,494

Age	Period	Present Value	Probability of Living	Participation Rate	Employment Rate	Adjusted Sum	Adjusted Total
98	61	5,857	.0000	.271	.962	0	368,494
99	62	5,747	0.0000	.271	.962	0	368,494

§19.09 Calculating Present Value of Fringe Benefits Using the Extended Analysis

The fringe benefits paid to Mr. Jones are $1.00 per hour, or $2,080 per year. Extended Worksheets 19-6A and Extended Worksheet 19-6B show the calculation of the present value of the future fringe benefits using the extended analysis. The present value totals $38,319. This loss would be in addition to the present value of the lost wages.

Extended Worksheet 19-6A
Extended Analysis
Present Value of Fringe Benefits

Age	Period	Current Income	Growth Rate	Future Income	Discount Rate	Present Value
37	0	2,080	(1+.04)	2,080	(1+.06)	2,080
38	1	2,080	(1+.04)	2,163	(1+.06)	2,041
39	2	2,080	(1+.04)	2,250	(1+.06)	2,002
40	3	2,080	(1+.04)	2,340	(1+.06)	1,964
41	4	2,080	(1+.04)	2,433	(1+.06)	1,927
42	5	2,080	(1+.04)	2,531	(1+.06)	1,891
43	6	2,080	(1+.04)	2,632	(1+.06)	1,855
44	7	2,080	(1+.04)	2,737	(1+.06)	1,820
45	8	2,080	(1+.04)	2,847	(1+.06)	1,786
46	9	2,080	(1+.04)	2,960	(1+.06)	1,752
47	10	2,080	(1+.04)	3,079	(1+.06)	1,719
48	11	2,080	(1+.04)	3,202	(1+.06)	1,687
49	12	2,080	(1+.04)	3,330	(1+.06)	1,655
50	13	2,080	(1+.04)	3,463	(1+.06)	1,624
51	14	2,080	(1+.04)	3,602	(1+.06)	1,593
52	15	2,080	(1+.04)	3,746	(1+.06)	1,563
53	16	2,080	(1+.04)	3,896	(1+.06)	1,534
54	17	2,080	(1+.04)	4,052	(1+.06)	1,505
55	18	2,080	(1+.04)	4,214	(1+.06)	1,476
56	19	2,080	(1+.04)	4,382	(1+.06)	1,448
57	20	2,080	(1+.04)	4,558	(1+.06)	1,421
58	21	2,080	(1+.04)	4,740	(1+.06)	1,394
59	22	2,080	(1+.04)	4,929	(1+.06)	1,368
60	23	2,080	(1+.04)	5,127	(1+.06)	1,342

Age	Period	Current Income	Growth Rate	Future Income	Discount Rate	Present Value
61	24	2,080	(1+.04)	5,332	(1+.06)	1,317
62	25	2,080	(1+.04)	5,545	(1+.06)	1,292
63	26	2,080	(1+.04)	5,767	(1+.06)	1,268
64	27	2,080	(1+.04)	5,997	(1+.06)	1,244
65	28	2,080	(1+.04)	6,237	(1+.06)	1,220
66	29	2,080	(1+.04)	6,487	(1+.06)	1,197
67	30	2,080	(1+.04)	6,746	(1+.06)	1,175
68	31	2,080	(1+.04)	7,016	(1+.06)	1,152
69	32	2,080	(1+.04)	7,297	(1+.06)	1,131
70	33	2,080	(1+.04)	7,589	(1+.06)	1,109
71	34	2,080	(1+.04)	7,892	(1+.06)	1,088
72	35	2,080	(1+.04)	8,208	(1+.06)	1,068
73	36	2,080	(1+.04)	8,536	(1+.06)	1,048
74	37	2,080	(1+.04)	8,878	(1+.06)	1,028
75	38	2,080	(1+.04)	9,233	(1+.06)	1,009
76	39	2,080	(1+.04)	9,602	(1+.06)	990
77	40	2,080	(1+.04)	9,986	(1+.06)	971
78	41	2,080	(1+.04)	10,386	(1+.06)	953
79	42	2,080	(1+.04)	10,801	(1+.06)	935
80	43	2,080	(1+.04)	11,233	(1+.06)	917
81	44	2,080	(1+.04)	11,682	(1+.06)	900
82	45	2,080	(1+.04)	12,150	(1+.06)	883
83	46	2,080	(1+.04)	12,636	(1+.06)	866
84	47	2,080	(1+.04)	13,141	(1+.06)	850
85	48	2,080	(1+.04)	13,667	(1+.06)	834
86	49	2,080	(1+.04)	14,213	(1+.06)	818
87	50	2,080	(1+.04)	14,782	(1+.06)	802
88	51	2,080	(1+.04)	15,373	(1+.06)	787
89	52	2,080	(1+.04)	15,988	(1+.06)	772
90	53	2,080	(1+.04)	16,628	(1+.06)	758
91	54	2,080	(1+.04)	17,293	(1+.06)	744
92	55	2,080	(1+.04)	17,984	(1+.06)	730
93	56	2,080	(1+.04)	18,704	(1+.06)	716
94	57	2,080	(1+.04)	19,452	(1+.06)	702
95	58	2,080	(1+.04)	20,230	(1+.06)	689
96	59	2,080	(1+.04)	21,039	(1+.06)	676
97	60	2,080	(1+.04)	21,881	(1+.06)	663
98	61	2,080	(1+.04)	22,756	(1+.06)	651
99	62	2,080	(1+.04)	23,666	(1+.06)	639

Extended Worksheet 19-6B
Extended Analysis
Present Value of Fringe Benefits

Age	Period	Present Value	Probability of Living	Participation Rate	Employment Rate	Adjusted Sum	Adjusted Total
37	0	2,080	1.00000	1.0000	1.0000	2,080	2,080
38	1	2,041	.99603	.9720	.9700	1,916	3,996
39	2	2,002	.99383	.9720	.9700	1,876	5,873
40	3	1,964	.99144	.9720	.9700	1,836	7,709
41	4	1,927	.98884	.9720	.9700	1,797	9,506
42	5	1,891	.98598	.9720	.9700	1,758	11,264
43	6	1,855	.98283	.9720	.9700	1,719	12,983
44	7	1,820	.97936	.9720	.9700	1,681	14,664
45	8	1,786	.97553	.9460	.9690	1,597	16,261
46	9	1,752	.97130	.9460	.9690	1,560	17,821
47	10	1,719	.96661	.9460	.9690	1,523	19,345
48	11	1,687	.96141	.9460	.9690	1,487	20,831
49	12	1,655	.95563	.9460	.9690	1,450	22,281
50	13	1,624	.94924	.9460	.9690	1,376	23,694
51	14	1,593	.94219	.9460	.9690	1,376	25,070
52	15	1,563	.93447	.9460	.9690	1,339	26,409
53	16	1,534	.92604	.9460	.9690	1,302	27,711
54	17	1,505	.91688	.9460	.9690	1,265	28,975
55	18	1,476	.90695	.8180	.9650	1,057	30,032
56	19	1,448	.89621	.8180	.9650	1,025	31,057
57	20	1,421	.88461	.8180	.9650	992	32,049
58	21	1,394	.87208	.8180	.9650	960	33,009
59	22	1,368	.85859	.8180	.9650	927	33,936
60	23	1,342	.84412	.8180	.9650	894	34,830
61	24	1,317	.82863	.8180	.9650	861	35,692
62	25	1,292	.81203	.8180	.9650	828	36,520
63	26	1,268	.79420	.8180	.9650	795	37,314
64	27	1,244	.77509	.8180	.9650	761	38,075
65	28	1,220	.75465	.2710	.9620	240	38,315
66	29	1,197	.73304	.2710	.9620	229	38,544
67	30	1,175	.71026	.2710	.9620	217	38,762
68	31	1,152	.68629	.2710	.9620	206	38,968
69	32	1,131	.66116	.2710	.9620	195	39,163
70	33	1,109	.63486	.2710	.9620	184	39,346
71	34	1,088	.60751	.2710	.9620	172	39,519
72	35	1,068	.57913	.2710	.9620	161	39,680
73	36	1,048	.54983	.2710	.9620	150	39,830
74	37	1,028	.51968	.2710	.9620	139	39,969
75	38	1,009	.48880	.2710	.9620	129	40,098
76	39	990	.45738	.2710	.9620	118	40,216
77	40	971	.42558	.2710	.9620	108	40,324

Age	Period	Present Value	Probability of Living	Participation Rate	Employment Rate	Adjusted Sum	Adjusted Total
78	41	953	.39358	.2710	.9620	98	40,421
79	42	935	.36157	.2710	.9620	88	40,509
80	43	917	.32975	.2710	.9620	79	40,588
81	44	900	.29677	.2710	.9620	70	40,658
82	45	883	.26304	.2710	.9620	61	40,718
83	46	866	.22906	.2710	.9620	52	40,770
84	47	850	.19544	.2710	.9620	43	40,813
85	48	834	.16284	.2710	.9620	35	40,849
86	49	818	.13198	.2710	.9620	28	40,877
87	50	802	.10355	.2710	.9620	22	40,899
88	51	787	.07820	.2710	.9620	16	40,915
89	52	772	.05645	.2710	.9620	11	40,926
90	53	758	.03861	.2710	.9620	8	40,934
91	54	744	.02474	.2710	.9620	5	40,939
92	55	730	.01464	.2710	.9620	3	40,941
93	56	716	.00785	.2710	.9620	1	40,943
94	57	702	.00371	.2710	.9620	1	40,943
95	58	689	.00149	.2710	.9620	0	40,944
96	59	676	.00047	.2710	.9620	0	40,944
97	60	663	.00011	.2710	.9620	0	40,944
98	61	651	.00001	.2710	.9620	0	40,944
99	62	639	0.00000	.2710	.9620	0	40,944

§19.10 —A Faster Method for Calculating Present Value of Fringe Benefits Using the Extended Analysis

Once the present value of the lost income, using the extended analysis, is computed, it is not necessary to go through the extended analysis to calculate the present value of the fringe benefits. The present value of future income is $369,195. Dividing this number by the beginning wage of $18,720 gives a present value factor of 19.72195.

The factor is the present value of $1 received each year starting today and extending for 62 future years, adjusted for the probability of living, the probability of seeking employment, and the probability of finding employment.

If the annual fringe benefit of $2,080 is multiplied by the present value factor of 19.72195, the present value of the fringe benefit is calculated to be $41,022.

This process can be followed for any calculation where the growth rate and discount rate are the same and when the probability of living, the probability of seeking, and the probability of finding employment are relevant.

§19.11 Calculating Present Value of Future Medical Expenses Using the Extended Analysis

Consider the situation where an individual has recurring annual medical expenses. From §19.02, recall that Mr. Jones was disabled. Assume that his annual medical costs are $10,000 and that the appropriate growth rate of medical expenses is 8 per cent annually. In calculating the present value of future medical expenses, only the probability of living would be included.

Extended worksheet 19-7A shows the calculation of the medical expenses, mortality-adjusted. The present value of the medical expenses is $542,208 after the mortality adjustment.

Extended Worksheet 19-7A
Extended Analysis
Present Value of Fringe Benefits

Age	Period	Current Income	Growth Rate	Future Income	Discount Rate	Present Value
37	0	$10,000	$(1+.08)^0$	$ 10,000	$1/(1+.06)^0$	$10,000
38	1	10,000	$(1+.08)^1$	10,800	$1/(1+.06)^1$	10,189
39	2	10,000	$(1+.08)^2$	11,664	$1/(1+.06)^2$	10,381
40	3	10,000	$(1+.08)^3$	12,597	$1/(1+.06)^3$	10,577
41	4	10,000	$(1+.08)^4$	13,605	$1/(1+.06)^4$	10,776
42	5	10,000	$(1+.08)^5$	14,693	$1/(1+.06)^5$	10,980
43	6	10,000	$(1+.08)^6$	15,869	$1/(1+.06)^6$	11,187
44	7	10,000	$(1+.08)^7$	17,138	$1/(1+.06)^7$	11,398
45	8	10,000	$(1+.08)^8$	18,509	$1/(1+.06)^8$	11,613
46	9	10,000	$(1+.08)^9$	19,990	$1/(1+.06)^9$	11,832
47	10	10,000	$(1+.08)^{10}$	21,589	$1/(1+.06)^{10}$	12,055
48	11	10,000	$(1+.08)^{11}$	23,316	$1/(1+.06)^{11}$	12,283
49	12	10,000	$(1+.08)^{12}$	25,182	$1/(1+.06)^{12}$	12,515
50	13	10,000	$(1+.08)^{13}$	27,196	$1/(1+.06)^{13}$	12,751
51	14	10,000	$(1+.08)^{14}$	29,372	$1/(1+.06)^{14}$	12,991
52	15	10,000	$(1+.08)^{15}$	31,722	$1/(1+.06)^{15}$	13,236
53	16	10,000	$(1+.08)^{16}$	34,259	$1/(1+.06)^{16}$	13,486
54	17	10,000	$(1+.08)^{17}$	37,000	$1/(1+.06)^{17}$	13,741
55	18	10,000	$(1+.08)^{18}$	39.960	$1/(1+.06)^{18}$	14,000
56	19	10,000	$(1+.08)^{19}$	43,157	$1/(1+.06)^{19}$	14,264
57	20	10,000	$(1+.08)^{20}$	46,610	$1/(1+.06)^{20}$	14,533
58	21	10,000	$(1+.08)^{21}$	50,338	$1/(1+.06)^{21}$	14,807
59	22	10,000	$(1+.08)^{22}$	54,365	$1/(1+.06)^{22}$	15,087
60	23	10,000	$(1+.08)^{23}$	58,715	$1/(1+.06)^{23}$	15,371
61	24	10,000	$(1+.08)^{24}$	63,412	$1/(1+.06)^{24}$	15,661
62	25	10,000	$(1+.08)^{25}$	68,485	$1/(1+.06)^{25}$	15,957
63	26	10,000	$(1+.08)^{26}$	73,964	$1/(1+.06)^{26}$	16,258
64	27	10,000	$(1+.08)^{27}$	79,881	$1/(1+.06)^{27}$	16,565

Age	Period	Current Income	Growth Rate	Future Income	Discount Rate	Present Value
65	28	10,000	$(1+.08)^{28}$	86,271	$1/(1+.06)^{28}$	16,877
66	29	10,000	$(1+.08)^{29}$	93,173	$1/(1+.06)^{29}$	17,196
67	30	10,000	$(1+.08)^{30}$	100,627	$1/(1+.06)^{30}$	17,520
68	31	10,000	$(1+.08)^{31}$	108,677	$1/(1+.06)^{31}$	17,851
69	32	10,000	$(1+.08)^{32}$	117,371	$1/(1+.06)^{32}$	18,187
70	33	10,000	$(1+.08)^{33}$	126,760	$1/(1+.06)^{33}$	18,531
71	34	10,000	$(1+.08)^{34}$	136,901	$1/(1+.06)^{34}$	18,880
72	35	10,000	$(1+.08)^{35}$	147,853	$1/(1+.06)^{35}$	19,237
73	36	10,000	$(1+.08)^{36}$	159,682	$1/(1+.06)^{36}$	19,599
74	37	10,000	$(1+.08)^{37}$	172,456	$1/(1+.06)^{37}$	19,969
75	38	10,000	$(1+.08)^{38}$	186,253	$1/(1+.06)^{38}$	20,346
76	39	10,000	$(1+.08)^{39}$	201,153	$1/(1+.06)^{39}$	20,730
77	40	10,000	$(1+.08)^{40}$	217,245	$1/(1+.06)^{40}$	21,121
78	41	10,000	$(1+.08)^{41}$	234,625	$1/(1+.06)^{41}$	21,520
79	42	10,000	$(1+.08)^{42}$	253,395	$1/(1+.06)^{42}$	21,926
80	43	10,000	$(1+.08)^{43}$	273,666	$1/(1+.06)^{43}$	22,339
81	44	10,000	$(1+.08)^{44}$	295,560	$1/(1+.06)^{44}$	22,761
82	45	10,000	$(1+.08)^{45}$	319,204	$1/(1+.06)^{45}$	23,190
83	46	10,000	$(1+.08)^{46}$	344,741	$1/(1+.06)^{46}$	23,628
84	47	10,000	$(1+.08)^{47}$	372,320	$1/(1+.06)^{47}$	24,074
85	48	10,000	$(1+.08)^{48}$	402,106	$1/(1+.06)^{48}$	24,528
86	49	10,000	$(1+.08)^{49}$	434,274	$1/(1+.06)^{49}$	24,991
87	50	10,000	$(1+.08)^{50}$	469,016	$1/(1+.06)^{50}$	25,462
88	51	10,000	$(1+.08)^{51}$	506,537	$1/(1+.06)^{51}$	25,943
89	52	10,000	$(1+.08)^{52}$	547,060	$1/(1+.06)^{52}$	26,432
90	53	10,000	$(1+.08)^{53}$	590,825	$1/(1+.06)^{53}$	26,931
91	54	10,000	$(1+.08)^{54}$	638,091	$1/(1+.06)^{54}$	27,439
92	55	10,000	$(1+.08)^{55}$	689,139	$1/(1+.06)^{55}$	27,957
93	56	10,000	$(1+.08)^{56}$	744,270	$1/(1+.06)^{56}$	28,484
94	57	10,000	$(1+.08)^{57}$	803,811	$1/(1+.06)^{57}$	29,021
95	58	10,000	$(1+.08)^{58}$	868,116	$1/(1+.06)^{58}$	29,569
96	59	10,000	$(1+.08)^{59}$	937,565	$1/(1+.06)^{59}$	30,127
97	60	10,000	$(1+.08)^{60}$	1,012,571	$1/(1+.06)^{60}$	30,695
98	61	10,000	$(1+.08)^{61}$	1,093,576	$1/(1+.06)^{61}$	31,275
99	62	10,000	$(1+.08)^{62}$	1,181,062	$1/(1+.06)^{62}$	31,865

Extended Worksheet 19-7B
Extended Analysis
Present Value of Fringe Benefits

Age	Period	Present Value	Probability of Living	Adjusted Value	Total Sum
37	0	$ 10,000	1.00000	$10,000	$ 10,000
38	1	10,189	.99603	10,148	20,148

Age	Period	Present Value	Probability of Living	Adjusted Value	Total Sum
39	2	10,381	.99383	10,317	30,465
40	3	10,577	.99144	10,486	40,951
41	4	10,776	.98884	10,656	51,607
42	5	10,980	.98598	10,826	62,433
43	6	11,187	.98283	10,995	73,428
44	7	11,398	.97936	11,163	84,591
45	8	11,613	.97553	11,329	95,919
46	9	11,832	.97130	11,493	107,412
47	10	12,055	.96661	11,653	119,065
48	11	12,283	.96141	11,809	130,874
49	12	12,515	.95563	11,959	142,833
50	13	12,751	.94924	12,103	154,936
51	14	12,991	.94219	12,240	167,176
52	15	13,236	.93447	12,369	179,545
53	16	13,486	.92604	13,486	192,034
54	17	13,741	.91688	12,598	204,633
55	18	14,000	.90695	12,697	217,330
56	19	14,264	.89621	12,784	230,113
57	20	14,533	.88461	12,856	242,969
58	21	14,807	.87208	12,913	255,882
59	22	15,087	.85859	12,953	268,836
60	23	15,371	.84412	12,975	281,811
61	24	15,661	.82863	12,978	294,788
62	25	15,957	.81203	12,957	307,746
63	26	16,258	.79420	12,912	320,658
64	27	16,565	.77509	12,839	333,497
65	28	16,877	.75465	12,736	346,233
66	29	17,196	.73304	12,605	358,839
67	30	17,520	.71026	12,444	371,282
68	31	17,851	.68629	12,251	383,533
69	32	18,187	.66116	12,025	395,558
70	33	18,531	.63486	11,764	407,322
71	34	18,880	.60751	11,470	418,792
72	35	19,237	.57913	11,141	429,933
73	36	19,599	.54983	10,776	440,709
74	37	19,969	.51968	10,378	451,087
75	38	20,346	.48880	9,945	461,032
76	39	20,730	.45738	9,481	470,513
77	40	21,121	.42558	8,989	479,502
78	41	21,520	.39358	8,470	487,972
79	42	21,926	.36157	7,928	495,899
80	43	22,339	.32975	7,366	503,266
81	44	22,761	.29677	6,755	510,020
82	45	23,190	.26304	6,100	516,120

Age	Period	Present Value	Probability of Living	Adjusted Value	Total Sum
83	46	23,628	.22906	5,412	521,532
84	47	24,074	.19544	4,705	526,237
85	48	24,528	.16284	3,994	530,232
86	49	24,991	.13198	3,298	533,530
87	50	25,462	.10355	2,637	536,166
88	51	25,943	.07820	2,029	538,195
89	52	26,432	.05645	1,492	539,687
90	53	26,931	.03861	1,040	540,727
91	54	27,439	.02474	679	541,406
92	55	27,957	.01464	409	541,815
93	56	28,484	.00785	224	542,039
94	57	29,021	.00371	108	542,146
95	58	29,569	.00149	44	542,190
96	59	30,127	.00047	14	542,205
97	60	30,695	.00011	3	542,208
98	61	31,275	.00001	0	542,208
99	62	31,865	.00000	0	542,208

§19.12   Summary

The calculation of the present value of a future income stream, using the extended analysis, includes the probability of living, the probability of seeking employment, and the probability of finding employment. The economist may choose different mortality tables to employ, but the choice of mortality table will have little impact on the present value calculation.

When using the extended analysis to calculate the present value of future medical expenses, it is appropriate to adjust the present value figures for mortality only.

20 Evaluating Structured Settlements

§20.01 Introduction

This chapter will define structured settlements and the terms used in discussing structured settlements. In addition, it will explain interest assumptions, growth assumptions, and mortality assumptions used in evaluating and designing structured settlements. The latter part of the chapter focuses on evaluating structured settlements and designing structured settlements.

§20.02 Defining the Terms: Structured Settlement

A structured settlement occurs whenever the plaintiff will receive a payment at some date in the future. A structured settlement might be one in which the plaintiff will receive $100,000 in 29 years. Or it may be in the form of an annuity; that is, the plaintiff will receive $1,000 per month for life. The fact that payments occur at dates other than at the time of settlement makes the settlement a structured settlement.

§20.03 Defining the Terms: Present Value

The present value of a structured settlement refers to the cost of providing the future payments. The present value will depend on the number of dollars being paid, when the dollars are being paid, the growth rate, the current rate of interest, and whether the payments are certain.

§20.04 Defining the Terms: Payout

The payout of a structured settlement is the number of dollars the plaintiff will receive over the life of the structured settlement. It has nothing to do with the cost or present value of providing the settlement.

For example, suppose a five-year-old female is bitten by a dog, and a settlement is to provide the girl with $1 million. The payout is $1 million. The cost, or present value, of the settlement will depend on when the $1 million is to be received. If the money is to be received today, then the present value is $1 million. If, on the other hand, the money is to be received at a future date, the present value will be less than $1 million. The longer the time until the money is to be received, the smaller the present value.

§20.05   Defining the Terms: Dollars Received

There are different types of payments which can be made to a plaintiff. Payments will be lump sums or in the form of annuities. A lump sum payment is a one-time payment. An annuity is a series of payments.

§20.06   Defining the Terms: Dollars Received as Lump Sums

A lump sum is a one-time payment. For instance, $10,000 received in 10 years is a lump sum payment, as is $50,000 received at age 65. There may be more than one lump sum payment in a settlement. For example, the settlement may in the following form:

Table 20-1 Structured Lump Sum Payments

$20,000 to be received in 5 years
$20,000 to be received in 10 years
$20,000 to be received in 15 years
$20,000 to be received in 20 years
$20,000 to be received in 25 years
$20,000 to be received in 30 years
$20,000 to be received in 35 years
$20,000 to be received in 40 years

This is a settlement containing eight lump sum payments. Rather than specify that a payment will occur in five, or ten years, the settlement may specify the money will be paid when the recipient reaches a certain age. Table 20-2 specifies when the money is to be paid based on age.

Table 20-2 Structured Lump Sum Payments

$20,000 to be paid at age 30
$20,000 to be paid at age 35
$20,000 to be paid at age 40
$20,000 to be paid at age 45
$20,000 to be paid at age 50
$20,000 to be paid at age 55
$20,000 to be paid at age 60
$20,000 to be paid at age 65

The examples in lump sum payouts in Tables 20-1 and 20-2 have the same number of payments, eight. Both have the same payout, $160,000 (eight payments times $20,000). The lump sum payments do not have to be the same amount. Table 20-3 presents a different lump sum package.

Table 20-3 Structured Lump Sum Payments

$20,000 to be paid at age 30
$25,000 to be paid at age 35
$30,000 to be paid at age 40
$35,000 to be paid at age 45
$40,000 to be paid at age 50
$45,000 to be paid at age 55
$50,000 to be paid at age 60
$55,000 to be paid at age 65

§20.07   Defining the Terms: Dollars Received as Annuities

An annuity was defined in **§20.05** as a series of payments. Annuity payments may be made annually or monthly. An annuity payment may be $1,000 per month for life, or $10,000 per year for life.

Suppose a college fund is to be established for a minor. The money to be received is $10,000 per year at ages 18, 19, 20, and 21. This could be a series of four lump sum payments or a four-year annuity of $10,000 per year.

§20.08   Defining the Terms: Certain or Uncertain Payments—The Mortality Adjustment

Payments are said to be *certain* or *uncertain,* depending on whether the recipient is living when the payment is to be made. Payments which are *certain* are made to the plaintiff or the plaintiff's estate. If the payments are *uncertain,* the payments are made only if the recipient is alive.

Using the example in Table 20-1, the settlement offer is modified to uncertain, as follows:

Table 20-4 Structured Lump Sum Payments Payments Made if Living

$20,000 to be received in 5 years if living
$20,000 to be received in 10 years if living
$20,000 to be received in 15 years if living
$20,000 to be received in 20 years if living
$20,000 to be received in 25 years if living
$20,000 to be received in 30 years if living
$20,000 to be received in 35 years if living
$20,000 to be received in 40 years if living

Certain and uncertain lump sum payments may be combined into the same offer. For example, the following offer might be made:

Table 20-5 Structured Lump Sum Payments

$20,000 to be received in 5 years
$20,000 to be received in 10 years
$20,000 to be received in 15 years
$20,000 to be received in 20 years
$20,000 to be received in 25 years if living
$20,000 to be received in 30 years if living
$20,000 to be received in 35 years if living
$20,000 to be received in 40 years if living

In this case the first five payments are certain. The payments are made to the individual or to the individual's estate. The last four payments are made to the individual only if he or she is living.

In a like fashion, annuities may be certain or uncertain. For example, an annuity of $1,000 per month for life is an uncertain annuity. The money will be paid to the recipient only if living.

Payment may be made where part of the payments are certain and part of the payments are uncertain. For example, an annuity may read as follows: "$1,000 per month, starting immediately, continuing for life, payments guaranteed to age 65." In this case $1,000 will be paid each month to the recipient for as long as he or she is alive. If the individual dies before age 65, then the $1,000 per month is paid to his or her estate. The payments to the estate continue until the individual would have reached age 65.

The calculation of the present value of uncertain payments requires estimating the probability of an individual being alive in the future years. This requires knowing the sex, race, and current age of the individual who is to receive the lump sum payments.

Many times the term *guaranteed* is used in the structured settlement discussion. *Guaranteed* usually means the same as *certain*.

Lump sum payments and annuities may be combined in a structured settlement. For example, the following structured settlement offer contains both:

Table 20-6 Structured Settlement Offer

Lump Sum Payments
$20,000 to be received in 5 years
$20,000 to be received in 10 years
$20,000 to be received in 15 years
$20,000 to be received in 20 years
$20,000 to be received in 25 years if living
$20,000 to be received in 30 years if living
$20,000 to be received in 35 years if living
$20,000 to be received in 40 years if living
Annuities
$1,000 per month for life guaranteed to age 65.

The structured settlement presented in Table 20-6 might be written as follows: "$20,000 every five years for 40 years, with the first four payments guaranteed, plus a life annuity of $1,000 per month guaranteed to age 65."

§20.09   Defining the Terms: Deferred Annuities

Annuities do not have to start immediately. An annuity which does not start immediately is a deferred annuity. Suppose the plaintiff is a 10-year-old child. The annuity offered might read: "$1,000 per month for life, starting at age 20, guaranteed to age 65."

This means that when the child reaches age 20 the monthly annuity will begin. The annuity will pay $1,000 per month and guarantee payments for 45 years.

§20.10   Defining the Terms: Growth Rate

When a structured settlement contains a growth rate, it usually refers to the annuity portion of the settlement. The growth rate is usually an annual growth rate. The growth rate can be whatever is agreed upon, but typically runs between 3 and 6 percent annually.

If the annuity is $1,000 per month starting immediately and growing at 4 percent annually, then during the first year the party will receive $1,000 per month. During the second year the annuity would grow by 4 percent and be $1,040 per month. During the third year the annuity again would be 4 percent larger, or $1,084. The annual growth is compounded.

If the annuity is a deferred annuity, the growth of the annuity does not take effect until the annuity begins. If the annuity is $2,000 per month starting in 20 years and growing at 3 per cent per year, then the monthly annuity will grow to $2,060 in 21 years.

§20.11   Defining the Terms: Interest Rate

The interest rate, or discount rate, is used to determine the cost, or present value, of a structured settlement. It is the fact that money can earn interest that makes the present value and the payout of a structured settlement different. The higher the interest rate in effect, the lower the cost of purchasing a given structured settlement package. The cost of a structured settlement and the present value of a structured settlement mean the same thing. An appropriate interest rate may be determined by examining a financial publication such as *The Wall Street Journal.*

The interest earned on an individual's investment is taxable income. If an individual purchases an annuity, the interest earned on the investment is not taxable. This point is of major importance to an individual considering settling a case. Suppose $100,000 has been offered to settle a case. The individual may take the $100,000 now or may receive $100,000 in the form of a structured settlement. Once the individual takes the $100,000 and invests it, for example, at 10 per cent annually, the interest income becomes taxable income. In this case the individual would pay tax on an interest income of $10,000. If a structured settlement is accepted, the interest income is not taxable.[1] The structure allows the principal left with the annuity company to compound at a higher rate.

§20.12 Overview of Evaluating Structured Settlements

To evaluate a structured settlement offer means to calculate the cost, or present value, of the offer. To determine the present value requires knowledge of (1) the date of birth of the recipient; (2) the race and sex of the recipient; (3) when the payments will occur; (4) the size of the payments; (5) how long the payment are to continue; (6) whether the payments are certain or uncertain; (7) the rate of growth of annuities; and (8) the current rate of interest.[1]

§20.13 Worksheet for Calculating Present Value of Certain Lump Sum Payments

The following structured settlement offer has been made:

$10,000 to be paid in 5 years
$20,000 to be paid in 10 years
$40,000 to be paid in 15 years
$80,000 to be paid in 20 years

In order to evaluate the present value of the offer, the current rate of interest must be known. Having determined the appropriate rate of interest to employ is 6 per cent, the present value can be calculated. Appendix B contains the present value factors for single payments. A portion of Appendix B appears below.

Table 20-7 Present Value of $1 Received in "t" Years

Period	Interest Rate				
	2%	4%	6%	8%	10%
0	1.0000	1.0000	1.0000	1.0000	1.0000

[1] IRC (a)(2) provides that gross income does not include the amount of any damages received whether by suit or agreement and whether by lump sums or as periodic payments on account of personal injuries or sickness.

[1] IRC (a)(2) provides that gross income does not include the amount of any damages received whether by suit or agreement and whether by lump sums or as periodic payments on account of personal injuries or sickness.

Period	Interest Rate				
	2%	4%	6%	8%	10%
1	.9804	.9615	.9434	.9259	.9091
2	.9612	.9246	.8900	.8573	.8264
3	.9423	.8890	.8396	.7938	.7513
4	.9238	.8548	.7921	.7350	.6830
5	.9057	.8219	.7473	.6806	.6209
6	.8880	.7903	.7050	.6302	.5645
7	.8706	.7599	.6651	.5835	.5132
8	.8535	.7307	.6274	.5403	.4665
9	.8368	.7026	.5919	.5002	.4241
10	.8203	.6756	.5584	.4632	.3855
11	.8043	.6496	.5268	.4289	.3505
12	.7885	.6246	.4970	.3971	.3186
13	.7730	.6006	.4688	.3677	.2897
14	.7579	.5775	.4423	.3405	.2633
15	.7430	.5553	.4173	.3152	.2394
16	.7284	.5339	.3936	.2919	.2176
17	.7142	.5134	.3714	.2703	.1978
18	.7002	.4936	.3503	.2502	.1799
19	.6864	.4746	.3305	.2317	.1635
20	.6730	.4564	.3118	.2145	.1486

Table 20-7 shows the present value factor of $1 received in five years to be .7473. The present value of $10,000 received in five years would be $7,473.

The present value of the lump sum payments can be estimated using the following form. The spaces filled in show the information that must be determined before the present value can be calculated.

Worksheet 20-1
Worksheet for Calculating the
Present Value of Lump Sum Payments
All Payments Certain
Using a 6% Interest Assumption

Dollars	In "t" Years	Present Value Factor	Present Value
$ 10,000	5	_____	$____
20,000	10	_____	____
40,000	15	_____	____
80,000	20	_____	____
$150,000 is the payout		Present Value	$____

The blank spaces have to be filled in. The present value factors are from Appendix B. The present value factors are where the column headed with the appropriate interest rate and the row representing when the payment is to be received intersect. Worksheet 20-2 shows the present value factors filled in.

Worksheet 20-2
Worksheet for Calculating the
Present Value of Lump Sum Payments
All Payments Certain
Using a 6% Interest Assumption

Dollars	In "t" Years	Present Value Factor	Present Value
$ 10,000	5	.7473	
20,000	10	.5584	
40,000	15	.4173	
80,000	20	.3118	
$150,000 is the payout		Present Value	

The calculation of the present value of the lump sum payments is the multiplication of the payment times the present value factor. The present value of the $10,000 received in five years is $7,473. Worksheet 20-3 completes the present value calculation. The present value of the four lump sum payments is $60,277. The structure has a payout of $150,000, but with a 6 per cent annual interest has a cost of $60,277.

Worksheet 20-3
Worksheet for Calculating the
Present Value of Lump Sum Payments
All Payments Certain
Using a 6% Interest Assumption

Dollars	In "t" Years	Present Value Factor	Present Value
$ 10,000	5	.7473	$ 7,473
20,000	10	.5584	11,168
40,000	15	.4173	16,692
80,000	20	.3118	24,944
$150,000 is the payout		Present Value	$60,277

The interest rate assumption is of critical importance in the cost of providing lump sum payments. If the appropriate interest rate increases, then the cost of providing the future payments decreases. Worksheet 20-4 presents the calculation of the present value of the same settlement offer but the interest assumption is 10 per cent.

Worksheet 20-4
Worksheet for Calculating the
Present Value of Lump Sum Payments
All Payments Certain
Using a 10% Interest Assumption

Dollars	In "t" Years	Present Value Factor	Present Value
$ 10,000	5	.6209	$ 6,209
20,000	10	.3855	7,710

Dollars	In "t" Years	Present Value Factor	Present Value
40,000	15	.2394	9,576
80,000	20	.1486	11,888
$150,000 is the payout		Present Value	$ 35,383

The payout of the structure is $150,000 regardless of the interest assumption. The cost of providing the settlement decreased from $60,277 to $35,383 because of the increase in the interest rate used to calculate the present value.

§20.14   Worksheet for Calculating Present Value of Uncertain Lump Sum Payments

When the payments are uncertain, the payments are made only if the recipient is alive. The payout and the present value are both adjusted for the probability of the recipient being alive when the payment is to occur.

When payments are uncertain, the race, sex, and current age of the recipient must be known. Worksheet 20-5 is the same lump sum payment schedule as in Worksheet 20-1, but the payments are uncertain. The worksheet has been modified to reflect the necessary adjustments to the present value and payout calculation.

The modification is to determine the probability of the individual living the number of years necessary to receive the payments. Assume the individual is a 20-year-old white male. The probability of living to age 25 is found in Appendix F. The probability of a 20-year-old white male living to age 25 is .99179. This value is entered in the column headed "Probability of Living." Likewise, from Appendix F, the probability of 20-year-old white male living to age 30 is .98407. The column is completed in this manner.

Worksheet 20-5
Worksheet for Calculating the
Present Value of Lump Sum Payments
For a 20-Year-Old White Male
All Payments Uncertain
Using a 6% Interest Assumption

Dollars	Received at Age	Present Value Factor	Probability of Living	Present Value
$ 10,000	25	.7473	.99179	$ 7,412
20,000	30	.5584	.98407	10,990
40,000	35	.4173	.97617	16,294
80,000	40	.3118	.96670	24,113
$145,982 is the payout			Present Value	$58,809

The payout is also adjusted to reflect the uncertainty of the payments. As seen on Worksheet 20-5, the payout decreased from $150,000 when all payments were guaranteed to $145,982 when the payments are uncertain. The older the recipient is, the lower the cost of providing the settlement. This is because of the decreasing chance of survival as one gets older. Worksheets

20-6 and 20-7 show the calculation of the present value of uncertain payments to 40- and 60-year-old white males, respectively.

Worksheet 20-6
Worksheet for Calculating the
Present Value of Lump Sum Payments
For a 40-Year-Old White Male
All Payments Uncertain
Using a 6% Interest Assumption

Dollars	Received at Age	Present Value Factor	Probability of Living	Present Value
$ 10,000	45	.7473	.98545	$ 7,364
20,000	50	.5584	.96156	10,739
40,000	55	.4173	.92257	15,400
80,000	60	.3118	.86392	21,550
$135,174 is the payout			Present Value	$55,053

Worksheet 20-7
Worksheet for Calculating the
Present Value of Lump Sum Payments
For a 60-Year-Old White Male
All Payments Uncertain
Using a 6% Interest Assumption

Dollars	In "t" Years	Present Value Factor	Probability of Living	Present Value
$ 10,000	5	.7473	.90274	$6,746
20,000	10	.5584	.77005	8,600
40,000	15	.4173	.60528	10,103
80,000	20	.3118	.42112	10,504
$82,429 is the payout			Present Value	$35,953

When the payments are certain, there are two things that influence the present value of the payments. They are the interest rate and the length of time until the payments are made. The higher the interest rate, the smaller the present value. The farther away the payments are, the lower the present value.

§20.15 Worksheet for Calculating Present Value of Certain Annuities with No Growth Rate

A no-growth certain annuity pays a stated amount of money each month, or each year. The payment is made for a specified number of years. The recipient may change since the annuity is certain.

To calculate the present value of a certain annuity, the annual payment, current rate of interest, and the number of years the payments will occur must be known. Assume the annuity will pay $1,000 per month for 20 years, and the current rate of interest is 8 per cent. Worksheet 20-8 presents the steps necessary to calculate the present value of the annuity, with the blanks which must be known in order to make the calculation filled in. Worksheet 20-9 shows the calculations. The present value of the annuity is $127,200.

Worksheet 20-8
Worksheet for Calculating the
Present Value of A No-Growth Annuity
All Payments Certain
Using 8% Interest Assumption

1. The monthly annuity of _____
    times _____ equals an annual annuity of   _____.
    The annuity payments will be made
    for _____ years in the future (Year number from Appendix C).
    The annual annuity will grow
    at _____ per year (Column
    Number).
    The interest rate, or discount
    rate, is _____ (Row Number).
2. The present value factor is
    found in Year 19____ of Appendix C where
    column _____ and row _____
    intersect.
3. Multiply the annual payment of
    _____ by the factor of _____.
    The present value of the future payments is $_____.
4. The present value of the future income
    is the sum of line
    1 and line 3. $_____.

Worksheet 20-9
Worksheet for Calculating the
Present Value of a No-Growth Annuity
All Payments Certain
Using a 8% Interest Assumption

1. The monthly annuity of $1,000
    times 12 equals an annual annuity of $12,000.
    The annuity payments will be made
    for   19   years in the future
    (Year number from Appendix C).
    The annual annuity will grow
    at   0%   per year (Column
    Number).
    The interest rate, or discount
    rate, is   8%   (Row Number).

2. The present value factor is found
    in Year   19   of Appendix C where
    column   0%   and row   8%
    intersect.
3. Multiply the annual payment of
    $12,000 by the factor of   9.60   .
    The present value of the future payments is $115,200

4. The present value of the future income is the sum of line 1 and line 3
    $127,200.

§20.16 Worksheet for Calculating Present Value of Certain Annuities with a Growth Rate

The calculation of the present value of annuities which have a growth rate is done in exactly the same manner as the no-growth annuity, except the column in which the present factor in Appendix C appears is different. If the annuity had a 2 per cent annual growth rate, the present value factor would increase to 11.26.

The changes made on the worksheet should reflect that there is a growth rate in the annuity, thus the present value factor changes. With a 2 per cent growth rate the present value of the annuity becomes $151,440 (see Worksheet 20-10).

Worksheet 20-10
Worksheet for Calculating the
Present Value of an Annuity Growing at 2% Annually
All Payments Certain
Using 8% Interest Assumption

1. The monthly annuity of $1,000
    times 12 equals an annual annuity of $12,000   .
    The annuity payments will be made
    for   19   years in the future
    (Year number from Appendix C).
    The annual annuity will grow
    at   2%   per year (Column
    Number).
    The interest rate, or discount
    rate, is   8%   (Row Number).
2. The present value factor is found
    in Year   19   of Appendix C where
    column   2%   and row   8%
    intersect.
3. Multiply the annual payment of
    $12,000 by the factor of   11.62 .
    The present value of the future payments is $139,440.
    4. The present value of the future income is the sum of line
        1 and line 3 $151,440.

§20.17 Worksheet for Calculating Present Value of Uncertain Annuities with No Growth Rate

When the annuity to be paid is paid only if the recipient is living, the present value of the annuity is adjusted to reflect the probability the individual will be alive to receive payment. To calculate the present value of a no-growth uncertain annuity, the age, sex, and race of the recipient must be known. Worksheets 20-11A and 20-11B show the calculation of an annuity paying $1,000 per month for 20 years. The recipient is a 25-year-old black male. The probabilities for living each year are obtained from Appendix F. As the worksheet indicates, the present value of the annuity, when interest rates are 8 per cent, is $123,419.

Worksheet 20-11A
Worksheet for Calculating the
Present Value of a No-Growth Annuity
All Payments Certain
Black Male (1982)
Using a 8% Interest Assumption

Period	Age	Current Income	Growth Factor	Future Value	Discount Factor	Present Value
0	25	$12,000	1,000	$12,000	1.000	$12,000
1	26	$12,000	1.000	$12,000	.926	11,112
2	27	$12,000	1.000	$12,000	.857	10,284
3	28	$12,000	1.000	$12,000	.794	9,528
4	29	$12,000	1.000	$12,000	.735	8,820
5	30	$12,000	1.000	$12,000	.681	8,172
6	31	$12,000	1.000	$12,000	.630	7,560
7	32	$12,000	1.000	$12,000	.583	6,996
8	33	$12,000	1.000	$12,000	.540	6,480
9	34	$12,000	1.000	$12,000	.500	6,000
10	35	$12,000	1.000	$12,000	.463	5,556
11	36	$12,000	1.000	$12,000	.429	5,148
12	37	$12,000	1.000	$12,000	.397	4,764
13	38	$12,000	1.000	$12,000	.368	4,416
14	39	$12,000	1.000	$12,000	.340	4,080
15	40	$12,000	1.000	$12,000	.315	3,780
16	41	$12,000	1.000	$12,000	.292	3,504
17	42	$12,000	1.000	$12,000	.270	3,240
18	43	$12,000	1.000	$12,000	.250	3,000
19	44	$12,000	1.000	$12,000	.232	2,784

Worksheet 20-11B
Worksheet for Calculating the
Present Value of a No-Growth Annuity
All Payments Uncertain
Black Male (1982)
Using 8% Interest Assumption

Period	Age	Present Value	Prob Living	Adjusted Pres Val	Sum Adj Pres Val
0	25	$12,000	1.00000	$12,000	$12,000
1	26	12,000	.99417	11,046	23,046
2	27	12,000	.99102	10,196	33,242
3	28	12,000	.98771	9,409	42,651
4	29	12,000	.98422	8,681	51,332
5	30	12,000	.98055	8.008	59,340
6	31	12,000	.97670	7,386	66,726
7	32	12,000	.97267	6,811	73,537
8	33	12,000	.96849	6,279	79,816
9	34	12,000	.96415	5,788	85,603
10	35	12,000	.95963	5,334	90,937
11	36	12,000	.95491	4,915	95,852
12	37	12,000	.94997	4,527	100,379
13	38	12,000	.94479	4,169	104,548
14	39	12,000	.93935	3,838	108,385
15	40	12,000	.93363	3,532	111,917
16	41	12,000	.92757	3,249	115,116
17	42	12,000	.92110	2,987	118,153
18	43	12,000	.91411	2,745	120,898
19	44	12,000	.90650	2,521	123,419

§20.18 Worksheet for Calculating Present Value of Uncertain Annuities with a Growth Rate

If the annuity is growing at 2 per cent annually, the present value increases to $145,192 (see Worksheet 20-12). As the worksheet shows, the annuity will grow to an annual payment of $17,482 in the last year.

Worksheet 20-12A
Worksheet for Calculating the
Present Value of 20 Year Annuity With a 2% Annual Growth
All Payments Certain
Using a 8% Interest Assumption
25 Year Old Black Male (1982)

Period	Age	Current Income	Growth Factor	Future Value	Discount Factor	Present Value
0	25	$12,000	1.000	$12,000	1.000	$12,000

Period	Age	Current Income	Growth Factor	Future Value	Discount Factor	Present Value
1	26	12,000	1.020	12,240	.926	11,334
2	27	12,000	1.040	12,480	.857	10,695
3	28	12,000	1.061	12,732	.794	10,109
4	29	12,000	1.082	12,984	.735	9,543
5	30	12,000	1.104	13,248	.681	9,022
6	31	12,000	1.126	13,512	.630	8,513
7	32	12,000	1.149	13,784	.583	8,043
8	33	12,000	1.172	14,060	.540	7,596
9	34	12,000	1.195	14,341	.500	7,174
10	35	12,000	1.219	14,628	.463	6,776
11	36	12,000	1.243	14,920	.429	6,399
12	37	12,000	1.268	15,219	.397	6,044
13	38	12,000	1.294	15,523	.368	5,708
14	39	12,000	1.319	15,834	.340	5,391
15	40	12,000	1.346	16,150	.315	5,091
16	41	12,000	1.373	16,473	.292	4,808
17	42	12,000	1,400	16,803	.270	4,541
18	43	12,000	1.428	17,139	.250	4,289
19	44	12,000	1.457	17,482	.232	4,051

Worksheet 20-12B
Worksheet for Calculating the
Present Value of 20-Year Annuity With a 2% Annual Growth
All Payments Uncertain
Using a 8% Interest Assumption
25-Year-Old Black Male (1982)

Period	Age	Present Value	Prob Living	Adjusted Pres Value	Sum Adj Pres Val
0	25	$12,000	1.00000	$12,000	$12,000
1	26	11,333	.99417	11,267	23,267
2	27	10,704	.99102	10,608	33,875
3	28	10,109	.98771	9,985	43,860
4	29	9,547	.98422	9,397	53,256
5	30	9,017	.98055	8,842	62,098
6	31	8,516	.97670	8,318	70,416
7	32	8,043	.97267	9,985	78,239
8	33	7,596	.96849	9,397	85,596
9	34	7,174	.96415	6,917	92,513
10	35	6,776	.95963	6,502	99,015
11	36	6,399	.95941	6,111	105,125
12	37	6,044	.94997	5,741	110,867
13	38	5,708	.94479	5,393	116,259
14	39	8,043	.97267	9,985	78,239
15	40	7,596	.96849	9,397	85,596

Period	Age	Present Value	Prob Living	Adjusted Pres Value	Sum Adj Pres Val
16	41	4,808	.92757	4,460	130,537
17	42	4,541	.92110	4,183	134,720
18	43	4,289	.91411	3,921	138,640
19	44	4,051	.90650	3,672	142,312

If the annuity is a life annuity, the calculation can be quite long. Worksheet 20-13 shows the present value calculation for a life annuity. The recipient is a 25-year-old black male. As the Worksheet shows, the present value of the annuity is $185,816.

Worksheet 20-13A
Worksheet for Calculating the
Present Value of a Life Annuity with 2% Annual Growth
All Payments Uncertain
Black Male (1982)
Using 8% Interest Assumption

Period	Age	Current Income	Growth Factor	Future Value	Discount Factor	Present Value
0	25	$12,000	1.000	12,000	1.000	12,000
1	26	12,000	1.020	12,240	.926	11,333
2	27	12,000	1.040	12,485	.857	10,704
3	28	12,000	1.061	12,734	.794	10,109
4	29	12,000	1.082	12,989	.735	9,547
5	30	12,000	1.104	13,249	.681	9,017
6	31	12,000	1.126	13,514	.630	8,516
7	32	12,000	1.149	13,784	.583	8,043
8	33	12,000	1.172	14,060	.540	7,596
9	34	12,000	1.195	14,341	.500	7,174
10	35	12,000	1.219	14,628	.463	6,776
11	36	12,000	1.243	14,920	.429	6,399
12	37	12,000	1.268	15,219	.397	6,044
13	38	12,000	1.294	15,523	.368	5,708
14	39	12,000	1.319	15,834	.340	5,391
15	40	12,000	1.346	16,150	.315	5,091
16	41	12,000	1.373	16,473	.292	4,808
17	42	12,000	1.400	16,803	.270	4,541
18	43	12,000	1.428	17,139	.250	4,289
19	44	12,000	1,457	17,482	.232	4,051
20	45	12,000	1.486	17,831	.215	3,826
21	46	12,000	1.516	18,188	.199	3,613
22	47	12,000	1,546	18,552	.184	3,412
23	48	12,000	1.577	18,923	.170	3,223
24	49	12,000	1.608	19,301	.158	3,044
25	50	12,000	1.641	19,687	.146	2,875

Period	Age	Current Income	Growth Factor	Future Value	Discount Factor	Present Value
26	51	12,000	1.673	20,081	.135	2,715
27	52	12,000	1.707	20,483	.125	2,564
28	53	12,000	1.741	20,892	.116	2,422
29	54	12,000	1.776	21,310	.107	2,287
30	55	12,000	1.811	21,736	.099	2,160
31	56	12,000	1.848	22,171	.092	2,040
32	57	12,000	1.885	22,614	.085	1,927
33	58	12,000	1.922	23,067	.079	1,820
34	59	12,000	1.961	23,528	.073	1,719
35	60	12,000	2.000	23,999	.068	1,623
36	61	12,000	2.040	24,479	.063	1,533
37	62	12,000	2.081	24,968	.058	1,448
38	63	12,000	2.122	25,468	.054	1,367
39	64	12,000	2.165	25,977	.050	1,291
40	65	12,000	2.208	26,496	.046	1,220
41	66	12,000	2.252	27,026	.043	1,152
42	67	12,000	2.297	27,567	.039	1,088
43	68	12,000	2.343	28,118	.037	1,027
44	69	12,000	2.390	28,681	.034	970
45	70	12,000	2.438	29,254	.031	916
46	71	12,000	2.487	29,839	.029	866
47	72	12,000	2.536	30,436	.027	817
48	73	12,000	2.587	31,045	.025	772
49	74	12,000	2.639	31,666	.023	729
50	75	12,000	2.692	32,299	.021	689
51	76	12,000	2.745	32,945	.020	650
52	77	12,000	2.800	33,604	.018	614
53	78	12,000	2.856	34,276	.017	580
54	79	12,000	2.913	34,962	.016	548
55	80	12,000	2.972	35,661	.015	517
56	81	12,000	3.031	36,374	.013	489
57	82	12,000	3.092	37,101	.012	462
58	83	12,000	3.154	37,843	.012	436
59	84	12,000	3.217	38,600	.011	412
60	85	12,000	3.281	39,372	.010	389
61	86	12,000	3.347	40,160	.009	367
62	87	12,000	3.414	40,963	.008	347
63	88	12,000	3.482	41,782	.008	328
64	89	12,000	3.551	42,618	.007	309
65	90	12,000	3.623	43,470	.007	292
66	91	12,000	3.695	44,340	.006	276
67	92	12,000	3.769	45,226	.006	261
68	93	12,000	3.844	46,131	.005	246
69	94	12,000	3.921	47,054	.005	232

Period	Age	Current Income	Growth Factor	Future Value	Discount Factor	Present Value
70	95	12,000	4.000	47,995	.005	220
71	96	12,000	4.080	48,955	.004	207
72	97	12,000	4.161	49,934	.004	196
73	98	12,000	4.244	50,932	.004	185
74	99	12,000	4.329	51,951	.003	175

Worksheet 20-13B
Worksheet for Calculating the
Present Value of a Life Annuity with a 2% Annual Growth
All Payments Uncertain
Black Male (1982)
Using 8% Interest Assumption

Period	Age	Present Value	Prob Living	Adjusted Pres Val	Sum Adj Pres Val
0	25	$12,000	1.00000	12,000	$12,000
1	26	11,333	.99417	11,267	23,267
2	27	10,704	.99102	10,608	33,875
3	28	10,109	.98771	9,985	43,860
4	29	9,547	.98422	9,397	53,256
5	30	9,017	.98055	8,842	62,098
6	31	8,516	.97670	8,318	70,416
7	32	8,043	.97267	7,823	78,239
8	33	7,596	.96849	7,357	85,596
9	34	7,174	.96415	6,917	92,513
10	35	6,776	.95963	6,502	99,015
11	36	6,399	.95491	6,111	105,125
12	37	6,044	.94997	5,741	110,867
13	38	5,708	.94479	5,393	116,259
14	39	5,391	.93935	5,064	121,323
15	40	5,091	.93363	4,753	126,076
16	41	4,808	.92757	4,460	130,537
17	42	4,541	.92110	4,183	134,720
18	43	4,289	.91411	3,921	138,640
19	44	4,051	.90650	3,672	142,312
20	45	3,826	.89824	3,436	145,749
21	46	3,613	.88930	3,213	148,962
22	47	3,412	.87966	3,002	151,964
23	48	3,223	.86929	2,802	154,765
24	49	3,044	.85817	2,612	157,377
25	50	2,875	.84628	2,433	159,810
26	51	2,715	.83359	2,263	162,073
27	52	2,564	.82012	2,103	164,176
28	53	2,422	.80585	1,952	166,128
29	54	2,287	.79078	1,809	167,936

Period	Age	Present Value	Prob Living	Adjusted Pres Val	Sum Adj Pres Val
30	55	2,160	.77494	1,674	169,610
31	56	2,040	.75832	1,547	171,157
32	57	1,927	.74091	1,428	172,585
33	58	1,820	.72268	1,315	173,900
34	59	1,719	.70363	1,209	175,109
35	60	1,623	.68377	1,110	176,219
36	61	1,533	.66316	1,017	177,236
37	62	1,448	.64185	929	178,165
38	63	1,367	.61989	848	179,013
39	64	1,291	.59736	771	179,784
40	65	1,220	.57433	700	180,484
41	66	1,152	.55087	635	181,119
42	67	1,088	.52704	573	181,692
43	68	1,027	.50289	517	182,209
44	69	970	.47848	464	182,673
45	70	916	.45388	416	183,089
46	71	866	.42939	372	183,461
47	72	817	.40509	331	183,792
48	73	772	.38103	294	184,086
49	74	729	.35729	261	184,347
50	75	689	.33394	230	184,577
51	76	650	.31091	202	184,779
52	77	614	.28829	177	184,956
53	78	580	.26617	154	185,111
54	79	548	.24461	134	185,245
55	80	517	.22372	116	185,360
56	81	489	.20196	99	185,459
57	82	462	.17961	83	185,542
58	83	436	.15698	68	185,610
59	84	412	.13447	55	185,666
60	85	389	.11252	44	185,709
61	86	367	.09162	34	185,743
62	87	347	.07224	25	185,768
63	88	328	.05486	18	185,786
64	89	309	.03983	12	185,798
65	90	292	.02741	8	185,806
66	91	276	.01768	5	185,811
67	92	261	.01054	3	185,814
68	93	246	.00569	1	185,816
69	94	232	.00271	1	185,816
70	95	220	.00110	0	185,816
71	96	207	.00035	0	185,816
72	97	196	.00008	0	185,816

Period	Age	Present Value	Prob Living	Adjusted Pres Val	Sum Adj Pres Val
73	98	185	.00001	0	185,816
74	99	175	0.00000	0	185,816

§20.19   Short Cut to Estimating Present Value of Life Annuities

Rather than go through all the calculations necessary to determine the present value of the life annuity, the present value may be estimated by considering the annuity a little differently. The annuity shown in Worksheet 20-13 is a life annuity paying $1,000 per month, growing at 2 per cent per year. It is being paid to a 25-year-old black male. The discount rate used is 8 per cent per year.

Instead of considering the annuity a life annuity, evaluate the annuity as though it is an annuity certain to life expectancy. Appendix F indicates the life expectancy for a 25-year-old black male is 42.7 years, or rounded off, the life expectancy is 43 years. Using Worksheet 20-14, which is the same as Worksheet 20-10, the present value of the annuity to life expectancy is $198,480. If the goal of the calculation is to ESTIMATE the present value, then treating the life annuity as an annuity certain to life expectancy is a much faster calculation.

Worksheet 20-14
Worksheet for Calculating the
Present Value of an Annuity Growing at 2% Annually
All Payments Certain
Using 8% Interest Assumption

1. The monthly annuity of $1,000
    times 12 equals an annual annuity of $ 12,000
    The annuity payments will be made
    for   43   years in the future
    (Year number from Appendix C).
    The annual annuity will grow
    at   2%   per year (Column
    Number).
    The interest rate, or discount
    rate, is   8%   (Row Number).
2. The present value factor is found
    in Year   43   of Appendix C where
    column   2%   and row   8%
    intersect.
3. Multiply the annual payment of
    $12,000 by the factor of 15.54.
    The present value of the future payments is $186,480

4. The present value of the future income is
the sum of line 1 and line 3 $198,480

§20.20   Evaluating Deferred Annuities

On occasion the offer may be an annuity that does not start for a period of years. The present value can be determined by considering this as two annuities, one of which the plaintiff receives and one he or she does not.

Consider the offer of a 20-year annuity certain paying $1,000 per month growing at 4 per cent annually. The annuity does not start for 10 years. The appropriate interest rate is deemed to be 10 per cent annually.

The annuity the individual receives is an annuity paying $1,000 per month growing at 4 per cent annually for 30 years. The individual does not receive any annuity for the first 10 years. The difference in the two present values is the present value of the deferred annuity. The present value of the 30-year annuity is shown on Worksheet 20-15. Worksheet 20-16 shows the 10-year annuity with the same conditions.

Worksheet 20-15
Worksheet for Calculating the
Present Value of a 30-Year Annuity Growing
at 4% Annually
All Payments Certain
Using 10% Interest Assumption

1. The monthly annuity of $1,000
times 12 equals an annual annuity of $ 12,000
The annuity payments will be made
for   29   years in the future
(Year number from Appendix C).
The annual annuity will grow
at   4%   per year (Column
Number).
The interest rate, or discount
rate, is   8%   (Row Number).
2. The present value factor is found
in Year   29   of Appendix C where
column   4%   and row   10%
intersect.
3. Multiply the annual payment of
$12,000 by the factor of   13.93.
The present value of the future payments is $167,160
_____

4. The present value of the future income is
the sum of line 1 and line 3 $179,160

Worksheet 20-16
Worksheet for Calculating the
Present Value of a 10-Year Annuity Growing
at 4% Annually
All Payments Certain
Using 10% Interest Assumption

1. The monthly annuity of $ 1,000
    times 12 equals an annual annuity of $ 12,000
    The annuity payments will be made
    for   9   years in the future
    (Year number from Appendix C).
    The annual annuity will grow
    at   4%   per year (Column
    Number).
    The interest rate, or discount
    rate, is   10%   (Row Number).
2. The present value factor is found
    in Year   9   of Appendix C where
    column   4%   and row   10%
    intersect.
3. Multiply the annual payment which
    is $12,000 by the factor of   6.87 .
    The present value of the future payments is $ 82,440

4. The present value of the future income is $ 94,440
The difference between the two present values is $84,720 and is the present
value of the deferred annuity.

§20.21 Evaluating Structured Settlement Offers: Example 1

An injured 30-year-old white male has been offered $100,000 plus one of
three different structures to settle his claim. If one of the three offers is to be
accepted which should be accepted? What is the present value of each offer?

1. $1,460 per month for life
2. $1,083.90 per month for life increasing at 2 per cent annually
3. $962.09 per month for life increasing at 4 per cent annually
4. $842.27 per month for life increasing at 6 per cent annually

To determine the present value of each offer the economist, or person
evaluating the offer, must know how long the annuity will be paid and what
the appropriate discount rate, or interest rate, is. Appendix F indicates the life
expectancy of a 30-year-old white male is 43.8 years. Assume the appropriate
interest rate is 10 per cent.

The calculation of the present value of each annuity is completed quickly if the annuity is considered as an annuity certain to life expectancy. Assume that Annuity 1 is certain and lasts for 44 years—this year and 43 future years. The present value factors can be found in Appendix C.

For Annuity 1 the present value factor is 9.83. Multiplying the factor by the annual income of $17,520 ($1,460 × 12) gives a present value of $172,221. Table 20-8 shows the present value of the four annuities. Worksheets 20-17 through 20-20 show the calculation of the present values.

Table 20-8 Present Value of Life Annuities Discount Rate of 10%

Monthly Payment	Annual Payment	Annual Growth Rate	Present Value Factor	Present Value of Annuity
$1,460.00	$17,520.00	0.0%	9.83	$172,221
1,083.90	13,006.80	2.0	12.25	159,333
962.09	11,545.08	4.0	15.78	182,181
842.27	10,107.24	6.0	21.11	213,364

Annuity 4 has the highest present value. However, other considerations may enter into the decision of which annuity to accept. The annual payout and the total payout of the four annuities are presented in Tables 20-9 and 20-10. Whichever annuity is accepted may be modified by the individual's family life expectancy.

Worksheet 20-17
Present Value
Life Annuity 1

1. The monthly annuity of $1,460.00
    times 12 equals an annual annuity of $ 17,520.00.
    The annuity payments will be made
    for   43   years in the future
    (Year number from Appendix C).
    The annual annuity will grow
    at   0%   per year (Column
    Number).
    The interest rate, or discount
    rate, is   10%   (Row Number).
2. The present value factor is found
    in Year   43   of Appendix C where
    column   0%   and row   10%
    intersect.
3. Multiply the annual payment which
    is $17,520 by the factor of   9.83.
    The present value of the future payments is $172,221.60
4. The present value of the future income is
    the sum of line 1 and line 3 $189,741.60

5. The money paid at settlement is $100,000.00
6. The present value of the offer is $289,741.60

Worksheet 20-18
Present Value
Life Annuity 2

1. The monthly annuity of $1,083.90
    times 12 equals an annual annuity of $13,006.80.
    The annuity payments will be made
    for   43   years in the future
    (Year number from Appendix C).
    The annual annuity will grow
    at   2%   per year (Column
    Number).
    The interest rate, or discount
    rate, is   10%   (Row Number).
2. The present value factor is found
    in Year   43   of Appendix C where
    column   2%   and row   10%
    intersect.
3. Multiply the annual payment of
    $13,006.80 by the factor of   12.25.
    The present value of the future payments is $159,333.30
4. The present value of the future income is
    the sum of line 1 and line 3. $172,340.10
5. The money paid at settlement is $100,000.00
6. The present value of the offer is $272,340.10

Worksheet 20-19
Present Value
Life Annuity 3

1. The monthly annuity of $ 962.09
    times 12 equals an annual annuity of $11,545.08.
    The annuity payments will be made
    for   43   years in the future
    (Year number from Appendix C).
    The annual annuity will grow
    at   4%   per year (Column
    Number).
    The interest rate, or discount
    rate, is   10%   (Row Number).
2. The present value factor is found
    in Year   43   of Appendix C where
    column   4%   and row   10%
    intersect.

3. Multiply the annual payment of
    $11,545.08 by the factor of   15.78.
    The present value of the future payments is $182,181.36
4. The present value of the future income is
    the sum of line 1 and line 3 $193,726.44
5. The money paid at settlement is $100,000.00
6. The present value of the offer is $293,726.44

Worksheet 20-20
Present Value
Life Annuity 4

1. The monthly annuity of $ 842.27
    times 12 equals an annual annuity of $10,107.24.
    The annuity payments will be made
    for   43   years in the future
    (Year number from Appendix C).
    The annual annuity will grow
    at   6%   per year (Column
    Number).
    The interest rate, or discount
    rate, is   10%   (Row Number).
2. The present value factor is found
    in Year   43   of Appendix C where
    column   6%   and row   10%
    intersect.
3. Multiply the annual payment of
    $10,107.24 by the factor of   21.11   .
    The present value of the future payments is $213,363.83
4. The present value of the future income is
    the sum of line 1 and line 3 $223,471.07
5. The money paid at settlement is $100,000.00
6. The present value of the offer is $323,471.07

Table 20-9 Annual Payout and Total Payout

Period	Age	Annual Payment 0% Growth	Total Payout	Annual Payment 2% Growth	Total Payout
0	30	$17,520	$ 17,520	$13,007	$ 13,007
1	31	17,520	35,040	13,267	26,274
2	32	17,520	52,560	13,532	39,806
3	33	17,520	70,080	13,803	53,609
4	34	17,520	87,600	14,079	67,688
5	35	17,520	105,120	14,361	82,048
6	36	17,520	122,640	14,648	96,696
7	37	17,520	140,160	14,941	111,637
8	38	17,520	157,680	15,240	126,877

Period	Age	Annual Payment 0% Growth	Total Payout	Annual Payment 2% Growth	Total Payout
9	39	17,520	175,200	15,544	142,421
10	40	17,520	192,720	15,855	158,276
11	41	17,520	210,240	16,172	174,448
12	42	17,520	227,760	16,496	190,944
13	43	17,520	245,280	16,826	207,770
14	44	17,520	262,800	17,162	224,932
15	45	17,520	280,320	17,505	242,437
16	46	17,520	297,840	17,856	260,293
17	47	17,520	315,360	18,213	278,506
18	48	17,520	332,880	18,577	297,083
19	49	17,520	350,400	18,948	316,031
20	50	17,520	367,920	19,327	335,358
21	51	17,520	385,440	19,714	355,072
22	52	17,520	402,960	20,108	375,181
23	53	17,520	420,480	20,510	395,691
24	54	17,520	438,000	20,921	416,612
25	55	17,520	455,520	21,339	437,951
26	56	17,520	473,040	21,766	459,717
27	57	17,520	490,560	22,201	481,918
28	58	17,520	508,080	22,645	504,563
29	59	17,520	525,600	23,098	527,661
30	60	17,520	543,120	23,560	551,221
31	61	17,520	560,640	24,031	575,252
32	62	17,520	578,160	24,512	599,764
33	63	17,520	595,680	25,002	624,766
34	64	17,520	613,200	25,502	650,268
35	65	17,520	630,720	26,012	676,280
36	66	17,520	648,240	26,532	702,813
37	67	17,520	665,760	27,063	729,876
38	68	17,520	683,280	27,604	757,480
39	69	17,520	700,800	28,156	785,637
40	70	17,520	718,320	28,720	814,356
41	71	17,520	735,840	29,294	843,650
42	72	17,520	753,360	29,880	873,530
43	73	17,520	770,880	30,477	904,007

Table 20-10 Annual Payout and Total Payout

Period	Age	Annual Payment 4% Growth	Total Payout	Annual Payment 6% Growth	Total Payout
0	30	$11,545	$ 11,545	$10,107	$ 10,107
1	31	12,007	23,552	10,714	20,821
2	32	12,487	36,039	11,356	32,177

Period	Age	Annual Payment 4% Growth	Total Payout	Annual Payment 6% Growth	Total Payout
3	33	12,987	49,026	12,038	44,215
4	34	13,506	62,532	12,760	56,975
5	35	14,046	76,578	13,526	70,501
6	36	14,608	91,186	14,337	84,839
7	37	15,193	106,379	15,198	100,036
8	38	15,800	122,179	16,109	116,145
9	39	16,432	138,611	17,076	133,221
10	40	17,090	155,701	18,101	151,322
11	41	17,773	173,474	19,187	170,509
12	42	18,484	191,958	20,338	190,846
13	43	19,223	211,182	21,558	212,404
14	44	19,992	231,174	22,851	235,256
15	45	20,792	251,966	24,223	259,478
16	46	21,624	273,590	25,676	285,154
17	47	22,489	296,078	27,217	312,371
18	48	23,388	319,467	28,849	341,220
19	49	24,324	343,790	30,580	371,801
20	50	25,297	369,087	32,415	404,216
21	51	26,309	395,396	34,360	438,576
22	52	27,361	422,756	36,422	474,998
23	53	28,455	451,212	38,607	513,605
24	54	29,594	480,805	40,924	554,529
25	55	30,777	511,583	43,379	597,908
26	56	32,008	543,591	45,982	643,889
27	57	33,289	576,880	48,741	692,630
28	58	34,620	611,500	51,665	744,295
29	59	36,005	647,505	54,765	799,060
30	60	37,445	684,950	58,051	857,111
31	61	38,943	723,893	61,534	918,645
32	62	40,501	764,394	65,226	983,871
33	63	42,121	806,515	69,139	1,053,010
34	64	43,806	850,321	73,288	1,126,298
35	65	45,558	895,879	77,685	1,203,983
36	66	47,380	943,259	82,346	1,286,329
37	67	49,275	992,534	87,287	1,373,616
38	68	51,246	1,043,781	92,524	1,466,141
39	69	53,296	1,097,077	98,076	1,564,216
40	70	55,428	1,152,505	103,960	1,668,177
41	71	57,645	1,210,151	110,198	1,778,374
42	72	59,951	1,270,102	116,810	1,895,184
43	73	62,349	1,332,451	123,818	2,019,002

Tables 20-9 and 20-10 show that, while the annual payment under Annuity

1 is the highest annual payment until the payments in the tenth year under Annuity 4, the total money received by the recipient is highest under Annuity 1 until the eighteenth year when the total dollars paid out under Annuity 4 exceed the money paid out under Annuity 1.

The point is that the highest present value may not always be in the best interest of the recipient. This is particularly true if the recipient has a family history of an unusually short life expectancy.

§20.22   Evaluating Structured Settlement Offers: Example 2

The plaintiff is an 40-year-old white male. He has been offered $150,000 when the case is settled, plus the following:

$ 25,000 in 5 years payment certain
50,000 in 10 years payment certain
100,000 in 25 years payment certain

In addition, he will receive a life annuity of $1,200 per month starting immediately and growing at 2 per cent annually, with payments guaranteed to age 65.

To calculate the present value of the offer, the life expectancy must be known. From Appendix F, the life expectancy is determined to be 34.5 years. This figure is of concern only in the estimation of the annuity payments since the lump sum payments are guaranteed. The appropriate interest rate is 8 per cent.

The present value of the offer is $427,553: $150,000 paid at the time of settlement plus the present value of the deferred payments, which totaled $277,553. Worksheets 20-21 and 20-22 present the calculation of the present value of the lump sum payments and the annuity, respectively. The present value factors for the lump sum value come from Appendix B, and the present value factor for the annuity comes from Appendix C.

Worksheet 20-21
Worksheet for Calculating the
Present Value of Lump Sum Payments
All Payments Certain
Using 8% Interest Assumption

Dollars	In "t" Years	Present Value Factor	Present Value
$ 25,000	5	.6807	$17,018
50,000	10	.3971	19,855
100,000	25	.1460	14,600
$175,000 is the payout		Present Value	$ 51,473

Worksheet 20-22
Present Value

1. The monthly annuity of $ 1,200
    times 12 equals an annual annuity of $ 14,400.
    The annuity payments will be made
    for   35   years in the future
    (Year number from Appendix C).
    The annual annuity will grow
    at   2%   per year (Column
    Number).
    The interest rate, or discount
    rate, is   8%   (Row Number).
2. The present value factor is found
    in Year   35   of Appendix C where
    column   2%   and row   8%
    intersect.
3. Multiply the annual payment of
    is $14,400 by the factor of   14.70.
    The present value of the future payments is $211,680.
4. The present value of the future income is
    the sum of line 1 and line 3 $226,080.

§20.23   Overview to Designing a Structured Settlement

If a structured settlement is desired, it can be designed by the attorney. What needs to be determined at the outset is the goal of the structured settlement. Is the structured settlement to replace a monthly income? Is the structured settlement to provide lump sums of money at some future date to provide a fund for education and training? Is the structured settlement to provide retirement benefits? Is the structured settlement to provide for future medical expenses? The purpose of the settlement will help determine how it should be designed.

The present value of the settlement is known. The present value is how much the settlement costs today. Suppose there is a $300,000 policy limit that is expected to be paid to plaintiff. Of the $300,000, one-third, or $100,000, is the plaintiff's attorney fees. This leaves $200,000 to structure for the plaintiff. The $200,000 is the present value of the structured settlement.

There are an infinite number of ways in which the $200,000 can be structured. One way to structure the settlement is to pay the entire amount, $200,000, to the plaintiff at the time of settlement. In this case the present value and the payout would be the same thing, since the payment of $200,000 is being made at the time of settlement.

The money could be paid in lump sums of so-many dollars every five years, or the money could be paid in the form of an annuity, or a combination of the two.

Suppose the plaintiff is a 22-year-old male. If the plaintiff wants a life annuity, then Appendix F can be used to estimate the dollar amount that can be received each year. From Appendix F, a 22-year-old white male has a life expectancy of 51.2 years, rounded to 51 years.

Using Appendix C, the present value factors of $1 received each year for 51 years can be found. Remember the money available for the structure is $200,000.

The size of the annual annuity will depend on the growth rate of the annuity and the market rate of interest when the annuity is purchased. The annual growth rate may be determined by the plaintiff, but the interest rate is determined by conditions in the financial markets. Assume the appropriate interest rate is 8 per cent.

If the growth rate desired is 0 per cent, then the present value factor is 12.25. This factor may be interpreted to mean that in order to receive $1 per year for 51 years, the annuity starting in one year requires an investment today of $12.25.

Since the plaintiff desires the annuity to start immediately, the value "1" must be added to the present value factor, making the factor 13.25. If $200,000 is available to buy the annual annuity, and each $1 of annual income costs $13.25, an annual annuity of $15,094.34 ($200,000 / 13.25) can be purchased. Dividing the $15,094.34 by 12 months gives a monthly annuity of approximately $1,257.86.

Had the plaintiff wanted a 2 per cent annual growth rate in the annuity, then the present value factor would have been 16.08. To this must be added "1" for the annuity to start immediately. The present value factor is 17.08. The $200,000 divided by 17.08 equals $11,709.60. This is the size of the annual annuity starting immediately and growing at 2 per cent annually. The monthly annuity is approximately $975.80.

Suppose the plaintiff wants some money at the time of settlement and the rest of the money in the form of a life annuity. If $50,000 is paid to the client at settlement, then $150,000 is available for the life annuity. If the growth rate of the annuity is 0 per cent, the annual annuity would equal $11,320.75 ($150,000 / 13.25). The monthly annuity is $943.40. If the growth of the annuity is 2 per cent annually, the annual annuity would be $8,782.20. The monthly annuity would be approximately $731.85.

When the plaintiff is receiving $50,000 at settlement, it means the total cash paid at settlement to the plaintiff is $150,000—$100,000 attorney fees and $50,000 for the plaintiff. The remaining $150,000 is used to purchase the life annuity.

Worksheets 20-23 and 20-24 present the data offered in the two structured settlements.

Worksheet 20-23
No-Growth Annuities

Proposal 1
Cash at Settlement

Attorney Fees	$100,000
Monthly Annuity	
$1,257.86 for life	$200,000
TOTAL PRESENT VALUE	$300,000

Proposal 2
Cash at Settlement

Attorney Fees	$100,000
To Plaintiff	50,000
Monthly Annuity	
$943.40 for life	$150,000
TOTAL PRESENT VALUE	$300,000

Worksheet 20-24
Annuities with 2% Annual Growth

Proposal 1
Cash at Settlement

Attorney Fees	$100,000
Monthly Annuity	
$975.80 for life	$200,000
TOTAL PRESENT VALUE	$300,000

Proposal 2
Cash at Settlement

Attorney Fees	$100,000
To Plaintiff	50,000
Monthly Annuity	
$731.85 for life	$150,000
TOTAL PRESENT VALUE	$300,000

The present value of future lump sum payments can be calculated in the same manner. Since these are only one-time payments, the present value factor can be found in Appendix B. Consider the situation where the plaintiff has $150,000 available at settlement. One-third is attorney fees, leaving $100,000 to structure. Plaintiff would like six payments starting in five years, with each payment five years apart. Thus, plaintiff will receive a payment in 5 years, 10 years, 15 years, 20 years, 25 years, and 30 years. The present value factor for each of the one-time payments is in Appendix B. Table 20-11 shows the present value factors for the six future payments.

Table 20-11 Calculating the Present Value of Future Lump Sum Payments

In "t" Year	Present Value Factor
5	.6806
10	.4632
15	.3152
20	.2145
25	.1460
30	.0994
TOTAL:	1.9189

By adding up all the present value factors, the total cost of providing $1 in each of the five years can be determined. In this case the cost of providing $1 in each of the years is 1.9189. Since there is $100,000 available to provide the future lump sums, $52,113.19 ($100,000 / 1.9189) can be provided as each of the six future payments. Table 20-12 presents the present value of the six payments.

Table 20-12 Present Value of Future Lump Sum Payments

In "t" Years	Payment	Present Value Factor	Present Value
5	$52,113.19	.6806	$35,468.23
10	52,113.19	.4632	24,138.83
15	52,113.19	.3152	16,426.08
20	52,113.19	.2145	11,178.28
25	52,113.19	.1460	7,608.53
30	52,113.19	.0994	5,180.05
Payout	$312,679.14	Present Value	$100,000.00

On the other hand, the client may prefer to specify how many dollars to receive at various points in the future. This is acceptable but one of the future payments will be the residual. That is, one of the payments will be determined by how much money is left in the fund after the five desired payments are determined.

Suppose the plaintiff would like payments of $30,000 in 5 years, $50,000 in 10 years, $70,000 in 15 years, $90,000 in 20 years, and $110,000 in 25 years. Is there any money available for the payment in 30 years, and, if there is money for a payment in 30 years, how large will the payment be? Table 20-13 shows the present value of the five future payments. The appropriate interest rate is again assumed to be 8 per cent.

Table 20-13 Calculating the Present Value of Future Lump Sum Payments

In "t" Years	Payment	8% Annual Interest Present Value Factor	Present Value
5	$20,000	.6806	$13,612
10	40,000	.4632	18,528
15	60,000	.3152	18,912
20	80,000	.2145	17,160
25	100,000	.1460	14,600
		Present Value	$82,812

Since the present value of the first five payments is $82,812, the entire present value of $100,000 has not been used. In fact, $17,188 remains to purchase a payment 30 years in the future. Recall the present value factor of $1 to be received 30 years in the future was .0994 when interest rates are 8 per cent. Therefore, $17,188 will purchase a lump sum payment of $172,918 to be received in 30 years. Table 20-14 presents the present value and the payout of the structured settlement. If the size of the payments or the timing of the payments are not acceptable to the plaintiff, he or she may wish to restructure the future payments.

Table 20-14 Calculating the Present Value of Future Lump Sum Payments

In "t" Years	Payment	8% Annual Interest Present Value Factor	Present Value
5	$20,000	.6806	$13,612
10	40,000	.4632	18,528
15	60,000	.3152	18,912
20	80,000	.2145	17,160
25	100,000	.1460	14,600
30	172,918	.0994	17,188
Payout	$472,918	Present Value	$100,000

§20.24   Concluding Structured Settlements

The designing of a structured settlement is left to the imagination, but many things should be considered when designing the settlement. What is the life expectancy of the plaintiff, what is the expected medical needs, what are the educational goals of the individual or the individual's dependents. Will a structured settlement relieve the plaintiff of the responsibility of handling large sums of money, meaning is a structure in the best interest of the individual.

Consider the question of an individual life expectancy. An individual has been offered 1 of 4 life annuities. They are (A) $17,520 per year for life; (B) $13,007 per year for life with a 2 per cent annual growth rate; (C) $11,545 per year for life with a 4 per cent annual growth rate; and (D) $10,107 per year for life with a 6 per cent annual growth rate. The annuity with the highest present value is Annuity D.

Tables 20-15 and 20-16 present the annual annuity and the total payout. As can be seen in Table 20-15, Annuity A has the highest annual annuity until the plaintiff receives age 45. After age 45 Annuity B has the highest annual annuity. Annuity C is higher than Annuity A after age 41, and Annuity D passes Annuity A after age 40.

The payout of Annuity B does not pass Annuity until the plaintiff is age 59. The payout of Annuity C is greater than a when plaintiff reaches age 50, and Annuity D's payout passes Annuity A when plaintiff is age 48.

Table 20-15 Annual Annuity And Total Payout

		$17,520 per year Annuity A		$13,007 per year Annuity B	
Period	Age	0 Growth	Payout	2% Growth	Payout
0	30	$17,520	$ 17,520	$13,007	$ 13,007
1	31	17,520	35,040	13,267	26,274
2	32	17,520	52,560	13,532	39,806
3	33	17,520	70,080	13,803	53,609
4	34	17,520	87,600	14,079	67,688
5	35	17,520	105,120	14,361	82,048
6	36	17,520	122,640	14,648	96,696
7	37	17,520	140,160	14,941	111,637
8	38	17,520	157,680	15,240	126,877
9	39	17,520	175,200	15,544	142,421
10	40	17,520	192,720	15,855	158,276
11	41	17,520	210,240	16,172	174,448
12	42	17,520	227,760	16,496	190,944
13	43	17,520	245,280	16,826	207,770
14	44	17,520	262,800	17,162	224,932
15	45	17,520	280,320	17,505	242,437
16	46	17,520	297,840	17,856	260,293
17	47	17,520	315,360	18,213	278,506
18	48	17,520	332,880	18,577	297,083
19	49	17,520	350,400	18,948	316,031
20	50	17,520	367,920	19,327	335,358
21	51	17,520	385,440	19,714	355,072
22	52	17,520	402,960	20,108	375,181
23	53	17,520	420,480	20,510	395,691
24	54	17,520	438,000	20,921	416,612
25	55	17,520	455,520	21,339	437,951
26	56	17,520	473,040	21,766	459,717
27	57	17,520	490,560	22,201	481,918
28	58	17,520	508,080	22,645	504,563
29	59	17,520	525,600	23,098	527,661

Period	Age	$17,520 per year Annuity A 0 Growth	Payout	$13,007 per year Annuity B 2% Growth	Payout
30	60	17,520	543,120	23,560	551,211
31	61	17,520	560,640	24,031	575,252
32	62	17,520	578,160	24,512	599,764
33	63	17,520	595,680	25,002	624,766
34	64	17,520	613,200	25,502	650,268
35	64	17,520	630,720	26,012	676,280
36	66	17,520	648,240	26,532	702,813
37	67	17,520	665,760	27,063	729,876
38	68	17,520	683,280	27,604	757,480
39	69	17,520	700,800	28,156	785,637
40	70	17,520	718,320	28,720	814,356
41	71	17,520	735,840	29,294	843,650
42	72	17,520	753,360	29,880	873,530
43	73	17,520	770,880	30,477	904,007

Table 20-16 Annual Annuity And Total Payout

Period	Age	$11,545 per year Annuity C 4% Growth	Payout	$10,107 per year Annuity D 6% Growth	Payout
0	30	$11,545	$11,545	$10,107	$10,107
1	31	12,007	23,552	10,714	20,821
2	32	12,487	36,039	11,356	32,177
3	33	12,987	49,026	12,038	44,215
4	34	13,506	62,532	12,760	56,975
5	35	14,046	76,578	13,526	70,501
6	36	14,608	91,186	14,337	84,839
7	37	15,193	106,379	15,198	100,036
8	38	15,800	122,179	16,109	116,145
9	39	16,432	138,611	17,076	133,211
10	40	17,090	155,701	18,101	151,322
11	41	17,773	173,474	19,187	170,509
12	42	18,484	191,958	20,338	190,846
13	43	19,223	211,182	21,558	212,404
14	44	19,992	231,174	22,851	235,256
15	45	20,792	251,966	24,223	259,478
16	46	21,624	273,590	25,676	285,154
17	47	22,489	296,078	27,217	312,371
18	48	23,388	319,467	28,849	341,220
19	49	24,324	343,790	30,580	371,801
20	50	25,297	369,087	32,415	404,216
21	51	26,309	395,396	34,360	438,576
22	52	27,361	422,756	36,422	474,998
23	53	28,455	451,212	38,607	513,605

Period	Age	$11,545 per year Annuity C 4% Growth	Payout	$10,107 per year Annuity D 6% Growth	Payout
24	54	29,594	480,805	40,924	554,529
25	55	30,777	511,583	43,379	597,908
26	56	32,008	543,591	45,982	643,889
27	57	33,289	576,880	48,741	692,630
28	58	34,620	611,500	51,665	744,295
29	59	36,005	647,505	54,765	799,060
30	60	37,445	684,950	58,051	857,111
31	61	38,943	723,893	61,534	918,645
32	62	40,501	764,394	65,226	983,871
33	63	42,121	806,515	69,139	1,053,010
34	64	43,806	850,321	73,288	1,126,298
35	65	45,558	895,879	77,685	1,203,983
36	66	47,380	943,259	82,346	1,286,329
37	67	49,275	992,534	87,287	1,373,616
38	68	51,246	1,043,781	92,524	1,466,141
39	69	53,296	1,097,077	98,076	1,564,216
40	70	55,428	1,152,505	103,960	1,668,177
41	71	57,645	1,210,151	110,198	1,778,374
42	72	59,951	1,270,102	116,810	1,895,184
43	73	62,349	1,332,451	123,818	2,019,002

While Annuity D has the highest present value, it does assume a normal life expectancy. Suppose the family history indicates that males in the plaintiff's family do not live beyond age 50. This may make Annuity A, with the highest current annual annuity, the most attractive.

§20.25 Summary

Structured settlements permit the money from a settlement to be paid over a period of time. Management of the funds not dispersed fall to the company from whom the annuity is purchased. The interest earned on an annuity is free of federal income tax. If a lump sum is paid to the plaintiff and plaintiff invests the money, interest earned on the investments are subject to federal income tax.

The purchasing of an annuity permits the reinvestment of funds at a tax free, or on a tax deferred basis. This permits a higher monthly annuity than the individual can probably provide through the management of his own funds.

The cost of an annuity is greatly affected by the current interest rates. The higher the interest rate the lower will be the cost of the annuity. This also means that the higher the interest rates, the larger the annuity or lump sum payments a given amount of money will purchase. Likewise, the lower the interest rates the higher the cost of the annuity.

21

Sample Testimony

§21.01   Introduction

This chapter presents a sample report of an economist and scripts of a direct examination, a cross-examination, and a redirect examination. The premise for the direct examination is two-fold. First, the quality of the expert's testimony is directly related to the quality of the direct examination, and, second, all things relating to the economic evidence should be initially presented by the plaintiff's attorney.

Section 21.02 is the economist's report to the plaintiff's attorney. The fact situation and all relevant variables should be presented in the report. The direct examination begins in **§21.03,** and the cross-examination in **§21.21.** The concluding section presents the redirect examination.

§21.02   The Economist's Report

Economic Consultants, Inc.
Street Address
City, State 00000

September 11, 1987

Attorney, Attorney, and Attorney
Attn: Senior Attorney
Street Address
City, State 00000

RE: Mr. John Jones

Dear Attorney:

The case involving Mr. John Jones has been evaluated. The present value of the loss is $670,949. This amount is the sum of the historic loss plus the present value of the future loss.

The historic loss represents the lost income from wages, supervisory differential, and fringe benefits from the date of the accident, September 1, 1986, to the date of the trial, October 10, 1987. This loss is $45,159.

The present value of the future loss, beginning October 10, 1987, and continuing to age 65, is $625,790.

This loss is the economic loss sustained by Mr. Brown's family and does not include loss of services, attention, marital care, advice, or protection to Mrs. Brown or any of the minor children. This figure is exclusive of the value of household services and is not reduced for personal consumption.

The economic evaluation is based on information received from your office as detailed in Part I of this report. The methodology and other sources of information employed in preparing this report appear in Parts II and III.

If there is an error in the information contained in Part I, please contact me immediately so a corrected copy may be provided to you.

Sincerely,

The Economist, Ph.D.

Summary of Losses to
Mr. John Jones

Historic Loss
From September 1, 1986, to October 10, 1987
Wages . . . . $ 45,159
Present Value of Future Loss
Beginning October 10, 1987
Wages to age 65 . . . . $625,790
Total Loss $670,949

Economic Analysis
Mr. John Jones

PART I.

Date of Birth:	July 4, 1946
Current Age:	41
Race:	Caucasian
Sex:	Male
Date of Accident:	September 1, 1986
Injury:	Permanent Partial Disability
Life Expectancy	
Absent the Accident:	33 years
Education:	High School Graduate

Earnings History:

Year	Income
1986	$ 34,512*
1985	42,116
1984	39,046
1983	37,816

* represents partial year

Age at Retirement:	65
Marital Status:	Married
Dependents:	No minor children
Date of Analysis:	September 10, 1987
Date of Present Value:	October 10, 1987

PART II. Calculation of Economic Loss

The present value of the loss is calculated by using the following formula:

$$\text{Present Value of Future Income} = \$ \sum_{t=0}^{n} [(1 + g)^t (1 + d)]^t$$

The four variables in this formula are $, t, g, and d.

- Represents the basis for calculating the economic loss resulting from the accident. The wage calculation is based on an hourly wage rate of $18.50 plus supervisory benefits of $1.00 per hour. The fringe benefits are calculated using an hourly cost of $2.11 per hour. The present value of the future income is reduced for current employment at $6.00 per hour.

t - Represents time and starts in period "t", on the present value date, October 10, 1987, and continues until period "t". Period "t" is when Mr. Jones reaches age 64. This means retirement occurs at age 65.

g - Represents the growth rate for wages. The growth rate is 4.39 per cent annually. This is the 1952-1985 historic rate of change in the Consumer Price Index.

d - Represents the discount rate or rate at which dollars received will earn interest. The discount rate is 5.99 per cent annually. This is the 1952-1985 historic yield on one-year Treasury Bills. There are many types of investments which can be made today, ranging from passbook savings to speculating in future markets. While there is no such thing as a risk-free investment, the United States One-Year Treasury Bill is used as a surrogate.

For example, if we are receiving $1,000 one year from today, we might be willing to receive some amount less than $1,000 today. This is true because we could invest the money for one year and earn interest. The rate of earnings is the interest rate, or discount rate.

PART III.   Bibliography

Probability of Living

    Life Expectancy Tables, U.S. National Center for Health Statistics, Vital Statistics of U.S. 1982, as cited in Statistical Abstracts of the United States, 1986.

Job Participation Rate

    Civilian Labor Force Participation Rate by Sex, Race, and Age, Handbook of Labor Statistics, U.S. Department of Labor, Bureau of Labor Statistics, December 1980, Bulletin 2070.

Probability of Employment

    Unemployment Rates by Sex, Race, and Age, Handbook of Labor Statistics, U.S. Department of Labor, Bureau of Labor Statistics, December 1980, Bulletin 2070.

Consumption

    Revised Equivalence Scale for Urban Families of Different Size, Age, and Composition, derived from the U.S. Department of Labor, Bureau of Labor Statistics of Consumer Expenditures - 1960-1961.

Value of Household Services

    The Dollar Value of Household Work, Wm. H. Gauger and Kathryn E. Walker, New York State College of Human Ecology, Cornell University, Ithaca, New York.

Present Value
as of October 10, 1987

Prepared: September 10, 1987
Name: John Jones
Birthdate: July 4, 1946
Age: 41

Life Expectancy at 41 is 33.6 years (U.S. Life Tables (1982) - White Males). The adjusted sum was computed using participation and employment rates (1978-1982) for white males.

Annual Income   = $ 38,480.00
Annual Growth Rate   =   4.00%
Annual Discount Rate =   6.00%

Age	Period	Present Value	Total Income	Prob Living	Part Rate	Emp Rate	Adjusted Sum
41	0	$38,480	$38,480	.99737	.9620	.9624	$ 35,532
42	1	37,754	76,234	.99449	.9620	.9624	70,293
43	2	37,042	113,276	.99132	.9620	.9624	104,290
44	3	36,343	149,618	.98782	.9620	.9624	137,527
45	4	35,657	185,275	.98395	.9220	.9656	168,762
46	5	34,984	220,260	.97968	.9220	.9656	199,275
47	6	34,324	254,584	.97495	.9220	.9656	229,068
48	7	33,677	288,260	.96971	.9220	.9656	258,141
49	8	33,041	321,301	.96388	.9220	.9656	286,495
50	9	32,418	353,719	.95743	.9220	.9656	314,127
51	10	31,806	385,525	.95033	.9220	.9656	341,037
52	11	31,206	416,731	.94253	.9220	.9656	367,223
53	12	30,617	447,348	.93403	.9220	.9656	392,682
54	13	30,039	477,388	.92479	.9220	.9656	417,415
55	14	29,473	506,860	.91478	.7262	.9666	436,340
56	15	28,917	535,777	.90395	.7262	.9666	454,688
57	16	28,371	564,148	.89224	.7262	.9666	472,457
58	17	27,836	591,984	.87961	.7262	.9666	489,644
59	18	27,310	619,294	.86600	.7262	.9666	506,245
60	19	26,795	646,089	.85141	.7262	.9666	522,259
61	20	26,290	672,379	.83578	.7262	.9666	537,683
62	21	25,794	698,173	.81903	.7262	.9666	552,512
63	22	25,307	723,480	.80106	.7262	.9666	566,742
64	23	24,829	748,309	.78178	.7262	.9666	580,367
65	24	24,361	772,670	.76116	.1920	.9698	583,820
66	25	23,901	796,571	.73937	.1920	.9698	587,110
67	26	23,450	820,022	.71639	.1920	.9698	590,239
68	27	23,008	843,030	.69222	.1920	.9698	593,204
69	28	22,574	865,603	.66686	.1920	.9698	596,007
70	29	22,148	887,751	.64034	.1920	.9698	598,648

Age	Period	Present Value	Total Income	Prob Living	Part Rate	Emp Rate	Adjusted Sum
71	30	21,730	909,481	.61275	.1920	.9698	601,127
72	31	21,320	930,801	.58413	.1920	.9698	603,446
73	32	20,918	951,719	.55458	.1920	.9698	605,606
74	33	20,523	972,242	.52417	.1920	.9698	607,609
75	34	20,136	992,378	.49302	.1920	.9698	609,458
76	35	19,756	1,012,134	.46133	.1920	.9698	611,155
77	36	19,383	1,031,517	.42925	.1920	.9698	612,704
78	37	19,017	1,050,534	.39697	.1920	.9698	614,110
79	38	18,659	1,069,193	.36469	.1920	.9698	615,377
80	39	18,307	1,087,499	.33259	.1920	.9698	616,510
81	40	17,961	1,105,460	.29933	.1920	.9698	617,511
82	41	17,622	1,123,083	.26531	.1920	.9698	618,382
83	42	17,290	1,140,372	.23104	.1920	.9698	619,126
84	43	16,964	1,157,336	.19713	.1920	.9698	619,748
85	44	16,643	1,173,979	.16425	.1920	.9698	620,257
86	45	16,329	1,190,309	.13311	.1920	.9698	620,662
87	46	16,021	1,206,330	.10444	.1920	.9698	620,974
88	47	15,719	1,222,049	.07888	.1920	.9698	621,205
89	48	15,422	1,237,472	.05694	.1920	.9698	621,368
90	49	15,131	1,252,603	.03894	.1920	.9698	621,478
91	50	14,846	1,267,449	.02495	.1920	.9698	621,547
92	51	14,566	1,282,015	.01477	.1920	.9698	621,587
93	52	14,291	1,296,306	.00792	.1920	.9698	621,608
94	53	14,021	1,310,328	.00374	.1920	.9698	621,618
95	54	13,757	1,324,084	.00150	.1920	.9698	621,622
96	55	13,497	1,337,582	.00048	.1920	.9698	621,623
97	56	13,243	1,350,824	.00011	.1920	.9698	621,623
98	57	12,993	1,363,817	.00001	.1920	.9698	621,623
99	58	12,748	1,376,565	0.00000	.1920	.9698	621,623

Employment Rates
White Males
1954 - 1982 Inclusive

Year	16-17	18-19	Ages 20-24	25-34	35-44	45-54	55-64	65+
1954	86.00	87.00	90.20	95.80	96.40	96.20	95.70	95.80
1955	87.80	89.60	93.00	97.30	97.40	97.10	96.10	96.20
1956	88.80	90.30	93.90	97.20	97.80	97.20	96.90	96.60
1957	88.10	88.80	92.90	97.30	97.50	97.00	96.60	91.80
1958	85.10	83.50	88.30	94.40	95.60	95.20	94.80	95.00
1959	85.00	87.00	92.50	96.20	96.80	96.30	95.80	95.50
1960	85.40	86.50	91.70	95.90	96.70	96.40	95.90	96.00
1961	83.50	84.90	90.00	95.10	96.00	95.60	94.70	94.80
1962	84.90	87.30	92.00	96.20	96.90	96.50	95.90	95.90

				Ages				
Year	16-17	18-19	20-24	25-34	35-44	45-54	55-64	65+
1963	82.20	85.80	92.20	96.10	97.10	96.70	96.00	95.90
1964	83.80	86.60	92.60	97.00	97.50	97.10	96.50	96.40
1965	85.30	88.60	94.10	97.40	97.70	97.70	96.90	97.00
1966	87.50	91.10	95.90	97.90	98.30	98.30	97.50	96.30
1967	87.30	91.00	95.80	98.10	98.40	98.20	97.80	97.20
1968	87.70	91.80	95.40	98.30	98.60	98.50	98.30	97.60
1969	87.50	92.10	95.40	98.30	98.60	98.60	98.30	97.90
1970	84.30	88.00	92.20	96.90	97.70	97.70	97.30	96.80
1971	82.90	86.50	90.60	96.00	97.10	97.20	96.80	96.60
1972	83.60	87.60	91.50	96.60	97.50	97.50	97.00	96.70
1973	84.90	90.00	93.50	97.00	98.20	98.00	97.60	97.10
1974	83.80	88.50	92.20	96.50	97.60	97.80	97.50	97.00
1975	80.30	82.80	86.80	93.70	95.50	95.60	95.90	95.00
1976	80.30	84.50	89.10	94.40	96.30	96.30	96.00	95.20
1977	82.40	87.00	90.70	95.00	96.90	97.00	96.70	95.10
1978	83.10	89.20	92.40	96.30	97.50	97.50	97.40	96.10
1979	83.90	87.70	92.60	96.40	97.50	97.50	97.50	96.90
1980	81.50	85.50	88.90	94.10	96.40	96.70	96.90	97.50
1981	80.10	83.60	88.40	93.90	96.00	96.40	96.60	97.60
1982	75.80	80.00	85.70	91.10	93.80	94.70	94.90	96.80
54-82 Ave	84.23	87.34	91.74	96.08	97.08	96.98	96.61	96.22
78-82 Ave	80.88	85.20	89.60	94.36	96.24	96.56	96.66	96.98

Participation Rates for White Males
1954 - 1982 Inclusive

				Ages				
Year	16-17	18-19	20-24	25-34	35-44	45-54	55-64	65+
1954	47.10	70.40	86.40	97.50	98.20	96.80	89.20	40.40
1955	48.00	71.70	85.60	97.80	98.30	96.70	88.40	39.50
1956	51.30	71.90	87.60	97.40	98.10	96.80	88.90	40.00
1957	49.60	71.60	86.70	97.20	98.00	96.60	88.00	37.70
1958	46.80	69.40	86.70	97.20	98.00	96.60	88.20	35.70
1959	45.40	70.30	87.30	97.50	98.00	96.30	87.90	34.30
1960	46.00	69.00	87.60	97.70	97.90	96.10	87.20	33.30
1961	44.30	66.20	87.60	97.70	97.90	95.90	87.80	31.90
1962	42.90	66.40	86.50	97.40	97.90	96.00	86.70	30.60
1963	42.40	67.80	85.80	97.40	97.80	96.20	86.60	28.40
1964	43.50	66.60	85.70	97.50	97.60	96.10	86.10	27.90
1965	44.60	65.80	85.30	97.40	97.70	95.90	85.20	27.90
1966	47.10	65.40	84.40	97.50	97.60	95.80	84.90	27.20
1967	47.90	66.10	84.00	97.50	97.70	95.60	84.90	27.10

				Ages				
Year	16-17	18-19	20-24	25-34	35-44	45-54	55-64	65+
1968	47.70	65.70	82.40	97.20	97.60	95.40	84.70	27.30
1969	48.80	66.30	82.60	97.00	97.40	95.10	83.90	27.30
1970	48.90	67.40	83.30	96.70	97.30	94.90	83.30	26.70
1971	49.20	67.80	83.20	96.30	97.00	94.70	82.60	25.60
1972	50.20	71.10	84.30	96.00	97.00	94.00	81.20	24.40
1973	52.70	72.30	85.80	96.30	96.80	93.50	79.00	22.50
1974	53.30	73.60	86.50	96.30	96.70	93.00	78.10	22.50
1975	51.80	72.80	85.50	95.80	96.40	92.90	76.50	21.80
1976	51.80	73.50	86.20	95.90	96.00	92.50	75.40	20.30
1977	53.80	74.90	86.80	96.00	96.20	92.20	74.70	20.20
1978	55.30	75.30	87.20	96.00	96.30	92.10	73.90	20.40
1979	55.30	74.50	87.60	96.10	96.40	92.20	73.60	20.10
1980	53.60	74.10	87.20	95.90	96.20	92.10	73.10	19.10
1981	51.50	73.50	87.00	95.80	96.10	92.40	71.50	18.50
1982	49.30	70.50	86.30	95.60	96.00	92.20	71.00	17.90
54-82								
Ave	48.97	70.07	85.83	96.81	97.24	94.71	82.16	27.47
78-82								
Ave	53.00	73.58	87.06	95.88	96.20	92.20	72.62	19.20

Dollar Value of Household Services
Wm. H. Gauger and Kathryn E. Walker
1979 Dollars

# of Children	Employed Wife Households				Nonemployed Wife Households		
	Age of Wife	Wife	Husband	Teen	Wife	Husband	Teen
0	Under 25	$4,700	$1,800		$7,000	$1,100	
	25-39	5,000	1,900		8,000	1,600	
	40-54	5,900	1,100		8,400	2,100	
	55 plus	6,000	1,500		7,400	2,700	
	Age of Youngest Child						
1	12-17	$6,700	$2,400	$1,400	$9,600	$2,700	$1,200
	6-11	8,000	1,500	†	9,400	2,000	†
	2-5	6,200	2,000	†	9,100	2,400	†
	1	8,300	600	†	9,900	2,300	†

† No cases.

# of Children	Age of Youngest Child	Employed Wife Households			Nonemployed Wife Households		
		Wife	Husband	Teen	Wife	Husband	Teen
	Under 1	*	*	†	10,900	2,100	†
2	12-17	$6,300	$2,100	$1,000	$10,000	$2,200	$1,100
	6-11	7,200	2,000	1,100	9,900	2,100	1,100
	2-5	8,300	2,400	1,500	1,100	2,200	900
	1	8,400	5,000	*	11,700	2,200	*
	Under 1	10,200	2,100	*	12,600	2,000	*
2	12-17	$5,000	$2,100	$1,100	$9,000	$1,400	$1,000
	6-11	8,600	2,000	1,700	9,900	2,200	1,600
	2-5	10,200	2,800	*	10,700	1,900	1,000
	1	11,500	3,200	*	11,600	2,200	1,400
	Under 1	8,700	2,800	*	13,300	2,000	*
4	12-17	$8,700	$1,900	$1,700	$8,400	$1,400	$1,000
	6-11	7,200	1,400	1,100	10,700	1,900	1,100
	2-5	*	*	*	12,000	2,000	1,100
	1	*	*	*	11,800	2,600	800
	Under 1	*	*	*	13,700	2,600	*
5 - 6	12-17	*	*	*	†	†	†
	6-11	*	*	*	$11,500	$2,000	$1,700
	2-5	*	*	*	12,200	2,100	900
	1	*	*	*	9,90	700	*
	Under 1	*	*	*	13,600	2,600	1,000
7 - 9							
	6-11	†	†	†	*	*	*
	2-5	*	*	*	$11,900	2,900	1,400
	1	†	†	†	*	*	*
	Under 1	†	†	†	15,200	2,600	*

Dollar Value of Household Services
Wm. H. Gauger and Kathryn E. Walker
1985 Dollars

# of Children	Employed Wife Households				Nonemployed Wife Households		
	Age of Wife	Wife	Husband	Teen	Wife	Husband	Teen
0	Under 25	$6,961	$2,666		$10,367	$1,629	
	25-39	7,405	2,814		11,848	2,370	

---

* Averages not calculated because there were fewer than 4 cases.
† No cases.

# of Children	Employed Wife Households Age of Wife	Wife	Husband	Teen	Nonemployed Wife Households Wife	Husband	Teen
	40-54	8,738	1,629		12,441	3,110	
	55 plus	8,886	2,222		10,960	3,999	

# of Children	Age of Youngest Child	Wife	Husband	Teen	Wife	Husband	Teen
1	12-17	$9,923	$3,555	$2,073	$14,218	$3,999	$1,777
	6-11	11,848	2,222	†	13,922	2,962	†
	2-5	9,183	2,962	†	13,478	3,555	†
	1	12,293	889	†	14,662	3,406	†
	Under 1	*	*	†	16,144	3,110	†
2	12-17	$9,331	$3,110	$1,481	$14,811	$3,258	$1,629
	6-11	10,664	2,962	1,629	14,662	3,110	1,629
	2-5	12,293	3,555	2,222	1,629	3,258	1,333
	1	12,441	7,405	*	17,328	3,258	*
	Under 1	15,107	3,110	*	18,661	2,962	*
3	12-17	$7,405	$3,110	$1,629	$13,330	$2,073	$1,481
	6-11	12,737	2,962	2,518	14,662	3,258	2,370
	2-5	15,107	4,147	*	15,847	2,814	1,481
	1	17,032	4,739	*	17,180	3,258	2,073
	Under 1	12,885	4,147	*	19,698	2,962	*
4	12-17	$12,885	$2,814	$2,518	$12,441	$2,073	$1,481
	6-11	10,664	2,073	1,629	15,847	2,814	1,629
	2-5	*	*	*	17,773	2,962	1,629
	1	*	*	*	17,477	3,851	1,185
	Under 1	*	*	*	20,291	3,851	*
5 - 6	12-17	*	*	*	†	†	†
	6-11	*	*	*	$17,032	$2,962	$2,518
	2-5	*	*	*	1,777	3,111	1,333
	1	*	*	*	14,662	1,037	*
	Under 1	*	*	*	20,142	3,851	1,481
7 - 9							
	6-11	†	†	†	*	*	*
	2-5	*	*	*	$17,625	$4,295	$2,073
	1	†	†	†	*	*	*
	Under 1	†	†	†	22,512	3,851	*

† No cases.

* Averages not calculated because there were fewer than 4 cases.

Consumer Price Index
Average Percentage Change

From To	1952	1953	1954	1955	1956	1957	1958	1959
1952								
1953	.75							
1954	.63	.50						
1955	.29	.06	−.37					
1956	.59	.54	.56	1.50				
1957	1.19	1.30	1.56	2.53	3.56			
1958	1.44	1.58	1.85	2.60	3.15	2.73		
1959	1.35	1.45	1.64	2.15	2.37	1.77	.81	
1960	1.39	1.48	1.64	2.04	2.18	1.71	1.21	1.60
1961	1.34	1.42	1.55	1.87	1.94	1.54	1.14	1.31
1962	1.32	1.38	1.49	1.76	1.81	1.45	1.14	1.24
1963	1.31	1.37	1.46	1.69	1.72	1.41	1.15	1.24
1964	1.31	1.36	1.45	1.65	1.67	1.40	1.18	1.25
1965	1.34	1.39	1.47	1.66	1.68	1.44	1.26	1.33
1966	1.45	1.50	1.59	1.77	1.79	1.60	1.46	1.55
1967	1.55	1.60	1.69	1.86	1.89	1.73	1.61	1.71
1968	1.71	1.78	1.87	2.04	2.08	1.95	1.87	1.99
1969	1.93	2.00	2.10	2.28	2.34	2.24	2.19	2.33
1970	2.15	2.23	2.34	2.52	2.59	2.52	2.50	2.66
1971	2.26	2.35	2.45	2.63	2.71	2.65	2.64	2.79
1972	2.31	2.40	2.50	2.67	2.74	2.69	2.69	2.83
1973	2.50	2.59	2.70	2.87	2.95	2.91	2.92	3.07
1974	2.89	2.99	3.11	3.29	3.39	3.38	3.43	3.60
1975	3.16	3.27	3.40	3.59	3.70	3.70	3.76	3.95
1976	3.27	3.38	3.51	3.69	3.80	3.81	3.87	4.05
1977	3.39	3.50	3.63	3.82	3.93	3.95	4.01	4.19
1978	3.56	3.67	3.80	3.98	4.10	4.12	4.19	4.37
1979	3.84	3.96	4.10	4.29	4.41	4.45	4.53	4.71
1980	4.19	4.32	4.46	4.66	4.79	4.84	4.94	5.13
1981	4.40	4.53	4.68	4.88	5.01	5.07	5.17	5.37
1982	4.46	4.59	4.73	4.92	5.05	5.11	5.21	5.40
1983	4.42	4.54	4.68	4.86	4.99	5.04	5.13	5.31
1984	4.41	4.53	4.67	4.84	4.96	5.01	5.10	5.27
1985	4.39	4.50	4.63	4.80	4.91	4.96	5.04	5.21

From To	1960	1961	1962	1963	1964	1965	1966	1967
1961	1.01							
1962	1.07	1.12						
1963	1.11	1.17	1.21					
1964	1.16	1.21	1.26	1.31				

From To	1960	1961	1962	1963	1964	1965	1966	1967
1965	1.28	1.34	1.42	1.52	1.72			
1966	1.54	1.64	1.78	1.96	2.29	2.86		
1967	1.73	1.85	2.00	2.19	2.49	2.87	2.88	
1968	2.04	2.19	2.36	2.59	2.92	3.31	3.54	4.20
1969	2.41	2.58	2.79	3.06	3.41	3.83	4.15	4.79
1970	2.76	2.95	3.18	3.47	3.83	4.25	4.59	5.16
1971	2.90	3.09	3.31	3.57	3.89	4.26	4.53	4.95
1972	2.93	3.11	3.31	3.54	3.82	4.12	4.33	4.62
1973	3.19	3.37	3.57	3.81	4.09	4.38	4.60	4.89
1974	3.74	3.95	4.19	4.46	4.77	5.11	5.40	5.76
1975	4.10	4.32	4.57	4.85	5.17	5.52	5.81	6.18
1976	4.21	4.42	4.66	4.92	5.22	5.54	5.81	6.13
1977	4.34	4.55	4.78	5.03	5.32	5.62	5.87	6.16
1978	4.52	4.73	4.96	5.20	5.48	5.77	6.02	6.30
1979	4.88	5.09	5.33	5.58	5.87	6.16	6.42	6.71
1980	5.31	5.54	5.78	6.05	6.35	6.65	6.93	7.24
1981	5.55	5.78	6.02	6.29	6.58	6.89	7.16	7.46
1982	5.58	5.79	6.03	6.28	6.56	6.84	7.09	7.37
1983	5.47	5.68	5.89	6.13	6.38	6.64	6.86	7.11
1984	5.42	5.62	5.82	6.04	6.28	6.52	6.72	6.94
1985	5.35	5.53	5.72	5.93	6.15	6.37	6.55	6.76

From To	1968	1969	1970	1971	1972	1973	1974	1975
1969	5.37							
1970	5.65	5.92						
1971	5.20	5.11	4.30					
1972	4.72	4.51	3.80	3.30				
1973	5.02	4.94	4.61	4.76	6.23			
1974	6.01	6.14	6.20	6.83	8.60	10.97		
1975	6.46	6.64	6.79	7.41	8.78	10.05	9.14	
1976	6.37	6.52	6.62	7.08	8.03	8.63	7.45	5.77
1977	6.38	6.51	6.59	6.98	7.71	8.08	7.12	6.11
1978	6.51	6.64	6.73	7.07	7.70	8.00	7.25	6.63
1979	6.94	7.10	7.23	7.60	8.21	8.54	8.06	7.78
1980	7.49	7.68	7.86	8.25	8.87	9.25	8.97	8.93
1981	7.71	7.91	8.09	8.47	9.04	9.39	9.17	9.17
1982	7.60	7.77	7.92	8.25	8.75	9.03	8.79	8.74
1983	7.31	7.45	7.56	7.83	8.25	8.45	8.17	8.05
1984	7.12	7.23	7.33	7.56	7.91	8.07	7.78	7.63
1985	6.91	7.00	7.08	7.27	7.58	7.69	7.40	7.22

From To	1976	1977	1978	1979	1980	1981	1982	1983
1977	6.45							
1978	7.06	7.66						
1979	8.46	9.46	11.26					
1980	9.72	10.81	12.39	13.52				
1981	9.85	10.70	11.72	11.95	10.37			
1982	9.23	9.79	10.32	10.01	8.25	6.13		
1983	8.37	8.69	8.90	8.31	6.57	4.67	3.22	
1984	7.86	8.06	8.13	7.50	5.99	4.53	3.74	4.26
1985	7.38	7.50	7.48	6.84	5.51	4.29	3.68	3.91

From To	1984	1985
1985	3.57	

Average Return 1 Year Treasury Bills

From	1952	1953	1954	1955	1956	1957	1958	1959
1952	1.84							
1953	1.98	2.11						
1954	1.63	1.52	.93					
1955	1.70	1.66	1.43	1.93				
1956	1.94	1.97	1.92	2.42	2.91			
1957	2.23	2.31	2.36	2.83	3.29	3.66		
1958	2.22	2.28	2.31	2.66	2.90	2.90	2.13	
1959	2.48	2.57	2.64	2.98	3.25	3.36	3.21	4.29
1960	2.61	2.70	2.79	3.10	3.33	3.44	3.36	3.98
1961	2.64	2.72	2.80	3.07	3.26	3.33	3.24	3.61
1962	2.68	2.76	2.83	3.07	3.23	3.29	3.21	3.49
1963	2.74	2.82	2.89	3.11	3.26	3.31	3.25	3.47
1964	2.83	2.91	2.98	3.19	3.33	3.38	3.34	3.54
1965	2.93	3.01	3.09	3.28	3.42	3.47	3.45	3.64
1966	3.09	3.18	3.26	3.45	3.59	3.66	3.66	3.85
1967	3.20	3.29	3.38	3.57	3.70	3.78	3.79	3.97
1968	3.35	3.45	3.54	3.72	3.86	3.94	3.97	4.15
1969	3.57	3.67	3.77	3.96	4.11	4.20	4.24	4.44
1970	3.75	3.86	3.96	4.15	4.30	4.39	4.45	4.64
1971	3.81	3.91	4.01	4.19	4.33	4.43	4.48	4.66
1972	3.86	3.97	4.06	4.24	4.37	4.46	4.52	4.69
1973	4.03	4.14	4.24	4.41	4.55	4.65	4.71	4.88
1974	4.22	4.33	4.43	4.61	4.75	4.85	4.92	5.10
1975	4.32	4.43	4.54	4.71	4.85	4.95	5.02	5.19
1976	4.38	4.49	4.59	4.76	4.89	4.99	5.06	5.23
1977	4.45	4.55	4.65	4.82	4.95	5.04	5.11	5.27
1978	4.59	4.70	4.80	4.97	5.10	5.20	5.27	5.43
1979	4.82	4.92	5.03	5.20	5.33	5.44	5.52	5.68

From	1952	1953	1954	1955	1956	1957	1958	1959
1980	5.07	5.19	5.30	5.47	5.61	5.72	5.81	5.98
1981	5.41	5.53	5.65	5.83	5.98	6.10	6.20	6.38
1982	5.63	5.76	5.89	6.06	6.22	6.34	6.45	6.63
1983	5.76	5.89	6.01	6.19	6.34	6.47	6.57	6.75
1984	5.92	6.05	6.17	6.35	6.50	6.63	6.74	6.92
1985	5.97	6.10	6.22	6.39	6.54	6.67	6.78	6.95

From To	1960	1961	1962	1963	1964	1965	1966	1967
1960	3.66							
1961	3.28	2.89						
1962	3.22	3.00	3.10					
1963	3.27	3.13	3.25	3.41				
1964	3.39	3.32	3.47	3.65	3.89			
1965	3.53	3.50	3.66	3.84	4.06	4.23		
1966	3.79	3.81	3.99	4.22	4.49	4.79	5.34	
1967	3.93	3.97	4.15	4.36	4.60	4.84	5.14	4.94
1968	4.14	4.20	4.38	4.59	4.83	5.07	5.35	5.35
1969	4.45	4.54	4.74	4.98	5.24	5.51	5.83	5.99
1970	4.68	4.78	4.99	5.22	5.48	5.75	6.05	6.23
1971	4.70	4.79	4.98	5.19	5.41	5.63	5.86	5.96
1972	4.72	4.81	4.98	5.17	5.37	5.55	5.74	5.80
1973	4.92	5.02	5.20	5.39	5.58	5.77	5.96	6.05
1974	5.15	5.26	5.44	5.63	5.83	6.03	6.23	6.34
1975	5.25	5.35	5.53	5.72	5.91	6.09	6.28	6.38
1976	5.28	5.38	5.55	5.72	5.90	6.07	6.24	6.33
1977	5.33	5.42	5.58	5.75	5.91	6.07	6.22	6.30
1978	5.49	5.59	5.75	5.91	6.08	6.24	6.39	6.48
1979	5.75	5.86	6.03	6.20	6.37	6.54	6.71	6.81
1980	6.06	6.18	6.35	6.53	6.72	6.90	7.07	7.20
1981	6.47	6.61	6.79	6.99	7.19	7.38	7.58	7.73
1982	6.73	6.87	7.06	7.26	7.46	7.66	7.86	8.02
1983	6.85	6.99	7.18	7.37	7.57	7.77	7.96	8.12
1984	7.02	7.16	7.35	7.54	7.74	7.93	8.12	8.28
1985	7.05	7.19	7.37	7.55	7.74	7.92	8.11	8.25

Average Return 1 Year Treasury Bills

From To	1968	1969	1970	1971	1972	1973	1974	1975
1952								
1953								
1954								
1955								

From	1968	1969	1970	1971	1972	1973	1974	1975
To								
1956								
1957								
1958								
1959								
1960								
1961								
1962								
1963								
1964								
1965								
1966								
1967								
1968	5.76							
1969	6.52	7.28						
1970	6.66	7.11	6.94					
1971	6.22	6.37	5.92	4.90				
1972	5.98	6.03	5.62	4.96	5.01			
1973	6.24	6.33	6.10	5.82	6.28	7.54		
1974	6.54	6.67	6.55	6.45	6.97	7.95	8.35	
1975	6.56	6.68	6.58	6.50	6.90	7.54	7.54	6.72
1976	6.48	6.57	6.47	6.39	6.69	7.11	6.97	6.28
1977	6.44	6.52	6.42	6.35	6.59	6.90	6.74	6.21
1978	6.62	6.70	6.64	6.60	6.84	7.15	7.07	6.75
1979	6.97	7.08	7.05	7.07	7.34	7.67	7.69	7.56
1980	7.37	7.50	7.52	7.58	7.88	8.24	8.34	8.34
1981	7.92	8.09	8.16	8.27	8.61	9.01	9.19	9.31
1982	8.23	8.40	8.49	8.62	8.96	9.35	9.55	9.70
1983	8.31	8.49	8.57	8.70	9.01	9.38	9.56	9.70
1984	8.47	8.64	8.73	8.86	9.17	9.51	9.69	9.83
1985	8.44	8.59	8.68	8.79	9.07	9.38	9.54	9.64

From	1976	1977	1978	1979	1980	1981	1982	1983
To								
1976	5.84							
1977	5.95	6.06						
1978	6.76	7.22	8.39					
1979	7.77	8.42	9.60	10.80				
1980	8.66	9.37	10.47	11.51	12.22			
1981	9.74	10.52	11.64	12.72	13.68	15.13		
1982	10.13	10.84	11.80	12.65	13.27	13.79	12.45	
1983	10.07	10.67	11.44	12.05	12.36	12.41	11.05	9.65
1984	10.17	10.71	11.38	11.88	12.09	12.06	11.04	10.33
1985	9.94	10.39	10.93	11.30	11.38	11.21	10.23	9.49

From	1984	1985
To		
1984	11.01	
1985	9.41	7.81

Revised Equivalency Scale for Urban
Families of Different Sizes,
Ages, and Composition

(A four-person family =husband, age 35 to 54; wife; two children, older child 6 to 15 years of age; equals 100%)

Size and Types of Family	Age of Head			
	Under 35	35-54	55-64	65+
One person	35	36	32	28
Two persons: Average	47	59	59	52
Husband, wife	49	60	59	51
One parent, one child	40	57	60	58
Three persons: Average	62	81	86	77
Husband, wife (child under 6)	62	69	—	—
Husband, wife (child 6-15)	62	82	88	81
Husband, wife (child 16-17)	—	91	88	77
Husband, wife (child over 18)	—	82	85	77
One parent, 2 children	67	76	82	75
Four persons: Average	74	99	109	91
Husband, wife (child under 6)	72	80	—	—
Husband, Wife (older child 6-15)	77	100	105	95
Husband, wife (older child 16-17)	—	113	125	—
Husband, wife (older child over 18)	—	96	110	89
One parent, three children	88	96	—	—
Five persons: Average	94	118	124	—
Husband, wife (child under 6)	87	97	—	—
Husband, wife (older child 6-15)	96	116	120	—
Husband, wife (older child 16-17)	—	128	138	—
Husband, wife (older child over 18)	—	119	124	—
One parent, four children	108	117	—	—

Size and Types of Family	Under 35	Age of Head 35-54	55-64	65+
Six persons: Average	111	138	143	—
Husband, wife (child under 6)	101	—	—	—
Husband, wife (older child 6-15)	110	132	140	—
Husband, wife (older child 16-17)	—	146	—	—
Husband, wife (older child over 18)	—	149	—	—
One parent, five children	125	137	—	—

Source: Derived from the Bureau of Labor Statistics Survey of Consumer Expenditures 1960-61

§21.03   Direct Examination: Identify the Expert

(Examination by plaintiff's attorney)

Q.   Please state your name for the court.

A.   My name is W. Economist.

Q.   Where are you employed?

A.   I am employed by the local university.

Q.   In what capacity are you employed?

A.   I am a Professor of Economics.

Q.   How long have you been employed in that capacity?

A.   I have been a Professor of Economics for seven years.

Q.   What courses do you currently teach at the University?

A.   My teaching responsibilities include teaching Principles of Economics, a graduate course in Economic Theory, and a course in Investments.

Q.   Have you taught other courses in the last three years?

A.   Yes, I have.

Q.   What are the other courses you have taught?

A.   In the last three years I have also taught the undergraduate course in Statistics, the undergraduate course in Personal Finance, and the undergraduate course in Business Finance.

Q.   Do you have other duties, responsibilities, or expectations as an employee of the University?

A.   Yes.

Q.   Would you please explain these other responsibilities.

A. Well, the School of Business, which employs me, expects performance in three areas. These areas are teaching, research and publication, and community service. It is expected that I contribute in all three areas.

Q. You have explained how you discharge your responsibilities in the teaching area. Please explain how you discharge your responsibilities in the other two areas.

A. In the area of research and publication I have presented papers and published articles in the area of forensic economics. In the area of community service I present seminars for the University concerning the use of economists in the area of forensic economics.

Q. Is this a list of the papers, articles, and seminars presented by you in the last five years?

A. Yes, it is.

§21.04 Direct Examination: Why the Expert Is Here

(Examination by plaintiff's attorney.)

Q. Just what is it that your type of research is attempting to determine?

A. The purpose of the analysis is to estimate the economic loss sustained by an individual, or family, as the result of an injury.

Q. What types of losses might an individual sustain as the result of an injury?

A. The losses to an individual and family can include the loss of wage or salary, the loss of fringe benefits, and the loss of household services.

Q. Do all parties disabled by an injury suffer the same degree of economic loss?

A. No, they do not. A person may be only partially disabled, or temporarily disabled. These types of disabilities result in economic losses very different from permanent and total disabilities.

Q. Did I retain you to do an economic calculation concerning the economic loss suffered by Mr. Jones as a result of an accident September 1, 1986?

A. Yes, you did.

Q. Do you do this type of analysis as part of the community service responsibilities at the University?

A. No, this type of work falls into consulting.

Q. Are you paid to do this type of work?

A. Yes, I am.

Q. Who pays you to do this type of analysis?

A. In this case, you will. The attorney who retains me to perform the economic analysis is responsible for my bill.

Q. Have you ever done this type of economic analysis before?

A. Yes, I have.

Q. How long have you been involved in this type of economic analysis?

A. I have been involved in this type of analysis for the last five years.

Q. Over that five-year period, how many cases have you handled?

A. I would estimate I have been involved in 40 to 50 cases.

Q. In the 40 to 50 cases you have handled, how many times have you been retained by the plaintiff's attorney and how many times have you been retained by the defendant's attorney?

A. I would estimate that 25 per cent of my work is done for the defendant.

Q. In the 40 to 50 cases you have handled, have you ever been asked to testify, either in court or by deposition?

A. Yes, I have testified approximately 20 times.

Q. How many times have you testified for the plaintiff?

A. Of the 20 times I have testified, all have been for the plaintiff.

Q. How is it you have never been asked to testify for the defense?

A. My analysis for the plaintiff is to determine the economic loss sustained by the plaintiff. My work for the defense is to assist in the cross-examination of the plaintiff's economist. As a defense economist I am required to estimate the loss to the plaintiff. This establishes a floor for the economic loss. The defense does not wish to have a high figure, from the plaintiff's economist, and a low figure from the defendant's econo-mist. Since this provides the jury with a high and low figure for a verdict, if the defendant is found at fault.

Q. So, you have been retained by me to estimate the economic loss sustained by Mr. Jones and his family as a result of the accident September 1, 1986. And for this you are to be compensated. Is this correct?

A. Yes, that is correct.

§21.05 —The Direct Examination: The Facts

Q. How does an economic analysis like this begin?

A. First it is necessary to establish certain facts.

Q. What facts do you need?

A. I need to know the client's name, date of birth, race, the date of the accident and the result of the accident. That is, was the accident fatal or disabling. The analysis also requires knowing the earnings history, educational attainment, marital status, and dates of birth of dependents. If the accident necessitates on-going medical care, it is necessary to know the current cost of the care and when the care will be required in the future.

Q. Were those facts provided to you?

A. Yes, they were.

Q. Who provided those facts to you?

A. Your office.

Q. Would you state the facts as you believe them to be?

A. Mr. Jones is a 41-year-old white male born July 4, 1946. He was permanently partially disabled in an accident September 1, 1986. He is a high school graduate. He is married and has no minor children. His earnings increased from $37,816 in 1983 to $42,116 in 1985. During the nine months prior to his accident, he earned $34,512.

§21.06 Direct Examination: The Time Frame

(Examination by plaintiff's attorney.)

Q. Using the information provided by my office, you were then able to make an economic forecast concerning the economic loss sustained by Mr. Jones?[1]

A. Yes.

Q. Please explain how the analysis proceeds.

A. In an analysis such as this there are two parts to the economic loss: the historic loss and the future loss. The historic loss is from the date of the accident until today, the date of the trial. The future loss is the loss from today until Mr. Jones retires.

Q. What do you mean until Mr. Jones retires?

A. When calculating the future loss it is necessary to determine when a loss stops. When the loss stops depends on what type of loss is being estimated. If the loss of wages is being estimated, then the future loss will terminate at retirement. If the loss being estimated is the retirement benefit then the beginning point in time is the retirement date and the termination date is the date Mr. Jones passes away. If medical expenses

---

[1] Rule 703 of the Federal Rule of Evidence permits the expert to base an opinion on facts or data perceived by or made known to him at or before the hearing. Thus, the expert need not testify in response to a hypothetical question given by the attorney in open court.

are being estimated, then the loss would begin today, the date of the trial, and continue throughout Mr. Jones' life.

Q. So, the historic loss begins at the date of the accident and continues until today, and the future loss starts today and continues until some date in the future. What future date depends on what is being estimated.

A. Yes.

§21.07 —The Direct Examination: The Historic Loss

Q. When calculating the historic loss, what sort of losses are considered by the economist?

A. The losses which can be calculated by an economist include the loss of wages, the loss of the supervisory differential, the loss of the fringe benefits received by the injured party, the loss resulting from the inability of the injured party to perform household services, and, finally, medical expenses.

Q. In this case what losses were you asked to calculate?

A. I was asked to calculate the economic loss resulting from the lost wages, the lost supervisory differential, and the lost fringe benefits. This loss was to be modified, or reduced, to reflect Mr. Jones's return to the labor force.

Q. How do you calculate the historic loss?

A. The calculation of the historic loss begins by establishing the date of the accident, which was September 1, 1986. After determining the loss which occurred from that date through the end of the year, I then determine size of the loss from January 1, 1987, through the day of the trial, October 10, 1987. The loss is based on the hourly earnings of $18 plus a $1 per hour supervisory benefit and a $2 per hour fringe benefit, which Mr. Jones was earning at the time of the accident. These rates were increased January 1, 1987, as per the union contract. The contract called for an hourly wage increase to $18.50 on January 1, but fringe and supervisory benefits remain the same. On July 1, 1987, the hourly wage remained at $18.50 with a $1 differential for supervisory responsibility. However, the fringe increased to $2.11 per hour. So, as the historic losses were calculated, these changes in hourly benefits and fringe benefits were incorporated into the analysis.

Q. How do you go about calculating the loss that occurred from September 1, 1986, through the end of 1987?

A. September 1, 1986, represents the 244th day of the year. That would mean that Mr. Jones was disabled 33.15 per cent of the year. Using the hourly wage rate of $18 per hour and the supervisory differential of $1 per hour, Mr. Jones would have suffered a lost wage in 1986 of $12,411. The supervisory loss would have been $690. The $2 per hour fringe benefit resulted in a loss of $1,379. The total loss, then, for 1986 would have been $14,480.

But Mr. Jones worked for two weeks following the accident starting November 1, 1986. He returned in a supervisory capacity and received full benefits. His earnings in that two-week period were $1,680. Thus, the total loss of income in 1986 was $12,800.

Beginning the first of January 1987 and running to the trial date of October 10, 1987, the loss is calculated for 77.53 per cent of the year. The loss is based on an $18.50 per hour wage plus a $1 per hour supervisory benefit and a $2 per hour fringe benefit. The fringe benefit is increased to $2.11 per hour on the first of July as per the union contract. Historic lost wage would be $29,834, the $1 per hour supervisory benefit would be $1,612, and the lost fringe benefits would be $3,306. The total loss from the 1st of January to today would be $34,752. However, Mr. Jones did return to work the first of August of 1987. So the work from the first of August until today, the trial date, would represent 70 days, or 19.18 per cent, of the year. He now earns only $6 per hour, thus he has earned $2,393 since returning to the labor force. Subtracting this from what he would have earned in his previous job, the 1987 loss is $32,359. The total loss from the date of the accident until today is $45,159.

Q. Would this historic loss include any medical expenses?

A. No, the $45,159 represents a loss of wages, supervisory differential, and fringe benefits.

Q. Did I ask you to calculate the loss of household services to Mr. Jones resulting from this accident?

A. No, you did not.

Q. So this figure, $45,159, would understate the loss experienced by Mr. Jones, is that correct?

A. Yes sir.

Q. Did I ask you to calculate the medical expenses suffered by Mr. Jones in connection with his injury?

A. No, you did not.

Q. So this figure, $45,159, does not include the medical expenses incurred by Mr. Jones as a result of this accident or the value of the household services which were lost as a result of this accident. Is that correct?

A. Yes, it is.

Q. You said earlier that there were two losses, an historic loss and the present value of the future loss. Is that correct?

A. That is correct.

§21.08 Direct Examination: Present Value

(Examination by plaintiff's attorney.)

Q. Just exactly what is meant by the concept of present value?

A. Let me use an example to explain the concept of present value. Suppose the individual is to receive $1,000 one year from today. That individual might be willing to accept something less than $1,000 today. How much less the individual would accept depends on interest rates and other factors. But the point is that $1,000 to be received one year from today has a present value which is less. Monies to be received in the future have a present value or a value today. What is attempting to be calculated in a case such as this is how many dollars Mr. Jones needs today in order to provide a stream of income over the remaining time that he would have been in the labor force.

Q. Then if I understand you correctly, the economist is attempting to determine the size of a fund, and this fund would be sufficient to provide an income for Mr. Jones each year until he reaches age 65. Is that correct?

A. That is correct.

Q. Is this concept of present value used only in the calculation of this income stream?

A. No. We use the concept of present value to determine the value of common stock. We can use the present value to determine the value of an asset by looking at the cash flows expected from the asset. We also use the concept of present value to determine the value of a business.

Q. Is there a formula which the economist uses in order the calculate the present value of a stream of income?

A. Yes, there is.

Q. What is that formula?

A. The formula is:

$$\text{Present value} = \$ * (1+g)^t/(1+d)^t$$

Q. What are the variables in this formula?

A. There are four variables in the formula. They are represented by the dollar sign, the letter "g," the letter "d," and the letter "t."

Q. What do each of those symbols represent?

§21.09 Direct Examination: The Dollar Amount

(Examination by plaintiff's attorney.)

A. The dollar sign represents the current income, current medical expense, or the current value of household services.

Q. Then the dollar sign is today's value or the current value of what is being estimated. Is that correct?

Q. Yes, sir, that is correct.

A. When you calculated a dollar loss for Mr. Jones, what was the dollar amount that you used in this formula?

Q. There were actually three different numbers that I used as I did this three different times. The first dollar amount was $38,480, the second dollar amount was $4,389, and the third dollar amount was $2,080.

Q. What does the $38,480 represent?

A. That would be the annual wage which would have been earned by Mr. Jones had the accident not occurred. It is $18.50 per hour as per the union contract times 2,080 hours per year.

Q. What does the $2,080 represent?

A. That represents the annual income resulting from the $1 per hour wage differential for the supervisor.

Q. What does the $4,389 represent?

A. That represents the $2.11 per hour in fringe benefits times 2,080 hours per year and would be the value of the fringe benefits Mr. Jones would have earned on that job.

§21.10 Direct Examination: The Time Factor

(Examination by plaintiff's attorney.)

Q. What does the letter "t" represent?

A. "T" represents the time frame in which the analysis occurs.

Q. What is that time frame?

A. As the formula indicates, "t" is equal to zero and runs out to a value "n," and we would say in this case "n" equals 24. The time frame starts today, meaning "t" is zero, and runs for 24 years, which would correspond to when Mr. Jones would be 64 years of age. Now there would be one calculation for each year until Mr. Jones' sixty-fourth birthday.

Q. Will the analysis always stop when Mr. Jones reaches age 65?

A. No. In this case the analysis stops at age 65 because it is assumed that Mr. Jones would retire at that age. Upon retirement, the wage, the fringe benefits, and the supervisory differential would cease. If the analysis were to encompass medical expenses on household services, then the analysis would continue past age 65.

Q. Then if I understand it correctly, the analysis stops when "t" is equal to 24 because it is assumed that the wage would stop at that point. Is that correct?

A. That is correct.

§21.11   Direct Examination: The Growth Rate

(Examination by plaintiff's attorney.)

Q.   You have a symbol "g" in the formula. What does this represent?

A.   "G" in the formula represents the growth rate of wages which Mr. Jones may expect. The growth rate is an annual growth rate.

Q.   On what is the growth rate of wage based?

A.   The growth rate is based on the historical average of . . . [the economist's rationale will be explained].

Q.   In this case what growth rate did you assume?

A.   The growth rate which I assumed in this analysis was 4 percent per year.

Q.   If I understand you correctly, then this would state that the wages would grow each year at 4 percent per year. Is that correct?

A.   That is correct.

Q.   How does the growth rate affect present value of the income stream?

A.   The larger the growth rate assumed in this analysis, the larger the present value of the future income.

Q.   If you would, let's assume different growth rates and see what would happen then to the value of future income. If you assume a 4 percent annual growth wages, and let's use the $38,480 which you said was the wage Mr. Jones would have earned, how much would the wage be in one year if the growth of wages were 4 percent per year?

A.   The wages would grow to $40,019.

Q.   And how much would wages grow to in the second year?

A.   In the second year, wages would grow to $41,620.

Q.   And using a 4 per cent growth rate in each successive year, that level of salary would increase by 4 per cent. Is that correct?

A.   That is correct.

Q.   And the growth rate would stop when Mr. Jones' income stopped; that is, income would stop after Mr. Jones retired at age 65. Is that correct?

A.   That is correct.

Q.   Please assume for me that the growth of wages was 0 per cent per year. What would the current wage be?

A.   Current wage would be $38,480.

Q.   With a zero growth rate, what would the wage be a year from now?

A.   The wage would be the same, $38,480, and each year thereafter it would remain at that level, assuming a zero growth rate.

Q.   So, as you indicated, the higher the growth rate, the higher the wage will be each successive year. Is that correct?

A.   That is correct.

§21.12   Direct Examination: The Discount Rate

(Examination by plaintiff's attorney.)

Q.   What is the significance of the discount rate?

A.   First, let's explain that the dollar amount, when multiplied by the expression "1 + g," gives a future value. For example, the $38,480, which is the current wage growing at 4 per cent per year, renders a wage or future value of $40,119 one year from now. It is the discount rate which reduces that future value to present value. The larger the discount rate or interest rate, then the smaller the present value of that future income.

Q.   What discount rate did you assume?

A.   I assumed a 6 per cent discount rate.

Q.   And what was the basis for that discount rate?

A.   That discount rate represents the . . . [economist's rationale is explained here].

Q.   How does the present value of that income stream change as the interest rate or discount rate changes?

A.   The larger the discount rate, the smaller the present value. The smaller the discount rate, the larger the present value.

Q.   If we used the example of zero growth rate, then according to what you have already told me, Mr. Jones could expect an income of $38,480 each year until he reaches age 65. Is that correct?

A.   Yes, sir.

Q.   And you further stated that the higher the discount rate, then the lower each of those future values would be today, or the smaller the present value. Is that correct?

A.   Yes, sir.

Q.   Assume, if you would, that Mr. Jones was to receive $38,480 one year from today. If that is to be discounted at 6 per cent, what would the present value of that $38,480 be?

A.   The present value would be $36,302.

Q.   That means that $36,302 today is the same as $38,480 received one year from today. Is that correct?

A.   That is correct, if you assume an interest rate of 6 per cent.

Q.   Assume for me, if you would, the discount rate of 10 per cent instead of 6 per cent. Would the present value of $38,480 received in one year be higher or lower than the $36,302 using a 6 per cent discount rate?

A.   The present value would be lower.

Q.   What would the present value be?

A.   Present value of $38,480 earning 10 per cent per year and received in one year would be $34,982.

§21.13   Direct Examination: Growth and Discount Together

(Examination by plaintiff's attorney.)

Q. You stated that you have used a growth rate of 4 per cent and a discount rate of 6 per cent. Is it your belief that the growth and discount rates will be the same each year until Mr. Jones retires at age 65?

A. No. What I believe to be correct is that the relationship between the growth and discount rates will be maintained. That is, historically we have seen a 2 per cent spread between the growth and discount rates, the discount rate exceeding the growth rate by 2 per cent. I would suggest that this spread will be maintained. As the growth rate may increase or decrease, then the discount rate will increase or decrease, maintaining approximately a 2 per cent difference between now and the time Mr. Jones retires at age 65.

Q. Please explain how the growth and discount rates, when taken together, project the present value of the income stream.

A. If we take as a given the dollar amount of the wages of $38,480 Mr. Jones would have earned, and we take the time frame as a given (that is, retirement at age 65), then the two variables, growth and discount, will determine present value. If the discount rate is held constant, then the higher the growth rate, the higher the present value. If the growth rate is held constant, then the lower the discount rate, the higher the present value; or, the higher the interest assumption, the lower the present value.

§21.14   —Direct Examination: Present Value of Future Income

Q. When I first contacted you to calculate the present value of the loss for Mr. Jones, what did I ask you to calculate?

A. You asked me to calculate the present value of the future wages, the present value of the loss due to giving up the supervisory differential, and the present value of the fringe benefits.

Q. What were the present values of those?

A. The present value of the wages beginning today and running until retirement at age 65 is $741,642. The present value of the supervisory differential is $40,089. The present value of the fringe benefit was $84,592. From this I subtracted the present value of future income resulting from the employment Mr. Jones currently enjoys. The present value of his future wage which he is currently earning is $240,533. So the total loss would be the present value of future wages at $18.50 per hour plus the $1 per hour supervisory benefit differential plus the $2.11 per hour fringe benefit, less the $6 per hour wage that he is currently earning. The present value of the future loss would be $625,790.

Q. What would the total loss suffered by Mr. Jones be?

A. The total loss would be $670,949. It would consist of the $45,159 historic loss plus the $625,790 present value of future loss.

Q. You earlier referred to this analysis as being a basic analysis. What does that mean?

A. Basic analysis means that the loss is calculated from today, the date of trial, to retirement at age 65.

Q. What assumptions are made in that basic analysis?

A. Basic assumptions made in this analysis are that Mr. Jones would work uninterrupted to age 65, or 25 future years. Additionally, the annual growth and discount rate are assumed to be 4 and 6 per cent, respectively.

Q. That means that under the basic analysis, there are four variables, the dollar amount, the time in which the analysis is to take place, the growth rate, and the discount rate. Is that correct?

A. That is correct.

Q. If one assumes that the dollar amount does not change, and if one assumes that the time frame is appropriate, then the other two variables would be growth and discount. How do those two relate to the dollar amount and the time frame?

A. If the time frame and the dollar amount are taken as constant, then the dollar amount can be multiplied by what is called a "present value factor." There is a present value factor for every growth and discount rate combination. The size of that factor depends on the number of years in which the analysis takes place.

For example, in this case we said that Mr. Jones would be working from age 41 to age 65. There would be a factor corresponding to a 4 per cent growth rate and a 6 per cent discount rate. That factor would be 19.2734. When multiplied by the current annual income, we would get the present value of the future income.

In this case the current income, had Mr. Jones not been injured, would have been $38,480. When multiplied by the factor of 19.2734, the present value of the future income is determined to be $741,642. If the analysis were to estimate the present value of alternative income, then the same factor would be employed.

Mr. Jones is working at $6 per hour. The current annual income is $12,480. Multiplying that number by the factor of 19.2734, we have a present value of future income of $240,532.

This money is subtracted from the previous number in order to determine the present value of the loss. In a like fashion, the present value of the annual amount received as a supervisory differential can be determined. The $2,080 annual differential, when multiplied by the factor of 19.2734, give a present value of the supervisory benefits equal to $40,089. In the same manner, when the fringe benefits of $2.11 per hour are multiplied by 2,080 hours, the current annual fringe benefit is $4,389. When multiplied by the factor of 19.2734, it gives a present value of future benefits of $84,592.

Q. That would mean, then, if we felt that the dollar amount was too high or too low, we could change the dollar amount in order to determine the present value of the future income stream. Is that correct?

A. Yes, it is.

Q. In similar fashion, if we felt that the growth and discount rates were inappropriate, we could then calculate the discount factor, or present value factor, for whatever combinations of growth or discount rates we felt would be appropriate. Is that correct?

A. Yes, it is.

Q. Let us modify the assumptions, then, in this analysis. Assume Mr. Jones would be working for 23 years (this year plus 23 future years), and further assume that the $38,480 current income is an appropriate figure. What would the present value factor be if you used a zero growth rate of wages and a 6 per cent discount rate?

A. The discount factor would become 13.303 and the present value of future income would be $511,899.

Q. Assume the growth rate was 8 per cent and the discount rate did not change. What would the present value factor be and what would the present value of future income be?

A. The present value factor would be 30.005. The present value of future income would be $1,154,592.

Q. In this scenario we have allowed the growth rate to change while the discount rate remains the same. I would like now to switch and leave the growth rate the same and let the discount rate increase. Assume for me that the growth rate was 0 per cent annually and that, initially, the discount rate was a zero rate, and then it increased to 10 per cent. What would the present value factors be and what would the present value of future income be?

A. If we have a growth rate of 0 and a discount rate of 0, the present value factor is 24. The present value of future income is $923,520. In the second scenario, if the growth rate is 0 and the discount rate is 10 percent, the present value factor declines to 9.883 and the present value of future income drops to $380,298.

Q. Would you please summarize the relationship between the growth and discount rates and the present value factor.

A. As the growth rate rises, assuming discount rate does not change, the present value factor will increase, which would mean the higher the growth rate the higher the present value factor. By the same token, if the growth rate is to remain constant, then higher discount rates will result in lower present value factors. This results in a lower present value for the future income stream.

Q. Then essentially what you have done is to determine the appropriate growth rate and appropriate discount rate. These two determine a factor. Multiply the factor by the current level of wages, fringe benefits, or supervisory benefits in order to determine the present value of the income stream. Is that essentially correct?

A. That is correct.

Q. When we started this discussion you said this was the basic analysis. How can the present value formula be modified to reflect what you called the extended analysis?

§21.15 Direct Examination: Present Value of Future Income—Extended Analysis

(Examination by plaintiff's attorney.)

A. To do the extended analysis one would consider the probability of Mr. Jones's living each successive year until age 99, the probability that he would seek employment, the probability of finding employment, the effect disability has on consumption, the effect on the delivery of household services, and, finally, the impact income taxes have on the present value of the income stream. The modified formula would look like this:

$$\text{Present Value} = \sum_{t=0}^{n} \$ * (1+g)^t/(1+d)^t * PL * PS * PF * C * HS * TX$$

§21.16 Direct Examination: Probability of Living

(Examination by plaintiff's attorney.)

Q. When you do the extended analysis and it is necessary to include the probability of living, where do you get the information concerning the probability of living?

A. The information on the probability of living is obtained from the U.S. National Center for Health Statistics, Vital Statistics of the United States. This data is published in the *Statistical Abstracts of the United States.*

Q. And how do you use the information?

A. This information permits us to construct a mortality table for an individual of a given age. For each year, from now until age 99, a probability of living is constructed. When using the extended analysis, there is no longer a terminal age at 65, rather the analysis extends to age 99, and each year now takes into account the probability of reaching the next year.

§21.17 Direct Examination: Probabilities of Seeking and Finding Employment

(Examination by plaintiff's attorney.)

Q. How do the probabilities of seeking and finding employment enter into the analysis?

A. For each age there is a probability that each individual will seek employment. Likewise, for each age there is a probability that an individual seeking employment will find employment. These probabilities are then multiplied by the annual dollar amounts established under the basic analysis. The probable income level through age 99 is thus determined.

Q. Taking into consideration just those three variables, that is, the probability of living, the probability of seeking employment, and the probability of finding employment, what would be the impact had those three variables been included in your analysis in Mr. Jones' future income?

A. It becomes important to compare the level of income if Mr. Jones were to work uninterrupted to age 65 and the growth rate of wages of 4 per cent and the discount rate of 6 per cent. Then, as we stated earlier, the present value of the future income would be $741,642. If this income level were to be modified for the probability of living, the probability of seeking employment, and the probability of finding employment, then in my judgment the analysis would run out to age 99. The present value of that income stream would become $617,910.

§21.18 Direct Examination: Consumption

(Examination by plaintiff's attorney.)

Q. In this analysis you also said that consumption could be effective. How has consumption entered into the extended analysis?

A. In this case there was no adjustment made to reflect altered consumption as a result of the accident.

Q. In a more general sense, then, how does consumption affect the present value of future income stream?

A. In a case where the party was killed, then it would be necessary to reduce the future income to reflect that portion of the income which the deceased would have consumed. In a situation such as this, where the party was injured, the assumption is that the disability does not alter the consumption.

Q. Is it possible that a disability could alter the income consumption of the individual?

A. Yes, it is.

Q. In what fashion?

A. One could argue either direction that the disability could cause the income consumed by the individual to increase, meaning there is a greater financial demand on the income due to the disability, such as a wheelchair, modifications to a vehicle, modifications to the home, clothing requirements, or what have you. On the same token, it could be argued that the disability may reduce the consumption; the disability may no longer permit the individual to do recreational boating, skiing, sky diving, and so forth. In that sense, the expenses may in fact decrease.

Q. Was there any attempt to determine if the consumption should be modified in any fashion?

A. No, there was not.

Q. To your knowledge, are there any studies available which address the question of consumption as related to disability?

A. No, sir, not to my knowledge.

§21.19 Direct Examination: Household Services

(Examination by plaintiff's attorney.)

Q. Under the extended analysis, how would household services affect the present value of the loss?

A. In the case of disability, it would be assumed that the individual would not be able to perform the household services after the accident that were performed prior to the accident. While it is possible the individual could perform the same services, it would be thought that it would take longer for the disabled person than for the nondisabled person. As a result of the disability, then, the loss occurs either because of the inability to perform the service, or because it takes longer to perform the service, thus making it impossible to perform the same amount of household services.

Q. When you speak of household services, what do you mean?

A. Household services would include things like painting the house, auto repair, mowing the yard, cooking meals, laundry, ironing, care and rearing of children, shopping, and chauffering. All these things would be considered household services.

Q. Are there any studies that indicate the value of household services?

A. Yes, there are.

Q. What are these studies?

A. Probably the best known studies are one by Gauger and Walker and a study done by the Jefferson Standard Insurance Company reported in the *Sylvia Porter Money Book for the Eighties*. The latter study, however, addresses only the value of housewife services. In this case, the housewife is not employed outside the home. The Gauger and Walker study addresses the value of household services in the broader sense. The values are determined for the housewife employed outside the home, and the value of the services when the wife is not employed outside the home. In a similar vein, the value of the household services of the spouse, the husband, are estimated, and they too are a function of whether or not the housewife is employed outside the home. The study also indicates that teenagers have an economic contribution about the home. Again, the value of the teenage services depend on whether or not the housewife or mother is employed outside the home.

Q.   How are the household services from the Gauger and Walker study presented?

A.   The study presents two pieces of information. One is the number of hours that the individual puts in about the home, and the second portion reports the dollar value of those household services.

Q.   What are the dollar values based on?

A.   The dollar values of household services is based on the wage rates prevailing in the Ithaca, New York, area.

Q.   Why was the Ithaca, New York, area chosen for this study?

A.   Gauger and Walker did the study at Cornell University, which is located in Ithica.

Q.   The dollar value of household services, if you use the dollar amount recorded in the study as an Ithica, New York, amount, is not necessarily correct for this region of the country. Is that correct?

A.   That is correct.

Q.   Could you modify the Cornell University study to reflect this area of the country?

A.   Yes, sir, I believe so.

Q.   How would you do that?

A.   There are probably two ways one might go about making that modification. The first way would be to treat all value of household services at the value of minimum wage, so the number of hours spent in household responsibility would be multiplied by minimum wage. The second way would be to try to determine just exactly what type of activities the individual was involved in and then multiply the number of hours by the current local wage rate in order to estimate the value of household services.

Q.   Nonetheless, in this case did I ask you to calculate the lost household services for Mr. Jones?

A.   No, you did not.

Q.   So when you stated earlier that the present value of lost income to Mr.

Jones was $670,949, that was exclusive of any loss in the value of household services to which he would be able to perform. Is that correct?

A. That is correct.

§21.20 Direct Examination: Taxes

(Examination by plaintiff's attorney.)

Q. Does this extended analysis allow for the reduction of present value of lost income for federal income tax purposes?

A. No, it does not.

Q. Why have you not reduced this present value judgment for taxes?

A. In my judgment, it is not necessarily true that federal income taxes would cause the present value of this loss to decline.

Q. Would you please explain that?

A. If the taxes to be paid to the federal government are taken into consideration, it becomes necessary to forecast the deductions that Mr. Jones would have each year in the future. For example, if the Jones' house is not currently paid for, the interest is a tax deductible item, and we must be able to determine how much interest will be paid each year before we can calculate the tax rate. In a like fashion, we would have to know if the Jones' plan to move, the annual interest the Jones' would be paying on their house, what year they plan to move, what the price of the house would be, how much they would put down on the house, and what the current mortgage interest rate would be in order to calculate the taxable income. In the same manner, since medical expenses are still deductible under the tax laws, we would have to know what medical expenses would be incurred, if those expenses exceeded the deductible, in what year the medical expenses occurred, the size of the medical expenses, whether or not it was insured, and how much of it was not insured. Consequently, the inclusion of taxes is almost prohibitive because of the additional knowledge and assumptions which are necessary. In another vein, if the Jones' were to receive the award of $625,790, which is the present value of the future income loss, and they were to invest that money at an interest rate of 10 percent, they would be earning $62,579 in the first year for interest. From this amount they should deduct one year's income. That would be $38,480, growing each year at 4 percent. So from the income of $62,579 they should deduct $40,020. The difference between the two should be reinvested at 10 percent. Under the tax laws it is possible that they would have to pay tax on the $62,579 at a rate which would be higher than what they would pay on the income of $40,000. Consequently, it would take more money than $625,790 would indicate. Stated a little differently, the inclusion of taxes would require a higher present value in order to leave the Jones' in the same position after inclusion of federal income tax in the judgment.

Q. In the extended analysis, then, you have considered the probability of living, the probability of seeking employment, the probability of finding employment, consumption, household services, and taxes. Is that correct?

A. Yes, it is.

Q. In your judgment, then, how does each of these variables effect the present value of the future income stream?

A. If we were to include the probability of living, then the present value of the future income stream would be reduced. If the probability of seeking employment and finding employment are included, again, the present value of the future income stream would be reduced. In this particular case, since Mr. Jones was disabled, there does not appear to be any impact on the present value of the income stream with the inclusion of consumption. If one were to include services, then the present value of the future loss would be increased. If one were to include taxes, the present value of the future income stream would be further increased.

Q. In summary, then, you believe it would be best to do the present value of the future loss using the basic analysis. Is that correct?

A. That is correct.

Q. In your judgment, if the basic analysis is used, what is the present value of the future income stream loss to Mr. Jones?

A. The present value of the future loss would be $625,790.

Q. Does that include historic loss?

A. No, the historic loss would be an additional $45,159.

Q. Then this loss would exclude any loss arising from the inability of Mr. Jones to continue to perform household services. Is that correct?

A. That is correct.

Q. No further questions.

§21.21   The Cross Examination: An Overview

The purpose of cross examining a witness is to discredit that witness. When the witness is an economist, there are three areas in which the economist can be attacked; the first area is personal integrity, the second area is the methodology employed by the economist, and the third area is the numbers provided to the economist and used in the analysis.

If the integrity is to be attacked, then it must be demonstrated that the economist has a bias in favor of the plaintiff, or that perhaps the economist is rewarded or compensated based on the size of the loss.

If the methodology is to be attacked, then one of two things must occur: (1) the methodology employed by the economist is conceptually incorrect; or (2) the methodology employed by the economist changes depending on the type of loss being evaluated. If the defense attorney is attempting to demonstrate that the methodology employed is conceptually incorrect, it may well be necessary to employ a defense economist. On the other hand, if the methodology has changed over time, perhaps the defense attorney can demonstrate different results using the different methods historically employed by the economist. One way to evaluate methodology is to retain a defense attorney to review reports which have been provided to various attorneys by the plaintiff's economist. **Sections 21.22** through **21.25** are designed to indicate questions which might be asked on cross-examination.

§21.22   Cross-Examination: The Introduction

(Examination by defense attorney.)

Q. Thank you, Mr. Economist, for that fine explanation of economic loss. Would you be more comfortable if I called your Dr.? I believe Dr. is an appropriate term, isn't it?

A. Yes, sir.

Q. Well would you be more comfortable if I called you Mr. or Dr.?

A. It really doesn't make any difference.

Q. Thank you, Mr. Economist. Let us proceed. I only have a few brief questions.

(What the defense attorney is attempting to do at this point is no longer refer to the witness as Dr. so-and-so, rather referring to the witness as Mr. so-and-so, and therefore reduce some of the credibility the witness may have with the jury.)

Q. Mr. Economist, have you ever met Mr. Jones?

A. No, I have not.

Q. Have you ever met Mr. Jones' family?

A. No, I have not.

(What the defense attorney has done at this point is establish that the plaintiff's economist does not know Mr. Jones or Mr. Jones' family. This means that the economist knows nothing about Mr. Jones' personal habits unless such information was provided to him by the plaintiff's attorney. This will permit the defense attorney to ask a whole series of questions about Mr. Jones which will require the plaintiff's economist to answer "no." The "no" answers underscore the "statistical" nature of the economist's analysis. An example of the questions about the personal habits of Mr. Jones are: "Did you take into consideration the impact of Mr. Jones' smoking?" "Did you know that Mr. Jones' family has a history of heart problems?")

Q. In your analysis I believe you indicated that the present value of the future loss when you used a zero growth rate and a 10 per cent discount rate was in the neighborhood of $380,000. Isn't that correct?

A. That is true.

Q. Within that analysis we would like to determine just exactly which formula you used in arriving at that dollar amount.

A.   I don't believe I understand the question, sir.

Q.   You mentioned earlier that there were two methods or formulas which you could employ, one being what I think you called a basic analysis, and the other being what I think you called an extended analysis. When you reached the $388,000 loss figure, what analysis were you using?

A.   I was using the basic analysis.

(Defense attorney has pointed out that the basic analysis was used to arrive at all the dollar losses stated by the plaintiff's economist. On later examination all the uncertain elements which were discussed in the extended analysis can be pointed out as having not been included in the analysis provided to plaintiff's attorney in the economist's report.)

Q.   Now in the basic analysis, you used a dollar amount for the wages of Mr. Jones. What was that dollar amount?

A.   I used $18.50 per hour for wages plus $1 for supervisory differential and $2.11 for fringe benefits.

Q.   When you arrived at the $380,000 loss, you were using the $18.50 an hour as the basis for the loss. Isn't that correct?

A.   Yes, I was.

(Since the defense attorney recognizes that if there is a loss the jury is going to award something, what may happen is that all references the defense attorney makes to a loss are to the $380,000 loss. While this does not reflect the economist's testimony, it was the lowest figure mentioned by the economist. It was calculated by using a zero growth rate and a 10 per cent discount rate. All future references to losses made by the defense attorney will be to the $380,000 figure, or some lower figure.)

Q.   Where did you get the $18.50 per hour wage rate earned by Mr. Jones?

A.   That information was provided to me through the plaintiff's attorney's office.

Q.   So that figure was not verified by yourself, but rather taken as information provided to you. Is that correct?

A.   That is correct.

Q.   Then where did you get the information on the growth and discount rates which you employed?

A.   I found those pieces of information in various government publications.

Q.   Would you tell us which publications you used?

A.   Yes, sir. The publications were . . . .

(The defense attorney or defense attorney's economist may wish to verify the accuracy of the data and the accuracy of the source.)

Q.   If I understand what you have done, then, you have taken the information from Mr. Jones' attorney's office and used that information as the dollar amount and then used government data to determine a growth rate and discount rate. Is that correct?

A. That is correct.

Q. Is it also correct that you assume that this individual, Mr. Jones, would work uninterrupted to age 65?

A. That is correct.

§21.23 Cross-Examination: The Dollar Amount

(Examination by defense attorney.)

Q. When you calculated the dollar loss, you used the $18.50 per hour as the basis for that loss. Isn't that correct?

A. That is correct.

Q. Assume for me, if you would, that following this trial, Mr. Jones was able to return to work, and further assume that he was able to return to the same job he had prior to the accident. In your judgment what would he be earning?

A. Well, sir, if it were the same job, he would be earning $18.50 per hour.

Q. That is correct. And if he were supervisor, how much would he be earning?

A. Well, sir, he would be earning an additional $1 per hour.

Q. Well, I agree with you. Further assume that he also received the benefit package. How much would he be earning in fringe benefits?

A. He would be earning the $2.11 per hour.

Q. I believe you are saying that if he returns to work in the same capacity following this trial, there would be no economic loss. Is that correct?

A. If he returned to work in the same capacity after the accident as before the accident, and he received the same compensation, that is correct, there would be no economic loss.

Q. So it is possible if Mr. Jones returns to work there would be no economic loss, that is, he was not injured economically. Let's turn to another issue. Suppose Mr. Jones was injured, and further suppose that Mr. Jones entered the university where you teach and graduated with a degree in accounting. Would it be possible for him to enter the labor market as an accountant?

A. Yes, I suppose that would be possible.

Q. What does a graduate in accounting earn when they first enter the job market?

A. Sir, I really don't know.

Q. But it would be reasonable to say that within a few years they would be making more than the $38,000 which you said Mr. Jones is currently earning.

A. I really don't know.

Q. Let me rephrase the question. If Mr. Jones were to retrain, is it possible that his new job, following training, would provide an income greater than the earnings he would experience on his current job?

A. Yes, sir, I suppose that is possible.

Q. So what you are saying is yes, it is possible that with training he would suffer no economic loss.

A. Yes, sir, that is possible.

Q. Assume it took four years to retrain, what is the tuition at the local university?

A. At our institution, tuition, books, and fees would run around $5,000 a year.

Q. So the retraining loss would be essentially $20,000.

A. No, sir, you would have to consider . . . .

Q. I withdraw the question. Let's continue, sir. Do you know the nature of the job which Mr. Jones held prior to this accident?

A. Yes, sir, I believe he was a sheet metal worker.

Q. Just exactly what is a sheet metal worker?

A. I believe they deal with thin metals which are used to build ducting for air conditioning, heating, things like that.

Q. Does this require a great deal of strength or little strength?

A. I am really not sure.

Q. Just how much do you really know about sheet metal workers?

A. Very little.

Q. So you really don't understand the nature of the occupation, or the union contract, just that Mr. Jones was in fact earning $18 or so per hour at the time of the accident.

A. Yes, sir.

Q. For some reason, you really don't know anything about Mr. Jones personally, you don't know him individually, you have never met his family, you really don't know what a sheet metalworker does, or what he was required to do as an employee or as a member of the union. Isn't that correct?

A. Yes, sir.

Q. Further, your analysis did not take into consideration the possibility that Mr. Jones could return to work following this trial, did it?

A. Well, sir, the disability information indicated that he would not be able to return to work.

Q. Was that your medical judgment, or how did you arrive at that fact?

A. That was not my decision. I was told by Mr. Jones' attorney that he was unable to return to work.

Q. So you relied nearly 100 per cent on the plaintiff's attorney saying that he was unable to return to work.

A. Yes, sir, that is correct.

Q. Do you think the plaintiff's attorney is biased in this area? I mean, the larger the award, the larger the compensation to . . .

I object, Your Honor.   Plaintiff's Attorney:

Q. I withdraw the question. Sir, when you calculated the present value of the economic loss, I believe you said you used $18 per hour and then multiplied it by 2,000 hours per year to get an annual income of $36,000. Isn't that essentially correct?

A. Yes, sir.

Q. Then you multiplied the $36,000 by the present value factor of nine point something-or-other and this resulted in a present value estimate of around $340,000, or something like that. Isn't that correct?

A. Yes, sir, that is correct.

Q. Sir, if you take the $18 per hour that you said Mr. Jones was earning at the time of the accident and deduct from that the $6 per hour which Mr. Jones is currently earning, you would have a $12 per hour income. Isn't that correct?

A. That is correct.

Q. If you multiply the $12 per hour, which you claim to be the loss, by 2,000 hours, you would have an earnings of $24,000 per year. Isn't that correct?

A. That is approximately correct, sir, there are 2,080 hours in the year.

Q. Well, using the approximately correct number of $24,000 and multiplying it by the discount factor that you talked about earlier with the zero growth rate and the 10 per cent discount rate, which I believe you said was approximately nine, isn't that correct?

A. I believe it was slightly over nine, but that was not the figure I used.

Q. Multiplying the $12 per hour times 2,000 gives $24,000 per year income times a factor of 9 would render a loss of $216,000. Isn't that correct?

A. The math is correct, sir, but that is not what I said the loss was.

Q. The loss of $216,000 is considerably less than what you testified to earlier, is it not?

A. It is.

§21.24 Cross-Examination: The Time Factor

(Examination by defense attorney.)

Q. Let's move on to the value which you assigned for "t." I believe "t" was the time factor in which the analysis occurred. Isn't that correct?

A. That is correct.

Q. You used the value "t" for 24 years, I believe. Isn't that correct?

A. That is correct.

Q. In your analysis, though, you assumed that the individual would work uninterrupted to age 65. Isn't that correct?

A. That is correct.

Q. Are you familiar with the unemployment rates in the area in which Mr. Jones is historically employed?

A. I don't believe I understand your question.

Q. My question is this: Do they work uninterrupted as sheet metal workers from age 41 until age 65?

A. I am not really sure.

Q. Isn't it a fact that there are seasonal unemployments in this trade, and that is one of the reasons they are paid $18 an hour?

A. I'm not sure.

Q. It is important that you be sure. You are attempting to estimate an economic loss here. Had you considered allowing this man to work less than full-time between now and age 65, isn't it true that the loss that you estimated would have been less?

A. Yes, that is true.

Q. Then the $216,000, which you just testified was the loss, should be less if Mr. Jones had not worked full-time to age 65.

A. Well, sir, . . .

Q. That was not a question, sir, that was just a statement that it would be less. Now, sir, did you consider the probability that Mr. Jones could die prior to age 65?

A. I did in the extended analysis.

Q. Sir, your report to the plaintiff's attorney did not have a figure for the extended analysis. It had only the basic analysis, as I recall. In that basic analysis, is there an adjustment for the probability of living each year or probability of premature death?

A. Not in the basic analysis.

Q. Then to properly reflect the loss that would have occurred to Mr. Jones, there should be an adjustment for the probability of premature death.

A. Sir, but . . . .

Q. Sir, that was not a question, that was a statement that there should have been an adjustment for premature death. So the fact that you did not include mortality means that you did not take into consideration or were not aware of the fact that Mr. Jones smokes, is that correct?

A. That is correct.

Q. Were you aware of Mr. Jones drinking habits?

A. No, I am not.

Q. Are you aware of Mr. Jones' smoking habits?

A. No.

Q. Can smoking reduce one's life expectancy?

A. Yes.

Q. Are you aware of Mr. Jones' heart problem?

A. No.

Q. Are you aware of Mr. Jones . . .

(This type of questioning is designed to show how little the economist knows about the plaintiff. All the factors mentioned can be used on summary to show reduced life expectancy.)

Q. Were you aware of Mr. Jones hobbies, whether or not they could alter his life expectancy?

A. I was not aware of his hobbies.

§21.25 The Cross Examination: The Discount Rate

Q. Sir, you said earlier that in your judgment the loss that Mr. Jones would sustain due to this disability was $380,000. You also said earlier that the discount rate was 10 percent. Suppose Mr. Jones were to invest $380,000 today at 10 percent. What would his annual income be?

A. The interest income from that investment would be $38,000.

Q. Just a minute ago we talked about the loss sustained by Mr. Jones and determined that it was more like $24,000 a year. Now if you subtracted the $24,000 a year from that interest income which you just stated, how much excess would there be?

A. Sir, I didn't say that the loss was $24,000 . . .

Q. Your Honor, please ask the witness to answer the question. The question was that if you took the $38,000 in interest income and subtracted the $24,000 lost income, how much excess interest would there be?

A. There would be an excess of $14,000.

Defense Attorney. So that means that if Mr. Jones had an investment of $380,000, that Mr. Jones could take $24,000 in interest income each year until he is age 65, have an excess of

$14,000 each year, and still never touch the principal. That award is excessive.

§21.26   The Cross Examination: Taxes

Q. Sir, did you consider in your analysis the impact of taxes on this judgment?

A. When I did the extended analysis . . .

Q. Sir, please answer the question. The question wasn't what you did in the extended analysis; the question was in your report to the plaintiff's attorney, which you testified the loss was determined by the basic analysis, did you consider the impact of taxes?

A. No, sir.

Q. You testified earlier that the lost income would be $24,000 per year, and that the present value factor was 9 something, for a present value of future loss of $216,000. If that money were invested at 10 percent a year, the income would be $21,600 per year. Isn't that correct?

A. Yes, sir, that is correct.

Q. Of the $24,000 income, if the individual were in, say, 40 percent—well, let's even use the current tax bracket. If the individual were in, say, a 28 percent tax bracket, and rather than use 28, let's just make it simple and use a 25 percent tax bracket. Then, out of the $24,000 annual loss which you stated earlier, the individual would receive $18,000 per year. Isn't that correct?

A. Well, sir, in my analysis . . .

Q. Please answer the question. If you are in $24,000 a year and in a 25 percent tax bracket, wouldn't you end up with $18,000 discretionary income?

A. It takes several things into consideration.

Q. I realize that, but in a basic and simple analysis, if we said you take away 25 per cent of the total income, and if they had $24,000, after we took away 25 per cent, they would have $18,000 left. Isn't that correct?

A. The math is correct, but there are certainly many other variables.

Q. I appreciate the other variables, but since you agree, let's just use that simple little concept. Out of that $18,000 per year is what would be necessary to replace the income. Now you testified earlier that the annual income would have been $21,600. That would be out of $216,000 earning 10 per cent a year, of which we only need $18,000 now. You keep reducing the amount of money which is lenient for this person, don't you?

A. No, sir, I . . .

Q. Nonetheless, if he had the $18,000 per year then from the $21,000 annual interest income, there is an excess of $3,000 year. Again, Mr. Jones never touches the principal. So a more appropriate figure would be in the neighborhood of perhaps $180,000 in terms of the future loss which Mr. Jones may have experienced. Isn't that correct?

A.   No, sir, that is not what I said.

Q.   That is what you said. Just a minute ago you said he would have earned $18,000 a year after we adjusted for taxes. His appropriate loss would be in the neighborhood of $180,000 per year.

A.   No, sir, that isn't what I said.

Q.   I believe it is what you said. I have no further questions.

§21.27   Redirect Examination

(Examination by plaintiff's attorney.)

Q.   Dr. _____, you have been cross-examined by one of the finest defense attorneys in this part of the country. After having been examined by someone as knowledgeable as the defense attorney . . .

Q.   Your Honor, I object to the form of the question.

Q.   Your Honor, if the defense attorney objects to being called a fine attorney, I respectfully withdraw that judgment. Dr. _, after having been cross-examined on the matter of the economic loss sustained by Mr. Jones, have you changed your opinion?

A.   No, sir, I have not.

Q.   In your judgment, sir, what is the total economic loss sustained by Mr. Jones as a result of this accident?

A.   In my judgment the total loss is $670,949.

Q.   In your judgment how did that loss break down; that is, what part was historical and what part was future?

A.   Sir, the present value of the future loss is $625,790, the historic loss is $45,159, and the total loss sustained by Mr. Jones is $670,949.

Q.   Thank you. I have no further questions.

Appendix A
Annual Growth Factors

Year	2%	4%	6%	8%	10%	12%
1	1.020	1.040	1.060	1.080	1.100	1.120
2	1.040	1.082	1.124	1.166	1.210	1.254
3	1.061	1.125	1.191	1.260	1.331	1.405
4	1.082	1.170	1.262	1.360	1.464	1.574
5	1.104	1.217	1.338	1.469	1.611	1.762
6	1.126	1.265	1.419	1.587	1.772	1.974
7	1.149	1.316	1.504	1.714	1.949	2.211
8	1.172	1.369	1.594	1.851	2.144	2.476
9	1.195	1.423	1.689	1.999	2.358	2.773
10	1.219	1.480	1.791	2.159	2.594	3.106
11	1.243	1.539	1.898	2.332	2.853	3.479
12	1.268	1.601	2.012	2.518	3.138	3.896
13	1.294	1.665	2.133	2.720	3.452	4.363
14	1.319	1.732	2.261	2.937	3.797	4.887
15	1.346	1.801	2.397	3.172	4.177	5.474
16	1.373	1.873	2.540	3.426	4.595	6.130
17	1.400	1.948	2.693	3.700	5.054	6.866
18	1.428	2.026	2.854	3.996	5.560	7.690
19	1.457	2.107	3.026	4.316	6.116	8.613
20	1.486	2.191	3.207	4.661	6.738	9.646
21	1.516	2.279	3.400	5.034	7.400	10.804
22	1.546	2.370	3.604	5.437	8.140	12.100
23	1.577	2.465	3.820	5.871	8.954	13.552
24	1.608	2.563	4.049	6.341	9.850	15.179
25	1.641	2.666	4.292	6.848	10.835	17.000
26	1.673	2.772	4.549	7.396	11.918	19.040
27	1.707	2.883	4.822	7.988	13.110	21.325
28	1.741	2.999	5.112	8.627	14.421	23.884
29	1.776	3.119	5.418	9.317	15.863	26.750
30	1.811	3.243	5.743	10.063	17.449	29.960

Appendix B
Annual Discount Factors

Year	2%	4%	6%	8%	10%	12%
1	.980	.962	.943	.926	.909	.893
2	.961	.962	.890	.857	.826	.797
3	.942	.962	.840	.794	.751	.712
4	.924	.962	.792	.735	.683	.636
5	.906	.962	.747	.681	.621	.567
6	.888	.962	.705	.630	.564	.507
7	.871	.962	.665	.583	.513	.452
8	.853	.962	.627	.540	.467	.404
9	.837	.962	.592	.500	.424	.361
10	.820	.962	.558	.463	.386	.322
11	.804	.962	.527	.429	.350	.287
12	.788	.962	.497	.397	.319	.257
13	.773	.962	.469	.368	.290	.229
14	.758	.962	.442	.340	.263	.205
15	.743	.962	.417	.315	.239	.183
16	.728	.962	.394	.292	.218	.163
17	.714	.962	.371	.270	.198	.146
18	.700	.962	.350	.250	.180	.130
19	.686	.962	.331	.232	.164	.116
20	.673	.962	.312	.215	.149	.104
21	.660	.962	.294	.199	.135	.093
22	.647	.962	.278	.184	.123	.083
23	.634	.962	.262	.170	.112	.074
24	.622	.962	.247	.158	.102	.066
25	.610	.962	.233	.146	.092	.059
26	.598	.962	.220	.135	.084	.053

Year	2%	4%	6%	8%	10%	12%
27	.586	.962	.207	.125	.076	.047
28	.574	.962	.196	.116	.069	.042
29	.563	.962	.185	.107	.063	.037
30	.552	.962	.174	.099	.057	.033
31	.541	.962	.164	.092	.052	.030
32	.531	.962	.155	.085	.047	.027
33	.520	.962	.146	.079	.043	.024
34	.510	.962	.138	.073	.039	.021
35	.500	.962	.130	.068	.036	.019
36	.490	.962	.123	.063	.032	.017
37	.481	.962	.116	.058	.029	.015
38	.471	.962	.109	.054	.027	.013
39	.462	.962	.103	.050	.024	.012
40	.453	.962	.097	.046	.022	.011
41	.444	.962	.092	.043	.020	.010
42	.435	.962	.087	.039	.018	.009
43	.427	.962	.082	.037	.017	.008
44	.418	.962	.077	.034	.015	.007
45	.410	.962	.073	.031	.014	.006
46	.402	.962	.069	.029	.012	.005
47	.394	.962	.065	.027	.011	.005
48	.387	.962	.061	.025	.010	.004
49	.379	.962	.058	.023	.009	.004
50	.372	.962	.054	.021	.009	.003
51	.364	.962	.051	.020	.008	.003
52	.357	.962	.048	.018	.007	.003
53	.350	.962	.046	.017	.006	.002
54	.343	.962	.043	.016	.006	.002
55	.337	.962	.041	.015	.005	.002
56	.330	.962	.038	.013	.005	.002
57	.323	.962	.036	.012	.004	.002
58	.317	.962	.034	.012	.004	.001
59	.311	.962	.032	.011	.004	.001
60	.305	.962	.030	.010	.003	.001
61	.299	.962	.029	.009	.003	.001
62	.293	.962	.027	.008	.003	.001
63	.287	.962	.025	.008	.002	.001
64	.282	.962	.024	.007	.002	.001
65	.276	.962	.023	.007	.002	.001
66	.271	.962	.021	.006	.002	.001
67	.265	.962	.020	.006	.002	.001
68	.260	.962	.019	.005	.002	.000
69	.255	.962	.018	.005	.001	.000
70	.250	.962	.017	.005	.001	.000
71	.245	.962	.016	.004	.001	.000

Year	2%	4%	6%	8%	10%	12%
72	.240	.962	.015	.004	.001	.000
73	.236	.962	.014	.004	.001	.000
74	.231	.962	.013	.003	.001	.000

Appendix C
Present Value Factors
When Growth Rates and
Discount Rates Are
Combined

**Year 1
Growth Rates
Per Cent**

Discount Rate	0%	2%	4%	6%	8%	10%
0%	1.000	1.020	1.040	1.060	1.080	1.100
2%	.980	1.000	1.020	1.039	1.059	1.078
4%	.962	.981	1.000	1.019	1.038	1.058
6%	.943	.962	.981	1.000	1.019	1.038
8%	.926	.944	.963	.981	1.000	1.019
10%	.909	.927	.945	.964	.982	1.000
12%	.893	.911	.929	.946	.964	.982
14%	.877	.895	.912	.930	.947	.965
16%	.862	.879	.897	.914	.931	.948
18%	.847	.864	.881	.898	.915	.932

Year 2
Growth Rates
Per Cent

Discount Rate	0%	2%	4%	6%	8%	10%
0%	2.000	2.060	2.122	2.184	2.246	2.310
2%	1.942	2.000	2.059	2.119	2.180	2.241
4%	1.886	1.943	2.000	2.058	2.117	2.176
6%	1.833	1.888	1.944	2.000	2.057	2.115
8%	1.783	1.836	1.890	1.945	2.000	2.056
10%	1.736	1.787	1.839	1.892	1.946	2.000
12%	1.690	1.740	1.791	1.842	1.894	1.947
14%	1.647	1.695	1.745	1.794	1.845	1.896
16%	1.605	1.652	1.700	1.749	1.798	1.848
18%	1.566	1.612	1.658	1.705	1.753	1.801

Year 3
Growth Rates
Per Cent

Discount Rate	0%	2%	4%	6%	8%	10%
0%	3.000	3.122	3.246	3.375	3.506	3.641
2%	2.884	3.000	3.119	3.242	3.367	3.496
4%	2.775	2.886	3.000	3.117	3.237	3.360
6%	2.673	2.779	2.888	3.000	3.115	3.232
8%	2.577	2.679	2.783	2.890	3.000	3.112
10%	2.487	2.584	2.684	2.787	2.892	3.000
12%	2.402	2.495	2.591	2.690	2.791	2.894
14%	2.332	2.412	2.504	2.598	2.695	2.794
16%	2.246	2.332	2.421	2.512	2.605	2.700
18%	2.174	2.257	2.343	2.430	2.520	2.611

Year 4
Growth Rates
Per Cent

Discount Rate	0%	2%	4%	6%	8%	10%
0%	4.000	4.204	4.416	4.637	4.867	5.105
2%	3.808	4.000	4.200	4.408	4.624	4.848
4%	3.630	3.811	4.000	4.196	4.400	4.611
6%	3.465	3.637	3.815	4.000	4.192	4.392
8%	3.312	3.474	3.643	3.818	4.000	4.189
10%	3.170	3.324	3.483	3.649	3.821	4.000
12%	3.037	3.183	3.335	3.492	3.655	3.825
14%	2.914	3.052	3.196	3.346	3.501	3.661
16%	2.798	2.930	3.067	3.209	3.356	3.509
18%	2.690	2.816	2.946	3.081	3.221	3.366

Year 5
Growth Rates
Per Cent

Discount Rate	0%	2%	4%	6%	8%	10%
0%	5.000	5.308	5.633	5.975	6.336	6.716
2%	4.713	5.000	5.302	5.620	5.955	6.307
4%	4.452	4.719	5.000	5.296	5.607	5.935
6%	4.212	4.462	4.724	5.000	5.290	5.595
8%	3.993	4.226	4.471	4.729	5.000	5.285
10%	3.791	4.009	4.239	4.480	4.734	5.000
12%	3.605	3.810	4.025	4.252	4.489	4.738
14%	3.433	3.626	3.828	4.041	4.264	4.498
16%	3.274	3.456	3.646	3.846	4.056	4.276
18%	3.127	3.298	3.478	3.666	3.864	4.070

Year 6
Growth Rates
Per Cent

Discount Rate	0%	2%	4%	6%	8%	10%
0%	6.000	6.434	6.989	7.394	7.923	8.487
2%	5.601	6.000	6.425	6.880	7.364	7.880
4%	5.242	5.609	6.000	6.417	6.862	7.335
6%	4.917	5.256	5.616	6.000	6.409	6.844
8%	4.623	4.936	5.268	5.623	6.000	6.401
10%	4.355	4.645	4.953	5.281	5.630	6.000
12%	4.111	4.380	4.666	4.970	5.293	5.636
14%	3.889	4.139	4.405	4.687	4.987	5.305
16%	3.685	3.918	4.166	4.428	4.707	5.003
18%	3.498	3.716	3.947	4.192	4.451	4.727

Year 7
Growth Rates
Per Cent

Discount Rate	0%	2%	4%	6%	8%	10%
0%	7.000	7.583	8.214	8.897	9.637	10.436
2%	6.472	7.000	7.571	8.189	8.856	9.577
4%	6.002	6.482	7.000	7.560	8.164	8.816
6%	5.582	6.019	6.491	7.000	7.549	8.140
8%	5.206	5.606	6.036	6.500	7.000	7.538
10%	4.868	5.234	5.628	6.053	6.509	7.000
12%	4.564	4.900	5.262	5.650	6.068	6.517
14%	4.288	4.598	4.931	5.288	5.672	6.084
16%	4.039	4.325	4.631	4.960	5.314	5.692
18%	3.812	4.076	4.360	4.664	4.989	5.338

Year 8
Growth Rates
Per Cent

Discount Rate	0%	2%	4%	6%	8%	10%
0%	8.000	8.755	9.583	10.491	11.488	12.579
2%	7.325	8.000	8.739	9.549	10.436	11.406
4%	6.733	7.338	8.000	8.724	9.516	10.382
6%	6.210	6.755	7.350	8.000	8.710	9.485
8%	5.747	6.239	6.776	7.361	8.000	8.696
10%	5.335	5.781	6.267	6.796	7.372	8.000
12%	4.968	5.373	5.814	6.294	6.816	7.383
14%	4.639	5.009	5.410	5.847	6.321	6.835
16%	4.344	4.682	5.049	5.447	5.878	6.346
18%	4.078	4.388	4.724	5.088	5.482	5.909

Year 9
Growth Rates
Per Cent

Discount Rate	0%	2%	4%	6%	8%	10%
0%	9.000	9.950	11.006	12.181	13.487	14.937
2%	8.162	9.000	9.930	10.963	12.108	13.379
4%	7.435	8.178	9.000	9.911	10.921	12.039
6%	6.802	7.462	8.192	9.000	9.893	10.881
8%	6.247	6.837	7.488	8.207	9.000	9.876
10%	5.759	6.288	6.871	7.513	8.220	9.000
12%	5.328	5.804	6.328	6.903	7.537	8.234
14%	4.946	5.376	5.848	6.366	6.935	7.560
16%	4.607	4.996	5.423	5.891	6.404	6.966
18%	4.303	4.657	5.045	5.469	5.933	6.440

Year 10
Growth Rates
Per Cent

Discount Rate	0%	2%	4%	6%	8%	10%
0%	10.000	11.169	12.486	13.972	15.645	17.531
2%	8.983	10.000	11.144	12.432	13.879	15.507
4%	8.111	9.001	10.000	11.121	12.379	13.791
6%	7.360	8.143	9.019	10.000	11.099	12.329
8%	6.710	7.401	8.173	9.036	10.000	11.077
10%	6.145	6.758	7.441	8.203	9.053	10.000
12%	5.650	6.197	6.804	7.480	8.232	9.069
14%	5.216	5.705	6.247	6.849	7.518	8.260
16%	4.833	5.272	5.759	6.297	6.893	7.554
18%	4.494	4.890	5.328	5.811	6.345	6.936

Year 11
Growth Rates
Per Cent

Discount Rate	0%	2%	4%	6%	8%	10%
0%	11.000	12.412	14.026	15.870	17.977	20.384
2%	9.787	11.000	12.383	13.958	15.755	17.802
4%	8.760	9.809	11.000	12.354	13.894	15.644
6%	7.887	8.798	9.830	11.000	12.327	13.832
8%	7.139	7.935	8.834	9.850	11.000	12.301
10%	6.495	7.194	7.981	8.868	9.870	11.000
12%	5.938	6.554	7.247	8.026	8.902	9.889
14%	5.453	5.999	6.612	7.298	8.069	8.935
16%	5.029	5.515	6.059	6.668	7.349	8.112
18%	4.656	5.092	5.577	6.118	6.723	7.398

Year 12
Growth Rates
Per Cent

Discount Rate	0%	2%	4%	6%	8%	10%
0%	12.000	13.680	15.627	17.882	20.495	23.523
2%	10.575	12.000	13.645	15.545	17.740	20.276
4%	9.385	10.601	12.000	13.611	15.467	17.605
6%	8.384	9.428	10.625	12.000	13.578	15.392
8%	7.536	8.438	9.469	10.649	12.000	13.547
10%	6.814	7.598	8.491	9.510	10.672	12.000
12%	6.194	6.880	7.658	8.542	9.549	10.694
14%	5.660	6.263	6.944	7.716	8.592	9.586
16%	5.197	5.729	6.329	7.007	7.773	8.640
18%	4.793	5.266	5.797	6.394	7.068	7.829

Year 13
Growth Rates
Per Cent

Discount Rate	0%	2%	4%	6%	8%	10%
0%	13.000	14.974	17.292	20.015	23.215	26.975
2%	11.348	13.000	14.932	17.194	19.842	22.945
4%	9.986	11.378	13.000	14.892	17.100	19.678
6%	8.853	10.034	11.406	13.000	14.854	17.010
8%	7.904	8.914	10.082	11.434	13.000	14.817
10%	7.103	7.972	8.973	10.127	11.460	13.000
12%	6.424	7.176	8.039	9.031	10.172	11.486
14%	5.842	6.498	7.247	8.104	9.087	10.215
16%	5.342	5.917	6.571	7.317	8.168	9.142
18%	4.910	5.416	5.990	6.642	7.384	8.230

Year 14
Growth Rates
Per Cent

Discount Rate	0%	2%	4%	6%	8%	10%
0%	14.000	16.293	19.024	22.276	26.152	30.772
2%	12.106	14.000	16.245	18.907	22.068	25.823
4%	10.563	12.140	14.000	16.198	18.796	21.871
6%	9.295	10.618	12.172	14.000	16.153	18.690
8%	8.244	9.363	10.671	12.203	14.000	16.110
10%	7.367	8.320	9.429	10.723	12.233	14.000
12%	6.628	7.446	8.394	9.494	10.773	12.263
14%	6.002	6.709	7.524	8.466	9.556	10.821
16%	5.468	6.082	6.788	7.600	8.536	9.617
18%	5.008	5.546	6.161	6.865	7.674	8.604

Year 15
Growth Rates
Per Cent

Discount Rate	0%	2%	4%	6%	8%	10%
0%	15.000	17.639	20.825	24.673	29.324	34.950
2%	12.849	15.000	17.583	20.688	24.425	28.927
4%	11.118	12.887	15.000	17.528	20.558	24.190
6%	9.712	11.180	12.924	15.000	17.476	20.433
8%	8.559	9.787	11.239	12.959	15.000	17.426
10%	7.606	8.642	9.860	11.297	12.993	15.000
12%	6.811	7.692	8.723	9.931	11.352	13.026
14%	6.142	6.897	7.776	8.801	10.001	11.407
16%	5.575	6.227	6.982	7.858	8.878	10.068
18%	5.092	5.658	6.311	7.065	7.939	8.953

Year 16
Growth Rates
Per Cent

Discount Rate	0%	2%	4%	6%	8%	10%
0%	16.000	19.012	22.698	27.213	32.750	39.545
2%	13.578	16.000	18.947	22.538	26.921	32.274
4%	11.652	13.620	16.000	18.885	22.387	26.644
6%	10.106	11.720	13.661	16.000	18.825	22.242
8%	8.851	10.188	11.786	13.700	16.000	18.768
10%	7.824	8.941	10.268	11.849	13.738	16.000
12%	6.974	7.916	9.028	10.346	11.911	13.775
14%	6.265	7.066	8.006	9.114	10.422	11.971
16%	5.668	6.355	7.156	8.095	9.197	10.495
18%	5.162	5.756	6.444	7.245	8.181	9.278

Year 17
Growth Rates
Per Cent

Discount Rate	0%	2%	4%	6%	8%	10%
0%	17.000	20.412	24.645	29.906	36.450	44.599
2%	14.292	17.000	20.338	24.462	29.563	35.884
4%	12.166	14.339	17.000	20.267	24.286	29.239
6%	10.477	12.240	14.384	17.000	20.199	24.119
8%	9.122	10.566	12.312	14.428	17.000	20.134
10%	8.022	9.218	10.653	12.382	14.470	17.000
12%	7.120	8.120	9.312	10.738	12.450	14.511
14%	6.373	7.217	8.216	9.404	10.821	12.516
16%	5.749	6.467	7.313	8.311	9.494	10.901
18%	5.222	5.840	6.561	7.407	8.403	9.581

Year 18
Growth Rates
Per Cent

Discount Rate	0%	1%	2%	3%	4%	5%	6%
0%	18.000	19.811	21.841	24.117	26.671	29.539	32.760
1%	16.398	18.000	19.792	21.798	24.045	26.564	29.389
2%	14.992	16.413	18.000	19.773	21.757	23.976	26.460
3%	13.754	15.018	16.428	18.000	19.755	21.716	23.907
4%	12.659	13.788	15.044	16.442	18.000	19.737	21.676
5%	11.690	12.700	13.822	15.069	16.456	18.000	19.720
6%	10.828	11.735	12.740	13.856	15.094	16.470	18.000
7%	10.059	10.876	11.780	12.780	13.889	15.118	16.483
8%	9.372	10.110	10.924	11.824	12.819	13.921	15.142
9%	8.756	9.424	10.160	10.971	11.867	12.858	13.953
10%	8.201	8.808	9.475	10.209	11.018	11.910	12.895
11%	7.702	8.254	8.860	9.525	10.258	11.064	11.952
12%	7.250	7.754	8.306	8.911	9.575	10.306	11.109
13%	6.840	7.301	7.805	8.357	8.962	9.625	10.353
14%	6.467	6.890	7.352	7.856	8.408	9.012	9.674
15%	6.128	6.517	6.941	7.403	7.907	8.458	9.061

Year 19
Growth Rates
Per Cent

Discount Rate	0%	2%	4%	6%	8%	10%
0%	19.000	23.297	28.778	35.786	44.762	56.275
2%	15.678	19.000	23.203	28.537	35.324	43.975
4%	13.134	15.735	19.000	23.112	28.307	34.886
6%	11.158	13.222	15.790	19.000	23.025	28.088
8%	9.604	11.261	13.307	15.843	19.000	22.942
10%	8.365	9.713	11.362	13.390	15.895	19.000
12%	7.366	8.475	9.820	11.460	13.471	15.945
14%	6.550	7.473	8.582	9.925	11.556	13.549
16%	5.877	6.653	7.578	8.688	10.027	11.650
18%	5.316	5.975	6.754	7.682	8.792	10.128

Year 20
Growth Rates
Per Cent

Discount Rate	0%	2%	4%	6%	8%	10%
0%	20.000	24.783	30.969	38.993	49.423	63.002
2%	16.351	20.000	24.677	30.695	38.460	48.502
4%	13.590	16.413	20.000	24.576	30.434	37.956
6%	11.470	13.685	16.473	20.000	24.479	30.186
8%	9.818	11.580	13.777	16.531	20.000	24.386
10%	8.514	9.934	11.688	13.867	16.588	20.000
12%	7.469	8.629	10.047	11.793	13.954	16.642
14%	6.623	7.581	8.742	10.158	11.895	14.039
16%	5.929	6.729	7.691	8.853	10.267	11.996
18%	5.353	6.029	6.834	7.799	8.962	10.373

Year 21
Growth Rates
Per Cent

Discount Rate	0%	2%	4%	6%	8%	10%
0%	21.000	26.299	33.248	42.392	54.457	70.403
2%	17.011	21.000	26.181	32.938	41.782	53.384
4%	14.029	17.079	21.000	26.068	32.643	41.204
6%	11.764	14.131	17.144	21.000	25.959	32.363
8%	10.017	11.881	14.230	17.207	21.000	25.856
10%	8.649	10.139	11.996	14.326	17.268	21.000
12%	7.562	8.769	10.258	12.108	14.420	17.327
14%	6.687	7.678	8.887	10.375	12.217	14.511
16%	5.973	6.797	7.792	9.004	10.490	12.323
18%	5.384	6.076	6.905	7.904	9.118	10.602

Year 22
Growth Rates
Per Cent

Discount Rate	0%	2%	4%	6%	8%	10%
0%	22.000	27.845	35.618	45.996	59.893	78.543
2%	17.658	22.000	27.714	35.269	45.298	58.650
4%	14.451	17.731	22.000	27.588	34.937	44.639
6%	12.042	14.560	17.801	22.000	27.468	34.622
8%	10.201	12.166	14.666	17.870	22.000	27.353
10%	8.772	10.329	12.287	14.769	17.936	22.000
12%	7.645	8.897	10.454	12.405	14.869	18.000
14%	6.743	7.764	9.020	10.577	12.521	14.967
16%	6.011	6.856	7.882	9.141	10.697	12.634
18%	5.410	6.117	6.967	7.999	9.261	10.815

Year 23
Growth Rates
Per Cent

Discount Rate	0%	2%	4%	6%	8%	10%
0%	23.000	29.422	38.083	49.816	65.765	87.497
2%	18.292	23.000	29.277	37.691	49.022	64.328
4%	14.857	18.371	23.000	29.138	37.320	48.272
6%	12.303	14.973	18.447	23.000	29.005	36.966
8%	10.371	12.434	15.086	18.520	23.000	28.878
10%	8.883	10.505	12.562	15.196	18.591	23.000
12%	7.718	9.013	10.636	12.687	15.302	18.660
14%	6.792	7.842	9.141	10.764	12.810	15.406
16%	6.044	6.907	7.963	9.267	10.891	12.929
18%	5.432	6.152	7.022	8.084	9.391	11.014

Year 24
Growth Rates
Per Cent

Discount Rate	0%	2%	4%	6%	8%	10%
0%	24.000	31.030	40.646	53.865	72.106	97.347
2%	18.914	24.000	30.870	40.209	52.964	70.452
4%	15.247	18.998	24.000	30.718	39.793	52.114
6%	12.550	15.370	19.080	24.000	30.571	39.398
8%	10.529	12.688	15.490	19.159	24.000	30.431
10%	8.985	10.668	12.822	15.607	19.235	24.000
12%	7.784	9.119	10.805	12.954	15.720	19.309
14%	6.835	7.911	9.252	10.939	13.083	15.831
16%	6.073	6.953	8.036	9.382	11.071	13.209
18%	5.451	6.182	7.070	8.160	9.510	11.200

Year 25
Growth Rates
Per Cent

Discount Rate	0%	2%	4%	6%	8%	10%
0%	25.000	32.671	43.312	58.156	78.954	108.182
2%	19.523	25.000	32.495	42.825	57.138	77.056
4%	15.622	19.614	25.000	32.327	42.362	56.178
6%	12.783	15.752	19.701	25.000	32.167	41.923
8%	10.675	12.928	15.879	19.785	25.000	32.013
10%	9.077	10.819	13.069	16.003	19.867	25.000
12%	7.843	9.216	10.961	13.207	16.123	19.947
14%	6.873	7.973	9.352	11.101	13.342	16.240
16%	6.097	6.993	8.101	9.487	11.238	13.474
18%	5.467	6.208	7.113	8.228	9.620	11.373

Year 26
Growth Rates
Per Cent

Discount Rate	0%	2%	4%	6%	8%	10%
0%	26.000	34.344	46.084	62.706	86.351	120.100
2%	20.121	26.000	34.152	45.543	61.558	84.178
4%	15.983	20.217	26.000	33.968	45.030	60.477
6%	13.003	16.120	20.310	26.000	33.793	44.543
8%	10.810	13.154	16.254	20.401	26.000	33.625
10%	9.161	10.960	13.301	16.384	20.488	26.000
12%	7.896	9.304	11.107	13.445	16.512	20.573
14%	6.906	8.028	9.444	11.252	13.587	16.635
16%	6.118	7.029	8.160	9.583	11.394	13.725
18%	5.480	6.231	7.150	8.290	9.720	11.534

Year 27
Growth Rates
Per Cent

Discount Rate	0%	2%	4%	6%	8%	10%
0%	27.000	36.051	48.968	67.528	94.339	133.210
2%	20.707	27.000	35.841	48.369	66.238	91.859
4%	16.330	20.809	27.000	35.641	47.801	65.024
6%	13.211	16.474	20.908	27.000	35.449	47.261
8%	10.935	13.367	16.615	21.004	27.000	35.266
10%	9.237	11.090	13.521	16.752	21.097	27.000
12%	7.943	9.384	11.242	13.672	16.886	21.187
14%	6.935	8.078	9.528	11.392	13.819	17.017
16%	6.136	7.060	8.212	9.671	11.539	13.963
18%	5.492	6.250	7.183	8.345	9.811	11.684

Year 28
Growth Rates
Per Cent

Discount Rate	0%	2%	4%	6%	8%	10%
0%	28.000	37.792	51.966	72.640	102.966	147.631
2%	21.281	28.000	37.564	51.305	71.193	100.142
4%	16.663	21.390	28.000	37.346	50.678	69.883
6%	13.406	16.815	21.495	28.000	37.137	50.082
8%	11.051	13.569	16.963	21.597	28.000	36.938
10%	9.307	11.211	13.729	17.107	21.695	28.000
12%	7.984	9.456	11.368	13.886	17.247	21.791
14%	6.961	8.123	9.605	11.522	14.039	17.384
16%	6.152	7.087	8.259	9.751	11.675	14.189
18%	5.502	6.267	7.212	8.395	9.895	11.824

Year 29
Growth Rates
Per Cent

Discount Rate	0%	2%	4%	6%	8%	10%
0%	29.000	39.568	55.085	78.058	112.283	163.494
2%	21.844	29.000	39.320	54.356	76.440	109.075
4%	16.984	21.959	29.000	39.083	53.665	74.920
6%	13.591	17.143	22.070	29.000	38.857	53.010
8%	11.158	13.760	17.297	22.178	29.000	38.640
10%	9.370	11.323	13.926	17.448	22.283	29.000
12%	8.022	9.523	11.484	14.088	17.596	22.384
14%	6.983	8.162	9.674	11.644	14.247	17.739
16%	6.166	7.111	8.301	9.824	11.800	14.404
18%	5.510	6.282	7.238	8.439	9.972	11.955

Year 30
Growth Rates
Per Cent

Discount Rate	0%	2%	4%	6%	8%	10%
0%	30.000	41.379	58.328	83.802	122.346	180.943
2%	22.396	30.000	41.110	57.527	81.995	118.708
4%	17.292	22.518	30.000	40.854	56.768	80.300
6%	13.765	17.458	22.635	30.000	40.609	56.048
8%	11.258	13.940	17.620	22.749	30.000	40.374
10%	9.427	11.426	14.112	17.777	22.859	30.000
12%	8.055	9.583	11.593	14.280	17.931	22.967
14%	7.003	8.198	9.738	11.756	14.445	18.082
16%	6.177	7.132	8.339	9.891	11.918	14.607
18%	5.517	6.294	7.261	8.479	10.042	12.077

Year 31
Growth Rates
Per Cent

Discount Rate	0%	2%	4%	6%	8%	10%
0%	31.000	43.227	61.701	89.890	133.214	200.138
2%	22.938	31.000	42.936	60.822	87.877	129.097
4%	17.588	23.065	31.000	42.659	59.989	85.990
6%	13.929	17.761	23.189	31.000	42.394	59.201
8%	11.350	14.110	17.930	23.309	31.000	42.140
10%	9.479	11.523	14.287	18.095	23.426	31.000
12%	8.085	9.638	11.693	14.461	18.255	23.539
14%	7.020	8.230	9.796	11.861	14.632	18.412
16%	6.187	7.151	8.373	9.952	12.027	14.800
18%	5.523	6.305	7.280	8.515	10.106	12.190

Year 32
Growth Rates
Per Cent

Discount Rate	0%	2%	4%	6%	8%	10%
0%	32.000	45.112	65.210	96.343	144.951	221.252
2%	23.468	32.000	44.798	64.246	94.106	140.301
4%	17.874	23.603	32.000	44.498	63.335	92.009
6%	14.084	18.053	23.733	32.000	44.212	62.473
8%	11.435	14.270	18.229	23.859	32.000	43.939
10%	9.526	11.612	14.453	18.400	23.982	32.000
12%	8.112	9.689	11.787	14.633	18.568	24.100
14%	7.035	8.258	9.849	11.959	14.809	18.731
16%	6.196	7.167	8.403	10.008	12.128	14.983
18%	5.528	6.315	7.298	8.548	10.165	12.296

Year 33
Growth Rates
Per Cent

Discount Rate	0%	2%	4%	6%	8%	10%
0%	33.000	47.034	68.858	103.184	157.627	244.477
2%	23.989	33.000	46.696	67.805	100.700	152.383
4%	18.148	24.130	33.000	46.373	66.810	98.374
6%	14.230	18.334	24.266	33.000	46.065	65.868
8%	11.514	14.422	18.517	24.399	33.000	45.771
10%	9.569	11.695	14.610	18.695	24.527	33.000
12%	8.135	9.734	11.873	14.796	18.869	24.652
14%	7.048	8.284	9.897	12.049	14.977	19.039
16%	6.203	7.181	8.431	10.059	12.223	15.156
18%	5.532	6.323	7.314	8.577	10.219	12.394

Year 34
Growth Rates
Per Cent

Discount Rate	0%	2%	4%	6%	8%	10%
0%	34.000	48.994	72.652	110.435	171.317	270.024
2%	24.499	34.000	48.631	71.503	107.682	165.413
4%	18.411	24.646	34.000	48.284	70.418	105.108
6%	14.368	18.605	24.789	34.000	47.953	69.391
8%	11.587	14.565	18.794	24.928	34.000	47.638
10%	9.609	11.771	14.759	18.979	25.063	34.000
12%	8.157	9.776	11.954	14.949	19.159	25.194
14%	7.060	8.306	9.941	12.134	15.136	19.336
16%	6.210	7.194	8.455	10.106	12.311	15.320
18%	5.536	6.330	7.327	8.603	10.268	12.486

Year 35
Growth Rates
Per Cent

Discount Rate	0%	2%	4%	6%	8%	10%
0%	35.000	50.994	76.598	118.121	186.102	298.127
2%	24.999	35.000	50.604	75.346	115.075	179.465
4%	18.665	25.153	35.000	50.232	74.165	112.229
6%	14.498	18.865	25.303	35.000	49.877	73.048
8%	11.655	14.701	19.061	25.448	35.000	49.538
10%	9.644	11.843	14.899	19.252	25.589	35.000
12%	8.176	9.814	12.028	15.095	19.439	25.726
14%	7.070	8.327	9.982	12.212	15.287	19.622
16%	6.215	7.205	8.477	10.148	12.393	15.476
18%	5.539	6.336	7.339	8.626	10.313	12.572

Year 36
Growth Rates
Per Cent

Discount Rate	0%	2%	4%	6%	8%	10%
0%	36.000	53.034	80.702	126.268	202.070	329.039
2%	25.489	36.000	52.616	79.340	122.903	194.619
4%	18.908	25.650	36.000	52.217	78.055	119.762
6%	14.621	19.115	25.807	86.000	51.837	76.842
8%	11.717	14.828	19.318	25.958	36.000	51.474
10%	9.677	11.909	15.032	19.516	26.106	36.000
12%	8.192	9.848	12.098	15.233	19.709	26.249
14%	7.079	8.345	10.018	12.285	15.430	19.899
16%	6.220	7.215	8.497	10.187	12.469	15.624
18%	5.541	6.341	7.350	8.647	10.354	12.652

Year 37
Growth Rates
Per Cent

Discount Rate	0%	2%	4%	6%	8%	10%
0%	37.000	55.115	84.970	134.904	219.316	363.043
2%	25.969	37.000	54.667	83.491	131.192	210.962
4%	19.143	26.138	37.000	54.241	82.096	127.729
6%	14.737	19.356	26.301	37.000	53.834	80.779
8%	11.775	14.949	19.565	26.459	37.000	53.446
10%	9.706	11.970	15.158	19.770	26.613	37.000
12%	8.208	9.890	12.162	15.363	19.970	26.763
14%	7.087	8.361	10.052	12.352	15.565	20.165
16%	6.224	7.223	8.514	10.223	12.540	15.764
18%	5.543	6.346	7.359	8.666	10.392	12.726

Year 38
Growth Rates
Per Cent

Discount Rate	0%	2%	4%	6%	8%	10%
0%	38.000	57.237	89.409	144.058	237.941	400.448
2%	26.441	38.000	56.759	87.804	139.968	228.586
4%	19.368	26.616	38.000	56.303	86.292	136.155
6%	14.846	19.588	26.786	38.000	55.869	84.865
8%	11.829	15.063	19.804	26.951	38.000	55.454
10%	9.733	12.027	15.276	20.014	27.111	38.000
12%	8.221	9.908	12.222	15.486	20.221	27.267
14%	7.094	8.376	10.082	12.415	15.693	20.423
16%	6.228	7.231	8.530	10.255	12.607	15.897
18%	5.545	6.350	7.367	8.683	10.427	12.796

Year 39
Growth Rates
Per Cent

Discount Rate	0%	2%	4%	6%	8%	10%
0%	39.000	59.402	94.026	153.762	258.057	441.593
2%	26.903	39.000	58.891	92.287	149.260	247.593
4%	19.584	27.085	39.000	58.405	90.649	145.068
6%	14.949	19.811	27.261	39.000	57.942	89.105
8%	11.879	15.171	20.033	27.433	39.000	57.500
10%	9.757	12.079	15.389	20.250	27.600	39.000
12%	8.233	9.934	12.278	15.603	20.463	27.762
14%	7.100	8.389	10.110	12.474	15.815	20.671
16%	6.231	7.237	8.544	10.285	12.668	16.023
18%	5.547	6.353	7.375	8.699	10.458	12.860

Year 40
Growth Rates
Per Cent

Discount Rate	0%	2%	4%	6%	8%	10%
0%	40.000	61.610	98.827	164.048	279.781	486.852
2%	27.355	40.000	61.065	96.945	159.099	268.090
4%	19.793	27.545	40.000	60.547	95.174	154.495
6%	15.046	20.026	27.728	40.000	60.054	93.506
8%	11.925	15.272	20.254	27.907	40.000	59.583
10%	9.779	12.128	15.495	20.478	28.080	40.000
12%	8.244	9.958	12.329	15.714	20.696	28.248
14%	7.105	8.401	10.136	12.528	15.930	20.911
16%	6.233	7.243	8.557	10.312	12.726	16.142
18%	5.548	6.356	7.381	8.712	10.487	12.921

Year 41
Growth Rates
Per Cent

Discount Rate	0%	2%	4%	6%	8%	10%
0%	41.000	63.862	103.820	174.951	303.244	536.637
2%	27.799	41.000	63.282	101.786	169.516	290.196
4%	19.993	27.996	41.000	62.731	99.873	164.466
6%	15.138	20.232	28.186	41.000	62.206	98.072
8%	11.967	15.368	20.467	28.371	41.000	61.705
10%	9.799	12.173	15.595	20.697	28.551	41.000
12%	8.253	9.980	12.377	15.818	20.921	28.726
14%	7.110	8.411	10.159	12.579	16.039	21.142
16%	6.236	7.248	8.568	10.337	12.779	16.256
18%	5.549	6.359	7.387	8.725	10.514	12.977

Year 42
Growth Rates
Per Cent

Discount Rate	0%	2%	4%	6%	8%	10%
0%	42.000	66.159	109.012	186.508	328.583	591.401
2%	28.235	42.000	65.543	106.817	180.547	314.034
4%	20.186	28.438	42.000	64.957	104.753	175.012
6%	15.225	20.431	28.635	42.000	64.398	102.810
8%	12.007	15.459	20.672	28.827	42.000	63.866
10%	9.817	12.215	15.690	20.908	29.014	42.000
12%	8.262	9.999	12.422	15.917	21.139	29.195
14%	7.114	8.420	10.180	12.626	16.142	21.365
16%	6.238	7.253	8.578	10.360	12.829	16.363
18%	5.550	6.361	7.392	8.736	10.538	13.029

Year 43
Growth Rates
Per Cent

Discount Rate	0%	2%	4%	6%	8%	10%
0%	43.000	68.503	114.413	198.758	355.950	651.641
2%	28.662	43.000	67.848	112.045	192.226	339.743
4%	20.371	28.872	43.000	67.225	109.821	186.167
6%	15.306	20.623	29.076	43.000	66.632	107.728
8%	12.043	15.544	20.869	29.275	43.000	66.067
10%	9.834	12.254	15.779	21.111	29.468	43.000
12%	8.270	10.017	12.463	16.011	21.348	29.656
14%	7.117	8.429	10.199	12.670	16.240	21.580
16%	6.239	7.257	8.587	10.380	12.875	16.465
18%	5.551	6.363	7.396	8.746	10.560	13.078

Year 44
Growth Rates
Per Cent

Discount Rate	0%	2%	4%	6%	8%	10%
0%	44.000	70.893	120.029	211.744	385.506	717.905
2%	29.080	44.000	70.198	117.478	204.592	367.468
4%	20.549	29.297	44.000	69.537	115.083	197.965
6%	15.383	20.807	29.509	44.000	68.908	112.831
8%	12.077	15.625	21.059	29.714	44.000	68.309
10%	9.849	12.290	15.864	21.307	29.914	44.000
12%	8.276	10.033	12.501	16.100	21.550	30.109
14%	7.120	8.436	10.217	12.711	16.332	21.788
16%	6.241	7.260	8.596	10.399	12.918	16.562
18%	5.552	6.365	7.400	8.754	10.581	13.124

Year 45
Growth Rates
Per Cent

Discount Rate	0%	2%	4%	6%	8%	10%
0%	45.000	73.331	125.871	225.508	417.426	790.795
2%	29.490	45.000	72.594	123.124	217.686	397.367
4%	20.720	29.715	45.000	71.893	120.548	210.443
6%	15.456	20.984	29.933	45.000	71.227	118.126
8%	12.108	15.702	21.242	30.146	45.000	70.593
10%	9.863	12.324	15.944	21.496	30.352	45.000
12%	8.283	10.048	12.537	16.184	21.744	30.553
14%	7.123	8.443	10.233	12.749	16.420	21.988
16%	6.242	7.263	8.603	10.417	12.958	16.653
18%	5.552	6.366	7.403	8.763	10.599	13.166

Year 46
Growth Rates
Per Cent

Discount Rate	0%	2%	4%	6%	8%	10%
0%	46.000	75.817	131.945	240.099	451.900	870.975
2%	29.892	46.000	75.037	128.992	231.550	429.612
4%	20.885	30.124	46.000	74.295	126.223	223.642
6%	15.524	21.154	30.350	46.000	73.590	123.622
8%	12.137	15.774	21.418	30.569	46.000	72.919
10%	9.875	12.355	16.020	21.678	30.782	46.000
12%	8.288	10.062	12.570	16.263	21.932	30.990
14%	7.126	8.449	10.248	12.784	16.503	22.182
16%	6.243	7.266	8.610	10.432	12.996	16.740
18%	5.553	6.367	7.406	8.770	10.616	13.206

Year 47
Growth Rates
Per Cent

Discount Rate	0%	1%	2%	3%	4%	5%	6%
0%	47.000	60.223	78.354	103.408	138.263	187.025	255.565
1%	37.354	47.000	60.070	77.935	102.540	136.650	184.203
2%	30.287	37.435	47.000	59.922	77.528	101.696	135.090
3%	25.025	30.407	37.515	47.000	59.776	77.130	100.877
4%	21.043	25.160	30.526	37.594	47.000	59.634	76.743
5%	17.981	21.181	25.295	30.643	37.671	47.000	59.495
6%	15.589	18.115	21.318	25.427	30.758	37.747	47.000
7%	13.692	15.716	18.248	21.454	25.558	30.872	37.822
8%	12.164	13.810	15.842	18.380	21.588	25.688	30.984
9%	10.918	12.274	13.928	15.967	18.511	21.721	25.816
10%	9.887	11.019	12.383	14.045	16.092	18.641	21.853
11%	9.024	9.981	11.120	12.492	14.162	16.215	18.770
12%	8.293	9.111	10.074	11.221	12.601	14.278	16.338
13%	7.668	8.374	9.197	10.168	11.322	12.709	14.393
14%	7.128	7.743	8.454	9.284	10.261	11.422	12.816
15%	6.657	7.198	7.818	8.535	9.371	10.354	11.522

Year 48
Growth Rates
Per Cent

Discount Rate	0%	2%	4%	6%	8%	10%
0%	48.000	80.941	144.834	271.958	529.343	1,056.190
2%	30.673	48.000	80.067	141.426	261.772	501.886
4%	21.195	30.919	48.000	79.238	138.236	252.368
6%	15.650	21.476	31.159	48.000	78.450	135.242
8%	12.189	15.906	21.752	31.392	48.000	77.700
10%	9.897	12.410	16.159	22.022	31.619	48.000
12%	8.297	10.085	12.629	16.410	22.288	31.840
14%	7.130	8.459	10.273	12.847	16.657	22.548
16%	6.245	7.271	8.621	10.460	13.063	16.901
18%	5.554	6.369	7.411	8.782	10.646	13.277

Year 49
Growth Rates
Per Cent

Discount Rate	0%	2%	4%	6%	8%	10%
0%	49.000	83.579	151.667	289.336	572.770	1,162.909
2%	31.052	49.000	82.657	148.012	278.229	542.328
4%	21.341	31.306	49.000	81.781	144.591	267.985
6%	15.708	21.628	31.552	49.000	80.949	141.383
8%	12.212	15.967	21.909	31.792	49.000	80.158
10%	9.906	12.435	16.223	22.185	32.026	49.000
12%	8.301	10.096	12.656	16.477	22.456	32.253
14%	7.131	8.463	10.284	12.875	16.727	22.722
16%	6.246	7.272	8.626	10.472	13.093	16.975
18%	5.554	6.370	7.413	8.787	10.659	13.309

Year 50
Growth Rates
Per Cent

Discount Rate	0%	2%	4%	6%	8%	10%
0%	50.000	86.271	158.774	307.756	619.672	1,280.299
2%	31.424	50.000	85.297	154.855	295.655	585.942
4%	21.482	31.684	50.000	84.373	151.191	284.504
6%	15.762	21.774	31.938	50.000	83.495	147.756
8%	12.233	16.024	22.060	32.185	50.000	82.660
10%	9.915	12.458	16.284	22.342	32.425	50.000
12%	8.304	10.105	12.680	16.541	22.618	32.659
14%	7.133	8.467	10.294	12.901	16.794	22.890
16%	6.246	7.274	8.630	10.483	13.121	17.045
18%	5.554	6.371	7.415	8.792	10.671	13.339

Year 51
Growth Rates
Per Cent

Discount Rate	0%	2%	4%	6%	8%	10%
0%	51.000	89.016	166.165	327.281	670.326	1,409.429
2%	31.788	51.000	87.989	161.967	314.105	632.977
4%	21.617	32.056	51.000	87.015	158.044	301.975
6%	15.813	21.914	32.316	51.000	86.090	154.370
8%	12.253	16.079	22.206	32.570	51.000	85.210
10%	9.923	12.479	16.341	22.493	32.817	51.000
12%	8.308	10.113	12.703	16.601	22.775	33.058
14%	7.134	8.471	10.304	12.926	16.858	23.052
16%	6.247	7.275	8.634	10.493	13.147	17.112
18%	5.554	6.371	7.417	8.796	10.682	13.367

Year 52
Growth Rates
Per Cent

Discount Rate	0%	1%	2%	3%	4%	5%	6%
0%	52.000	68.447	91.817	125.347	173.851	244.499	347.978
1%	40.394	52.000	68.254	91.268	124.164	171.566	240.335
2%	32.145	40.490	52.000	68.066	90.734	123.017	169.358
3%	26.166	32.283	40.585	52.000	67.882	90.214	121.903
4%	21.748	26.319	32.420	40.678	52.000	67.703	89.708
5%	18.418	21.899	26.469	32.555	40.770	52.000	67.527
6%	15.861	18.563	22.050	26.618	32.688	40.860	52.000
7%	13.862	15.996	18.706	22.199	26.766	32.819	40.949
8%	12.272	13.986	16.130	18.849	22.347	26.911	32.949
9%	10.985	12.385	14.110	16.263	18.990	22.493	27.056
10%	9.930	11.090	12.499	14.232	16.395	19.131	22.639
11%	9.051	10.025	11.194	12.612	14.355	16.527	19.270
12%	8.310	9.139	10.121	11.298	12.724	14.477	16.658
13%	7.679	8.392	9.228	10.217	11.401	12.837	14.598
14%	7.135	7.755	8.474	9.316	10.312	11.505	12.949
15%	6.662	7.206	7.831	8.555	9.404	10.407	11.608

Year 53
Growth Rates
Per Cent

Discount Rate	0%	2%	4%	6%	8%	10%
0%	53.000	94.673	181.845	369.917	784.114	1,707.720
2%	32.495	53.000	93.533	177.039	354.325	738.403
4%	21.873	32.777	53.000	92.452	172.552	340.000
6%	15.907	22.180	33.052	53.000	91.426	168.355
8%	12.288	16.178	22.482	33.320	53.000	90.451
10%	9.936	12.517	16.447	22.779	33.581	53.000
12%	8.313	10.128	12.744	16.712	23.071	33.835
14%	7.136	8.477	10.320	12.970	16.975	23.358
16%	6.248	7.278	8.640	10.511	13.194	17.235
18%	5.555	6.372	7.419	8.803	10.701	13.417

Year 54
Growth Rates
Per Cent

Discount Rate	0%	2%	4%	6%	8%	10%
0%	54.000	97.587	190.159	393.172	847.923	1,879.591
2%	32.838	54.000	96.386	185.021	376.227	797.395
4%	21.993	33.128	54.000	95.249	180.227	360.673
6%	15.950	22.305	33.410	54.000	94.170	175.746
8%	12.304	16.224	22.612	33.684	54.000	93.144
10%	9.942	12.534	16.495	22.914	33.952	54.000
12%	8.315	10.135	12.762	16.763	23.211	34.213
14%	7.137	8.479	10.327	12.989	17.029	23.504
16%	6.248	7.279	8.643	10.519	13.215	17.292
18%	5.555	6.373	7.420	8.806	10.709	13.440

Year 55
Growth Rates
Per Cent

Discount Rate	0%	2%	4%	6%	8%	10%
0%	55.000	100.558	198.806	417.822	916.837	2,068.651
2%	33.175	55.000	99.296	193.316	399.416	861.014
4%	22.109	33.471	55.000	98.100	188.197	382.538
6%	15.991	22.426	33.760	55.000	96.966	183.415
8%	12.319	16.267	22.738	34.042	55.000	95.888
10%	9.947	12.550	16.541	23.045	34.316	55.000
12%	8.317	10.140	12.779	16.812	23.347	34.584
14%	7.138	8.481	10.333	13.008	17.080	23.644
16%	6.248	7.280	8.645	10.526	13.235	17.346
18%	5.555	6.373	7.421	8.809	10.717	13.461

Year 56
Growth Rates
Per Cent

Discount Rate	0%	2%	4%	6%	8%	10%
0%	56.000	103.589	207.798	443.952	991.264	2,276.616
2%	33.505	56.000	102.263	201.936	423.970	929.623
4%	22.220	33.809	56.000	101.006	196.474	405.666
6%	16.029	22.542	34.105	56.000	99.814	191.374
8%	12.332	16.308	22.859	34.393	56.000	98.682
10%	9.952	12.564	16.584	23.170	34.674	56.000
12%	8.319	10.146	12.795	16.857	23.477	34.949
14%	7.138	8.483	10.339	13.025	17.128	23.779
16%	6.248	7.280	8.648	10.532	13.253	17.397
18%	5.555	6.373	7.422	8.812	10.724	13.480

Year 57
Growth Rates
Per Cent

Discount Rate	0%	2%	4%	6%	8%	10%
0%	57.000	106.681	217.150	471.649	1,071.645	2,505.377
2%	33.828	57.000	105.287	210.894	449.969	1,003.613
4%	22.327	34.139	57.000	103.968	205.069	430.127
6%	16.065	22.653	34.442	57.000	102.716	199.634
8%	12.344	16.346	22.975	34.738	57.000	101.528
10%	9.956	12.578	16.625	23.292	35.026	57.000
12%	8.320	10.151	12.810	16.901	23.603	35.307
14%	7.139	8.485	10.344	13.041	17.174	23.910
16%	6.249	7.281	8.650	10.538	13.270	17.445
18%	5.555	6.373	7.423	8.814	10.731	13.499

Year 58
Growth Rates
Per Cent

Discount Rate	0%	2%	4%	6%	8%	10%
0%	58.000	109.835	226.876	501.008	1,158.457	2,757.015
2%	34.145	58.000	108.371	220.204	477.496	1,083.406
4%	22.430	34.463	58.000	106.986	213.995	456.000
6%	16.099	22.761	34.774	58.000	105.673	208.205
8%	12.356	16.382	23.087	35.076	58.000	104.427
10%	9.960	12.590	16.663	23.408	35.371	58.000
12%	8.322	10.155	12.823	16.942	23.724	35.658
14%	7.139	8.487	10.349	13.055	17.218	24.036
16%	6.249	7.282	8.651	10.543	13.286	17.491
18%	5.555	6.374	7.424	8.816	10.736	13.516

Year 59
Growth Rates
Per Cent

Discount Rate	0%	2%	4%	6%	8%	10%
0%	59.000	113.052	236.991	532.128	1,252.213	3,033.816
2%	34.456	59.000	111.516	229.879	506.643	1,169.458
4%	22.528	34.781	59.000	110.063	223.264	483.365
6%	16.131	22.864	35.099	59.000	108.686	217.099
8%	12.367	16.417	23.195	35.408	59.000	107.379
10%	9.964	12.602	16.700	23.521	35.709	59.000
12%	8.323	10.159	12.836	16.981	23.841	36.004
14%	7.140	8.488	10.354	13.069	17.259	24.157
16%	6.249	7.282	8.653	10.548	13.301	17.535
18%	5.555	6.374	7.424	8.818	10.742	13.532

Year 60
Growth Rates
Per Cent

Discount Rate	0%	2%	4%	6%	8%	10%
0%	60.000	116.333	247.510	565.116	1,353.470	3,338.298
2%	34.761	60.000	114.722	239.933	537.504	1,262.258
4%	22.623	35.093	60.000	113.199	232.890	512.309
6%	16.161	22.964	35.417	60.000	111.755	226.329
8%	12.377	16.449	23.299	35.734	60.000	110.386
10%	9.967	12.613	16.734	23.629	36.042	60.000
12%	8.324	10.163	12.848	17.017	23.954	36.343
14%	7.140	8.489	10.358	13.082	17.298	24.274
16%	6.249	7.282	8.654	10.553	13.315	17.576
18%	5.555	6.374	7.425	8.819	10.747	13.546

Year 61
Growth Rates
Per Cent

Discount Rate	0%	2%	4%	6%	8%	10%
0%	61.000	119.679	258.451	600.083	1,462.828	3,673.228
2%	35.060	61.000	117.991	250.381	570.181	1,362.337
4%	22.715	35.399	61.000	116.395	242.885	542.923
6%	16.190	23.059	35.730	61.000	114.883	235.908
8%	12.386	16.480	23.399	36.053	61.000	113.449
10%	9.970	12.623	16.767	23.733	36.369	61.000
12%	8.325	10.166	12.859	17.052	24.063	36.676
14%	7.140	8.490	10.362	13.093	17.335	24.388
16%	6.249	7.283	8.656	10.557	13.327	17.615
18%	5.555	6.374	7.425	8.821	10.751	13.560

Year 62
Growth Rates
Per Cent

Discount Rate	0%	2%	4%	6%	8%	10%
0%	62.000	123.093	269.829	637.148	1,580.934	4,041.651
2%	35.353	62.000	121.324	261.239	604.780	1,470.266
4%	22.803	35.699	62.000	119.652	253.265	575.304
6%	16.217	23.152	36.037	62.000	118.069	245.848
8%	12.394	16.509	23.495	36.367	62.000	116.568
10%	9.973	12.632	16.798	23.834	36.689	62.000
12%	8.326	10.169	12.869	17.085	24.168	37.003
14%	7.141	8.491	10.365	13.104	17.370	24.497
16%	6.249	7.283	8.657	10.560	13.339	17.652
18%	5.555	6.374	7.426	8.822	10.755	13.573

Year 63
Growth Rates
Per Cent

Discount Rate	0%	2%	4%	6%	8%	10%
0%	63.000	126.575	281.662	676.437	1,708.489	4,446.916
2%	35.640	63.000	124.723	272.523	641.414	1,586.659
4%	22.887	35.993	63.000	122.973	264.045	609.552
6%	16.242	23.240	36.338	63.000	121.316	256.163
8%	12.402	16.536	23.588	36.675	63.000	119.745
10%	9.975	12.640	16.827	23.931	37.004	63.000
12%	8.327	10.172	12.878	17.116	24.269	37.325
14%	7.141	8.492	10.368	13.115	17.403	24.602
16%	6.249	7.284	8.658	10.564	13.350	17.687
18%	5.555	6.374	7.426	8.823	10.759	13.585

Year 64
Growth Rates
Per Cent

Discount Rate	0%	2%	4%	6%	8%	10%
0%	64.000	130.126	293.968	718.083	1,846.248	4,892.707
2%	35.921	64.000	128.188	284.249	680.203	1,712.181
4%	22.969	36.282	64.000	126.357	275.239	645.776
6%	16.266	23.325	36.634	64.000	124.624	266.867
8%	12.409	16.562	23.677	36.977	64.000	122.981
10%	9.978	12.648	16.855	24.024	37.313	64.000
12%	8.327	10.174	12.887	17.146	24.367	37.640
14%	7.141	8.493	10.371	13.124	17.434	24.704
16%	6.250	7.284	8.659	10.567	13.361	17.721
18%	5.555	6.374	7.426	8.824	10.763	13.596

Year 65
Growth Rates
Per Cent

Discount Rate	0%	2%	4%	6%	8%	10%
0%	65.000	133.749	306.767	762.228	1,995.028	5,383.078
2%	36.197	65.000	131.721	296.436	721.274	1,847.549
4%	23.047	36.565	65.000	129.806	286.864	684.090
6%	16.289	23.407	36.924	65.000	127.994	277.975
8%	12.416	16.586	23.763	37.274	65.000	126.277
10%	9.980	12.656	16.881	24.114	37.616	65.000
12%	8.328	10.177	12.895	17.174	24.461	37.950
14%	7.141	8.494	10.373	13.133	17.464	24.802
16%	6.250	7.284	8.660	10.570	13.370	17.753
18%	5.555	6.375	7.427	8.825	10.766	13.607

Year 66
Growth Rates
Per Cent

Discount Rate	0%	2%	4%	6%	8%	10%
0%	66.000	137.444	320.078	809.022	2,155.710	5,922.486
2%	36.468	66.000	135.324	309.100	764.761	1,993.533
4%	23.122	36.843	66.000	133.321	298.935	724.614
6%	16.310	23.486	37.208	66.000	131.428	289.503
8%	12.422	16.609	23.846	37.565	66.000	129.634
10%	9.981	12.663	16.906	24.201	37.914	66.000
12%	8.329	10.179	12.902	17.200	24.551	38.255
14%	7.142	8.494	10.376	13.141	17.492	24.897
16%	6.250	7.284	8.660	10.572	13.379	17.783
18%	5.555	6.375	7.427	8.826	10.769	13.616

Year 67
Growth Rates
Per Cent

Discount Rate	0%	2%	4%	6%	8%	10%
0%	67.000	141.213	333.921	858.623	2,329.247	6,515.835
2%	36.733	67.000	138.997	322.261	810.805	2,150.967
4%	23.194	37.115	67.000	136.904	311.471	767.477
6%	16.331	23.562	37.487	67.000	134.926	301.465
8%	12.428	16.631	23.926	37.851	67.000	133.053
10%	9.983	12.669	16.929	24.285	38.207	67.000
12%	8.329	10.181	12.909	17.225	24.639	38.554
14%	7.142	8.495	10.378	13.149	17.519	24.988
16%	6.250	7.284	8.661	10.575	13.388	17.811
18%	5.555	6.375	7.427	8.827	10.771	13.625

Year 68
Growth Rates
Per Cent

Discount Rate	0%	2%	4%	6%	8%	10%
0%	68.000	145.057	348.318	911.200	2,516.667	7,168.518
2%	36.994	68.000	142.742	335.937	859.559	2,320.749
4%	23.264	37.382	68.000	140.556	324.489	812.812
6%	16.350	23.636	37.761	68.000	138.491	313.879
8%	12.433	16.651	24.003	38.132	68.000	136.536
10%	9.985	12.675	16.951	24.365	38.494	68.000
12%	8.330	10.182	12.916	17.249	24.723	38.848
14%	7.142	8.496	10.380	13.156	17.544	25.076
16%	6.250	7.285	8.662	10.577	13.395	17.838
18%	5.555	6.375	7.427	8.827	10.774	13.634

Year 69
Growth Rates
Per Cent

Discount Rate	0%	1%	2%	3%	4%	5%	6%
0%	69.000	99.676	148.978	229.594	363.290	587.529	966.932
1%	49.670	69.000	99.297	147.751	226.572	356.589	573.456
2%	37.249	49.822	69.000	98.927	146.560	223.653	350.151
3%	28.997	37.447	49.971	69.000	98.565	145.403	220.832
4%	23.330	29.199	37.644	50.118	69.000	98.213	144.279
5%	19.310	23.519	29.399	37.838	50.263	69.000	97.868
6%	16.368	19.480	23.706	29.598	38.030	50.406	69.000
7%	14.152	16.519	19.649	23.892	29.794	38.220	50.546
8%	12.438	14.287	16.671	19.818	24.077	29.989	38.407
9%	11.082	12.559	14.422	16.822	19.985	24.260	30.183
10%	9.986	11.191	12.680	14.557	16.972	20.152	24.443
11%	9.084	10.085	11.300	12.801	14.691	17.122	20.319
12%	8.330	9.174	10.184	11.409	12.922	14.825	17.271
13%	7.691	8.413	9.265	10.283	11.518	13.042	14.959
14%	7.142	7.767	8.496	9.355	10.382	11.627	13.163
15%	6.666	7.213	7.844	8.579	9.445	10.480	11.735

Year 70
Growth Rates
Per Cent

Discount Rate	0%	2%	4%	6%	8%	10%
0%	70.000	152.977	378.862	1,026.008	2,937.687	8,676.217
2%	37.499	70.000	150.453	364.921	965.837	2,701.305
4%	23.395	37.901	70.000	148.073	352.047	911.480
6%	16.385	23.774	38.294	70.000	145.823	340.129
8%	12.443	16.689	24.148	38.677	70.000	143.695
10%	9.987	12.685	16.992	24.518	39.052	70.000
12%	8.330	10.185	12.927	17.292	24.883	39.419
14%	7.142	8.496	10.383	13.169	17.591	25.243
16%	6.250	7.285	8.663	10.581	13.409	17.888
18%	5.556	6.375	7.427	8.828	10.778	13.649

Year 71
Growth Rates
Per Cent

Discount Rate	0%	2%	4%	6%	8%	10%
0%	71.000	157.057	395.057	1,088.629	3,173.781	9,544.939
2%	37.744	71.000	154.423	380.271	1,023.710	2,914.251
4%	23.456	38.153	71.000	151.939	366.626	965.123
6%	16.401	23.839	38.552	71.000	149.594	354.002
8%	12.447	16.706	24.217	38.943	71.000	147.375
10%	9.988	12.690	17.010	24.590	39.324	71.000
12%	8.331	10.187	12.933	17.312	24.958	39.697
14%	7.142	8.497	10.385	13.174	17.613	25.322
16%	6.250	7.285	8.663	10.582	13.415	17.911
18%	5.556	6.375	7.428	8.829	10.780	13.656

Year 72
Growth Rates
Per Cent

Discount Rate	0%	2%	4%	6%	8%	10%
0%	72.000	161.218	411.899	1,155.006	3,428.764	10,500.532
2%	37.984	72.000	158.471	396.223	1,084.987	3,143.898
4%	23.516	38.400	72.000	155.880	381.765	1,021.861
6%	16.416	23.901	38.806	72.000	153.435	368.398
8%	12.451	16.723	24.283	39.203	72.000	151.123
10%	9.990	12.694	17.028	24.659	39.591	72.000
12%	8.331	10.188	12.937	17.331	25.031	39.971
14%	7.142	8.497	10.386	13.180	17.633	25.399
16%	6.250	7.285	8.663	10.584	13.421	17.933
18%	5.556	6.375	7.428	8.829	10.782	13.662

Year 73
Growth Rates
Per Cent

Discount Rate	0%	2%	4%	6%	8%	10%
0%	73.000	165.463	429.415	1,225.367	3,704.145	11,551.686
2%	38.220	73.000	162.597	412.800	1,149.869	3,391.556
4%	23.573	38.642	73.000	159.897	397.487	1,081.872
6%	16.430	23.962	39.055	73.000	157.349	383.338
8%	12.455	16.738	24.346	39.458	73.000	154.940
10%	9.990	12.699	17.044	24.726	39.853	73.000
12%	8.331	10.189	12.942	17.349	25.102	40.239
14%	7.142	8.497	10.387	13.185	17.652	25.473
16%	6.250	7.285	8.664	10.585	13.427	17.954
18%	5.556	6.375	7.428	8.830	10.783	13.668

Year 74
Growth Rates
Per Cent

Discount Rate	0%	2%	4%	6%	8%	10%
0%	74.000	169.792	447.631	1,299.949	4,001.557	12,707.954
2%	38.451	74.000	166.805	430.028	1,218.567	3,658.639
4%	23.628	38.880	74.000	163.992	413.813	1,145.345
6%	16.443	24.020	39.299	74.000	161.336	398.841
8%	12.458	16.753	24.407	39.709	74.000	158.827
10%	9.991	12.702	17.060	24.791	40.110	74.000
12%	8.331	10.190	12.946	17.366	25.169	40.503
14%	7.142	8.498	10.388	13.189	17.671	25.544
16%	6.250	7.285	8.664	10.587	13.432	17.973
18%	5.556	6.375	7.428	8.830	10.785	13.674

Year 75
Growth Rates
Per Cent

Discount Rate	0%	2%	4%	6%	8%	10%
0%	75,000	174.208	466.577	1,379.006	4,322.761	13,979.850
2%	38.677	75.000	171.096	447.931	1,291.306	3,946.670
4%	23.680	39.113	75.000	168.164	430.768	1,212.481
6%	16.456	24.076	39.539	75.000	165.399	414.930
8%	12.461	16.766	24.466	39.955	75.000	162.787
10%	9.992	12.706	17.075	24.853	40.363	75.000
12%	8.332	10.191	12.950	17.382	25.235	40.762
14%	7.142	8.498	10.389	13.193	17.688	25.612
16%	6.250	7.285	8.664	10.588	13.437	17.992
18%	5.556	6.375	7.428	8.830	10.786	13.679

Year 76
Growth Rates
Per Cent

Discount Rate	0%	2%	4%	6%	8%	10%
0%	76.000	178.712	486.280	1,462.806	4,669.662	15,378.935
2%	38.899	76.000	175.470	466.536	1,368.324	4,257.291
4%	23.731	39.341	76.000	172.418	448.374	1,283.489
6%	16.468	24.129	39.774	76.000	169.539	431.625
8%	12.464	16.779	24.523	40.197	76.000	166.820
10%	9.993	12.709	17.089	24.913	40.611	76.000
12%	8.332	10.192	12.953	17.398	25.298	41.016
14%	7.143	8.498	10.390	13.197	17.704	25.679
16%	6.250	7.285	8.665	10.589	13.441	18.010
18%	5.556	6.375	7.428	8.831	10.787	13.684

Year 77
Growth Rates
Per Cent

Discount Rate	0%	2%	4%	6%	8%	10%
0%	77.000	183.306	506.771	1,551.634	5,044.315	16,917.928
2%	39.117	77.000	179.930	485.871	1,449.873	4,592.274
4%	23.780	39.566	77.000	176.753	466.658	1,358.594
6%	16.479	24.181	40.004	77.000	173.757	448.951
8%	12.467	16.792	24.578	40.434	77.000	170.928
10%	9.994	12.712	17.103	24.970	40.854	77.000
12%	8.332	10.192	12.957	17.412	25.359	41.266
14%	7.143	8.498	10.391	13.201	17.720	25.742
16%	6.250	7.285	8.665	10.590	13.445	18.026
18%	5.556	6.375	7.428	8.831	10.788	13.688

Year 78
Growth Rates
Per Cent

Discount Rate	0%	2%	4%	6%	8%	10%
0%	78.000	187.992	528.082	1,645.792	5,448.940	18,610.821
2%	39.330	78.000	184.478	505.964	1,536.218	4,953.531
4%	23.827	39.785	78.000	181.171	485.644	1,438.032
6%	16.490	24.231	40.231	78.000	178.054	466.930
8%	12.469	16.803	24.631	40.667	78.000	175.112
10%	9.994	12.715	17.115	25.026	41.093	78.000
12%	8.332	10.193	12.960	17.426	25.417	41.511
14%	7.143	8.499	10.392	13.205	17.735	25.804
16%	6.250	7.285	8.665	10.591	13.449	18.042
18%	5.556	6.375	7.428	8.831	10.789	13.692

Year 79
Growth Rates
Per Cent

Discount Rate	0%	2%	4%	6%	8%	10%
0%	79.000	192.772	550.245	1,745.600	5,885.936	20,473.003
2%	39.539	79.000	189.115	526.845	1,627.643	5,343.122
4%	23.872	40.001	79.000	185.674	505.362	1,522.053
6%	16.500	24.279	40.453	79.000	182.432	485.588
8%	12.471	16.814	24.681	40.895	79.000	179.373
10%	9.995	12.717	17.127	25.080	41.328	79.000
12%	8.332	10.194	12.963	17.439	25.474	41.752
14%	7.143	8.499	10.393	13.208	17.749	25.864
16%	6.250	7.285	8.665	10.591	13.452	18.057
18%	5.556	6.375	7.428	8.831	10.790	13.696

Year 80
Growth Rates
Per Cent

Discount Rate	0%	2%	4%	6%	8%	10%
0%	80.000	197.647	573.295	1,851.396	6,357.890	22,521.403
2%	39.745	80.000	193.842	548.544	1,724.445	5,763.269
4%	23.915	40.213	80.000	190.264	525.837	1,610.922
6%	16.509	24.325	40.671	80.000	186.893	504.949
8%	12.474	16.824	24.730	41.119	80.000	183.714
10%	9.995	12.720	17.138	25.131	41.558	80.000
12%	8.332	10.194	12.965	17.451	25.528	41.988
14%	7.143	8.499	10.393	13.211	17.762	25.921
16%	6.250	7.285	8.665	10.592	13.456	18.072
18%	5.556	6.375	7.428	8.832	10.791	13.700

Year 81
Growth Rates
Per Cent

Discount Rate	0%	2%	4%	6%	8%	10%
0%	81.000	202.620	597.267	1,963.540	6,867.602	24,774.644
2%	39.946	81.000	198.663	571.095	1,826.942	6,216.368
4%	23.957	40.420	81.000	194.942	547.100	1,704.917
6%	16.518	24.369	40.885	81.000	191.439	525.042
8%	12.475	16.834	24.777	41.339	81.000	188.134
10%	9.996	12.722	17.149	25.181	41.785	81.000
12%	8.332	10.195	12.968	17.462	25.581	42.221
14%	7.143	8.499	10.394	13.213	17.774	25.976
16%	6.250	7.285	8.665	10.593	13.459	18.085
18%	5.556	6.375	7.428	8.832	10.792	13.703

Year 82
Growth Rates
Per Cent

Discount Rate	0%	2%	4%	6%	8%	10%
0%	82.000	207.693	622.197	2,082.412	7,418.090	27,253.208
2%	40.143	82.000	203.578	594.530	1,935.468	6,705.005
4%	23.997	40.624	82.000	199.710	569.181	1,804.336
6%	16.526	24.412	41.094	82.000	196.070	545.892
8%	12.477	16.843	24.823	41.555	82.000	192.637
10%	9.996	12.724	17.159	25.229	42.007	82.000
12%	8.333	10.195	12.970	17.473	25.632	42.449
14%	7.143	8.499	10.394	13.216	17.786	26.030
16%	6.250	7.286	8.666	10.593	13.461	18.098
18%	5.556	6.375	7.428	8.832	10.792	13.707

Year 83
Growth Rates
Per Cent

Discount Rate	0%	2%	4%	6%	8%	10%
0%	83.000	212.867	648.125	2,208.417	8,012.617	29,979.629
2%	40.336	83.000	208.589	618.884	2,050.378	7,231.966
4%	24.036	40.823	83.000	204.570	592.111	1,909.490
6%	16.534	24.453	41.300	83.000	200.788	567.530
8%	12.479	16.852	24.866	41.767	83.000	197.223
10%	9.996	12.726	17.168	25.275	42.225	83.000
12%	8.333	10.196	12.972	17.484	25.680	42.673
14%	7.143	8.499	10.395	13.218	17.798	26.082
16%	6.250	7.286	8.666	10.594	13.464	18.110
18%	5.556	6.375	7.428	8.832	10.793	13.709

Year 84
Growth Rates
Per Cent

Discount Rate	0%	2%	4%	6%	8%	10%
0%	84.000	218.144	675.090	2,341.982	8,654.706	32,978.692
2%	40.526	84.000	213.699	644.194	2,172.047	7,800.257
4%	24.073	41.019	84.000	209.523	615.923	2,020.710
6%	16.542	24.492	41.502	84.000	205.595	589.984
8%	12.481	16.860	24.908	41.975	84.000	201.893
10%	9.997	12.728	17.177	25.320	42.439	84.000
12%	8.333	10.196	12.974	17.493	25.729	42.893
14%	7.143	8.499	10.395	13.221	17.808	26.131
16%	6.250	7.286	8.666	10.595	13.467	18.122
18%	5.556	6.375	7.428	8.832	10.794	13.712

Year 85
Growth Rates
Per Cent

Discount Rate	0%	2%	4%	6%	8%	10%
0%	85.000	223.527	703.134	2,483.561	9,348.163	36,277.661
2%	40.711	85.000	218.908	670.495	2,300.874	8,413.121
4%	24.109	41.211	85.000	214.572	640.650	2,138.347
6%	16.549	24.530	41.700	85.000	210.493	613.285
8%	12.482	16.868	24.949	42.179	85.000	206.651
10%	9.997	12.729	17.186	25.363	42.649	85.000
12%	8.333	10.196	12.976	17.503	25.773	43.109
14%	7.143	8.499	10.396	13.223	17.818	26.179
16%	6.250	7.286	8.666	10.595	13.469	18.133
18%	5.556	6.375	7.428	8.832	10.794	13.715

Year 86
Growth Rates
Per Cent

Discount Rate	0%	2%	4%	6%	8%	10%
0%	86.000	229.017	732.299	2,633.634	10,097.096	39,906.527
2%	40.893	86.000	224.220	697.828	2,437.278	9,074.052
4%	24.143	41.399	86.000	219.718	666.329	2,262.771
6%	16.556	24.567	41.894	86.000	215.484	637.466
8%	12.483	16.875	24.987	42.380	86.000	211.496
10%	9.997	12.731	17.194	25.404	42.855	86.000
12%	8.333	10.197	12.978	17.512	25.817	43.322
14%	7.143	8.499	10.396	13.225	17.828	26.226
16%	6.250	7.286	8.666	10.595	13.471	18.143
18%	5.556	6.375	7.428	8.832	10.795	13.717

Year 87
Growth Rates
Per Cent

Discount Rate	0%	2%	4%	6%	8%	10%
0%	87.000	234.618	762.631	2,792.712	10,905.943	43,898.280
2%	41.072	87.000	229.636	726.233	2,581.706	9,786.821
4%	24.176	41.584	87.000	224.962	692.996	2,394.373
6%	16.562	24.602	42.085	87.000	220.568	662.559
8%	12.485	16.882	25.025	42.576	87.000	216.431
10%	9.997	12.732	17.202	25.444	43.058	87.000
12%	8.333	10.197	12.979	17.520	25.859	43.530
14%	7.143	8.499	10.396	13.226	17.837	26.270
16%	6.250	7.286	8.666	10.596	13.473	18.153
18%	5.556	6.375	7.428	8.833	10.795	13.719

Year 88
Growth Rates
Per Cent

Discount Rate	0%	2%	4%	6%	8%	10%
0%	88.000	240.330	794.176	2,961.335	11,779.499	48,289.208
2%	41.247	88.000	235.159	755.752	2,734.630	10,555.493
4%	24.207	41.765	88.000	230.308	720.688	2,533.568
6%	16.568	24.636	42.272	88.000	225.749	688.599
8%	12.486	16.889	25.061	42.769	88.000	221.458
10%	9.998	12.733	17.209	25.482	43.257	88.000
12%	8.333	10.197	12.981	17.528	25.900	43.735
14%	7.143	8.500	10.397	13.228	17.845	26.314
16%	6.250	7.286	8.666	10.596	13.475	18.162
18%	5.556	6.375	7.428	8.833	10.796	13.721

Year 89
Growth Rates
Per Cent

Discount Rate	0%	2%	4%	6%	8%	10%
0%	89.000	246.157	826.983	3,140.075	12,722.939	53,119.228
2%	41.419	89.000	240.789	786.429	2,896.550	11,384.453
4%	24.238	41.942	89.000	235.756	749.445	2,680.793
6%	16.573	24.669	42.456	89.000	231.027	715.621
8%	12.487	16.895	25.096	42.959	89.000	226.577
10%	9.998	12.735	17.216	25.519	43.452	89.000
12%	8.333	10.198	12.982	17.535	25.939	43.936
14%	7.143	8.500	10.397	13.230	17.854	26.355
16%	6.250	7.286	8.666	10.597	13.477	18.171
18%	5.556	6.375	7.428	8.833	10.796	13.723

Year 90
Growth Rates
Per Cent

Discount Rate	0%	2%	4%	6%	8%	10%
0%	90.000	252.100	861.103	3,329.540	13,741.854	58,432.251
2%	41.587	90.000	246.530	818.309	3,067.994	12,278.430
4%	24.267	42.116	90.000	241.309	779.308	2,836.512
6%	16.579	24.700	42.636	90.000	236.405	743.664
8%	12.488	16.901	25.129	43.145	90.000	231.792
10%	9.998	12.736	17.222	25.555	43.644	90.000
12%	8.333	10.198	12.984	17.542	25.977	44.134
14%	7.143	8.500	10.397	13.231	17.861	26.395
16%	6.250	7.286	8.666	10.597	13.478	18.179
18%	5.556	6.375	7.428	8.833	10.796	13.725

Year 91
Growth Rates
Per Cent

Discount Rate	0%	2%	4%	6%	8%	10%
0%	91.000	258.1C2	896.587	3,530.372	14,842.282	64,276.577
2%	41.752	91.000	252.384	851.438	3,249.523	13,242.522
4%	24.295	42.287	91.000	246.969	810.320	3,001.215
6%	16.584	24.730	42.812	91.000	241.884	772.764
8%	12.489	16.906	25.162	43.327	91.000	237.103
10%	9.998	12.737	17.228	25.589	43.832	91.000
12%	8.333	10.198	12.985	17.549	26.014	44.328
14%	7.143	8.500	10.398	13.232	17.869	26.434
16%	6.250	7.286	8.666	10.597	13.480	18.187
18%	5.556	6.375	7.428	8.833	10.797	13.727

Year 92
Growth Rates
Per Cent

Discount Rate	0%	2%	4%	6%	8%	10%
0%	92.000	264.345	933.490	3,743.255	16,030.745	70,705.334
2%	41.914	92.000	258.352	885.867	3,441.730	14,282.230
4%	24.323	42.455	92.000	252.737	842.525	3,175.419
6%	16.588	24.759	42.986	92.000	247.467	802.963
8%	12.489	16.912	25.193	43.506	92.000	242.512
10%	9.998	12.738	17.234	25.622	44.017	92.000
12%	8.333	10.198	12.986	17.555	26.049	44.518
14%	7.143	8.500	10.398	13.234	17.876	26.471
16%	6.250	7.286	8.666	10.597	13.481	18.195
18%	5.556	6.375	7.429	8.833	10.797	13.728

Year 93
Growth Rates
Per Cent

Discount Rate	0%	2%	4%	6%	8%	10%
0%	93,000	270.652	971.870	3,968.910	17,314.284	77,776.968
2%	42.072	93.000	264.437	921.646	3,645.243	15,403.483
4%	24.349	42.619	93.000	258.617	875.968	3,359.674
6%	16.593	24.787	43.156	93.000	253.155	834.301
8%	12.490	16.916	25.223	43,682	93.000	248.021
10%	9.999	12.739	17.239	25.654	44.199	93.000
12%	8.333	10.198	12.987	17.561	26.083	44.705
14%	7.143	8.500	10.398	13.235	17.882	26.508
16%	6.250	7.286	8.666	10.598	13.482	18.202
18%	5.556	6.375	7.429	8.833	10.797	13.730

Year 94
Growth Rates
Per Cent

Discount Rate	0%	2%	4%	6%	8%	10%
0%	94.000	277.085	1,011.785	4,208.104	18,700.507	85,555.764
2%	42.228	94.000	270.642	958.829	3,860.728	16,612.678
4%	24.374	42.780	94.000	264.609	910.698	3,554.559
6%	16.597	24.814	43.323	94.000	258.950	866.822
8%	12.491	16.921	25.251	43.855	94.000	253.633
10%	9.999	12.739	17.244	25.685	44.377	94.000
12%	8.333	10.198	12.988	17.567	26.115	44.889
14%	7.143	8.500	10.398	13.236	17.888	26.542
16%	6.250	7.286	8.666	10.598	13.484	18.209
18%	5.556	6.375	7.429	8.833	10.797	13.731

Year 95
Growth Rates
Per Cent

Discount Rate	0%	2%	4%	6%	8%	10%
0%	95,000	283.647	1,053.296	4,461.651	20,197.628	94,112.441
2%	42.380	95.000	276.968	977.469	4,088.889	17,916.712
4%	24.398	42.938	95.000	270.717	946.763	3,760.688
6%	16.601	24.840	43.486	95.000	264.855	900.570
8%	12.492	16.925	25.279	44,024	95.000	259.348
10%	9.999	12.740	17.249	25.715	44.552	95.000
12%	8.333	10.199	12.989	17.572	26.147	45.070
14%	7.143	8.500	10.398	13.237	17.894	26.576
16%	6.250	7.286	8.666	10.598	13.485	18.215
18%	5.556	6.375	7.429	8.833	10.798	13.733

Year 96
Growth Rates
Per Cent

Discount Rate	0%	2%	4%	6%	8%	10%
0%	96.000	290.340	1,096.468	4,730.410	21,814.518	103,524.785
2%	42.529	96.000	283.419	1,037.625	4,330.471	19,323.022
4%	24.421	43.093	96.000	276.943	984.216	3,978.708
6%	16.605	24.865	43.647	96.000	270.871	935.591
8%	12.492	16.930	25.306	44.190	96.000	265.169
10%	9.999	12.741	17.254	25.743	44.724	96.000
12%	8.333	10.199	12.989	17.577	26.178	45.247
14%	7.143	8.500	10.398	13.238	17.900	26.608
16%	6.250	7.286	8.666	10.598	13.486	18.221
18%	5.556	6.375	7.429	8.833	10.798	13.734

Year 97
Growth Rates
Per Cent

Discount Rate	0%	2%	4%	6%	8%	10%
0%	97,000	297.166	1,141.367	5,015.294	23,560.760	113,878.364
2%	42.676	97.000	289.996	1,079.355	4,586.263	20,839.632
4%	24.443	43.246	97.000	283.288	1,023.108	4,209.307
6%	16.608	24.889	43.805	97.000	277.001	971.934
8%	12.493	16.934	25.331	44,353	97.000	271.099
10%	9.999	12.742	17.258	25.771	44.892	97.000
12%	8.333	10.199	12.990	17.582	26.207	45.421
14%	7.143	8.500	10.399	13.239	17.905	26.640
16%	6.250	7.286	8.666	10.598	13.487	18.227
18%	5.556	6.375	7.429	8.833	10.798	13.735

Year 98
Growth Rates
Per Cent

Discount Rate	0%	2%	4%	6%	8%	10%
0%	98.000	304.130	1,188.061	5,317.272	25,446.700	125,267.300
2%	42.820	98.000	296.701	1,122.722	4,857.102	22,475.191
4%	24.465	43.395	98.000	289.755	1,063.497	4,453.209
6%	16.611	24.912	43.959	98.000	283.246	1,009.649
8%	12.493	16.937	25.356	44.514	98.000	277.137
10%	9.999	12.742	17.262	25.797	45.058	98.000
12%	8.333	10.199	12.991	17.587	26.235	45.592
14%	7.143	8.500	10.399	13.239	17.910	26.670
16%	6.250	7.286	8.666	10.598	13.488	18.233
18%	5.556	6.375	7.429	8.833	10.798	13.736

Year 99
Growth Rates
Per Cent

Discount Rate	0%	2%	4%	6%	8%	10%
0%	99.000	311.232	1,236.624	5,637.368	27,483.516	137,795.130
2%	42.960	99.000	303.539	1,167.789	5,143,873	24,239.030
4%	24.485	43.541	99.000	296.346	1,105.439	4,711.183
6%	16.615	24.934	44.111	99.000	289.609	1,048.786
8%	12.494	16.941	25.380	44.671	99.000	283.288
10%	9.999	12.743	17.266	25.823	45.221	99.000
12%	8.333	10.199	12.992	17.591	26.263	45.760
14%	7.143	8.500	10.399	13.240	17.915	26.699
16%	6.250	7.286	8.666	10.599	13.489	18.238
18%	5.556	6.375	7.429	8.833	10.798	13.737

Year 100
Growth Rates
Per Cent

Discount Rate	0%	2%	4%	6%	8%	10%
0%	100.000	318.477	1,287.129	5,976.670	29,683.278	151,575.743
2%	43.098	100.000	310.510	1,214.624	5,447.512	26,141.209
4%	24.505	43.684	100.000	303.064	1,148.995	4,984.039
6%	16.618	24.956	44.260	100.000	296.092	1,089.401
8%	12.494	16.944	25.403	44.825	100.000	289.553
10%	9.999	12.743	17.270	25.848	45.380	100.000
12%	8.333	10.199	12.992	17.595	26.289	45.925
14%	7.143	8.500	10.399	13.241	17.919	26.727
16%	6.250	7.286	8.667	10.599	13.489	18.243
18%	5.556	6.375	7.429	8.833	10.798	13.738

Appendix D
Employment Participation Rates

Participation Rates
White Males
1954—1983

Year	16-17	18-19	20-24	Age 25-34	35-44	45-54	55-64	65+
1983	46.9	71.3	86.1	95.2	96.0	91.9	70.0	17.1
1982	49.3	70.5	86.3	95.6	96.0	92.2	71.0	17.9
1981	51.5	73.5	87.0	95.8	96.1	92.4	71.5	18.5
1980	53.6	74.1	87.2	95.9	96.2	92.1	73.1	19.1
1979	55.3	74.5	87.6	96.1	96.4	92.2	73.6	20.1
1978	55.3	75.3	87.2	96.0	96.3	92.1	73.9	20.4
1977	53.8	74.9	86.8	96.0	96.2	92.2	74.7	20.2
1976	51.8	73.5	86.2	95.9	96.0	92.5	75.4	20.3
1975	51.8	72.8	85.5	95.8	96.4	92.9	76.5	21.8
1974	53.3	73.6	86.5	96.3	96.7	93.0	78.1	22.5
1973	52.7	72.3	85.8	96.3	96.8	93.5	79.0	22.5
1972	50.2	71.0	84.3	96.0	97.0	94.0	81.2	24.4
1971	49.2	67.8	83.2	96.3	97.0	94.7	82.6	25.6
1970	48.9	67.4	83.3	96.7	97.3	94.9	83.3	26.7
1969	48.8	66.3	82.6	97.0	97.4	95.1	83.9	27.3
1968	47.7	65.7	82.4	97.2	97.6	95.4	84.7	27.3
1967	47.9	66.1	84.0	97.5	97.7	95.6	84.9	27.1
1966	47.1	65.4	84.4	97.5	97.6	95.8	84.9	27.2
1965	44.6	65.8	85.3	97.4	97.7	95.9	85.2	27.9
1964	43.5	66.6	85.7	97.5	97.6	96.1	86.1	27.9
1963	42.4	67.8	85.8	97.4	97.8	96.2	86.6	28.4
1962	42.9	66.4	86.5	97.4	97.9	96.0	86.7	30.6
1961	44.3	66.2	87.6	97.7	97.9	95.9	87.8	31.9
1960	46.0	69.0	87.6	97.7	97.9	96.1	87.2	33.3
1959	45.4	70.3	87.3	97.5	98.0	96.3	87.9	34.3

446

Year	16-17	18-19	20-24	Age 25-34	35-44	45-54	55-64	65+
1958	46.8	69.4	86.7	97.2	98.0	96.6	88.2	35.7
1957	49.6	71.6	86.7	97.2	98.0	96.6	88.0	37.7
1956	51.3	71.9	87.6	97.4	98.1	96.8	88.9	40.0
1955	48.0	71.7	85.6	97.8	98.3	96.7	88.4	39.5
1954	47.1	70.4	86.4	97.5	98.2	96.8	89.2	40.4
Ave	48.9	70.1	85.8	96.8	97.2	94.6	81.8	27.1

Source: US Dept of Labor, Bureau of Labor Statistics, Handbook of Labor Statistics 20 (1985).

Participation Rates
White Females
1954—1983

Year	16-17	18-19	20-24	Age 25-34	35-44	45-54	55-64	65+
1954	29.3	52.1	44.4	32.5	32.5	39.8	29.1	9.1
1955	29.9	52.0	45.8	32.8	32.8	42.7	31.8	10.5
1956	33.5	53.0	46.5	33.2	33.2	44.4	34.0	10.6
1957	32.1	52.6	45.8	33.6	33.6	45.4	33.7	10.2
1958	28.8	52.3	46.0	33.6	33.6	46.5	34.5	10.1
1959	29.9	50.8	44.5	33.4	33.4	47.8	35.7	10.0
1960	30.0	51.9	45.7	34.1	34.1	48.6	36.2	10.6
1961	29.4	51.9	46.9	34.3	34.3	48.9	37.2	10.5
1962	27.9	51.6	47.1	34.1	34.1	48.9	38.0	9.8
1963	27.8	51.3	47.3	34.8	34.8	49.5	38.9	9.4
1964	28.4	49.6	48.8	35.0	35.0	50.2	39.4	9.9
1965	28.7	50.6	49.2	36.3	36.3	49.9	40.3	9.7
1966	31.8	53.1	50.0	37.7	37.7	50.6	41.1	9.4
1967	32.3	52.7	53.1	39.7	39.7	50.9	41.9	9.3
1968	33.0	53.3	54.0	40.6	40.6	51.5	42.0	9.4
1969	35.2	54.6	56.4	41.7	41.7	53.0	42.6	9.7
1970	36.6	55.0	57.7	43.2	43.2	53.7	42.6	9.5
1971	36.3	55.0	58.0	43.7	43.7	53.6	42.5	9.3
1972	39.3	57.4	59.4	46.0	46.0	53.4	41.9	0.0
1973	41.7	58.8	61.7	48.7	48.7	53.4	40.7	8.7
1974	43.3	60.4	63.9	51.3	51.3	53.6	40.4	8.0
1975	42.7	60.4	65.5	53.8	53.8	54.9	40.6	8.0
1976	43.8	61.7	66.3	56.0	56.0	57.1	40.7	7.9
1977	45.8	63.3	67.8	58.5	58.5	58.9	40.7	7.9
1978	48.8	64.6	69.3	61.2	61.2	60.7	41.1	8.1

Year	16-17	18-19	20-24	Age 25-34	35-44	45-54	55-64	65+
1979	49.0	65.7	70.5	63.1	63.1	63.0	41.5	8.1
1980	47.2	65.1	70.6	64.8	64.8	65.0	40.9	7.9
1981	46.1	64.2	71.5	66.4	66.4	66.4	40.9	7.9
1982	44.6	64.6	71.8	67.8	67.8	67.5	41.5	7.8
1983	43.9	64.1	72.1	68.7	68.7	68.2	41.1	7.8
Ave	36.6	56.5	56.6	45.4	45.4	53.3	39.1	8.8

Source: US Dept of Labor, Bureau of Labor Statistics, Handbook of Labor Statistics 20, 21 (June 1985).

Participation Rates
Black Males
1972—1983

Year	16-17	18-19	20-24	Age 25-34	35-44	45-54	55-64	65+
1983	24.7	55.0	79.4	89.0	89.7	84.5	62.6	14.0
1982	24.6	55.3	78.7	89.2	89.8	82.2	61.9	15.9
1981	29.2	55.0	79.2	88.9	89.3	82.7	62.1	16.0
1980	31.0	56.7	79.8	90.8	89.1	83.1	61.7	16.3
1979	30.8	57.9	80.6	90.7	90.4	84.6	64.8	19.4
1978	32.1	59.6	78.8	90.8	90.6	83.3	67.9	21.0
1977	30.4	57.9	79.3	90.7	90.9	82.0	65.5	19.9
1976	29.0	55.0	79.1	90.9	89.9	82.4	65.1	19.7
1975	29.7	57.4	78.8	91.5	89.3	83.5	67.6	20.5
1974	34.1	61.7	83.5	92.7	90.3	84.1	68.9	21.5
1973	32.5	61.1	83.7	91.8	91.0	87.5	69.5	22.4
1972	34.3	60.0	82.6	92.6	91.0	85.6	72.5	24.3
Ave	30.2	57.7	80.3	90.8	90.1	83.8	65.8	19.2

Source: US Dept of Labor, Bureau of Labor Statistics, Handbook of Labor Statistics 21 (June 1985).

Participation Rates
Black Females
1972—1983

Year	16-17	18-19	20-24	Age 25-34	35-44	45-54	55-64	65+
1983	20.8	44.4	59.1	72.3	72.6	62.3	44.8	8.2
1982	23.3	43.3	60.1	70.2	71.7	62.4	44.8	8.5
1981	23.9	44.0	61.1	70.0	69.8	62.0	45.4	9.3
1980	24.6	45.0	60.2	70.5	68.1	61.4	44.8	10.2

Year	16-17	18-19	20-24	Age 25-34	35-44	45-54	55-64	65+
1979	27.5	45.9	61.5	70.1	68.0	59.6	44.0	10.9
1978	26.4	48.3	62.7	70.6	67.2	59.4	43.8	11.1
1977	21.5	44.3	59.3	68.5	64.1	57.9	43.7	10.5
1976	23.2	42.6	56.9	66.7	63.0	56.8	43.7	11.3
1975	25.0	43.8	55.9	62.8	62.0	56.6	43.1	10.7
1974	22.7	44.6	58.8	62.4	62.2	56.4	42.8	10.4
1973	23.9	45.1	58.0	62.7	61.7	56.1	44.7	11.4
1972	21.0	44.3	57.0	60.8	61.4	57.2	44.0	12.6
Ave	23.6	44.6	59.2	67.3	66.0	59.0	44.1	10.4

Source: US Dept of Labor, Bureau of Labor Statistics, Handbook of Labor Statistics 21 (June 1985).

Appendix E
Employment Rates

Employment Rates
White Males
1954—1983

Year	16-17	18-19	20-24	Age 25-34	35-44	45-54	55-64	65+
1983	77.4	81.3	86.2	91.0	93.6	94.3	94.4	96.8
1982	75.8	80.0	85.7	91.1	93.8	94.7	94.9	96.8
1981	80.1	83.6	88.4	93.9	96.0	96.4	96.6	97.6
1980	81.5	85.5	88.9	94.1	96.4	96.7	96.9	97.5
1979	83.9	87.7	92.6	96.4	97.5	97.5	97.5	96.9
1978	83.1	89.2	92.4	96.3	97.5	97.5	97.4	96.1
1977	82.4	87.0	90.7	95.0	96.9	97.0	96.7	95.1
1976	80.3	84.5	89.1	94.4	96.3	96.3	96.0	95.2
1975	80.3	82.8	86.8	93.7	95.5	95.6	95.9	95.0
1974	83.8	88.5	92.2	95.5	97.6	97.8	97.5	97.0
1973	84.9	90.0	93.5	97.0	98.2	98.0	97.6	97.1
1972	83.6	87.6	91.5	96.6	97.5	97.5	97.0	96.7
1971	82.9	86.5	90.6	96.0	97.1	97.2	96.8	96.6
1970	84.3	88.0	92.2	96.9	97.7	97.7	97.3	96.8
1969	87.5	92.1	95.4	98.3	98.6	98.6	98.3	97.9
1968	87.7	91.8	95.4	98.3	98.6	98.5	98.3	97.6
1967	87.3	91.0	95.8	98.1	98.4	98.2	97.8	97.2
1966	87.5	91.1	95.9	97.9	98.3	98.3	97.5	96.3
1965	85.3	88.6	94.1	97.4	97.7	97.7	96.9	97.0
1964	83.8	86.6	92.6	97.0	97.5	97.1	96.5	96.4
1963	82.2	85.8	92.2	96.1	97.1	96.7	96.0	95.9
1962	84.9	87.3	92.0	96.2	96.9	96.5	95.9	95.9
1961	83.5	84.9	90.0	95.1	96.0	95.6	94.7	94.8
1960	85.4	86.5	91.7	95.9	96.7	96.4	95.9	96.0
1959	85.0	87.0	92.5	96.2	96.8	96.3	95.8	95.5

Year	16-17	18-19	20-24	Age 25-34	35-44	45-54	55-64	65+
1958	85.1	83.5	88.3	94.4	95.6	95.2	94.8	95.0
1957	88.1	88.9	92.9	97.3	97.5	97.0	96.6	91.8
1956	88.8	90.3	93.9	97.2	97.8	97.2	96.9	96.6
1955	87.8	89.6	93.0	97.3	97.4	97.1	96.1	96.2
1954	86.0	87.0	90.2	95.8	96.4	96.2	95.7	95.8
Ave	84.0	87.1	91.6	95.9	97.0	96.9	96.5	96.2

Source: US Dept of Labor, Bureau of Labor Statistics, Handbook of Labor Statistics 71 (June 1985).

Employment Rates
White Females
1954—1983

Year	16-17	18-19	20-24	Age 25-34	35-44	45-54	55-64	65+
1983	79.6	83.6	89.7	92.4	93.8	94.5	95.3	96.9
1982	78.8	82.4	89.1	92.0	93.6	94.5	95.0	96.9
1981	81.6	84.7	90.9	93.4	94.9	95.8	96.3	96.6
1980	82.7	86.9	91.5	93.7	95.1	95.7	96.9	97.0
1979	84.1	87.5	92.2	94.4	95.8	96.3	97.0	96.9
1978	82.9	87.6	91.7	94.2	95.5	96.2	97.0	96.3
1977	81.8	85.8	90.7	93.3	94.7	95.0	95.6	95.1
1976	81.8	84.9	89.6	92.4	94.2	95.0	95.2	94.7
1975	80.8	83.9	88.8	91.5	93.4	94.2	94.9	94.7
1974	83.6	87.0	91.8	94.3	95.7	96.4	96.7	96.1
1973	84.3	89.1	93.0	94.9	96.3	96.9	97.2	97.2
1972	83.0	87.7	91.8	94.5	95.5	96.5	96.7	96.3
1971	83.4	85.9	91.5	93.7	95.1	96.1	96.7	96.4
1970	84.7	88.1	93.1	94.7	95.7	96.6	97.4	96.8
1969	86.2	90.0	94.5	95.8	96.8	97.6	97.9	97.6
1968	86.1	89.0	94.1	96.1	96.9	97.7	97.9	97.3
1967	87.1	89.4	94.0	95.3	96.3	97.1	97.7	97.4
1966	85.5	89.3	94.7	96.3	96.7	97.3	97.8	97.3
1965	85.0	86.6	93.6	52.0	95.9	97.0	97.3	97.3
1964	82.9	86.8	92.9	94.8	95.5	96.4	96.5	96.6
1963	81.9	86.8	92.6	94.2	95.4	96.1	96.5	97.0
1962	84.4	88.7	92.3	94.6	95.5	96.3	96.6	96.0
1961	83.0	86.4	91.6	93.4	94.4	95.2	95.7	96.3
1960	85.5	88.5	92.8	94.3	95.8	96.0	96.7	97.2
1959	86.7	88.9	93.3	95.0	95.3	96.0	96.0	96.6
1958	84.4	89.0	92.6	93.4	94.4	95.1	95.7	96.5
1957	88.1	92.1	94.9	95.3	96.3	97.0	97.0	96.5

Year	16-17	18-19	20-24	Age 25-34	35-44	45-54	55-64	65+
1956	87.9	91.7	94.9	96.0	96.5	96.7	96.5	97.7
1955	88.4	92.3	94.9	95.7	96.2	96.6	96.4	97.8
1954	88.0	90.6	93.6	94.3	95.1	95.6	95.5	97.2
Ave	84.1	87.7	92.4	92.9	95.4	96.1	96.5	96.7

Source: US Dept of Labor, Bureau of Labor Statistics, Handbook of Labor Statistics 71, 72 (June 1985).

Employment Rates
Black Males
1972—1983

Year	16-17	18-19	20-24	Age 25-34	35-44	45-54	55-64	65+
1983	47.3	52.7	68.6	80.6	86.5	88.6	89.0	88.2
1982	47.3	52.9	68.5	79.9	86.6	91.0	89.7	90.7
1981	56.8	60.8	73.6	85.6	90.7	92.2	93.9	92.5
1980	60.3	63.8	76.3	86.6	91.8	92.8	93.8	91.3
1979	62.1	67.8	81.3	90.4	93.7	94.8	94.9	93.6
1978	57.0	67.1	79.0	90.2	94.9	95.1	95.6	93.4
1977	59.0	61.8	77.0	88.2	93.8	95.1	94.0	92.2
1976	59.2	64.0	77.4	88.0	92.5	92.7	93.7	91.3
1975	58.1	64.1	75.3	87.3	91.3	90.7	93.7	91.3
1974	60.1	71.7	83.8	91.9	95.7	95.8	96.4	94.7
1973	64.3	77.0	86.8	93.8	96.1	96.8	96.8	96.7
1972	63.3	71.6	85.1	92.8	95.2	96.2	95.6	94.6
Ave	57.9	64.6	77.7	87.9	92.4	93.5	93.9	92.5

Source: US Dept of Labor, Bureau of Labor Statistics, Handbook of Labor Statistics 72 (June 1985).

Employment Rates
Black Females
1972—1983

Year	16-17	18-19	20-24	Age 25-34	35-44	45-54	55-64	65+
1983	51.4	52.0	68.2	81.4	88.6	90.1	92.7	93.7
1982	55.8	51.4	70.4	82.2	89.3	91.5	93.9	95.5
1981	53.5	60.2	73.6	85.1	90.2	93.1	95.3	94.0
1980	57.1	61.8	76.5	86.8	91.8	93.6	95.5	95.0
1979	57.3	63.1	77.4	87.9	92.8	94.8	95.3	96.0

Year	16-17	18-19	20-24	Age 25-34	35-44	45-54	55-64	65+
1978	55.0	61.3	77.3	88.1	92.2	94.4	94.8	95.2
1977	50.5	59.6	74.5	86.4	91.3	94.2	95.2	96.5
1976	51.6	62.4	77.2	86.4	91.5	94.1	94.6	96.6
1975	58.8	59.4	75.7	86.6	91.0	93.0	94.7	96.3
1974	59.8	64.0	81.0	91.0	93.4	95.6	96.4	98.0
1973	61.4	65.8	81.6	89.7	94.4	96.1	96.7	96.2
1972	58.0	59.9	82.1	89.5	92.4	95.4	96.3	97.4
Ave	55.9	60.1	76.3	86.8	91.6	93.8	95.1	95.9

Source: US Dept of Labor, Bureau of Labor Statistics, Handbook of Labor Statistics 72, 73 (June 1985).

Appendix F
Probability of Surviving

Probability of surviving through age X staring from age 0

| | CSO (1980) | | Total Population | U. S. Life Tables (1982) | | | |
Age	Male	Female		White Male	White Female	Black Male	Black Female
Life Expectancy	70.83	75.83	70.75	71.50	78.80	64.90	73.50
0	99.582	99.711	97.998	98.874	99.112	97.841	98.229
1	99.475	99.624	97.876	98.793	99.050	97.726	98.134
2	99.377	99.544	97.791	98.733	99.000	97.631	98.054
3	99.280	99.465	97.724	98.685	98.960	97.552	97.989
4	99.185	99.388	97.668	98.646	98.928	97.484	97.935
5	99.096	99.313	97.618	98.610	98.900	97.427	97.890
6	99.011	99.240	97.573	98.577	98.876	97.377	97.852
7	98.932	99.169	97.531	98.545	98.856	97.333	97.821
8	98.856	99.099	97.493	98.518	98.837	97.294	97.794
9	98.783	99.031	97.460	98.494	98.820	97.260	97.769
10	98.711	98.964	97.430	98.474	98.804	97.229	97.747
11	98.635	98.895	97.401	98.456	98.788	97.198	97.724
12	98.551	98.824	97.367	98.430	98.770	97.161	97.701
13	98.454	98.750	97.322	98.389	98.747	97.114	97.674
14	98.340	98.671	97.261	98.326	98.718	97.050	97.644
15	98.210	98.587	97.181	98.238	98.682	96.970	97.609
16	98.061	98.498	97.083	98.128	98.639	96.871	97.568
17	97.898	98.405	96.969	98.000	98.591	96.753	97.521
18	97.723	98.308	96.845	97.858	98.541	96.613	97.469
19	97.542	98.208	96.715	97.711	98.489	96.453	97.410
20	97.356	98.105	96.580	97.556	98.438	96.271	97.346
21	97.170	98.000	96.438	97.396	98.387	96.066	97.276

| | CSO (1980) | | Total Population | U. S. Life Tables (1982) | | | |
	Male	Female		White Male	White Female	Black Male	Black Female
Life Expectancy	70.83	75.83	70.75	71.50	78.80	64.90	73.50
Age							
22	96.987	97.893	96.291	97.233	98.335	95.840	97.199
23	96.806	97.785	96.144	97.069	98.283	95.598	97.115
24	96.630	97.673	95.999	96.908	98.231	95.340	97.025
25	96.459	97.560	95.858	96.751	98.178	95.070	96.928
26	96.292	97.444	95.721	96.600	98.125	94.784	96.832
27	96.128	97.325	95.585	96.451	98.071	94.484	96.711
28	95.964	97.202	95.447	96.302	98.016	94.168	96.592
29	95.800	97.076	95.305	96.154	97.959	93.836	96.466
30	95.634	96.945	95.157	96.004	97.899	93.486	96.333
31	95.464	96.809	95.002	95.852	97.836	93.119	96.193
32	95.289	96.669	94.839	95.699	97.771	92.735	96.043
33	95.107	96.524	94.665	95.543	97.702	92.336	95.882
34	94.917	96.371	94.480	95.382	97.627	91.922	95.710
35	94.717	96.212	94.283	95.216	97.547	91.491	95.524
36	94.505	96.043	94.071	95.043	97.460	91.401	95.324
37	94.278	95.861	94.841	94.860	97.366	90.571	95.109
38	94.035	95.666	93.592	94.666	97.262	90.077	94.876
39	93.772	95.453	93.320	94.457	97.147	89.558	94.623
40	93.489	95.222	93.027	94.230	97.020	89.013	94.350
41	93.182	94.971	92.710	93.982	96.878	88.435	94.053
42	92.850	94.698	92.367	93.711	96.722	87.818	93.729
43	92.490	94.406	91.994	93.412	96.549	87.151	93.376
44	92.103	94.092	91.586	93.082	96.358	86.426	92.991

| | CSO (1980) | | Total | U. S. Life Tables (1982) | | | |
	Male	Female	Population	White Male	White Female	Black Male	Black Female
Life Expectancy	70.83	75.83	70.75	71.50	78.80	64.90	73.50
Age							
45	91.684	93.757	91.143	92.718	96.147	85.639	92.572
46	91.233	93.401	90.662	92.316	95.914	84.787	92.115
47	90.747	93.023	90.141	91.870	95.658	83.868	91.619
48	90.227	92.620	89.579	91.375	95.376	82.879	91.076
49	89.666	92.191	88.972	90.826	95.066	81.819	90.484
50	89.065	91.734	88.315	90.219	94.725	80.685	89.839
51	88.414	91.247	87.605	89.549	94.352	79.475	89.139
52	87.711	90.727	86.837	88.815	93.944	78.190	88.384
53	86.947	90.169	86.006	88.014	93.498	76.830	87.576
54	86.115	89.573	85.109	87.143	93.015	75.394	86.715
55	85.214	88.938	84.143	86.200	92.489	73.884	85.802
56	84.237	88.264	83.103	85.179	91.919	72.299	84.833
57	83.185	87.556	81.988	84.076	91.299	70.639	83.802
58	82.055	86.814	80.798	82.885	90.628	68.900	82.697
59	80.843	86.038	79.529	81.603	89.901	67.084	81.514
60	79.543	85.223	78.181	80.228	89.116	65.191	80.247
61	78.148	84.360	76.751	78.756	88.267	63.226	78.900
62	76.648	83.435	75.236	77.178	87.350	61.194	77.479
63	75.034	82.432	73.631	75.484	86.360	59.101	75.996
64	73.297	81.340	71.933	73.667	85.290	56.953	74.459
65	71.434	80.153	70.139	71.724	84.136	54.757	72.872
66	69.445	78.871	68.246	69.641	82.878	52.505	71.201
67	67.331	77.496	66.254	67.431	81.521	50.210	69.455

Life Expectancy Age	CSO (1980)		Total Population	U.S. Life Tables (1982)			
	Male	Female		White Male	White Female	Black Male	Black Female
	70.83	75.83	70.75	71.50	78.80	64.90	73.50
68	65.096	76.036	64.166	65.111	80.070	47.886	67.641
69	62.742	74.488	61.984	62.696	78.531	45.547	65.766
70	60.263	72.841	59.715	60.202	76.910	43.205	63.838
71	57.653	71.076	57.360	57.571	75.141	40.863	61.827
72	54.906	69.166	54.913	54.829	73.236	38.534	59.745
73	52.016	67.084	52.363	52.002	71.206	36.230	57.604
74	48.989	64.808	49.706	49.116	69.064	33.963	55.413
75	45.844	62.329	46.946	46.197	66.823	31.743	53.186
76	42.611	59.651	44.101	43.187	64.387	29.541	50.851
77	39.325	56.786	41.192	40.127	61.781	27.373	48.430
78	36.026	53.750	38.246	37.054	59.031	25.255	45.946
79	32.745	50.560	35.285	34.005	56.166	23.198	43.419
80	29.509	47.224	32.323	31.012	53.214	21.217	40.870
81	26.337	43.748	29.375	26.868	47.897	18.434	36.547
82	23.249	40.143	26.469	22.053	40.842	15.173	30.962
83	20.267	36.429	23.638	17.096	32.892	11.795	24.773
84	17.425	32.647	20.908	12.473	24.931	8.630	18.655
85	14.760	28.857	18.282	8.531	17.715	5.920	13.170
86	12.308	25.126	15.769	5.446	11.749	3.790	8.678
87	10.098	21.525	13.407	3.228	7.236	2.253	5.309
88	8.147	18.120	11.240	1.767	4.113	1.236	2.999
89	6.458	14.968	9.297	0.886	2.143	0.622	1.552
90	5.026	12.113	7.577	0.404	1.015	0.284	0.731

		CSO (1980)			U. S. Life Tables (1982)			
Life Expectancy		Male	Female	Total Population	White Male	White Female	Black Male	Black Female
		70.83	75.83	70.75	71.50	78.80	64.90	73.50
Age								
91		3.835	9.583	6.070	0.166	0.433	0.117	0.309
92		2.863	7.390	4.773	0.060	0.164	0.043	0.117
93		2.084	5.532	3.682	0.019	0.054	0.014	0.038
94		1.467	3.987	2.786	0.005	0.015	0.004	0.011
95		0.983	2.722	2.068	0.001	0.004	0.001	0.003
96		0.605	1.699	1.511	> 0.001	0.001	> 0.001	> 0.001
97		0.315	0.892	1.087	> 0.001	> 0.001	> 0.001	> 0.001
98		0.108	0.307	0.772	> 0.001	> 0.001	> 0.001	> 0.001
99		> 0.001	> 0.001	0.542	> 0.001	> 0.001	> 0.001	> 0.001

Probability of surviving through age X starting from age 1

		CSO (1980)			U. S. Life Tables (1982)			
Expectancy		Male	Female	Total Population Life	White Male	White Female	Black Male	Black Female
		70.13	75.04	71.19	71.30	78.50	65.40	73.80
Age								
1		99.893	99.913	99.875	99.918	99.937	99.882	99.903
2		99.794	99.832	99.789	99.857	99.887	99.785	99.822
3		99.696	99.753	99.720	99.809	99.847	99.704	99.755
4		99.602	99.676	99.663	99.769	99.814	99.635	99.700
5		99.512	99.601	99.613	99.733	99.786	99.577	99.654

| | CSO (1980) | | | U. S. Life Tables (1982) | | | |
Age	Male	Female	Total Population Life	White Male	White Female	Black Male	Black Female
Expectancy	70.13	75.04	71.19	71.30	78.50	65.40	73.80
6	99.426	99.528	99.567	99.699	99.762	99.526	99.617
7	99.347	99.456	99.524	99.667	99.741	99.481	99.585
8	99.271	99.387	99.485	99.640	99.722	99.441	99.557
9	99.198	99.318	99.451	99.616	99.705	99.407	99.532
10	99.125	99.251	99.420	99.596	99.689	99.375	99.509
11	99.049	99.182	99.391	99.577	99.673	99.343	99.486
12	98.965	99.111	99.356	99.551	99.655	99.305	99.462
13	98.867	99.036	99.310	99.509	99.632	99.257	99.435
14	98.753	98.957	99.248	99.445	99.603	99.192	99.405
15	98.622	98.873	99.166	99.357	99.566	99.110	99.369
16	98.473	98.784	99.066	99.246	99.523	99.009	99.327
17	98.309	98.690	98.950	99.116	99.474	98.888	99.279
18	98.134	98.593	98.823	98.973	99.424	98.745	99.226
19	97.951	98.493	98.691	98.823	99.372	98.581	99.166
20	97.765	98.389	98.553	98.667	99.320	98.395	99.101
21	97.578	98.284	98.408	98.505	99.269	98.186	99.029
22	97.394	98.177	98.258	98.340	99.216	97.955	98.951
23	97.213	98.068	98.108	98.175	99.163	97.707	98.866
24	97.036	97.956	97.960	98.012	99.111	97.444	98.774
25	96.864	97.843	97.816	97.853	99.057	97.167	98.675
26	96.696	97.726	97.676	97.700	99.004	96.876	98.569
27	96.531	97.607	97.537	97.549	98.949	96.569	98.455
28	96.367	97.484	97.397	97.399	98.894	96.246	98.333

	CSO (1980)		Total Population Life	U. S. Life Tables (1982)			
	Male	Female		White Male	White Female	Black Male	Black Female
Expectancy	70.13	75.04	71.19	71.30	78.50	65.40	73.80
Age							
29	96.202	97.357	97.252	97.249	98.837	95.907	98.206
30	96.036	97.226	97.101	97.097	98.776	95.549	98.070
31	95.865	97.090	96.943	96.944	98.713	95.173	97.927
32	95.689	96.949	96.776	96.788	98.647	94.781	97.774
33	95.507	96.804	96.599	96.631	98.577	94.374	97.611
34	95.316	96.651	96.411	96.468	98.502	93.951	97.435
35	95.114	96.491	96.209	96.301	98.421	93.510	97.246
36	94.901	96.321	95.993	96.125	98.334	93.050	97.043
37	94.674	96.139	95.758	95.941	98.238	92.569	96.824
38	94.429	95.943	95.504	95.744	98.133	92.065	96.586
39	94.166	95.730	95.227	95.532	98.017	91.534	96.329
40	93.882	95.498	94.928	95.303	97.889	90.977	96.051
41	93.573	95.246	94.604	95.053	97.746	90.386	95.748
42	93.240	94.973	94.254	94.778	97.589	89.756	95.419
43	92.879	94.679	93.873	94.475	97.414	89.074	95.059
44	92.490	94.365	93.457	94.142	97.221	88.333	94.668
45	92.069	94.029	93.005	93.774	97.008	87.528	94.241
46	91.616	93.672	92.514	93.367	96.773	86.658	93.776
47	91.128	93.293	91.983	92.916	96.515	85.718	93.271
48	90.605	92.889	91.409	92.416	96.230	84.708	92.719
49	90.043	92.458	90.789	91.861	95.918	83.624	92.116
50	89.438	92.000	90.119	91.246	95.574	82.465	91.459
51	88.785	91.511	89.395	90.569	95.198	81.229	90.746

Age	CSO (1980) Male	CSO (1980) Female	Total Population Life	U. S. Life Tables (1982) White Male	White Female	Black Male	Black Female
Expectancy	70.13	75.04	71.19	71.30	78.50	65.40	73.80
52	88.079	90.990	88.611	89.826	94.785	79.915	89.977
53	87.312	90.430	87.763	89.016	94.336	78.525	89.155
54	86.477	89.832	86.848	88.136	93.848	77.057	88.278
55	85.571	89.196	85.862	87.181	93.318	75.514	87.349
56	84.591	88.520	84.800	86.149	92.742	73.894	86.363
57	83.534	87.809	83.663	85.033	92.117	72.197	85.312
58	82.399	87.066	82.448	83.829	91.440	70.421	84.188
59	81.182	86.287	81.154	82.532	90.707	68.564	82.983
60	79.877	85.470	79.778	81.142	89.914	66.630	81.694
61	78.476	84.604	78.319	79.653	89.058	64.621	80.322
62	76.970	83.677	76.773	78.057	88.133	62.544	78.875
63	75.349	82.671	75.136	76.343	87.133	60.405	77.366
64	73.605	81.576	73.403	74.506	86.054	58.210	75.801
65	71.734	80.386	71.572	72.541	84.889	55.965	74.185
66	69.736	79.100	69.640	70.434	83.620	53.663	72.485
67	67.613	77.721	67.608	68.199	82.251	51.318	70.708
68	65.369	76.257	65.477	65.852	80.787	48.943	68.861
69	63.005	74.704	63.251	63.410	79.235	46.552	66.952
70	60.516	73.052	60.935	60.888	77.599	44.159	64.989
71	57.895	71.282	58.532	58.227	75.814	41.765	62.942
72	55.137	69.367	56.035	55.454	73.892	39.384	60.823
73	52.234	67.278	53.433	52.594	71.844	37.030	58.642
74	49.195	64.996	50.721	49.675	69.683	34.713	56.412

| | CSO (1980) | | Total Population Life | U. S. Life Tables (1982) | | | |
	Male	Female		White Male	White Female	Black Male	Black Female
Expectancy	70.13	75.04	71.19	71.30	78.50	65.40	73.80
Age							
75	46.037	62.510	47.905	46.723	67.422	32.444	54.145
76	42.790	59.824	45.002	43.679	64.964	30.193	51.768
77	39.490	56.950	42.034	40.584	62.334	27.977	49.304
78	36.177	53.906	39.027	37.476	59.560	25.812	46.774
79	32.883	50.707	36.006	34.392	56.669	23.710	44.202
80	29.633	47.361	32.984	31.365	53.691	21.685	41.607
81	26.448	43.875	29.975	27.174	48.326	18.841	37.206
82	23.347	40.260	27.010	22.304	41.208	15.508	31.520
83	20.352	36.534	24.121	17.290	33.186	12.056	25.219
84	17.498	32.742	21.336	12.615	25.154	8.821	18.991
85	14.822	28.940	18.656	8.628	17.874	6.050	13.407
86	12.360	25.199	16.091	5.508	11.854	3.873	8.834
87	10.141	21.587	13.681	3.265	7.300	2.303	5.405
88	8.181	18.173	11.470	1.787	4.150	1.264	3.053
89	6.485	15.012	9.487	0.896	2.163	0.636	1.580
90	5.047	12.148	7.731	0.409	1.024	0.291	0.744
91	3.851	9.611	6.194	0.168	0.437	0.120	0.315
92	2.875	7.412	4.871	0.061	0.166	0.044	0.119
93	2.093	5.548	3.757	0.020	0.055	0.014	0.039
94	1.473	3.998	2.842	0.005	0.016	0.004	0.011
95	0.987	2.729	2.111	0.001	0.004	0.001	0.003
96	0.608	1.704	1.542	>0.001	0.001	>0.001	>0.001
97	0.316	0.895	1.110	>0.001	>0.001	>0.001	>0.001

	CSO (1980)		Total Population Life	U. S. Life Tables (1982)			
	Male	Female		White Male	White Female	Black Male	Black Female
Expectancy	70.13	75.04	71.19	71.30	78.50	65.40	73.80
Age							
98	0.108	0.308	0.788	> 0.001	> 0.001	> 0.001	> 0.001
99	> 0.001	> 0.001	0.553	> 0.001	> 0.001	> 0.001	> 0.001.

Probability of surviving through age X starting from age 2

	CSO (1980)		Total Population	U. S. Life Tables (1982)			
	Male	Female		White Male	White Female	Black Male	Black Female
Life Expectancy	69.20	74.11	70.28	70.40	77.50	64.40	72.90
Age							
2	99.901	99.919	99.914	99.939	99.950	99.903	99.919
3	99.803	99.840	99.845	99.891	99.910	99.822	99.852
4	99.708	99.763	99.788	99.851	99.877	99.753	99.797
5	99.619	99.687	99.737	99.815	99.849	99.694	99.751
6	99.533	99.615	99.691	99.781	99.825	99.644	99.713
7	99.453	99.543	99.649	99.749	99.804	99.599	99.681
8	99.378	99.473	99.610	99.721	99.785	99.559	99.654
9	99.304	99.405	99.576	99.697	99.768	99.524	99.629
10	99.232	99.337	99.545	99.677	99.752	99.492	99.606
11	99.155	99.268	99.515	99.659	99.736	99.460	99.583
12	99.071	99.197	99.480	99.633	99.717	99.422	99.559
13	98.973	99.123	99.434	99.591	99.694	99.374	99.532

	CSO (1980)		Total Population	U. S. Life Tables (1982)			
	Male	Female		White Male	White Female	Black Male	Black Female
Life Expectancy	69.20	74.11	70.28	70.40	77.50	64.40	72.90
Age							
14	98.859	99.043	99.372	99.527	99.666	99.309	99.501
15	98.728	98.959	99.290	99.438	99.629	99.227	99.465
16	98.578	98.870	99.190	99.327	99.586	99.126	99.424
17	98.414	98.776	99.074	99.197	99.537	99.005	99.376
18	98.239	98.679	98.947	99.054	99.486	98.862	99.322
19	98.056	98.579	98.815	98.905	99.435	98.698	99.263
20	97.870	98.475	98.676	98.748	99.383	98.511	99.197
21	97.683	98.370	98.531	98.586	99.331	98.302	99.126
22	97.498	98.263	98.381	98.421	99.278	98.071	99.047
23	97.317	98.153	98.231	98.255	99.226	97.822	98.962
24	97.140	98.042	98.083	98.092	99.173	97.559	98.870
25	96.968	97.928	97.938	97.933	99.120	97.282	98.771
26	96.800	97.811	97.798	97.781	99.066	96.990	98.665
27	96.634	97.692	97.659	97.629	99.012	96.683	98.550
28	96.470	97.569	97.519	97.479	98.956	96.360	98.429
29	96.305	97.442	97.374	97.329	98.899	96.020	98.301
30	96.139	97.310	97.223	97.177	98.839	95.662	98.165
31	95.967	97.174	97.064	97.023	98.775	95.286	98.022
32	95.792	97.033	96.897	96.868	98.709	94.893	97.869
33	95.609	96.888	96.720	96.710	98.639	94.485	97.706
34	95.418	96.735	96.531	96.548	98.564	94.062	97.530
35	95.216	96.575	96.330	96.380	98.483	93.621	97.341
36	95.003	96.405	96.113	96.204	98.396	93.160	97.137

| | CSO (1980) | | | U. S. Life Tables (1982) | | | |
	Male	Female	Total Population	White Male	White Female	Black Male	Black Female
Life Expectancy	69.20	74.11	70.28	70.40	77.50	64.40	72.90
Age							
37	94.775	96.223	95.878	96.019	98.300	92.678	96.918
38	94.530	96.027	95.623	95.823	98.195	92.173	96.680
39	94.267	95.813	95.346	95.611	98.079	91.642	96.423
40	93.982	95.582	95.047	95.381	97.951	91.084	96.144
41	93.673	95.329	94.722	95.131	97.808	90.493	95.841
42	93.339	95.056	94.372	94.856	97.650	89.862	95.512
43	92.978	94.762	93.991	94.553	97.475	89.179	95.152
44	92.589	94.447	93.574	94.219	97.282	88.438	94.760
45	92.167	94.111	93.121	93.851	97.069	87.632	94.332
46	91.714	93.753	92.630	93.444	96.834	86.760	93.867
47	91.226	93.374	92.098	92.992	96.576	85.819	93.361
48	90.702	92.969	91.523	92.492	96.291	84.808	92.809
49	90.139	92.539	90.903	91.936	95.978	83.723	92.205
50	89.534	92.080	90.232	91.321	95.634	82.563	91.548
51	88.881	91.591	89.506	90.643	95.258	81.325	90.834
52	88.173	91.069	88.722	89.900	94.845	80.010	90.064
53	87.405	90.509	87.873	89.089	94.396	78.618	89.241
54	86.570	89.911	86.957	88.208	93.908	77.148	88.364
55	85.663	89.273	85.969	87.253	93.377	75.603	87.434
56	84.681	88.597	84.906	86.220	92.801	73.981	86.446
57	83.624	87.886	83.768	85.103	92.175	72.283	85.395
58	82.487	87.142	82.551	83.898	91.498	70.504	84.270
59	81.269	86.363	81.255	82.600	90.764	68.645	83.064

	CSO (1980)		Total Population	U. S. Life Tables (1982)			
	Male	Female		White Male	White Female	Black Male	Black Female
Life Expectancy	69.20	74.11	70.28	70.40	77.50	64.40	72.90
Age							
60	79.962	85.545	79.878	81.208	89.971	66.708	81.773
61	78.560	84.678	78.417	79.718	89.114	64.698	80.400
62	77.052	83.750	76.869	78.121	88.188	62.618	78.952
63	75.429	82.743	75.230	76.406	87.188	60.476	77.441
64	73.684	81.647	73.495	74.567	86.108	58.278	75.875
65	71.811	80.456	71.661	72.601	84.943	56.031	74.257
66	69.811	79.168	69.727	70.491	83.673	53.727	72.555
67	67.686	77.789	67.692	68.255	82.303	51.379	70.776
68	65.439	76.323	65.559	65.906	80.838	49.001	68.928
69	63.072	74.769	63.330	63.462	79.285	46.607	67.017
70	60.580	73.116	61.011	60.938	77.648	44.211	65.052
71	57.957	71.344	58.606	58.275	75.862	41.814	63.003
72	55.196	69.427	56.105	55.499	73.938	39.431	60.882
73	52.290	67.337	53.500	52.637	71.889	37.073	58.699
74	49.247	65.052	50.785	49.716	69.726	34.754	56.467
75	46.086	62.565	47.965	46.761	67.465	32.482	54.197
76	42.836	59.876	45.058	43.715	65.005	30.229	51.818
77	39.532	57.000	42.086	40.617	62.373	28.010	49.351
78	36.216	53.953	39.076	37.507	59.597	25.842	46.820
79	32.918	50.751	36.051	34.420	56.705	23.738	44.245
80	29.664	47.402	33.025	31.391	53.725	21.710	41.647

	CSO (1980)		Total Population	U. S. Life Tables (1982)			
	Male	Female		White Male	White Female	Black Male	Black Female
Life Expectancy	69.20	74.11	70.28	70.40	77.50	64.40	72.90
Age							
81	26.476	43.913	30.012	27.197	48.357	18.863	37.242
82	23.372	40.295	27.044	22.323	41.234	15.526	31.551
83	20.374	36.566	24.151	17.304	33.207	12.070	25.244
84	17.517	32.770	21.362	12.625	25.170	8.831	19.010
85	14.837	28.966	18.679	8.635	17.885	6.057	13.420
86	12.373	25.221	16.111	5.513	11.862	3.878	8.843
87	10.152	21.606	13.698	3.268	7.305	2.305	5.410
88	8.190	18.188	11.484	1.788	4.153	1.265	3.056
89	6.492	15.025	9.499	0.897	2.164	0.636	1.582
90	5.052	12.159	7.741	0.409	1.025	0.291	0.745
91	3.855	9.619	6.202	0.168	0.437	0.120	0.315
92	2.878	7.418	4.877	0.061	0.166	0.044	0.119
93	2.095	5.552	3.761	0.020	0.055	0.014	0.039
94	1.475	4.002	2.846	0.005	0.016	0.004	0.011
95	0.988	2.732	2.113	0.001	0.004	0.001	0.003
96	0.608	1.705	1.544	> 0.001	0.001	> 0.001	> 0.001
97	0.316	0.895	1.111	> 0.001	> 0.001	> 0.001	> 0.001
98	0.108	0.308	0.789	> 0.001	> 0.001	> 0.001	> 0.001
99	> 0.001	> 0.001	0.553	> 0.001	> 0.001	> 0.001	> 0.001

Probability of surviving through age X starting from age 3

| | CSO (1980) | | | U. S. Life Tables (1982) | | | |
Age	Male	Female	Total Population	White Male	White Female	Black Male	Black Female
Life Expectancy	68.27	73.17	69.34	69.40	76.50	63.50	71.90
3	99.902	99.921	99.931	99.952	99.960	99.919	99.933
4	99.807	99.844	99.874	99.912	99.927	99.850	99.878
5	99.717	99.768	99.823	99.876	99.899	99.791	99.832
6	99.632	99.695	99.777	99.842	99.875	99.740	99.794
7	99.552	99.624	99.734	99.810	99.854	99.695	99.762
8	99.476	99.554	99.695	99.782	99.835	99.655	99.734
9	99.403	99.485	99.661	99.758	99.818	99.621	99.709
10	99.330	99.417	99.631	99.738	99.802	99.589	99.686
11	99.253	99.349	99.601	99.719	99.786	99.557	99.663
12	99.169	99.277	99.566	99.693	99.767	99.519	99.640
13	99.071	99.203	99.520	99.652	99.744	99.470	99.613
14	98.957	99.124	99.457	99.588	99.715	99.406	99.582
15	98.825	99.039	99.376	99.499	99.678	99.323	99.546
16	98.676	98.950	99.275	99.388	99.636	99.222	99.504
17	98.511	98.856	99.159	99.258	99.587	99.101	99.456
18	98.336	98.759	99.032	99.115	99.536	98.958	99.403
19	98.153	98.659	98.900	98.965	99.484	98.794	99.343
20	97.967	98.555	98.761	98.809	99.433	98.607	99.277
21	97.780	98.449	98.616	98.646	99.381	98.397	99.206
22	97.595	98.342	98.466	98.481	99.328	98.166	99.128
23	97.413	98.233	98.315	98.315	99.275	97.917	99.042
24	97.236	98.121	98.167	98.152	99.223	97.654	98.950

| | CSO (1980) | | | | U. S. Life Tables (1982) | | | |
	Male	Female	Total Population	White Male	White Female	Black Male	Black Female
Life Expectancy	68.27	73.17	69.34	69.40	76.50	63.50	71.90
Age							
25	97.064	98.007	98.023	97.993	99.169	97.377	98.851
26	96.896	97.891	97.883	97.840	99.116	97.085	98.745
27	96.730	97.771	97.744	97.689	99.061	96.777	98.630
28	96.566	97.648	97.603	97.538	99.006	96.454	98.509
29	96.401	97.521	97.457	97.388	98.948	96.113	98.381
30	96.234	97.389	97.306	97.236	98.888	95.755	98.245
31	96.063	97.253	97.148	97.082	98.825	95.378	98.101
32	95.887	97.112	96.981	96.927	98.758	94.985	97.948
33	95.704	96.966	96.803	96.769	98.688	94.577	97.785
34	95.512	96.813	96.614	96.606	98.613	94.153	97.609
35	95.311	96.653	96.412	96.438	98.532	93.712	97.419
36	95.097	96.483	96.195	96.263	98.445	93.251	97.216
37	94.869	96.301	95.961	96.078	98.349	92.768	96.996
38	94.624	96.104	95.706	95.881	98.244	92.263	96.758
39	94.360	95.891	95.428	95.669	98.128	91.731	96.501
40	94.075	95.659	95.128	95.440	98.000	91.173	96.222
41	93.766	95.407	94.804	95.189	97.857	90.581	95.919
42	93.432	95.133	94.453	94.913	97.699	89.949	95.589
43	93.070	94.839	94.072	94.611	97.524	89.266	95.229
44	92.680	94.524	93.655	94.277	97.331	88.523	94.836
45	92.259	94.187	93.202	93.908	97.118	87.717	94.409
46	91.805	93.829	92.709	93.501	96.883	86.844	93.943
47	91.316	93.449	92.177	93.049	96.624	85.903	93.437

| | CSO (1980) | | Total Population | U. S. Life Tables (1982) | | | |
Life Expectancy	Male	Female		White Male	White Female	Black Male	Black Female
	68.27	73.17	69.34	69.40	76.50	63.50	71.90
Age							
48	90.792	93.045	91.602	92.548	96.339	84.890	92.884
49	90.228	92.614	90.981	91.992	96.026	83.804	92.280
50	89.632	92.155	90.310	91.377	95.682	82.643	91.622
51	88.969	91.665	89.584	90.699	95.305	81.404	90.907
52	88.260	91.143	88.799	89.955	94.893	80.088	90.137
53	87.492	90.582	87.949	89.144	94.443	78.694	89.314
54	86.655	89.984	87.032	88.262	93.954	77.223	88.436
55	85.748	89.346	86.043	87.306	93.424	75.676	87.504
56	84.765	88.669	84.979	86.272	92.847	74.053	86.516
57	83.707	87.957	83.840	85.155	92.221	72.353	85.464
58	82.569	87.212	82.623	83.949	91.544	70.572	84.338
59	81.350	86.433	81.325	82.651	90.809	68.712	83.131
60	80.041	85.614	79.947	81.258	90.016	66.773	81.839
61	78.638	84.747	78.485	79.767	89.159	64.760	80.465
62	77.128	83.818	76.935	78.168	88.232	62.679	79.016
63	75.504	82.810	75.294	76.453	87.232	60.535	77.504
64	73.757	81.713	73.558	74.612	86.151	58.335	75.937
65	71.882	80.521	71.723	72.645	84.985	56.086	74.318
66	69.880	79.233	69.787	70.534	83.715	53.779	72.614
67	67.753	77.852	67.751	68.296	82.345	51.429	70.834
68	65.504	76.385	65.615	65.946	80.879	49.049	68.984
69	63.135	74.830	63.384	63.500	79.324	46.653	67.071
70	60.641	73.175	61.064	60.975	77.687	44.254	65.105

| | CSO (1980) | | Total | U. S. Life Tables (1982) | | | |
Life Expectancy	Male	Female	Population	White Male	White Female	Black Male	Black Female
	68.27	73.17	69.34	69.40	76.50	63.50	71.90
Age							
71	58.015	71.402	58.656	58.310	75.900	41.855	63.054
72	55.250	69.484	56.154	55.533	73.975	39.469	60.931
73	52.342	67.391	53.546	52.669	71.925	37.109	58.747
74	49.296	65.105	50.828	49.756	69.761	34.788	56.513
75	46.132	62.615	48.006	46.790	67.498	32.514	54.241
76	42.878	59.925	45.097	43.741	65.037	30.258	51.860
77	39.571	57.046	42.123	40.642	62.405	28.038	49.391
78	36.251	53.997	39.110	37.529	59.627	25.868	46.858
79	32.951	50.792	36.082	34.441	56.733	23.761	44.281
80	29.694	47.440	33.053	31.410	53.752	21.731	41.681
81	26.502	43.949	30.038	27.213	48.381	18.881	37.273
82	23.395	40.327	27.067	22.336	41.255	15.541	31.576
83	20.394	36.596	24.172	17.315	33.224	12.081	25.264
84	17.534	32.797	21.381	12.633	25.182	8.840	19.025
85	14.852	28.989	18.695	8.641	17.894	6.063	13.431
86	12.385	25.241	16.125	5.516	11.868	3.882	8.850
87	10.162	21.624	13.710	3.270	7.309	2.308	5.415
88	8.198	18.203	11.494	1.789	4.155	1.266	3.058
89	6.498	15.037	9.507	0.897	2.165	0.637	3.583
90	5.057	12.169	7.748	0.409	1.026	0.291	0.745
91	3.859	9.627	6.207	0.168	0.437	0.120	0.316
92	2.881	7.424	4.881	0.061	0.166	0.044	0.119
93	2.097	5.557	3.765	0.020	0.055	0.014	0.039

| | CSO (1980) | | Total | U. S. Life Tables (1982) | | | |
	Male	Female	Population	White Male	White Female	Black Male	Black Female
Life Expectancy	68.27	73.17	69.34	69.40	76.50	63.50	71.90
Age							
94	1.476	4.005	2.848	0.005	0.016	0.004	0.011
95	0.989	2.734	2.115	0.001	0.004	0.001	0.003
96	0.609	1.707	1.545	> 0.001	0.001	> 0.001	> 0.001
97	0.316	0.896	1.112	> 0.001	> 0.001	> 0.001	> 0.001
98	0.108	0.308	0.790	> 0.001	> 0.001	> 0.001	> 0.001
99	> 0.001	> 0.001	0.554	> 0.001	> 0.001	> 0.001	> 0.001

Probability of surviving through age X starting from age 4

| | CSO (1980) | | Total | U. S. Life Tables (1982) | | | |
	Male	Female	Population	White Male	White Female	Black Male	Black Female
Life Expectancy	67.34	72.23	68.39	68.40	75.60	62.60	71.00
Age							
4	99.905	99.923	99.943	99.960	99.967	99.931	99.945
5	99.815	99.847	99.892	99.924	99.939	99.872	99.899
6	99.729	99.774	99.846	99.890	99.915	99.821	99.861
7	99.649	99.702	99.803	99.858	99.894	99.776	99.829
8	99.574	99.633	99.764	99.830	99.875	99.736	99.801
9	99.500	99.564	99.730	99.806	99.858	99.701	99.776
10	99.427	99.496	99.699	99.786	99.842	99.669	99.753
11	99.351	99.427	99.669	99.767	99.826	99.638	99.730

	CSO (1980)		Total Population	U. S. Life Tables (1982)			
	Male	Female		White Male	White Female	Black Male	Black Female
Life Expectancy	67.34	72.23	68.39	68.40	75.60	62.60	71.00
Age							
12	99.266	99.356	99.635	99.741	99.807	99.600	99.706
13	99.168	99.281	99.589	99.699	99.784	99.551	99.679
14	99.054	99.202	99.526	99.636	99.755	99.486	99.649
15	98.922	99.118	99.444	99.547	99.718	99.404	99.613
16	98.773	99.028	99.344	99.435	99.675	99.302	99.571
17	98.608	98.934	99.228	99.305	99.627	99.181	99.523
18	98.432	98.837	99.101	99.162	99.576	99.038	99.469
19	98.249	98.737	98.968	99.012	99.524	98.874	99.410
20	98.063	98.633	98.829	98.856	99.472	98.687	99.344
21	97.875	98.527	98.684	98.694	99.421	98.477	99.272
22	97.690	98.420	98.534	98.528	99.368	98.245	99.194
23	97.509	98.311	98.383	98.363	99.315	97.997	99.109
24	97.331	98.199	98.235	98.199	99.263	97.733	99.017
25	97.159	98.085	98.090	98.040	99.209	97.456	98.918
26	96.991	97.968	97.950	97.887	99.155	97.163	98.811
27	96.825	97.848	97.811	97.736	99.101	96.855	98.696
28	96.660	97.725	97.670	97.585	99.045	96.532	98.575
29	96.495	97.598	97.525	97.435	98.988	96.191	98.447
30	96.328	97.466	97.373	97.283	98.928	95.832	98.311
31	96.157	97.330	97.215	97.129	98.864	95.456	98.167
32	95.981	97.189	97.048	96.974	98.798	95.062	98.014
33	95.797	97.043	96.870	96.816	98.728	94.654	97.850
34	95.606	96.890	96.681	96.653	98.653	94.229	97.674

| | CSO (1980) | | Total Population | U. S. Life Tables (1982) | | | |
	Male	Female		White Male	White Female	Black Male	Black Female
Life Expectancy	67.34	72.23	68.39	68.40	75.60	62.60	71.00
Age							
35	95.404	96.730	96.479	96.485	98.572	93.788	97.485
36	95.190	96.560	96.262	96.309	98.484	93.326	97.281
37	94.962	96.377	96.027	96.124	98.389	92.844	97.061
38	94.717	96.180	95.772	95.927	98.283	92.338	96.823
39	94.453	95.967	95.494	95.715	98.167	91.806	96.566
40	94.167	95.735	95.194	95.485	98.039	91.247	96.287
41	93.858	95.482	94.869	95.234	97.896	90.654	95.983
42	93.524	95.208	94.518	94.959	97.738	90.022	95.653
43	93.162	94.914	94.137	94.656	97.563	89.338	95.293
44	92.771	94.599	93.720	94.322	97.370	88.595	94.900
45	92.349	94.262	93.266	93.953	97.157	87.788	94.472
46	91.895	93.904	92.773	93.545	96.922	86.915	94.006
47	91.406	93.523	92.241	93.094	96.663	85.972	93.500
48	90.881	93.118	91.665	92.593	96.378	84.959	92.946
49	90.317	92.687	91.044	92.036	96.064	83.872	92.342
50	89.711	92.228	90.372	91.421	95.721	82.710	91.684
51	89.056	91.738	89.645	90.742	95.343	81.470	90.968
52	88.347	91.215	88.860	89.998	94.931	80.153	90.198
53	87.578	90.654	88.010	89.186	94.481	78.758	89.373
54	86.740	90.055	87.092	88.304	93.992	77.286	88.495
55	85.832	89.416	86.102	87.348	93.461	75.738	87.563
56	84.849	88.739	85.038	86.314	92.884	74.113	86.574
57	83.789	88.027	83.898	85.196	92.258	72.412	85.522

	CSO (1980)			U. S. Life Tables (1982)			
Life Expectancy	Male	Female	Total Population	White Male	White Female	Black Male	Black Female
	67.34	72.23	68.39	68.40	75.60	62.60	71.00
Age							
58	82.650	87.281	82.680	83.990	91.580	70.630	84.395
59	81.429	86.501	81.382	82.690	90.846	68.768	83.187
60	80.120	85.682	80.002	81.297	90.052	66.827	81.894
61	78.715	84.814	78.539	79.805	89.194	64.813	80.519
62	77.204	83.884	76.989	78.206	88.268	62.730	79.069
63	75.578	82.876	75.346	76.489	87.267	60.584	77.556
64	73.829	81.778	73.609	74.648	86.186	58.382	75.987
65	71.953	80.585	71.772	72.680	85.019	56.131	74.367
66	69.949	79.295	69.835	70.568	83.748	53.822	72.663
67	67.819	77.913	67.797	68.329	82.377	51.470	70.881
68	65.569	76.445	65.660	65.978	80.911	49.088	69.030
69	63.197	74.889	63.428	63.531	79.356	46.690	67.116
70	60.700	73.233	61.106	61.004	77.718	44.290	65.148
71	58.072	71.459	58.696	58.338	75.931	41.889	63.096
72	55.305	69.539	56.192	55.560	74.005	39.501	60.972
73	52.393	67.445	53.583	52.695	71.954	37.140	58.786
74	49.345	65.156	50.864	49.770	69.789	34.816	56.551
75	46.177	62.665	48.040	46.812	67.525	32.540	54.278
76	42.920	59.972	45.128	43.762	65.063	30.283	51.895
77	39.610	57.091	42.152	40.661	62.430	28.060	49.425
78	36.287	54.039	39.137	37.547	59.651	25.889	46.889
79	32.983	50.832	36.107	34.458	56.756	23.781	44.310
80	29.723	47.478	33.076	31.425	53.773	21.749	41.709

| | CSO (1980) | | | U. S. Life Tables (1982) | | | |
	Male	Female	Total Population	White Male	White Female	Black Male	Black Female
Life Expectancy	67.34	72.23	68.39	68.40	75.60	62.60	71.00
Age							
81	26.528	43.983	30.059	27.226	48.400	18.896	37.298
82	23.418	40.359	27.086	22.347	41.271	15.554	31.597
83	20.414	36.625	24.189	17.323	33.237	12.091	25.281
84	17.551	32.823	21.395	12.639	25.192	8.847	19.038
85	14.867	29.012	18.708	8.645	17.901	6.068	13.440
86	12.398	25.261	16.136	5.519	11.873	3.885	8.856
87	10.172	21.641	13.719	3.271	7.312	2.309	5.418
88	8.206	18.218	11.502	1.790	4.156	1.267	3.060
89	6.505	15.049	9.513	0.898	2.166	0.637	1.584
90	5.062	12.178	7.753	0.409	1.026	0.291	0.746
91	3.863	9.635	6.211	0.168	0.437	0.120	0.316
92	2.884	7.430	4.884	0.061	0.166	0.044	0.119
93	2.099	5.561	3.767	0.020	0.055	0.014	0.039
94	1.478	4.008	2.850	0.005	0.016	0.004	0.011
95	0.990	2.736	2.117	0.001	0.004	0.001	0.003
96	0.609	1.708	1.546	> 0.001	0.001	> 0.001	> 0.001
97	0.317	0.897	1.113	> 0.001	> 0.001	> 0.001	> 0.001
98	0.108	0.309	0.790	> 0.001	> 0.001	> 0.001	> 0.001
99	> 0.001	> 0.001	0.554	> 0.001	> 0.001	> 0.001	> 0.001

Probability of surviving through age X starting from age 5

Age	CSO (1980) Male	CSO (1980) Female	Total Population Life	U. S. Life Tables (1982) White Male	White Female	Black Male	Black Female
Expectancy	66.40	71.28	67.43	67.50	74.60	61.60	70.00
5	99.910	99.924	99.949	99.964	99.972	99.941	99.954
6	99.824	99.851	99.903	99.930	99.948	99.890	99.916
7	99.744	99.779	99.860	99.898	99.927	99.845	99.884
8	99.668	99.709	99.821	99.870	99.908	99.805	99.856
9	99.595	99.641	99.787	99.846	99.891	99.770	99.831
10	99.522	99.573	99.756	99.826	99.875	99.738	99.808
11	99.445	99.504	99.726	99.807	99.859	99.706	99.785
12	99.361	99.432	99.691	99.781	99.840	99.668	99.761
13	99.262	99.358	99.646	99.739	99.817	99.620	99.734
14	99.148	99.278	99.583	99.675	99.788	99.555	99.703
15	99.016	99.194	99.501	99.587	99.751	99.472	99.668
16	98.876	99.105	99.401	99.475	99.708	99.371	99.626
17	98.702	99.011	99.284	99.345	99.660	99.250	99.578
18	98.526	98.914	99.157	99.202	99.609	99.107	99.524
19	98.343	98.813	99.024	99.052	99.557	98.942	99.464
20	98.156	98.709	98.886	98.896	99.505	98.755	99.399
21	97.969	98.603	98.740	98.733	99.453	98.545	99.327
22	97.783	98.496	98.590	98.567	99.401	98.313	99.249
23	97.601	98.386	98.439	98.402	99.348	98.064	99.163
24	97.424	98.274	98.291	98.239	99.295	97.801	99.071
25	97.251	98.160	98.146	98.079	99.242	97.523	98.972
26	97.083	98.043	98.006	97.926	99.188	97.230	98.865

	CSO (1980)		Total Population Life	U. S. Life Tables (1982)			
	Male	Female		White Male	White Female	Black Male	Black Female
Expectancy	66.40	71.28	67.43	67.50	74.60	61.60	70.00
Age							
27	96.917	97.924	97.867	97.775	99.134	96.922	98.750
28	96.752	97.800	97.726	97.624	99.078	96.598	98.629
29	96.587	97.673	97.580	97.474	99.021	96.257	98.501
30	96.420	97.541	97.429	97.322	98.960	95.898	98.365
31	96.248	97.405	97.270	97.168	98.897	95.521	98.221
32	96.072	97.264	97.103	97.012	98.831	95.128	98.068
33	95.889	97.118	96.925	96.854	98.760	94.719	97.904
34	95.697	96.964	96.736	96.692	98.685	94.295	97.728
35	95.495	96.804	96.534	96.523	98.604	93.852	97.538
36	95.281	96.634	96.317	96.348	98.517	93.391	97.335
37	95.052	96.451	96.082	96.163	98.421	92.908	97.115
38	94.807	96.255	95.826	95.966	98.316	92.401	96.877
39	94.543	96.041	95.548	95.753	98.200	91.869	96.619
40	94.257	95.808	95.248	95.524	98.071	91.310	96.340
41	93.947	95.556	94.924	95.272	97.928	90.717	96.036
42	93.612	95.281	94.572	94.997	97.770	90.084	95.706
43	93.250	94.987	94.190	94.694	97.595	89.400	95.345
44	92.859	94.672	93.773	94.360	97.402	88.656	94.952
45	92.437	94.334	93.319	93.991	97.189	87.849	94.524
46	91.982	93.976	92.826	93.583	96.954	86.975	94.058
47	91.493	93.595	92.294	93.131	96.695	86.032	93.551
48	90.968	93.190	91.718	92.630	96.409	85.017	92.997
49	90.403	92.759	91.096	92.073	96.096	83.930	92.393

| | CSO (1980) | | Total Population Life | U.S. Life Tables (1982) | | | |
	Male	Female		White Male	White Female	Black Male	Black Female
Expectancy	66.40	71.28	67.43	67.50	74.60	61.60	70.00
Age							
50	89.796	92.299	90.424	91.457	95.752	82.767	91.734
51	89.141	91.808	89.696	90.779	95.375	81.526	91.018
52	88.431	91.285	88.911	90.034	94.962	80.208	90.248
53	87.661	90.724	88.060	89.222	94.512	78.812	89.423
54	86.823	90.124	87.141	88.340	94.023	77.339	88.544
55	85.914	89.485	86.151	87.383	93.492	75.790	87.611
56	84.929	88.808	85.087	86.348	92.915	74.164	86.622
57	83.868	88.095	83.946	85.230	92.289	72.462	85.569
58	82.729	87.348	82.727	84.023	91.610	70.678	84.441
59	81.507	86.568	81.428	82.723	90.876	68.815	83.233
60	80.196	85.748	80.048	81.330	90.082	66.873	81.939
61	78.789	84.879	78.584	79.837	89.224	64.858	80.563
62	77.278	83.949	77.032	78.237	88.297	62.773	79.113
63	75.650	82.940	75.389	76.520	87.296	60.626	77.598
64	73.900	81.841	73.651	74.678	86.214	58.423	76.029
65	72.021	80.647	71.813	72.709	85.048	56.170	74.408
66	70.015	79.356	69.875	70.597	83.776	53.860	72.703
67	67.884	77.973	67.836	68.357	82.405	51.506	70.920
68	65.631	76.504	65.698	66.004	80.938	49.122	69.068
69	63.257	74.947	63.464	63.556	79.382	46.723	67.153
70	60.758	73.290	61.141	61.029	77.744	44.320	65.184
71	58.127	71.514	58.730	58.362	75.956	41.918	63.131
72	55.357	69.592	56.225	55.582	74.029	39.528	61.005

	CSO (1980)		Total Population Life	U. S. Life Tables (1982)			
	Male	Female		White Male	White Female	Black Male	Black Female
Expectancy	66.40	71.28	67.43	67.50	74.60	61.60	70.00
Age							
73	52.443	67.497	53.613	52.716	71.977	37.165	58.818
74	49.391	65.207	50.893	49.790	69.812	34.840	56.582
75	46.221	62.713	48.067	46.831	67.548	32.563	54.307
76	42.961	60.018	45.154	43.780	65.085	30.304	51.923
77	39.648	57.135	42.176	40.678	62.450	28.080	49.452
78	36.321	54.081	39.159	37.563	59.670	25.906	46.915
79	33.014	50.871	36.128	34.471	56.775	23.797	44.335
80	29.751	47.514	33.095	31.438	53.791	21.764	41.732
81	26.554	44.017	30.076	27.237	48.416	18.910	37.318
82	23.440	40.390	27.101	22.356	41.285	15.565	31.615
83	20.434	36.653	24.203	17.330	33.248	12.100	25.295
84	17.568	32.848	21.408	12.644	25.201	8.853	19.048
85	14.881	29.034	18.719	8.648	17.907	6.072	13.447
86	12.409	25.281	16.145	5.521	11.877	3.888	8.861
87	10.181	21.657	13.727	3.273	7.314	2.311	5.421
88	8.214	18.232	11.509	1.791	4.158	1.268	3.062
89	6.511	15.060	9.519	0.898	2.167	0.638	1.585
90	5.067	12.188	7.758	0.410	1.026	0.292	0.746
91	3.866	9.642	6.215	0.168	0.438	0.120	0.316
92	2.886	7.436	4.887	0.061	0.166	0.044	0.119
93	2.101	5.566	3.769	0.020	0.055	0.014	0.039
94	1.479	4.011	2.852	0.005	0.016	0.004	0.011
95	0.991	2.738	2.118	0.001	0.004	0.001	0.003

	CSO (1980)		Total Population Life	U. S. Life Tables (1982)			
	Male	Female		White Male	White Female	Black Male	Black Female
Expectancy	66.40	71.28	67.43	67.50	74.60	61.60	70.00
Age							
96	0.610	1.709	1.547	> 0.001	0.001	> 0.001	> 0.001
97	0.317	0.897	1.113	> 0.001	> 0.001	> 0.001	> 0.001
98	0.108	0.309	0.791	> 0.001	> 0.001	> 0.001	> 0.001
99	> 0.001	> 0.001	0.555	> 0.001	> 0.001	> 0.001	> 0.001

Probability of surviving through age X starting from age 6

	CSO (1980)		Total Population	U. S. Life Tables (1982)			
	Male	Female		White Male	White Female	Black Male	Black Female
Life Expectancy	65.46	70.34	66.46	66.50	73.60	60.60	69.10
Age							
6	99.914	99.927	99.954	99.966	99.976	99.949	99.962
7	99.834	99.855	99.911	99.934	99.955	99.904	99.930
8	99.758	99.785	99.872	99.906	99.936	99.864	99.902
9	99.684	99.716	99.838	99.882	99.919	99.829	99.877
10	99.612	99.648	99.807	99.862	99.903	99.797	99.854
11	99.535	99.580	99.777	99.843	99.887	99.765	99.831
12	99.450	99.508	99.742	99.817	99.868	99.727	99.807
13	99.352	99.433	99.696	99.775	99.845	99.678	99.780
14	99.238	99.354	99.634	99.711	99.816	99.614	99.749
15	99.106	99.269	99.552	99.623	99.779	99.531	99.713

| | CSO (1980) | | Total Population | U. S. Life Tables (1982) | | | |
Life Expectancy	Male	Female		White Male	White Female	Black Male	Black Female
	65.46	70.34	66.46	66.50	73.60	60.60	69.10
Age							
16	98.956	99.180	99.451	99.511	99.736	99.429	99.671
17	98.791	99.086	99.335	99.381	99.687	99.308	99.624
18	98.615	98.989	99.208	99.238	99.637	99.165	99.570
19	98.431	98.888	99.075	99.088	99.585	99.001	99.510
20	98.244	98.784	98.936	98.931	99.533	98.813	99.444
21	98.057	98.678	98.791	98.769	99.481	98.603	99.373
22	97.871	98.571	98.641	98.603	99.429	98.371	99.294
23	97.689	98.461	98.490	98.437	99.376	98.122	99.209
24	97.512	98.349	98.341	98.274	99.323	97.858	99.117
25	97.339	98.235	98.196	98.115	99.270	97.580	99.018
26	97.171	98.118	98.056	97.962	99.216	97.288	98.911
27	97.004	97.998	97.917	97.810	99.161	96.979	98.796
28	96.840	97.875	97.776	97.659	99.106	96.655	98.674
29	96.674	97.748	97.630	97.509	99.048	96.314	98.546
30	96.507	97.616	97.479	97.357	98.988	95.955	98.410
31	96.335	97.479	97.320	97.203	98.925	95.578	98.266
32	96.159	97.338	97.152	97.047	98.858	95.184	98.113
33	95.975	97.192	96.975	96.889	98.788	94.775	97.949
34	95.783	97.038	96.786	96.726	98.713	94.350	97.773
35	95.581	96.878	96.583	96.558	98.632	93.908	97.583
36	95.367	96.707	96.366	96.382	98.544	93.446	97.379

| Life Expectancy | CSO (1980) | | Total Population | U. S. Life Tables (1982) | | | |
	Male	Female		White Male	White Female	Black Male	Black Female
	65.46	70.34	66.46	66.50	73.60	60.60	69.10
Age							
37	95.138	96.525	96.131	96.197	98.449	92.963	97.159
38	94.892	96.328	95.875	96.000	98.343	92.456	96.921
39	94.628	96.114	95.597	95.788	98.227	91.923	96.663
40	94.342	95.881	95.297	95.558	98.099	91.364	96.384
41	94.032	95.628	94.972	95.307	97.955	90.771	96.080
42	93.697	95.354	94.621	95.031	97.798	90.137	95.750
43	93.334	95.059	94.238	94.728	97.623	89.453	95.389
44	92.943	94.744	93.821	94.394	97.429	88.709	94.996
45	92.520	94.406	93.367	94.025	97.216	87.901	94.568
46	92.065	94.047	92.874	93.617	96.981	87.026	94.101
47	91.575	93.667	92.341	93.164	96.722	86.083	93.594
48	91.050	93.261	91.764	92.663	96.436	85.068	93.040
49	90.484	92.829	91.142	92.106	96.123	83.980	92.435
50	89.877	92.369	90.470	91.490	95.779	82.816	91.776
51	89.221	91.878	89.742	90.811	95.402	81.574	91.060
52	88.511	91.355	88.956	90.067	94.988	80.255	90.289
53	87.740	90.793	88.105	89.254	94.538	78.859	89.464
54	86.901	90.193	87.186	88.371	94.049	77.385	88.584
55	85.991	89.553	86.195	87.414	93.518	75.835	87.652
56	85.006	88.875	85.130	86.379	92.941	74.208	86.662
57	83.944	88.162	83.988	85.261	92.315	72.504	85.608

	CSO (1980)		Total Population	U. S. Life Tables (1982)			
	Male	Female		White Male	White Female	Black Male	Black Female
Life Expectancy	65.46	70.34	66.46	66.50	73.60	60.60	69.10
Age							
58	82.803	87.415	82.769	84.054	91.636	70.720	84.480
59	81.580	86.633	81.469	82.753	90.901	68.856	83.271
60	80.268	85.813	80.089	81.359	90.107	66.913	81.977
61	78.860	84.944	78.624	79.866	89.249	64.896	80.601
62	77.347	84.013	77.072	78.265	88.322	62.810	79.149
63	75.718	83.003	75.428	76.547	87.320	60.662	77.634
64	73.966	81.903	73.688	74.705	86.238	58.457	76.064
65	72.086	80.708	71.850	72.735	85.071	56.203	74.443
66	70.078	79.417	69.911	70.622	83.800	53.891	72.736
67	67.945	78.033	67.871	68.381	82.428	51.536	70.953
68	65.690	76.562	65.731	66.028	80.961	49.151	69.100
69	63.314	75.004	63.497	63.579	79.404	46.750	67.184
70	60.812	73.345	61.172	61.051	77.766	44.346	65.214
71	58.179	71.568	58.760	58.383	75.977	41.942	63.160
72	55.407	69.645	56.253	55.602	74.050	39.552	61.033
73	52.490	67.548	53.641	52.735	71.998	37.187	58.845
74	49.436	65.256	50.919	49.808	69.832	34.860	56.608
75	46.263	62.761	48.092	46.848	67.566	32.582	54.332
76	43.000	60.064	45.177	43.796	65.103	30.322	51.947
77	39.684	57.178	42.197	40.692	62.468	28.096	49.475
78	36.354	54.122	39.179	37.576	59.687	25.922	46.937

| | CSO (1980) | | Total Population | U. S. Life Tables (1982) | | | |
Age	Male	Female		White Male	White Female	Black Male	Black Female
Life Expectancy	65.46	70.34	66.46	66.50	73.60	60.60	69.10
79	33.044	50.910	36.146	34.484	56.791	23.811	44.355
80	29.778	47.551	33.112	31.449	53.806	21.777	41.751
81	26.578	44.051	30.092	27.247	48.430	18.921	37.335
82	23.461	40.421	27.115	22.364	41.297	15.574	31.629
83	20.452	36.681	24.215	17.336	33.257	12.107	25.307
84	17.584	32.873	21.419	12.648	25.208	8.858	19.057
85	14.894	29.056	18.728	8.651	17.912	6.076	13.454
86	12.421	25.300	16.153	5.523	11.880	3.890	8.865
87	10.190	21.674	13.734	3.274	7.316	2.312	5.424
88	8.221	18.245	11.515	1.791	4.159	1.269	3.063
89	6.517	15.072	9.524	0.899	2.167	0.638	1.586
90	5.072	12.197	7.762	0.410	1.027	0.292	0.746
91	3.870	9.649	6.218	0.168	0.438	0.120	0.316
92	2.889	7.441	4.890	0.061	0.166	0.044	0.119
93	2.103	5.570	3.771	0.020	0.055	0.014	0.039
94	1.481	4.014	2.854	0.005	0.016	0.004	0.011
95	0.992	2.740	2.119	0.001	0.004	0.001	0.003
96	0.611	1.711	1.548	> 0.001	0.001	> 0.001	> 0.001
97	0.317	0.898	1.114	> 0.001	> 0.001	> 0.001	> 0.001
98	0.109	0.309	0.791	> 0.001	> 0.001	> 0.001	> 0.001
99	> 0.001	> 0.001	0.555	> 0.001	> 0.001	> 0.001	> 0.001

Probability of surviving through age X starting from age 7

| | CSO (1980) | | | U. S. Life Tables (1982) | | | |
	Male	Female	Total Population	White Male	White Female	Black Male	Black Female
Life Expectancy	64.52	69.39	65.49	65.50	72.60	59.70	68.10
Age							
7	99.920	99.928	99.957	99.968	99.979	99.955	99.968
8	99.844	99.858	99.918	99.940	99.960	99.915	99.940
9	99.770	99.789	99.884	99.916	99.943	99.880	99.915
10	99.697	99.721	99.853	99.896	99.927	99.848	99.892
11	99.621	99.652	99.823	99.877	99.911	99.816	99.869
12	99.536	99.581	99.788	99.851	99.892	99.778	99.845
13	99.437	99.506	99.742	99.809	99.869	99.729	99.818
14	99.323	99.426	99.679	99.745	99.840	99.664	99.787
15	99.191	99.342	99.598	99.657	99.803	99.582	99.751
16	99.041	99.253	99.497	99.545	99.760	99.480	99.709
17	98.876	99.158	99.381	99.414	99.711	99.359	99.662
18	98.700	99.061	99.253	99.271	99.661	99.216	99.608
19	98.516	98.960	99.120	99.121	99.609	99.051	99.548
20	98.329	98.856	98.982	98.965	99.557	98.864	99.482
21	98.141	98.750	98.836	98.803	99.505	98.653	99.411
22	97.956	98.643	98.686	98.637	99.452	98.421	99.332
23	97.773	98.533	98.535	98.471	99.400	98.172	99.247
24	97.596	98.421	98.386	98.307	99.347	97.908	99.154
25	97.423	98.307	98.242	98.148	99.293	97.630	99.055
26	97.254	98.190	98.101	97.995	99.240	97.337	98.948
27	97.088	98.070	97.962	97.843	99.185	97.029	98.833
28	96.923	97.946	97.821	97.692	99.130	96.705	98.712

	CSO (1980)		Total Population	U. S. Life Tables (1982)			
	Male	Female		White Male	White Female	Black Male	Black Female
Life Expectancy	64.52	69.39	65.49	65.50	72.60	59.70	68.10
Age							
29	96.757	97.819	97.675	97.542	99.072	96.363	98.584
30	96.590	97.687	97.524	97.390	99.012	96.004	98.447
31	96.418	97.550	97.365	97.236	98.948	95.627	98.304
32	96.241	97.409	97.197	97.080	98.882	95.233	98.150
33	96.058	97.263	97.019	96.922	98.812	94.823	97.987
34	95.865	97.109	96.830	96.759	98.737	94.398	97.810
35	95.663	96.949	96.628	96.591	98.656	93.956	97.620
36	95.449	96.778	96.410	96.415	98.568	93.493	97.416
37	95.220	96.595	96.175	96.230	98.472	93.010	97.196
38	94.974	96.398	95.919	96.033	98.367	92.503	96.958
39	94.709	96.184	95.641	95.821	98.251	91.970	96.700
40	94.423	95.951	95.341	95.591	98.122	91.410	96.421
41	94.112	95.698	95.016	95.339	97.979	90.817	96.117
42	93.777	95.423	94.664	95.064	97.821	90.183	95.786
43	93.415	95.129	94.282	94.760	97.646	89.499	95.425
44	93.023	94.813	93.864	94.426	97.453	88.754	95.032
45	92.600	94.475	93.410	94.057	97.239	87.945	94.603
46	92.144	94.116	92.916	93.648	97.004	87.070	94.137
47	91.645	93.735	92.383	93.196	96.745	86.126	93.630
48	91.128	93.329	91.807	92.695	96.460	85.111	93.075
49	90.562	92.897	91.184	92.138	96.146	84.022	92.470
50	89.954	92.436	90.511	91.521	95.802	82.858	91.811
51	89.298	91.945	89.784	90.842	95.424	81.616	91.095

Age	CSO (1980)			U. S. Life Tables (1982)			
---	Male	Female	Total Population	White Male	White Female	Black Male	Black Female
Life Expectancy	64.52	69.39	65.49	65.50	72.60	59.70	68.10
52	88.587	91.421	88.997	90.097	95.011	80.296	90.323
53	87.815	90.859	88.145	89.285	94.561	78.899	89.498
54	86.976	90.259	87.226	88.402	94.072	77.424	88.618
55	86.065	89.619	86.235	87.444	93.541	75.874	87.685
56	85.079	88.940	85.169	86.409	92.963	74.246	86.695
57	84.016	88.226	84.027	85.290	92.337	72.541	85.641
58	82.874	87.479	82.807	84.082	91.658	70.756	84.512
59	81.650	86.697	81.507	82.781	90.923	68.891	83.303
60	80.337	85.876	80.125	81.386	90.128	66.947	82.008
61	78.928	85.006	78.660	79.893	89.270	64.929	80.631
62	77.414	84.074	77.107	78.292	88.343	62.842	79.179
63	75.783	83.063	75.463	76.573	87.341	60.692	77.664
64	74.030	81.963	73.722	74.730	86.259	58.487	76.093
65	72.148	80.767	71.883	72.760	85.092	56.232	74.471
66	70.139	79.475	69.943	70.646	83.820	53.919	72.764
67	68.004	78.090	67.902	68.404	82.448	51.563	70.980
68	65.747	76.618	65.762	66.051	80.980	49.176	69.126
69	63.368	75.058	63.526	63.601	79.424	46.774	67.210
70	60.865	73.399	61.200	61.071	77.784	44.369	65.239
71	58.229	71.620	58.787	58.403	75.995	41.964	63.184
72	55.455	69.696	56.279	55.621	74.068	39.572	61.057
73	52.536	67.597	53.666	52.753	72.015	37.206	58.868
74	49.479	65.304	50.942	49.825	69.849	34.878	56.630

| | CSO (1980) | | | U. S. Life Tables (1982) | | | |
Life Expectancy	Male	Female	Total Population	White Male	White Female	Black Male	Black Female
	64.52	69.39	65.49	65.50	72.60	59.70	68.10
Age							
75	46.303	62.807	48.114	46.864	67.583	32.599	54.353
76	43.037	60.108	45.198	43.811	65.119	30.337	51.967
77	39.718	57.220	42.217	40.706	62.483	28.111	49.493
78	36.385	54.162	39.197	37.589	59.702	25.935	46.954
79	33.073	50.947	36.163	34.496	56.804	23.823	44.372
80	29.804	47.585	33.127	31.460	53.819	21.788	41.767
81	26.600	44.083	30.105	27.256	48.442	18.930	37.350
82	23.481	40.451	27.127	22.372	41.307	15.582	31.641
83	20.470	36.708	24.226	17.342	33.265	12.113	25.316
84	17.599	32.897	21.428	12.653	25.214	8.863	19.064
85	14.907	29.078	18.737	8.654	17.917	6.079	13.459
86	12.431	25.318	16.161	5.525	11.883	3.892	8.868
87	10.199	21.690	13.740	3.275	7.318	2.314	5.426
88	8.228	18.259	11.520	1.792	4.160	1.270	3.064
89	6.522	15.083	9.528	0.899	2.168	0.639	1.586
90	5.076	12.206	7.765	0.410	1.027	0.292	0.747
91	3.873	9.656	6.221	0.168	0.438	0.120	0.316
92	2.891	7.447	4.892	0.061	0.166	0.044	0.119
93	2.105	5.574	3.773	0.020	0.055	0.014	0.039
94	1.482	4.017	2.855	0.005	0.016	0.004	0.011
95	0.993	2.742	2.120	0.001	0.004	0.001	0.003
96	0.611	1.712	1.548	> 0.001	0.001	> 0.001	> 0.001
97	0.318	0.899	1.114	> 0.001	> 0.001	> 0.001	> 0.001

	CSO (1980)			U. S. Life Tables (1982)			
	Male	Female	Total Population	White Male	White Female	Black Male	Black Female
Life Expectancy	64.52	69.39	65.49	65.50	72.60	59.70	68.10
Age							
98	0.109	0.309	0.792	> 0.001	> 0.001	> 0.001	> 0.001
99	> 0.001	> 0.001	0.555	> 0.001	> 0.001	> 0.001	> 0.001

Probability of surviving through age X starting from age 8

	CSO (1980)			U. S. Life Tables (1982)			
	Male	Female	Total Population	White Male	White Female	Black Male	Black Female
Life Expectancy	63.57	68.44	64.52	64.50	71.70	58.70	67.10
Age							
8	99.924	99.930	99.961	99.972	99.981	99.960	99.972
9	99.850	99.861	99.927	99.948	99.964	99.925	99.947
10	99.777	99.793	99.896	99.928	99.948	99.893	99.924
11	99.700	99.724	99.866	99.909	99.932	99.861	99.901
12	99.616	99.652	99.831	99.883	99.913	99.823	99.877
13	99.517	99.578	99.785	99.841	99.890	99.774	99.850
14	99.403	99.498	99.722	99.777	99.861	99.709	99.819
15	99.270	99.414	99.641	99.688	99.824	99.627	99.783
16	99.120	99.324	99.540	99.577	99.781	99.525	99.741
17	98.955	99.230	99.423	99.446	99.732	99.404	99.693
18	98.779	99.132	99.296	99.303	99.681	99.260	99.640
19	98.595	99.031	99.163	99.153	99.630	99.096	99.580

	CSO (1980)		U. S. Life Tables (1982)				
Life Expectancy	Male	Female	Total Population	White Male	White Female	Black Male	Black Female
	63.57	68.44	64.52	64.50	71.70	58.70	67.10
Age							
20	98.408	98.927	99.024	98.996	99.578	98.908	99.514
21	98.220	98.821	98.879	98.834	99.526	98.698	99.442
22	98.034	98.714	98.728	98.668	99.473	98.466	99.364
23	97.852	98.604	98.577	98.502	99.421	98.217	99.278
24	97.674	98.492	98.429	98.339	99.368	97.952	99.186
25	97.501	98.378	98.284	98.180	99.314	97.674	99.087
26	97.332	98.260	98.143	98.026	99.261	97.381	98.980
27	97.166	98.141	98.004	97.874	99.206	97.073	98.865
28	97.000	98.017	97.863	97.724	99.150	96.748	98.743
29	96.835	97.890	97.717	97.573	99.093	96.407	98.615
30	96.667	97.757	97.566	97.421	99.032	96.047	98.479
31	96.495	97.620	97.407	97.267	98.969	95.670	98.335
32	96.318	97.479	97.239	97.111	98.903	95.276	98.182
33	96.134	97.333	97.061	96.953	98.833	94.866	98.018
34	95.942	97.179	96.872	96.790	98.757	94.441	97.841
35	95.740	97.019	96.669	96.622	98.676	93.998	97.652
36	95.525	96.848	96.452	96.446	98.589	93.535	97.448
37	95.296	96.665	96.216	96.261	98.493	93.052	97.227
38	95.050	96.468	95.961	96.063	98.388	92.545	96.989
39	94.785	96.253	95.682	95.851	98.272	92.012	96.731
40	94.499	96.021	95.382	95.621	98.143	91.451	96.452
41	94.188	95.767	95.057	95.370	98.000	90.858	96.148
42	93.853	95.492	94.705	95.094	97.842	90.224	95.817

	CSO (1980)		Total Population	U. S. Life Tables (1982)			
	Male	Female		White Male	White Female	Black Male	Black Female
Life Expectancy	63.57	68.44	64.52	64.50	71.70	58.70	67.10
Age							
43	93.489	95.197	94.322	94.791	97.667	89.539	95.456
44	93.098	94.881	93.904	94.456	97.473	88.794	95.062
45	92.674	94.543	93.450	94.087	97.260	87.985	94.634
46	92.218	94.184	92.956	93.678	97.024	87.110	94.167
47	91.727	93.803	92.423	93.226	96.765	86.165	93.660
48	91.201	93.396	91.846	92.724	96.480	85.149	93.105
49	90.635	92.964	91.223	92.167	96.166	84.060	92.500
50	90.026	92.503	90.550	91.551	95.822	82.895	91.840
51	89.369	92.012	89.822	90.871	95.444	81.653	91.124
52	88.658	91.487	89.035	90.126	95.031	80.332	90.352
53	87.886	90.925	88.183	89.313	94.581	78.935	89.526
54	87.045	90.324	87.264	88.430	94.092	77.459	88.646
55	86.134	89.683	86.272	87.472	93.560	75.908	87.713
56	85.147	89.004	85.206	86.436	92.983	74.280	86.723
57	84.084	88.290	84.063	85.317	92.356	72.574	85.668
58	82.941	87.542	82.843	84.109	91.677	70.788	84.539
59	81.716	86.759	81.542	82.808	90.942	68.922	83.329
60	80.402	85.938	80.160	81.413	90.147	66.977	82.034
61	78.992	85.067	78.694	79.919	89.289	64.958	80.657
62	77.476	84.135	77.140	78.317	88.361	62.871	79.204
63	75.844	83.123	75.495	76.598	87.359	60.720	77.688
64	74.089	82.022	73.754	74.754	86.277	58.513	76.118
65	72.206	80.825	71.914	72.783	85.110	56.257	74.495

	CSO (1980)			U. S. Life Tables (1982)			
	Male	Female	Total Population	White Male	White Female	Black Male	Black Female
Life Expectancy	63.57	68.44	64.52	64.50	71.70	58.70	67.10
Age							
66	70.195	79.532	69.973	70.669	83.837	53.943	72.787
67	68.058	78.146	67.931	68.426	82.465	51.586	71.003
68	65.799	76.674	65.790	66.072	80.997	49.198	69.148
69	63.419	75.112	63.553	63.621	79.440	46.795	67.231
70	60.914	73.452	61.226	61.091	77.801	44.389	65.260
71	58.276	71.672	58.812	58.421	76.011	41.983	63.204
72	55.499	69.746	56.303	55.639	74.084	39.590	61.076
73	52.578	67.646	53.689	52.769	72.030	37.223	58.887
74	49.518	65.351	50.964	49.841	69.863	34.894	56.648
75	46.340	62.852	48.134	46.879	67.597	32.613	54.370
76	43.071	60.151	45.217	43.825	65.132	30.351	51.984
77	39.750	57.261	42.235	40.719	62.496	28.123	49.509
78	36.415	54.201	39.214	37.601	59.714	25.947	46.969
79	33.099	50.984	36.178	34.507	56.816	23.834	44.386
80	29.828	47.620	33.141	31.470	53.830	21.798	41.781
81	26.622	44.115	30.118	27.265	48.452	18.939	37.361
82	23.500	40.480	27.139	22.379	41.315	15.589	31.652
83	20.486	36.734	24.236	17.348	33.272	12.118	25.324
84	17.613	32.921	21.438	12.657	25.219	8.867	19.070
85	14.919	29.099	18.745	8.657	17.920	6.082	13.463
86	12.441	25.336	16.168	5.527	11.885	3.894	8.871
87	10.207	21.705	13.746	3.276	7.319	2.315	5.428
88	8.235	18.272	11.525	1.793	4.161	1.270	3.065

	CSO (1980)			U. S. Life Tables (1982)			
	Male	Female	Total Population	White Male	White Female	Black Male	Black Female
Life Expectancy	63.57	68.44	64.52	64.50	71.70	58.70	67.10
Age							
89	6.528	15.094	9.532	0.899	2.168	0.639	1.587
90	5.080	12.215	7.768	0.410	1.027	0.292	0.747
91	3.876	9.663	6.223	0.168	0.438	0.120	0.316
92	2.894	7.452	4.894	0.061	0.166	0.044	0.119
93	2.106	5.578	3.775	0.020	0.055	0.014	0.039
94	1.483	4.020	2.856	0.005	0.016	0.004	0.011
95	0.994	2.744	2.121	0.001	0.004	0.001	0.003
96	0.612	1.713	1.549	> 0.001	0.001	> 0.001	> 0.001
97	0.318	0.899	1.115	> 0.001	> 0.001	> 0.001	> 0.001
98	0.109	0.310	0.792	> 0.001	> 0.001	> 0.001	> 0.001
99	> 0.001	> 0.001	0.555	> 0.001	> 0.001	> 0.001	> 0.001

Probability of surviving through age X starting from age 9

	CSO (1980)			U. S. Life Tables (1982)			
	Male	Female	Total Population	White Male	White Female	Black Male	Black Female
Life Expectancy	62.62	67.48	63.54	63.60	70.70	57.70	66.10
Age							
9	99.926	99.931	99.966	99.976	99.983	99.965	99.975
10	99.853	99.863	99.935	99.956	99.967	99.933	99.952
11	99.776	99.794	99.905	99.937	99.951	99.901	99.929

Age	CSO (1980) Male	CSO (1980) Female	Total Population	U.S. Life Tables (1982) White Male	U.S. Life Tables (1982) White Female	U.S. Life Tables (1982) Black Male	U.S. Life Tables (1982) Black Female
Life Expectancy	62.62	67.48	63.54	63.60	70.70	57.70	66.10
12	99.691	99.722	99.870	99.911	99.932	99.863	99.905
13	99.593	99.647	99.824	99.869	99.909	99.814	99.878
14	99.478	99.568	99.761	99.805	99.880	99.749	99.847
15	99.346	99.483	99.679	99.716	99.843	99.666	99.811
16	99.196	99.394	99.579	99.605	99.800	99.565	99.769
17	99.030	99.299	99.462	99.474	99.751	99.443	99.721
18	98.854	99.202	99.335	99.331	99.700	99.300	99.667
19	98.670	99.101	99.202	99.181	99.649	99.135	99.608
20	98.483	98.997	99.063	99.024	99.597	98.948	99.542
21	98.294	98.891	98.917	98.862	99.545	98.737	99.470
22	98.109	98.783	98.767	98.696	99.492	98.505	99.392
23	97.926	98.673	98.616	98.530	99.439	98.256	99.306
24	97.748	98.561	98.467	98.366	99.387	97.992	99.214
25	97.575	98.446	98.322	98.207	99.333	97.713	99.115
26	97.406	98.329	98.182	98.054	99.279	97.420	99.008
27	94.240	98.209	98.042	97.902	99.225	97.111	98.893
28	97.074	98.086	97.901	97.751	99.169	96.787	98.771
29	96.908	97.958	97.755	97.601	99.112	96.445	98.643
30	96.741	97.826	97.604	97.448	99.051	96.086	98.507
31	96.568	97.689	97.445	97.294	98.988	95.708	98.363
32	96.392	97.547	97.277	97.139	98.922	95.314	98.209
33	96.208	97.401	97.099	96.980	98.851	94.904	98.045
34	96.015	97.247	96.910	96.817	98.776	94.479	97.869

| | CSO (1980) | | | U. S. Life Tables (1982) | | | |
	Male	Female	Total Population	White Male	White Female	Black Male	Black Female
Life Expectancy	62.62	67.48	63.54	63.60	70.70	57.70	66.10
Age							
35	95.813	97.087	96.707	96.649	98.695	94.036	97.679
36	95.598	96.916	96.489	96.473	98.607	93.573	97.475
37	95.369	96.733	96.254	96.288	98.512	93.089	97.255
38	95.122	96.535	95.998	96.090	98.406	92.582	97.016
39	94.857	96.321	95.720	95.878	98.290	92.049	96.758
40	94.571	96.088	95.419	95.648	98.161	91.488	96.479
41	94.259	95.834	95.094	95.396	98.018	90.894	96.175
42	93.924	95.559	94.742	95.121	97.860	90.260	95.844
43	93.560	95.264	94.359	94.817	97.685	89.575	95.482
44	93.168	94.948	93.941	94.483	97.492	88.829	95.089
45	92.744	94.609	93.486	94.113	97.278	88.020	94.660
46	92.288	94.250	92.993	93.705	97.043	87.144	94.194
47	91.797	93.868	92.459	93.252	96.784	86.200	93.686
48	91.270	93.462	91.882	92.750	96.498	85.183	93.131
49	90.704	93.029	91.259	92.193	96.185	84.094	92.526
50	90.095	92.568	90.586	91.576	95.840	82.928	91.866
51	89.437	92.076	89.857	90.897	95.463	81.685	91.150
52	88.725	91.551	89.070	90.151	95.049	80.364	90.378
53	87.952	90.988	88.218	89.338	94.599	78.966	89.552
54	87.112	90.387	87.298	88.455	94.110	77.490	88.671
55	86.200	89.746	86.306	87.497	93.578	75.938	87.738
56	85.212	89.067	85.239	86.461	93.001	74.309	86.747
57	84.147	88.351	84.096	85.341	92.374	72.603	85.692

	CSO (1980)			U. S. Life Tables (1982)			
	Male	Female	Total Population	White Male	White Female	Black Male	Black Female
Life Expectancy	62.62	67.48	63.54	63.60	70.70	57.70	66.10
Age							
58	83.004	87.603	82.875	84.133	91.695	70.816	84.563
59	81.778	86.820	81.574	82.831	90.959	68.950	83.353
60	80.463	85.998	80.191	81.435	90.164	67.004	82.057
61	79.052	85.127	78.724	79.941	89.306	64.984	80.680
62	77.535	84.194	77.170	78.339	88.378	62.896	79.227
63	75.902	83.182	75.524	76.619	87.376	60.744	77.710
64	74.145	82.079	73.783	74.775	86.293	58.537	76.139
65	72.261	80.882	71.942	72.803	85.126	56.279	74.516
66	70.248	79.588	70.000	70.688	83.853	53.965	72.808
67	68.110	78.201	67.958	68.446	82.481	51.606	71.022
68	65.849	76.727	65.816	66.090	81.012	49.218	69.167
69	63.467	75.165	63.578	63.639	79.455	46.814	67.250
70	60.960	73.503	61.250	61.108	77.815	44.407	65.278
71	58.320	71.722	58.835	58.438	76.026	41.999	63.222
72	55.541	69.795	56.325	55.654	74.098	39.605	61.093
73	52.618	67.693	53.710	52.784	72.044	37.238	58.903
74	49.556	65.397	50.984	49.855	69.877	34.908	56.664
75	46.375	62.896	48.153	46.892	67.610	32.626	54.386
76	43.104	60.193	45.235	43.837	65.145	30.363	51.998
77	39.780	57.302	42.251	40.731	62.508	28.135	49.523
78	36.442	54.239	39.229	37.611	59.725	25.957	46.983
79	33.124	51.020	36.192	34.516	56.827	23.844	44.398
80	29.850	47.653	33.154	31.479	53.841	21.807	41.792

| | CSO (1980) | | Total Population | U. S. Life Tables (1982) | | | |
	Male	Female		White Male	White Female	Black Male	Black Female
Life Expectancy	62.62	67.48	63.54	63.60	70.70	57.70	66.10
Age							
81	26.642	44.146	30.130	27.273	48.461	18.946	37.372
82	23.518	40.508	27.150	22.385	41.323	15.595	31.660
83	20.502	36.760	24.246	17.353	33.279	12.123	25.331
84	17.626	32.944	21.446	12.660	25.224	8.870	19.076
85	14.930	29.119	18.752	8.660	17.924	6.084	13.467
86	12.451	25.354	16.174	5.528	11.887	3.895	8.873
87	10.215	21.720	13.751	3.277	7.321	2.316	5.429
88	8.241	18.285	11.529	1.793	4.162	1.271	3.066
89	6.533	15.104	9.536	0.899	2.169	0.639	1.587
90	5.084	12.223	7.771	0.410	1.027	0.292	0.747
91	3.879	9.670	6.226	0.168	0.438	0.120	0.316
92	2.896	7.457	4.896	0.061	0.166	0.044	0.119
93	2.108	5.582	3.776	0.020	0.055	0.014	0.039
94	1.484	4.023	2.857	0.005	0.016	0.004	0.011
95	0.994	2.746	2.122	0.001	0.004	0.001	0.003
96	0.612	1.714	1.550	> 0.001	0.001	> 0.001	> 0.001
97	0.318	0.900	1.115	> 0.001	> 0.001	> 0.001	> 0.001
98	0.109	0.310	0.792	> 0.001	> 0.001	> 0.001	> 0.001
99	> 0.001	> 0.001	0.556	> 0.001	> 0.001	> 0.001	> 0.001

Probability of surviving through age X starting from age 10

| | CSO (1980) | | Total Population | U. S. Life Tables (1982) | | | |
	Male	Female		White Male	White Female	Black Male	Black Female
Life Expectancy	61.66	66.53	62.57	62.60	69.70	56.70	65.10
Age							
10	99.927	99.932	99.969	99.980	99.984	99.968	99.977
11	99.850	99.863	99.939	99.961	99.968	99.936	99.954
12	99.765	99.791	99.904	99.935	99.949	99.898	99.930
13	99.666	99.716	99.858	99.893	99.926	99.849	99.903
14	99.552	99.637	99.795	99.829	99.897	99.784	99.872
15	99.419	99.552	99.713	99.740	99.860	99.701	99.836
16	99.269	99.462	99.613	99.629	99.817	99.600	99.794
17	99.103	99.368	99.496	99.498	99.768	99.478	99.746
18	98.927	99.270	99.369	99.355	99.717	99.335	99.692
19	98.743	99.169	99.236	99.205	99.665	99.170	99.633
20	98.555	99.065	99.097	99.048	99.614	98.983	99.567
21	98.367	98.959	98.951	98.886	99.562	98.772	99.495
22	98.181	98.851	98.801	98.719	99.509	98.540	99.417
23	97.999	98.741	98.649	98.554	99.456	98.290	99.331
24	97.820	98.629	98.500	98.390	99.404	98.026	99.239
25	97.647	98.514	98.356	98.231	99.350	97.748	99.139
26	97.478	98.397	98.215	98.077	99.296	97.454	99.032
27	97.312	98.277	98.076	97.925	99.242	97.145	98.917
28	97.146	98.153	97.934	97.775	99.186	96.821	98.796
29	96.980	98.026	97.788	97.624	99.129	96.479	98.667
30	96.812	97.893	97.637	97.472	99.068	96.119	98.531
31	96.640	97.756	97.478	97.318	99.005	95.742	98.387

| | CSO (1980) | | Total Population | U. S. Life Tables (1982) | | | |
	Male	Female		White Male	White Female	Black Male	Black Female
Life Expectancy	61.66	66.53	62.57	62.60	69.70	56.70	65.10
Age							
32	96.463	97.615	97.310	97.162	98.938	95.347	98.234
33	96.279	97.468	97.132	97.004	98.868	94.937	98.070
34	96.086	97.314	96.943	96.841	98.793	94.512	97.893
35	95.884	97.154	96.740	96.672	98.712	94.068	97.703
36	95.669	96.983	96.522	96.496	98.624	93.606	97.499
37	95.439	96.799	96.287	96.311	98.528	93.122	97.279
38	95.193	96.602	96.031	96.113	98.423	92.614	97.041
39	94.927	96.387	95.752	95.901	98.307	92.081	96.782
40	94.641	96.154	95.451	95.671	98.178	91.520	96.503
41	94.329	95.900	95.126	95.419	98.035	90.926	96.199
42	93.993	95.625	94.774	95.143	97.877	90.291	95.868
43	93.630	95.330	94.391	94.840	97.702	89.606	95.506
44	93.237	95.013	93.973	94.505	97.508	88.861	95.113
45	92.813	94.675	93.518	94.136	97.295	88.051	94.684
46	92.357	94.315	93.024	93.727	97.059	87.175	94.217
47	91.865	93.933	92.490	93.274	96.800	86.230	93.709
48	91.338	93.526	91.913	92.773	96.515	85.213	93.155
49	90.771	93.093	91.290	92.215	96.201	84.123	92.549
50	90.162	92.632	90.616	91.598	95.857	82.957	91.889
51	89.503	92.140	89.888	90.918	95.479	81.714	91.172
52	88.791	91.615	89.100	90.173	95.065	80.393	90.400
53	88.018	91.051	88.248	89.360	94.615	78.994	89.574
54	87.176	90.449	87.327	88.476	94.126	77.517	88.693

Life Expectancy Age	CSO (1980)		Total Population	U. S. Life Tables (1982)			
	Male	Female		White Male	White Female	Black Male	Black Female
	61.66	66.53	62.57	62.60	69.70	56.70	65.10
55	86.263	89.808	86.335	87.518	93.594	75.965	87.759
56	85.275	89.128	85.268	86.481	93.016	74.335	86.769
57	84.210	88.412	84.125	85.361	92.389	72.629	85.714
58	83.065	87.664	82.903	84.153	91.710	70.841	84.584
59	81.838	86.880	81.602	82.851	90.975	68.974	83.373
60	80.523	86.057	80.218	81.455	90.180	67.027	82.078
61	79.110	85.185	78.751	79.960	89.321	65.007	80.700
62	77.592	84.252	77.197	78.358	88.393	62.918	79.246
63	75.958	83.239	75.550	76.638	87.391	60.765	77.730
64	74.200	82.136	73.808	74.793	86.308	58.557	76.158
65	72.314	80.938	71.966	72.821	85.140	56.299	74.534
66	70.300	79.643	70.024	70.705	83.867	53.984	72.826
67	68.160	78.255	67.981	68.462	82.495	51.625	71.040
68	65.898	76.780	65.838	66.106	81.026	49.235	69.185
69	63.514	75.217	63.599	63.654	79.469	46.830	67.267
70	61.005	73.554	61.271	61.123	77.829	44.422	65.295
71	58.363	71.772	58.855	58.452	76.039	42.014	63.238
72	55.582	69.843	56.344	55.668	74.110	39.619	61.109
73	52.657	67.740	53.728	52.797	72.056	37.251	58.918
74	49.593	65.442	51.001	49.867	69.888	34.920	56.678
75	46.409	62.939	48.170	46.903	67.621	32.638	54.399
76	43.136	60.235	45.250	43.847	65.156	30.374	52.011
77	39.809	57.341	42.266	40.740	62.518	28.144	49.535

| | CSO (1980) | | | U. S. Life Tables (1982) | | | |
	Male	Female	Total Population	White Male	White Female	Black Male	Black Female
Life Expectancy	61.66	66.53	62.57	62.60	69.70	56.70	65.10
Age							
78	36.469	54.276	39.242	37.620	59.736	25.966	46.994
79	33.149	51.055	36.205	34.525	56.837	23.852	44.410
80	29.872	47.686	33.166	31.486	53.850	21.814	41.803
81	26.662	44.176	30.140	27.279	48.469	18.953	37.381
82	23.536	40.536	27.159	22.391	41.330	15.600	31.668
83	20.517	36.785	24.254	17.357	33.284	12.128	25.338
84	17.639	32.967	21.453	12.663	25.228	8.873	19.080
85	14.941	29.139	18.759	8.662	17.927	6.086	13.470
86	12.460	25.372	16.180	5.530	11.890	3.897	8.876
87	10.223	21.735	13.756	3.278	7.322	1.316	5.430
88	8.247	18.297	11.533	1.794	4.162	1.271	3.067
89	6.537	15.115	9.539	0.900	2.169	0.639	1.588
90	5.088	12.232	7.774	0.410	1.028	0.292	0.747
91	3.882	9.677	6.228	0.168	0.438	0.120	0.317
92	2.898	7.463	4.898	0.061	0.166	0.044	0.119
93	2.109	5.586	3.777	0.020	0.055	0.014	0.039
94	1.485	4.026	2.858	0.005	0.016	0.004	0.011
95	0.995	2.748	2.122	0.001	0.004	0.001	0.003
96	0.612	1.716	1.550	< 0.001	0.001	< 0.001	< 0.001
97	0.318	0.901	1.116	< 0.001	< 0.001	< 0.001	< 0.001
98	0.109	0.310	0.792	< 0.001	< 0.001	< 0.001	< 0.001
99	< 0.001	< 0.001	0.556	< 0.001	< 0.001	< 0.001	< 0.001

Probability of surviving through age X starting from age 11

	CSO (1980)		Total Population	U. S. Life Tables (1982)			
	Male	Female		White Male	White Female	Black Male	Black Female
Life Expectancy	60.71	65.58	61.58	61.60	68.70	55.80	64.20
Age							
11	99.923	99.931	99.970	99.981	99.984	99.968	99.977
12	99.838	99.859	99.935	99.955	99.965	99.930	99.953
13	99.739	99.784	99.889	99.913	99.942	99.881	99.926
14	99.625	99.704	99.826	99.849	99.913	99.816	99.895
15	99.492	99.620	99.744	99.760	99.876	99.733	99.859
16	99.342	99.530	99.644	99.648	99.833	99.632	99.817
17	99.176	99.435	99.527	99.518	99.784	99.510	99.769
18	98.999	99.338	99.400	99.375	99.733	99.367	99.715
19	98.815	99.237	99.266	99.225	99.681	99.202	99.656
20	98.627	99.132	99.127	99.068	99.630	99.014	99.590
21	98.439	99.026	98.982	98.905	99.578	98.803	99.518
22	98.253	98.918	98.831	98.739	99.525	98.571	99.439
23	98.070	98.809	98.680	98.573	99.472	98.322	99.354
24	97.892	98.696	98.531	98.410	99.420	98.057	99.262
25	97.719	98.581	98.386	98.250	99.366	97.779	99.162
26	97.549	98.464	98.245	98.097	99.312	97.485	99.055
27	97.383	98.344	98.106	97.945	99.258	97.176	98.940
28	97.217	98.220	97.965	97.794	99.202	96.852	98.819
29	97.051	98.092	97.819	97.643	99.144	96.510	98.690
30	96.883	97.960	97.667	97.491	99.084	96.150	98.554
31	96.711	97.823	97.508	97.337	99.021	95.772	98.410
32	96.534	97.681	97.340	97.181	98.954	95.378	98.256

Life Expectancy Age	CSO (1980) Male	CSO (1980) Female	Total Population	U.S. Life Tables (1982) White Male	White Female	Black Male	Black Female
	60.71	65.58	61.58	61.60	68.70	55.80	64.20
33	96.349	97.534	97.162	97.023	98.884	94.967	98.092
34	96.156	97.380	96.973	96.860	98.809	94.542	97.916
35	95.954	97.220	96.770	96.691	98.728	94.099	97.726
36	95.739	97.049	96.552	96.515	98.640	93.636	97.522
37	95.509	96.865	96.317	96.330	98.544	93.152	97.301
38	95.262	96.668	96.060	96.133	98.439	92.644	97.063
39	94.997	96.453	95.782	95.920	98.323	92.110	96.805
40	94.710	96.220	95.481	95.690	98.194	91.549	96.525
41	94.398	95.966	95.155	95.438	98.050	90.955	96.221
42	94.062	95.690	94.803	95.163	97.893	90.320	95.890
43	93.698	95.394	94.420	94.859	97.717	89.635	95.528
44	93.306	95.078	94.002	94.524	97.524	88.889	95.135
45	92.881	94.739	93.547	94.155	97.310	88.079	94.706
46	92.424	94.379	93.053	93.746	97.075	87.203	94.239
47	91.932	93.997	92.519	93.293	96.816	86.258	93.731
48	91.405	93.590	91.942	92.791	96.530	85.241	93.176
49	90.837	93.157	91.318	92.234	96.216	84.150	92.570
50	90.227	92.695	90.644	91.616	95.872	82.984	91.910
51	89.569	92.202	89.916	90.937	95.494	81.740	91.193
52	88.856	91.677	89.128	90.191	95.081	80.418	90.421
53	88.082	91.113	88.275	89.377	94.630	79.019	89.595
54	87.240	90.511	87.354	88.494	94.141	77.542	88.714
55	86.326	89.869	86.362	87.535	93.609	75.989	87.780

	CSO (1980)		Total Population	U. S. Life Tables (1982)			
	Male	Female		White Male	White Female	Black Male	Black Female
Life Expectancy	60.71	65.58	61.58	61.60	68.70	55.80	64.20
Age							
56	85.337	89.189	85.295	86.499	93.031	74.359	86.789
57	84.271	88.473	84.151	85.379	92.404	72.652	85.733
58	83.126	87.723	82.929	84.170	91.725	70.864	84.603
59	81.898	86.939	81.627	82.867	90.989	68.996	83.393
60	80.581	86.116	80.243	81.471	90.194	67.049	82.097
61	79.168	85.243	78.776	79.976	89.336	65.028	80.718
62	77.649	84.309	77.221	78.373	88.407	62.938	79.265
63	76.013	83.296	75.574	76.653	87.405	60.785	77.747
64	74.254	82.192	73.831	74.808	86.322	58.576	76.175
65	72.367	80.933	71.989	72.835	85.154	56.317	74.551
66	70.352	79.697	70.046	70.720	83.881	54.001	72.843
67	68.210	78.308	68.002	68.476	82.508	51.641	71.057
68	65.946	76.832	65.858	66.119	81.039	49.251	69.201
69	63.561	75.268	63.619	63.667	79.482	46.845	67.282
70	61.050	73.604	61.290	61.135	77.841	44.436	65.310
71	58.406	71.821	58.873	58.463	76.051	42.028	63.252
72	55.623	69.891	56.362	55.679	74.122	39.632	61.123
73	52.695	67.786	53.744	52.807	72.067	37.263	58.931
74	49.629	65.486	51.017	49.877	69.900	34.931	56.691
75	46.443	62.982	48.184	46.912	67.632	32.648	54.412
76	43.167	60.276	45.264	43.856	65.166	30.383	52.023
77	39.838	57.380	42.279	40.748	62.528	28.153	49.547
78	36.496	54.313	39.255	37.628	59.745	25.974	47.005

	CSO (1980)		Total Population	U. S. Life Tables (1982)			
	Male	Female		White Male	White Female	Black Male	Black Female
Life Expectancy	60.71	65.58	61.58	61.60	68.70	55.80	64.20
Age							
79	33.173	51.090	36.216	34.532	56.846	23.860	44.420
80	29.894	47.718	33.176	31.492	53.858	21.821	41.812
81	26.681	44.206	30.150	27.285	48.477	18.959	37.390
82	23.553	40.564	27.167	22.395	41.337	15.605	31.676
83	20.532	36.810	24.262	17.360	33.290	12.131	25.344
84	17.652	32.989	21.460	12.666	25.232	8.876	19.085
85	14.952	29.159	18.764	8.663	17.930	6.088	13.473
86	12.469	25.389	16.185	5.531	11.891	3.898	8.878
87	10.230	21.750	13.760	3.278	7.323	2.317	5.432
88	8.253	18.310	11.537	1.794	4.163	1.271	3.068
89	6.542	15.125	9.542	0.900	2.169	0.640	1.588
90	5.091	12.240	7.777	0.410	1.028	0.292	0.747
91	3.885	9.683	6.230	0.168	0.438	0.120	0.317
92	2.900	7.468	4.899	0.061	0.166	0.044	0.119
93	2.111	5.590	3.779	0.020	0.055	0.014	0.039
94	1.486	4.028	2.859	0.005	0.016	0.004	0.011
95	0.996	2.750	2.123	0.001	0.004	0.001	0.003
96	0.613	1.717	1.551	> 0.001	0.001	> 0.001	> 0.001
97	0.319	0.901	1.116	> 0.001	> 0.001	> 0.001	> 0.001
98	0.109	0.310	0.793	> 0.001	> 0.001	> 0.001	> 0.001
99	> 0.001	> 0.001	0.556	> 0.001	> 0.001	> 0.001	> 0.001

Probability of surviving through age X starting from age 12

| | CSO (1980) | | Total Population | U. S. Life Tables (1982) | | | |
	Male	Female		White Male	White Female	Black Male	Black Female
Life Expectancy	59.75	64.62	60.60	60.60	67.70	54.80	63.20
Age							
12	99.915	99.928	99.965	99.974	99.981	99.962	99.976
13	99.816	99.853	99.919	99.932	99.958	99.913	99.949
14	99.701	99.773	99.856	99.868	99.929	99.848	99.918
15	99.569	99.688	99.774	99.779	99.892	99.765	99.882
16	99.418	99.599	99.673	99.667	99.849	99.663	99.840
17	99.252	99.504	99.557	99.537	99.800	99.542	99.792
18	99.076	99.407	99.429	99.394	99.749	99.399	99.738
19	98.891	99.305	99.296	99.243	99.697	99.234	99.678
20	98.703	99.201	99.157	99.087	99.646	99.046	99.613
21	98.515	99.095	99.011	98.924	99.594	98.835	99.541
22	98.329	98.987	98.861	98.758	99.541	98.603	99.462
23	98.146	98.877	98.710	98.592	99.488	98.353	99.377
24	97.967	98.764	98.561	98.428	99.435	98.089	99.284
25	97.794	98.650	98.416	98.269	99.382	97.810	99.185
26	97.625	98.532	98.275	98.116	99.328	97.517	99.078
27	97.458	98.412	98.135	97.964	99.273	97.208	98.963
28	97.292	98.288	97.994	97.813	99.218	96.883	98.841
29	97.126	98.160	97.848	97.662	99.160	96.541	98.713
30	96.958	98.028	97.696	97.510	99.100	96.181	98.577
31	96.785	97.890	97.537	97.356	99.036	95.803	98.433
32	96.608	97.748	97.369	97.200	98.970	95.408	98.279
33	96.423	97.602	97.191	97.014	98.900	94.998	98.115

| | CSO (1980) | | | U. S. Life Tables (1982) | | | |
Life Expectancy	Male	Female	Total Population	White Male	White Female	Black Male	Black Female
	59.75	64.62	60.60	60.60	67.70	54.80	63.20
Age							
34	96.231	97.448	97.002	96.878	98.825	94.572	97.938
35	96.028	97.287	96.799	96.710	98.744	94.129	97.748
36	95.812	97.116	96.581	96.534	98.656	93.666	97.544
37	95.582	96.932	96.345	96.348	98.560	93.181	97.324
38	95.336	96.734	96.089	96.151	98.455	92.674	97.085
39	95.070	96.520	95.811	95.938	98.338	92.140	96.827
40	94.783	96.286	95.510	95.708	98.210	91.579	96.547
41	94.471	96.032	95.184	95.456	98.066	90.984	96.243
42	94.135	95.756	94.832	95.181	97.908	90.349	95.912
43	93.770	95.460	94.449	94.877	97.733	89.663	95.550
44	93.377	95.143	94.030	94.542	97.540	88.917	95.157
45	92.953	94.805	93.575	94.172	97.326	88.107	94.727
46	92.495	94.444	93.081	93.764	97.090	87.231	94.260
47	92.003	94.062	92.547	93.311	96.831	86.285	93.752
48	91.475	93.655	91.969	92.809	96.546	85.268	93.197
49	90.907	93.221	91.346	92.251	96.232	84.177	92.592
50	90.297	92.759	90.672	91.634	95.887	83.011	91.931
51	89.638	92.266	89.943	90.954	95.509	81.766	91.214
52	88.924	91.740	89.155	90.208	95.096	80.444	90.442
53	88.150	91.176	88.302	89.394	94.645	79.044	89.615
54	87.307	90.573	87.381	88.510	94.156	77.567	88.734
55	86.393	89.931	86.388	87.552	93.624	76.013	87.800
56	85.403	89.250	85.320	86.515	93.046	74.383	86.809

	CSO (1980)		Total Population	U. S. Life Tables (1982)			
Life Expectancy	Male	Female		White Male	White Female	Black Male	Black Female
	59.75	64.62	60.60	60.60	67.70	54.80	63.20
Age							
57	84.336	88.534	84.176	85.395	92.419	72.675	85.753
58	83.190	87.784	82.954	84.186	91.740	70.886	84.623
59	81.961	86.999	81.651	82.883	91.004	69.018	83.412
60	80.643	86.175	80.267	81.487	90.209	67.070	82.116
61	79.229	85.302	78.799	79.991	89.350	65.049	80.737
62	77.709	84.367	77.244	78.388	88.421	62.958	79.283
63	76.072	83.353	75.596	76.668	87.419	60.804	77.765
64	74.312	82.249	73.853	74.822	86.336	58.595	76.193
65	72.423	81.049	72.010	72.849	85.168	56.335	74.568
66	70.406	79.752	70.067	70.733	83.894	54.018	72.859
67	68.263	78.362	68.022	68.489	82.521	51.658	71.073
68	65.997	76.886	65.878	66.132	81.052	49.267	69.216
69	63.610	75.320	63.638	63.679	79.494	46.860	67.298
70	61.097	73.655	61.309	61.147	77.853	44.451	65.325
71	58.451	71.870	58.891	58.474	76.063	42.041	63.267
72	55.666	69.939	56.379	55.689	74.134	39.645	61.137
73	52.736	67.833	53.761	52.817	72.079	37.275	58.945
74	49.667	65.532	51.032	49.886	69.911	34.942	56.704
75	46.479	63.026	48.199	46.921	67.643	32.659	54.424
76	43.201	60.317	45.278	43.864	65.177	30.393	52.035
77	39.869	57.420	42.292	40.756	62.538	28.162	49.558
78	36.524	54.351	39.266	37.635	59.755	25.983	47.016
79	33.199	51.125	36.227	34.538	56.855	23.867	44.430

| | CSO (1980) | | Total | U. S. Life Tables (1982) | | | |
Life Expectancy	Male	Female	Population	White Male	White Female	Black Male	Black Female
	59.75	64.62	60.60	60.60	67.70	54.80	63.20
Age							
80	29.917	47.751	33.186	31.498	53.867	21.828	41.822
81	26.702	44.237	30.159	27.290	48.485	18.965	37.398
82	23.571	40.592	27.175	22.399	41.343	15.610	31.683
83	20.548	36.836	24.269	17.364	33.295	12.135	25.349
84	17.666	33.012	21.466	12.668	25.236	8.879	19.089
85	14.964	29.179	18.770	8.665	17.933	6.090	13.476
86	12.479	25.407	16.190	5.532	11.893	3.899	8.880
87	10.238	21.765	13.764	3.279	7.324	2.318	5.433
88	8.259	18.322	11.540	1.794	4.164	1.272	3.068
89	6.547	15.135	9.545	0.900	2.170	0.640	1.589
90	5.095	12.248	7.779	0.410	1.028	0.293	0.748
91	3.888	9.690	6.232	0.168	0.438	0.120	0.317
92	2.902	7.473	4.901	0.061	0.166	0.044	0.119
93	2.113	5.593	3.780	0.020	0.055	0.014	0.039
94	1.488	4.031	2.860	0.005	0.016	0.004	0.011
95	0.997	2.752	2.124	0.001	0.004	0.001	0.003
96	0.613	1.718	1.551	> 0.001	0.001	> 0.001	> 0.001
97	0.319	0.902	1.116	> 0.001	> 0.001	> 0.001	> 0.001
98	0.109	0.310	0.793	> 0.001	> 0.001	> 0.001	> 0.001
99	> 0.001	> 0.001	0.556	> 0.001	> 0.001	> 0.001	> 0.001

Probability of surviving through age X starting from age 13

| | CSO (1980) | | Total Population | U. S. Life Tables (1982) | | | |
	Male	Female		White Male	White Female	Black Male	Black Female
Life Expectancy	58.80	63.67	59.62	59.60	66.70	53.80	62.20
Age							
13	99.901	99.925	99.954	99.958	99.977	99.951	99.973
14	99.786	99.845	99.891	99.894	99.948	99.886	99.942
15	99.653	99.760	99.809	99.805	99.911	99.803	99.906
16	99.503	99.670	99.708	99.693	99.868	99.701	99.864
17	99.337	99.576	99.592	99.563	99.819	99.580	98.816
18	99.160	99.478	99.464	99.419	99.768	99.436	99.762
19	98.975	99.377	99.331	99.269	99.716	99.271	99.702
20	98.787	99.272	99.192	99.112	99.664	99.084	99.637
21	98.599	99.166	99.046	98.950	99.613	98.873	99.565
22	98.412	99.058	98.895	98.784	99.560	98.640	99.486
23	98.229	98.948	98.744	98.618	99.507	98.391	99.401
24	98.051	98.835	98.595	98.454	99.454	98.126	99.308
25	97.877	98.721	98.450	98.294	99.401	97.847	99.209
26	97.708	98.603	98.309	98.141	99.347	97.554	99.102
27	97.541	98.483	98.170	97.989	99.292	97.245	98.987
28	97.375	98.359	98.028	97.838	99.237	96.920	98.865
29	97.208	98.231	97.882	97.687	99.179	96.578	98.736
30	97.040	98.098	97.731	97.535	99.119	96.217	98.600
31	96.867	97.961	97.571	97.381	99.055	95.839	98.456
32	96.690	97.819	97.403	97.225	98.989	95.444	98.303
33	96.505	97.672	97.225	97.067	98.919	95.034	98.139
34	96.312	97.518	97.036	96.904	98.843	94.608	97.962

| | CSO (1980) | | Total Population | U. S. Life Tables (1982) | | | |
	Male	Female		White Male	White Female	Black Male	Black Female
Life Expectancy	58.80	63.67	59.62	59.60	66.70	53.80	62.20
Age							
35	96.109	97.357	96.833	96.735	98.762	94.164	97.772
36	95.894	97.186	96.615	96.559	98.674	93.701	97.567
37	95.664	97.002	96.379	96.374	98.579	93.217	97.347
38	95.417	96.804	96.123	96.176	98.473	92.709	97.108
39	95.151	96.589	95.844	95.963	98.357	92.175	96.850
40	94.863	96.355	95.543	95.733	98.228	91.613	96.570
41	94.551	96.101	95.217	95.481	98.085	91.019	96.266
42	94.215	95.825	94.865	95.205	97.927	90.384	95.935
43	93.850	95.529	94.482	94.902	97.752	89.697	95.573
44	93.457	95.212	94.063	94.567	97.558	88.951	95.179
45	93.032	94.873	93.608	94.197	97.344	88.141	94.750
46	92.574	94.512	93.114	93.788	97.109	87.264	94.283
47	92.081	94.130	92.579	93.335	96.850	86.318	93.775
48	91.553	93.722	92.002	92.833	96.564	85.300	93.220
49	90.984	93.288	91.378	92.275	96.250	84.209	92.614
50	90.374	92.825	90.703	91.658	95.905	83.042	91.954
51	89.714	92.333	89.974	90.978	95.528	81.797	91.236
52	89.000	91.806	89.186	90.232	95.114	80.475	90.463
53	88.225	91.242	88.332	89.418	94.663	79.074	89.637
54	87.381	90.639	87.411	88.533	94.174	77.596	88.756
55	86.466	89.996	86.418	87.575	93.642	76.042	87.821
56	85.476	89.315	85.350	86.538	93.064	74.411	86.829
57	84.408	88.597	84.205	85.417	92.437	72.703	85.774

| | CSO (1980) | | Total Population | U. S. Life Tables (1982) | | | |
	Male	Female		White Male	White Female	Black Male	Black Female
Life Expectancy	58.80	63.67	59.62	59.60	66.70	53.80	62.20
Age							
58	83.261	87.847	82.983	84.207	91.757	70.913	84.643
59	82.031	87.062	81.680	82.905	91.021	69.044	83.432
60	80.712	86.237	80.296	81.508	90.226	67.096	82.135
61	79.296	85.364	78.827	80.012	89.367	65.073	80.756
62	77.775	84.428	77.271	78.409	88.438	62.982	79.302
63	76.137	83.413	75.623	76.688	87.435	60.827	77.784
64	74.375	82.308	73.879	74.842	86.352	58.617	76.211
65	72.484	81.107	72.036	72.868	85.184	56.357	74.586
66	70.466	79.809	70.091	70.751	83.910	54.039	72.877
67	68.321	78.418	68.046	68.506	82.537	51.677	71.090
68	66.053	76.941	65.901	66.149	81.067	49.286	69.233
69	63.664	75.374	63.661	63.696	79.509	46.878	67.314
70	61.149	73.708	61.330	61.163	77.868	44.468	65.340
71	58.501	71.922	58.912	58.490	76.077	42.057	63.282
72	55.713	69.989	56.399	55.704	74.148	39.660	61.151
73	52.781	67.882	53.779	52.831	72.093	37.289	58.959
74	49.709	65.579	51.050	49.899	69.924	34.956	56.717
75	46.518	63.071	48.216	46.934	67.656	32.671	54.437
76	43.237	60.361	45.294	43.876	65.189	30.405	52.048
77	39.903	57.461	42.306	40.767	62.550	28.173	49.570
78	36.555	54.390	39.280	37.645	59.766	25.993	47.027
79	33.227	51.162	36.239	34.547	56.866	23.876	44.441
80	29.943	47.786	33.198	31.507	53.877	21.837	41.832

Age	CSO (1980) Male	CSO (1980) Female	Total Population	U.S. Life Tables (1982) White Male	White Female	Black Male	Black Female
Life Expectancy	58.80	63.67	59.62	59.60	66.70	53.80	62.20
81	26.724	44.269	30.169	27.297	48.494	18.972	37.407
82	23.591	40.621	27.185	22.405	41.351	15.616	31.690
83	20.565	36.862	24.277	17.368	33.301	12.140	25.356
84	17.681	33.036	21.474	12.672	25.241	8.882	19.094
85	14.977	29.200	18.777	8.667	17.936	6.093	13.480
86	12.489	25.425	16.195	5.533	11.896	3.900	8.882
87	10.247	21.781	13.769	3.280	7.326	2.319	5.434
88	8.266	18.336	11.544	1.795	4.164	1.272	3.069
89	6.553	15.146	9.548	0.900	2.170	0.640	1.589
90	5.100	12.257	7.782	0.411	1.028	0.293	0.748
91	3.891	9.697	6.234	0.168	0.438	0.120	0.317
92	2.905	7.478	4.902	0.061	0.166	0.044	0.119
93	2.114	5.597	3.781	0.020	0.055	0.014	0.039
94	1.489	4.034	2.861	0.005	0.016	0.004	0.011
95	0.998	2.754	2.124	0.001	0.004	0.001	0.003
96	0.614	1.719	1.552	> 0.001	0.001	> 0.001	> 0.001
97	0.319	0.903	1.117	> 0.001	> 0.001	> 0.001	> 0.001
98	0.109	0.311	0.793	> 0.001	> 0.001	> 0.001	> 0.001
99	> 0.001	> 0.001	0.556	> 0.001	> 0.001	> 0.001	> 0.001

Probability of surviving through age X starting from age 14

	CSO (1980)			U. S. Life Tables (1982)			
	Male	Female	Total Population	White Male	White Female	Black Male	Black Female
Life Expectancy	57.86	62.71	58.65	58.60	65.70	52.80	61.20
Age							
14	99.885	99.920	99.937	99.936	99.971	99.935	99.969
15	99.752	99.835	99.855	99.847	99.934	99.852	99.933
16	99.602	99.745	99.754	99.735	99.891	99.750	99.891
17	99.435	99.650	99.637	99.605	99.842	99.629	99.843
18	99.258	99.553	99.510	99.461	99.791	99.485	99.789
19	99.074	99.451	99.377	99.311	99.739	99.320	99.729
20	98.885	99.347	99.237	99.154	99.687	99.132	99.663
21	98.696	99.241	99.092	98.991	99.636	98.921	99.592
22	98.510	99.132	98.941	98.825	99.583	98.689	99.513
23	98.327	99.022	98.790	98.659	99.530	98.439	99.427
24	98.148	98.909	98.640	98.495	99.477	98.174	99.335
25	97.974	98.795	98.495	98.336	99.424	97.895	99.236
26	97.805	98.677	98.355	98.182	99.370	97.602	99.128
27	97.637	98.557	98.215	98.030	99.315	97.292	99.013
28	97.471	98.433	98.073	97.879	99.260	96.967	98.892
29	97.305	98.305	97.927	97.728	99.202	96.625	98.763
30	97.136	98.172	97.776	97.576	99.141	96.265	98.627
31	96.963	98.034	97.616	97.422	99.078	95.886	98.483
32	96.786	97.892	97.448	97.266	99.012	95.491	98.329
33	96.601	97.745	97.270	97.107	98.941	95.081	98.165
34	96.408	97.591	97.080	96.944	98.866	94.655	97.988
35	96.204	97.430	96.877	96.776	98.785	94.211	97.798

	CSO (1980)		Total Population	U. S. Life Tables (1982)			
	Male	Female		White Male	White Female	Black Male	Black Female
Life Expectancy	57.86	62.71	58.65	58.60	65.70	52.80	61.20
Age							
36	95.989	97.259	96.659	96.599	98.697	93.747	97.594
37	95.759	97.075	96.424	96.414	98.601	93.262	97.373
38	95.512	96.877	96.167	96.216	98.496	92.754	97.135
39	95.245	96.662	95.888	96.004	98.380	92.220	96.876
40	94.957	96.428	95.587	95.773	98.251	91.658	96.596
41	94.645	96.173	95.261	95.521	98.107	91.063	96.292
42	94.308	95.897	94.909	95.245	97.949	90.428	95.961
43	93.943	95.601	94.525	94.942	97.774	89.741	95.599
44	93.549	95.283	94.107	94.606	97.581	88.995	95.205
45	93.124	94.944	93.651	94.236	97.367	88.184	94.776
46	92.666	94.583	93.157	93.827	97.131	87.307	94.309
47	92.173	94.200	92.622	93.374	96.872	86.360	93.800
48	91.644	93.792	92.044	92.872	96.586	85.342	93.245
49	91.074	93.358	91.420	92.314	96.272	84.251	92.639
50	90.463	92.895	90.745	91.696	95.928	83.083	91.978
51	89.803	92.402	90.016	91.016	95.550	81.837	91.261
52	89.088	91.875	89.227	90.270	95.136	80.514	90.488
53	88.312	91.310	88.373	89.455	94.685	79.113	89.661
54	87.468	90.707	87.451	88.571	94.195	77.635	88.780
55	86.552	90.063	86.458	87.611	93.663	76.080	87.845
56	85.560	89.382	85.389	86.574	93.085	74.448	86.853
57	84.492	88.664	84.244	85.453	92.458	72.738	85.797
58	83.343	87.913	83.021	84.243	91.778	70.948	84.666

Age	CSO (1980) Male	CSO (1980) Female	Total Population	U.S. Life Tables (1982) White Male	U.S. Life Tables (1982) White Female	U.S. Life Tables (1982) Black Male	U.S. Life Tables (1982) Black Female
Life Expectancy	57.86	62.71	58.65	58.60	65.70	52.80	61.20
59	82.112	87.127	81.718	82.940	91.042	69.078	83.454
60	80.792	86.302	80.332	81.542	90.247	67.129	82.158
61	79.375	85.428	78.863	80.046	89.387	65.105	80.778
62	77.852	84.491	77.306	78.442	88.459	63.013	79.323
63	76.212	83.476	75.657	76.720	87.456	60.857	77.805
64	74.449	82.370	73.913	74.873	86.372	58.646	76.232
65	72.556	81.168	72.069	72.899	85.203	56.384	74.607
66	70.535	79.869	70.124	70.781	83.930	54.065	72.897
67	68.388	78.477	68.077	68.535	82.556	51.703	71.109
68	66.119	76.999	65.932	66.177	81.086	49.310	69.252
69	63.727	75.431	63.690	63.722	79.528	46.901	67.332
70	61.209	73.763	61.358	61.188	77.886	44.489	65.358
71	58.559	71.976	58.939	58.514	76.095	42.078	63.299
72	55.768	70.042	56.425	55.727	74.165	39.679	61.168
73	52.833	67.933	53.804	52.853	72.109	37.307	58.975
74	49.759	65.628	51.074	49.920	69.940	34.973	56.733
75	46.565	63.118	48.238	46.953	67.671	32.687	54.452
76	43.280	60.406	45.315	43.894	65.204	30.419	52.062
77	39.943	57.504	42.326	40.784	62.565	28.187	49.584
78	36.591	54.431	39.298	37.661	59.780	26.005	47.040
79	33.260	51.200	36.256	34.562	56.879	23.888	44.453

	CSO (1980)		Total Population	U. S. Life Tables (1982)			
	Male	Female		White Male	White Female	Black Male	Black Female
Life Expectancy	57.86	62.71	58.65	58.60	65.70	52.80	61.20
Age							
80	29.972	47.822	33.213	31.520	53.890	21.847	41.843
81	26.751	44.302	30.183	27.308	48.505	18.982	37.418
82	23.614	40.651	27.197	22.415	41.361	15.624	31.699
83	20.586	36.890	24.289	17.376	33.309	12.146	25.362
84	17.698	33.060	21.484	12.677	25.247	8.887	19.099
85	14.991	29.222	18.785	8.671	17.940	6.096	13.483
86	12.502	25.444	16.203	5.535	11.898	3.902	8.884
87	10.257	21.797	13.776	3.281	7.327	2.320	5.436
88	8.275	18.349	11.550	1.796	4.165	1.273	3.070
89	6.559	15.158	9.553	0.901	2.171	0.640	1.589
90	5.105	12.266	7.785	0.411	1.028	0.293	0.748
91	3.895	9.704	6.237	0.169	0.438	0.121	0.317
92	2.908	7.484	4.904	0.061	0.166	0.044	0.119
93	2.117	5.602	3.783	0.020	0.055	0.014	0.039
94	1.490	4.037	2.862	0.005	0.016	0.004	0.011
95	0.999	2.756	2.125	0.001	0.004	0.001	0.003
96	0.615	1.720	1.552	> 0.001	0.001	> 0.001	> 0.001
97	0.319	0.903	1.117	> 0.001	> 0.001	> 0.001	> 0.001
98	0.109	0.311	0.794	> 0.001	> 0.001	> 0.001	> 0.001
99	> 0.001	> 0.001	0.557	> 0.001	> 0.001	> 0.001	> 0.001

Probability of surviving through age X starting from age 15

	CSO (1980)			U. S. Life Tables (1982)			
	Male	Female	Total Population	White Male	White Female	Black Male	Black Female
Life Expectancy	56.93	61.76	57.69	57.70	64.70	51.90	60.20
Age							
15	99.867	99.915	99.918	99.911	99.963	99.917	99.964
16	99.716	99.825	99.817	99.799	99.920	99.815	99.922
17	99.550	99.730	99.700	99.668	99.871	99.693	99.874
18	99.372	99.633	99.573	99.525	99.820	99.550	99.820
19	99.188	99.531	99.439	99.375	99.768	99.384	99.760
20	98.999	99.426	99.300	99.218	99.716	99.197	99.694
21	98.810	99.320	99.154	99.055	99.664	98.985	99.623
22	98.623	99.212	99.003	98.888	99.612	98.753	99.544
23	98.440	99.102	98.852	98.722	99.559	98.503	99.458
24	98.261	98.989	98.703	98.558	99.506	98.238	99.366
25	98.087	98.874	98.558	98.399	99.452	97.959	99.266
26	97.917	98.756	98.417	98.245	99.399	97.665	99.159
27	97.750	98.636	98.277	98.093	99.344	97.355	99.044
28	97.584	98.511	98.135	97.942	99.288	97.030	98.922
29	97.417	98.383	97.989	97.791	99.231	96.688	98.794
30	97.248	98.250	97.837	97.639	99.170	96.327	98.657
31	97.075	98.113	97.678	97.484	99.107	95.949	98.513
32	96.897	97.971	97.510	97.328	99.040	95.553	98.360
33	96.712	97.824	97.331	97.170	98.970	95.142	98.195
34	96.519	97.669	97.141	97.006	98.895	94.716	98.019
35	96.315	97.508	96.938	96.838	98.814	94.272	97.829
36	96.099	97.336	96.720	96.661	98.726	93.808	97.624

	CSO (1980)		Total Population	U. S. Life Tables (1982)			
	Male	Female		White Male	White Female	Black Male	Black Female
Life Expectancy	56.93	61.76	57.69	57.70	64.70	51.90	60.20
Age							
37	95.869	97.152	96.484	96.476	98.630	93.323	97.403
38	95.621	96.954	96.228	96.278	98.524	92.815	97.165
39	95.355	96.739	95.949	96.065	98.408	92.280	96.906
40	95.067	96.505	95.647	95.835	98.279	91.718	96.626
41	94.754	96.250	95.321	95.583	98.136	91.123	96.322
42	94.417	95.974	94.969	95.306	97.978	90.487	95.991
43	94.051	95.677	94.585	95.002	97.802	89.800	95.629
44	93.657	95.360	94.166	94.667	97.609	89.053	95.235
45	93.231	95.020	93.710	94.297	97.395	88.241	94.805
46	92.772	94.659	93.215	93.888	97.159	87.363	94.338
47	92.279	94.276	92.680	93.434	96.900	86.416	93.829
48	91.749	93.868	92.102	92.931	96.614	85.398	93.274
49	91.179	93.433	91.477	92.373	96.300	84.305	92.668
50	90.568	92.969	90.802	91.755	95.955	83.137	92.007
51	89.906	92.476	90.072	91.074	95.577	81.891	91.289
52	89.191	91.949	89.283	90.327	95.163	80.566	90.516
53	88.414	91.383	88.429	89.513	94.712	79.165	89.689
54	87.569	90.779	87.507	88.627	94.223	77.685	88.807
55	86.652	90.136	86.512	87.667	93.690	76.129	87.872
56	85.659	89.453	85.443	86.629	93.112	74.496	86.880
57	84.589	88.735	84.297	85.508	92.485	72.786	85.823
58	83.439	87.983	83.073	84.297	91.805	70.994	84.692
59	82.207	87.197	81.769	82.993	91.069	69.123	83.480

| | CSO (1980) | | Total | U. S. Life Tables (1982) | | | |
	Male	Female	Population	White Male	White Female	Black Male	Black Female
Life Expectancy	56.93	61.76	57.69	57.70	64.70	51.90	60.20
Age							
60	80.885	86.371	80.383	81.594	90.273	67.172	82.183
61	79.466	85.496	78.913	80.097	89.413	65.148	80.803
62	77.941	84.559	77.355	78.492	88.484	63.054	79.348
63	76.300	83.543	75.705	76.769	87.481	60.897	77.829
64	74.534	82.436	73.959	74.921	86.397	58.684	76.255
65	72.640	81.233	72.114	72.946	85.228	56.421	74.630
66	70.617	79.933	70.168	70.826	83.954	54.100	72.919
67	68.467	78.540	68.120	68.579	82.580	51.736	71.131
68	66.195	77.060	65.973	66.219	81.110	49.342	69.273
69	63.800	75.491	63.730	63.763	79.551	46.931	67.353
70	61.280	73.822	61.397	61.227	77.909	44.518	65.378
71	58.626	72.034	58.976	58.552	76.117	42.105	63.319
72	55.833	70.098	56.460	55.763	74.187	39.705	61.187
73	52.894	67.987	53.838	52.887	72.130	37.331	58.993
74	49.816	65.681	51.106	49.952	69.960	34.996	56.750
75	46.618	63.169	48.268	46.983	67.691	32.708	54.469
76	43.330	60.455	45.343	43.922	65.223	30.439	52.078
77	39.989	57.550	42.352	40.810	62.583	28.205	49.599
78	36.633	54.474	39.323	37.685	59.797	26.022	47.054
79	33.298	51.241	36.279	34.584	56.895	23.904	44.466
80	30.007	47.860	33.234	31.540	53.905	21.861	41.856

	CSO (1980)		Total Population	U. S. Life Tables (1982)			
	Male	Female		White Male	White Female	Black Male	Black Female
Life Expectancy	56.93	61.76	57.69	57.70	64.70	51.90	60.20
Age							
81	26.782	44.337	30.202	27.326	48.519	18.994	37.429
82	23.642	40.684	27.215	22.429	41.373	15.634	31.709
83	20.609	36.919	24.304	17.387	33.319	12.154	25.370
84	17.719	33.087	21.497	12.685	25.254	8.892	19.105
85	15.009	29.245	18.797	8.676	17.945	6.100	13.487
86	12.516	25.464	16.213	5.539	11.902	3.905	8.887
87	10.269	21.815	13.784	3.283	7.330	2.321	5.437
88	8.284	18.364	11.557	1.797	4.167	1.274	3.071
89	6.567	15.170	9.559	0.901	2.171	0.641	1.590
90	5.111	12.276	7.790	0.411	1.029	0.293	0.748
91	3.899	9.712	6.241	0.169	0.439	0.121	0.317
92	2.911	7.490	4.908	0.062	0.166	0.044	0.119
93	2.119	5.606	3.785	0.020	0.055	0.014	0.039
94	1.492	4.040	2.864	0.005	0.016	0.004	0.011
95	1.000	2.758	2.127	0.001	0.004	0.001	0.003
96	0.615	1.722	1.553	> 0.001	0.001	> 0.001	> 0.001
97	0.320	0.904	1.118	> 0.001	> 0.001	> 0.001	> 0.001
98	0.109	0.311	0.794	> 0.001	> 0.001	> 0.001	> 0.001
99	> 0.001	> 0.001	0.557	> 0.001	> 0.001	> 0.001	> 0.001

Probability of surviving through age X starting from age 16

	CSO (1980)		Total Population	U. S. Life Tables (1982)			
	Male	Female		White Male	White Female	Black Male	Black Female
Life Expectancy	56.00	60.82	56.73	56.70	63.80	50.90	59.20
Age							
16	99.849	99.910	99.899	99.888	99.957	99.898	99.958
17	99.682	99.815	99.782	99.757	99.908	99.776	99.910
18	99.505	99.717	99.654	99.613	99.857	99.632	99.856
19	99.320	99.616	99.521	99.463	99.805	99.467	99.796
20	99.131	99.511	99.382	99.306	99.753	99.279	99.730
21	98.942	99.404	99.235	99.143	99.701	99.068	99.658
22	98.755	99.296	99.085	98.977	99.649	98.835	99.580
23	98.571	99.186	98.933	98.810	99.596	98.585	99.494
24	98.392	99.073	98.784	98.646	99.543	98.320	99.402
25	98.217	98.958	98.638	98.486	99.489	98.040	99.302
26	98.048	98.840	98.497	98.333	99.435	97.746	99.195
27	97.880	98.720	98.357	98.180	99.381	97.436	99.080
28	97.713	98.595	98.216	98.029	99.325	97.111	98.958
29	97.546	98.467	98.070	97.878	99.268	96.768	98.829
30	97.378	98.334	97.917	97.725	99.207	96.407	98.693
31	97.204	98.196	97.758	97.571	99.143	96.028	98.549
32	97.026	98.054	97.590	97.415	99.077	95.633	98.395
33	96.841	97.907	97.411	97.256	99.007	95.221	98.231
34	96.647	97.752	97.221	97.093	98.931	94.795	98.054
35	96.443	97.591	97.018	96.924	98.850	94.350	97.864
36	96.227	97.419	96.800	96.747	98.762	93.886	97.659
37	95.997	97.235	96.564	96.562	98.667	93.401	97.439

| | CSO (1980) | | Total Population | U.S. Life Tables (1982) | | | |
	Male	Female		White Male	White Female	Black Male	Black Female
Life Expectancy	56.00	60.82	56.73	56.70	63.80	50.90	59.20
Age							
38	95.749	97.037	96.307	96.364	98.561	92.892	97.200
39	95.482	96.821	96.027	96.151	98.445	92.357	96.941
40	95.193	96.587	95.726	95.920	98.316	91.794	96.661
41	94.880	96.332	95.399	95.668	98.172	91.198	96.357
42	94.542	96.056	95.046	95.391	98.014	90.562	96.025
43	94.177	95.759	94.662	95.087	97.839	89.874	95.663
44	93.782	95.441	94.243	94.751	97.645	89.127	95.269
45	93.355	95.101	93.787	94.381	97.431	88.315	94.839
46	92.896	94.740	93.292	93.971	97.195	87.436	94.372
47	92.402	94.356	92.756	93.517	96.936	86.488	93.863
48	91.871	93.947	92.177	93.014	96.650	85.469	93.307
49	91.301	93.512	91.553	92.455	96.336	84.375	92.701
50	90.688	93.049	90.877	91.837	95.991	83.206	92.040
51	90.026	92.555	90.146	91.155	95.613	81.959	91.322
52	89.310	92.027	89.357	90.408	95.199	80.633	90.549
53	88.532	91.461	88.501	89.592	94.747	79.230	89.721
54	87.685	90.856	87.578	88.706	94.258	77.750	88.839
55	86.767	90.212	86.583	87.746	93.725	76.192	87.904
56	85.773	89.529	85.513	86.707	93.147	74.558	86.911
57	84.702	88.810	84.367	85.584	92.519	72.846	85.854
58	83.550	88.058	83.142	84.372	91.839	71.053	84.723

| | CSO (1980) | | | U. S. Life Tables (1982) | | | |
	Male	Female	Total Population	White Male	White Female	Black Male	Black Female
Life Expectancy	56.00	60.82	56.73	56.70	63.80	50.90	59.20
Age							
59	82.316	87.271	81.836	83.067	91.102	69.180	83.510
60	80.993	86.444	80.449	81.667	90.306	67.228	82.213
61	79.572	85.569	78.978	80.168	89.446	65.202	80.832
62	78.045	84.631	77.419	78.562	88.517	63.106	79.376
63	76.402	83.614	75.767	76.837	87.513	60.947	77.857
64	74.634	82.506	74.020	74.988	86.429	58.733	76.283
65	72.736	81.302	72.173	73.011	85.260	56.468	74.657
66	70.711	80.001	70.225	70.920	84.005	54.162	72.960
67	68.558	78.607	68.176	68.716	82.659	51.819	71.194
68	66.283	77.126	66.027	66.398	81.218	49.444	69.357
69	63.885	75.556	63.782	63.965	79.677	47.044	67.450
70	61.361	73.885	61.447	61.421	78.033	44.625	65.472
71	58.704	72.095	59.024	58.775	76.270	42.217	63.428
72	55.907	70.158	56.506	56.030	74.384	39.828	61.318
73	52.964	68.045	53.882	53.195	72.370	37.463	59.145
74	49.882	65.736	51.148	50.278	70.226	35.129	56.914
75	46.680	63.223	48.308	47.290	67.948	32.833	54.626
76	43.388	60.506	45.381	44.250	65.521	30.569	52.257
77	40.042	57.599	42.387	41.174	62.943	28.345	49.813
78	36.682	54.521	39.355	38.078	60.216	26.169	47.301
79	33.342	51.285	36.309	34.981	57.344	24.050	44.727

	CSO (1980)		Total Population	U. S. Life Tables (1982)			
	Male	Female		White Male	White Female	Black Male	Black Female
Life Expectancy	56.00	60.82	56.73	56.70	63.80	50.90	59.20
Age							
80	30.047	47.901	33.261	31.902	54.331	21.996	42.102
81	26.817	44.375	30.227	28.712	50.997	19.857	39.233
82	23.673	40.719	27.237	25.467	47.343	17.659	36.129
83	20.637	36.951	24.324	22.178	43.382	15.434	32.811
84	17.742	33.115	21.515	18.923	39.143	13.221	29.313
85	15.029	29.270	18.812	15.766	34.678	11.063	25.685
86	12.533	25.486	16.226	12.778	30.058	9.008	21.995
87	10.282	21.833	13.796	10.026	25.382	7.103	18.326
88	8.295	18.380	11.567	7.571	20.772	5.393	14.777
89	6.576	15.183	9.566	5.465	16.366	3.916	11.455
90	5.117	12.287	7.796	3.738	12.312	2.695	8.466
91	3.905	9.720	6.246	0.169	0.439	0.121	0.317
92	2.915	7.496	4.912	0.062	0.166	0.044	0.119
93	2.122	5.611	3.788	0.020	0.055	0.014	0.039
94	1.494	4.044	2.866	0.005	0.016	0.004	0.011
95	1.001	2.761	2.128	0.001	0.004	0.001	0.003
96	0.616	1.723	1.555	< 0.001	0.001	< 0.001	< 0.001
97	0.320	0.905	1.119	< 0.001	< 0.001	< 0.001	< 0.001
98	0.110	0.311	0.795	< 0.001	< 0.001	< 0.001	< 0.001
99	< 0.001	< 0.001	0.557	< 0.001	< 0.001	< 0.001	< 0.001

Probability of surviving through age 'X' starting from age 17

	CSO (1980)		Total Population	U. S. Life Tables (1982)			
	Male	Female		White Male	White Female	Black Male	Black Female
Life Expectancy	55.09	59.87	55.79	55.80	62.80	50.00	58.30
Age							
17	99.833	99.905	99.883	99.869	99.951	99.878	99.952
18	99.655	99.807	99.755	99.725	99.900	99.734	99.898
19	99.470	99.705	99.621	99.575	99.848	99.569	99.838
20	99.281	99.601	99.482	99.417	99.796	99.380	99.772
21	99.091	99.494	99.336	99.254	99.744	99.169	99.700
22	98.904	99.386	99.185	99.087	99.691	98.936	99.622
23	98.720	99.275	99.033	98.921	99.639	98.685	99.536
24	98.540	99.162	98.883	98.757	99.586	98.420	99.443
25	98.366	99.047	98.738	98.597	99.532	98.140	99.344
26	98.196	98.929	98.597	98.443	99.478	97.846	99.237
27	98.028	98.808	98.457	98.290	99.424	97.536	99.122
28	97.861	98.684	98.315	98.139	99.368	97.210	99.000
29	97.694	98.556	98.169	97.988	99.310	96.867	98.871
30	97.525	98.423	98.016	97.835	99.250	96.506	98.734
31	97.351	98.285	97.857	97.680	99.186	96.126	98.590
32	97.173	98.142	97.688	97.524	99.120	95.730	98.436
33	96.988	97.995	97.510	97.365	99.049	95.319	98.272
34	96.794	97.840	97.320	97.202	98.974	94.892	98.095
35	96.589	97.679	97.116	97.033	98.893	94.447	97.905
36	96.373	97.507	96.898	96.856	98.805	93.982	97.700
37	96.142	97.323	96.661	96.670	98.709	93.496	97.479

| | CSO (1980) | | Total Population | U. S. Life Tables (1982) | | | |
	Male	Female		White Male	White Female	Black Male	Black Female
Life Expectancy	55.09	59.87	55.79	55.80	62.80	50.00	58.30
Age							
38	95.894	97.124	96.404	96.472	98.603	92.986	97.241
39	95.626	96.909	96.124	96.259	98.487	92.451	96.982
40	95.337	96.674	95.823	96.028	98.358	91.888	96.702
41	95.024	96.419	95.496	95.775	98.214	91.291	96.397
42	94.685	96.142	95.143	95.498	98.056	90.654	96.066
43	94.319	95.845	94.758	95.194	97.881	89.966	95.703
44	93.924	95.527	94.338	94.858	97.687	89.218	95.309
45	93.496	95.187	93.882	94.487	97.473	88.405	94.879
46	93.036	94.825	93.386	94.077	97.237	87.525	94.411
47	92.541	94.441	92.850	93.622	96.978	86.577	93.903
48	92.010	94.032	92.271	93.119	96.691	85.556	93.347
49	91.439	93.597	91.645	92.559	96.377	84.462	92.740
50	90.825	93.132	90.969	91.940	96.032	83.291	92.079
51	90.162	92.638	90.237	91.257	95.654	82.042	91.360
52	89.445	92.110	89.447	90.509	95.240	80.716	90.587
53	88.666	91.543	88.591	89.693	94.788	79.311	89.759
54	87.818	90.938	87.667	88.806	94.298	77.829	88.876
55	86.898	90.294	86.671	87.844	93.765	76.270	87.940
56	85.903	89.610	85.600	86.804	93.187	74.634	86.948
57	84.830	88.890	84.452	85.680	92.559	72.920	85.890
58	83.677	88.138	83.226	84.467	91.878	71.126	84.758

	CSO (1980)		Total Population	U. S. Life Tables (1982)			
	Male	Female		White Male	White Female	Black Male	Black Female
Life Expectancy	55.09	59.87	55.79	55.80	62.80	50.00	58.30
Age							
59	82.441	87.350	81.919	83.160	91.142	69.251	83.545
60	81.115	86.522	80.530	81.759	90.345	67.297	82.247
61	79.692	85.646	79.058	80.258	89.485	65.268	80.866
62	78.163	84.707	77.497	79.650	88.555	63.171	79.410
63	76.517	83.689	75.844	76.924	87.551	61.010	77.890
64	74.746	82.580	74.095	75.072	86.466	58.793	76.315
65	72.846	81.375	72.246	73.092	85.296	56.525	74.688
66	70.818	80.073	70.296	70.969	84.021	54.201	72.976
67	68.662	78.678	68.245	68.717	82.646	51.832	71.187
68	66.383	77.195	66.094	66.353	81.175	49.433	69.327
69	63.982	75.624	63.847	63.892	79.614	47.018	67.406
70	61.454	73.952	61.509	61.351	77.971	44.601	65.429
71	58.793	72.160	59.084	58.670	76.178	42.183	63.368
72	55.992	70.221	56.564	55.875	74.246	39.778	61.235
73	53.044	68.106	53.937	52.994	72.188	37.401	59.039
74	49.958	65.796	51.199	50.053	70.016	35.060	56.795
75	46.751	63.280	48.357	47.078	67.745	32.769	54.512
76	43.453	60.560	45.426	44.011	65.275	30.496	52.118
77	40.102	57.651	42.430	40.892	62.633	28.258	49.638
78	36.738	54.570	39.395	37.761	59.845	26.070	47.091
79	33.393	51.331	36.346	34.653	56.941	23.948	44.501

| | CSO (1980) | | Total Population | U. S. Life Tables (1982) | | | |
	Male	Female		White Male	White Female	Black Male	Black Female
Life Expectancy	55.09	59.87	55.79	55.80	62.80	50.00	58.30
Age							
80	30.092	47.944	33.295	31.604	53.948	21.902	41.889
81	26.858	44.415	30.258	27.381	48.558	19.029	37.458
82	23.709	40.755	27.264	22.474	41.406	15.663	31.734
83	20.668	36.984	24.349	17.422	33.345	12.176	25.390
84	17.769	33.145	21.537	12.711	25.274	8.909	19.120
85	15.051	29.297	18.832	8.694	17.960	6.111	13.498
86	12.552	25.509	16.243	5.550	11.911	3.912	8.894
87	10.298	21.853	13.810	3.290	7.335	2.326	5.442
88	8.308	18.396	11.578	1.800	4.170	1.276	3.073
89	6.586	15.196	9.576	0.903	2.173	0.642	1.591
90	5.125	12.298	7.804	0.412	1.029	0.294	0.749
91	3.911	9.729	6.252	0.169	0.439	0.121	0.317
92	2.919	7.503	4.917	0.062	0.166	0.044	0.119
93	2.125	5.616	3.792	0.020	0.055	0.014	0.039
94	1.496	4.047	2.869	0.005	0.016	0.004	0.011
95	1.003	2.763	2.131	0.001	0.004	0.001	0.003
96	0.617	1.725	1.556	<0.001	0.001	<0.001	<0.001
97	0.321	0.906	1.120	<0.001	<0.001	<0.001	<0.001
98	0.110	0.312	0.796	<0.001	<0.001	<0.001	<0.001
99	<0.001	<0.001	0.558	<0.001	<0.001	<0.001	<0.001

Probability of surviving through age X starting from age 18

| | CSO (1980) | | | U. S. Life Tables (1982) | | | |
Age	Male	Female	Total Population	White Male	White Female	Black Male	Black Female
Life Expectancy	54.18	58.93	54.86	54.90	61.80	49.00	57.30
18	99.822	99.902	99.872	99.856	99.949	99.856	99.946
19	99.636	99.800	99.738	99.705	99.897	99.690	99.886
20	99.447	99.695	99.599	99.548	99.845	99.502	99.820
21	99.257	99.589	99.452	99.384	99.793	99.290	99.748
22	99.069	99.480	99.301	99.217	99.740	99.057	99.669
23	98.885	99.370	99.149	99.051	99.687	98.806	99.584
24	98.705	99.256	98.999	98.886	99.635	98.540	99.491
25	98.531	99.141	98.854	98.726	99.581	98.260	99.392
26	98.360	99.023	98.712	98.572	99.527	97.966	99.284
27	98.192	98.902	98.572	98.419	99.472	97.655	99.169
28	98.025	98.778	98.430	98.268	99.417	97.329	99.047
29	97.857	98.649	98.284	98.116	99.359	96.985	98.918
30	97.688	98.516	98.131	97.963	99.298	96.623	98.782
31	97.514	98.378	97.971	97.809	99.235	96.244	98.638
32	97.336	98.236	97.803	97.652	99.168	95.847	98.484
33	97.150	98.088	97.624	97.493	99.098	95.435	98.319
34	96.955	97.933	97.433	97.329	99.023	95.008	98.142
35	96.751	97.772	97.230	97.160	98.941	94.562	97.952
36	96.534	97.600	97.011	96.983	98.853	94.097	97.747
37	96.303	97.415	96.774	96.797	98.757	93.610	97.526

Age	CSO (1980)		Total Population	U. S. Life Tables (1982)			
	Male	Female		White Male	White Female	Black Male	Black Female
Life Expectancy	54.18	58.93	54.86	54.90	61.80	49.00	57.30
38	96.054	97.216	96.517	96.598	98.652	93.100	97.287
39	95.786	97.001	96.237	96.385	98.535	92.564	97.029
40	95.497	96.766	95.935	96.154	98.406	92.000	96.748
41	95.183	96.510	95.608	95.901	98.263	91.403	96.443
42	94.844	96.233	95.254	95.623	98.104	90.765	96.112
43	94.477	95.936	94.869	95.318	97.929	90.076	95.749
44	94.081	95.618	94.449	94.982	97.735	89.327	95.355
45	93.653	95.277	93.992	94.611	97.521	88.513	94.925
46	93.192	94.915	93.495	94.200	97.285	87.632	94.457
47	92.696	94.531	92.959	93.745	97.025	86.682	93.948
48	92.164	94.121	92.379	93.241	96.739	85.660	93.391
49	91.592	93.686	91.752	92.680	96.424	84.565	92.784
50	90.977	93.221	91.075	92.060	96.079	83.393	92.123
51	90.313	92.726	90.343	91.377	95.701	82.143	91.404
52	89.594	92.197	89.552	90.628	95.286	80.814	90.630
53	88.814	91.630	88.695	89.810	94.835	79.408	89.802
54	87.965	91.025	87.770	88.922	94.344	77.924	88.919
55	87.044	90.379	86.772	87.959	93.811	76.363	87.983
56	86.046	89.695	85.700	86.918	93.232	74.725	86.989
57	84.972	88.975	84.551	85.792	92.604	73.010	85.932
58	83.817	88.221	83.323	84.577	91.923	71.213	84.799

| | CSO (1980) | | | U. S. Life Tables (1982) | | | |
	Male	Female	Total Population	White Male	White Female	Black Male	Black Female
Life Expectancy	54.18	58.93	54.86	54.90	61.80	49.00	57.30
Age							
59	82.579	87.433	82.015	83.269	91.186	69.336	83.586
60	81.251	86.605	80.625	81.866	90.389	67.379	82.287
61	79.826	85.727	79.150	80.364	89.529	65.348	80.905
62	78.294	84.788	77.588	78.753	88.599	63.248	79.448
63	76.645	83.769	75.933	77.024	87.594	61.084	77.927
64	74.872	82.659	74.182	75.170	86.509	58.864	76.352
65	72.968	81.453	72.331	73.188	85.338	56.595	74.724
66	70.936	80.149	70.379	71.062	84.062	54.267	73.011
67	68.777	78.752	68.325	68.807	82.686	51.895	71.221
68	66.494	77.269	66.171	66.559	81.293	49.555	69.420
69	64.089	75.696	63.922	64.121	79.751	47.149	67.511
70	61.557	74.022	61.581	61.571	78.105	44.725	65.531
71	58.891	72.228	59.153	58.918	76.340	42.312	63.485
72	56.085	70.288	56.630	56.166	74.452	39.917	61.373
73	53.133	68.171	54.000	53.324	72.437	37.547	59.199
74	50.041	65.858	51.249	50.401	70.291	35.208	56.965
75	46.829	63.340	48.414	47.405	68.010	32.907	54.675
76	43.526	60.618	45.480	44.358	65.581	30.637	52.304
77	40.169	57.706	42.480	41.274	63.001	28.408	49.858
78	36.799	54.622	39.441	38.171	60.272	26.228	47.343
79	33.449	51.380	36.388	35.066	57.397	24.104	44.767

	CSO (1980)		Total Population	U. S. Life Tables (1982)			
	Male	Female		White Male	White Female	Black Male	Black Female
Life Expectancy	54.18	58.93	54.86	54.90	61.80	49.00	57.30
Age							
80	30.143	47.989	33.334	31.980	54.381	22.045	42.140
81	26.903	44.457	30.293	28.782	51.044	19.901	39.268
82	23.748	40.794	27.296	25.529	47.387	17.699	36.162
83	20.703	37.019	24.377	22.232	43.422	15.469	32.841
84	17.799	33.176	21.562	18.969	39.179	13.251	29.339
85	15.077	29.325	18.854	15.805	34.710	11.088	25.708
86	12.573	25.533	16.262	12.809	30.086	9.028	22.014
87	10.315	21.874	13.826	10.050	25.406	7.119	18.342
88	8.322	18.414	11.592	7.590	20.791	5.406	14.791
89	6.597	15.211	9.587	5.479	16.381	3.925	11.466
90	5.134	12.309	7.813	3.747	12.324	2.701	8.473
91	3.917	9.738	6.260	2.401	8.760	1.742	5.906
92	2.924	7.510	4.922	1.421	5.801	1.038	3.833
93	2.129	5.621	3.797	0.020	0.055	0.014	0.039
94	1.499	4.051	2.873	0.005	0.016	0.004	0.011
95	1.004	2.766	2.133	0.001	0.004	0.001	0.003
96	0.618	1.726	1.558	< 0.001	0.001	< 0.001	< 0.001
97	0.321	0.906	1.121	< 0.001	< 0.001	< 0.001	< 0.001
98	0.110	0.312	0.796	< 0.001	< 0.001	< 0.001	< 0.001
99	< 0.001	< 0.001	0.559	< 0.001	< 0.001	< 0.001	< 0.001

Probability of surviving through age X starting from age 19

	CSO (1980)		Total Population	U. S. Life Tables (1982)			
	Male	Female		White Male	White Female	Black Male	Black Female
Life Expectancy	53.27	57.98	53.93	53.90	60.90	48.10	56.30
Age							
19	99.814	99.898	99.866	99.849	99.948	99.834	99.940
20	99.624	99.793	99.726	99.691	99.896	99.645	99.874
21	99.434	99.686	99.580	99.528	99.844	99.433	99.802
22	99.246	99.578	99.428	99.361	99.791	99.199	99.723
23	99.062	99.467	99.276	99.194	99.738	98.948	99.638
24	98.881	99.354	99.126	99.029	99.685	98.682	99.545
25	98.706	99.238	98.980	98.869	99.632	98.402	99.445
26	98.535	99.120	98.839	98.714	99.578	98.107	99.338
27	98.367	98.999	98.699	98.561	99.523	97.796	99.223
28	98.200	98.875	98.556	98.409	99.467	97.469	99.101
29	98.032	98.746	98.410	98.258	99.410	97.125	98.972
30	97.862	98.613	98.257	98.105	99.349	96.763	98.835
31	97.688	98.475	98.097	97.950	99.285	96.383	98.691
32	97.509	98.332	97.928	97.793	99.219	95.985	98.537
33	97.323	98.185	97.749	97.634	99.148	95.573	98.372
34	97.128	98.029	97.558	97.470	99.073	95.145	98.195
35	96.923	97.868	97.354	97.300	98.992	94.698	98.005
36	96.706	97.695	97.135	97.123	98.904	94.232	97.800
37	96.474	97.511	96.898	96.936	98.808	93.745	97.579
38	96.225	97.312	96.641	96.738	98.702	93.234	97.340
39	95.957	97.096	96.360	96.524	98.586	92.697	97.081
40	95.667	96.861	96.058	96.292	98.456	92.133	96.800

	CSO (1980)		U. S. Life Tables (1982)				
	Male	Female	Total Population	White Male	White Female	Black Male	Black Female
Life Expectancy	53.27	57.98	53.93	53.90	60.90	48.10	56.30
Age							
41	95.352	96.605	95.730	96.039	98.313	91.555	96.496
42	95.013	96.328	95.376	95.761	98.154	90.896	96.164
43	94.645	96.030	94.991	95.456	97.979	90.206	95.801
44	94.249	95.711	94.570	95.119	97.785	89.455	95.406
45	93.820	95.371	94.112	94.747	97.571	88.641	94.976
46	93.358	95.008	93.615	94.336	97.334	87.759	94.508
47	92.862	94.623	93.078	93.880	97.075	86.807	93.998
48	92.328	94.214	92.497	93.375	96.788	85.784	93.442
49	91.755	93.778	91.870	92.814	96.474	84.687	92.835
50	91.139	93.312	91.192	92.193	96.128	83.513	92.173
51	90.474	92.817	90.459	91.509	95.750	82.261	91.454
52	89.754	92.288	89.666	90.759	95.335	80.931	90.679
53	88.972	91.720	88.808	89.940	94.883	79.523	89.850
54	88.122	91.114	87.882	89.050	94.392	78.036	88.967
55	87.199	90.468	86.884	88.086	93.859	76.473	88.030
56	86.200	89.783	85.810	87.043	93.280	74.833	87.036
57	85.123	89.062	84.659	85.916	92.651	73.115	85.978
58	83.966	88.308	83.430	84.699	91.970	71.315	84.845
59	82.726	87.518	82.120	83.389	91.233	69.436	83.631
60	81.396	86.690	80.728	81.984	90.435	67.476	82.331
61	79.968	85.811	79.252	80.479	89.574	65.442	80.949
62	78.434	84.871	77.687	78.867	88.644	63.339	79.491
63	76.782	83.851	76.030	77.136	87.639	61.172	77.969

Life Expectancy	CSO (1980)		Total Population	U. S. Life Tables (1982)			
	Male	Female		White Male	White Female	Black Male	Black Female
	53.27	57.98	53.93	53.90	60.90	48.10	56.30
Age							
64	75.005	82.740	74.277	75.279	86.553	58.949	76.393
65	73.098	81.533	72.424	73.294	85.382	56.676	74.764
66	71.063	80.228	70.469	71.165	84.105	54.345	73.051
67	68.899	78.830	68.413	68.907	82.728	51.970	71.259
68	66.613	77.345	66.256	66.535	81.256	49.565	69.398
69	64.203	75.770	64.004	64.068	79.694	47.144	67.474
70	61.667	74.095	61.660	61.520	78.049	44.720	65.496
71	58.996	72.299	59.229	58.831	76.254	42.295	63.433
72	56.185	70.357	56.702	56.029	74.320	39.885	61.297
73	53.228	68.238	54.069	53.140	72.260	37.500	59.100
74	50.130	65.923	51.325	50.190	70.087	35.154	56.853
75	46.913	63.402	48.476	47.208	67.813	32.856	54.567
76	43.604	60.678	45.538	44.132	65.340	30.577	52.172
77	40.241	57.763	42.534	41.005	62.695	28.333	49.688
78	36.865	54.675	39.492	37.865	59.905	26.140	47.139
79	33.508	51.430	36.435	34.749	56.998	24.012	44.547
80	30.196	48.036	33.376	31.691	54.002	21.960	41.932
81	26.951	44.501	30.332	27.456	48.607	19.080	37.497
82	23.791	40.834	27.331	22.536	41.447	15.705	31.766
83	20.739	37.056	24.408	17.470	33.379	12.209	25.416
84	17.831	33.209	21.590	12.746	25.300	8.933	19.139
85	15.104	29.353	18.878	8.718	17.978	6.127	13.512
86	12.595	25.558	16.282	5.565	11.923	3.923	8.903

	CSO (1980)			U. S. Life Tables (1982)			
	Male	Female	Total Population	White Male	White Female	Black Male	Black Female
Life Expectancy	53.27	57.98	53.93	53.90	60.90	48.10	56.30
Age							
87	10.334	21.895	13.843	3.299	7.343	2.332	5.447
88	8.336	18.432	11.607	1.805	4.174	1.280	3.076
89	6.608	15.226	9.600	0.905	2.175	0.644	1.593
90	5.143	12.321	7.824	0.413	1.030	0.294	0.750
91	3.924	9.748	6.268	0.169	0.439	0.121	0.318
92	2.930	7.517	4.929	0.062	0.166	0.044	0.120
93	2.132	5.627	3.801	0.020	0.055	0.014	0.039
94	1.501	4.055	2.876	0.005	0.016	0.004	0.011
95	1.006	2.768	2.136	0.001	0.004	0.001	0.003
96	0.619	1.728	1.560	> 0.001	0.001	> 0.001	> 0.001
97	0.322	0.907	1.123	> 0.001	> 0.001	> 0.001	> 0.001
98	0.110	0.312	0.797	> 0.001	> 0.001	> 0.001	> 0.001
99	> 0.001	> 0.001	0.559	> 0.001	> 0.001	> 0.001	> 0.001

Probability of surviving through age X starting from age 20

	CSO (1980)			U. S. Life Tables (1982)			
	Male	Female	Total Population	White Male	White Female	Black Male	Black Female
Life Expectancy	52.37	57.04	53.00	53.00	59.90	47.20	55.40
Age							
20	99.810	99.895	99.860	99.842	99.948	99.811	99.934

	CSO (1980)		Total Population	U. S. Life Tables (1982)			
	Male	Female		White Male	White Female	Black Male	Black Female
Life Expectancy	52.37	57.04	53.00	53.00	59.90	47.20	55.40
Age							
21	99.619	99.788	99.713	99.678	99.896	99.598	99.862
22	99.431	99.679	99.562	99.511	99.843	99.364	99.783
23	99.246	99.569	99.409	99.344	99.790	99.113	99.697
24	99.066	99.455	99.259	99.179	99.737	98.846	99.605
25	98.890	99.340	99.113	99.018	99.683	98.566	99.505
26	98.719	99.222	98.972	98.864	99.630	98.270	99.398
27	98.550	99.101	98.831	98.710	99.575	97.958	99.282
28	98.383	98.976	98.689	98.558	99.519	97.631	99.160
29	98.215	98.847	98.542	98.407	99.461	97.287	99.031
30	98.045	98.714	98.389	98.253	99.401	96.924	98.895
31	97.870	98.575	98.229	98.098	99.337	96.543	98.750
32	97.691	98.432	98.060	97.941	99.270	96.145	98.596
33	97.504	98.285	97.880	97.781	99.200	95.732	98.431
34	97.309	98.130	97.689	97.617	99.125	95.303	98.254
35	97.104	97.968	97.485	97.447	99.043	94.856	98.064
36	96.887	97.795	97.266	97.270	98.955	94.389	97.859
37	96.654	97.610	97.028	97.083	98.859	93.901	97.638
39	96.405	97.411	96.770	96.884	98.753	93.389	97.398
39	96.136	97.195	96.490	96.670	98.637	92.851	97.139
40	95.845	96.960	96.187	96.438	98.508	92.286	96.859
41	95.530	96.704	95.859	96.184	98.364	91.687	96.553
42	95.190	96.426	95.504	95.906	98.205	91.047	96.221
43	94.822	96.128	95.118	95.600	98.030	90.356	95.859

| | CSO (1980) | | Total Population | U. S. Life Tables (1982) | | | |
	Male	Female		White Male	White Female	Black Male	Black Female
Life Expectancy	52.37	57.04	53.00	53.00	59.90	47.20	55.40
Age							
44	94.424	95.809	94.697	95.263	97.836	89.604	95.464
45	93.995	95.468	94.239	94.890	97.621	88.788	95.033
46	93.532	95.105	93.741	94.478	97.385	87.904	94.565
47	93.035	94.720	93.203	94.022	97.125	86.952	94.055
48	92.501	94.310	92.621	93.516	96.839	85.926	93.498
49	91.926	93.873	91.993	92.954	96.524	84.827	92.890
50	91.309	93.408	91.314	92.332	96.178	83.652	92.228
51	90.643	92.912	90.580	91.647	95.799	82.398	91.509
52	89.921	92.382	89.787	90.896	95.385	81.065	90.734
53	89.138	91.814	88.927	90.076	94.932	79.655	89.904
54	88.286	91.207	88.000	89.185	94.442	78.166	89.020
55	87.361	90.560	87.000	88.219	93.908	76.600	88.083
56	86.360	89.875	85.925	87.175	93.329	74.957	87.089
57	85.282	89.153	84.773	86.046	92.700	73.236	86.030
58	84.123	88.398	83.542	84.827	92.018	71.434	84.896
59	82.880	87.608	82.230	83.515	91.280	69.551	83.681
60	81.548	86.778	80.836	82.108	90.482	67.588	82.381
61	80.117	85.899	79.358	80.601	89.621	65.551	80.997
62	78.580	84.958	77.791	78.986	88.690	63.444	79.539
63	76.925	83.936	76.132	77.252	87.684	61.274	78.016
64	75.145	82.824	74.376	75.393	86.598	59.047	76.439
65	73.235	81.616	72.521	73.405	85.426	56.770	74.809
66	71.195	80.310	70.563	71.272	84.149	54.435	73.094

Life Expectancy	CSO (1980)		Total Population	U. S. Life Tables (1982)			
	Male	Female		White Male	White Female	Black Male	Black Female
	52.37	57.04	53.00	53.00	59.90	47.20	55.40
Age							
67	69.028	78.910	68.504	69.011	82.771	52.057	71.302
68	66.737	77.424	66.345	66.636	81.298	49.647	69.440
69	64.323	75.847	64.089	64.165	79.736	47.222	67.515
70	61.782	74.170	61.743	61.613	78.090	44.794	65.535
71	59.106	72.373	59.309	58.920	76.294	42.366	63.471
72	56.290	70.428	56.778	56.114	74.359	39.951	61.334
73	53.327	68.308	54.142	53.220	72.298	37.563	59.135
74	50.224	65.990	51.394	50.266	70.123	35.212	56.887
75	47.000	63.467	48.541	47.279	67.848	32.911	54.600
76	43.685	60.739	45.599	44.199	65.374	30.628	52.203
77	40.316	57.822	42.591	41.067	62.728	28.380	49.718
78	36.934	54.731	39.545	37.922	59.936	26.183	47.168
79	33.571	51.483	36.484	34.801	57.027	24.052	44.573
80	30.253	48.085	33.421	31.739	54.031	21.997	41.957
81	27.001	44.546	30.372	27.498	48.632	19.112	37.519
82	23.835	40.876	27.368	22.570	41.469	15.731	31.785
83	20.778	37.093	24.441	17.496	33.396	12.229	25.431
84	17.864	33.243	21.519	12.765	25.313	8.947	19.151
85	15.132	29.383	18.903	8.731	17.987	6.137	13.520
86	12.618	25.584	16.304	5.574	11.929	3.929	8.908
87	10.353	21.918	13.862	3.304	7.347	2.336	5.450
88	8.352	18.451	11.622	1.808	4.176	1.282	3.078
89	6.621	15.241	9.613	0.907	2.176	0.645	1.594

| | CSO (1980) | | Total | U. S. Life Tables (1982) | | | |
	Male	Female	Population	White Male	White Female	Black Male	Black Female
Life Expectancy	52.37	57.04	53.00	53.00	59.90	47.20	55.40
Age							
90	5.152	12.334	7.834	0.414	1.031	0.295	0.750
91	3.931	9.758	6.276	0.170	0.440	0.121	0.318
92	2.935	7.525	4.935	0.062	0.167	0.044	0.120
93	2.136	5.633	3.807	0.020	0.055	0.014	0.039
94	1.504	4.059	2.880	0.005	0.016	0.004	0.011
95	1.008	2.771	2.139	0.001	0.004	0.001	0.003
96	0.620	1.730	1.562	> 0.001	0.001	> 0.001	> 0.001
97	0.322	0.908	1.124	> 0.001	> 0.001	> 0.001	> 0.001
98	0.110	0.313	0.799	> 0.001	> 0.001	> 0.001	> 0.001
99	> 0.001	> 0.001	0.560	> 0.001	> 0.001	> 0.001	> 0.001

Probability of surviving through age X starting from age 21

| | CSO (1980) | | Total | U. S. Life Tables (1982) | | | |
	Male	Female	Population	White Male	White Female	Black Male	Black Female
Life Expectancy	51.47	56.10	52.07	52.10	58.90	46.20	54.40
Age							
21	99.809	99.893	99.853	99.836	99.948	99.787	99.928
22	99.620	99.784	99.701	99.668	99.895	99.553	99.849
23	99.435	99.673	99.549	99.501	99.842	99.301	99.763
24	99.254	99.560	99.398	99.336	99.789	99.034	99.670

	CSO (1980)		Total Population	U.S. Life Tables (1982)			
	Male	Female		White Male	White Female	Black Male	Black Female
Life Expectancy	51.47	56.10	52.07	52.10	58.90	46.20	54.40
Age							
25	99.078	99.444	99.252	99.175	99.735	98.752	99.571
26	98.907	99.326	99.110	99.020	99.681	98.456	99.463
27	98.738	99.205	98.970	98.867	99.627	98.144	99.348
28	98.570	99.080	98.827	98.714	99.571	97.816	99.226
29	98.401	98.951	98.680	98.562	99.513	97.471	99.097
30	98.231	98.817	98.527	98.409	99.452	97.107	98.960
31	98.056	98.679	98.366	98.253	99.389	96.726	98.815
32	97.877	98.536	98.197	98.096	99.322	96.327	98.661
33	97.690	98.388	98.017	97.936	99.252	95.913	98.496
34	97.495	98.233	97.826	97.771	99.176	95.483	98.319
35	97.289	98.071	97.622	97.601	99.095	95.035	98.128
36	97.071	97.898	97.402	97.424	99.007	94.568	97.923
37	96.838	97.713	97.164	97.237	98.911	94.079	97.702
38	96.588	97.514	96.906	97.037	98.805	93.566	97.463
39	96.319	97.297	96.625	96.823	98.688	93.027	97.203
40	96.028	97.062	96.322	96.590	98.559	92.461	96.923
41	95.712	96.805	95.993	96.336	98.415	91.861	96.617
42	95.371	96.528	95.638	96.058	98.257	91.219	96.285
43	95.002	96.229	95.252	95.752	98.081	90.527	95.922
44	94.604	95.910	94.830	95.414	97.886	89.774	95.527
45	94.174	95.568	94.371	95.040	97.672	88.956	95.096
46	93.710	95.205	93.872	94.628	97.436	88.071	94.627
47	93.212	94.820	93.334	94.171	97.176	87.116	94.117

| | CSO (1980) | | | U. S. Life Tables (1982) | | | |
	Male	Female	Total Population	White Male	White Female	Black Male	Black Female
Life Expectancy	51.47	56.10	52.07	52.10	58.90	46.20	54.40
Age							
48	92.677	94.409	92.751	93.664	86.889	86.089	93.560
49	92.101	93.972	92.122	93.101	96.574	84.988	92.952
50	91.483	93.506	91.442	92.479	96.228	83.810	92.289
51	90.815	93.009	90.707	91.792	95.849	82.554	91.569
52	90.092	92.479	89.913	91.040	95.434	81.219	90.793
53	89.308	91.910	89.052	90.218	94.982	79.806	89.964
54	88.454	91.303	88.123	89.326	94.491	78.314	89.079
55	87.528	90.656	87.122	88.359	93.957	76.746	88.141
56	86.525	89.969	86.045	87.313	93.377	75.099	87.146
57	85.444	89.247	84.892	86.182	92.748	73.375	86.086
58	84.283	88.491	83.659	84.962	92.066	71.569	84.952
59	83.038	87.700	82.345	83.647	91.328	69.683	83.736
60	81.703	86.869	80.950	82.238	90.529	67.716	82.435
61	80.270	85.989	79.469	80.729	89.668	65.675	81.051
62	78.729	85.047	77.900	79.111	88.736	63.564	79.591
63	77.071	84.025	76.239	77.374	87.730	61.390	78.068
64	75.288	82.911	74.481	75.512	86.643	59.159	76.489
65	73.374	81.702	72.622	73.521	85.470	56.878	74.858
66	71.331	80.394	70.662	71.385	84.193	54.538	73.143
67	69.159	78.993	68.600	69.120	82.814	52.155	71.349
68	66.864	77.505	66.438	66.742	81.340	49.741	69.486
69	64.445	75.927	64.179	64.266	79.777	47.312	67.559
70	61.899	74.248	61.830	61.710	78.130	44.879	65.579

| | CSO (1980) | | Total Population | U. S. Life Tables (1982) | | | |
	Male	Female		White Male	White Female	Black Male	Black Female
Life Expectancy	51.47	56.10	52.07	52.10	58.90	46.20	54.40
Age							
71	59.219	72.449	59.392	59.186	76.459	42.524	63.599
72	56.397	70.502	56.858	56.422	74.568	40.117	61.484
73	53.428	68.380	54.218	53.567	72.549	37.735	59.305
74	50.319	66.059	51.466	50.630	70.400	35.384	57.068
75	47.089	63.533	48.609	47.621	68.116	33.071	54.774
76	43.768	60.803	45.663	44.560	65.683	30.791	52.399
77	40.393	57.882	42.651	41.462	63.099	28.551	49.948
78	37.004	54.789	39.600	38.344	60.365	26.359	47.429
79	33.635	51.537	36.535	35.225	57.486	24.225	44.848
80	30.310	48.136	33.468	32.125	54.465	22.156	42.215
81	27.052	44.593	30.415	28.912	51.123	20.001	39.339
82	23.881	40.919	27.406	25.645	47.460	17.787	36.227
83	20.818	37.132	24.475	22.333	43.489	15.547	32.900
84	17.898	33.278	21.649	19.055	39.240	13.317	29.392
85	15.160	29.414	18.930	15.877	34.764	11.144	25.754
86	12.642	25.611	16.327	12.867	30.133	9.073	22.054
87	10.373	21.941	13.881	10.096	25.445	7.155	18.375
88	8.368	18.470	11.639	7.624	20.823	5.433	14.817
89	6.633	15.257	9.626	5.504	16.406	3.944	11.486
90	5.162	12.347	7.845	3.764	12.343	2.714	8.489
91	3.939	9.768	6.285	2.412	8.773	1.751	5.917
92	2.941	7.533	4.942	1.427	5.810	1.044	3.840
93	2.140	5.638	3.812	0.765	3.519	0.564	2.272

	CSO (1980)		Total Population	U. S. Life Tables (1982)			
	Male	Female		White Male	White Female	Black Male	Black Female
Life Expectancy	51.47	56.10	52.07	52.10	58.90	46.20	54.40
Age							
94	1.507	4.064	2.884	0.362	1.899	0.269	1.195
95	1.010	2.774	2.142	0.145	0.878	0.109	0.538
96	0.621	1.732	1.564	> 0.001	0.001	> 0.001	> 0.001
97	0.323	0.909	1.126	> 0.001	> 0.001	> 0.001	> 0.001
98	0.110	0.313	0.800	> 0.001	> 0.001	> 0.001	> 0.001
99	> 0.001	> 0.001	0.561	> 0.001	> 0.001	> 0.001	> 0.001

Probability of surviving through age X starting from age 22

	CSO (1980)		Total Population	U. S. Life Tables (1982)			
	Male	Female		White Male	White Female	Black Male	Black Female
Life Expectancy	50.57	55.16	51.15	51.20	58.00	45.30	53.40
Age							
22	99.811	99.891	99.848	99.832	99.947	99.765	99.921
23	99.625	99.780	99.695	99.664	99.894	99.513	99.835
24	99.444	99.666	99.545	99.499	99.841	99.245	99.742
25	99.268	99.551	99.398	99.338	99.787	98.963	99.642
26	99.096	99.432	99.256	99.183	99.733	98.666	99.535
27	98.927	99.311	99.115	99.029	99.678	98.353	99.419
28	98.759	99.186	98.973	98.876	99.623	98.025	99.297
29	98.590	99.057	98.825	98.724	99.565	97.679	99.168

	CSO (1980)		Total Population	U. S. Life Tables (1982)			
Life Expectancy	Male	Female		White Male	White Female	Black Male	Black Female
	50.57	55.16	51.15	51.20	58.00	45.30	53.40
Age							
30	98.419	98.923	98.672	98.570	99.504	97.315	99.031
31	98.244	98.785	98.511	98.414	99.440	96.932	98.887
32	98.064	98.641	98.342	98.257	99.374	96.533	98.732
33	97.877	98.493	98.162	98.097	99.303	96.118	98.567
34	97.681	98.338	97.970	97.932	99.228	95.687	98.390
35	97.475	98.176	97.765	97.762	99.146	95.238	98.199
36	97.257	98.003	97.546	97.584	99.058	94.770	97.994
37	97.023	97.818	97.308	97.396	98.962	94.280	97.772
38	96.773	97.618	97.049	97.197	98.856	93.766	97.533
39	96.503	97.401	96.767	96.982	98.740	93.226	97.273
40	96.212	97.155	96.463	96.749	98.610	92.658	96.992
41	95.895	96.909	96.134	96.495	98.466	92.057	96.687
42	95.554	96.631	95.779	96.216	98.308	91.414	96.354
43	95.184	96.332	95.392	95.909	98.132	90.720	95.991
44	94.785	96.013	94.969	95.570	97.937	89.966	95.595
45	94.354	95.671	94.510	95.197	97.723	89.146	95.164
46	93.890	95.307	94.011	94.783	97.486	88.259	94.695
47	93.390	94.921	93.471	94.326	97.226	87.302	94.185
48	92.854	94.510	92.888	93.818	96.939	86.273	93.627
49	92.277	94.073	92.258	93.254	96.624	85.169	93.019
50	91.658	93.606	91.577	92.630	96.278	83.989	92.355
51	90.989	93.109	90.841	91.943	95.899	82.730	91.635
52	90.265	92.578	90.045	91.189	95.484	81.392	90.859

	CSO (1980)		Total	U. S. Life Tables (1982)			
	Male	Female	Population	White Male	White Female	Black Male	Black Female
Life Expectancy	50.57	55.16	51.15	51.20	58.00	45.30	53.40
Age							
53	89.479	92.009	89.183	90.367	95.031	79.976	90.028
54	88.623	91.401	88.253	89.473	94.540	78.481	89.143
55	87.695	90.753	87.251	88.504	94.006	76.909	88.205
56	86.690	90.066	86.172	87.456	93.426	75.260	87.209
57	85.608	89.342	85.017	86.324	92.796	73.532	86.148
58	84.444	88.586	83.782	85.101	92.114	71.722	85.013
59	83.197	87.794	82.467	83.785	91.375	69.831	83.797
60	81.859	86.962	81.069	82.373	90.577	67.861	82.494
61	80.423	86.081	79.586	80.861	89.714	65.815	81.109
62	78.880	85.138	78.015	79.241	88.782	63.700	79.648
63	77.219	84.115	76.351	77.502	87.775	61.521	78.124
64	75.432	83.000	74.590	75.636	86.688	59.285	76.544
65	73.514	81.789	72.729	73.642	85.515	56.999	74.912
66	71.467	80.481	70.766	71.533	84.256	54.671	73.210
67	69.292	79.078	68.701	69.310	82.906	52.306	71.438
68	66.992	77.588	66.536	66.971	81.461	49.909	69.595
69	64.569	76.008	64.274	64.518	79.916	47.487	67.681
70	62.018	74.328	61.921	61.952	78.267	45.045	65.697
71	59.332	72.527	59.479	59.283	76.499	42.614	63.645
72	56.505	70.578	56.942	56.295	74.436	40.112	61.419
73	53.531	68.453	54.297	53.392	72.373	37.714	59.217
74	50.416	66.130	51.542	50.429	70.196	35.354	56.965
75	47.180	63.601	48.680	47.432	67.919	33.044	54.675

Life Expectancy	CSO (1980)		Total Population	U. S. Life Tables (1982)			
	Male	Female		White Male	White Female	Black Male	Black Female
	50.57	55.16	51.15	51.20	58.00	45.30	53.40
Age							
76	43.852	60.868	45.730	44.341	65.442	30.751	52.275
77	40.470	57.944	42.714	41.199	62.793	28.494	49.787
78	37.075	54.847	39.659	38.044	59.998	26.289	47.233
79	33.699	51.592	36.589	34.914	57.087	24.149	44.635
80	30.368	48.187	33.517	31.841	54.087	22.086	42.015
81	27.104	44.641	30.460	27.587	48.682	19.189	37.571
82	23.926	40.962	27.447	22.643	41.512	15.794	31.829
83	20.857	37.172	24.511	17.553	33.431	12.278	25.466
84	17.932	33.313	21.681	12.806	25.339	8.984	19.177
85	15.189	29.446	18.957	8.759	18.006	6.162	13.539
86	12.667	25.639	16.351	5.592	11.942	3.945	8.921
87	10.392	21.964	13.902	3.315	7.354	2.345	5.458
88	8.384	18.490	11.656	1.814	4.181	1.287	3.083
89	6.646	15.274	9.640	0.910	2.179	0.647	1.596
90	5.172	12.360	7.857	0.415	1.032	0.296	0.751
91	3.946	9.779	6.294	0.170	0.440	0.122	0.318
92	2.946	7.541	4.949	0.062	0.167	0.045	0.120
93	2.144	5.644	3.817	0.020	0.055	0.014	0.039
94	1.510	4.068	2.888	0.005	0.016	0.004	0.011
95	1.012	2.777	2.145	0.001	0.004	0.001	0.003
96	0.623	1.734	1.567	> 0.001	0.001	> 0.001	> 0.001
97	0.324	0.910	1.128	0.010	0.087	0.008	0.050
98	0.111	0.313	0.801	0.001	0.013	0.001	0.007

	CSO (1980)		Total Population	U. S. Life Tables (1982)			
	Male	Female		White Male	White Female	Black Male	Black Female
Life Expectancy	50.57	55.16	51.15	51.20	58.00	45.30	53.40
Age 99	> 0.001	> 0.001	0.562	> 0.001	> 0.001	> 0.001	> 0.001

Probability of surviving through age X starting from age 23

	CSO (1980)		Total Population	U. S. Life Tables (1982)			
	Male	Female		White Male	White Female	Black Male	Black Female
Life Expectancy	49.66	54.22	50.22	50.30	57.00	44.50	52.50
Age							
23	99.814	99.889	99.847	99.832	99.947	99.747	99.914
24	99.632	99.775	99.696	99.666	99.894	99.479	99.821
25	99.456	99.659	99.550	99.505	99.840	99.196	99.721
26	99.284	99.541	99.407	99.350	99.786	98.899	99.614
27	99.114	99.419	99.266	99.196	99.731	98.585	99.498
28	98.946	99.294	99.123	99.043	99.675	98.256	99.376
29	98.776	99.165	98.976	98.890	99.618	97.909	99.246
30	98.606	99.031	98.822	98.736	99.557	97.544	99.109
31	98.430	98.892	98.661	98.580	99.493	97.160	98.965
32	98.250	98.749	98.491	98.422	99.426	96.760	98.810
33	98.062	98.601	98.311	98.262	99.356	96.344	98.645
34	97.866	98.445	98.119	98.097	99.280	95.912	98.468
35	97.660	98.283	97.914	97.926	99.199	95.463	98.277

| | CSO (1980) | | | U. S. Life Tables (1982) | | | |
	Male	Female	Total Population	White Male	White Female	Black Male	Black Female
Life Expectancy	49.66	54.22	50.22	50.30	57.00	44.50	52.50
Age							
36	97.441	98.110	97.694	97.748	99.111	94.993	98.071
37	97.207	97.924	97.456	97.560	99.015	94.502	97.850
38	96.956	97.725	97.196	97.360	98.909	93.987	97.610
39	96.686	97.508	96.915	97.145	98.792	93.445	97.350
40	96.394	97.272	96.610	96.912	98.662	92.876	97.069
41	96.077	97.015	96.281	96.657	98.518	92.274	96.763
42	95.735	96.736	95.925	96.378	98.360	91.629	96.430
43	95.364	96.438	95.537	96.070	98.184	90.934	96.067
44	94.965	96.117	95.114	95.731	97.989	90.177	95.671
45	94.532	95.775	94.653	95.357	97.775	89.356	95.240
46	94.067	95.411	94.154	94.943	97.538	88.467	94.770
47	93.567	95.025	93.613	94.484	97.278	87.508	94.259
48	93.030	94.613	93.029	93.976	96.991	86.476	93.701
49	92.452	94.175	92.398	93.411	96.676	85.370	93.092
50	91.832	93.708	91.716	92.786	96.329	84.187	92.428
51	91.151	93.211	90.979	92.098	95.950	82.925	91.707
52	90.436	92.679	90.182	91.343	95.534	81.584	90.931
53	89.648	92.109	89.319	90.519	95.082	80.164	90.100
54	88.791	91.500	88.387	89.624	94.590	78.666	89.214
55	87.861	90.852	87.383	88.653	94.056	77.090	88.275
56	86.854	90.164	86.303	87.603	93.475	75.437	87.278
57	85.770	89.440	85.146	86.469	92.845	73.705	86.217
58	84.604	88.682	83.910	85.244	92.163	71.891	85.080

| | CSO (1980) | | Total Population | U. S. Life Tables (1982) | | | |
	Male	Female		White Male	White Female	Black Male	Black Female
Life Expectancy	49.66	54.22	50.22	50.30	57.00	44.50	52.50
Age							
59	83.354	87.890	82.592	83.926	91.424	69.996	83.863
60	82.014	87.057	81.192	82.512	90.625	68.021	82.560
61	80.576	86.175	79.707	80.997	89.762	65.971	81.173
62	79.029	85.231	78.134	79.374	88.829	63.850	79.711
63	77.365	84.206	76.467	77.632	87.822	61.666	78.186
64	75.575	83.091	74.704	75.763	86.734	59.425	76.605
65	73.654	81.878	72.840	73.765	85.560	57.134	74.972
66	71.602	80.568	70.874	71.654	84.301	54.800	73.268
67	69.423	79.164	68.806	69.427	82.950	52.430	71.494
68	67.119	77.673	66.637	67.084	81.505	50.027	69.650
69	64.691	76.091	64.372	64.627	79.958	47.598	67.735
70	62.135	74.409	62.015	62.057	78.308	45.151	65.749
71	59.445	72.505	59.570	59.383	76.539	42.715	63.695
72	56.612	70.655	57.028	56.609	74.646	40.297	61.577
73	53.632	68.528	54.380	53.482	72.411	37.803	59.264
74	50.511	66.202	51.620	50.513	70.233	35.438	57.010
75	47.269	63.671	48.754	47.511	67.955	33.121	54.719
76	43.935	60.935	45.800	44.416	65.477	30.824	52.316
77	40.547	58.008	42.779	41.269	62.827	28.562	49.826
78	37.145	54.907	39.719	38.108	60.030	26.351	47.270
79	33.763	51.648	36.644	34.972	57.117	24.205	44.670
80	30.426	48.240	33.568	31.895	54.115	22.138	42.048
81	27.156	44.690	30.506	27.633	48.708	19.234	37.601

	CSO (1980)		Total Population	U. S. Life Tables (1982)			
	Male	Female		White Male	White Female	Black Male	Black Female
Life Expectancy	49.66	54.22	50.22	50.30	57.00	44.50	52.50
Age							
82	23.972	41.007	27.489	22.681	41.534	15.832	31.854
83	20.897	37.213	24.549	17.582	33.449	12.307	25.487
84	17.966	33.350	21.714	12.828	25.353	9.005	19.192
85	15.218	29.478	18.986	8.774	18.015	6.177	13.549
86	12.691	25.667	16.376	5.601	11.948	3.954	8.928
87	10.412	21.988	13.923	3.320	7.358	2.351	5.462
88	8.400	18.510	11.673	1.817	4.183	1.290	3.085
89	6.659	15.290	9.655	0.911	2.180	0.649	1.597
90	5.182	12.374	7.868	0.416	1.033	0.297	0.752
91	3.954	9.789	6.304	0.171	0.440	0.122	0.318
92	2.952	7.549	4.957	0.062	0.167	0.045	0.120
93	2.149	5.651	3.823	0.020	0.005	0.014	0.039
94	1.513	4.072	2.893	0.005	0.016	0.004	0.011
95	1.014	2.780	2.148	0.001	0.004	0.001	0.003
96	0.624	1.736	1.569	> 0.001	0.001	> 0.001	> 0.001
97	0.324	0.911	1.129	> 0.001	> 0.001	> 0.001	> 0.001
98	0.111	0.314	0.802	> 0.001	> 0.001	> 0.001	> 0.001
99	> 0.001	> 0.001	0.562	> 0.001	> 0.001	> 0.001	> 0.001

Probability of surviving through age X starting from age 24

| | CSO (1980) | | | U. S. Life Tables (1982) | | | |
	Male	Female	Total Population	White Male	White Female	Black Male	Black Female
Life Expectancy	48.75	53.28	49.30	49.40	56.00	43.60	51.50
Age							
24	99.818	99.886	99.849	99.834	99.947	99.731	99.907
25	99.641	99.770	99.702	99.672	99.893	99.448	99.807
26	99.469	99.651	99.560	99.517	99.839	99.149	99.699
27	99.299	99.530	99.418	99.363	99.784	98.835	99.584
28	99.130	99.404	99.275	99.210	99.728	98.505	99.461
29	98.961	99.275	99.127	99.057	99.670	98.157	99.332
30	98.789	99.141	98.974	98.902	99.610	97.791	99.195
31	98.613	99.002	98.812	98.746	99.546	97.407	99.050
32	98.433	98.859	98.642	98.588	99.479	97.006	98.895
33	98.245	98.711	98.462	98.427	99.409	96.588	98.730
34	98.049	98.555	98.270	98.262	99.333	96.156	98.553
35	97.842	98.392	98.064	98.091	99.252	95.705	98.361
36	97.622	98.219	97.844	97.912	99.163	95.234	98.156
37	97.388	98.033	97.605	97.724	99.067	94.741	97.934
38	97.137	97.833	97.345	97.524	98.961	94.225	97.694
39	96.866	97.616	97.063	97.309	98.844	93.682	97.434
40	96.573	97.380	96.758	97.075	98.715	93.112	97.153
41	96.256	97.123	96.428	96.820	98.571	92.508	96.847
42	95.913	96.844	96.072	96.540	98.412	91.862	96.513
43	95.542	96.545	95.683	96.232	98.236	91.165	96.150
44	95.141	96.224	95.260	95.892	98.041	90.406	95.753
45	94.709	95.882	94.798	95.517	97.827	89.583	95.322

Age	CSO (1980) Male	CSO (1980) Female	Total Population	White Male	White Female	Black Male	Black Female
Life Expectancy	48.75	53.28	49.30	49.40	56.00	43.60	51.50
46	94.243	95.517	94.298	95.103	97.590	88.691	94.852
47	93.741	95.130	93.757	94.643	97.329	87.730	94.340
48	93.203	94.718	93.172	94.134	97.042	86.695	93.782
49	92.624	94.280	92.540	93.568	96.727	85.587	93.172
50	92.003	93.812	91.857	92.942	96.380	84.400	92.508
51	91.331	93.314	91.118	92.253	96.001	83.135	91.786
52	90.604	92.782	90.320	91.496	95.585	81.791	91.009
53	89.815	92.212	89.456	90.671	95.132	80.368	90.177
54	88.956	91.602	88.523	89.774	94.640	78.866	89.291
55	88.025	90.953	87.517	88.802	94.105	77.286	88.350
56	87.016	90.264	86.436	87.751	93.525	75.628	87.353
57	85.929	89.539	85.276	86.614	92.894	73.892	86.291
58	84.762	88.781	84.038	85.388	92.212	72.073	85.153
59	83.510	87.987	82.719	84.067	91.472	70.173	83.935
60	82.167	87.154	81.317	82.650	90.673	68.193	82.631
61	80.726	86.271	79.829	81.134	89.809	66.138	81.243
62	79.177	85.326	78.254	79.508	88.876	64.012	79.780
63	77.509	84.300	76.584	77.763	87.869	61.822	78.253
64	75.716	83.183	74.818	75.891	86.780	59.576	76.671
65	73.791	81.969	72.952	73.890	85.606	57.278	75.036
66	71.736	80.658	70.983	71.743	84.326	54.923	73.316
67	69.552	79.252	68.911	69.467	82.945	52.522	71.519
68	67.244	77.759	66.739	67.076	81.469	50.092	69.651

U. S. Life Tables (1982): White Male, White Female, Black Male, Black Female

	CSO (1980)			U. S. Life Tables (1982)			
	Male	Female	Total Population	White Male	White Female	Black Male	Black Female
Life Expectancy	48.75	53.28	49.30	49.40	56.00	43.60	51.50
Age							
69	64.812	76.176	64.470	64.589	79.903	47.645	67.720
70	62.251	74.491	62.110	62.020	78.254	45.195	65.734
71	59.555	72.687	59.661	59.310	76.454	42.745	63.664
72	56.718	70.733	57.116	56.485	74.515	40.308	61.520
73	53.732	68.604	54.463	53.572	72.450	37.899	59.315
74	50.605	66.276	51.699	50.598	70.270	35.527	57.059
75	47.357	63.742	48.829	47.591	67.991	33.205	54.766
76	44.017	61.003	45.870	44.491	65.512	30.902	52.361
77	40.622	58.072	42.844	41.338	62.860	28.634	49.869
78	37.214	54.968	39.780	38.173	60.062	26.418	47.311
79	33.826	51.706	36.700	35.031	57.147	24.267	44.709
80	30.482	48.294	33.620	31.948	54.144	22.194	42.084
81	27.206	44.739	30.553	27.680	48.734	19.283	37.633
82	24.016	41.053	27.531	22.719	41.556	15.872	31.882
83	20.936	37.254	24.586	17.612	33.466	12.338	25.508
84	18.000	33.387	21.747	12.849	25.366	9.028	19.209
85	15.247	29.511	19.015	8.789	18.025	6.192	13.561
86	12.714	25.695	16.401	5.611	11.954	3.964	8.935
87	10.431	22.013	13.944	3.326	7.362	2.357	5.467
88	8.415	18.531	11.691	1.820	4.185	1.293	3.088
89	6.671	15.307	9.670	0.913	2.181	0.650	1.599
90	5.192	12.387	7.881	0.416	1.033	0.297	0.752
91	3.961	9.800	6.313	0.171	0.440	0.122	0.319

	CSO (1980)			U. S. Life Tables (1982)			
	Male	Female	Total Population	White Male	White Female	Black Male	Black Female
Life Expectancy	48.75	53.28	49.30	49.40	56.00	43.60	51.50
Age							
92	2.957	7.558	4.965	0.062	0.167	0.045	0.120
93	2.153	5.657	3.829	0.020	0.055	0.014	0.040
94	1.516	4.077	2.897	0.005	0.016	0.004	0.011
95	1.016	2.783	2.151	0.001	0.004	0.001	0.003
96	0.625	1.737	1.571	> 0.001	0.001	> 0.001	> 0.001
97	0.325	0.912	1.131	> 0.001	> 0.001	> 0.001	> 0.001
98	0.111	0.314	0.803	> 0.001	> 0.001	> 0.001	> 0.001
99	> 0.001	> 0.001	0.563	> 0.001	> 0.001	> 0.001	> 0.001

Probability of surviving through age X starting from age 25

	CSO (1980)			U. S. Life Tables (1982)			
	Male	Female	Total Population	White Male	White Female	Black Male	Black Female
Life Expectancy	47.84	52.34	48.37	48.40	55.00	42.70	50.60
Age							
25	99.823	99.884	99.853	99.838	99.946	99.716	99.900
26	99.650	99.765	99.710	99.682	99.892	99.417	99.792
27	99.480	99.643	99.569	99.528	99.837	99.102	99.676
28	99.311	99.518	99.425	99.347	99.781	98.771	99.554
29	99.141	99.389	99.277	99.221	99.723	98.422	99.424
30	98.969	99.254	99.123	99.067	99.662	98.055	99.287

| | CSO (1980) | | Total Population | U. S. Life Tables (1982) | | | |
Life Expectancy	Male	Female		White Male	White Female	Black Male	Black Female
	47.84	52.34	48.37	48.40	55.00	42.70	50.60
Age							
31	98.793	99.115	98.962	98.910	99.599	97.670	99.142
32	98.612	98.972	98.791	98.752	99.532	97.267	98.988
33	98.424	98.823	98.611	98.591	99.461	96.849	98.822
34	98.227	98.667	98.418	98.425	99.386	96.415	98.644
35	98.020	98.504	98.213	98.254	99.304	95.963	98.453
36	97.800	98.331	97.992	98.075	99.216	95.491	98.247
37	97.566	98.145	97.753	97.887	99.120	94.997	98.025
38	97.314	97.945	97.493	97.686	99.014	94.479	97.785
39	97.043	97.727	97.210	97.470	98.897	93.935	97.525
40	96.749	97.491	96.905	97.236	98.767	93.363	97.243
41	96.431	97.234	96.574	96.981	98.623	92.757	96.937
42	96.088	96.954	96.217	96.700	98.464	92.110	96.603
43	95.716	96.655	95.828	96.392	98.288	91.411	96.239
44	95.315	96.334	95.404	96.052	98.093	90.650	95.843
45	94.881	95.991	94.942	95.676	97.878	89.824	95.410
46	94.414	95.626	94.441	95.261	97.642	88.930	94.940
47	93.912	95.239	93.898	94.801	97.381	87.966	94.428
48	93.373	94.827	93.313	94.291	97.094	86.929	93.869
49	92.793	94.388	92.680	93.724	96.778	85.817	93.259
50	92.171	93.919	91.996	93.097	96.432	84.628	92.594
51	91.498	93.421	91.256	92.406	96.052	83.359	91.872
52	90.769	92.888	90.457	91.649	95.636	82.012	91.094
53	89.979	92.317	89.591	90.822	95.182	80.585	90.261

Age / Life Expectancy	CSO (1980)		Total Population	U. S. Life Tables (1982)			
	Male	Female		White Male	White Female	Black Male	Black Female
Life Expectancy	47.84	52.34	48.37	48.40	55.00	42.70	50.60
54	89.119	91.707	88.657	89.924	94.690	79.078	89.374
55	88.186	91.056	87.650	88.950	94.155	77.494	88.433
56	87.175	90.367	86.566	87.897	93.574	75.832	87.434
57	86.086	89.642	85.405	86.758	92.944	74.091	86.371
58	84.916	88.882	84.165	85.530	92.261	72.268	85.233
59	83.662	88.088	82.844	84.207	91.521	70.363	84.013
60	82.317	87.253	81.440	82.788	90.721	68.377	82.708
61	80.873	86.370	79.950	81.269	89.857	66.316	81.319
62	79.321	85.423	78.372	79.640	88.923	64.185	79.854
63	77.650	84.396	76.700	77.892	87.915	61.989	78.326
64	75.854	83.278	74.932	76.017	86.826	59.736	76.742
65	73.925	82.063	73.062	74.012	85.651	57.433	75.106
66	71.867	80.750	71.090	71.862	84.371	55.071	73.385
67	69.679	79.342	69.016	69.582	82.989	52.664	71.585
68	67.366	77.848	66.840	67.188	81.512	50.227	69.715
69	64.930	76.263	64.568	64.696	79.946	47.773	67.783
70	62.364	74.576	62.204	62.123	78.295	45.317	65.795
71	59.664	72.770	59.751	59.408	76.495	42.860	63.723
72	56.821	70.814	57.202	56.579	74.555	40.417	61.577
73	53.830	68.682	54.546	53.661	72.488	38.001	59.370
74	50.698	66.352	51.778	50.683	70.308	35.623	57.113
75	47.443	63.814	48.903	47.671	68.027	33.295	54.815
76	44.097	61.072	45.939	44.565	65.547	30.985	52.410

	CSO (1980)			U. S. Life Tables (1982)			
	Male	Female	Total Population	White Male	White Female	Black Male	Black Female
Life Expectancy	47.84	52.34	48.37	48.40	55.00	42.70	50.60
Age							
77	40.696	58.138	42.909	41.407	62.893	28.711	49.915
78	37.282	55.031	39.840	38.236	60.094	26.489	47.355
79	33.887	51.765	36.756	35.090	57.178	24.332	44.750
80	30.538	48.349	33.671	32.001	54.173	22.254	42.123
81	27.256	44.790	30.599	27.726	48.760	19.335	37.668
82	24.060	41.100	27.572	22.757	41.578	15.915	31.911
83	20.974	37.297	24.623	17.641	33.484	12.372	25.532
84	18.032	33.425	21.780	12.871	25.380	9.052	19.227
85	15.274	29.544	19.044	8.803	18.034	6.209	13.574
86	12.737	25.724	16.426	5.620	11.961	3.975	8.944
87	10.450	22.038	13.966	3.331	7.366	2.363	5.472
88	8.431	18.552	11.709	1.823	4.187	1.297	3.091
89	6.683	15.325	9.684	0.914	2.182	0.652	1.600
90	5.201	12.402	7.892	0.417	1.034	0.298	0.753
91	3.968	9.811	6.323	0.171	0.441	0.123	0.319
92	2.963	7.566	4.972	0.062	0.167	0.045	0.120
93	2.156	5.663	3.835	0.020	0.055	0.014	0.040
94	1.518	4.082	2.902	0.005	0.016	0.004	0.011
95	1.017	2.786	2.155	0.001	0.004	0.001	0.003
96	0.626	1.739	1.574	< 0.001	0.001	< 0.001	< 0.001
97	0.325	0.913	1.133	< 0.001	< 0.001	< 0.001	< 0.001
98	0.111	0.314	0.805	< 0.001	< 0.001	< 0.001	< 0.001
99	< 0.001	< 0.001	0.564	< 0.001	< 0.001	< 0.001	< 0.001

Probability of surviving through age X starting from age 26

| | CSO (1980) | | U. S. Life Tables (1982) | | | | |
	Male	Female	Total Population	White Male	White Female	Black Male	Black Female
Life Expectancy	46.93	51.40	47.44	47.50	54.10	41.80	49.60
Age							
26	99.827	99.881	99.857	99.844	99.946	99.700	99.892
27	99.656	99.759	99.715	99.689	99.891	99.384	99.776
28	99.487	99.633	99.572	99.536	99.835	99.052	99.653
29	99.317	99.504	99.423	99.382	99.777	98.702	99.524
30	99.145	99.370	99.269	99.227	99.716	98.334	99.387
31	98.968	99.230	99.107	99.071	99.653	97.948	99.241
32	98.787	99.087	98.937	98.912	99.586	97.544	99.087
33	98.599	98.938	98.756	98.751	99.515	97.125	98.921
34	98.401	98.782	98.563	98.585	99.439	96.690	98.743
35	98.194	98.619	98.357	98.413	99.358	96.236	98.551
36	97.974	98.445	98.136	98.234	99.269	95.763	98.346
37	97.739	98.259	97.896	98.046	99.173	95.268	98.123
38	97.487	98.059	97.636	97.845	99.067	94.748	97.883
39	97.215	97.841	97.353	97.628	98.950	94.203	97.622
40	96.921	97.604	97.047	97.394	98.821	93.629	97.340
41	96.602	97.346	96.716	97.138	98.676	93.021	97.034
42	96.258	97.067	96.358	96.857	98.517	92.372	96.700
43	95.886	96.767	95.969	96.548	98.341	91.671	96.335
44	95.484	96.446	95.544	96.208	98.146	90.908	95.938
45	95.050	96.102	95.082	95.831	97.931	90.080	95.506

| | CSO (1980) | | U. S. Life Tables (1982) | | | | |
Age	Male	Female	Total Population	White Male	White Female	Black Male	Black Female
Life Expectancy	46.93	51.40	47.44	47.50	54.10	41.80	49.60
46	94.582	95.737	94.580	95.415	97.694	89.184	95.035
47	94.079	95.350	94.037	94.955	97.434	88.217	94.523
48	93.539	94.937	93.450	94.444	97.146	87.177	93.963
49	92.958	94.497	92.816	93.876	96.830	86.062	93.352
50	92.334	94.028	92.131	93.248	96.484	84.869	92.687
51	91.660	93.529	91.391	92.556	96.104	83.597	91.964
52	90.930	92.996	90.590	91.797	95.687	82.245	91.185
53	90.138	92.424	89.723	90.969	95.234	80.814	90.351
54	89.277	91.813	88.787	90.070	94.742	79.304	89.463
55	88.342	91.162	87.779	89.094	94.206	77.715	88.521
56	87.330	90.472	86.694	88.039	93.625	76.048	87.522
57	86.239	89.746	85.531	86.899	92.994	74.302	86.458
58	85.067	88.985	84.289	85.669	92.310	72.474	85.318
59	83.810	88.190	82.966	84.343	91.570	70.563	84.097
60	82.463	87.355	81.560	82.922	90.770	68.572	82.790
61	81.016	86.470	80.068	81.401	89.906	66.505	81.400
62	79.462	85.522	78.487	79.769	88.972	64.368	79.934
63	77.788	84.494	76.813	78.018	87.963	62.166	78.404
64	75.988	83.375	75.042	76.140	86.873	59.907	76.819
65	74.057	82.158	73.170	74.133	85.697	57.597	75.181
66	71.994	80.844	71.195	71.979	84.416	55.228	73.458

Age	CSO (1980) Male	CSO (1980) Female	Total Population	U. S. Life Tables (1982) White Male	White Female	Black Male	Black Female
Life Expectancy	46.93	51.40	47.44	47.50	54.10	41.80	49.60
67	69.803	79.435	69.117	69.695	83.034	52.814	71.657
68	67.486	77.938	66.939	67.297	81.556	50.370	69.785
69	65.045	76.351	64.663	64.801	79.989	47.909	67.851
70	62.475	74.663	62.295	62.224	78.338	45.446	65.861
71	59.770	72.854	59.839	59.505	76.536	42.982	63.787
72	56.922	70.896	57.286	56.670	74.595	40.532	61.639
73	53.925	68.762	54.626	53.748	72.527	38.109	59.429
74	50.787	66.429	51.854	50.765	70.346	35.725	57.170
75	47.527	63.888	48.975	47.748	68.064	33.390	54.872
76	44.175	61.143	46.007	44.637	65.582	31.074	52.463
77	40.768	58.206	42.972	41.474	62.927	28.793	49.965
78	37.348	55.095	39.899	38.298	60.126	26.564	47.402
79	33.947	51.825	36.810	35.147	57.208	24.402	44.795
80	30.592	48.405	33.720	32.053	54.202	22.317	42.166
81	27.304	44.842	30.644	27.771	48.786	19.390	37.706
82	24.103	41.147	27.613	22.794	41.601	15.960	31.943
83	21.011	37.340	24.660	17.670	33.502	12.407	25.558
84	18.064	33.464	21.812	12.892	25.393	9.078	19.246
85	15.301	29.579	19.072	8.818	18.044	6.227	13.587
86	12.760	25.754	16.450	5.629	11.967	3.986	8.953
87	10.469	22.063	13.986	3.337	7.370	2.370	5.478

	CSO (1980)			U. S. Life Tables (1982)			
	Male	Female	Total Population	White Male	White Female	Black Male	Black Female
Life Expectancy	46.93	51.40	47.44	47.50	54.10	41.80	49.60
Age							
88	8.446	18.573	11.726	1.826	4.190	1.300	3.094
89	6.695	15.343	9.699	0.916	2.183	0.654	1.602
90	5.210	12.416	7.904	0.418	1.034	0.299	0.754
91	3.975	9.823	6.332	0.171	0.441	0.123	0.319
92	2.968	7.575	4.979	0.063	0.167	0.045	0.120
93	2.160	5.670	3.841	0.020	0.055	0.014	0.040
94	1.521	4.086	2.906	0.005	0.016	0.004	0.011
95	1.019	2.790	2.158	0.001	0.004	0.001	0.003
96	0.627	1.741	1.576	> 0.001	0.001	> 0.001	> 0.001
97	0.326	0.914	1.134	> 0.001	> 0.001	> 0.001	> 0.001
98	0.112	0.315	0.806	> 0.001	> 0.001	> 0.001	> 0.001
99	> 0.001	> 0.001	0.565	> 0.001	> 0.001	> 0.001	> 0.001

Probability of surviving through age X starting from age 27

	CSO (1980)			U. S. Life Tables (1982)			
	Male	Female	Total Population	White Male	White Female	Black Male	Black Female
Life Expectancy	46.01	50.46	46.51	46.60	53.10	40.90	48.70
Age							
27	99.829	99.878	99.858	99.845	99.945	99.683	99.884

| | CSO (1980) | | Total Population | U. S. Life Tables (1982) | | | |
Age	Male	Female		White Male	White Female	Black Male	Black Female
Life Expectancy	46.01	50.46	46.51	46.60	53.10	40.90	48.70
28	99.659	99.752	99.714	99.691	99.889	99.350	99.761
29	99.489	99.622	99.566	99.538	99.831	98.999	99.631
30	99.317	99.488	99.411	99.382	99.770	98.630	99.494
31	99.140	99.349	99.249	99.225	99.706	98.242	99.349
32	98.959	99.205	99.079	99.067	99.640	97.838	99.194
33	98.770	99.056	98.897	98.905	99.569	97.417	99.028
34	98.572	98.899	98.704	98.739	99.493	96.981	98.850
35	98.364	98.736	98.498	98.567	99.412	96.526	98.658
36	98.144	98.562	98.276	98.388	99.323	96.051	98.452
37	97.908	98.376	98.037	98.199	99.227	95.554	98.229
38	97.656	98.175	97.776	97.998	99.121	95.033	97.989
39	97.383	97.957	97.492	97.781	99.004	94.486	97.728
40	97.089	97.720	97.186	97.546	98.874	93.911	97.446
41	96.770	97.462	96.855	97.290	98.730	93.301	97.139
42	96.425	97.183	96.496	97.009	98.571	92.650	96.804
43	96.052	96.882	96.107	96.699	98.394	91.947	96.440
44	95.649	96.561	95.681	96.358	98.199	91.182	96.042
45	95.214	96.217	95.218	95.981	97.984	90.351	95.609
46	94.746	95.851	94.715	95.565	97.747	89.452	95.138
47	94.243	95.463	94.171	95.103	97.486	88.482	94.625
48	93.701	95.050	93.584	94.591	97.199	87.439	94.065
49	93.119	94.610	92.949	94.023	96.883	86.321	93.453
50	92.494	94.140	92.263	93.394	96.536	85.124	92.787

| | CSO (1980) | | Total Population | U. S. Life Tables (1982) | | | |
	Male	Female		White Male	White Female	Black Male	Black Female
Life Expectancy	46.01	50.46	46.51	46.60	53.10	40.90	48.70
Age							
51	91.819	93.641	91.521	92.701	96.155	83.848	92.063
52	91.088	93.107	90.720	91.941	95.739	82.493	91.283
53	90.295	92.534	89.852	91.111	95.285	81.057	90.449
54	89.431	91.923	88.914	90.210	94.793	79.542	89.560
55	88.495	91.271	87.904	89.233	94.257	77.949	88.617
56	87.481	90.580	86.818	88.177	93.676	76.277	87.616
57	86.388	89.853	85.654	87.035	93.044	74.526	86.551
58	85.214	89.092	84.410	85.802	92.360	72.692	85.410
59	83.956	88.295	83.085	84.475	91.620	70.775	84.188
60	82.606	87.459	81.676	83.052	90.819	68.778	82.880
61	81.157	86.573	80.183	81.528	89.954	66.705	81.488
62	79.599	85.624	78.600	79.894	89.020	64.561	80.021
63	77.923	84.595	76.923	78.140	88.010	62.353	78.489
64	76.120	83.474	75.149	76.259	86.920	60.087	76.902
65	74.185	82.256	73.274	74.248	85.744	57.770	75.262
66	72.119	80.940	71.297	72.091	84.462	55.394	73.537
67	69.924	79.529	69.216	69.804	83.079	52.973	71.734
68	67.603	78.031	67.035	67.402	81.600	50.521	69.861
69	65.158	76.442	64.755	64.902	80.032	48.053	67.924
70	62.583	74.752	62.385	62.321	78.380	45.583	65.933
71	59.873	72.941	59.925	59.598	76.577	43.112	63.856
72	57.020	70.981	57.368	56.759	74.635	40.654	61.706
73	54.019	68.844	54.704	53.832	72.566	38.224	59.493

| | CSO (1980) | | | U. S. Life Tables (1982) | | | |
Age	Male	Female	Total Population	White Male	White Female	Black Male	Black Female
Life Expectancy	46.01	50.46	46.51	46.60	53.10	40.90	48.70
74	50.875	66.508	51.928	50.844	70.384	35.832	57.232
75	47.610	63.965	49.045	47.823	68.100	33.490	54.931
76	44.252	61.216	46.073	44.707	65.617	31.167	52.519
77	40.839	58.275	43.034	41.539	62.961	28.880	50.019
78	37.413	55.160	39.956	38.358	60.159	26.644	47.453
79	34.006	51.887	36.863	35.201	57.239	24.475	44.844
80	30.645	48.463	33.768	32.103	54.231	22.384	42.211
81	27.351	44.896	30.688	27.814	48.813	19.448	37.747
82	24.144	41.196	27.652	22.829	41.623	16.008	31.978
83	21.048	37.384	24.695	17.697	33.520	12.444	25.585
84	18.096	33.504	21.843	12.912	25.407	9.105	19.267
85	15.328	29.614	19.099	8.831	18.054	6.245	13.602
86	12.782	25.785	16.474	5.638	11.974	3.998	8.962
87	10.487	22.090	14.006	3.342	7.374	2.377	5.484
88	8.460	18.595	11.743	1.829	4.192	1.304	3.097
89	6.707	15.361	9.712	0.917	2.184	0.656	1.603
90	5.219	12.431	7.915	0.418	1.035	0.300	0.755
91	3.982	9.834	6.341	0.172	0.441	0.123	0.320
92	2.973	7.584	4.987	0.063	0.167	0.045	0.120
93	2.164	5.677	3.846	0.020	0.055	0.014	0.040
94	1.524	4.091	2.910	0.005	0.016	0.004	0.011
95	1.021	2.793	2.161	0.001	0.004	0.001	0.003
96	0.628	1.744	1.578	> 0.001	0.001	> 0.001	> 0.001

	CSO (1980)			U. S. Life Tables (1982)			
	Male	Female	Total Population	White Male	White Female	Black Male	Black Female
Life Expectancy	46.01	50.46	46.51	46.60	53.10	40.90	48.70
Age							
97	0.327	0.915	1.136	> 0.001	> 0.001	> 0.001	> 0.001
98	0.112	0.315	0.807	> 0.001	> 0.001	> 0.001	> 0.001
99	> 0.001	> 0.001	0.566	> 0.001	> 0.001	> 0.001	> 0.001

Probability of surviving through age X starting from age 28

	CSO (1980)			U. S. Life Tables (1982)			
	Male	Female	Total Population	White Male	White Female	Black Male	Black Female
Life Expectancy	45.09	49.52	45.58	45.70	52.10	40.10	47.70
Age							
28	99.830	99.874	99.856	99.846	99.944	99.666	99.877
29	99.659	99.744	99.707	99.692	99.886	99.314	99.747
30	99.487	99.610	99.553	99.537	99.825	98.944	99.610
31	99.310	99.470	99.390	99.379	99.761	98.555	99.464
32	99.128	99.326	99.219	99.220	99.694	98.149	99.309
33	98.939	99.177	99.038	99.059	99.624	97.727	99.143
34	98.741	99.020	98.845	98.892	99.548	97.289	98.965
35	98.533	98.857	98.638	98.720	99.466	96.833	98.773
36	98.312	98.683	98.416	98.541	99.378	96.356	98.566
37	98.076	98.496	98.176	98.351	99.281	95.858	98.343
38	97.823	98.295	97.915	98.150	99.175	95.336	98.102

| | CSO (1980) | | Total Population | U. S. Life Tables (1982) | | | |
	Male	Female		White Male	White Female	Black Male	Black Female
Life Expectancy	45.09	49.52	45.58	45.70	52.10	40.10	47.70
Age							
39	97.550	98.077	97.631	97.933	99.058	94.787	97.842
40	97.255	97.840	97.324	97.698	98.928	94.209	97.559
41	96.935	97.581	96.993	97.441	98.784	93.598	97.251
42	96.590	97.301	96.634	97.159	98.625	92.945	96.917
43	96.216	97.001	96.243	96.849	98.448	92.239	96.552
44	95.813	96.679	95.817	96.507	98.253	91.472	96.154
45	95.377	96.335	95.353	96.130	98.038	90.638	95.720
46	94.908	95.968	94.850	95.713	97.801	89.737	95.248
47	94.403	95.580	94.305	95.251	97.540	88.764	94.735
48	93.861	95.166	93.717	94.738	97.252	87.717	94.174
49	93.278	94.725	93.081	94.169	96.936	86.595	93.562
50	92.652	94.255	92.394	93.539	96.589	85.395	92.895
51	91.976	93.755	91.652	92.845	96.208	84.115	92.170
52	91.244	93.221	90.849	92.083	95.792	82.755	91.389
53	90.449	92.647	89.979	91.253	95.338	81.315	90.554
54	89.585	92.035	89.041	90.350	94.845	79.795	89.664
55	88.647	91.382	88.029	89.372	94.309	78.197	88.720
56	87.631	90.691	86.941	88.314	93.727	76.520	87.718
57	86.536	89.962	85.775	87.170	93.095	74.763	86.652
58	85.360	89.200	84.530	85.936	92.411	72.923	85.510
59	84.099	88.403	83.203	84.606	91.670	71.001	84.286

| | CSO (1980) | | | U. S. Life Tables (1982) | | | |
	Male	Female	Total Population	White Male	White Female	Black Male	Black Female
Life Expectancy	45.09	49.52	45.58	45.70	52.10	40.10	47.70
Age							
60	82.747	87.566	81.793	83.181	90.869	68.997	82.976
61	81.296	86.679	80.297	81.654	90.004	66.917	81.583
62	79.736	85.729	78.712	80.018	89.069	64.767	80.114
63	78.056	84.698	77.033	78.262	88.059	62.551	78.580
64	76.250	83.576	75.256	76.378	86.968	60.278	76.991
65	74.312	82.357	73.379	74.364	85.791	57.954	75.350
66	72.242	81.039	71.398	72.203	84.508	55.570	73.623
67	70.043	79.626	69.315	69.912	83.125	53.142	71.818
68	67.719	78.126	67.130	67.507	81.645	50.682	69.942
69	65.269	76.536	64.847	65.003	80.076	48.206	68.003
70	62.690	74.843	62.473	62.418	78.423	45.728	66.009
71	59.976	73.030	60.010	59.690	76.620	43.249	63.930
72	57.118	71.068	57.450	56.847	74.676	40.783	61.777
73	54.111	68.928	54.782	53.915	72.606	38.345	59.563
74	50.963	66.589	52.002	50.923	70.422	35.946	57.298
75	47.691	64.043	49.115	47.897	68.138	33.597	54.995
76	44.328	61.291	46.138	44.776	65.654	31.266	52.580
77	40.909	58.346	43.095	41.603	62.996	28.971	50.078
78	37.477	55.228	40.013	38.417	60.192	26.729	47.509
79	34.065	51.950	36.915	35.256	57.271	24.553	44.896
80	30.698	48.522	33.816	32.153	54.261	22.455	42.260

U. S. Life Tables (1982)

	CSO (1980)		Total	White	White	Black	Black
	Male	Female	Population	Male	Female	Male	Female
Life Expectancy	45.09	49.52	45.58	45.70	52.10	40.10	47.70
Age							
81	27.398	44.951	30.732	27.857	48.840	19.510	37.790
82	24.186	41.247	27.692	22.865	41.646	16.059	32.015
83	21.084	37.430	24.730	17.725	33.539	12.484	25.615
84	18.127	33.544	21.874	12.932	25.421	9.134	19.289
85	15.354	29.650	19.127	8.845	18.064	6.265	13.618
86	12.804	25.817	16.497	5.647	11.980	4.011	8.973
87	10.505	22.117	14.026	3.347	7.378	2.384	5.490
88	8.475	18.618	11.760	1.832	4.194	1.308	3.101
89	6.718	15.380	9.726	0.919	2.186	0.658	1.605
90	5.228	12.446	7.927	0.419	1.035	0.301	0.755
91	3.989	9.846	6.350	0.172	0.441	0.124	0.320
92	2.978	7.593	4.994	0.063	0.167	0.045	0.120
93	2.168	5.684	3.852	0.020	0.055	0.015	0.040
94	1.526	4.096	2.914	0.005	0.016	0.004	0.011
95	1.023	2.796	2.164	0.001	0.004	0.001	0.003
96	0.629	1.746	1.581	>0.001	0.001	>0.001	>0.001
97	0.327	0.917	1.138	>0.001	>0.001	>0.001	>0.001
98	0.112	0.315	0.808	>0.001	>0.001	>0.001	>0.001
99	>0.001	>0.001	0.567	>0.001	>0.001	>0.001	>0.001

Probability of surviving through age X starting from age 29

| | CSO (1980) | | U. S. Life Tables (1982) | | | | |
	Male	Female	Total Population	White Male	White Female	Black Male	Black Female
Life Expectancy	44.16	48.59	44.64	44.70	51.20	39.20	46.80
Age							
29	99.829	99.870	99.851	99.846	99.942	99.647	99.870
30	99.656	99.735	99.696	99.690	99.881	99.275	99.732
31	99.479	99.596	99.534	99.533	99.817	98.885	99.587
32	99.297	99.451	99.363	99.373	99.750	98.478	99.431
33	99.107	99.302	99.181	99.211	99.679	98.054	99.265
34	98.909	99.145	98.987	99.045	99.604	97.615	99.086
35	98.700	98.981	98.780	98.872	99.522	97.157	98.894
36	98.479	98.807	98.558	98.693	99.433	96.679	98.688
37	98.243	98.621	98.318	98.503	99.337	96.179	98.465
38	97.989	98.419	98.056	98.301	99.231	95.655	98.223
39	97.716	98.201	97.772	98.084	99.114	95.104	97.962
40	97.421	97.963	97.465	97.848	98.984	94.525	97.679
41	97.100	97.705	97.123	97.591	98.839	93.912	97.371
42	96.755	97.424	96.773	97.309	98.680	93.256	97.036
43	96.380	97.123	96.382	96.999	98.503	92.548	96.670
44	95.976	96.801	95.955	96.656	98.308	91.778	96.272
45	95.540	96.456	95.491	96.278	98.093	90.942	95.838
46	95.070	96.090	94.986	95.860	97.856	90.037	95.365
47	94.564	95.700	94.441	95.397	97.594	89.061	94.851
48	94.021	95.286	93.852	94.884	97.307	88.011	94.290
49	93.437	94.845	93.216	94.314	96.990	86.886	93.677
50	92.810	94.374	92.528	93.683	96.643	85.681	93.009

	CSO (1980)		Total	U. S. Life Tables (1982)			
	Male	Female	Population	White Male	White Female	Black Male	Black Female
Life Expectancy	44.16	48.59	44.64	44.70	51.20	39.20	46.80
Age							
51	92.133	93.873	91.784	92.988	96.262	84.397	92.284
52	91.399	93.338	90.980	92.225	95.845	83.032	91.502
53	90.603	92.764	90.109	91.394	95.391	81.588	90.666
54	89.737	92.151	89.169	90.490	94.898	80.063	89.774
55	88.798	91.498	88.156	89.510	94.362	78.459	88.829
56	87.780	90.805	87.067	88.450	93.780	76.776	87.826
57	86.684	90.076	85.899	87.304	93.148	75.013	86.758
58	85.506	89.313	84.652	86.068	92.463	73.167	85.615
59	84.243	88.514	83.323	84.737	91.721	71.238	84.390
60	82.888	87.676	81.910	83.309	90.920	69.228	83.078
61	81.434	86.788	80.412	81.780	90.054	67.142	81.683
62	79.871	85.837	78.825	80.141	89.119	64.984	80.212
63	78.189	84.805	77.144	78.382	88.108	62.761	78.677
64	76.380	83.681	75.365	76.496	87.016	60.480	77.086
65	74.438	82.450	73.484	74.478	85.839	58.148	75.443
66	72.365	81.141	71.501	72.315	84.556	55.756	73.714
67	70.163	79.727	69.415	70.020	83.171	53.320	71.906
68	67.834	78.225	67.227	67.611	81.691	50.852	70.028
69	65.380	76.632	64.941	65.103	80.121	48.368	68.087
70	62.797	74.938	62.563	62.514	78.467	45.881	66.090
71	60.078	73.122	60.097	59.782	76.662	43.394	64.009
72	57.215	71.157	57.533	56.935	74.718	40.920	61.853
73	54.203	69.015	54.861	53.999	72.647	38.474	59.636

| | CSO (1980) | | | U. S. Life Tables (1982) | | | |
	Male	Female	Total Population	White Male	White Female	Black Male	Black Female
Life Expectancy	44.16	48.59	44.64	44.70	51.20	39.20	46.80
Age							
74	51.049	66.673	52.077	51.002	70.462	36.067	57.369
75	47.773	64.123	49.186	47.971	68.176	33.709	55.062
76	44.403	61.368	46.205	44.845	65.690	31.371	52.645
77	40.979	58.420	43.157	41.668	63.031	29.069	50.139
78	37.541	55.297	40.070	38.477	60.226	26.819	47.567
79	34.123	52.016	36.968	35.310	57.303	24.635	44.951
80	30.750	48.583	33.865	32.203	54.292	22.531	42.312
81	27.445	45.007	30.776	27.900	48.867	19.575	37.837
82	24.227	41.299	27.732	22.900	41.669	16.113	32.054
83	21.120	37.477	24.766	17.752	33.558	12.526	25.647
84	18.158	33.587	21.906	12.952	25.435	9.165	19.313
85	15.380	29.687	19.154	8.859	18.074	6.286	13.634
86	12.826	25.849	16.521	5.655	11.987	4.024	8.984
87	10.523	22.144	14.046	3.352	7.382	2.392	5.497
88	8.489	18.642	11.777	1.834	4.197	1.313	3.104
89	6.729	15.399	9.740	0.920	2.187	0.660	1.607
90	5.237	12.462	7.938	0.420	1.036	0.302	0.756
91	3.996	9.859	6.359	0.172	0.442	0.124	0.320
92	2.983	7.603	5.001	0.063	0.167	0.045	0.121
93	2.171	5.691	3.857	0.020	0.056	0.015	0.040
94	1.529	4.101	2.918	0.005	0.016	0.004	0.011
95	1.024	2.800	2.167	0.001	0.004	0.001	0.003
96	0.630	1.748	1.583	> 0.001	0.001	> 0.001	> 0.001

	CSO (1980)		Total Population	U. S. Life Tables (1982)			
	Male	Female		White Male	White Female	Black Male	Black Female
Life Expectancy	44.16	48.59	44.64	44.70	51.20	39.20	46.80
Age							
97	0.328	0.918	1.139	> 0.001	> 0.001	> 0.001	> 0.001
98	0.112	0.316	0.809	> 0.001	> 0.001	> 0.001	> 0.001
99	> 0.001	> 0.001	0.567	> 0.001	> 0.001	> 0.001	> 0.001

Probability of surviving through age X starting from age 30

	CSO (1980)		Total Population	U. S. Life Tables (1982)			
	Male	Female		White Male	White Female	Black Male	Black Female
Life Expectancy	43.24	47.65	43.71	43.80	50.20	38.30	45.80
Age							
30	99.827	99.865	99.845	99.844	99.939	99.627	99.862
31	99.649	99.725	99.682	99.686	99.875	99.235	99.716
32	99.467	99.581	99.511	99.527	99.808	98.827	99.561
33	99.277	99.431	99.329	99.365	99.737	98.402	99.394
34	99.078	99.274	99.135	99.198	99.661	97.961	99.215
35	98.869	99.110	98.928	99.025	99.580	97.501	99.023
36	98.648	98.936	98.705	98.845	99.491	97.022	98.816
37	98.411	98.749	98.464	98.655	99.395	96.520	98.593
38	98.157	98.547	98.202	98.453	99.288	95.994	98.351
39	97.883	98.329	97.918	98.235	99.171	95.441	98.090
40	97.588	98.091	97.610	97.999	99.041	94.860	97.806

| | CSO (1980) | | Total Population | U. S. Life Tables (1982) | | | |
	Male	Female		White Male	White Female	Black Male	Black Female
Life Expectancy	43.24	47.65	43.71	43.80	50.20	38.30	45.80
Age							
41	97.267	97.832	97.277	97.742	98.897	94.244	97.498
42	96.920	97.551	96.917	97.459	98.737	93.586	97.163
43	96.545	97.250	96.526	97.148	98.561	92.876	96.796
44	96.141	96.927	96.098	96.805	98.365	92.103	96.397
45	95.703	96.582	95.633	96.427	98.150	91.264	95.963
46	95.233	96.215	95.128	96.008	97.913	90.356	95.490
47	94.726	95.825	94.582	95.545	97.651	89.377	94.975
48	94.182	95.410	93.992	95.031	97.363	88.323	94.413
49	93.597	94.968	93.355	94.459	97.047	87.193	93.799
50	92.969	94.497	92.666	93.828	96.699	85.985	93.130
51	92.291	93.995	91.921	93.131	96.318	84.696	92.404
52	91.556	93.460	91.116	92.368	95.901	83.326	91.621
53	90.758	92.885	90.244	91.534	95.447	81.877	90.784
54	89.891	92.271	89.302	90.629	94.953	80.346	89.891
55	88.950	91.617	88.288	89.648	94.417	78.737	88.945
56	87.930	90.923	87.197	88.586	93.834	77.048	87.941
57	86.832	90.193	86.027	87.439	93.202	75.279	86.871
58	85.652	89.429	84.778	86.201	92.517	73.426	85.726
59	84.387	88.630	83.447	84.867	91.775	71.491	84.500
60	83.030	87.790	82.033	83.437	90.972	69.473	83.186
61	81.574	86.901	80.532	81.906	90.106	67.379	81.790
62	80.008	85.949	78.943	80.265	89.170	65.214	80.317
63	78.323	84.915	77.259	78.503	88.159	62.983	78.779

	CSO (1980)		Total Population	U. S. Life Tables (1982)			
	Male	Female		White Male	White Female	Black Male	Black Female
Life Expectancy	43.24	47.65	43.71	43.80	50.20	38.30	45.80
Age							
64	76.511	83.790	75.477	76.614	87.067	60.694	77.186
65	74.566	82.568	73.594	74.593	85.889	58.354	75.541
66	72.489	81.247	71.608	72.426	84.605	55.954	73.809
67	70.283	79.831	69.518	70.128	83.220	53.508	72.000
68	67.950	78.327	67.327	67.715	81.738	51.032	70.119
69	65.492	76.732	65.038	65.204	80.167	48.539	68.175
70	62.905	75.035	62.657	62.610	78.513	46.043	66.176
71	60.181	73.217	60.186	59.874	76.707	43.547	64.092
72	57.313	71.250	57.619	57.023	74.762	41.065	61.934
73	54.296	69.105	54.943	54.082	72.689	38.610	59.714
74	51.137	66.760	52.155	51.080	70.503	36.194	57.443
75	47.854	64.207	49.259	48.045	68.216	33.829	55.134
76	44.479	61.448	46.274	44.915	65.729	31.482	52.714
77	41.049	58.496	43.222	41.732	63.068	29.172	50.204
78	37.605	55.369	40.130	38.536	60.261	26.914	47.629
79	34.181	52.083	37.024	35.365	57.336	24.722	45.009
80	30.803	48.646	33.916	32.252	54.323	22.610	42.367
81	27.492	45.066	30.822	27.943	48.895	19.645	37.886
82	24.268	41.352	27.773	22.935	41.693	16.170	32.096
83	21.156	37.526	24.803	17.779	33.577	12.570	25.680
84	18.189	33.631	21.939	12.972	25.450	9.197	19.338
85	15.407	29.726	19.183	8.872	18.085	6.309	13.652
86	12.848	25.883	16.546	5.664	11.994	4.039	8.996

Age	CSO (1980) Male	Female	Total Population	White Male	White Female	Black Male	Black Female
Life Expectancy	43.24	47.65	43.71	43.80	50.20	38.30	45.80
87	10.541	22.173	14.067	3.358	7.386	2.401	5.504
88	8.504	18.666	11.794	1.837	4.199	1.317	3.108
89	6.741	15.419	9.755	0.922	2.188	0.663	1.609
90	5.246	12.478	7.950	0.420	1.037	0.303	0.757
91	4.003	9.872	6.369	0.172	0.442	0.125	0.321
92	2.988	7.613	5.008	0.063	0.167	0.046	0.121
93	2.175	5.698	3.863	0.020	0.056	0.015	0.040
94	1.532	4.107	2.923	0.005	0.016	0.004	0.011
95	1.026	2.804	2.170	0.001	0.004	0.001	0.003
96	0.632	1.750	1.585	> 0.001	0.001	> 0.001	> 0.001
97	0.328	0.919	1.141	> 0.001	> 0.001	> 0.001	> 0.001
98	0.112	0.316	0.810	> 0.001	> 0.001	> 0.001	> 0.001
99	> 0.001	> 0.001	0.568	> 0.001	> 0.001	> 0.001	> 0.001

Probability of surviving through age X starting from age 31

Age	CSO (1980) Male	Female	Total Population	White Male	White Female	Black Male	Black Female
Life Expectancy	42.31	46.71	42.77	42.90	49.20	37.50	44.90
31	99.822	99.860	99.837	99.842	99.936	99.607	99.854

| | CSO (1980) | | | U. S. Life Tables (1982) | | | |
Age	Male	Female	Total Population	White Male	White Female	Black Male	Black Female
Life Expectancy	42.31	46.71	42.77	42.90	49.20	37.50	44.90
32	99.639	99.715	99.665	99.682	99.869	99.197	99.698
33	99.449	99.566	99.483	99.520	99.798	98.770	99.532
34	99.250	99.408	99.289	99.353	99.722	98.328	99.353
35	99.041	99.244	99.081	99.180	99.641	97.866	99.160
36	98.819	99.070	98.858	98.999	99.552	97.385	98.953
37	98.582	98.882	98.617	98.809	99.455	96.881	98.729
38	98.327	98.681	98.355	98.607	99.349	96.353	98.487
39	98.053	98.462	98.070	98.389	99.232	95.798	98.225
40	97.757	98.223	97.762	98.153	99.102	95.215	97.941
41	97.435	97.964	97.428	97.894	98.957	94.597	97.633
42	97.088	97.683	97.068	97.611	98.798	93.937	97.297
43	96.713	97.381	96.676	97.300	98.621	93.224	96.930
44	96.307	97.058	96.247	96.957	98.426	92.448	96.531
45	95.869	96.712	95.782	96.578	98.210	91.606	96.095
46	95.398	96.345	95.276	96.158	97.972	90.695	95.622
47	94.890	95.954	94.729	95.694	97.711	89.711	95.106
48	94.345	95.539	94.138	95.179	97.422	88.654	94.543
49	93.759	95.097	93.500	94.607	97.106	87.520	93.929
50	93.130	94.625	92.810	93.974	96.758	86.307	93.259
51	92.451	94.123	92.063	93.277	96.377	85.013	92.531
52	91.715	93.586	91.257	92.512	95.960	83.638	91.748
53	90.916	93.010	90.384	91.678	95.505	82.183	90.909
54	90.047	92.396	89.441	90.771	95.011	80.647	90.016

| | CSO (1980) | | Total Population | U. S. Life Tables (1982) | | | |
	Male	Female		White Male	White Female	Black Male	Black Female
Life Expectancy	42.31	46.71	42.77	42.90	49.20	37.50	44.90
Age							
55	89.104	91.741	88.425	89.788	94.474	79.023	89.068
56	88.083	91.046	87.332	88.725	93.891	77.336	88.062
57	86.983	90.315	86.161	87.576	93.258	75.561	86.991
58	85.800	89.550	84.910	86.336	92.573	73.701	85.845
59	84.533	88.749	83.577	85.000	91.831	71.759	84.616
60	83.174	87.909	82.160	83.568	91.028	69.733	83.301
61	81.715	87.018	80.657	82.034	90.161	67.632	81.903
62	80.147	86.065	79.065	80.390	89.225	65.458	80.428
63	78.459	85.030	77.379	78.626	88.213	63.219	78.888
64	76.643	83.904	75.594	76.733	87.120	60.921	77.293
65	74.695	82.679	73.708	74.710	85.941	58.572	75.645
66	72.615	81.357	71.719	72.539	84.656	56.163	73.911
67	70.405	79.939	69.626	70.238	83.271	53.709	72.099
68	68.068	78.432	67.432	67.821	81.788	51.223	70.216
69	65.606	76.836	65.139	65.305	80.216	48.721	68.270
70	63.014	75.137	62.754	62.708	78.561	46.216	66.268
71	60.285	73.316	60.280	59.968	76.754	43.710	64.180
72	57.413	71.346	57.708	57.112	74.807	41.219	62.019
73	54.390	69.198	55.028	54.166	72.734	38.755	59.796
74	51.225	66.850	52.236	51.160	70.546	36.330	57.523
75	47.937	64.294	49.335	48.120	68.257	33.955	55.210
76	44.556	61.531	46.346	44.985	65.769	31.600	52.787
77	41.120	58.575	43.289	41.797	63.106	29.281	50.274

| | CSO (1980) | | | U. S. Life Tables (1982) | | | |
	Male	Female	Total Population	White Male	White Female	Black Male	Black Female
Life Expectancy	42.31	46.71	42.77	42.90	49.20	37.50	44.90
Age							
78	37.670	55.444	40.192	38.596	60.297	27.014	47.695
79	34.240	52.154	37.081	35.420	57.371	24.815	45.072
80	30.856	48.712	33.968	32.303	54.356	22.695	42.426
81	27.540	45.127	30.870	27.987	48.925	19.718	37.939
82	24.311	41.408	27.816	22.971	41.719	16.230	32.140
83	21.192	37.577	24.841	17.807	33.597	12.617	25.716
84	18.220	33.676	21.973	12.992	25.466	9.231	19.365
85	15.433	29.766	19.213	8.886	18.096	6.332	13.671
86	12.870	25.918	16.571	5.673	12.001	4.054	9.008
87	10.559	22.203	14.089	3.363	7.391	2.410	5.511
88	8.518	18.691	11.813	1.840	4.202	1.322	3.113
89	6.753	15.440	9.770	0.923	2.189	0.665	1.611
90	5.255	12.495	7.962	0.421	1.037	0.304	0.758
91	4.010	9.885	6.379	0.173	0.442	0.125	0.321
92	2.994	7.623	5.016	0.063	0.168	0.046	0.121
93	2.179	5.706	3.869	0.020	0.056	0.015	0.040
94	1.534	4.112	2.927	0.006	0.016	0.004	0.011
95	1.028	2.807	2.174	0.001	0.004	0.001	0.003
96	0.633	1.752	1.588	> 0.001	0.001	> 0.001	> 0.001
97	0.329	0.920	1.143	> 0.001	> 0.001	> 0.001	> 0.001
98	0.112	0.317	0.812	> 0.001	> 0.001	> 0.001	> 0.001
99	> 0.001	> 0.001	0.569	> 0.001	> 0.001	> 0.001	> 0.001

Probability of surviving through age X starting from age 32

	CSO (1980)		Total Population	U. S. Life Tables (1982)			
	Male	Female		White Male	White Female	Black Male	Black Female
Life Expectancy	41.38	45.78	41.84	41.90	48.20	36.60	44.00
Age							
32	99.817	99.855	99.828	99.840	99.933	99.588	99.844
33	99.626	99.705	99.645	99.677	99.862	99.160	99.677
34	99.427	99.548	99.451	99.510	99.786	98.716	99.498
35	99.217	99.383	99.243	99.337	99.704	98.253	99.305
36	98.995	99.209	99.020	99.156	99.616	97.769	99.097
37	98.757	99.021	98.778	98.965	99.519	97.264	98.873
38	98.503	98.819	98.515	98.763	99.412	96.734	98.631
39	98.228	98.600	98.230	98.544	99.295	96.176	98.369
40	97.931	98.361	97.921	98.308	99.165	95.591	98.084
41	97.609	98.101	97.587	98.049	99.020	94.970	97.775
42	97.262	97.820	97.226	97.766	98.861	94.307	97.439
43	96.885	97.518	96.834	97.454	98.684	93.592	97.072
44	96.479	97.194	96.405	97.110	98.489	92.813	96.672
45	96.040	96.848	95.938	96.730	98.273	91.967	96.236
46	95.568	96.480	95.431	96.311	98.035	91.052	95.761
47	95.059	96.089	94.884	95.845	97.773	90.065	95.245
48	94.514	95.673	94.292	95.330	97.458	89.003	94.681
49	93.927	95.230	93.652	94.757	97.168	87.865	94.066
50	93.296	94.758	92.961	94.123	96.820	86.647	93.395
51	92.615	94.254	92.214	93.424	96.439	85.348	92.667
52	91.878	93.717	91.406	92.658	96.021	83.968	91.882
53	91.078	93.141	90.531	91.823	95.566	82.507	91.042

Age	CSO (1980) Male	CSO (1980) Female	Total Population	U. S. Life Tables (1982) White Male	White Female	Black Male	Black Female
Life Expectancy	41.38	45.78	41.84	41.90	48.20	36.60	44.00
54	90.207	92.525	89.587	90.914	95.072	80.965	90.147
55	89.263	91.869	88.569	89.930	94.535	79.344	89.198
56	88.240	91.174	87.475	88.865	93.951	77.642	88.191
57	87.138	90.442	86.302	87.714	93.318	75.859	87.118
58	85.953	89.676	85.048	86.472	92.632	73.992	85.970
59	84.684	88.874	83.713	85.135	91.889	72.042	84.740
60	83.322	88.032	82.294	83.700	91.086	70.009	83.423
61	81.861	87.140	80.789	82.164	90.219	67.899	82.022
62	80.290	86.185	79.194	80.518	89.282	65.716	80.545
63	78.599	85.149	77.505	78.750	88.269	63.468	79.004
64	76.780	84.021	75.718	76.855	87.176	61.162	77.406
65	74.828	82.795	73.829	74.828	85.996	58.803	75.756
66	72.744	81.471	71.836	72.654	84.711	56.385	74.020
67	70.530	80.051	69.740	70.349	83.324	53.921	72.205
68	68.189	78.542	67.542	67.928	81.841	51.425	70.319
69	65.723	76.943	65.245	65.409	80.268	48.913	68.369
70	63.126	75.242	62.857	62.807	78.611	46.398	66.365
71	60.393	73.419	60.378	60.063	76.803	43.883	64.274
72	57.515	71.446	57.802	57.202	74.855	41.381	62.110
73	54.487	69.295	55.118	54.252	72.780	38.908	59.884
74	51.317	66.944	52.321	51.241	70.591	36.473	57.607
75	48.023	64.384	49.416	48.196	68.301	34.089	55.291
76	44.636	61.617	46.421	45.056	65.811	31.725	52.864

Life Expectancy	CSO (1980) Male	CSO (1980) Female	Total Population	White Male	White Female	Black Male	Black Female
	41.38	45.78	41.84	41.90	48.20	36.60	44.00
Age							
77	41.193	58.657	43.359	41.863	63.147	29.396	50.347
78	37.737	55.522	40.258	38.657	60.336	27.121	47.765
79	34.301	52.227	37.142	35.476	57.408	24.913	45.137
80	30.911	48.780	34.024	32.354	54.391	22.785	42.488
81	27.589	45.190	30.920	28.031	48.956	19.796	37.994
82	24.354	41.466	27.862	23.008	41.746	16.294	32.187
83	21.230	37.630	24.882	17.835	33.619	12.667	25.753
84	18.253	33.723	22.008	13.012	25.482	9.268	19.393
85	15.461	29.808	19.244	8.900	18.107	6.357	13.691
86	12.893	25.954	16.598	5.682	12.009	4.070	9.021
87	10.578	22.234	14.112	3.368	7.396	2.419	5.519
88	8.534	18.717	11.832	1.843	4.204	1.328	3.117
89	6.765	15.462	9.786	0.924	2.191	0.668	1.614
90	5.265	12.512	7.975	0.422	1.038	0.305	0.760
91	4.017	9.899	6.389	0.173	0.442	0.126	0.322
92	2.999	7.634	5.024	0.063	0.168	0.046	0.121
93	2.183	5.714	3.875	0.020	0.056	0.015	0.040
94	1.537	4.118	2.932	0.006	0.016	0.004	0.011
95	1.030	2.811	2.177	0.001	0.004	0.001	0.003
96	0.634	1.755	1.590	<0.001	0.001	<0.001	<0.001
97	0.329	0.921	1.145	<0.001	<0.001	<0.001	<0.001
98	0.113	0.317	0.813	<0.001	<0.001	<0.001	<0.001
99	<0.001	<0.001	0.570	<0.001	<0.001	<0.001	<0.001

Probability of surviving through age X starting from age 33

	CSO (1980)		Total Population	U. S. Life Tables (1982)			
	Male	Female		White Male	White Female	Black Male	Black Female
Life Expectancy	40.46	44.84	40.92	41.00	47.30	35.80	43.00
Age							
33	99.809	99.850	99.817	99.837	99.929	99.570	99.833
34	99.609	99.692	99.622	99.669	99.853	99.124	99.653
35	99.399	99.528	99.414	99.496	99.771	98.659	99.460
36	99.177	99.352	99.190	99.315	99.682	98.174	99.252
37	98.939	99.165	98.948	99.124	99.586	97.666	99.028
38	98.683	98.963	98.685	98.921	99.479	97.134	98.785
39	98.408	98.743	98.399	98.702	99.362	96.574	98.522
40	98.111	98.504	98.090	98.465	99.232	95.986	98.238
41	97.788	98.244	97.756	98.206	99.087	95.363	97.928
42	97.440	97.962	97.394	97.923	98.927	94.698	97.591
43	97.063	97.659	97.000	97.610	98.750	93.979	97.223
44	96.656	97.335	96.571	97.266	98.555	93.197	96.823
45	96.216	96.988	96.103	96.885	98.339	92.348	96.386
46	95.743	96.620	95.596	96.465	98.101	91.429	95.911
47	95.234	96.229	95.047	95.999	97.839	90.438	95.394
48	94.687	95.812	94.454	95.482	97.550	89.372	94.829
49	94.099	95.368	93.814	94.909	97.233	88.229	94.213
50	93.467	94.895	93.121	94.274	96.885	87.006	93.541
51	92.785	94.391	92.373	93.574	96.503	85.702	92.812

Life Expectancy	CSO (1980)		Total Population	U. S. Life Tables (1982)			
	Male	Female		White Male	White Female	Black Male	Black Female
	40.46	44.84	40.92	41.00	47.30	35.80	43.00
Age							
52	92.047	93.853	91.563	92.807	96.085	84.316	92.025
53	91.245	93.276	90.687	91.970	95.630	82.849	91.184
54	90.373	92.660	89.741	91.060	95.136	81.300	90.288
55	89.426	92.003	88.722	90.074	94.598	79.672	89.337
56	88.402	91.306	87.625	89.008	94.014	77.963	88.329
57	87.297	90.573	86.450	87.855	93.381	76.173	87.255
58	86.111	89.806	85.195	86.611	92.694	74.298	86.105
59	84.839	89.003	83.857	85.271	91.951	72.340	84.872
60	83.475	88.160	82.436	83.834	91.147	70.298	83.553
61	82.011	87.267	80.928	82.296	90.280	68.179	82.151
62	80.437	86.311	79.331	80.647	89.342	65.988	80.671
63	78.743	85.273	77.639	78.876	88.329	63.731	79.127
64	76.921	84.143	75.848	76.978	87.234	61.415	77.527
65	74.966	82.916	73.956	74.948	86.054	59.047	75.874
66	72.878	81.589	71.960	72.771	84.767	56.618	74.135
67	70.659	80.167	69.860	70.462	83.380	54.144	72.317
68	68.314	78.657	67.658	68.037	81.896	51.638	70.428
69	65.843	77.055	65.358	65.514	80.322	49.116	68.476
70	63.242	75.351	62.965	62.908	78.664	46.590	66.468
71	60.503	73.526	60.482	60.159	76.854	44.064	64.375
72	57.620	71.550	57.902	57.294	74.905	41.553	62.207

Life Expectancy	CSO (1980)			U. S. Life Tables (1982)			
	Male	Female	Total Population	White Male	White Female	Black Male	Black Female
	40.46	44.84	40.92	41.00	47.30	35.80	43.00
Age							
73	54.587	69.396	55.213	54.339	72.829	39.069	59.977
74	51.411	67.041	52.411	51.323	70.638	36.624	57.697
75	48.111	64.477	49.501	48.273	68.347	34.230	55.377
76	44.718	61.707	46.501	45.128	65.855	31.856	52.946
77	41.269	58.742	43.434	41.930	63.189	29.518	50.426
78	37.806	55.603	40.327	38.719	60.377	27.233	47.839
79	34.364	52.303	37.206	35.533	57.446	25.016	45.208
80	30.968	48.851	34.083	32.406	54.428	22.879	42.554
81	27.639	45.256	30.974	28.076	48.989	19.878	38.053
82	24.399	41.527	27.910	23.045	41.774	16.362	32.238
83	21.269	37.684	24.925	17.864	33.642	12.719	25.793
84	18.286	33.772	22.046	13.033	25.499	9.306	19.423
85	15.489	29.851	19.277	8.915	18.119	6.383	13.712
86	12.917	25.992	16.627	5.691	12.017	4.087	9.035
87	10.597	22.267	14.136	3.374	7.401	2.429	5.528
88	8.549	18.744	11.852	1.846	4.207	1.333	3.122
89	6.777	15.484	9.803	0.926	2.192	0.671	1.616
90	5.274	12.530	7.989	0.422	1.039	0.307	0.761
91	4.024	9.913	6.400	0.173	0.443	0.126	0.322
92	3.004	7.645	5.033	0.063	0.168	0.046	0.121
93	2.187	5.722	3.882	0.020	0.056	0.015	0.040

| | CSO (1980) | | | U. S. Life Tables (1982) | | | |
	Male	Female	Total Population	White Male	White Female	Black Male	Black Female
Life Expectancy	40.46	44.84	40.92	41.00	47.30	35.80	43.00
Age							
94	1.540	4.124	2.937	0.006	0.016	0.004	0.011
95	1.032	2.815	2.181	0.001	0.004	0.001	0.003
96	0.635	1.757	1.593	> 0.001	0.001	> 0.001	0.001
97	0.330	0.923	1.147	> 0.001	> 0.001	> 0.001	> 0.001
98	0.113	0.318	0.814	> 0.001	> 0.001	> 0.001	> 0.001
99	> 0.001	> 0.001	0.571	> 0.001	> 0.001	> 0.001	> 0.001

Probability of surviving through age X starting from age 34

| | CSO (1980) | | | U. S. Life Tables (1982) | | | |
	Male	Female	Total Population	White Male	White Female	Black Male	Black Female
Life Expectancy	39.54	43.91	39.99	40.10	46.30	34.90	42.10
Age							
34	99.800	99.842	99.805	99.832	99.924	99.552	99.820
35	99.589	99.677	99.596	99.658	99.842	99.085	99.626
36	99.366	99.502	99.372	99.477	99.753	98.598	99.418
37	99.128	99.314	99.130	99.286	99.656	98.088	99.193
38	98.872	99.111	98.866	99.082	99.550	97.553	98.950
39	98.596	98.891	98.579	98.863	99.432	96.991	98.687
40	98.298	98.652	98.270	98.626	99.302	96.401	98.402
41	97.975	98.391	97.935	98.367	99.157	95.775	98.092

	CSO (1980)			U. S. Life Tables (1982)			
	Male	Female	Total Population	White Male	White Female	Black Male	Black Female
Life Expectancy	39.54	43.91	39.99	40.10	46.30	34.90	42.10
Age							
42	97.626	98.109	97.572	98.082	98.977	95.107	97.755
43	97.248	97.806	97.178	97.770	98.820	94.385	97.386
44	96.841	97.481	96.748	97.424	98.625	93.599	96.985
45	96.400	97.134	96.279	97.044	98.409	92.747	96.547
46	95.926	96.765	95.771	96.622	98.170	91.824	96.071
47	95.416	96.373	95.221	96.156	97.908	90.829	95.554
48	94.868	95.956	94.627	95.638	97.620	89.758	94.988
49	94.279	95.512	93.986	95.064	97.302	88.610	94.371
50	93.646	95.038	93.292	94.428	96.954	87.382	93.698
51	92.963	94.533	92.542	93.727	96.572	86.072	92.967
52	92.223	93.994	91.731	92.958	96.154	84.680	92.179
53	91.419	93.416	90.853	92.120	95.698	83.206	91.337
54	90.546	92.799	89.906	91.209	95.203	81.651	90.439
55	89.598	92.141	88.885	90.221	94.665	80.016	89.487
56	88.571	91.443	87.786	89.153	94.081	78.300	88.476
57	87.464	90.709	86.609	87.998	93.447	76.502	87.401
58	86.276	89.941	85.351	86.752	92.760	74.619	86.249
59	85.002	89.137	84.011	85.410	92.016	72.652	85.014
60	83.635	88.293	82.587	83.971	91.212	70.602	83.693
61	82.168	87.398	81.077	82.430	90.344	68.474	82.288
62	80.591	86.440	79.476	80.778	89.405	66.273	80.806
63	78.894	85.401	77.781	79.005	88.391	64.006	79.259
64	77.068	84.270	75.987	77.104	87.296	61.680	77.657

Age	CSO (1980) Male	CSO (1980) Female	Total Population	U. S. Life Tables (1982) White Male	White Female	Black Male	Black Female
Life Expectancy	39.54	43.91	39.99	40.10	46.30	34.90	42.10
65	75.109	83.040	74.091	75.070	86.115	59.302	76.001
66	73.017	81.712	72.092	72.890	84.828	56.863	74.259
67	70.795	80.287	69.988	70.577	83.439	54.378	72.438
68	68.445	78.775	67.782	68.148	81.954	51.861	70.546
69	65.969	77.171	65.477	65.621	80.379	49.328	68.591
70	63.363	75.465	63.080	63.011	78.720	46.791	66.580
71	60.619	73.636	60.593	60.257	76.909	44.255	64.482
72	57.731	71.657	58.008	57.387	74.959	41.732	62.311
73	54.692	69.500	55.314	54.428	72.881	39.237	60.077
74	51.509	67.142	52.507	51.407	70.688	36.782	57.793
75	48.203	64.574	49.592	48.352	68.395	34.378	55.470
76	44.803	61.799	46.587	45.202	65.902	31.993	53.035
77	41.348	58.831	43.514	41.999	63.234	29.645	50.510
78	37.879	55.686	40.401	38.782	60.419	27.351	47.919
79	34.430	52.381	37.274	35.591	57.487	25.124	45.284
80	31.027	48.925	34.145	32.459	54.466	22.978	42.625
81	27.692	45.324	31.030	28.122	49.024	19.964	38.117
82	24.445	41.589	27.961	23.082	41.803	16.432	32.292
83	21.310	37.741	24.970	17.893	33.665	12.774	25.836
84	18.321	33.823	22.087	13.055	25.517	9.346	19.456
85	15.519	29.896	19.312	8.929	18.123	6.411	13.735
86	12.941	26.031	16.657	5.700	12.026	4.104	9.050
87	10.618	22.300	14.162	3.379	7.406	2.440	5.537

CSO (1980) / U. S. Life Tables (1982)

| | CSO (1980) | | | U. S. Life Tables (1982) | | | |
	Male	Female	Total Population	White Male	White Female	Black Male	Black Female
Life Expectancy	39.54	43.91	39.99	40.10	46.30	34.90	42.10
Age							
88	8.566	18.773	11.874	1.849	4.210	1.339	3.127
89	6.790	15.507	9.821	0.927	2.194	0.673	1.619
90	5.284	12.549	8.004	0.423	1.039	0.308	0.762
91	4.032	9.928	6.412	0.174	0.443	0.127	0.323
92	3.010	7.656	5.042	0.063	0.168	0.046	0.122
93	2.191	5.731	3.889	0.020	0.056	0.015	0.040
94	1.543	4.130	2.943	0.006	0.016	0.004	0.011
95	1.034	2.820	2.185	0.001	0.004	0.001	0.003
96	0.636	1.760	1.596	> 0.001	0.001	> 0.001	0.001
97	0.331	0.924	1.149	> 0.001	> 0.001	> 0.001	> 0.001
98	0.113	0.318	0.816	> 0.001	> 0.001	> 0.001	> 0.001
99	> 0.001	> 0.001	0.572	> 0.001	> 0.001	> 0.001	> 0.001

Probability of surviving through age X starting from age 35

| | CSO (1980) | | | U. S. Life Tables (1982) | | | |
	Male	Female	Total Population	White Male	White Female	Black Male	Black Female
Life Expectancy	38.61	42.98	39.07	39.10	45.30	34.10	41.20
Age							
35	99.789	99.835	99.791	99.826	99.918	99.531	99.806
36	99.565	99.659	99.566	99.644	99.829	99.041	99.597

	CSO (1980)		U. S. Life Tables (1982)				
	Male	Female	Total Population	White Male	White Female	Black Male	Black Female
Life Expectancy	38.61	42.98	39.07	39.10	45.30	34.10	41.20
Age							
37	99.327	99.471	99.324	99.453	99.732	98.529	99.372
38	99.070	99.268	99.059	99.249	99.626	97.992	99.129
39	98.794	99.048	98.772	99.030	99.508	97.428	98.865
40	98.495	98.808	98.462	98.792	99.378	96.835	98.579
41	98.171	98.547	98.126	98.532	99.233	96.206	98.269
42	97.822	98.264	97.763	98.248	99.073	95.535	97.931
43	97.443	97.961	97.368	97.934	98.895	94.809	97.562
44	97.035	97.635	96.937	97.588	98.700	94.021	97.160
45	96.594	97.288	96.468	97.207	98.483	93.164	96.722
46	96.118	96.918	95.958	96.785	98.245	92.237	96.245
47	95.607	96.526	95.407	96.317	97.983	91.237	95.726
48	95.058	96.108	94.812	95.799	97.694	90.162	95.159
49	94.468	95.663	94.169	95.224	97.376	89.008	94.541
50	93.834	95.188	93.474	94.587	97.028	87.775	93.867
51	93.149	94.683	92.723	93.885	96.645	86.459	93.134
52	92.408	94.143	91.911	93.115	96.227	85.061	92.346
53	91.603	93.564	91.031	92.275	95.771	83.581	91.502
54	90.727	92.946	90.082	91.362	95.276	82.019	90.602
55	89.777	92.287	89.058	90.373	94.737	80.376	89.648
56	88.748	91.588	87.957	89.303	94.153	78.652	88.636
57	87.640	90.853	86.778	88.146	93.518	76.846	87.558
58	86.449	90.083	85.518	86.898	92.831	74.955	86.404
59	85.172	89.278	84.175	85.554	92.086	72.979	85.168

| | CSO (1980) | | Total Population | U. S. Life Tables (1982) | | | |
	Male	Female		White Male	White Female	Black Male	Black Female
Life Expectancy	38.61	42.98	39.07	39.10	45.30	34.10	41.20
Age							
60	83.802	88.432	82.748	84.112	91.282	70.920	83.844
61	82.332	87.536	81.235	82.569	90.413	68.782	82.436
62	80.752	86.577	79.631	80.914	89.473	66.571	80.952
63	79.052	85.536	77.933	79.138	88.458	64.294	79.402
64	77.223	84.403	76.136	77.233	87.362	61.958	77.797
65	75.260	83.172	74.236	75.197	86.180	59.568	76.138
66	73.164	81.841	72.233	73.012	84.892	57.118	74.393
67	70.936	80.414	70.125	70.695	83.502	54.622	72.569
68	68.582	78.899	67.914	68.263	82.016	52.094	70.673
69	66.101	77.293	65.605	65.731	80.440	49.550	68.714
70	63.490	75.584	63.204	63.117	78.779	47.002	66.700
71	60.741	73.753	60.711	60.359	76.968	44.454	64.599
72	57.846	71.771	58.121	57.484	75.016	41.920	62.424
73	54.801	69.610	55.422	54.519	72.936	39.414	60.186
74	51.612	67.248	52.610	51.494	70.742	36.948	57.897
75	48.299	64.676	49.689	48.433	68.447	34.533	55.570
76	44.893	61.897	46.678	45.278	65.952	32.137	53.130
77	41.431	58.924	43.599	42.069	63.282	29.779	50.601
78	37.955	55.774	40.480	38.848	60.465	27.474	48.006
79	34.499	52.464	37.347	35.651	57.531	25.237	45.365
80	31.089	49.002	34.212	32.513	54.508	23.081	42.702

Age	CSO (1980) Male	CSO (1980) Female	Total Population	White Male	White Female	Black Male	Black Female
Life Expectancy	38.61	42.98	39.07	39.10	45.30	34.10	41.20
81	27.748	45.395	31.091	28.169	49.061	20.054	38.186
82	24.494	41.655	28.015	23.121	41.835	16.506	32.350
83	21.353	37.800	25.019	17.923	33.691	12.832	25.883
84	18.358	33.876	22.130	13.077	25.536	9.388	19.491
85	15.550	29.943	19.350	8.944	18.146	6.440	13.760
86	12.967	26.072	16.690	5.710	12.035	4.123	9.067
87	10.639	22.335	14.190	3.385	7.411	2.451	5.547
88	8.583	18.802	11.897	1.852	4.213	1.345	3.133
89	6.804	15.532	9.840	0.929	2.196	0.676	1.622
90	5.295	12.569	8.019	0.424	1.040	0.309	0.763
91	4.040	9.944	6.424	0.174	0.443	0.127	0.323
92	3.016	7.669	5.052	0.063	0.168	0.047	0.122
93	2.195	5.740	3.897	0.020	0.056	0.015	0.040
94	1.546	4.137	2.948	0.006	0.016	0.004	0.011
95	1.036	2.824	2.189	0.001	0.004	0.001	0.003
96	0.637	1.763	1.599	> 0.001	0.001	> 0.001	0.001
97	0.331	0.926	1.151	> 0.001	> 0.001	> 0.001	> 0.001
98	0.113	0.319	0.817	> 0.001	> 0.001	> 0.001	> 0.001
99	> 0.001	> 0.001	0.573	> 0.001	> 0.001	> 0.001	> 0.001

U. S. Life Tables (1982)

Probability of surviving through age X starting from age 36

| | CSO (1980) | | Total Population | U. S. Life Tables (1982) | | | |
	Male	Female		White Male	White Female	Black Male	Black Female
Life Expectancy	37.69	42.05	38.15	38.20	44.40	33.20	40.30
Age							
36	99.776	99.824	99.775	99.818	99.911	99.508	99.791
37	99.537	99.635	99.532	99.626	99.814	98.994	99.565
38	99.280	99.432	99.267	99.422	99.707	98.454	99.322
39	99.003	99.211	98.979	99.202	99.590	97.887	99.057
40	98.704	98.971	98.668	98.964	99.459	97.291	98.771
41	98.379	98.710	98.332	98.704	99.314	96.659	98.460
42	98.029	98.427	97.968	98.419	99.154	95.985	98.121
43	97.649	98.123	97.572	98.105	98.977	95.256	97.751
44	97.240	97.797	97.140	97.759	98.781	94.464	97.349
45	96.798	97.449	96.670	97.376	98.564	93.603	96.910
46	96.322	97.078	96.159	96.954	98.326	92.672	96.432
47	95.809	96.685	95.607	96.485	98.063	91.667	95.912
48	95.259	96.266	95.011	95.966	97.774	90.586	95.344
49	94.668	95.821	94.367	95.390	97.456	89.428	94.724
50	94.032	95.345	93.670	94.751	97.107	88.188	94.049
51	93.346	94.839	92.917	94.048	96.725	86.866	93.316
52	92.603	94.299	92.103	93.277	96.306	85.462	92.525
53	91.796	93.719	91.222	92.436	95.849	83.975	91.679
54	90.919	93.099	90.270	91.522	95.354	82.405	90.778
55	89.967	92.439	89.245	90.530	94.815	80.755	89.822
56	88.936	91.739	88.142	89.459	94.230	79.022	88.808
57	87.825	91.003	86.960	88.300	93.595	77.208	87.728

| | CSO (1980) | | | U. S. Life Tables (1982) | | | |
Age	Male	Female	Total Population	White Male	White Female	Black Male	Black Female
Life Expectancy	37.69	42.05	38.15	38.20	44.40	33.20	40.30
58	86.632	90.232	85.697	87.050	92.907	75.308	86.572
59	85.352	89.425	84.352	85.703	92.162	73.323	85.333
60	83.980	88.578	82.922	84.259	91.356	71.254	84.007
61	82.507	87.681	81.405	82.713	90.487	69.106	82.597
62	80.923	86.720	79.798	81.055	89.547	66.885	81.109
63	79.219	85.678	78.096	79.276	88.531	64.597	79.557
64	77.386	84.542	76.295	77.368	87.434	62.249	77.948
65	75.419	83.309	74.392	75.328	86.251	59.849	76.286
66	73.318	81.976	72.384	73.139	84.962	57.388	74.538
67	71.086	80.547	70.272	70.819	83.571	54.880	72.710
68	68.727	79.030	68.057	68.382	82.083	52.340	70.811
69	66.241	77.421	65.743	65.846	80.506	49.783	68.848
70	63.624	75.709	63.336	63.227	78.844	47.223	66.829
71	60.869	73.874	60.839	60.464	77.031	44.663	64.724
72	57.969	71.889	58.243	57.584	75.077	42.117	62.545
73	54.917	69.725	55.538	54.614	72.996	39.600	60.303
74	51.722	67.359	52.720	51.583	70.800	37.122	58.010
75	48.402	64.783	49.793	48.518	68.504	34.696	55.678
76	44.988	62.000	46.775	45.357	66.006	32.289	53.234
77	41.518	59.021	43.690	42.143	63.334	29.919	50.700
78	38.035	55.866	40.565	38.915	60.515	27.603	48.099
79	34.572	52.551	37.425	35.713	57.578	25.356	45.453
80	31.155	49.083	34.283	32.570	54.552	23.190	42.785

| | CSO (1980) | | Total Population | U. S. Life Tables (1982) | | | |
Age	Male	Female		White Male	White Female	Black Male	Black Female
Life Expectancy	37.69	42.05	38.15	38.20	44.40	33.20	40.30
81	27.806	45.470	31.156	28.218	49.102	20.148	38.260
82	24.546	41.724	28.074	23.161	41.869	16.584	32.413
83	21.398	37.863	25.072	17.954	33.719	12.892	25.933
84	18.397	33.932	22.176	13.099	25.557	9.433	19.529
85	15.583	29.993	19.391	8.960	18.161	6.470	13.787
86	12.995	26.115	16.725	5.720	12.045	4.142	9.084
87	10.662	22.372	14.220	3.391	7.418	2.462	5.558
88	8.601	18.833	11.922	1.855	4.217	1.351	3.139
89	6.818	15.558	9.860	0.931	2.197	0.680	1.625
90	5.306	12.590	8.036	0.424	1.041	0.311	0.765
91	4.049	9.960	6.438	0.174	0.444	0.128	0.324
92	3.022	7.681	5.063	0.064	0.168	0.047	0.122
93	2.200	5.749	3.905	0.020	0.056	0.015	0.040
94	1.549	4.144	2.954	0.006	0.016	0.004	0.011
95	1.038	2.829	2.194	0.001	0.004	0.004	0.003
96	0.639	1.766	1.602	> 0.001	0.001	0.001	0.001
97	0.332	0.927	1.153	> 0.001	> 0.001	> 0.001	> 0.001
98	0.114	0.319	0.819	> 0.001	> 0.001	> 0.001	> 0.001
99	> 0.001	> 0.001	0.574	> 0.001	> 0.001	> 0.001	> 0.001

Probability of surviving through age X starting from age 37

| | CSO (1980) | | | U. S. Life Tables (1982) | | | |
	Male	Female	Total Population	White Male	White Female	Black Male	Black Female
Life Expectancy	36.78	41.12	37.23	37.30	43.40	32.40	39.30
Age							
37	99.760	99.811	99.756	99.808	99.903	99.483	99.774
38	99.503	99.607	99.491	99.603	99.796	98.941	99.530
39	99.225	99.386	99.202	99.383	99.678	98.371	99.265
40	98.925	99.146	98.891	99.145	99.548	97.772	98.978
41	98.600	98.884	98.553	98.884	99.402	97.137	98.666
42	98.249	98.600	98.189	98.598	99.242	96.459	98.327
43	97.869	98.296	97.792	98.284	99.065	95.727	97.956
44	97.459	97.969	97.359	97.937	98.869	94.931	97.552
45	97.015	97.620	96.888	97.554	98.652	94.066	97.113
46	96.538	97.249	96.376	97.130	98.413	93.130	96.634
47	96.024	96.856	95.823	96.661	98.151	92.120	96.113
48	95.473	96.436	95.225	96.141	97.861	91.034	95.544
49	94.880	95.990	94.579	95.563	97.543	89.870	94.923
50	94.244	95.514	93.881	94.924	97.194	88.624	94.246
51	93.556	95.006	93.127	94.220	96.811	87.296	93.511
52	92.811	94.465	92.311	93.447	96.392	85.884	92.719
53	92.002	93.884	91.427	92.604	95.935	84.390	91.871
54	91.123	93.263	90.474	91.688	95.439	82.813	90.968
55	90.169	92.602	89.446	90.695	94.900	81.154	90.010
56	89.136	91.901	88.340	89.622	94.314	79.413	88.994
57	88.022	91.163	87.156	88.461	93.678	77.590	87.912
58	86.826	90.391	85.890	87.208	92.990	75.680	86.753

| | CSO (1980) | | Total Population | U. S. Life Tables (1982) | | | |
	Male	Female		White Male	White Female	Black Male	Black Female
Life Expectancy	36.78	41.12	37.23	37.30	43.40	32.40	39.30
Age							
59	85.544	89.583	84.542	85.859	92.244	73.685	85.512
60	84.168	88.735	83.109	84.413	91.438	71.606	84.183
61	82.692	87.836	81.589	82.864	90.567	69.448	82.770
62	81.105	86.873	79.978	81.203	89.626	67.216	81.279
63	79.397	85.829	78.272	79.421	88.610	64.916	79.723
64	77.560	84.692	76.467	77.509	87.512	62.557	78.111
65	75.588	83.456	74.559	75.465	86.328	60.145	76.446
66	73.483	82.121	72.547	73.273	85.037	57.671	74.694
67	71.246	80.689	70.430	70.948	83.645	55.151	72.862
68	68.881	79.169	68.210	68.507	82.156	52.599	70.959
69	66.390	77.557	65.891	65.966	80.577	50.029	68.992
70	63.767	75.842	63.479	63.342	78.914	47.457	66.969
71	61.006	74.005	60.976	60.574	77.099	44.884	64.860
72	58.099	72.016	58.375	57.689	75.144	42.326	62.676
73	55.041	69.848	55.664	54.714	73.061	39.795	60.429
74	51.838	67.478	52.839	51.677	70.863	37.305	58.132
75	48.510	64.898	49.905	48.606	68.565	34.867	55.795
76	45.089	62.109	46.881	45.439	66.065	32.448	53.345
77	41.612	59.125	43.789	42.220	63.390	30.067	50.806
78	38.120	55.965	40.656	38.986	60.569	27.740	48.200
79	34.650	52.643	37.509	35.778	57.629	25.481	45.549
80	31.225	49.169	34.361	32.629	54.601	23.304	42.875

Age	CSO (1980) Male	CSO (1980) Female	Total Population	U. S. Life Tables (1982) White Male	White Female	Black Male	Black Female
Life Expectancy	36.78	41.12	37.23	37.30	43.40	32.40	39.30
81	27.869	45.551	31.226	28.270	49.145	20.248	38.340
82	24.601	41.797	28.137	23.204	41.907	16.666	32.481
83	21.446	37.930	25.128	17.987	33.749	12.956	25.988
84	18.438	33.992	22.226	13.123	25.580	9.479	19.570
85	15.618	30.046	19.434	8.976	18.177	6.502	13.816
86	13.024	26.161	16.763	5.730	12.055	4.163	9.103
87	10.685	22.412	14.252	3.397	7.424	2.475	5.570
88	8.620	18.867	11.949	1.859	4.220	1.358	3.146
89	6.833	15.585	9.883	0.932	2.199	0.683	1.629
90	5.318	12.612	8.054	0.425	1.042	0.312	0.766
91	4.058	9.978	6.452	0.174	0.444	0.129	0.325
92	3.029	7.695	5.074	0.064	0.168	0.047	0.122
93	2.205	5.759	3.914	0.020	0.056	0.015	0.040
94	1.553	4.151	2.961	0.006	0.016	0.004	0.011
95	1.040	2.834	2.199	0.001	0.004	0.001	0.003
96	0.640	1.769	1.606	> 0.001	0.001	> 0.001	0.001
97	0.333	0.929	1.156	> 0.001	> 0.001	> 0.001	> 0.001
98	0.114	0.320	0.821	> 0.001	> 0.001	> 0.001	> 0.001
99	> 0.001	> 0.001	0.576	> 0.001	> 0.001	> 0.001	> 0.001

Probability of surviving through age X starting from age 38

	CSO (1980)		Total Population	U. S. Life Tables (1982)			
	Male	Female		White Male	White Female	Black Male	Black Female
Life Expectancy	35.87	40.20	36.32	36.30	42.50	31.60	38.40
Age							
38	99.742	99.796	99.734	99.795	99.893	99.455	99.755
39	99.464	99.574	99.445	99.574	99.775	98.882	99.490
40	99.163	99.333	99.133	99.335	99.644	98.280	99.202
41	98.837	99.071	98.794	99.074	99.499	97.642	98.890
42	98.485	98.787	98.429	98.788	99.339	96.961	98.549
43	98.104	98.482	98.031	98.473	99.161	96.225	98.178
44	97.693	98.155	97.597	98.125	98.965	95.424	97.773
45	97.249	97.805	97.125	97.741	98.748	94.555	97.332
46	96.770	97.434	96.612	97.317	98.509	93.614	96.853
47	96.255	97.039	96.057	96.847	98.246	92.599	96.331
48	95.703	96.619	95.458	96.326	97.956	91.507	95.760
49	95.108	96.171	94.811	95.747	97.638	90.337	95.138
50	94.470	95.694	94.111	95.107	97.288	89.085	94.460
51	93.781	95.186	93.354	94.401	96.905	87.750	93.723
52	93.034	94.644	92.537	93.627	96.485	86.331	92.929
53	92.224	94.062	91.651	92.782	96.028	84.828	92.080
54	91.342	93.440	90.695	91.865	95.531	83.243	91.174
55	90.386	92.777	89.665	90.870	94.992	81.576	90.214
56	89.350	92.075	88.556	89.794	94.406	79.826	89.196
57	88.234	91.336	87.369	88.631	93.769	77.993	88.111
58	87.035	90.562	86.100	87.376	93.080	76.074	86.950
59	85.749	89.753	84.749	86.024	92.334	74.068	85.706

| | CSO (1980) | | Total Population | U. S. Life Tables (1982) | | | |
	Male	Female		White Male	White Female	Black Male	Black Female
Life Expectancy	35.87	40.20	36.32	36.30	42.50	31.60	38.40
Age							
60	84.371	88.903	83.312	84.575	91.527	71.978	84.374
61	82.891	88.002	81.788	83.023	90.655	69.809	82.957
62	81.300	87.037	80.174	81.359	89.713	67.565	81.463
63	79.588	85.991	78.464	79.573	88.696	65.254	79.904
64	77.746	84.852	76.654	77.658	87.597	62.882	78.288
65	75.770	83.614	74.742	75.610	86.412	60.458	76.619
66	73.660	82.276	72.725	73.414	85.120	57.971	74.863
67	71.417	80.842	70.602	71.084	83.727	55.438	73.027
68	69.047	79.319	68.377	68.638	82.236	52.872	71.120
69	66.550	77.704	66.052	66.093	80.656	50.289	69.148
70	63.920	75.986	63.634	63.464	78.991	47.703	67.121
71	61.153	74.145	61.125	60.691	77.174	45.117	65.007
72	58.239	72.153	58.517	57.800	75.217	42.546	62.818
73	55.173	69.980	55.800	54.819	73.132	40.002	60.566
74	51.962	67.606	52.968	51.777	70.932	37.499	58.263
75	48.627	65.020	50.027	48.700	68.631	35.048	55.921
76	45.197	62.226	46.996	45.527	66.129	32.617	53.466
77	41.712	59.237	43.896	42.301	63.452	30.223	50.921
78	38.212	56.071	40.756	39.061	60.628	27.884	48.309
79	34.733	52.743	37.601	35.847	57.685	25.614	45.652
80	31.300	49.263	34.445	32.692	54.654	23.426	42.972

	CSO (1980)		Total Population	U. S. Life Tables (1982)			
	Male	Female		White Male	White Female	Black Male	Black Female
Life Expectancy	35.87	40.20	36.32	36.30	42.50	31.60	38.40
Age							
81	27.936	45.637	31.303	28.324	49.193	20.353	38.427
82	24.660	41.876	28.206	23.248	41.947	16.753	32.554
83	21.497	38.002	25.190	18.022	33.781	13.023	26.047
84	18.482	34.057	22.281	13.148	25.605	9.529	19.614
85	15.655	30.103	19.482	8.993	18.195	6.536	13.847
86	13.055	26.211	16.804	5.741	12.067	4.184	9.124
87	10.711	22.454	14.287	3.403	7.431	2.487	5.582
88	8.641	18.902	11.978	1.862	4.225	1.365	3.153
89	6.850	15.614	9.907	0.934	2.201	0.687	1.632
90	5.331	12.636	8.074	0.426	1.043	0.314	0.768
91	4.067	9.997	6.468	0.175	0.445	0.129	0.325
92	3.037	7.709	5.086	0.064	0.169	0.047	0.123
93	2.210	5.770	3.923	0.020	0.056	0.015	0.040
94	1.556	4.159	2.968	0.006	0.016	0.004	0.011
95	1.043	2.839	2.204	0.001	0.004	0.001	0.003
96	0.642	1.772	1.610	> 0.001	0.001	> 0.001	0.001
97	0.334	0.931	1.159	> 0.001	> 0.001	> 0.001	> 0.001
98	0.114	0.320	0.823	> 0.001	> 0.001	> 0.001	> 0.001
99	> 0.001	> 0.001	0.577	> 0.001	> 0.001	> 0.001	> 0.001

Probability of surviving through age X starting from age 39

| | CSO (1980) | | Total Population | U. S. Life Table (1982) | | | |
	Male	Female		White Male	White Female	Black Male	Black Female
Life Expectancy	34.96	39.28	35.42	35.40	41.50	30.70	37.50
Age							
39	99.721	99.778	99.710	99.779	99.882	99.424	99.734
40	99.420	99.537	99.397	99.540	99.751	98.819	99.446
41	99.093	99.274	99.058	99.278	99.606	98.177	99.133
42	98.740	98.989	98.691	98.991	99.445	97.492	98.791
43	98.358	98.683	98.293	98.675	99.267	96.752	98.419
44	97.946	98.355	97.857	98.327	99.071	95.947	98.014
45	97.500	98.005	97.384	97.942	98.854	95.073	97.572
46	97.020	97.633	96.869	97.517	98.614	94.127	97.090
47	96.504	97.237	96.313	97.046	98.351	93.107	96.567
48	95.950	96.816	95.712	96.524	98.061	92.009	95.996
49	95.354	96.368	95.064	95.944	97.742	90.832	95.372
50	94.715	95.890	94.362	95.302	97.392	89.573	94.692
51	94.023	95.381	93.603	94.595	97.009	88.230	93.953
52	93.275	94.837	92.783	93.819	96.589	86.804	93.157
53	92.462	94.254	91.895	92.973	96.131	85.293	92.306
54	91.578	93.631	90.937	92.054	95.634	83.699	91.398
55	90.620	92.967	89.904	91.057	95.093	82.023	90.436
56	89.581	92.263	88.793	89.978	94.507	80.263	89.415
57	88.462	91.522	87.602	88.813	93.870	78.420	88.328
58	87.260	90.747	86.330	87.556	93.180	76.491	87.163
59	85.971	89.936	84.975	86.201	92.432	74.474	85.916

| Life Expectancy | CSO (1980) | | Total Population | U. S. Life Table (1982) | | | |
	Male	Female		White Male	White Female	Black Male	Black Female
	34.96	39.28	35.42	35.40	41.50	30.70	37.50
Age							
60	84.589	89.084	83.534	84.749	91.625	72.373	84.581
61	83.105	88.182	82.006	83.194	90.752	70.191	83.161
62	81.510	87.215	80.388	81.526	89.809	67.935	81.663
63	79.794	86.167	78.673	79.737	88.791	65.611	80.100
64	77.947	85.025	76.859	77.818	87.691	63.227	78.481
65	75.966	83.785	74.941	75.766	86.504	60.789	76.807
66	73.850	82.444	72.918	73.565	85.211	58.289	75.047
67	71.602	81.007	70.791	71.230	83.816	55.741	73.207
68	69.226	79.481	68.559	68.779	82.324	53.162	71.295
69	66.722	77.863	66.228	66.228	80.742	50.565	69.318
70	64.086	76.141	63.804	63.594	79.076	47.965	67.286
71	61.311	74.296	61.288	60.815	77.257	45.365	65.166
72	58.389	72.300	58.673	57.919	75.298	42.779	62.972
73	55.316	70.123	55.949	54.932	73.210	40.221	60.715
74	52.097	67.744	53.109	51.883	71.008	37.705	58.406
75	48.753	65.153	50.161	48.800	68.705	35.240	56.058
76	45.314	62.354	47.121	45.620	66.200	32.796	53.597
77	41.820	59.358	44.013	42.388	63.520	30.389	51.046
78	38.311	56.186	40.865	39.142	60.693	28.037	48.427
79	34.823	52.851	37.701	35.921	57.747	25.754	45.764
80	31.381	49.363	34.537	32.759	54.713	23.554	43.078

Life Expectancy	CSO (1980)		Total Population	U. S. Life Table (1982)			
Age	Male	Female		White Male	White Female	Black Male	Black Female
	34.96	39.28	35.42	35.40	41.50	30.70	37.50
81	28.008	45.730	31.386	28.382	49.246	20.465	38.521
82	24.724	41.962	28.281	23.296	41.992	16.845	32.634
83	21.553	38.079	25.257	18.059	33.818	13.095	26.111
84	18.530	34.126	22.340	13.176	25.632	9.581	19.662
85	15.696	30.164	19.534	9.012	18.214	6.572	13.881
86	13.089	26.264	16.848	5.753	12.080	4.207	9.146
87	10.739	22.500	14.325	3.410	7.439	2.501	5.596
88	8.663	18.941	12.010	1.866	4.229	1.372	3.161
89	6.868	15.646	9.933	0.936	2.204	0.690	1.636
90	5.345	12.662	8.095	0.427	1.044	0.316	0.770
91	4.078	10.017	6.485	0.175	0.445	0.130	0.326
92	3.044	7.725	5.100	0.064	0.169	0.048	0.123
93	2.216	5.782	3.934	0.020	0.056	0.015	0.040
94	1.560	4.167	2.976	0.006	0.016	0.004	0.011
95	1.045	2.845	2.210	0.001	0.004	0.001	0.003
96	0.643	1.776	1.614	> 0.001	0.001	> 0.001	0.001
97	0.334	0.932	1.162	> 0.001	> 0.001	> 0.001	> 0.001
98	0.114	0.321	0.825	> 0.001	> 0.001	> 0.001	> 0.001
99	> 0.001	> 0.001	0.579	> 0.001	> 0.001	> 0.001	> 0.001

Probability of surviving through age X starting from age 40

| | CSO (1980) | | | U. S. Life Tables (1982) | | | |
	Male	Female	Total Population	White Male	White Female	Black Male	Black Female
Life Expectancy	34.05	38.36	34.52	34.50	40.60	29.90	36.60
Age							
40	99.698	99.758	99.686	99.760	99.869	99.391	99.711
41	99.370	99.495	99.346	99.498	99.723	98.746	99.397
42	99.016	99.209	98.978	99.210	99.563	98.057	99.055
43	98.633	98.903	98.579	98.894	99.384	97.312	98.682
44	98.220	98.574	98.142	98.545	99.188	96.503	98.275
45	97.773	98.223	97.667	98.159	98.970	95.624	97.832
46	97.292	97.850	97.151	97.733	98.731	94.672	97.349
47	96.774	97.454	96.594	97.261	98.467	93.646	96.825
48	96.219	97.032	95.991	96.738	98.177	92.542	96.252
49	95.621	96.582	95.340	96.156	97.858	91.358	95.626
50	94.980	96.103	94.636	95.513	97.507	90.092	94.944
51	94.286	95.593	93.876	94.804	97.123	88.742	94.204
52	93.536	95.048	93.053	94.027	96.703	87.307	93.406
53	92.721	94.464	92.163	93.179	96.244	85.787	92.552
54	91.835	93.839	91.201	92.257	95.747	84.184	91.642
55	90.873	93.174	90.165	91.258	95.206	82.498	90.677
56	89.832	92.469	89.051	90.178	94.618	80.728	89.653
57	88.710	91.726	87.857	89.010	93.981	78.875	88.563
58	87.504	90.949	86.581	87.750	93.290	76.934	87.396
59	86.212	90.136	85.222	86.392	92.542	74.906	86.145

Age	CSO (1980) Male	CSO (1980) Female	Total Population	U. S. Life Tables (1982) White Male	U. S. Life Tables (1982) White Female	U. S. Life Tables (1982) Black Male	U. S. Life Tables (1982) Black Female
Life Expectancy	34.05	38.36	34.52	34.50	40.60	29.90	36.60
60	84.825	89.283	83.777	84.936	91.733	72.792	84.807
61	83.338	88.378	82.245	83.378	90.860	70.598	83.383
62	81.738	87.409	80.621	81.707	89.916	68.329	81.881
63	80.017	86.359	78.902	79.913	88.896	65.991	80.314
64	78.165	85.215	77.082	77.990	87.794	63.593	78.690
65	76.178	83.971	75.159	75.933	86.607	61.141	77.012
66	74.057	82.628	73.131	73.727	85.312	58.626	75.247
67	71.803	81.188	70.997	71.388	83.915	56.064	73.402
68	69.419	79.658	68.759	68.932	82.422	53.470	71.485
69	66.909	78.036	66.421	66.375	80.837	50.858	69.503
70	64.265	76.311	63.989	63.735	79.169	48.243	67.465
71	61.482	74.462	61.466	60.950	77.348	45.627	65.340
72	58.553	72.461	58.844	58.047	75.387	43.027	63.140
73	55.470	70.279	56.111	55.053	73.297	40.455	60.877
74	52.243	67.895	53.264	51.998	71.092	37.923	58.562
75	48.889	65.298	50.306	48.908	68.786	35.445	56.208
76	45.441	62.492	47.258	45.721	66.278	32.986	53.740
77	41.937	59.490	44.141	42.482	63.595	30.565	51.182
78	38.418	56.311	40.983	39.228	60.764	28.199	48.557
79	34.920	52.968	37.811	36.000	57.815	25.903	45.886
80	31.469	49.473	34.637	32.832	54.777	23.690	43.193

| | CSO (1980) | | Total | U. S. Life Tables (1982) | | | |
	Male	Female	Population	White Male	White Female	Black Male	Black Female
Life Expectancy	34.05	38.36	34.52	34.50	40.60	29.90	36.60
Age							
81	28.086	45.832	31.477	28.445	49.304	20.583	38.624
82	24.793	42.055	28.364	23.348	42.042	16.942	32.721
83	21.613	38.164	25.330	18.099	33.858	13.171	26.180
84	18.582	34.202	22.405	13.205	25.663	9.636	19.715
85	15.740	30.231	19.591	9.032	18.236	6.610	13.918
86	13.126	26.323	16.897	5.766	12.094	4.232	9.171
87	10.769	22.550	14.366	3.418	7.448	2.516	5.611
88	8.688	18.983	12.045	1.870	4.234	1.380	3.169
89	6.887	15.681	9.962	0.938	2.206	0.694	1.641
90	5.359	12.690	8.119	0.428	1.045	0.318	0.772
91	4.089	10.039	6.504	0.176	0.446	0.131	0.327
92	3.053	7.742	5.115	0.064	0.169	0.048	0.123
93	2.222	5.795	3.945	0.020	0.056	0.015	0.041
94	1.565	4.176	2.985	0.006	0.016	0.004	0.011
95	1.048	2.851	2.216	0.001	0.004	0.001	0.003
96	0.645	1.780	1.619	> 0.001	0.001	> 0.001	0.001
97	0.335	0.934	1.165	> 0.001	> 0.001	> 0.001	> 0.001
98	0.115	0.322	0.828	> 0.001	> 0.001	> 0.001	> 0.001
99	> 0.001	> 0.001	0.580	> 0.001	> 0.001	> 0.001	> 0.001

Probability of surviving through age X starting from age 41

| | CSO (1980) | | Total Population | U. S. Life Tables (1982) | | | |
	Male	Female		White Male	White Female	Black Male	Black Female
Life Expectancy	33.16	37.46	33.63	33.60	39.60	29.10	35.70
Age							
41	99.671	99.736	99.659	99.737	99.854	99.351	99.685
42	99.316	99.450	99.290	99.449	99.693	98.658	99.342
43	98.932	99.142	98.889	99.132	99.515	97.909	98.968
44	98.517	98.813	98.451	98.782	99.318	97.094	98.560
45	98.069	98.462	97.975	98.395	99.100	96.210	98.115
46	97.587	98.087	97.457	97.968	98.860	95.252	97.632
47	97.067	97.690	96.898	97.495	98.596	94.220	97.105
48	96.510	97.267	96.293	96.971	98.306	93.109	96.531
49	95.911	96.817	95.640	96.388	97.986	91.918	95.903
50	95.267	96.337	94.935	95.743	97.635	90.644	95.219
51	94.572	95.825	94.171	95.033	97.251	89.285	94.477
52	93.819	95.279	93.346	94.253	96.830	87.842	93.676
53	93.002	94.693	92.453	93.403	96.371	86.313	92.820
54	92.113	94.067	91.489	92.479	95.872	84.700	91.908
55	91.148	93.400	90.449	91.478	95.331	83.003	90.940
56	90.104	92.693	89.331	90.395	94.742	81.223	89.913
57	88.978	91.949	88.133	89.224	94.104	79.358	88.820
58	87.769	91.170	86.854	87.961	93.412	77.405	87.649
59	86.473	90.355	85.490	86.600	92.663	75.365	86.395

	CSO (1980)			U. S. Life Tables (1982)			
Life Expectancy	**Male**	**Female**	**Total Population**	**White Male**	**White Female**	**Black Male**	**Black Female**
	33.16	37.46	33.63	33.60	39.60	29.10	35.70
Age							
60	85.082	89.499	84.041	85.141	91.853	73.238	85.052
61	83.590	88.592	82.504	83.578	90.979	71.031	83.624
62	81.986	87.622	80.875	81.903	90.033	68.748	82.118
63	80.259	86.568	79.150	80.106	89.013	66.396	80.547
64	78.402	85.421	77.325	78.178	87.910	63.983	78.918
65	76.409	84.175	75.396	76.116	86.720	61.516	77.235
66	74.281	82.828	73.361	73.905	85.424	58.986	75.465
67	72.020	81.384	71.220	71.560	84.025	56.408	73.615
68	69.630	79.851	68.975	69.097	82.530	53.797	71.692
69	67.111	78.225	66.630	66.535	80.943	51.169	69.705
70	64.460	76.496	64.191	63.889	79.273	48.538	67.661
71	61.669	74.642	61.660	61.097	77.450	45.907	65.530
72	58.730	72.637	59.029	58.187	75.485	43.290	63.323
73	55.638	70.450	56.288	55.186	73.393	40.702	61.053
74	52.401	68.059	53.431	52.123	71.185	38.156	58.732
75	49.037	65.457	50.465	49.025	68.876	35.662	56.371
76	45.579	62.644	47.407	45.831	66.365	33.188	53.896
77	42.064	59.635	44.280	42.584	63.678	30.752	51.331
78	38.534	56.447	41.112	39.323	60.844	28.372	48.697
79	35.026	53.097	37.930	36.087	57.891	26.062	46.019
80	31.564	49.593	34.746	32.911	54.849	23.836	43.318

	CSO (1980)		U. S. Life Tables (1982)				
	Male	Female	Total Population	White Male	White Female	Black Male	Black Female
Life Expectancy	33.16	37.46	33.63	33.60	39.60	29.10	35.70
Age							
81	28.171	45.943	31.577	28.514	49.369	20.709	38.736
82	24.868	42.157	28.453	23.404	42.097	17.046	32.816
83	21.679	38.257	25.410	18.142	33.902	13.251	26.256
84	18.638	34.285	22.476	13.236	25.696	9.695	19.772
85	15.788	30.305	19.652	9.054	18.260	6.650	13.958
86	13.165	26.387	16.951	5.780	12.110	4.258	9.197
87	10.802	22.605	14.412	3.426	7.458	2.531	5.627
88	8.714	19.029	12.083	1.875	4.240	1.389	3.178
89	6.908	15.719	9.994	0.940	2.209	0.699	1.645
90	5.376	12.721	8.145	0.429	1.047	0.319	0.774
91	4.102	10.064	6.525	0.176	0.446	0.131	0.328
92	3.062	7.761	5.131	0.064	0.169	0.048	0.124
93	2.229	5.809	3.957	0.020	0.056	0.015	0.041
94	1.569	4.187	2.994	0.006	0.016	0.004	0.011
95	1.052	2.858	2.223	0.001	0.004	0.001	0.003
96	0.647	1.784	1.624	< 0.001	0.001	< 0.001	0.001
97	0.336	0.937	1.169	< 0.001	< 0.001	< 0.001	< 0.001
98	0.115	0.322	0.830	< 0.001	< 0.001	< 0.001	< 0.001
99	< 0.001	< 0.001	0.582	< 0.001	< 0.001	< 0.001	< 0.001

Probability of surviving through age X starting from age 42

| | CSO (1980) | | | U. S. Life Tables (1982) | | | |
	Male	Female	Total Population	White Male	White Female	Black Male	Black Female
Life Expectancy	32.26	36.55	32.74	32.70	38.70	28.30	34.80
Age							
42	99.644	99.713	99.630	99.711	99.839	99.302	99.656
43	99.258	99.405	99.227	99.393	99.660	98.548	99.280
44	98.842	99.075	98.788	99.042	99.463	97.728	98.871
45	98.393	98.722	98.310	98.655	99.245	96.838	98.425
46	97.909	98.347	97.791	98.227	99.005	95.875	97.940
47	97.388	97.949	97.229	97.752	98.741	94.835	97.412
48	96.829	97.525	96.623	97.226	98.449	93.717	96.836
49	96.227	97.073	95.968	96.642	98.129	92.519	96.206
50	95.582	96.592	95.259	95.995	97.778	91.236	95.520
51	94.884	96.079	94.493	95.283	97.393	89.869	94.775
52	94.129	95.531	93.666	94.502	96.971	88.415	93.972
53	93.309	94.944	92.769	93.649	96.511	86.877	93.113
54	92.417	94.316	91.802	92.723	96.013	85.253	92.198
55	91.449	93.647	90.759	91.719	95.470	83.546	91.227
56	90.401	92.938	89.637	90.633	94.881	81.754	90.197
57	89.272	92.192	88.435	89.459	94.241	79.876	89.101
58	88.059	91.411	87.151	88.193	93.549	77.911	87.926
59	86.758	90.594	85.783	86.828	92.799	75.857	86.668
60	85.363	89.736	84.329	85.365	91.987	73.716	85.321
61	83.866	88.827	82.786	83.799	91.112	71.495	83.889
62	82.257	87.853	81.152	82.119	90.165	69.197	82.378
63	80.524	86.797	79.421	80.317	89.143	66.829	80.801

Age	CSO (1980)		Total Population	U. S. Life Tables (1982)			
	Male	Female		White Male	White Female	Black Male	Black Female
Life Expectancy	32.26	36.55	32.74	32.70	38.70	28.30	34.80
64	78.661	85.647	77.590	78.384	88.038	64.401	79.167
65	76.661	84.398	75.654	76.317	86.847	61.918	77.479
66	74.526	83.047	73.612	74.100	85.549	59.371	75.704
67	72.258	81.600	71.464	71.749	84.148	56.776	73.847
68	69.860	80.063	69.211	69.280	82.650	54.149	71.918
69	67.333	78.432	66.858	66.710	81.062	51.504	69.925
70	64.672	76.698	64.411	64.057	79.389	48.855	67.875
71	61.872	74.840	61.871	61.258	77.563	46.207	65.737
72	58.924	72.829	59.231	58.340	75.596	43.573	63.523
73	55.822	70.636	56.481	55.331	73.500	40.968	61.246
74	52.574	68.239	53.614	52.261	71.289	38.405	58.917
75	49.199	65.630	50.638	49.155	68.977	35.895	56.549
76	45.729	62.810	47.569	45.952	66.462	33.405	54.066
77	42.202	59.792	44.431	42.696	63.771	30.953	51.493
78	38.662	56.597	41.253	39.426	60.933	28.557	48.851
79	35.142	53.238	38.060	36.182	57.976	26.232	46.164
80	31.668	49.724	34.865	32.998	54.929	23.991	43.455
81	28.264	46.065	31.685	28.589	49.441	20.845	38.858
82	24.950	42.269	28.550	23.465	42.159	17.157	32.920
83	21.750	38.358	25.497	18.190	33.952	13.338	26.339
84	18.700	34.376	22.553	13.271	25.734	9.759	19.834
85	15.840	30.385	19.720	9.077	18.286	6.694	14.002
86	13.209	26.456	17.009	5.795	12.128	4.285	9.226

	CSO (1980)		Total Population	U. S. Life Tables (1982)			
	Male	Female		White Male	White Female	Black Male	Black Female
Life Expectancy	32.26	36.55	32.74	32.70	38.70	28.30	34.80
Age							
87	10.837	22.665	14.461	3.435	7.469	2.548	5.645
88	8.743	19.080	12.124	1.880	4.246	1.398	3.188
89	6.930	15.761	10.028	0.943	2.212	0.703	1.651
90	5.393	12.754	8.172	0.430	1.048	0.322	0.777
91	4.115	10.090	6.547	0.176	0.447	0.132	0.329
92	3.072	7.782	5.148	0.064	0.169	0.048	0.124
93	2.236	5.824	3.971	0.021	0.056	0.015	0.041
94	1.575	4.198	3.005	0.006	0.016	0.004	0.012
95	1.055	2.866	2.231	0.001	0.004	0.001	0.003
96	0.649	1.789	1.630	> 0.001	0.001	> 0.001	0.001
97	0.338	0.939	1.173	> 0.001	> 0.001	> 0.001	> 0.001
98	0.115	0.323	0.833	> 0.001	> 0.001	> 0.001	> 0.001
99	> 0.001	> 0.001	0.584	> 0.001	> 0.001	> 0.001	> 0.001

Probability of surviving through age X starting from age 43

	CSO (1980)		Total Population	U. S. Life Tables (1982)			
	Male	Female		White Male	White Female	Black Male	Black Female
Life Expectancy	31.38	35.66	31.86	31.80	37.70	27.50	34.00
Age							
43	99.613	99.691	99.596	99.681	99.821	99.241	99.623

	CSO (1980)		Total	U. S. Life Tables (1982)			
	Male	Female	Population	White Male	White Female	Black Male	Black Female
Life Expectancy	31.38	35.66	31.86	31.80	37.70	27.50	34.00
Age							
44	99.196	99.360	99.155	99.329	99.623	98.415	99.213
45	98.744	99.006	98.675	98.941	99.405	97.519	98.765
46	98.258	98.630	98.154	98.511	99.165	96.548	98.278
47	97.736	98.231	97.590	98.036	98.900	95.502	97.748
48	97.175	97.805	96.982	97.508	98.608	94.376	97.170
49	96.571	97.352	96.324	96.922	98.288	93.169	96.538
50	95.923	96.870	95.613	96.274	97.936	91.878	95.850
51	95.223	96.355	94.844	95.559	97.550	90.500	95.102
52	94.465	95.806	94.014	94.776	97.127	89.037	94.297
53	93.642	95.217	93.114	93.921	96.667	87.488	93.435
54	92.747	94.587	92.143	92.992	96.167	85.852	92.516
55	91.776	93.917	91.096	91.985	95.624	84.133	91.542
56	90.724	93.206	89.970	90.896	95.034	82.328	90.509
57	89.591	92.457	88.763	89.719	94.393	80.438	89.408
58	88.374	91.674	87.475	88.448	93.700	78.458	88.230
59	87.068	90.855	86.101	87.080	92.948	76.390	86.967
60	85.668	89.994	84.642	85.613	92.136	74.234	85.616
61	84.166	89.083	83.094	84.042	91.259	71.997	84.178
62	82.550	88.106	81.453	82.357	90.311	69.683	82.662
63	80.812	87.047	79.716	80.550	89.286	67.299	81.080
64	78.942	85.894	77.878	78.611	88.180	64.854	79.441
65	76.935	84.641	75.935	76.538	86.987	62.353	77.747
66	74.793	83.286	73.885	74.315	85.687	59.788	75.965

Life Expectancy	CSO (1980)			U. S. Life Tables (1982)			
	Male	Female	Total Population	White Male	White Female	Black Male	Black Female
	31.38	35.66	31.86	31.80	37.70	27.50	34.00
Age							
67	72.516	81.835	71.729	71.957	84.284	57.175	74.102
68	70.109	80.293	69.468	69.480	82.784	54.529	72.167
69	67.573	78.658	67.106	66.903	81.193	51.866	70.166
70	64.903	76.919	64.650	64.243	79.517	49.199	68.109
71	62.093	75.055	62.101	61.435	77.688	46.532	65.964
72	59.134	73.039	59.451	58.509	75.718	43.879	63.743
73	56.022	70.839	56.690	55.492	73.619	41.256	61.457
74	52.762	68.436	53.813	52.412	71.404	38.675	59.121
75	49.375	65.819	50.826	49.297	69.088	36.147	56.744
76	45.892	62.991	47.746	46.085	66.569	33.640	54.253
77	42.353	59.965	44.596	42.820	63.874	31.171	51.671
78	38.800	56.759	41.406	39.541	61.031	28.758	49.020
79	35.267	53.391	38.201	36.287	58.069	26.417	46.324
80	31.781	49.868	34.995	33.093	55.018	24.160	43.605
81	28.365	46.197	31.802	28.672	49.520	20.991	38.993
82	25.040	42.391	28.656	23.533	42.227	17.278	33.033
83	21.828	38.468	25.592	18.243	34.006	13.432	26.430
84	18.767	34.475	22.636	13.310	25.775	9.827	19.903
85	15.896	30.472	19.793	9.104	18.316	6.741	14.051
86	13.256	26.533	17.072	5.812	12.147	4.315	9.258
87	10.876	22.730	14.515	3.445	7.481	2.565	5.665
88	8.774	19.134	12.169	1.885	4.253	1.408	3.199
89	6.955	15.806	10.065	0.946	2.216	0.708	1.656

	CSO (1980)			U. S. Life Tables (1982)			
	Male	Female	Total Population	White Male	White Female	Black Male	Black Female
Life Expectancy	31.38	35.66	31.86	31.80	37.70	27.50	34.00
Age							
90	5.413	12.791	8.203	0.431	1.050	0.324	0.780
91	4.130	10.119	6.571	0.177	0.448	0.133	0.330
92	3.083	7.804	5.168	0.065	0.170	0.049	0.124
93	2.244	5.841	3.986	0.021	0.056	0.016	0.041
94	1.580	4.210	3.016	0.006	0.016	0.004	0.012
95	1.059	2.874	2.239	0.001	0.004	0.001	0.003
96	0.652	1.794	1.636	> 0.001	0.001	> 0.001	0.001
97	0.339	0.942	1.177	> 0.001	> 0.001	> 0.001	> 0.001
98	0.116	0.324	0.836	> 0.001	> 0.001	> 0.001	> 0.001
99	> 0.001	> 0.001	0.586	> 0.001	> 0.001	> 0.001	> 0.001

Probability of surviving through age X starting from age 44

	CSO (1980)			U. S. Life Table (1982)			
	Male	Female	Total Population	White Male	White Female	Black Male	Black Female
Life Expectancy	30.50	34.77	30.99	30.90	36.80	26.70	33.10
Age							
44	99.581	99.668	99.557	99.647	99.802	99.168	99.588
45	99.128	99.313	99.075	99.257	99.583	98.265	99.139
46	98.640	98.936	98.552	98.827	99.342	97.287	98.650
47	98.115	98.535	97.986	98.349	99.077	96.232	98.118

Life Expectancy	CSO (1980) Male	CSO (1980) Female	Total Population	U.S. Life Table (1982) White Male	White Female	Black Male	Black Female
	30.50	34.77	30.99	30.90	36.80	26.70	33.10
Age							
48	97.552	98.108	97.375	97.820	98.785	95.098	97.538
49	96.946	97.654	96.715	97.232	98.464	93.881	96.904
50	96.296	97.170	96.001	96.582	98.111	92.580	96.213
51	95.593	96.654	95.229	95.865	97.725	91.192	95.462
52	94.832	96.103	94.395	95.079	97.302	89.718	94.654
53	94.006	95.512	93.492	94.221	96.840	88.157	93.788
54	93.107	94.881	92.516	93.290	96.340	86.509	92.867
55	92.133	94.208	91.465	92.279	95.795	84.776	91.889
56	91.077	93.495	90.335	91.187	95.204	82.958	90.851
57	89.939	92.744	89.124	90.006	94.563	81.053	89.746
58	88.717	91.958	87.829	88.731	93.868	79.058	88.564
59	87.407	91.136	86.451	87.359	93.115	76.974	87.296
60	86.001	90.273	84.985	85.887	92.301	74.802	85.940
61	84.493	89.359	83.431	84.311	91.422	72.548	84.497
62	82.871	88.379	81.784	82.621	90.472	70.216	82.975
63	81.126	87.317	80.039	80.808	89.447	67.814	81.387
64	79.249	86.160	78.194	78.862	88.338	65.350	79.741
65	77.234	84.903	76.243	76.783	87.143	62.830	78.041
66	75.083	83.545	74.185	74.552	85.840	60.245	76.252
67	72.798	82.088	72.020	72.187	84.435	57.613	74.383
68	70.381	80.542	69.750	69.703	82.932	54.946	72.440
69	67.836	78.902	67.379	67.118	81.338	52.262	70.432
70	65.156	77.158	64.912	64.448	79.659	49.575	68.367

| | CSO (1980) | | Total Population | U. S. Life Tables (1982) | | | |
Age	Male	Female		White Male	White Female	Black Male	Black Female
Life Expectancy	29.62	33.88	30.12	30.00	35.90	25.90	32.20
53	94.402	95.830	93.908	94.555	97.033	88.896	94.176
54	93.499	95.197	92.928	93.620	96.531	87.235	93.251
55	92.520	94.522	91.872	92.606	95.986	85.488	92.269
56	91.460	93.806	90.737	91.510	95.393	83.654	91.227
57	90.318	93.053	89.520	90.325	94.750	81.733	90.118
58	89.090	92.265	88.220	89.046	94.054	79.722	88.930
59	87.774	91.440	86.835	87.668	93.300	77.620	87.657
60	86.363	90.574	85.363	86.191	92.484	75.430	86.295
61	84.848	89.656	83.802	84.609	91.604	73.156	84.846
62	83.220	88.674	82.148	82.914	90.652	70.805	83.318
63	81.467	87.608	80.396	81.094	89.624	68.383	81.724
64	79.582	86.447	78.542	79.142	88.514	65.898	80.071
65	77.559	85.186	76.582	77.055	87.316	63.357	78.364
66	75.399	83.823	74.515	74.816	86.011	60.751	76.568
67	73.104	82.362	72.341	72.443	84.603	58.096	74.690
68	70.678	80.810	70.061	69.950	83.097	55.407	72.739
69	68.121	79.165	67.679	67.355	81.500	52.701	70.723
70	65.430	77.415	65.201	64.677	79.817	49.991	68.650
71	62.597	75.539	62.630	61.850	77.982	47.281	66.487
72	59.614	73.509	59.958	58.904	76.004	44.586	64.248
73	56.476	71.296	57.174	55.867	73.897	41.921	61.945
74	53.190	68.877	54.272	52.766	71.674	39.298	59.590
75	49.775	66.243	51.259	49.630	69.349	36.729	57.194

| | CSO (1980) | | | U. S. Life Tables (1982) | | | |
Age	Male	Female	Total Population	White Male	White Female	Black Male	Black Female
Life Expectancy	29.62	33.88	30.12	30.00	35.90	25.90	32.20
76	46.265	63.396	48.153	46.397	66.821	34.181	54.684
77	42.697	60.351	44.976	43.109	64.116	31.673	52.081
78	39.114	57.125	41.759	39.808	61.262	29.221	49.409
79	35.553	53.735	38.527	36.532	58.289	26.842	46.691
80	32.039	50.189	35.293	33.317	55.226	24.549	43.951
81	28.595	46.495	32.073	28.865	49.708	21.329	39.302
82	25.243	42.664	28.901	23.692	42.386	17.556	33.295
83	22.005	38.716	25.810	18.366	34.135	13.648	26.640
84	18.919	34.697	22.829	13.400	25.873	9.986	20.061
85	16.025	30.669	19.962	9.165	18.385	6.849	14.162
86	13.364	26.703	17.217	5.851	12.193	4.385	9.332
87	10.964	22.876	14.638	3.468	7.509	2.607	5.709
88	8.845	19.258	12.273	1.898	4.269	1.430	3.225
89	7.012	15.908	10.151	0.952	2.224	0.720	1.669
90	5.457	12.874	8.273	0.434	1.054	0.329	0.786
91	4.164	10.185	6.627	0.178	0.449	0.135	0.333
92	3.108	7.854	5.212	0.065	0.170	0.050	0.125
93	2.262	5.879	4.020	0.021	0.056	0.016	0.041
94	1.593	4.237	3.041	0.006	0.016	0.004	0.012
95	1.067	2.892	2.258	0.001	0.004	0.001	0.003
96	0.657	1.806	1.650	> 0.001	0.001	> 0.001	0.001
97	0.341	0.948	1.187	> 0.001	> 0.001	> 0.001	> 0.001
98	0.117	0.326	0.843	> 0.001	> 0.001	> 0.001	> 0.001

	CSO (1980)			U. S. Life Tables (1982)			
	Male	Female	Total Population	White Male	White Female	Black Male	Black Female
Life Expectancy	29.62	33.88	30.12	30.00	35.90	25.90	32.20
Age 99	> 0.001	> 0.001	0.591	> 0.001	> 0.001	> 0.001	> 0.001

Probability of surviving through age X starting from age 46

	CSO (1980)			U. S. Life Tables (1982)			
	Male	Female	Total Population	White Male	White Female	Black Male	Black Female
Life Expectancy	28.76	33.00	29.27	29.10	34.90	25.10	31.40
Age							
46	99.508	99.620	99.472	99.566	99.758	99.005	99.507
47	98.979	99.217	98.901	99.085	99.492	97.932	98.971
48	98.410	98.787	98.284	98.552	99.198	96.777	98.385
49	97.799	98.330	97.618	97.960	98.876	95.539	97.745
50	97.143	97.842	96.897	97.304	98.522	94.215	97.048
51	96.434	97.322	96.118	96.582	98.134	92.803	96.291
52	95.666	96.768	95.276	95.790	97.709	91.302	95.476
53	94.833	96.172	94.364	94.926	97.246	89.714	94.603
54	93.926	95.537	93.380	93.988	96.743	88.037	93.673
55	92.943	94.859	92.319	92.970	96.196	86.274	92.687
56	91.878	94.141	91.178	91.869	95.603	84.423	91.640
57	90.730	93.385	89.955	90.679	94.958	82.485	90.526
58	89.497	92.594	88.649	89.395	94.260	80.455	89.333

| | CSO (1980) | | Total Population | U. S. Life Tables (1982) | | | |
Life Expectancy	Male	Female		White Male	White Female	Black Male	Black Female
	28.76	33.00	29.27	29.10	34.90	25.10	31.40
Age							
59	88.176	91.767	87.258	88.012	93.504	78.334	88.055
60	86.758	90.898	85.779	86.529	92.687	76.123	86.686
61	85.236	89.977	84.210	84.941	91.805	73.829	85.231
62	83.600	88.991	82.547	83.239	90.851	71.456	83.696
63	81.840	87.921	80.787	81.412	89.821	69.012	82.094
64	79.946	86.756	78.924	79.453	88.708	66.504	80.434
65	77.914	85.490	76.955	77.357	87.508	63.939	78.719
66	75.744	84.122	74.878	75.110	86.199	61.309	76.915
67	73.438	82.656	72.693	72.727	84.788	58.630	75.029
68	71.001	81.099	70.401	70.224	83.279	55.917	73.069
69	68.433	79.448	68.008	67.620	81.678	53.185	71.044
70	65.729	77.691	65.518	64.930	79.993	50.451	68.961
71	62.883	75.809	62.935	62.093	78.153	47.716	66.788
72	59.886	73.772	60.250	59.136	76.171	44.996	64.540
73	56.734	71.550	57.452	56.086	74.059	42.306	62.226
74	53.433	69.123	54.536	52.973	71.832	39.659	59.860
75	50.003	66.479	51.508	49.825	69.501	37.067	57.454
76	46.476	63.623	48.387	46.579	66.967	34.495	54.931
77	42.892	60.566	45.195	43.278	64.257	31.964	52.317
78	39.293	57.329	41.962	39.964	61.396	29.490	49.633
79	35.716	53.927	38.714	36.675	58.417	27.089	46.903
80	32.185	50.368	35.464	33.448	55.347	24.775	44.150

| | CSO (1980) | | Total | U. S. Life Tables (1982) | | | |
	Male	Female	Population	White Male	White Female	Black Male	Black Female
Life Expectancy	28.76	33.00	29.27	29.10	34.90	25.10	31.40
Age							
81	28.726	46.661	32.229	28.979	49.817	21.525	39.480
82	25.358	42.816	29.041	23.785	42.479	17.718	33.446
83	22.106	38.854	25.935	18.438	34.210	13.773	26.760
84	19.005	34.821	22.940	13.452	25.930	10.077	20.152
85	16.098	30.778	20.059	9.201	18.425	6.912	14.226
86	13.425	26.799	17.301	5.874	12.220	4.425	9.374
87	11.014	22.958	14.710	3.482	7.526	2.631	5.735
88	8.886	19.327	12.333	1.905	4.278	1.444	3.239
89	7.044	15.965	10.200	0.956	2.229	0.726	1.677
90	5.482	12.920	8.313	0.436	1.056	0.332	0.789
91	4.183	10.221	6.660	0.179	0.450	0.137	0.334
92	3.122	7.882	5.237	0.065	0.171	0.050	0.126
93	2.273	5.900	4.039	0.021	0.057	0.016	0.041
94	1.600	4.252	3.056	0.006	0.016	0.004	0.012
95	1.072	2.903	2.269	0.001	0.004	0.001	0.003
96	0.660	1.812	1.658	> 0.001	0.001	> 0.001	0.001
97	0.343	0.951	1.193	> 0.001	> 0.001	> 0.001	> 0.001
98	0.117	0.327	0.847	> 0.001	> 0.001	> 0.001	> 0.001
99	> 0.001	> 0.001	0.594	> 0.001	> 0.001	> 0.001	> 0.001

Probability of surviving through age X starting from age 47

	CSO (1980)		Total Population	U. S. Life Tables (1982)			
	Male	Female		White Male	White Female	Black Male	Black Female
Life Expectancy	27.90	32.12	28.42	28.20	34.00	24.40	30.50
Age							
47	99.468	99.595	99.426	99.517	99.733	98.916	99.461
48	98.897	99.164	98.806	98.982	99.439	97.750	98.872
49	98.283	98.705	98.136	98.387	99.116	96.500	98.230
50	97.623	98.215	97.411	97.729	98.761	95.162	97.529
51	96.911	97.694	96.628	97.003	98.372	93.736	96.768
52	96.139	97.137	95.782	96.208	97.946	92.220	95.949
53	95.302	96.539	94.865	95.340	97.481	90.615	95.072
54	94.391	95.901	93.876	94.397	96.977	88.922	94.137
55	93.403	95.221	92.809	93.375	96.430	87.141	93.146
56	92.332	94.500	91.662	92.269	95.835	85.271	92.094
57	91.179	93.742	90.433	91.074	95.189	83.314	90.975
58	89.940	92.948	89.120	89.785	94.489	81.263	89.775
59	88.611	92.117	87.721	88.396	93.731	79.121	88.491
60	87.187	91.244	86.234	86.906	92.912	76.888	87.116
61	85.657	90.320	84.657	85.312	92.027	74.571	85.653
62	84.014	89.330	82.985	83.602	91.071	72.174	84.110
63	82.244	88.256	81.215	81.767	90.039	69.705	82.500
64	80.341	87.087	79.343	79.799	88.923	67.172	80.832
65	78.299	85.816	77.363	77.695	87.720	64.582	79.109
66	76.118	84.443	75.275	75.438	86.408	61.926	77.296

	CSO (1980)			U. S. Life Tables (1982)			
	Male	Female	Total Population	White Male	White Female	Black Male	Black Female
Life Expectancy	27.90	32.12	28.42	28.20	34.00	24.40	30.50
Age							
67	73.801	82.971	73.078	73.044	84.994	59.219	75.401
68	71.352	81.408	70.775	70.530	83.481	56.479	73.431
69	68.771	79.751	68.369	67.914	81.877	53.720	71.396
70	66.054	77.987	65.866	65.214	80.187	50.958	69.302
71	63.194	76.098	63.269	62.364	78.342	48.195	67.119
72	60.182	74.053	60.570	59.393	76.356	45.448	64.859
73	57.014	71.823	57.757	56.330	74.239	42.731	62.534
74	53.697	69.386	54.826	53.204	72.006	40.057	60.157
75	50.250	66.733	51.782	50.042	69.670	37.439	57.738
76	46.706	63.866	48.644	46.782	67.130	34.842	55.204
77	43.104	60.797	45.435	43.467	64.412	32.285	52.576
78	39.488	57.548	42.185	40.138	61.545	29.786	49.879
79	35.892	54.132	38.920	36.835	58.559	27.361	47.135
80	32.345	50.560	35.653	33.593	55.481	25.024	44.369
81	28.868	46.839	32.400	29.105	49.938	21.741	39.676
82	25.483	42.979	29.195	23.889	42.582	17.896	33.612
83	22.215	39.003	26.073	18.519	34.293	13.912	26.893
84	19.099	34.954	23.062	13.511	25.993	10.179	20.252
85	16.178	30.896	20.165	9.241	18.470	6.982	14.297
86	13.491	26.901	17.393	5.900	12.250	4.470	9.420
87	11.069	23.046	14.788	3.497	7.544	2.657	5.764
88	8.929	19.400	12.398	1.914	4.288	1.458	3.255

	CSO (1980)			U. S. Life Tables (1982)			
	Male	Female	Total Population	White Male	White Female	Black Male	Black Female
Life Expectancy	27.90	32.12	28.42	28.20	34.00	24.40	30.50
Age							
89	7.078	16.026	10.254	0.960	2.235	0.733	1.685
90	5.509	12.969	8.357	0.438	1.059	0.335	0.793
91	4.203	10.260	6.695	0.180	0.451	0.138	0.336
92	3.138	7.912	5.265	0.066	0.171	0.050	0.127
93	2.284	5.922	4.061	0.021	0.057	0.016	0.042
94	1.608	4.268	3.072	0.006	0.016	0.004	0.012
95	1.078	2.914	2.281	0.001	0.004	0.001	0.003
96	0.663	1.819	1.666	> 0.001	0.001	0.001	0.001
97	0.345	0.955	1.199	> 0.001	> 0.001	> 0.001	> 0.001
98	0.118	0.329	0.852	> 0.001	> 0.001	> 0.001	> 0.001
99	> 0.001	> 0.001	0.597	> 0.001	> 0.001	> 0.001	> 0.001

Probability of surviving through age X starting from age 48

	CSO (1980)			U. S. Life Tables (1982)			
	Male	Female	Total Population	White Male	White Female	Black Male	Black Female
Life Expectancy	27.04	31.25	27.58	27.30	31.10	23.60	29.70
Age							
48	99.426	99.567	99.376	99.462	99.705	98.821	99.408
49	98.809	99.106	98.702	98.864	99.381	97.557	98.762
50	98.146	98.614	97.974	98.203	99.025	96.205	98.058

| | CSO (1980) | | Total Population | U. S. Life Tables (1982) | | | |
Life Expectancy	Male	Female		White Male	White Female	Black Male	Black Female
	27.04	31.25	27.58	27.30	31.10	23.60	29.70
Age							
51	97.429	98.091	97.186	97.474	98.635	94.763	97.293
52	96.654	97.532	96.335	96.675	98.208	93.231	96.469
53	95.812	96.932	95.413	95.803	97.742	91.608	95.587
54	94.896	96.291	94.418	94.855	97.237	89.896	94.647
55	93.902	95.608	93.345	93.828	96.688	88.096	93.651
56	92.826	94.885	92.191	92.717	96.091	86.206	92.593
57	91.667	94.123	90.955	91.516	95.443	84.227	91.468
58	90.421	93.326	89.634	90.221	94.742	82.154	90.262
59	89.085	92.491	88.227	88.825	93.982	79.988	88.970
60	87.653	91.615	86.732	87.328	93.161	77.731	87.588
61	86.115	90.687	85.145	85.726	92.274	75.388	86.117
62	84.463	89.693	83.465	84.008	91.315	72.965	84.566
63	82.684	88.615	81.684	82.164	90.280	70.469	82.948
64	80.771	87.441	79.801	80.186	89.161	67.908	81.270
65	78.718	86.165	77.810	78.072	87.955	65.290	79.538
66	76.525	84.787	75.710	75.804	86.640	62.604	77.715
67	74.196	83.309	73.500	73.398	85.221	59.868	75.809
68	71.733	81.739	71.184	70.873	83.705	57.098	73.829
69	69.139	80.075	68.763	68.244	82.096	54.309	71.782
70	66.407	78.305	66.246	65.530	80.401	51.516	69.678
71	63.532	76.407	63.634	62.666	78.552	48.723	67.483
72	60.504	74.354	60.919	59.682	76.560	45.946	65.211
73	57.319	72.115	58.090	56.604	74.438	43.199	62.873

	CSO (1980)			U. S. Life Tables (1982)			
Life Expectancy	Male	Female	Total Population	White Male	White Female	Black Male	Black Female
	27.04	31.25	27.58	27.30	31.10	23.60	29.70
Age							
74	53.984	69.669	55.142	53.462	72.199	40.496	60.483
75	50.519	67.004	52.081	50.285	69.857	37.850	58.051
76	46.956	64.125	48.925	47.009	67.310	35.224	55.503
77	43.334	61.045	45.697	43.678	64.585	32.639	52.861
78	39.699	57.782	42.429	40.333	61.710	30.113	50.149
79	36.084	54.352	39.144	37.014	58.715	27.661	47.391
80	32.518	50.766	35.859	33.756	55.630	25.298	44.609
81	29.023	47.029	32.588	29.246	50.071	21.980	39.891
82	25.620	43.154	29.364	24.005	42.696	18.092	33.794
83	22.334	39.161	26.223	18.608	34.385	14.064	27.039
84	19.201	35.096	23.195	13.577	26.062	10.290	20.361
85	16.265	31.021	20.282	9.286	18.520	7.058	14.374
86	13.563	27.010	17.493	5.928	12.283	4.519	9.471
87	11.128	23.139	14.873	3.514	7.564	2.686	5.795
88	8.977	19.479	12.470	1.923	4.300	1.474	3.273
89	7.116	16.091	10.314	0.965	2.241	0.741	1.694
90	5.538	13.022	8.405	0.440	1.061	0.339	0.797
91	4.226	10.302	6.734	0.181	0.453	0.140	0.338
92	3.155	7.945	5.295	0.066	0.172	0.051	0.127
93	2.296	5.946	4.084	0.021	0.057	0.016	0.042
94	1.617	4.286	3.090	0.006	0.016	0.004	0.012
95	1.083	2.926	2.295	0.001	0.004	0.001	0.003
96	0.667	1.826	1.676	> 0.001	0.001	> 0.001	0.001

	CSO (1980)			U. S. Life Tables (1982)			
	Male	Female	Total Population	White Male	White Female	Black Male	Black Female
Life Expectancy	27.04	31.25	27.58	27.30	31.10	23.60	29.70
Age							
97	0.347	0.959	1.206	> 0.001	> 0.001	> 0.001	> 0.001
98	0.119	0.330	0.857	> 0.001	> 0.001	> 0.001	> 0.001
99	> 0.001	> 0.001	0.601	> 0.001	> 0.001	> 0.001	> 0.001

Probability of surviving through age X starting from age 49

	CSO (1980)			U. S. Life Tables (1982)			
	Male	Female	Total Population	White Male	White Female	Black Male	Black Female
Life Expectancy	26.20	30.39	26.75	26.50	32.20	22.90	28.90
Age							
49	99.379	99.537	99.322	99.399	99.675	98.721	99.350
50	98.712	99.043	98.589	98.734	99.318	97.353	98.642
51	97.992	98.517	97.796	98.001	98.927	95.893	97.872
52	97.212	97.956	96.940	97.198	98.498	94.343	97.043
53	96.365	97.353	96.012	96.321	98.032	92.701	96.156
54	95.444	96.710	95.011	95.368	97.525	90.969	95.211
55	94.444	96.024	93.931	94.336	96.974	89.147	94.208
56	93.362	95.297	92.770	93.219	96.375	87.234	93.145
57	92.196	94.532	91.526	92.012	95.726	85.231	92.012
58	90.943	93.731	90.197	90.709	95.022	83.134	90.800
59	89.600	92.893	88.781	89.305	94.260	80.943	89.500

	CSO (1980)			U. S. Life Tables (1982)			
Life Expectancy	Male	Female	Total Population	White Male	White Female	Black Male	Black Female
	26.20	30.39	26.75	26.50	32.20	22.90	28.90
Age							
60	88.159	92.014	87.276	87.801	93.436	78.658	88.109
61	86.613	91.082	85.680	86.189	92.547	76.288	86.630
62	84.951	90.083	83.989	84.462	91.585	73.836	85.070
63	83.161	89.001	82.197	82.608	90.547	71.310	83.442
64	81.237	87.821	80.302	80.620	89.425	68.718	81.754
65	79.172	86.540	78.298	78.494	88.215	66.069	80.011
66	76.967	85.155	76.185	76.214	86.896	63.351	78.177
67	74.624	83.671	73.962	73.795	85.474	60.583	76.261
68	72.147	82.095	71.631	71.256	83.952	57.779	74.269
69	69.538	80.423	69.195	68.613	82.339	54.956	72.210
70	66.790	78.645	66.662	65.884	80.639	52.131	70.093
71	63.898	76.740	64.033	63.005	78.784	49.305	67.885
72	60.854	74.678	61.302	60.004	76.786	46.494	65.599
73	57.650	72.429	58.455	56.910	74.658	43.715	63.247
74	54.296	69.972	55.488	53.751	72.412	40.980	60.843
75	50.810	67.296	52.408	50.557	70.063	38.301	58.397
76	47.227	64.404	49.232	47.263	67.509	35.644	55.833
77	43.585	61.310	45.984	43.914	64.776	33.028	53.176
78	39.928	58.033	42.695	40.551	61.893	30.472	50.448
79	36.292	54.589	39.390	37.214	58.889	27.991	47.673
80	32.705	50.987	36.084	33.939	55.794	25.600	44.875

| | CSO (1980) | | Total | U. S. Life Tables (1982) | | | |
	Male	Female	Population	White Male	White Female	Black Male	Black Female
Life Expectancy	26.20	30.39	26.75	26.50	32.20	22.90	28.90
Age							
81	29.190	47.234	32.792	29.404	50.220	22.242	40.128
82	25.768	43.342	29.548	24.135	42.823	18.308	33.995
83	22.463	39.331	26.388	18.709	34.486	14.232	27.200
84	19.312	35.248	23.341	13.650	26.139	10.413	20.483
85	16.358	31.156	20.409	9.336	18.574	7.143	14.460
86	13.641	27.128	17.603	5.960	12.319	4.573	9.528
87	11.192	23.240	14.966	3.533	7.586	2.718	5.830
88	9.029	19.564	12.548	1.933	4.313	1.492	3.292
89	7.157	16.161	10.378	0.970	2.247	0.750	1.705
90	5.570	13.078	8.458	0.442	1.065	0.343	0.802
91	4.250	10.347	6.776	0.181	0.454	0.141	0.340
92	3.173	7.979	5.328	0.066	0.172	0.052	0.128
93	2.310	5.972	4.110	0.021	0.057	0.017	0.042
94	1.626	4.304	3.110	0.006	0.016	0.005	0.012
95	1.090	2.938	2.309	0.001	0.004	0.001	0.003
96	0.671	1.834	1.687	> 0.001	0.001	> 0.001	0.001
97	0.349	0.963	1.214	> 0.001	> 0.001	> 0.001	> 0.001
98	0.119	0.331	0.862	> 0.001	> 0.001	> 0.001	> 0.001
99	> 0.001	> 0.001	0.605	> 0.001	> 0.001	> 0.001	> 0.001

Probability of surviving through age X starting from age 50

	CSO (1980)		Total Population	U. S. Life Tables (1982)			
	Male	Female		White Male	White Female	Black Male	Black Female
Life Expectancy	25.36	29.53	25.93	25.60	33.10	22.20	28.00
Age							
50	99.329	99.504	99.262	99.331	99.642	98.614	99.287
51	98.604	98.976	98.464	98.594	99.249	97.136	98.513
52	97.819	98.411	97.601	97.785	98.820	95.565	97.678
53	96.967	97.806	96.667	96.903	98.351	93.902	96.785
54	96.040	97.160	95.659	95.945	97.843	92.147	95.834
55	95.034	96.471	94.572	94.906	97.290	90.302	94.825
56	93.945	95.741	93.404	93.782	96.690	88.365	93.754
57	92.772	94.972	92.151	92.568	96.038	86.336	92.614
58	91.511	94.167	90.813	91.257	95.332	84.211	91.394
59	90.160	93.326	89.387	89.845	94.568	81.991	90.086
60	88.710	92.442	87.872	88.331	93.741	79.677	88.686
61	87.154	91.505	86.265	86.711	92.849	77.276	87.197
62	85.481	90.502	84.562	84.973	91.884	74.792	85.626
63	83.681	89.415	82.758	83.108	90.842	72.234	83.987
64	81.745	88.230	80.850	81.107	89.716	69.609	82.289
65	79.667	86.943	78.833	78.969	88.503	66.925	80.535
66	77.448	85.551	76.705	76.674	87.179	64.172	78.689
67	75.091	84.060	74.467	74.242	85.752	61.368	76.760
68	72.598	82.477	72.120	71.687	84.226	58.528	74.755
69	69.972	80.797	69.667	69.028	82.607	55.668	72.682
70	67.208	79.011	67.117	66.283	80.902	52.806	70.551
71	64.298	77.097	64.471	63.386	79.041	49.943	68.329

	CSO (1980)		Total Population	U. S. Life Tables (1982)			
	Male	Female		White Male	White Female	Black Male	Black Female
Life Expectancy	25.36	29.53	25.93	25.60	33.10	22.20	28.00
Age							
72	61.234	75.025	61.720	60.367	77.037	47.097	66.028
73	58.011	72.766	58.854	57.254	74.901	44.281	63.661
74	54.635	70.297	55.867	54.076	72.648	41.510	61.241
75	51.128	67.609	52.765	50.863	70.292	38.797	58.779
76	47.522	64.704	49.568	47.549	67.729	36.106	56.199
77	43.857	61.595	46.298	44.180	64.987	33.456	53.523
78	40.177	58.303	42.987	40.796	62.095	30.867	50.778
79	36.519	54.843	39.659	37.439	59.081	28.354	47.985
80	32.910	51.224	36.330	34.144	55.976	25.931	45.168
81	29.373	47.454	33.016	29.582	50.383	22.530	40.391
82	25.929	43.543	29.750	24.281	42.962	18.545	34.218
83	22.603	39.514	26.568	18.822	34.599	14.416	27.378
84	19.433	35.412	23.500	13.733	26.225	10.548	20.617
85	16.461	31.301	20.548	9.393	18.635	7.235	14.555
86	13.727	27.254	17.723	5.996	12.359	4.632	9.590
87	11.262	23.348	15.069	3.555	7.611	2.754	5.868
88	9.085	19.655	12.634	1.945	4.327	1.511	3.314
89	7.202	16.236	10.449	0.976	2.255	0.760	1.716
90	5.605	13.139	8.516	0.445	1.068	0.348	0.807
91	4.277	10.395	6.822	0.183	0.455	0.143	0.342
92	3.193	8.016	5.365	0.067	0.173	0.052	0.129
93	2.324	6.000	4.138	0.021	0.057	0.017	0.042
94	1.636	4.324	3.131	0.006	0.016	0.005	0.012

CSO (1980)

Age	CSO (1980) Male	CSO (1980) Female	Total Population	U.S. Life Tables (1982) White Male	U.S. Life Tables (1982) White Female	U.S. Life Tables (1982) Black Male	U.S. Life Tables (1982) Black Female
Life Expectancy	25.36	29.53	25.93	25.60	33.10	22.20	28.00
Age							
95	1.096	2.952	2.325	0.001	0.004	0.001	0.003
96	0.675	1.843	1.698	> 0.001	0.001	> 0.001	0.001
97	0.351	0.968	1.222	> 0.001	> 0.001	> 0.001	> 0.001
98	0.120	0.333	0.868	> 0.001	> 0.001	> 0.001	> 0.001
99	> 0.001	> 0.001	0.609	> 0.001	> 0.001	> 0.001	> 0.001

Probability of surviving through age X starting from age 51

Age	CSO (1980) Male	CSO (1980) Female	Total Population	U.S. Life Tables (1982) White Male	U.S. Life Tables (1982) White Female	U.S. Life Tables (1982) Black Male	U.S. Life Tables (1982) Black Female
Life Expectancy	24.52	28.67	25.12	24.80	30.40	21.50	27.20
Age							
51	99.270	99.469	99.196	99.258	99.606	98.501	99.220
52	98.480	98.902	98.327	98.444	99.175	96.908	98.380
53	97.622	98.294	97.386	97.556	98.705	95.222	97.480
54	96.689	97.644	96.370	96.591	98.194	93.442	96.522
55	95.676	96.952	95.276	95.545	97.640	91.571	95.506
56	94.580	96.218	94.098	94.414	97.037	89.606	94.428
57	93.399	95.445	92.836	93.191	96.383	87.549	93.279
58	92.129	94.637	91.488	91.872	95.675	85.395	92.050
59	90.769	93.791	90.052	90.450	94.907	83.144	90.733

| | CSO (1980) | | Total | U. S. Life Tables (1982) | | | |
Age	Male	Female	Population	White Male	White Female	Black Male	Black Female
Life Expectancy	24.52	28.67	25.12	24.80	30.40	21.50	27.20
60	89.309	92.903	88.525	88.926	94.078	80.797	89.323
61	87.743	91.961	86.906	87.295	93.182	78.362	87.823
62	86.059	90.954	85.191	85.545	92.214	75.843	86.241
63	84.246	89.860	83.374	83.667	91.168	73.249	84.591
64	82.297	88.670	81.451	81.654	90.039	70.587	82.880
65	80.205	87.376	79.419	79.500	88.821	67.865	81.113
66	77.971	85.978	77.275	77.191	87.493	65.074	79.254
67	75.598	84.479	75.020	74.742	86.060	62.230	77.311
68	73.089	82.888	72.656	72.170	84.529	59.350	75.291
69	70.445	81.200	70.185	69.493	82.904	56.451	73.204
70	67.662	79.405	67.616	66.729	81.193	53.548	71.058
71	64.732	77.481	64.950	63.813	79.325	50.645	68.820
72	61.648	75.399	62.179	60.774	77.314	47.759	66.502
73	58.402	73.129	59.292	57.640	75.171	44.904	64.118
74	55.004	70.647	56.282	54.441	72.909	42.094	61.681
75	51.473	67.946	53.158	51.205	70.544	39.343	59.201
76	47.843	65.026	49.936	47.869	67.972	36.613	56.602
77	44.153	61.902	46.643	44.477	65.221	33.926	53.908
78	40.449	58.594	43.306	41.071	62.318	31.300	51.142
79	36.766	55.116	39.954	37.691	59.293	28.752	48.330
80	33.132	51.479	36.600	34.374	56.178	26.296	45.493

Age	CSO (1980)		Total Population	U. S. Life Tables (1982)			
	Male	Female		White Male	White Female	Black Male	Black Female
Life Expectancy	24.52	28.67	25.12	24.80	30.40	21.50	27.20
81	29.571	47.690	33.261	29.781	50.564	22.847	40.681
82	26.104	43.760	29.971	24.444	43.117	18.805	34.464
83	22.756	39.711	26.766	18.949	34.723	14.619	27.574
84	19.564	35.589	23.675	13.825	26.319	10.696	20.765
85	16.572	31.457	20.701	9.456	18.702	7.337	14.659
86	13.819	27.390	17.855	6.037	12.403	4.697	9.659
87	11.338	23.464	15.181	3.579	7.639	2.792	5.910
88	9.147	19.753	12.728	1.958	4.342	1.532	3.338
89	7.251	16.317	10.527	0.982	2.263	0.771	1.728
90	5.643	13.205	8.579	0.448	1.072	0.352	0.813
91	4.306	10.447	6.873	0.184	0.457	0.145	0.344
92	3.214	8.056	5.405	0.067	0.173	0.053	0.130
93	2.340	6.030	4.169	0.021	0.057	0.017	0.043
94	1.647	4.346	3.154	0.006	0.016	0.005	0.012
95	1.104	2.967	2.342	0.001	0.004	0.001	0.003
96	0.679	1.852	1.711	> 0.001	0.001	> 0.001	0.001
97	0.353	0.972	1.231	> 0.001	> 0.001	> 0.001	> 0.001
98	0.121	0.335	0.875	> 0.001	> 0.001	> 0.001	> 0.001
99	> 0.001	> 0.001	0.613	> 0.001	> 0.001	> 0.001	> 0.001

Probability of surviving through age X starting from age 52

| | CSO (1980) | | | U. S. Life Tables (1982) | | | |
	Male	Female	Total Population	White Male	White Female	Black Male	Black Female
Life Expectancy	23.70	27.82	24.32	24.00	29.60	20.80	26.50
Age							
52	99.204	99.430	99.124	99.180	99.567	98.383	99.153
53	98.340	98.819	98.175	98.285	99.095	96.671	98.247
54	97.400	98.165	97.151	97.313	98.583	94.864	97.281
55	96.380	97.469	96.048	96.259	98.026	92.964	96.257
56	95.276	96.731	94.861	95.120	97.421	90.970	95.170
57	94.086	95.955	93.589	93.888	96.764	88.881	94.013
58	92.807	95.142	92.230	92.558	96.053	86.694	92.774
59	91.436	94.291	90.782	91.127	95.283	84.409	91.446
60	89.966	93.398	89.243	89.591	94.450	82.027	90.025
61	88.388	92.452	87.611	87.947	93.551	79.555	88.513
62	86.692	91.439	85.881	86.185	92.579	76.998	86.919
63	84.866	90.340	84.049	84.293	91.529	74.364	85.256
64	82.902	89.143	82.111	82.264	90.395	71.661	83.532
65	80.795	87.842	80.062	80.095	89.172	68.898	81.751
66	78.545	86.437	77.902	77.768	87.839	66.064	79.877
67	76.154	84.930	75.628	75.300	86.401	63.177	77.919
68	73.626	83.330	73.245	72.709	84.863	60.253	75.883
69	70.963	81.634	70.754	70.012	83.232	57.310	73.780
70	68.159	79.829	68.164	67.228	81.514	54.363	71.617
71	65.208	77.894	65.476	64.290	79.639	51.416	69.361
72	62.101	75.801	62.683	61.228	77.619	48.485	67.025
73	58.832	73.519	59.772	58.071	75.468	45.587	64.622

	CSO (1980)		Total Population	U. S. Life Tables (1982)			
Life Expectancy	Male	Female		White Male	White Female	Black Male	Black Female
	23.70	27.82	24.32	24.00	29.60	20.80	26.50
Age							
74	55.409	71.025	56.739	54.848	73.198	42.735	62.165
75	51.852	68.309	53.589	51.588	70.823	39.941	59.666
76	48.195	65.373	50.341	48.227	68.241	37.171	57.047
77	44.478	62.233	47.021	44.810	65.479	34.443	54.332
78	40.746	58.906	43.657	41.378	62.564	31.777	51.544
79	37.036	55.410	40.278	37.973	59.528	29.190	48.709
80	33.376	51.754	36.897	34.631	56.400	26.696	45.850
81	29.788	47.945	33.531	30.004	50.764	23.194	41.001
82	26.296	43.994	30.214	24.627	43.287	19.092	34.735
83	22.923	39.923	26.983	19.091	34.860	14.841	27.791
84	19.708	35.779	23.867	13.928	26.423	10.859	20.928
85	16.694	31.625	20.869	9.527	18.776	7.448	14.774
86	13.921	27.536	18.000	6.082	12.452	4.768	9.735
87	11.422	23.590	15.304	3.605	7.669	2.835	5.956
88	9.214	19.858	12.831	1.973	4.359	1.556	3.364
89	7.304	16.404	10.612	0.990	2.272	0.782	1.742
90	5.684	13.275	8.649	0.451	1.076	0.358	0.820
91	4.337	10.502	6.929	0.185	0.459	0.147	0.347
92	3.238	8.099	5.448	0.068	0.174	0.054	0.131
93	2.357	6.062	4.202	0.022	0.058	0.017	0.043
94	1.659	4.369	3.180	0.006	0.016	0.005	0.012
95	1.112	2.983	2.361	0.001	0.004	0.001	0.003
96	0.684	1.862	1.725	> 0.001	0.001	> 0.001	0.001

	CSO (1980)		Total Population	U.S. Life Tables (1982)			
	Male	Female		White Male	White Female	Black Male	Black Female
Life Expectancy	23.70	27.82	24.32	24.00	29.60	20.80	26.50
Age							
97	0.356	0.978	1.241	> 0.001	> 0.001	> 0.001	> 0.001
98	0.122	0.336	0.882	> 0.001	> 0.001	> 0.001	> 0.001
99	> 0.001	> 0.001	0.618	> 0.001	> 0.001	> 0.001	> 0.001

Probability of surviving through age X starting from age 53

	CSO (1980)		Total Population	U.S. Life Tables (1982)			
	Male	Female		White Male	White Female	Black Male	Black Female
Life Expectancy	22.89	26.98	23.53	23.20	28.70	20.20	25.70
Age							
53	99.129	99.385	99.043	99.098	99.526	98.260	99.086
54	98.181	98.728	98.010	98.118	99.011	96.424	98.112
55	97.153	98.028	96.897	97.055	98.452	94.492	97.079
56	96.040	97.286	95.699	95.906	97.845	92.465	95.983
57	94.840	96.505	94.416	94.664	97.185	90.342	94.816
58	93.552	95.687	93.045	93.324	96.471	88.119	93.566
59	92.170	94.832	91.584	91.880	95.697	85.796	92.227
60	90.688	93.934	90.032	90.332	94.861	83.375	90.794
61	89.097	92.982	88.385	88.674	93.958	80.862	89.269
62	87.387	91.963	86.640	86.897	92.981	78.263	87.662
63	85.547	90.858	84.792	84.990	91.927	75.586	85.984

Life Expectancy	CSO (1980)		Total Population	U. S. Life Tables (1982)			
	Male	Female		White Male	White Female	Black Male	Black Female
	22.89	26.98	23.53	23.20	28.70	20.20	25.70
Age							
64	83.567	89.654	82.837	82.944	90.788	72.839	84.245
65	81.443	88.346	80.770	80.757	89.560	70.030	82.449
66	79.175	86.932	78.590	78.411	88.221	67.150	80.559
67	76.765	85.417	76.297	75.923	86.777	64.216	78.584
68	74.217	83.808	73.892	73.310	85.232	61.244	76.531
69	71.533	82.102	71.380	70.591	83.594	58.252	74.410
70	68.706	80.286	68.766	67.784	81.868	55.257	72.228
71	65.731	78.341	66.055	64.822	79.985	52.261	69.953
72	62.599	76.236	63.237	61.734	77.957	49.282	67.598
73	59.304	73.941	60.300	58.551	75.796	46.336	65.174
74	55.853	71.432	57.240	55.301	73.516	43.437	62.697
75	52.268	68.700	54.062	52.015	71.131	40.598	60.176
76	48.581	65.748	50.786	48.626	68.538	37.782	57.534
77	44.835	62.590	47.436	45.180	65.763	35.009	54.796
78	41.073	59.244	44.043	41.720	62.836	32.299	51.985
79	37.333	55.728	40.634	38.287	59.787	29.669	49.126
80	33.643	52.051	37.223	34.917	56.645	27.135	46.242
81	30.027	48.220	33.827	30.252	50.985	23.576	41.351
82	26.507	44.246	30.481	24.831	43.475	19.405	35.031
83	23.107	40.152	27.221	19.248	35.012	15.085	28.028
84	19.866	35.984	24.078	14.043	26.538	11.037	21.107
85	16.828	31.806	21.053	9.606	18.857	7.571	14.901
86	14.033	27.694	18.159	6.132	12.507	4.847	9.818

CSO (1980) / U. S. Life Tables (1982)

	CSO (1980)			U. S. Life Tables (1982)			
	Male	Female	Total Population	White Male	White Female	Black Male	Black Female
Life Expectancy	22.89	26.98	23.53	23.20	28.70	20.20	25.70
Age							
87	11.513	23.725	15.439	3.635	7.702	2.881	6.007
88	9.288	19.972	12.944	1.989	4.378	1.581	3.393
89	7.363	16.498	10.706	0.998	2.282	0.795	1.756
90	5.730	13.351	8.725	0.455	1.081	0.364	0.827
91	4.372	10.562	6.990	0.187	0.461	0.150	0.350
92	3.264	8.146	5.497	0.068	0.175	0.055	0.132
93	2.376	6.097	4.240	0.022	0.058	0.018	0.043
94	1.673	4.394	3.208	0.006	0.016	0.005	0.012
95	1.121	3.000	2.382	0.001	0.004	0.001	0.003
96	0.690	1.873	1.740	$>$ 0.001	0.001	$>$ 0.001	0.001
97	0.359	0.983	1.252	$>$ 0.001	$>$ 0.001	$>$ 0.001	$>$ 0.001
98	0.123	0.338	0.889	$>$ 0.001	$>$ 0.001	$>$ 0.001	$>$ 0.001
99	$>$ 0.001	$>$ 0.001	0.624	$>$ 0.001	$>$ 0.001	$>$ 0.001	$>$ 0.001

Probability of surviving through age X starting from age 54

	CSO (1980)			U. S. Life Tables (1982)			
	Male	Female	Total Population	White Male	White Female	Black Male	Black Female
Life Expectancy	22.08	26.14	22.75	22.40	27.80	19.50	24.90
Age							
54	99.044	99.339	98.957	99.011	99.483	98.131	99.017

| | CSO (1980) | | Total | U. S. Life Tables (1982) | | | |
Age	Male	Female	Population	White Male	White Female	Black Male	Black Female
Life Expectancy	22.08	26.14	22.75	22.40	27.80	19.50	24.90
55	98.007	98.635	97.833	97.939	98.921	96.165	97.974
56	96.884	97.888	96.624	96.779	98.311	94.103	96.868
57	95.674	97.102	95.328	95.526	97.648	91.942	95.690
58	94.374	96.280	93.944	94.173	96.930	89.679	94.429
59	92.980	95.419	92.469	92.716	96.153	87.315	93.078
60	91.485	94.515	90.901	91.154	95.312	84.851	91.631
61	89.880	93.558	89.239	89.481	94.405	82.294	90.093
62	88.155	92.532	87.477	87.688	93.424	79.649	88.470
63	86.299	91.420	85.611	85.673	92.365	76.924	86.777
64	84.302	90.209	83.367	83.699	91.220	74.129	85.022
65	82.159	88.893	81.550	81.492	89.986	71.270	83.210
66	79.871	87.470	79.349	79.125	88.641	68.339	81.303
67	77.439	85.946	77.034	76.614	87.190	65.353	79.309
68	74.869	84.327	74.606	73.978	85.638	62.328	77.237
69	72.161	82.610	72.069	71.234	83.992	59.283	75.096
70	69.310	80.783	69.431	68.401	82.258	56.235	72.895
71	66.309	78.826	66.693	65.412	80.366	53.187	70.598
72	63.149	76.708	63.848	62.296	78.328	50.155	68.221
73	59.825	74.398	60.883	59.084	76.157	47.157	65.776
74	56.344	71.874	57.793	55.804	73.866	44.206	63.275
75	52.727	69.125	54.584	52.488	71.470	41.317	60.731
76	49.008	66.155	51.277	49.068	68.864	38.451	58.065
77	45.229	62.977	47.894	45.591	66.077	35.629	55.301

	CSO (1980)			U. S. Life Tables (1982)			
	Male	Female	Total Population	White Male	White Female	Black Male	Black Female
Life Expectancy	22.08	26.14	22.75	22.40	27.80	19.50	24.90
Age							
78	41.434	59.611	44.469	42.100	63.136	32.871	52.464
79	37.662	56.073	41.026	38.636	60.072	30.195	49.579
80	33.939	52.373	37.582	35.235	59.915	27.615	46.668
81	30.291	48.518	34.154	30.528	51.228	23.993	41.732
82	26.740	44.520	30.776	25.057	43.683	19.749	35.354
83	23.310	40.401	27.484	19.424	35.179	15.352	28.287
84	20.041	36.207	24.310	14.171	26.664	11.233	21.301
85	16.976	32.003	21.257	9.693	18.947	7.705	15.038
86	14.156	27.865	18.334	6.188	12.566	4.933	9.909
87	11.614	23.872	15.588	3.668	7.739	2.932	6.063
88	9.370	20.096	13.069	2.007	4.399	1.609	3.424
89	7.427	16.600	10.809	1.007	2.292	0.809	1.773
90	5.780	13.434	8.809	0.459	1.086	0.370	0.834
91	4.410	10.628	7.057	0.188	0.463	0.152	0.353
92	3.293	8.196	5.550	0.069	0.175	0.056	0.133
93	2.397	6.135	4.281	0.022	0.058	0.018	0.044
94	1.687	4.421	3.239	0.006	0.017	0.005	0.012
95	1.131	3.018	2.405	0.001	0.004	0.001	0.003
96	0.696	1.884	1.757	< 0.001	0.001	< 0.001	0.001
97	0.362	0.989	1.264	< 0.001	< 0.001	< 0.001	< 0.001
98	0.124	0.340	0.898	< 0.001	< 0.001	< 0.001	< 0.001
99	< 0.001	< 0.001	0.630	< 0.001	< 0.001	< 0.001	< 0.001

Probability of surviving through age X starting from age 55

	CSO (1980)		Total Population	U. S. Life Tables (1982)			
	Male	Female		White Male	White Female	Black Male	Black Female
Life Expectancy	21.29	25.31	21.99	21.60	27.00	18.90	24.10
Age							
55	98.953	99.291	98.864	98.917	99.435	97.997	98.947
56	97.819	98.539	97.642	97.746	98.821	95.895	97.830
57	96.597	97.748	96.333	96.480	98.155	93.693	96.640
58	95.284	96.920	94.934	95.114	97.434	91.387	95.367
59	93.877	96.054	93.443	93.642	96.653	88.978	94.002
60	92.368	95.144	91.860	92.065	95.808	86.467	92.541
61	90.747	94.180	90.179	90.375	94.896	83.861	90.987
62	90.006	93.148	88.399	88.564	93.910	81.166	89.349
63	87.132	92.028	86.514	86.620	92.845	78.389	87.638
64	85.115	90.809	84.519	84.535	91.694	75.541	85.866
65	82.952	89.484	82.410	82.306	90.454	72.628	84.036
66	80.641	88.052	80.186	79.915	89.102	69.641	82.110
67	78.187	86.518	77.846	77.379	87.643	66.597	80.096
68	75.592	84.888	75.392	74.717	86.083	63.515	78.004
69	72.858	83.159	72.829	71.945	84.428	60.413	75.842
70	69.979	81.321	70.163	69.084	82.686	57.306	73.618
71	66.949	79.350	67.396	66.065	80.784	54.200	71.299
72	63.759	77.218	64.521	62.918	78.735	51.110	68.899
73	60.403	74.893	61.525	59.674	76.553	48.055	66.429
74	56.888	72.352	58.402	56.362	74.250	45.048	63.903
75	53.236	69.585	55.160	53.012	71.841	42.104	61.334
76	49.481	66.595	51.817	49.559	69.222	39.183	58.642

| | CSO (1980) | | Total | U. S. Life Tables (1982) | | | |
	Male	Female	Population	White Male	White Female	Black Male	Black Female
Life Expectancy	21.29	25.31	21.99	21.60	27.00	18.90	24.10
Age							
77	45.665	63.396	48.399	46.047	66.420	36.307	55.850
78	41.834	60.007	44.937	42.521	63.464	33.497	52.985
79	38.025	56.446	41.459	39.022	60.384	30.770	50.071
80	34.267	52.721	37.979	35.587	57.211	28.141	47.132
81	30.584	48.841	34.514	30.832	51.494	24.450	42.147
82	26.998	44.816	31.100	25.307	43.910	20.125	35.705
83	23.535	40.669	27.774	19.618	35.362	15.645	28.568
84	20.234	36.448	24.567	14.313	26.803	11.447	21.513
85	17.139	32.216	21.481	9.790	19.046	7.852	15.187
86	14.293	28.051	18.528	6.250	12.632	5.027	10.007
87	11.726	24.031	15.752	3.705	7.779	2.988	6.123
88	9.460	20.229	13.207	2.027	4.422	1.640	3.458
89	7.499	16.711	10.923	1.017	2.304	0.825	1.790
90	5.836	13.523	8.902	0.464	1.092	0.377	0.843
91	4.453	10.699	7.132	0.190	0.465	0.155	0.357
92	3.324	8.251	5.608	0.069	0.176	0.057	0.134
93	2.420	6.176	4.326	0.022	0.058	0.018	0.044
94	1.704	4.451	3.273	0.006	0.017	0.005	0.013
95	1.142	3.038	2.430	0.001	0.004	0.001	0.003
96	0.703	1.897	1.775	> 0.001	0.001	0.001	0.001
97	0.365	0.996	1.278	> 0.001	> 0.001	> 0.001	> 0.001
98	0.125	0.343	0.907	> 0.001	> 0.001	> 0.001	> 0.001
99	> 0.001	> 0.001	0.636	> 0.001	> 0.001	> 0.001	> 0.001

Probability of surviving through age X starting from age 56

Age	CSO (1980) Male	CSO (1980) Female	Total Population	U. S. Life Tables (1982) White Male	White Female	Black Male	Black Female
Life Expectancy	20.51	24.49	21.23	20.80	26.10	18.20	23.40
56	98.854	99.243	98.764	98.816	99.383	97.855	98.871
57	97.619	98.446	97.440	97.536	98.713	95.608	97.669
58	96.293	97.612	96.025	96.155	97.988	93.255	96.381
59	94.870	96.740	94.517	94.668	97.202	90.797	95.002
60	93.345	95.823	92.915	93.073	96.352	88.235	93.526
61	91.708	94.853	91.216	91.365	95.435	85.575	91.956
62	89.948	93.813	89.415	89.534	94.443	82.825	90.299
63	88.053	92.686	87.508	87.568	93.372	79.992	88.571
64	86.016	91.457	85.490	85.461	92.215	77.085	86.780
65	83.829	90.123	83.357	83.207	90.968	74.112	84.930
66	81.495	88.681	81.107	80.790	89.608	71.064	82.983
67	79.014	87.135	78.740	78.226	88.141	67.959	80.949
68	76.392	85.494	76.259	75.535	86.572	64.813	78.834
69	73.628	83.753	73.666	72.733	84.908	61.647	76.649
70	70.719	81.901	70.969	69.841	83.156	58.477	74.402
71	67.657	79.917	68.171	66.788	81.243	55.307	72.058
72	64.433	77.770	65.262	63.607	79.183	52.155	69.632
73	61.042	75.428	62.232	60.327	76.988	49.037	67.136
74	57.490	72.869	59.073	56.979	74.672	45.969	64.583

	CSO (1980)			U. S. Life Tables (1982)			
	Male	Female	Total Population	White Male	White Female	Black Male	Black Female
Life Expectancy	20.51	24.49	21.23	20.80	26.10	18.20	23.40
Age							
75	53.799	70.082	55.794	53.593	72.250	42.964	61.987
76	50.005	67.071	52.413	50.101	69.615	39.984	59.266
77	46.149	63.849	48.955	46.551	66.797	37.049	56.445
78	42.277	60.436	45.454	42.986	63.824	34.182	53.549
79	38.427	56.849	41.935	39.449	60.727	31.399	50.604
80	34.629	53.098	38.415	35.977	57.536	28.716	47.633
81	30.907	49.190	34.911	31.170	51.787	24.950	42.595
82	27.283	45.136	31.457	25.584	44.159	20.536	36.085
83	23.784	40.960	28.093	19.832	35.563	15.965	28.872
84	20.448	36.708	24.849	14.470	26.955	11.681	21.742
85	17.321	32.446	21.728	9.897	19.154	8.012	15.349
86	14.444	28.251	18.740	6.318	12.703	5.129	10.114
87	11.851	24.202	15.933	3.745	7.823	3.049	6.188
88	9.560	20.374	13.359	2.049	4.447	1.673	3.495
89	7.578	16.830	11.049	1.028	2.317	0.842	1.809
90	5.898	13.620	9.005	0.469	1.098	0.385	0.852
91	4.500	10.775	7.214	0.192	0.468	0.158	0.361
92	3.360	8.310	5.673	0.070	0.177	0.058	0.136
93	2.445	6.220	4.375	0.022	0.059	0.019	0.045
94	1.722	4.482	3.311	0.006	0.017	0.005	0.013
95	1.154	3.060	2.458	0.001	0.004	0.001	0.003

| | CSO (1980) | | Total | U. S. Life Tables (1982) | | | |
	Male	Female	Population	White Male	White Female	Black Male	Black Female
Life Expectancy	20.51	24.49	21.23	20.80	26.10	18.20	23.40
Age							
96	0.710	1.910	1.796	< 0.001	0.001	< 0.001	0.001
97	0.369	1.003	1.292	< 0.001	< 0.001	< 0.001	< 0.001
98	0.126	0.345	0.918	< 0.001	< 0.001	< 0.001	< 0.001
99	< 0.001	< 0.001	0.644	< 0.001	< 0.001	< 0.001	< 0.001

Probability of surviving through age X starting from age 57

| | CSO (1980) | | Total | U. S. Life Tables (1982) | | | |
	Male	Female	Population	White Male	White Female	Black Male	Black Female
Life Expectancy	19.74	23.67	20.49	20.10	25.30	17.60	22.70
Age							
57	98.751	99.197	98.659	98.705	99.326	97.704	98.784
58	97.409	98.357	97.226	97.307	98.596	95.300	97.482
59	95.970	97.477	95.700	95.802	97.805	92.787	96.087
60	94.427	96.554	94.078	94.188	96.950	90.169	94.594
61	92.771	95.576	92.357	92.459	96.027	87.451	93.006
62	90.991	94.529	90.534	90.606	95.030	84.641	91.331
63	89.074	93.393	88.603	88.618	93.952	81.745	89.583
64	87.013	92.155	86.560	86.485	92.788	78.774	87.771

Life Expectancy	CSO (1980) Male	CSO (1980) Female	Total Population	U.S. Life Tables (1982) White Male	White Female	Black Male	Black Female
	19.74	23.67	20.49	20.10	25.30	17.60	22.70
Age							
65	84.801	90.811	84.400	84.204	91.533	75.737	85.900
66	82.439	89.358	82.122	81.758	90.164	72.622	83.931
67	79.930	87.800	79.726	79.164	88.688	69.448	81.873
68	77.277	86.146	77.213	76.440	87.110	66.234	79.735
69	74.482	84.392	74.588	73.605	85.435	62.999	77.524
70	71.539	82.526	71.857	70.677	83.672	59.759	75.251
71	68.442	80.526	69.024	67.589	81.747	56.520	72.881
72	65.180	78.363	66.079	64.369	79.674	53.298	70.427
73	61.749	76.003	63.010	61.050	77.466	50.112	67.902
74	58.156	73.424	59.813	57.662	75.136	46.976	65.321
75	54.423	70.617	56.492	54.235	72.698	43.906	62.695
76	50.585	67.582	53.068	50.701	70.048	40.860	59.942
77	46.684	64.336	49.568	47.109	67.212	37.862	57.089
78	42.767	60.897	46.022	43.501	64.220	34.931	54.160
79	38.873	57.283	42.460	39.921	61.104	32.087	51.182
80	35.031	53.503	38.896	36.408	57.893	29.346	48.177
81	31.266	49.565	35.348	31.543	52.108	25.497	43.082
82	27.600	45.481	31.851	25.891	44.433	20.987	36.497
83	24.060	41.272	28.445	20.070	35.783	16.315	29.202
84	20.685	36.988	25.160	14.643	27.122	11.937	21.990
85	17.522	32.694	22.000	10.016	19.273	8.188	15.524
86	14.611	28.467	18.975	6.394	12.782	5.242	10.229
87	11.988	24.387	16.133	3.790	7.872	3.116	6.259

CSO (1980) / U. S. Life Tables (1982)

| | CSO (1980) | | | U. S. Life Tables (1982) | | | |
	Male	Female	Total Population	White Male	White Female	Black Male	Black Female
Life Expectancy	19.74	23.67	20.49	20.10	25.30	17.60	22.70
Age							
88	9.671	20.529	13.526	2.074	4.475	1.710	3.535
89	7.666	16.958	11.187	1.040	2.332	0.860	1.830
90	5.966	13.724	9.117	0.474	1.105	0.393	0.861
91	4.552	10.857	7.304	0.195	0.471	0.162	0.365
92	3.399	8.373	5.744	0.071	0.178	0.059	0.137
93	2.474	6.267	4.430	0.023	0.059	0.019	0.045
94	1.742	4.517	3.352	0.006	0.017	0.005	0.013
95	1.167	3.083	2.489	0.001	0.004	0.001	0.003
96	0.718	1.925	1.818	> 0.001	0.001	> 0.001	> 0.001
97	0.373	1.011	1.309	> 0.001	> 0.001	> 0.001	> 0.001
98	0.128	0.348	0.929	> 0.001	> 0.001	> 0.001	> 0.001
99	> 0.001	> 0.001	0.652	> 0.001	> 0.001	> 0.001	> 0.001

Probability of surviving through age X starting from age 57

| | CSO (1980) | | | U. S. Life Tables (1982) | | | |
	Male	Female	Total Population	White Male	White Female	Black Male	Black Female
Life Expectancy	19.74	23.67	20.49	20.10	25.30	17.60	22.70
Age							
57	98.751	99.197	98.659	98.705	99.326	97.704	98.784
58	97.409	98.357	97.226	97.307	98.596	95.300	97.482

	CSO (1980)		Total Population	U. S. Life Tables (1982)			
	Male	Female		White Male	White Female	Black Male	Black Female
Life Expectancy	19.74	23.67	20.49	20.10	25.30	17.60	22.70
Age							
59	95.970	97.477	95.700	95.802	97.805	92.787	96.087
60	94.427	96.554	94.078	94.188	96.950	90.169	94.594
61	92.771	95.576	92.357	92.459	96.027	87.451	93.006
62	90.991	94.529	90.534	90.606	95.030	84.641	81.331
63	89.074	93.393	88.603	88.618	93.952	81.745	89.583
64	87.013	92.155	86.560	86.485	92.788	78.774	87.771
65	84.801	90.811	84.400	84.204	91.533	75.737	85.900
66	82.439	89.358	82.122	81.758	90.164	72.622	83.931
67	79.930	87.800	79.726	79.164	88.688	69.448	81.873
68	77.277	86.146	77.213	76.440	87.110	66.234	79.735
69	74.482	84.392	74.588	73.605	85.435	62.999	77.524
70	71.539	82.526	71.857	70.677	83.672	59.759	75.251
71	68.442	80.526	69.024	67.589	81.747	56.520	72.881
72	65.180	78.363	66.079	64.369	79.674	53.298	70.427
73	61.749	76.003	63.010	61.050	77.466	50.112	67.902
74	58.156	73.424	59.813	57.662	75.136	46.976	65.321
75	54.423	70.617	56.492	54.235	72.698	43.906	62.695
76	50.585	67.582	53.068	50.701	70.048	40.860	59.942
77	46.684	64.336	49.568	47.109	67.212	37.862	57.089
78	42.767	60.897	46.022	43.501	64.220	34.931	54.160
79	38.873	57.283	42.460	39.921	61.104	32.087	51.182
80	35.031	53.503	38.896	36.408	57.893	29.346	48.177

Life Expectancy Age	CSO (1980) Male	CSO (1980) Female	Total Population	U.S. Life Tables (1982) White Male	U.S. Life Tables (1982) White Female	U.S. Life Tables (1982) Black Male	U.S. Life Tables (1982) Black Female
	19.74	23.67	20.49	20.10	25.30	17.60	22.70
81	31.266	49.565	35.348	31.543	52.108	25.497	43.082
82	27.600	45.481	31.851	25.891	44.433	20.987	36.497
83	24.060	41.272	28.445	20.070	35.783	16.315	29.202
84	20.684	36.988	25.160	14.643	27.122	11.937	21.990
85	17.522	32.694	22.000	10.016	19.273	8.188	15.524
86	14.611	28.467	18.975	6.394	12.782	5.242	10.229
87	11.988	24.387	16.133	3.790	7.872	3.116	6.259
88	9.671	20.529	13.526	2.074	4.475	1.710	3.535
89	7.666	16.958	11.187	1.050	2.332	0.860	1.830
90	5.966	13.724	9.117	0.474	1.105	0.393	0.861
91	4.552	10.857	7.304	0.195	0.471	0.162	0.365
92	3.399	8.373	5.744	0.071	0.178	0.059	0.137
93	2.474	6.267	4.430	0.023	0.059	0.019	0.045
94	1.742	4.517	3.352	0.006	0.017	0.005	0.013
95	1.167	3.083	2.489	0.001	0.004	0.001	0.003
96	0.718	1.925	1.818	< 0.001	0.001	< 0.001	0.001
97	0.373	1.011	1.309	< 0.001	< 0.001	< 0.001	< 0.001
98	0.128	0.348	0.929	< 0.001	< 0.001	< 0.001	< 0.001
99	< 0.001	< 0.001	0.652	< 0.001	< 0.001	< 0.001	< 0.001

Probability of surviving through age X starting from age 58

Age	CSO (1980) Male	CSO (1980) Female	Total Population	U.S. Life Tables (1982) White Male	U.S. Life Tables (1982) White Female	U.S. Life Tables (1982) Black Male	U.S. Life Tables (1982) Black Female
Life Expectancy	18.99	22.86	19.76	19.30	24.40	17.00	21.90
58	98.641	99.153	98.548	98.584	99.265	97.539	98.682
59	97.184	98.267	97.001	97.059	98.469	94.968	97.270
60	95.621	97.336	95.357	95.423	97.608	92.288	95.758
61	93.944	96.350	93.613	93.672	96.679	89.506	94.151
62	92.141	95.294	91.765	91.795	95.675	86.630	92.455
63	90.201	94.149	89.807	89.780	94.590	83.666	90.685
64	88.114	92.901	87.736	87.619	93.418	80.626	88.852
65	85.874	91.546	85.547	85.309	92.154	77.517	86.957
66	83.482	90.081	82.238	82.831	90.776	74.328	84.964
67	80.941	88.511	80.810	80.202	89.290	71.080	82.881
68	78.255	86.843	78.262	77.443	87.701	67.791	80.716
69	75.424	85.075	75.601	74.570	86.015	64.479	78.479
70	72.444	83.194	72.834	71.605	84.240	61.164	76.178
71	69.307	81.178	69.962	68.475	82.302	57.848	73.778
72	66.005	78.997	66.977	65.214	80.215	54.551	71.294
73	62.530	76.618	63.867	61.851	77.991	51.290	68.738
74	58.892	74.019	60.626	58.418	75.645	48.080	66.125
75	55.111	71.188	57.260	54.946	73.192	44.938	63.466
76	51.224	68.129	53.790	51.367	70.523	41.820	60.680
77	47.274	64.856	50.242	47.727	67.668	38.751	57.792
78	43.308	61.390	46.648	44.072	64.656	35.752	54.827
79	39.365	57.746	43.037	40.445	61.518	32.841	51.812

| | CSO (1980) | | Total Population | U. S. Life Tables (1982) | | | |
	Male	Female		White Male	White Female	Black Male	Black Female
Life Expectancy	18.99	22.86	19.76	19.30	24.40	17.00	21.90
Age							
80	35.474	53.936	39.424	36.886	58.286	30.035	48.770
81	31.661	49.966	35.828	31.957	52.462	26.096	43.612
82	27.949	45.849	32.284	26.230	44.735	21.480	36.947
83	24.364	41.606	28.831	20.333	36.026	16.698	29.561
84	20.947	37.287	25.502	14.835	27.306	12.217	22.261
85	17.743	32.958	22.299	10.147	19.404	8.380	15.715
86	14.796	28.697	19.233	6.478	12.869	5.365	10.355
87	12.140	24.584	16.352	3.840	7.925	3.189	6.336
88	9.793	20.695	13.710	2.101	4.505	1.750	3.578
89	7.763	17.096	11.339	1.054	2.348	0.880	1.852
90	6.042	13.835	9.241	0.481	1.112	0.403	0.872
91	4.610	10.945	7.403	0.197	0.474	0.166	0.369
92	3.441	8.441	5.822	0.072	0.180	0.061	0.139
93	2.505	6.318	4.490	0.023	0.060	0.019	0.046
94	1.764	4.553	3.398	0.006	0.017	0.005	0.013
95	1.182	3.108	2.523	0.001	0.004	0.001	0.003
96	0.727	1.940	1.843	<0.001	0.001	<0.001	0.001
97	0.378	1.019	1.326	<0.001	<0.001	<0.001	<0.001
98	0.129	0.351	0.942	<0.001	<0.001	<0.001	<0.001
99	<0.001	<0.001	0.661	<0.001	<0.001	<0.001	<0.001

Probability of surviving through age X starting from age 59

| | CSO (1980) | | Total Population | U. S. Life Tables (1982) | | | |
	Male	Female		White Male	White Female	Black Male	Black Female
Life Expectancy	18.24	22.05	19.05	18.60	23.60	16.50	21.20
Age							
59	98.523	99.106	98.430	98.453	99.198	97.364	98.569
60	96.939	98.167	96.762	96.794	98.331	94.616	97.037
61	95.238	97.173	94.992	95.018	97.395	91.765	95.408
62	93.411	96.108	93.117	93.114	96.383	88.815	93.690
63	91.444	94.953	91.131	91.070	95.290	85.777	91.896
64	89.328	93.695	89.029	88.878	94.109	82.660	90.038
65	87.057	92.328	86.808	86.534	92.836	79.472	88.119
66	84.632	90.850	84.465	84.020	91.448	76.204	86.099
67	82.056	89.267	82.000	81.354	89.951	72.874	83.988
68	79.333	87.585	79.416	78.555	88.350	69.501	81.794
69	76.463	85.802	76.715	75.641	86.652	66.106	79.527
70	73.442	83.905	73.907	72.633	84.863	62.707	77.195
71	70.262	81.872	70.993	69.459	82.912	59.307	74.763
72	66.914	79.672	67.964	66.151	80.809	55.927	72.246
73	63.392	77.273	64.808	62.739	78.569	52.584	69.656
74	59.703	74.651	61.519	59.257	76.206	49.293	67.008
75	55.871	71.796	58.103	55.736	73.733	46.072	64.314
76	51.930	68.711	54.582	52.104	71.045	42.876	61.491
77	47.925	65.410	50.982	48.412	68.169	39.729	58.564
78	43.904	61.914	47.335	44.705	65.135	36.654	55.559
79	39.907	58.240	43.671	41.026	61.974	33.670	52.504
80	35.962	54.396	40.005	37.415	58.717	30.793	49.422

Life Expectancy	CSO (1980)		Total Population	U. S. Life Tables (1982)			
	Male	Female		White Male	White Female	Black Male	Black Female
	18.24	22.05	19.05	18.60	23.60	16.50	21.20
Age							
81	32.097	50.393	36.356	32.416	52.850	26.754	44.194
82	28.334	46.240	32.760	26.607	45.066	22.022	37.440
83	24.700	41.962	29.256	20.625	36.293	17.119	29.956
84	21.236	37.606	25.878	15.048	27.509	12.526	22.558
85	17.988	33.240	22.627	10.293	19.547	8.592	15.925
86	15.000	28.942	19.516	6.571	12.964	5.500	10.493
87	12.307	24.794	16.593	3.895	7.984	3.270	6.420
88	9.928	20.872	13.912	2.131	4.539	1.794	3.626
89	7.870	17.242	11.506	1.069	2.365	0.903	1.877
90	6.125	13.953	9.377	0.487	1.120	0.413	0.884
91	4.673	11.039	7.512	0.200	0.478	0.170	0.374
92	3.489	8.513	5.908	0.073	0.181	0.062	0.141
93	2.540	6.372	4.556	0.023	0.060	0.020	0.046
94	1.788	4.592	3.448	0.006	0.017	0.005	0.013
95	1.198	3.135	2.560	0.001	0.004	0.001	0.003
96	0.737	1.957	1.870	> 0.001	0.001	> 0.001	0.001
97	0.383	1.027	1.346	> 0.001	> 0.001	> 0.001	> 0.001
98	0.131	0.354	0.956	> 0.001	> 0.001	> 0.001	> 0.001
99	> 0.001	> 0.001	0.670	> 0.001	> 0.001	> 0.001	> 0.001

Probability of surviving through age X starting from age 60

	CSO (1980)		Total Population	U. S. Life Tables (1982)			
	Male	Female		White Male	White Female	Black Male	Black Female
Life Expectancy	17.51	21.25	18.34	17.90	22.80	15.90	20.50
Age							
60	98.392	99.053	98.305	98.315	99.126	97.178	98.446
61	96.666	98.050	96.507	96.511	98.182	94.249	96.793
62	94.811	96.975	94.602	94.577	97.162	91.220	95.050
63	92.814	95.809	92.584	92.501	96.060	88.099	93.231
64	90.667	94.540	90.449	90.274	94.870	84.898	91.345
65	88.362	93.161	88.192	87.894	93.587	81.624	89.398
66	85.901	91.670	85.812	85.341	92.187	78.267	87.349
67	83.286	90.072	83.308	82.633	90.678	74.847	85.207
68	80.522	88.375	80.682	79.789	89.064	71.383	82.982
69	77.610	86.576	77.939	76.830	87.352	67.896	80.681
70	74.543	84.662	75.086	73.774	85.550	64.404	78.316
71	71.315	82.610	72.125	70.550	83.582	60.913	75.849
72	67.917	80.391	69.048	67.190	81.462	57.441	73.295
73	64.342	77.970	65.842	63.725	79.204	54.007	70.667
74	60.598	75.324	62.500	60.188	76.822	50.628	67.981
75	56.708	72.444	59.030	56.611	74.330	47.319	65.248
76	52.709	69.331	55.453	52.923	71.620	44.036	62.383
77	48.644	66.000	51.795	49.173	68.720	40.805	59.414
78	44.563	62.473	48.090	45.407	65.662	37.646	56.366
79	40.505	58.765	44.368	41.671	62.475	34.581	53.266
80	36.502	54.887	40.643	38.003	59.192	31.627	50.139

| | CSO (1980) | | Total Population | U. S. Life Tables (1982) | | | |
Age	Male	Female		White Male	White Female	Black Male	Black Female
Life Expectancy	17.51	21.25	18.34	17.90	22.80	15.90	20.50
81	32.578	50.847	36.936	32.926	53.278	27.479	44.836
82	28.759	46.658	33.282	27.025	45.430	22.618	37.984
83	25.070	42.340	29.723	20.950	36.586	17.583	30.391
84	21.554	37.945	26.290	15.285	27.731	12.865	22.885
85	18.257	33.540	22.988	10.455	19.705	8.824	16.156
86	15.225	29.203	19.828	6.674	13.069	5.649	10.646
87	12.491	25.018	16.858	3.956	8.048	3.358	6.513
88	10.077	21.061	14.134	2.165	4.575	1.843	3.679
89	7.988	17.397	11.690	1.086	2.384	0.927	1.904
90	6.217	14.079	9.527	0.495	1.129	0.424	0.896
91	4.743	11.138	7.632	0.203	0.482	0.174	0.380
92	3.541	8.590	6.002	0.074	0.182	0.064	0.143
93	2.578	6.429	4.629	0.024	0.061	0.020	0.047
94	1.815	4.633	3.503	0.006	0.017	0.006	0.013
95	1.216	3.163	2.601	0.001	0.004	0.001	0.003
96	0.748	1.975	1.900	> 0.001	0.001	0.001	0.001
97	0.389	1.037	1.367	> 0.001	> 0.001	> 0.001	> 0.001
98	0.133	0.357	0.971	> 0.001	> 0.001	> 0.001	> 0.001
99	> 0.001	> 0.001	0.681	> 0.001	> 0.001	> 0.001	> 0.001

Probability of surviving through age X starting from age 61

| | CSO (1980) | | Total Population | U. S. Life Tables (1982) | | | |
	Male	Female		White Male	White Female	Black Male	Black Female
Life Expectancy	16.79	20.44	17.65	17.20	22.00	15.30	19.80
Age							
61	98.246	98.987	98.171	98.165	99.048	96.986	98.321
62	96.361	97.902	96.233	96.198	98.019	93.869	96.550
63	94.331	96.725	94.180	94.086	96.907	90.658	94.702
64	92.148	95.444	92.009	91.822	95.707	87.363	92.787
65	89.806	94.051	89.713	89.400	94.412	83.994	90.809
66	87.305	92.546	87.292	86.803	93.000	80.540	88.728
67	84.647	90.933	84.745	84.049	91.478	77.020	86.552
68	81.838	89.220	82.073	81.157	89.850	73.456	84.291
69	78.878	87.404	79.283	78.147	88.123	69.867	81.955
70	75.761	85.471	76.380	75.039	86.304	66.275	79.552
71	72.481	83.400	73.369	71.760	84.319	62.682	77.046
72	69.027	81.159	70.239	68.342	82.181	59.109	74.452
73	65.394	78.715	66.977	64.817	79.902	55.576	71.783
74	61.588	76.045	63.578	61.220	77.499	52.098	69.054
75	57.635	73.137	60.048	57.582	74.985	48.693	66.278
76	53.570	69.994	56.409	53.830	72.251	45.315	63.368
77	49.439	66.631	52.688	50.016	69.326	41.990	60.352
78	45.291	63.070	48.920	46.186	66.241	38.740	57.256
79	41.167	59.327	45.133	42.385	63.026	35.585	54.107
80	37.098	55.412	41.344	38.655	59.714	32.545	50.931

	CSO (1980)			U. S. Life Tables (1982)			
Life Expectancy	Male	Female	Total Population	White Male	White Female	Black Male	Black Female
	16.79	20.44	17.65	17.20	22.00	15.30	19.80
Age							
81	33.111	51.334	37.573	33.490	53.747	28.277	45.544
82	29.229	47.104	33.856	27.488	45.831	23.275	38.583
83	25.480	42.745	30.235	21.309	36.909	18.093	30.870
84	21.906	38.308	26.744	15.547	27.976	13.238	23.247
85	18.556	33.860	23.384	10.634	19.879	9.080	16.411
86	15.474	29.482	20.169	6.788	13.184	5.813	10.814
87	12.695	25.257	17.148	4.024	8.119	3.456	6.616
88	10.242	21.262	14.377	2.202	4.616	1.896	3.737
89	8.119	17.564	11.891	1.104	2.405	0.954	1.935
90	6.318	14.213	9.691	0.504	1.139	0.436	0.910
91	4.821	11.245	7.764	0.207	0.486	0.180	0.386
92	3.599	8.672	6.105	0.075	0.184	0.066	0.145
93	2.620	6.491	4.709	0.024	0.061	0.021	0.048
94	1.845	4.678	3.563	0.007	0.017	0.006	0.014
95	1.236	3.193	2.646	0.002	0.004	0.001	0.003
96	0.761	1.994	1.932	> 0.001	0.001	> 0.001	0.001
97	0.395	1.047	1.391	> 0.001	> 0.001	> 0.001	0.001
98	0.135	0.360	0.988	> 0.001	> 0.001	> 0.001	0.001
99	> 0.001	> 0.001	0.693	> 0.001	> 0.001	> 0.001	0.001

Probability of surviving through age X starting from age 62

	CSO (1980)		Total Population	U. S. Life Tables (1982)			
	Male	Female		White Male	White Female	Black Male	Black Female
Life Expectancy	16.08	19.65	16.97	16.50	21.20	14.80	19.20
Age							
62	98.081	98.904	98.026	97.996	98.961	96.786	98.199
63	96.015	97.715	95.935	95.845	97.839	93.475	96.319
64	93.794	96.420	93.723	93.538	96.627	90.078	94.372
65	91.409	95.014	91.384	91.071	95.319	86.605	92.360
66	88.864	93.493	88.918	88.426	93.894	83.043	90.243
67	86.159	91.864	86.323	85.620	92.357	79.414	88.030
68	83.299	90.133	83.602	82.674	90.713	75.738	85.731
69	80.286	88.298	80.760	79.607	88.970	72.039	83.354
70	77.114	86.346	77.803	76.441	87.133	68.334	80.910
71	73.775	84.254	74.736	73.101	85.129	64.630	78.362
72	70.260	81.990	71.547	69.619	82.970	60.946	75.723
73	66.561	79.521	68.225	66.029	80.670	57.303	73.009
74	62.688	76.823	64.762	62.364	78.244	53.717	70.233
75	58.664	73.885	61.167	58.658	75.706	50.206	67.410
76	54.526	70.710	57.460	54.836	72.945	46.723	64.450
77	50.321	67.313	53.670	50.951	69.993	43.294	61.382
78	46.099	63.715	49.831	47.049	66.877	39.943	58.233
79	41.902	59.934	45.973	43.177	63.632	36.691	55.031
80	37.760	55.979	42.114	39.377	60.288	33.557	51.800

| | CSO (1980) | | | U. S. Life Tables (1982) | | | |
Life Expectancy	Male	Female	Total Population	White Male	White Female	Black Male	Black Female
	16.08	19.65	16.97	16.50	21.20	14.80	19.20
Age							
81	33.702	51.859	38.273	34.116	54.264	29.155	46.321
82	29.750	47.586	34.487	28.002	46.271	23.998	39.242
83	25.935	43.183	30.798	21.707	37.264	18.656	31.398
84	22.297	38.700	27.242	15.837	28.244	13.650	23.644
85	18.887	34.207	23.820	10.832	20.070	9.363	16.692
86	15.750	29.784	20.545	6.915	13.311	5.994	10.998
87	12.922	25.516	17.468	4.099	8.197	3.563	6.729
88	10.425	21.479	14.645	2.243	4.660	1.955	3.801
89	8.264	17.743	12.113	1.125	2.428	0.984	1.968
90	6.431	14.359	9.872	0.513	1.150	0.450	0.926
91	4.907	11.360	7.908	0.211	0.490	0.185	0.392
92	3.663	8.760	6.219	0.077	0.186	0.068	0.148
93	2.667	6.557	4.797	0.025	0.062	0.022	0.049
94	1.877	4.726	3.629	0.007	0.018	0.006	0.014
95	1.258	3.226	2.695	0.002	0.004	0.001	0.003
96	0.774	2.014	1.968	> 0.001	0.001	0.001	0.001
97	0.402	1.057	1.417	> 0.001	> 0.001	> 0.001	> 0.001
98	0.138	0.364	1.006	> 0.001	> 0.001	> 0.001	> 0.001
99	> 0.001	> 0.001	0.706	> 0.001	> 0.001	> 0.001	> 0.001

Probability of surviving through age X starting from age 63

	CSO (1980)		Total Population	U.S. Life Tables (1982)			
	Male	Female		White Male	White Female	Black Male	Black Female
Life Expectancy	15.38	18.86	16.30	15.80	20.40	14.30	18.50
Age							
63	97.894	98.798	97.867	97.805	98.866	96.579	98.086
64	95.629	97.489	95.610	95.451	97.641	93.069	96.103
65	93.198	96.067	93.225	92.934	96.320	89.481	94.054
66	90.602	94.529	90.709	90.234	94.880	85.800	91.898
67	87.844	92.882	88.062	87.371	93.327	82.051	89.645
68	84.929	91.132	85.286	84.365	91.666	78.253	87.303
69	81.857	89.277	82.386	81.235	89.904	74.431	84.883
70	78.623	87.303	79.370	78.005	88.048	70.604	82.394
71	75.218	85.187	76.241	74.596	86.023	66.776	79.799
72	71.634	82.898	72.988	71.043	83.842	62.970	77.112
73	67.863	80.402	69.599	67.379	81.517	59.206	74.348
74	63.914	77.674	66.066	63.640	79.065	55.501	71.521
75	59.812	74.704	62.398	59.858	76.500	51.874	68.646
76	55.593	71.494	58.617	55.958	73.711	48.275	65.632
77	51.306	68.059	54.751	51.993	70.727	44.732	62.508
78	47.001	64.422	50.834	48.011	67.579	41.270	59.302
79	42.722	60.598	46.899	44.060	64.300	37.910	56.040
80	38.499	56.599	42.963	40.182	60.921	34.671	52.750
81	34.361	52.434	39.044	34.814	54.834	30.124	47.171

	CSO (1980)		U. S. Life Tables (1982)				
	Male	Female	Total Population	White Male	White Female	Black Male	Black Female
Life Expectancy	15.38	18.86	16.30	15.80	20.40	14.30	18.50
Age							
82	30.332	48.113	35.181	28.575	46.757	24.795	39.962
83	26.442	43.661	31.419	22.151	37.655	19.275	31.973
84	22.734	39.129	27.790	16.161	28.541	14.103	24.077
85	19.256	34.586	24.300	11.054	20.281	9.674	16.998
86	16.058	30.114	20.959	7.057	13.451	6.193	11.200
87	13.175	25.798	17.820	4.183	8.283	3.682	6.853
88	10.629	21.717	14.940	2.289	4.709	2.020	3.870
89	8.425	17.940	12.357	1.148	2.454	1.016	2.004
90	6.557	14.518	10.071	0.524	1.162	0.465	0.943
91	5.003	11.486	8.068	0.215	0.496	0.191	0.399
92	3.735	8.858	6.344	0.078	0.188	0.070	0.150
93	2.719	6.630	4.893	0.025	0.062	0.022	0.050
94	1.914	4.778	3.702	0.007	0.018	0.006	0.014
95	1.283	3.262	2.749	0.002	0.004	0.001	0.003
96	0.789	2.036	2.008	> 0.001	0.001	> 0.001	0.001
97	0.410	1.069	1.445	> 0.001	> 0.001	> 0.001	> 0.001
98	0.140	0.368	1.027	> 0.001	> 0.001	> 0.001	> 0.001
99	> 0.001	> 0.001	0.720	> 0.001	> 0.001	> 0.001	> 0.001

Probability of surviving through age X starting from age 64

| | CSO (1980) | | Total Population | U. S. Life Tables (1982) | | | |
	Male	Female		White Male	White Female	Black Male	Black Female
Life Expectancy	14.70	18.08	15.65	15.20	19.60	13.80	17.90
Age							
64	97.686	98.675	97.694	97.593	98.761	96.366	97.978
65	95.203	97.235	95.257	95.019	97.425	92.650	95.889
66	92.551	95.680	92.686	92.259	95.968	88.839	93.691
67	89.734	94.012	89.981	89.332	94.397	84.957	91.394
68	86.756	92.241	87.145	86.258	92.717	81.025	89.007
69	83.618	90.363	84.182	83.059	90.935	77.067	86.540
70	80.314	88.365	81.100	79.755	89.058	73.104	84.002
71	76.837	86.224	77.902	76.270	87.010	69.141	81.356
72	73.175	83.907	74.579	72.637	84.803	65.200	78.617
73	69.323	81.380	71.115	68.891	82.452	61.303	75.798
74	65.289	78.619	67.506	65.068	79.972	57.467	72.917
75	61.099	75.613	63.758	61.201	77.378	53.711	69.985
76	56.789	72.364	59.895	57.214	74.557	49.985	66.913
77	52.410	68.887	55.944	53.160	71.539	46.317	63.728
78	48.012	65.205	51.942	49.089	68.355	42.732	60.459
79	43.641	61.335	47.921	45.049	65.037	39.253	57.133
80	39.327	57.288	43.899	41.084	61.620	35.899	53.780
81	35.101	53.071	39.894	35.595	55.463	31.191	48.091
82	30.985	48.698	35.948	29.216	47.293	25.673	40.742
83	27.011	44.192	32.103	22.648	38.087	19.958	32.597
84	23.223	39.605	28.396	16.524	28.868	14.602	24.547
85	19.671	35.007	24.829	11.302	20.514	10.016	17.330

| | CSO (1980) | | | U. S. Life Tables (1982) | | | |
Age	Male	Female	Total Population	White Male	White Female	Black Male	Black Female
Life Expectancy	14.70	18.08	15.65	15.20	19.60	13.80	17.90
86	16.404	30.481	21.416	7.215	13.605	6.412	11.419
87	13.458	26.112	18.208	4.277	8.378	3.812	6.986
88	10.857	21.982	15.266	2.340	4.763	2.092	3.946
89	8.607	18.158	12.626	1.174	2.482	1.052	2.043
90	6.698	14.695	10.290	0.535	1.176	0.481	0.961
91	5.111	11.625	8.244	0.220	0.501	0.198	0.407
92	3.815	8.965	6.482	0.080	0.190	0.072	0.153
93	2.777	6.710	5.000	0.026	0.063	0.023	0.051
94	1.955	4.836	3.783	0.007	0.018	0.006	0.014
95	1.310	3.302	2.809	0.002	0.004	0.001	0.003
96	0.806	2.061	2.052	> 0.001	0.001	> 0.001	0.001
97	0.419	1.082	1.477	> 0.001	> 0.001	> 0.001	> 0.001
98	0.143	0.372	1.049	> 0.001	> 0.001	> 0.001	> 0.001
99	> 0.001	> 0.001	0.736	> 0.001	> 0.001	> 0.001	> 0.001

Probability of surviving through age X starting from age 65

| | CSO (1980) | | Total Population | U. S. Life Tables (1982) | | | |
	Male	Female		White Male	White Female	Black Male	Black Female
Life Expectancy	14.04	17.32	15.00	14.50	18.90	13.30	17.20
Age							
65	97.458	98.541	97.505	97.363	98.647	96.144	97.868
66	94.744	96.964	94.873	94.535	97.172	92.190	95.625
67	91.860	95.274	92.105	91.535	95.582	88.161	93.280
68	88.811	93.479	89.202	88.385	93.880	84.081	90.844
69	85.599	91.576	86.169	85.107	92.076	79.973	88.325
70	82.217	89.551	83.014	81.722	90.175	75.861	85.736
71	78.657	87.381	79.741	78.151	88.101	71.749	83.035
72	74.909	85.034	76.339	74.429	85.867	67.659	80.239
73	70.966	82.473	72.794	70.590	83.487	63.614	77.363
74	66.836	79.675	69.100	66.673	80.976	59.634	74.421
75	62.546	76.628	65.263	62.710	78.349	55.736	71.430
76	58.134	73.335	61.308	58.625	75.492	51.870	68.294
77	53.651	69.812	57.265	54.471	72.436	48.063	65.043
78	49.150	66.081	53.168	50.299	69.212	44.343	61.706
79	44.675	62.159	49.053	46.160	65.853	40.733	58.313
80	40.259	58.057	44.935	42.098	62.393	37.253	54.890
81	35.932	53.784	40.836	36.473	56.158	32.367	49.084
82	31.719	49.352	36.797	29.937	47.887	26.641	41.582
83	27.651	44.786	32.861	23.207	38.565	20.711	33.270
84	23.773	40.137	29.066	16.931	29.230	15.153	25.054
85	20.137	35.477	25.415	11.581	20.771	10.394	17.687
86	16.792	30.890	21.921	7.393	13.776	6.654	11.654

| | CSO (1980) | | Total Population | U. S. Life Tables (1982) | | | |
	Male	Female		White Male	White Female	Black Male	Black Female
Life Expectancy	14.04	17.32	15.00	14.50	18.90	13.30	17.20
Age							
87	13.777	26.463	18.638	4.383	8.484	3.956	7.131
88	11.114	22.277	15.626	2.398	4.823	2.171	4.027
89	8.811	18.402	12.924	1.203	2.513	1.092	2.085
90	6.857	14.892	10.533	0.549	1.191	0.499	0.981
91	5.232	11.781	8.438	0.225	0.508	0.205	0.416
92	3.906	9.086	6.635	0.082	0.192	0.075	0.156
93	2.843	6.801	5.118	0.026	0.064	0.024	0.052
94	2.002	4.901	3.872	0.007	0.018	0.007	0.015
95	1.341	3.346	2.875	0.002	0.004	0.002	0.003
96	0.825	2.089	2.100	> 0.001	0.001	> 0.001	0.001
97	0.429	1.097	1.512	> 0.001	> 0.001	> 0.001	> 0.001
98	0.147	0.377	1.074	> 0.001	> 0.001	> 0.001	> 0.001
99	> 0.001	> 0.001	0.753	> 0.001	> 0.001	> 0.001	> 0.001

Probability of surviving through age X starting from age 66

| | CSO (1980) | | Total Population | U. S. Life Tables (1982) | | | |
	Male	Female		White Male	White Female	Black Male	Black Female
Life Expectancy	13.39	16.57	14.38	13.90	18.20	12.80	16.60
Age							
66	97.215	98.400	97.301	97.095	98.505	95.887	97.708

| | CSO (1980) | | | U. S. Life Tables (1982) | | | |
	Male	Female	Total Population	White Male	White Female	Black Male	Black Female
Life Expectancy	13.39	16.57	14.38	13.90	18.20	12.80	16.60
Age							
67	94.256	96.685	94.462	94.014	96.892	91.697	95.312
68	91.127	94.863	91.484	90.779	95.168	87.453	92.823
69	87.831	92.932	88.374	87.412	93.339	83.181	90.250
70	84.361	90.877	85.138	83.936	91.412	78.904	87.603
71	80.708	88.675	81.781	80.268	89.310	74.626	84.844
72	76.863	86.293	78.293	76.445	87.045	70.373	81.987
73	72.816	83.694	74.657	72.502	84.632	66.166	79.048
74	68.579	80.855	70.868	68.478	82.086	62.026	76.043
75	64.177	77.763	66.933	64.409	79.423	57.972	72.986
76	59.651	74.421	62.877	60.213	76.528	53.950	69.782
77	55.051	70.846	58.730	55.946	73.430	49.991	66.460
78	50.432	67.069	54.529	51.662	70.161	46.122	63.051
79	45.840	63.079	50.308	47.410	66.756	42.366	59.583
80	41.309	58.917	46.085	43.238	63.248	38.747	56.085
81	36.869	54.580	41.881	37.461	56.929	33.665	50.153
82	32.546	50.083	37.738	30.747	48.544	27.710	42.488
83	28.372	45.449	33.702	23.835	39.094	21.541	33.995
84	24.393	40.731	29.810	17.390	29.631	15.761	25.599
85	20.662	36.002	26.066	11.894	21.056	10.811	18.072
86	17.230	31.347	22.482	7.593	13.965	6.921	11.908
87	14.136	26.855	19.115	4.501	8.600	4.114	7.286
88	11.404	22.607	16.026	2.463	4.889	2.258	4.115
89	9.040	18.674	13.255	1.235	2.548	1.136	2.130

	CSO (1980)		Total	U. S. Life Tables (1982)			
	Male	Female	Population	White Male	White Female	Black Male	Black Female
Life Expectancy	13.39	16.57	14.38	13.90	18.20	12.80	16.60
Age							
90	7.035	15.112	10.802	0.563	1.207	0.519	1.003
91	5.368	11.956	8.654	0.231	0.515	0.214	0.425
92	4.008	9.220	6.805	0.084	0.195	0.078	0.160
93	2.917	6.901	5.249	0.027	0.065	0.025	0.053
94	2.054	4.974	3.972	0.007	0.018	0.007	0.015
95	1.376	3.395	2.949	0.002	0.004	0.002	0.004
96	0.847	2.120	2.154	> 0.001	0.001	> 0.001	0.001
97	0.440	1.113	1.550	> 0.001	> 0.001	> 0.001	> 0.001
98	0.151	0.383	1.101	> 0.001	> 0.001	> 0.001	> 0.001
99	> 0.001	> 0.001	0.772	> 0.001	> 0.001	> 0.001	> 0.001

Probability of surviving through age X starting from age 67

	CSO (1980)		Total	U. S. Life Tables (1982)			
	Male	Female	Population	White Male	White Female	Black Male	Black Female
Life Expectancy	12.76	15.83	13.76	13.30	17.50	12.30	16.00
Age							
67	96.956	98.257	97.082	96.827	98.363	95.630	97.548
68	93.738	96.406	94.022	93.495	96.612	91.204	95.000
69	90.348	94.443	90.825	90.027	94.755	86.749	92.367
70	86.778	92.355	87.500	86.447	92.800	82.288	89.658

	CSO (1980)			U. S. Life Tables (1982)			
	Male	Female	Total Population	White Male	White Female	Black Male	Black Female
Life Expectancy	12.76	15.83	13.76	13.30	17.50	12.30	16.00
Age							
71	83.020	90.117	84.050	82.669	90.665	77.827	86.834
72	79.064	87.696	80.464	78.732	88.366	73.391	83.911
73	74.903	85.055	76.728	74.672	85.916	69.004	80.902
74	70.544	82.169	72.834	70.527	83.332	64.686	77.826
75	66.016	79.027	68.790	66.336	80.629	60.458	74.698
76	61.360	75.631	64.621	62.014	77.689	56.264	71.419
77	56.628	71.998	60.359	57.620	74.544	52.135	68.019
78	51.877	68.150	56.041	53.207	71.226	48.100	64.530
79	47.153	64.105	51.703	48.829	67.770	44.184	60.981
80	42.493	59.875	47.363	44.531	64.208	40.409	57.401
81	37.925	55.468	43.043	38.582	57.793	35.109	51.330
82	33.479	50.897	38.785	31.667	49.280	28.899	43.485
83	29.185	46.188	34.637	24.548	39.687	22.465	34.792
84	25.092	41.393	30.637	17.910	30.081	16.437	26.200
85	21.254	36.587	26.789	12.250	21.375	11.275	18.496
86	17.724	31.857	23.106	7.821	14.177	7.218	12.187
87	14.541	27.291	19.645	4.636	8.730	4.291	7.457
88	11.731	22.974	16.471	2.537	4.963	2.355	4.211
89	9.299	18.978	13.623	1.272	2.586	1.184	2.180
90	7.237	15.358	11.102	0.580	1.225	0.542	1.026
91	5.522	12.150	8.894	0.238	0.522	0.223	0.435
92	4.122	9.370	6.994	0.087	0.198	0.082	0.164
93	3.001	7.013	5.395	0.028	0.066	0.026	0.054

	CSO (1980)			U. S. Life Tables (1982)			
	Male	Female	Total Population	White Male	White Female	Black Male	Black Female
Life Expectancy	12.76	15.83	13.76	13.30	17.50	12.30	16.00
Age							
94	2.113	5.055	4.082	0.008	0.019	0.007	0.015
95	1.416	3.451	3.031	0.002	0.004	0.002	0.004
96	0.871	2.154	2.214	> 0.001	0.001	> 0.001	0.001
97	0.453	1.131	1.593	> 0.001	> 0.001	> 0.001	> 0.001
98	0.155	0.389	1.132	> 0.001	> 0.001	> 0.001	> 0.001
99	> 0.001	> 0.001	0.794	> 0.001	> 0.001	> 0.001	> 0.001

Probability of surviving through age X starting from age 68

	CSO (1980)			U. S. Life Tables (1982)			
	Male	Female	Total Population	White Male	White Female	Black Male	Black Female
Life Expectancy	12.14	15.10	13.16	12.80	16.70	11.90	15.30
Age							
68	96.681	98.116	96.848	96.559	98.220	95.372	97.388
69	93.184	96.118	93.555	92.978	96.332	90.713	94.688
70	89.502	93.993	90.130	89.280	94.344	86.049	91.912
71	85.627	91.716	86.576	85.378	92.174	81.384	89.017
72	81.547	89.251	82.883	81.312	89.836	76.745	86.020
73	77.254	86.564	79.034	77.119	87.346	72.157	82.936
74	72.759	83.627	75.023	72.838	84.719	67.642	79.783
75	68.088	80.429	70.858	68.510	81.971	63.221	76.575

	CSO (1980)			U. S. Life Tables (1982)			
	Male	Female	Total Population	White Male	White Female	Black Male	Black Female
Life Expectancy	12.14	15.10	13.16	12.80	16.70	11.90	15.30
Age							
76	63.286	76.973	66.564	64.046	78.982	58.836	73.214
77	58.405	73.275	62.173	59.508	75.785	54.518	69.729
78	53.505	69.359	57.726	54.951	72.412	50.298	66.152
79	48.634	65.242	53.257	50.429	68.897	46.203	62.513
80	43.827	60.937	48.787	45.991	65.277	42.256	58.844
81	39.116	56.452	44.337	39.846	58.754	36.713	52.620
82	34.530	51.800	39.951	32.705	50.100	30.219	44.578
83	30.101	47.007	35.678	25.353	40.347	23.492	35.667
84	25.879	42.127	31.558	18.497	30.582	17.188	26.859
85	21.921	37.236	27.594	12.652	21.731	11.790	18.961
86	18.280	32.422	23.800	8.077	14.412	7.548	12.494
87	14.998	27.775	20.235	4.788	8.876	4.487	7.644
88	12.099	23.382	16.966	2.620	5.046	2.462	4.317
89	9.591	19.315	14.032	1.314	2.629	1.238	2.235
90	7.464	15.631	11.436	0.599	1.246	0.566	1.052
91	5.695	12.366	9.161	0.246	0.531	0.233	0.446
92	4.252	9.536	7.204	0.090	0.201	0.085	0.168
93	3.095	7.138	5.557	0.029	0.067	0.027	0.055
94	2.179	5.144	4.204	0.008	0.019	0.007	0.016
95	1.460	3.512	3.122	0.002	0.004	0.002	0.004
96	0.899	2.192	2.280	< 0.001	< 0.001	< 0.001	0.001
97	0.467	1.151	1.641	< 0.001	< 0.001	< 0.001	< 0.001
98	0.160	0.396	1.166	< 0.001	< 0.001	< 0.001	< 0.001

	CSO (1980)			U. S. Life Tables (1982)			
	Male	Female	Total Population	White Male	White Female	Black Male	Black Female
Life Expectancy	12.14	15.10	13.16	12.80	16.70	11.90	15.30
Age 99	> 0.001	> 0.001	0.818	> 0.001	> 0.001	> 0.001	> 0.001

Probability of surviving through age X starting from age 69

	CSO (1980)			U. S. Life Tables (1982)			
	Male	Female	Total Population	White Male	White Female	Black Male	Black Female
Life Expectancy	11.54	14.38	12.57	12.20	16.00	11.40	14.70
Age							
69	96.383	97.964	96.600	96.291	98.078	95.115	97.228
70	92.575	95.798	93.063	92.462	96.054	90.224	94.377
71	88.566	93.477	89.394	88.421	93.844	85.333	91.404
72	84.346	90.965	85.580	84.209	91.465	80.469	88.327
73	79.906	88.226	81.606	79.867	88.929	75.659	85.160
74	75.256	85.233	77.465	75.434	86.254	70.925	81.922
75	70.426	81.973	73.164	70.951	83.456	66.289	78.629
76	65.459	78.451	68.730	66.329	80.413	61.691	75.177
77	60.410	74.682	64.197	61.629	77.158	57.163	71.599
78	55.342	70.690	59.605	56.909	73.724	52.739	67.926
79	50.303	66.495	54.991	52.226	70.146	48.445	64.190
80	45.331	62.107	50.375	47.630	66.460	44.306	60.422

| | CSO (1980) | | | U. S. Life Tables (1982) | | | |
	Male	Female	Total Population	White Male	White Female	Black Male	Black Female
Life Expectancy	11.54	14.38	12.57	12.20	16.00	11.40	14.70
Age							
81	40.459	57.536	45.780	41.266	59.819	38.495	54.031
82	35.715	52.795	41.251	33.871	51.008	31.686	45.774
83	31.134	47.910	36.839	26.256	41.079	24.632	36.623
84	26.768	42.936	32.585	19.156	31.136	18.022	27.579
85	22.674	37.951	28.492	13.103	22.126	12.362	19.470
86	18.908	33.045	24.575	8.365	14.674	7.914	12.829
87	15.513	28.309	20.894	4.958	9.037	4.705	7.849
88	12.515	23.831	17.518	2.713	5.137	2.582	4.433
89	9.921	19.686	14.489	1.361	2.677	1.299	2.295
90	7.720	15.931	11.808	0.621	1.268	0.594	1.080
91	5.891	12.603	9.460	0.255	0.541	0.244	0.458
92	4.398	9.719	7.439	0.093	0.205	0.089	0.172
93	3.201	7.275	5.737	0.030	0.068	0.029	0.057
94	2.254	5.243	4.341	0.008	0.019	0.008	0.016
95	1.510	3.579	3.224	0.002	0.005	0.002	0.004
96	0.929	2.234	2.355	> 0.001	0.001	> 0.001	0.001
97	0.483	1.173	1.695	> 0.001	> 0.001	> 0.001	> 0.001
98	0.165	0.404	1.204	> 0.001	> 0.001	> 0.001	> 0.001
99	> 0.001	> 0.001	0.844	> 0.001	> 0.001	> 0.001	> 0.001

Probability of surviving through age X starting from age 70

	CSO (1980)		Total Population	U. S. Life Tables (1982)			
	Male	Female		White Male	White Female	Black Male	Black Female
Life Expectancy	10.96	13.67	12.00	11.60	15.30	10.90	14.10
Age							
70	96.049	97.789	96.339	96.023	97.936	94.858	97.068
71	91.890	95.420	92.540	91.827	95.683	89.716	94.010
72	87.512	92.856	88.593	87.453	93.257	84.602	90.845
73	82.905	90.060	84.478	82.943	90.672	79.544	87.588
74	78.081	87.004	80.191	78.340	87.944	74.567	84.258
75	73.069	83.677	75.739	73.684	85.092	69.694	80.871
76	67.915	80.081	71.149	68.884	81.989	64.859	77.321
77	62.678	76.234	66.456	64.002	78.670	60.099	73.640
78	57.419	72.160	61.702	59.101	75.169	55.447	69.863
79	52.191	67.877	56.926	54.238	71.521	50.933	66.020
80	47.032	63.398	52.148	49.464	67.762	46.582	62.145
81	41.977	58.732	47.391	42.855	60.991	40.472	55.572
82	37.055	53.892	42.703	35.175	52.008	33.313	47.079
83	32.303	48.906	38.136	27.267	41.884	25.897	37.668
84	27.772	43.829	33.732	19.894	31.746	18.948	28.365
85	23.525	38.740	29.495	13.607	22.558	12.997	20.025
86	19.617	33.731	25.440	8.687	14.961	8.321	13.195
87	16.095	28.897	21.629	5.149	9.214	4.946	8.073
88	12.984	24.326	18.134	2.818	5.238	2.714	4.559
89	10.293	20.095	14.999	1.413	2.729	1.365	2.360
90	8.010	16.262	12.224	0.644	1.293	0.624	1.111
91	6.112	12.865	9.793	0.264	0.551	0.257	0.471

	CSO (1980)			U. S. Life Tables (1982)			
	Male	Female	Total Population	White Male	White Female	Black Male	Black Female
Life Expectancy	10.96	13.67	12.00	11.60	15.30	10.90	14.10
Age							
92	4.563	9.921	7.701	0.096	0.209	0.094	0.177
93	3.321	7.426	5.939	0.031	0.069	0.030	0.058
94	2.338	5.352	4.494	0.008	0.020	0.008	0.016
95	1.567	3.654	3.337	0.002	0.006	0.002	0.004
96	0.964	2.281	2.437	> 0.001	0.001	> 0.001	0.001
97	0.501	1.198	1.754	> 0.001	> 0.001	> 0.001	> 0.001
98	0.171	0.412	1.246	> 0.001	> 0.001	> 0.001	> 0.001
99	> 0.001	> 0.001	0.874	> 0.001	> 0.001	> 0.001	> 0.001

Probability of surviving through age X starting from age 71

	CSO (1980)			U. S. Life Tables (1982)			
	Male	Female	Total Population	White Male	White Female	Black Male	Black Female
Life Expectancy	10.39	12.97	11.43	111.10	14.60	10.50	13.50
Age							
71	95.670	97.577	96.057	95.630	97.700	94.579	96.850
72	91.111	94.955	91.959	91.075	95.222	89.188	93.589
73	86.315	92.096	87.689	86.378	92.583	83.856	90.234
74	81.293	88.971	83.238	81.584	89.798	78.609	86.803
75	76.074	85.569	78.617	76.736	86.885	73.472	83.314
76	70.709	81.892	73.853	71.736	83.717	68.375	79.656

| | CSO (1980) | | | U. S. Life Tables (1982) | | | |
	Male	Female	Total Population	White Male	White Female	Black Male	Black Female
Life Expectancy	10.39	12.97	11.43	111.10	14.60	10.50	13.50
Age							
77	65.256	77.958	68.982	66.653	80.328	63.357	75.865
78	59.781	73.791	64.047	61.549	76.753	58.453	71.973
79	54.338	69.412	59.089	56.484	73.028	53.694	68.014
80	48.967	64.831	54.129	51.513	69.190	49.107	64.022
81	43.704	60.060	49.192	44.630	62.277	42.666	57.250
82	38.580	55.111	44.326	36.632	53.104	35.119	48.501
83	33.632	50.011	39.585	28.397	42.766	27.301	38.805
84	28.915	44.820	35.014	20.718	32.415	19.975	29.222
85	24.492	39.616	30.616	14.171	23.034	13.701	20.630
86	20.424	34.494	26.407	9.047	15.277	8.772	13.593
87	16.757	29.550	22.451	5.363	9.408	5.214	8.317
88	13.518	24.876	18.824	2.934	5.348	2.861	4.697
89	10.716	20.549	15.569	1.472	2.787	1.439	2.432
90	8.340	16.629	12.688	0.671	1.320	0.658	1.145
91	6.363	13.156	10.165	0.275	0.563	0.271	0.485
92	4.751	10.146	7.993	0.100	0.213	0.099	0.183
93	3.458	7.594	6.165	0.032	0.071	0.032	0.060
94	2.435	5.473	4.665	0.009	0.020	0.009	0.017
95	1.631	3.736	3.464	0.002	0.005	0.002	0.004
96	1.004	2.332	2.530	> 0.001	0.001	> 0.001	0.001
97	0.522	1.225	1.821	> 0.001	> 0.001	> 0.001	> 0.001
98	0.178	0.421	1.293	> 0.001	> 0.001	> 0.001	> 0.001
99	> 0.001	> 0.001	0.907	> 0.001	> 0.001	> 0.001	> 0.001

Probability of surviving through age X starting from age 72

	CSO (1980)			U. S. Life Tables (1982)			
	Male	Female	Total Population	White Male	White Female	Black Male	Black Female
Life Expectancy	9.84	12.28	10.88	10.60	14.00	10.10	13.00
Age							
72	95.235	97.313	95.734	95.237	97.464	94.300	96.633
73	90.222	94.383	91.288	90.326	94.762	88.663	93.169
74	84.972	91.180	86.655	85.313	91.912	83.115	89.626
75	79.517	87.694	81.844	80.242	88.930	77.683	86.023
76	73.909	83.926	76.884	75.015	85.688	72.294	82.247
77	68.209	79.894	71.813	69.699	82.219	66.988	78.332
78	62.486	75.623	66.676	64.362	78.560	61.803	74.314
79	56.797	71.135	61.515	59.065	74.747	56.771	70.226
80	51.183	66.441	56.351	53.867	70.819	51.921	66.104
81	45.682	61.551	51.211	46.670	63.743	45.111	59.112
82	40.326	56.479	46.145	38.306	54.354	37.132	50.078
83	35.154	51.253	41.210	29.694	43.773	28.865	40.068
84	30.223	45.933	36.451	21.665	33.178	21.120	30.172
85	25.601	40.600	31.872	14.819	23.576	14.487	21.301
86	21.349	35.351	27.491	9.460	15.636	9.274	14.035
87	17.516	30.284	23.373	5.608	9.629	5.513	8.587
88	14.130	25.494	19.596	3.069	5.474	3.025	4.850
89	11.201	21.059	16.208	1.539	2.853	1.522	2.511
90	8.717	17.042	13.209	0.702	1.351	0.696	1.182

	CSO (1980)			U. S. Life Tables (1982)			
	Male	Female	Total Population	White Male	White Female	Black Male	Black Female
Life Expectancy	9.84	12.28	10.88	10.60	14.00	10.10	13.00
Age							
91	6.651	13.483	10.582	0.288	0.576	0.286	0.501
92	4.966	10.398	8.321	0.105	0.218	0.105	0.188
93	3.614	7.783	6.418	0.034	0.072	0.034	0.062
94	2.545	5.609	4.856	0.009	0.021	0.009	0.018
95	1.705	3.829	3.606	0.002	0.005	0.002	0.004
96	1.049	2.390	2.634	> 0.001	0.001	> 0.001	0.001
97	0.546	1.255	1.896	> 0.001	> 0.001	> 0.001	> 0.001
98	0.187	0.432	1.346	> 0.001	> 0.001	> 0.001	> 0.001
99	> 0.001	> 0.001	0.944	> 0.001	> 0.001	> 0.001	> 0.001

Probability of surviving through age X starting from age 73

	CSO (1980)			U. S. Life Tables (1982)			
	Male	Female	Total Population	White Male	White Female	Black Male	Black Female
Life Expectancy	9.30	11.60	10.34	10.10	13.30	9.60	12.40
Age							
73	94.736	96.989	95.356	94.843	97.228	94.022	96.0415
74	89.223	93.698	90.517	89.579	94.303	88.139	92.749
75	83.496	90.115	85.491	84.256	91.244	82.378	89.021

	CSO (1980)		Total Population	U. S. Life Tables (1982)			
	Male	Female		White Male	White Female	Black Male	Black Female
Life Expectancy	9.30	11.60	10.34	10.10	13.30	9.60	12.40
Age							
76	77.607	86.243	80.310	78.766	87.917	76.664	85.113
77	71.622	82.100	75.013	73.185	84.359	71.037	81.061
78	65.613	77.712	69.647	67.580	80.604	65.539	76.903
79	59.639	73.099	64.256	62.019	76.692	60.203	72.673
80	53.744	68.276	58.862	56.561	72.662	55.060	68.407
81	47.968	63.250	53.493	49.004	65.401	47.838	61.172
82	42.344	58.039	48.201	40.222	55.769	39.376	51.823
83	36.913	52.668	43.046	31.180	44.912	30.610	41.464
84	31.736	47.201	38.075	22.748	34.042	22.396	31.224
85	26.882	41.721	33.293	15.560	24.190	15.362	22.043
86	22.417	36.327	28.716	9.933	16.043	9.835	14.524
87	18.392	31.120	24.414	5.888	9.880	5.847	8.887
88	14.837	26.198	20.469	3.222	5.616	3.208	5.019
89	11.762	21.641	16.930	1.616	2.927	1.614	2.598
90	9.153	17.513	13.797	0.737	1.386	0.738	1.223
91	6.984	13.855	11.053	0.302	0.591	0.304	0.518
92	5.214	10.685	8.692	0.110	0.224	0.111	0.195
93	3.795	7.997	6.704	0.035	0.074	0.036	0.064
94	2.672	5.764	5.073	0.010	0.021	0.010	0.018
95	1.790	3.935	3.767	0.002	0.005	0.002	0.004
96	1.102	2.456	2.751	> 0.001	0.001	> 0.001	0.001

| | CSO (1980) | | Total | U. S. Life Tables (1982) | | | |
	Male	Female	Population	White Male	White Female	Black Male	Black Female
Life Expectancy	9.30	11.60	10.34	10.10	13.30	9.60	12.40
Age							
97	0.573	1.290	1.980	> 0.001	> 0.001	> 0.001	> 0.001
98	0.196	0.444	1.406	> 0.001	> 0.001	> 0.001	> 0.001
99	> 0.001	> 0.001	0.986	> 0.001	> 0.001	> 0.001	> 0.001

Probability of surviving through age X starting from age 74

| | CSO (1980) | | Total | U. S. Life Tables (1982) | | | |
	Male	Female	Population	White Male	White Female	Black Male	Black Female
Life Expectancy	8.79	10.95	9.82	9.60	12.70	9.20	11.90
Age							
74	94.181	96.607	94.925	94.450	96.992	93.743	96.198
75	88.136	92.913	89.655	88.837	93.846	87.616	92.331
76	81.919	88.920	84.222	83.049	90.424	81.538	88.278
77	75.602	84.649	78.666	77.164	86.764	75.554	84.076
78	69.259	80.124	73.039	71.255	82.902	69.706	79.762
79	62.953	75.369	67.385	65.391	78.879	64.031	75.375
80	56.730	70.395	61.729	59.636	74.733	58.560	70.951
81	50.633	65.214	56.098	51.668	67.266	50.880	63.446
82	44.696	59.840	50.549	42.409	57.358	41.880	53.750
83	38.964	54.303	45.143	32.875	46.193	32.556	43.005
84	33.499	48.666	39.930	23.985	35.012	23.820	32.385

	CSO (1980)		Total Population	U. S. Life Tables (1982)			
	Male	Female		White Male	White Female	Black Male	Black Female
Life Expectancy	8.79	10.95	9.82	9.60	12.70	9.20	11.90
Age							
85	28.375	43.016	34.914	16.406	24.879	16.339	22.863
86	23.662	37.454	30.114	10.473	16.500	10.460	15.064
87	19.414	32.086	25.603	6.208	10.162	6.218	9.217
88	15.662	27.011	21.466	3.397	5.777	3.412	5.206
89	12.415	22.313	17.754	1.704	3.010	1.716	2.695
90	9.662	18.057	14.469	0.777	1.426	0.785	1.268
91	7.372	14.285	11.592	0.319	0.608	0.323	0.537
92	5.504	11.017	9.115	0.116	0.230	0.118	0.202
93	4.006	8.246	7.031	0.037	0.076	0.038	0.067
94	2.821	5.943	5.320	0.010	0.022	0.010	0.019
95	1.890	4.057	3.950	0.002	0.005	0.002	0.004
96	1.163	2.533	2.885	> 0.001	0.001	> 0.001	0.001
97	0.605	1.330	2.077	> 0.001	> 0.001	> 0.001	> 0.001
98	0.207	0.458	1.475	> 0.001	> 0.001	> 0.001	> 0.001
99	> 0.001	> 0.001	1.034	> 0.001	> 0.001	> 0.001	> 0.001

Probability of surviving through age X starting from age 75

| | CSO (1980) | | Total Population | U. S. Life Tables (1982) | | | |
	Male	Female		White Male	White Female	Black Male	Black Female
Life Expectancy	8.31	10.32	9.32	9.10	12.00	8.80	11.30
Age							
75	93.581	96.176	94.448	94.057	96.756	93.464	95.980
76	86.981	92.043	88.724	87.929	93.228	86.980	91.766
77	80.273	87.622	82.872	81.699	89.454	80.597	87.398
78	73.538	82.938	76.944	75.442	85.473	74.359	82.915
79	66.842	78.016	70.988	69.234	81.325	68.304	78.355
80	60.236	72.868	65.029	63.141	77.051	62.469	73.755
81	53.761	67.504	59.097	54.704	69.352	54.276	65.954
82	47.458	61.942	53.251	44.901	59.137	44.675	55.874
83	41.371	56.211	47.556	34.807	47.625	34.729	44.705
84	35.569	50.375	42.064	25.395	36.098	25.410	33.665
85	30.128	44.527	36.781	17.370	25.651	17.430	23.766
86	25.124	38.770	31.724	11.089	17.012	11.158	15.660
87	20.613	33.213	26.972	6.573	10.477	6.633	9.581
88	16.629	27.960	22.614	3.597	5.956	3.640	5.411
89	13.182	23.096	18.704	1.804	3.104	1.831	2.801
90	10.259	18.691	15.243	0.823	1.470	0.837	1.319
91	7.828	14.787	12.212	0.338	0.627	0.345	0.559
92	5.844	11.403	9.603	0.123	0.238	0.126	0.210
93	4.254	8.535	7.407	0.039	0.079	0.040	0.069
94	2.995	6.151	5.604	0.011	0.022	0.011	0.020
95	2.007	4.199	4.161	0.002	0.005	0.003	0.005
96	1.235	2.622	3.039	> 0.001	0.001	> 0.001	0.001

	CSO (1980)		Total Population	U. S. Life Tables (1982)			
	Male	Female		White Male	White Female	Black Male	Black Female
Life Expectancy	8.31	10.32	9.32	9.10	12.00	8.80	11.30
Age							
97	0.642	1.376	2.188	> 0.001	> 0.001	> 0.001	> 0.001
98	0.220	0.474	1.554	> 0.001	> 0.001	> 0.001	> 0.001
99	> 0.001	> 0.001	1.090	> 0.001	> 0.001	> 0.001	> 0.001

Probability of surviving through age X starting from age 76

	CSO (1980)		Total Population	U. S. Life Tables (1982)			
	Male	Female		White Male	White Female	Black Male	Black Female
Life Expectancy	7.84	9.71	8.84	8.70	11.40	8.40	10.80
Age							
76	92.947	95.703	93.940	93.485	96.354	93.063	95.610
77	85.779	91.105	87.744	86.861	92.454	86.233	91.059
78	78.582	86.236	81.467	80.209	88.338	79.559	86.388
79	71.427	81.118	75.161	73.608	84.051	73.081	81.636
80	64.367	75.765	68.852	67.130	79.635	66.838	76.844
81	57.449	70.188	62.571	58.161	71.677	58.071	68.716
82	50.713	64.405	56.382	47.738	61.120	47.799	58.215
83	44.209	58.446	50.352	37.006	49.222	37.158	46.577
84	38.008	52.378	44.537	26.999	37.308	27.187	35.075
85	32.195	46.297	38.943	18.467	26.511	18.648	24.762
86	26.848	40.311	33.589	11.789	17.583	11.939	16.316

| | CSO (1980) | | | U. S. Life Tables (1982) | | | |
	Male	Female	Total Population	White Male	White Female	Black Male	Black Female
Life Expectancy	7.84	9.71	8.84	8.70	11.40	8.40	10.80
Age							
87	22.027	34.534	28.558	6.989	10.828	7.097	9.983
88	17.770	29.071	23.943	3.824	6.155	3.895	5.638
89	14.087	24.015	19.803	1.918	3.208	1.959	2.919
90	10.963	19.434	16.139	0.875	1.520	0.896	1.374
91	8.365	15.375	12.929	0.359	0.648	0.369	0.582
92	6.245	11.857	10.167	0.131	0.246	0.135	0.219
93	4.545	8.875	7.842	0.042	0.081	0.043	0.072
94	3.200	6.396	5.934	0.011	0.023	0.012	0.020
95	2.144	4.366	4.406	0.003	0.005	0.003	0.005
96	1.320	2.726	3.218	> 0.001	0.001	> 0.001	0.001
97	0.686	1.431	2.316	> 0.001	> 0.001	> 0.001	> 0.001
98	0.235	0.493	1.645	> 0.001	> 0.001	> 0.001	> 0.001
99	> 0.001	> 0.001	1.154	> 0.001	> 0.001	> 0.001	> 0.001

Probability of surviving through age X starting from age 77

| | CSO (1980) | | | U. S. Life Tables (1982) | | | |
	Male	Female	Total Population	White Male	White Female	Black Male	Black Female
Life Expectancy	7.40	9.12	8.38	8.30	10.80	8.00	10.20
Age							
77	92.288	95.196	93.404	92.914	95.952	92.661	95.240

| | CSO (1980) | | Total Population | U. S. Life Tables (1982) | | | |
	Male	Female		White Male	White Female	Black Male	Black Female
Life Expectancy	7.40	9.12	8.38	8.30	10.80	8.00	10.20
Age							
78	84.545	90.108	86.723	85.799	91.681	85.489	90.354
79	76.847	84.760	80.010	78.738	87.232	78.529	85.385
80	69.252	79.167	73.294	71.809	82.648	71.820	80.373
81	61.808	73.340	66.608	62.214	74.390	62.400	71.872
82	54.561	67.297	60.019	51.065	63.433	51.362	60.887
83	47.563	61.070	53.600	39.585	51.084	39.928	48.716
84	40.893	54.730	47.410	28.881	38.720	29.214	36.685
85	34.638	48.376	41.455	19.754	27.514	20.038	25.899
86	28.885	42.121	35.756	12.611	18.248	12.829	17.065
87	23.699	36.085	30.400	7.476	11.238	7.626	10.441
88	19.118	30.377	25.488	4.091	6.388	4.185	5.897
89	15.155	25.093	21.081	2.052	3.329	2.105	3.053
90	11.794	20.306	17.180	0.936	1.577	0.963	1.437
91	8.999	16.065	13.763	0.384	0.672	0.396	0.609
92	6.718	12.389	10.823	0.140	0.255	0.145	0.229
93	4.890	9.273	8.348	0.045	0.084	0.046	0.075
94	3.443	6.683	6.316	0.012	0.024	0.013	0.021
95	2.307	4.562	4.690	0.003	0.006	0.003	0.005
96	1.420	2.848	3.426	0.001	0.001	0.001	0.001
97	0.738	1.495	2.466	> 0.001	> 0.001	> 0.001	> 0.001
98	0.252	0.515	1.751	> 0.001	> 0.001	> 0.001	> 0.001
99	> 0.001	> 0.001	1.228	> 0.001	> 0.001	> 0.001	> 0.001

Probability of surviving through age X starting from Age 78

| | CSO (1980) | | Total Population | U. S. Life Tables (1982) | | | |
Age	Male	Female		White Male	White Female	Black Male	Black Female
Life Expectancy	6.97	8.55	7.93	7.80	10.20	7.50	9.70
78	91.610	94.655	92.847	92.342	95.549	92.260	94.870
79	83.269	89.037	85.660	84.743	90.912	84.748	89.652
80	75.039	83.162	78.469	77.285	86.135	77.508	84.390
81	66.973	77.041	71.311	66.959	77.528	67.342	75.464
82	59.121	70.693	64.257	54.959	66.109	55.430	63.931
83	51.538	64.152	57.385	42.604	53.239	43.090	51.151
84	44.310	57.492	50.758	31.083	40.353	31.527	38.519
85	37.533	50.817	44.382	21.261	28.675	21.626	27.193
86	31.299	44.247	38.281	13.573	19.018	13.845	17.918
87	25.679	37.906	32.547	8.046	11.712	8.230	10.963
88	20.716	31.910	27.288	4.403	6.658	4.516	6.192
89	16.422	26.359	22.569	2.208	3.469	2.272	3.205
90	12.780	21.331	18.393	1.007	1.644	1.039	1.509
91	9.751	16.876	14.735	0.413	0.701	0.428	0.639
92	7.280	13.014	11.587	0.151	0.266	0.156	0.241
93	5.299	9.741	8.937	0.048	0.088	0.050	0.079
94	3.731	7.020	6.762	0.013	0.025	0.014	0.022
95	2.500	4.793	5.021	0.003	0.006	0.003	0.005
96	1.539	2.992	3.668	0.001	0.001	0.001	0.001
97	0.800	1.571	2.640	> 0.001	> 0.001	> 0.001	> 0.001
98	0.274	0.541	1.875	> 0.001	> 0.001	> 0.001	> 0.001
99	> 0.001	> 0.001	1.315	> 0.001	> 0.001	> 0.001	> 0.001

Probability of surviving through age X starting from age 79

| | CSO (1980) | | | U. S. Life Tables (1982) | | | |
	Male	Female	Total Population	White Male	White Female	Black Male	Black Female
Life Expectancy	6.57	8.01	7.51	7.40	9.60	7.10	9.10
Age							
79	90.895	94.065	92.259	91.771	95.147	91.858	94.500
80	81.911	87.858	84.515	83.694	90.147	84.011	88.953
81	73.107	81.391	76.805	72.512	81.140	72.992	79.544
82	64.535	74.685	69.208	59.417	69.188	60.080	67.388
83	56.258	67.774	61.806	46.137	55.720	46.705	53.917
84	48.368	60.738	54.669	33.661	42.233	34.172	40.601
85	40.970	53.687	47.802	23.024	30.010	23.440	28.663
86	34.165	46.746	41.230	14.698	19.904	15.006	18.887
87	28.031	40.046	35.054	8.713	12.257	8.921	11.556
88	22.613	33.712	29.390	4.768	6.968	4.895	6.526
89	17.926	27.848	24.308	2.391	3.631	2.462	3.379
90	13.950	22.536	19.810	1.090	1.720	1.126	1.590
91	10.644	17.829	15.871	0.448	0.733	0.463	0.674
92	7.947	13.749	12.480	0.163	0.278	0.170	0.254
93	5.784	10.291	9.626	0.052	0.092	0.054	0.084
94	4.073	7.417	7.283	0.014	0.026	0.015	0.024
95	2.729	5.063	5.408	0.003	0.006	0.003	0.006
96	1.679	3.161	3.950	0.001	0.001	0.001	0.001
97	0.873	1.660	2.843	> 0.001	> 0.001	> 0.001	> 0.001

CSO (1980) / U. S. Life Tables (1982)

	Male	Female	Total Population	White Male	White Female	Black Male	Black Female
Life Expectancy	6.57	8.01	7.51	7.40	9.60	7.10	9.10
Age							
98	0.299	0.571	2.019	> 0.001	> 0.001	> 0.001	> 0.001
99	> 0.001	> 0.001	1.416	> 0.001	> 0.001	> 0.001	> 0.001

Probability of surviving through age X starting from age 80

CSO (1980) / U. S. Life Tables (1982)

	Male	Female	Total Population	White Male	White Female	Black Male	Black Female
Life Expectancy	6.18	7.48	7.10	7.00	9.00	6.70	8.60
Age							
80	90.116	93.401	91.606	91.199	94.745	91.457	94.130
81	80.430	86.527	83.250	79.014	85.278	79.461	84.174
82	71.000	79.397	75.015	64.854	72.717	65.406	71.310
83	61.893	72.050	66.992	50.274	58.562	50.845	57.055
84	53.213	64.571	59.256	36.679	44.387	37.201	42.965
85	45.074	57.074	51.813	25.088	31.541	25.517	30.332
86	37.588	49.695	44.689	16.016	20.919	16.336	19.986
87	30.839	42.573	37.995	9.494	12.883	9.711	12.228
88	24.879	35.839	31.856	5.195	7.323	5.329	6.906
89	19.721	29.605	26.347	2.606	3.816	2.681	3.575

	CSO (1980)			U. S. Life Tables (1982)			
	Male	Female	Total Population	White Male	White Female	Black Male	Black Female
Life Expectancy	6.18	7.48	7.10	7.00	9.00	6.70	8.60
Age							
90	15.348	23.958	21.473	1.188	1.808	1.226	1.683
91	11.711	18.954	17.202	0.488	0.771	0.504	0.713
92	8.743	14.617	13.527	0.178	0.292	0.185	0.268
93	6.364	10.941	10.434	0.057	0.097	0.059	0.088
94	4.481	7.885	7.894	0.016	0.028	0.016	0.025
95	3.002	5.383	5.862	0.004	0.007	0.004	0.006
96	1.848	3.360	4.282	0.001	0.001	0.001	0.001
97	0.960	1.764	3.082	> 0.001	> 0.001	> 0.001	> 0.001
98	0.328	0.607	2.189	> 0.001	> 0.001	> 0.001	> 0.001
99	> 0.001	> 0.001	1.535	> 0.001	> 0.001	> 0.001	> 0.001

Probability of surviving through age X starting from age 81

	CSO (1980)			U. S. Life Tables (1982)			
	Male	Female	Total Population	White Male	White Female	Black Male	Black Female
Life Expectancy	5.80	6.98	6.70	6.70	8.60	6.40	8.20
Age							
81	89.252	92.640	90.878	86.639	90.008	86.884	89.423
82	78.787	85.006	81.888	71.112	76.751	71.515	75.756

		CSO (1980)		Total Population	U. S. Life Tables (1982)			
		Male	Female		White Male	White Female	Black Male	Black Female
Life Expectancy		5.80	6.98	6.70	6.70	8.60	6.40	8.20
Age								
83		68.682	77.141	73.130	55.126	61.810	55.594	60.613
84		59.049	69.133	64.685	40.219	46.849	40.676	45.644
85		50.018	61.107	56.560	27.509	33.291	27.901	32.223
86		41.710	53.206	48.784	17.562	22.079	17.862	21.232
87		34.221	45.581	41.477	10.410	13.597	10.619	12.991
88		27.607	38.371	34.775	5.696	7.730	5.827	7.337
89		21.885	31.696	28.762	2.857	4.028	2.931	3.798
90		17.031	25.650	23.440	1.303	1.908	1.340	1.788
91		12.995	20.293	18.778	0.535	0.814	0.552	0.757
92		9.702	15.650	14.767	0.195	0.308	0.202	0.285
93		7.062	11.714	11.390	0.062	0.102	0.065	0.094
94		4.972	8.442	8.618	0.017	0.029	0.018	0.027
95		3.332	5.763	6.399	0.004	0.007	0.004	0.006
96		2.050	3.598	4.675	0.001	0.001	0.001	0.001
97		1.066	1.889	3.364	> 0.001	> 0.001	> 0.001	> 0.001
98		0.365	0.650	2.389	> 0.001	> 0.001	> 0.001	> 0.001
99		> 0.001	> 0.001	1.676	> 0.001	> 0.001	> 0.001	> 0.001

Probability of surviving through age X starting from age 82

	CSO (1980)		Total Population	U.S. Life Tables (1982)			
	Male	Female		White Male	White Female	Black Male	Black Female
Life Expectancy	5.44	6.49	6.32	6.30	8.10	6.00	7.70
Age							
82	88.275	91.760	90.108	82.079	85.271	82.311	84.717
83	76.953	83.269	80.471	63.627	68.671	63.987	67.782
84	66.160	74.625	71.178	46.421	52.050	46.817	51.043
85	56.041	65.961	62.237	31.752	36.986	32.113	36.035
86	46.733	57.433	53.681	20.270	24.530	20.559	23.744
87	38.342	49.202	45.640	12.016	15.107	12.222	14.527
88	30.932	41.419	38.266	6.575	8.588	6.706	8.205
89	24.520	34.215	31.649	3.298	4.475	3.373	4.248
90	19.082	27.688	25.793	1.504	2.120	1.543	1.999
91	14.560	21.905	20.663	0.617	0.904	0.635	0.847
92	10.870	16.893	16.249	0.225	0.343	0.232	0.319
93	7.912	12.644	12.533	0.072	0.114	0.075	0.105
94	5.571	9.113	9.483	0.020	0.032	0.020	0.030
95	3.733	6.221	7.042	0.004	0.008	0.005	0.007
96	2.297	3.883	5.143	0.001	0.001	0.001	0.001
97	1.194	2.039	3.702	> 0.001	> 0.001	> 0.001	> 0.001
98	0.408	0.702	2.629	> 0.001	> 0.001	> 0.001	> 0.001
99	> 0.001	> 0.001	1.844	> 0.001	> 0.001	> 0.001	> 0.001

Probability of surviving through age X starting from age 83

	CSO (1980)		Total Population	U. S. Life Tables (1982)			
	Male	Female		White Male	White Female	Black Male	Black Female
Life Expectancy	5.09	6.03	5.96	6.00	7.70	5.70	7.30
Age							
83	87.174	90.747	89.305	77.519	80.533	77.738	80.010
84	74.948	81.327	78.992	56.557	61.041	56.878	60.251
85	63.485	71.885	69.070	38.684	43.375	39.014	42.534
86	52.940	62.591	59.574	24.696	28.767	24.977	28.027
87	43.435	53.620	50.651	14.639	17.716	14.848	17.148
88	35.040	45.138	42.466	8.011	10.071	8.148	9.685
89	27.777	37.287	35.123	4.018	5.248	4.098	5.014
90	21.617	30.175	28.625	1.832	2.486	1.874	2.360
91	16.494	23.872	22.932	0.752	1.060	0.771	1.000
92	12.314	18.410	18.033	0.274	0.402	0.282	0.376
93	8.963	13.780	13.909	0.088	0.133	0.090	0.124
94	6.311	9.931	10.524	0.024	0.038	0.025	0.035
95	4.228	6.780	7.815	0.005	0.009	0.006	0.008
96	2.602	4.232	5.708	0.001	0.002	0.001	0.002
97	1.353	2.222	4.108	> 0.001	> 0.001	> 0.001	> 0.001
98	0.463	0.765	2.918	> 0.001	> 0.001	> 0.001	> 0.001
99	> 0.001	> 0.001	2.046	> 0.001	> 0.001	> 0.001	> 0.001

Probability of surviving through age X starting from age 84

Age	CSO (1980)		Total Population	U. S. Life Tables (1982)			
	Male	Female		White Male	White Female	Black Male	Black Female
Life Expectancy	4.77	5.59	5.62	5.60	7.20	5.40	6.90
84	85.975	89.619	88.452	72.959	75.796	73.166	75.304
85	72.825	79.214	77.342	49.903	53.860	50.187	53.162
86	60.730	68.973	66.709	31.858	35.721	32.130	35.029
87	49.826	59.087	56.716	18.885	21.998	19.100	21.432
88	40.196	49.741	47.552	10.334	12.505	10.481	12.105
89	31.864	41.089	39.329	5.183	6.517	5.272	6.267
90	24.797	33.251	32.053	2.364	3.087	2.411	2.949
91	18.921	26.306	25.678	0.970	1.316	0.992	1.249
92	14.125	20.287	20.192	0.354	0.499	0.363	0.470
93	10.282	15.185	15.574	0.113	0.165	0.116	0.155
94	7.239	10.943	11.784	0.031	0.047	0.032	0.044
95	4.851	7.471	8.740	0.007	0.011	0.007	0.010
96	2.985	4.664	6.391	0.001	0.002	0.001	0.002
97	1.552	2.449	4.600	> 0.001	> 0.001	> 0.001	> 0.001
98	0.531	0.843	3.267	> 0.001	> 0.001	> 0.001	> 0.001
99	> 0.001	> 0.001	2.291	> 0.001	> 0.001	> 0.001	> 0.001

Probability of surviving through age X starting from age 85

| | CSO (1980) | | Total Population | U. S. Life Tables (1982) | | | |
	Male	Female		White Male	White Female	Black Male	Black Female
Life Expectancy	4.46	5.18	5.28	5.30	6.70	5.00	6.50
Age							
85	84.705	88.390	87.439	68.399	71.059	68.593	70.597
86	70.636	76.962	75.418	43.665	47.128	43.913	46.517
87	57.954	65.932	64.121	25.884	29.023	26.105	28.461
88	46.753	55.503	53.760	14.164	16.499	14.325	16.074
89	37.061	45.849	44.464	7.104	8.598	7.206	8.322
90	28.842	37.103	36.237	3.240	4.073	3.295	3.917
91	22.007	29.353	29.030	1.330	1.736	1.356	1.659
92	16.430	22.637	22.829	0.485	0.658	0.496	0.625
93	11.959	16.944	17.608	0.155	0.218	0.159	0.206
94	8.420	12.211	13.323	0.042	0.062	0.044	0.058
95	5.642	8.336	9.893	0.010	0.015	0.010	0.014
96	3.472	5.204	7.226	0.002	0.003	0.002	0.003
97	1.805	2.732	5.201	> 0.001	> 0.001	> 0.001	> 0.001
98	0.617	0.940	3.694	> 0.001	> 0.001	> 0.001	> 0.001
99	> 0.001	> 0.001	2.590	> 0.001	> 0.001	> 0.001	> 0.001

Probability of surviving through age X starting from age 86

| | CSO (1980) | | Total Population | U. S. Life Tables (1982) | | | |
	Male	Female		White Male	White Female	Black Male	Black Female
Life Expectancy	4.18	4.80	4.97	4.90	6.30	4.70	6.00
Age							
86	83.391	87.071	86.252	63.839	66.322	64.020	65.891
87	68.418	74.592	73.332	37.843	40.844	38.058	40.315
88	55.195	62.793	61.483	20.707	23.218	20.884	22.769
89	43.754	51.871	50.852	10.387	12.099	10.505	11.788
90	34.050	41.976	41.443	4.736	5.732	4.804	5.548
91	25.981	33.209	33.201	1.944	2.444	1.977	2.350
92	19.396	25.610	26.108	0.709	0.926	0.723	0.885
93	14.118	19.169	20.137	0.226	0.307	0.232	0.292
94	9.941	13.815	15.237	0.062	0.087	0.064	0.082
95	6.661	9.431	11.314	0.014	0.021	0.015	0.019
96	4.099	5.888	8.264	0.003	0.004	0.003	0.004
97	2.131	3.091	5.948	> 0.001	0.001	> 0.001	0.001
98	0.729	1.064	4.224	> 0.001	> 0.001	> 0.001	> 0.001
99	> 0.001	> 0.001	2.963	> 0.001	> 0.001	> 0.001	> 0.001

Probability of surviving through age X starting from age 87

| | CSO (1980) | | Total Population | U. S. Life Tables (1982) | | | |
	Male	Female		White Male	White Female	Black Male	Black Female
Life Expectancy	3.91	4.43	4.68	4.60	5.90	4.40	5.60
Age							
87	82.045	85.668	85.021	59.279	61.584	59.447	61.184
88	66.188	72.117	71.283	32.437	35.009	32.621	34.555
89	52.468	59.573	58.957	16.270	18.243	16.409	17.890
90	40.832	48.209	48.049	7.419	8.642	7.503	8.420
91	31.156	38.140	38.493	3.045	3.685	3.088	3.566
92	23.259	29.413	30.270	1.111	1.396	1.130	1.343
93	16.930	22.015	23.347	0.355	0.463	0.362	0.442
94	11.921	15.866	17.665	0.097	0.132	0.099	0.125
95	7.987	10.832	13.117	0.022	0.031	0.023	0.029
96	4.916	6.762	9.581	0.004	0.006	0.004	0.006
97	2.555	3.550	6.896	0.001	0.001	0.001	0.001
98	0.874	1.222	4.898	> 0.001	> 0.001	> 0.001	> 0.001
99	> 0.001	> 0.001	3.435	> 0.001	> 0.001	> 0.001	> 0.001

Probability of surviving through age X starting from age 88

| | CSO (1980) | | | U. S. Life Tables (1982) | | | |
	Male	Female	Total Population	White Male	White Female	Black Male	Black Female
Life Expectancy	3.66	4.09	4.42	4.20	5.40	4.00	5.20
Age							
88	80.673	84.182	83.842	54.719	56.847	54.874	56.478
89	63.950	69.539	69.344	27.447	29.623	27.602	29.239
90	49.768	56.275	56.514	12.516	14.033	12.622	13.761
91	37.974	44.521	45.275	5.136	5.983	5.195	5.829
92	28.349	34.334	35.603	1.874	2.267	1.900	2.195
93	20.635	25.699	27.460	0.598	0.752	0.608	0.723
94	14.529	18.521	20.777	0.164	0.214	0.167	0.204
95	9.735	12.644	15.428	0.037	0.051	0.038	0.048
96	5.992	7.893	11.269	0.007	0.010	0.007	0.009
97	3.114	4.144	8.111	0.001	0.001	0.001	0.001
98	1.065	1.426	5.761	> 0.001	> 0.001	> 0.001	> 0.001
99	> 0.001	> 0.001	4.040	> 0.001	> 0.001	> 0.001	> 0.001

Probability of surviving through age X starting from age 89

| | CSO (1980) | | | U. S. Life Tables (1982) | | | |
	Male	Female	Total Population	White Male	White Female	Black Male	Black Female
Life Expectancy	3.41	3.77	4.18	3.90	5.00	3.70	4.70
Age							
89	79.271	82.606	82.708	50.159	52.110	50.301	51.771

	CSO (1980)		Total Population	U. S. Life Tables (1982)			
	Male	Female		White Male	White Female	Black Male	Black Female
Life Expectancy	3.41	3.77	4.18	3.90	5.00	3.70	4.70
Age							
90	61.691	66.849	67.405	22.873	24.686	23.002	24.366
91	47.072	52.886	54.000	9.387	10.525	9.467	10.321
92	35.141	40.785	42.464	3.424	3.989	3.463	3.886
93	25.579	30.527	32.752	1.093	1.323	1.109	1.280
94	18.010	22.001	24.782	0.299	0.376	0.304	0.362
95	12.068	15.019	18.402	0.068	0.089	0.070	0.085
96	7.427	9.376	13.441	0.012	0.017	0.013	0.016
97	3.861	4.923	9.674	0.002	0.002	0.002	0.002
98	1.320	1.694	6.871	> 0.001	> 0.001	> 0.001	> 0.001
99	> 0.001	> 0.001	4.819	> 0.001	> 0.001	> 0.001	> 0.001

Probability of surviving through age X starting from age 90

	CSO (1980)		Total Population Life	U. S. Life Tables (1982)			
	Male	Female		White Male	White Female	Black Male	Black Female
Expectancy	3.18	3.45	3.94	3.50	4.50	3.40	4.30
Age							
90	77.823	80.925	81.498	45.600	47.373	45.728	47.065
91	59.381	64.022	65.290	18.714	20.197	18.820	19.936
92	44.331	49.373	51.342	6.827	7.654	6.885	7.506
93	32.268	36.955	39.600	2.179	2.538	2.207	2.473

	CSO (1980)			U. S. Life Tables (1982)			
	Male	Female	Total Population Life	White Male	White Female	Black Male	Black Female
Expectancy	3.18	3.45	3.94	3.50	4.50	3.40	4.30
Age							
94	22.720	26.633	29.963	0.596	0.721	0.605	0.698
95	15.223	18.182	22.249	0.136	0.171	0.138	0.164
96	9.369	11.350	16.251	0.025	0.032	0.025	0.031
97	4.870	5.959	11.697	0.003	0.005	0.003	0.004
98	1.666	2.051	8.307	> 0.001	> 0.001	> 0.001	> 0.001
99	> 0.001	> 0.001	5.826	> 0.001	> 0.001	> 0.001	> 0.001

Probability of surviving through age X starting from age 91

	CSO (1980)			U. S. Life Tables (1982)			
	Male	Female	Total Population	White Male	White Female	Black Male	Black Female
Life Expectancy	2.94	3.15	3.73	3.20	4.00	3.00	3.90
Age							
91	76.302	79.113	80.112	41.040	42.635	41.156	42.358
92	56.963	61.011	62.998	14.971	16.158	15.056	15.949
93	41.463	45.666	48.590	4.779	5.358	4.819	5.254
94	29.194	32.911	36.765	1.307	1.523	1.322	1.484
95	19.561	22.468	27.300	0.298	0.361	0.302	0.349
96	12.039	14.026	19.940	9.054	0.068	0.055	0.066

	CSO (1980)			U. S. Life Tables (1982)			
	Male	Female	Total Population	White Male	White Female	Black Male	Black Female
Life Expectancy	2.94	3.15	3.73	3.20	4.00	3.00	3.90
Age							
97	6.258	7.364	14.352	0.007	0.010	0.008	0.009
98	2.140	2.534	10.193	0.001	0.001	0.001	0.001
99	> 0.001	> 0.001	7.149	> 0.001	> 0.001	> 0.001	> 0.001

Probability of surviving through age X starting from age 92

	CSO (1980)			U. S. Life Tables (1982)			
	Male	Female	Total Population	White Male	White Female	Black Male	Black Female
Life Expectancy	2.70	2.85	3.53	2.80	3.60	2.70	3.40
Age							
92	74.655	77.119	78.637	36.480	37.898	36.583	37.652
93	54.341	57.723	60.653	11.644	12.567	11.710	12.404
94	38.261	41.600	45.892	3.186	3.572	3.213	3.503
95	25.637	28.400	34.077	0.726	0.846	0.735	0.824
96	15.778	17.729	24.890	0.132	0.160	0.134	0.155
97	8.201	9.308	17.915	0.018	0.023	0.018	0.022
98	2.805	3.203	12.724	0.002	0.002	0.002	0.002
99	> 0.001	> 0.001	8.923	> 0.001	> 0.001	> 0.001	> 0.001

Probability of surviving through age X starting from age 93

| | CSO (1980) | | Total Population | U. S. Life Tables (1982) | | | |
	Male	Female		White Male	White Female	Black Male	Black Female
Life Expectancy	2.44	2.55	3.35	2.50	3.10	2.30	3.00
Age							
93	72.789	74.849	77.130	31.920	33.161	32.010	32.945
94	51.251	53.943	58.360	8.733	9.426	8.783	9.303
95	34.340	36.826	43.335	1.991	2.233	2.008	2.189
96	21.135	22.989	31.652	0.363	0.423	0.367	0.412
97	10.986	12.070	22.782	0.050	0.060	0.050	0.058
98	3.757	4.154	16.180	0.005	0.004	0.005	0.005
99	> 0.001	> 0.002	11.348	> 0.001	> 0.001	> 0.001	> 0.001

Probability of surviving through age X starting from age 94

| | CSO (1980) | | Total Population | U. S. Life Tables (1982) | | | |
	Male	Female		White Male	White Female	Black Male	Black Female
Life Expectancy	2.17	2.24	3.19	2.10	2.70	2.00	2.60
Age							
94	70.410	72.069	75.664	27.360	28.424	27.437	28.239
95	47.178	49.200	56.184	6.238	6.733	6.273	6.645
96	29.035	30.714	41.038	1.138	1.276	1.147	1.251
97	15.093	16.126	29.537	0.156	0.181	0.157	0.177
98	5.162	5.550	20.978	0.014	0.014	0.014	0.017
99	> 0.001	> 0.001	14.712	0.001	> 0.001	0.001	0.001

Probability of surviving through age X starting from age 95

	CSO (1980)			U. S. Life Tables (1982)			
	Male	Female	Total Population	White Male	White Female	Black Male	Black Female
Life Expectancy	1.87	1.91	3.06	1.80	2.20	1.70	2.20
Age							
95	67.004	68.268	74.255	22.800	23.686	22.864	23.532
96	41.238	42.617	54.237	4.159	4.488	4.182	4.430
97	21.435	22.375	39.037	0.569	0.638	0.574	0.625
98	7.331	7.700	27.725	0.052	0.048	0.052	0.059
99	> 0.001	> 0.001	19.444	0.002	> 0.001	0.002	0.003

Probability of surviving through age X starting from age 96

	CSO (1980)			U. S. Life Tables (1982)			
	Male	Female	Total Population	White Male	White Female	Black Male	Black Female
Life Expectancy	1.54	1.56	2.95	1.40	1.80	1.30	1.70
Age							
96	61.545	62.426	73.041	18.240	18.949	18.291	18.826
97	31.991	32.776	52.572	2.495	2.693	2.509	2.658
98	10.942	11.280	37.338	0.228	0.201	0.230	0.250
99	> 0.001	> 0.001	26.186	0.010	> 0.001	0.010	0.012

Probability of surviving through age X starting from age 97

| | CSO (1980) | | | U. S. Life Tables (1982) | | | |
	Male	Female	Total Population	White Male	White Female	Black Male	Black Female
Life Expectancy	1.20	1.21	2.85	1.10	1.30	1.00	1.30
Age							
97	51.980	52.503	71.976	13.680	14.212	13.719	14.119
98	17.778	18.069	51.120	1.248	1.062	1.255	1.329
99	> 0.001	> 0.001	35.851	0.057	> 0.001	0.057	0.063

Probability of surviving through age X starting from age 98

| | CSO (1980) | | | U. S. Life Tables (1982) | | | |
	Male	Female	Total Population	White Male	White Female	Black Male	Black Female
Life Expectancy	0.84	0.84	2.76	0.70	0.90	0.70	0.90
Age							
98	34.202	34.415	71.023	9.120	7.475	9.146	9.413
99	> 0.001	> 0.001	49.809	0.415	> 0.001	0.418	0.443

Probability of surviving through age X starting from age 99

	CSO (1980)		Total Population	U. S. Life Tables (1982)			
Life Expectancy	Male	Female		White Male	White Female	Black Male	Black Female
	0.50	0.50	2.69	0.50	0.50	0.50	0.50
Age 99	> 0.001	> 0.001	70.131	4.550	> 0.001	4.573	4.706

Cases

B

Baulieu v Elliot, 434 P2d 665 (Alaska 1967) §§**6.02, 15.01**

C

Chesapeake & Ohio RR Co v Kelly, 241 US 485 (1916) §**6.02**

H

Higgins v Kinnebrew Motors, 547 F2d 1223, 1225–26 (5th Cir 1977) §**12.10**

K

Kuczkowski v Bolubasz, 491 Pa 561, 421 A2d 1027 (1980) §§**6.02, 15.01**

N

Norfolk & Western Railway Co v Liepelt, 444 US 490, *rehg denied,* 445 US 972 (1980) §**14.01**

Statutes

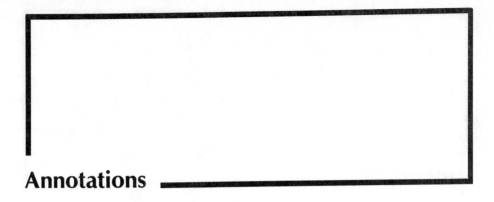

Annotations

Annotation, *Propriety of Taking Income into Consideration in Fixing Damages in Personal Injury or Death Action,* 16 ALR4th 589 (1983) **§14.01**

Annotation, *Validity and Construction of State Statute or Rule Allowing or Changing Rate of Prejudgement Interest in Tort Actions,* 40 ALR4th 147 (1985) **§4.11**

Annotation, *Propriety of Considering Future Income Taxes in Awarding Damages Under Federal Tort Claims Act,* 47 ALR Fed 735 (1980) **§14.01**

Authorities

American Medical Association, Guide to the Evaluation of Permanent Impairment (2d ed 1977) **§3.05**

L. Basset, The Use of Economists In Personal Injury Actions (Vol 1984, No 2) **§8.02**

W. Baumol & A. Blinder, Economics 114 (3rd ed 1985) **§12.02**

K. Black, Jr. & H. Skipper, Jr., Insurance 317 (11th ed 1987) **§10.03**

Bradshaw, *The Scope of 'Pecuniary Loss' Since Wentling v. M.A.S.*, 9, No 2 J Kan Trial Law Assn 7–11 (1985–86) **§13.08**

R. Brealey & S. Myers, Principles of Corporate Finance 31 (McGraw-Hill, Inc 1981) **§8.05**

Bureau of Labor Statistics, US Dept of Labor, Special Labor Force Report, Lenth of Working Life for Men and Women 187 (1970 rev ed 1976) **§9.03**

Chapman, *The Consumer Price Index: A History and Source List*, 13, No 4 Reference Servs Rev 47–51 (Winter 1985) **§5.17**

E. Cheit, Injury and Recovery in the Course of Employment (1961) **§12.04**

Committee of Rating of Mental & Physical Impairment, Manual for Orthopedic Surgeons for the Evaluation of Permanent Physical Impairment (2d ed 1977) **§3.05**

Durham, *The Valuation of the Production of a Deceased Housewife*, 4, No 5 J Kan Trial Law Assn 18 (1980–81) **§§2.16, 13.08**

Franz, *Should Income Taxes Be Included When Calculating Lost Earnigs*, Trial, Oct 1982, at 53–57 **§12.03**

Franz, *Simplied Calculation of Future Lost Earnings*, Trial, Aug 1977, at 34–37 **§15.02**

Gauger & Walker, *The Dollar Value of Household Work*, 60 Info Bull (New York State College of Human Ecology 1980) **§§2.16, 4.10, 13.03, 13.06**

Hunt & Kiker, *Valuation of Household Services: Methodology and Estimation*, 46, No 4 J Risk & Ins 697, 697–706 (1980) **§13.08**

N. Jacob & R. Pettit, Investments 504 (1984) **§6.07**

G. Kaufman, The Financial System, Money, Markets and Institutions (1980) **§5.17**

Kiker, *Evaluating Household Services,* Trial, Feb 1980, at 34–35 (1980) **§§2.16, 13.08**

Kirby, *The Economic Expert,* 31, No 3 J Mo B 201 (Apr-May 1975) **§§2.16, 13.08**

R. Kolb, Investments 44 (1986) **§6.16**

C. McConnell, Economics: Principles, Problems and Policies 744 (McGraw-Hill, Inc 10th ed 1987) **§2.03**

S. Porter, New Money Book For The 80's 621 (1980) **§§2.16, 4.10, 13.02**

G. Reynolds, The Mortality Merchants 46 (1978) **§10.02**

P. Rose & D. Fraser, Financial Institutions (2d ed 1985) **§4.16**

Standard & Poor's Corp, Bond Guide 10 (Mar 1985) **§6.15**

Standard & Poor's, Register of Corporations (McGraw-Hill, Inc 1987). Dun's Marketing Service, Million Dollar Directory (Div of Dun & Bradstreet, NJ 1987) **§2.10**

Stewart & Greenhalgh, *Work History Patterns and the Occupational Attainment of Women,* 94 Econ J 498–519 (Sept 1984) **§13.02**

US Government Printing Office, Standard Industrial Classification Tables Manual (Washington, DC) **§2.10**

US Dept of Commerce, Bureau of the Census, Statistical Abstracts of the United States 469 (104th ed 1984) **§§2.11, 8.04, 10.02**

US Dept of Labor, Bureau of Labor Statistics, Worklife Estimates: Effects of Race and Education, Bulletin 2254 (Feb 1986) **§9.01**

US Dept of Labor, Technical Notes, Current Population Survey (Household Survey), Handbook of Labor Statistics, Bulletin 2217 at 1–3 (June 1985) **§11.02**

US Dept of Labor, Revised Equilvalency Scale for Urban Families of Different Size, Age and Composition, Derived from the Bureau of Labor Statistics of Consumer Expenditures (1960–61) **§12.04**

R. Vukas, Description of SIC Codes (Washburn Univ 1987)(unpublished manuscript) **§§2.10, 5.17**

J. Viscione & G. Roberts, Contemporary Financial Management 65 (1987) **§10.04**

T. Yamane, Statistics, an Introductory Analysis 368 (1964) **§8.03**

Index

A

ACTUARIES
  Economists' roles §1.01
AGE EARNINGS PROFILE
  Generally §§1.14, 8.01, 8.02, 8.15
  Construction of profile with
    equations §8.06
  Current data, formation of §8.08
  Data sources §8.04
  Earnings history
  –generally §8.09
  –future income calculations when
    individual has an earnings
    history §8.11
  –present value calculations of
    future income when individual
    has no earnings history §8.10
  Effects of §8.07
  Estimated losses, observation of
    §8.14
  Equations for calculations §8.05
  Median income calculations §8.03
  Proper use of profile §8.13
  Shortcoming of profile §8.12
AGGREGATE MORTALITY TABLES
  Mortality adjustments, types of
    tables §10.03

ALASKA PLAN
  Present value of future income,
    quick estimation method. See
    PRESENT VALUE OF FUTURE
    INCOME, QUICK ESTIMATION
    METHOD
ALIMONY
  Family structures, federal income
    taxes §14.07
AMORTIZATION
  Expenditure forecasting §14.08
ANNUITIES
  Discount rates, present value
    calculations §§6.06, 6.07
  Economists' estimate of present
    value §§16.04, 16.05
  Growth and discount rates §7.04
  Mortality adjustments §§10.04,
    10.05
  Present value of retirement
    benefits, defined contribution
    plan §§15.04, 15.05
  Probability of living calculations
    §10.06
  Structured settlements. See
    STRUCTURED SETTLEMENTS
ASSETS
  Estimable types of losses by
    economists §1.03

G

Insurance Claims and Disputes

Representation of Insurance Companies and Insureds

Second Edition

1991 Cumulative Supplement
Current through December 1, 1990

Allan D. Windt
Law Offices of Allan D. Windt
Philadelphia, Pennsylvania
Member of the Pennsylvania,
   Florida, District of Columbia,
   and North Carolina Bars

*Insert in the pocket at the back
of the bound volume. Discard
supplement dated 1990.*

SHEPARD'S/McGRAW-HILL, INC.
P.O. Box 35300
Colorado Springs, Colorado 80935-3530

Supplement ISBN 0-07-172218-1

ICD1

New sections appearing in this supplement

Notice of Claim

1

§1.01   Notice Requirement

Add to note 6, page 2:

   E.g., Losi v Hanover Ins Co, 527 NYS2d 458, 459 (App Div 1988).

§1.02   Circumstances Under Which Failure to Comply with Notice Requirement Will Be Excused

Add to note 10, page 3:

   It has been held that futility—a belief that the insurer would deny the claim—does not constitute a valid excuse for tardy notice. *See* New York v Amro Realty Corp, 697 F Supp 99, 104 (NDNY 1988).

Add to first paragraph of note 11, page 4:

See West Am Ins Co v Bank of Isle of Wight, 673 F Supp 760, 766 (ED Va 1987).

Add to note 12, page 4:

E.g., Southern Guar Ins Co v Miller, 183 Ga App 261, 358 SE2d 611, 612 (1987); Stonewall Ins Co v Hamilton, 727 F Supp 271, 273 (WD Va 1989).

Add to first paragraph of note 13, page 5:

E.g., Powell v Fireman's Fund Ins Cos, 26 Mass App Ct 508, 529 NE2d 1228, 1231 (1988); Sandefer Oil & Gas, Inc v Aig Oil Rig Inc, 846 F2d 319, 325 (5th Cir 1988) (Texas law).

Add to first paragraph of note 14, page 5:

Contra Shipley v Kentucky Farm Bureau Ins Co, 747 SW2d 596, 597-98 (Ky 1988).

Add to note 21, page 6:

E.g., Virtuoso Aetna Cas & Sur Co, 134 AD2d 252, 520 NYS2d 439, 440 (1987); *see generally* Hovdestad v Interboro Mut Indem Ins Co, 135 AD2d 783, 522 NYS2d 895, 897 (1987) ("the infancy of [the insured] did not create an automatic tolling provision" with regard to giving of notice of a claim).

§1.03   Notice to Excess Insurers

Add to note 32, page 9:

But see Harbor Ins Co v Trammell Crow Co, 854 F2d 94, 98-99 (5th Cir 1988) (Texas law) (insured obligated to put excess insurer on notice when: (1) a reasonably prudent person in the insured's position would have concluded that the damages were likely to involve the excess policy; not (2) the insured had information from which it could reasonably conclude that the amount of the claim exceeded the primary policy).

§1.04   Effect of Unexcused Delay

Add following first sentence of section, page 10:

A breach of the notice provision relieves the insurer not only of its duty to indemnify, but also of its duty to defend. *See, e.g., Commercial Union Insurance Co v International Flavors & Fragrances, Inc,* 822 F2d 267, 272-73 (2d Cir 1987) (New York law).

Add to first paragraph of note 38, page 11:

E.g., North River Ins Co v Johnson, 757 SW2d 334, 335-36 (Tenn Ct App 1988); State Farm Fire & Cas Co v Scott, 372 SE2d 383, 385 (Va 1988); Reliance Ins Co v County Line Place, 692 F Supp 694, 697 (SD Miss 1988); State Farm Mut Auto Ins Co v Hollingsworth, 668 F Supp 1476, 1479 (D Wyo 1987); MGIC Indem Corp v Central Bank, 838 F2d 1382, 1386-87 (5th Cir 1988) (Louisiana law) (no prejudice required if policy is written so as to make giving of timely notice a condition precedent to coverage).

Add to second paragraph of note 38, page 11:

E.g., Fletcher v Palos Community Consol School Dist No 118, 164 Ill App 3d 921, 518 NE2d 363, 368 (1987).

Add to note 40, page 12:

E.g., Ruby v Midwestern Indem Co, 40 Ohio St 3d 159, 532 NE2d 730, 732 (1988); Aetna Cas & Sur Co v Murphy, 206 Conn 409, 538 A2d 219, 224 (1988); UNR Indus v Continental Ins Co, 682 F Supp 1434, 1444 (ND Ill 1988).

Add to first paragraph of note 41, page 13:

E.g., Seaway Port Auth v Midland Ins Co, 430 NW2d 242, 251 (Minn Ct App 1988).

Add to note 41, page 13:

See, e.g., South Carolina Ins Co v Hallmark Enters, 364 SE2d 678, 680-82 (NC Ct App 1988) (insurer is required to show prejudice if the insured first shows that it acted in good faith; i.e., if the insured can show either that it was unaware of its possible fault or that it did not purposefully and knowingly fail to notify the insurer); Darcy v Hartford Ins Co, 407 Mass 481, 554 NE2d 28, 32 (1990).

Add to note 44, page 14:

See, e.g., Molyneaux v Molyneaux, 230 NJ Super 169, 553 A2d 49, 54 (1989) ("conjecture and suspicions" may not "form the basis to establish appreciable prejudice").

Add to first paragraph of note 51, page 15:

See Holt v Utica Mut Ins Co, 157 Ariz 477, 759 P2d 623, 630 (1988) (indicating that insurer is not prejudiced by entry of default judgment against insured unless insured would have had good defense to claim).

Accord, e.g., Sinton v Hartford Accident & Indem Co, 261 Cal Rptr 163, 169 (Ct App 1989) (insurer not prejudiced even though it did not receive notice until after trial and an adverse judgment because, inter alia, it did not participate in attempt to obtain new trial or in appeal).

§1.05   To Whom Notice Must Be Given

Add to note 52, page 16:

See Kimble v Aetna Cas & Sur Co, 767 SW2d 846, 851 (Tex Ct App 1989) (because "under the facts of this case, it is by no means certain" that insurer could have opened default, insurer was prejudiced by late notice).

Add to note 55, page 17:

Accord Todd v Bankers Life & Cas Co, 523 NYS2d 206, 207 (App Div 1987) ("oral notification insufficient when written notice required").

Add to first paragraph of note 56, page 17:

See generally Todd v Bankers Life & Cas Co, 523 NYS2d 206, 207-208 (App Div 1987).

§1.06   Notice Received from Source Other Than the Insured

Add to first paragraph of note 58, page 18:

E.g., Mahone v State Farm Mut Auto Ins Co, 188 Ga App 664, 373 SE2d 809, 811 (1988) (notice requirement "satisfied if the insurer receives notice of the suit either from an insured or from a third party"); Hanson v Barmore, 779 P2d 1360, 1362-63 (Colo Ct App 1989).

§1.07   Notice Under a Claims-Made Policy

Add to second paragraph of note 67, page 21:

See National Union Fire Ins Co v Continental Ill Corp, 673 F Supp 300, 303-04 (ND Ill 1987).

Add at end of note 67, page 21:

See generally Yancey v Floyd West & Co, 755 SW2d 914, 923-25 (Tex Ct App 1988) (explaining why claims-made policies are not against public policy, and why use of retroactive date can be reasonable); Langley v Mutual Fire Marine & Inland Ins Co, 512 So 2d 752, 756-63 (Ala 1987) (discussing validity of claims-made policies, and holding that they are not against public policy); Poirier v National Union Fire Ins Co, 517 So 2d 225, 227 (La Ct App 1987) (claims-made policy not against public policy).

Add to note 68, page 21:

The court in Village Escrow Co v National Union Fire Ins Co, 248 Cal Rptr 687, 693 n 2 (Ct App 1988), indicated, in dictum, that a restrictive claims-made policy may be ambiguous (resulting in abrogating the need for notice within the policy period) if the policy "advertises itself as a 'claims made' policy, not a 'claims made and reported' policy."

Add to note 70, page 22:

E.g., Safeco Title Ins Co v Gannon, 54 Wash App 330, 774 P2d 30, 34-35 (1989). *Contra* Mt Hawley Ins Co v Federal Sav & Loan Ins Corp, 695 F Supp 469, 480 (CD Cal 1987); St Paul Fire & Marine Ins Co v House, 73 Md App 118, 533 A2d 301, 309 (1987) (statute interpreted to require prejudice with regard to late notice under claims made policies); Village Escrow Co v National Union Fire Ins Co, 248 Cal Rptr 687, 692 (Ct App 1988) (prejudice defense could be asserted); Slatten v St Paul Fire & Marine Ins Co, 780 P2d 428, 430 (Ariz Ct App 1989); Chas T Main, Inc v Fireman's Fund Ins Co, 551 NE2d 28, 30 (Mass 1990).

Add to note 75, page 23:

Note that, if the insured gives a broad notice of potential claims and the insurer does not object to the sufficiency of the notice within a reasonable time, the insurer may later be precluded from arguing that the notice was insufficient. *See* Federal Sav & Loan Ins Corp v Burdette, 718 F Supp 649, 653-54 (ED Tenn 1989).

In Home Ins Co v Cooper & Cooper, Ltd, 889 F2d 746, 750 (7th Cir 1989) (Illinois law), the insured put the carrier on notice, prior to the expiration of the policy, as to every matter that the insured had ever handled. The notice was held to be ineffective.

Obligations of Insurer Following Notice of Claim

2

§2.02 Failure Promptly to Respond to Notice of Claim—Estoppel to Deny Coverage

Add to note 3, page 27:

See, e.g., Guilford Indus v Liberty Mut Ins Co, 688 F Supp 792, 796 (D Me 1988) (insurer not estopped by failing sooner to notify insured of absence of coverage, because insured had not been misled to his injury).

Add to note 6, page 27:

In Rodgers v Missouri Ins Guar Assn, 841 F2d 858, 861-62 (8th Cir 1988) (Missouri law), the court held that notice to an insurer three days before a motion for summary judgment against the insured was decided was insufficient.

§2.03 —Insurer's Loss of Rights

Add to note 11, page 29:

Holt v Utica Mut Ins Co, 157 Ariz 477, 759 P2d 623, 628-29 (1988) ("even absent an express refusal to defend, an unreasonable delay in taking action after receiving notice of a claim may constitute a breach of the duty to defend").

§2.06 Notification of Insurer's Preliminary Coverage Position Under Policy Containing Duty to Defend Provision—Reservation of Rights Letter

Add following first full sentence on page 33:

In *St Paul Fire & Marine Insurance Co v Children's Hospital National Medical Center,* 670 F Supp 393, 402 (DDC 1987), the insurer provided both primary and excess insurance, and provided a defense without reserving its rights. The court held that the insurer did not lose any defenses that it had under the excess policy because the defense was provided solely pursuant to the primary policy.

A few courts have indicated that an insurer will also be precluded from requiring an insured to pay a deductible or retained limit if the insurer assumes a defense without a reservation of rights. *See Arkwright-Boston Manufacturers Mutual Insurance Co v Aries Marine Corp,* 736 F Supp 1447, 1449-50 (SD Tex 1990).

§2.07 Necessity of Reservation of Rights Letter Prior to Institution of a Lawsuit Against Insured

Add to note 37, page 37:

See also Battista v Western World Ins Co, 227 NJ Super 135, 545 A2d 841, 845 (1988).

§2.08 Insurer Precluded from Denying Coverage Because of Failure to Issue a Reservation of Rights Letter—In General

Add to note 40, page 38:

There should not be a waiver absent knowledge of the material facts. *See, e.g.,* Manzanita Park v Insurance Co of N Am, 857 F2d 549, 555-56 (9th Cir 1988) (Arizona law). *See* **§2.24**; Ara v Erie Ins Co, 387 SE2d 320, 323 (W Va 1989); Edmondson v Pennsylvania Natl Mut Cas Ins Co, 781 SW2d 753, 756 (Ky 1989).

Add to note 41, page 38:

See, e.g., National Union Fire Ins Co v Siliconix, Inc, 726 F Supp 264, 270 (ND Cal 1989).

Add to note 46, page 39:

Wis Stat Ann 631.11(4) (West) provides that an insurer must notify an insured within 60 days after "acquir[ing] knowledge of sufficient facts to constitute a general defense to all claims under the policy." The court in Estate of Logan v Northwestern Natl Cas Co, 144 Wis 2d 318, 424 NW2d 179, 189 (1988), held that the statute applied if the insurer was attempting to avoid the entire policy, not if the insurer was simply denying coverage for a particular claim.

§2.09   Insurer Estopped from Denying Coverage Because of Failure to Issue a Reservation of Rights Letter

Add to first paragraph of note 47, page 40:

See, e.g., Commercial Union Ins Co v International Flavors & Fragrances, Inc, 822 F2d 267, 274 (2d Cir 1987) (New York law). *See generally* Guaranty Natl Ins Co v Chester County Hous Auth, 714 F Supp 747, 752 (ED Pa 1989).

§2.10   —Absence of Control of Insured's Defense

Add to note 61, page 43:

National Union Fire Ins Co v Siliconix, Inc, 726 F Supp 264, 270-71 (ND Cal 1989).

In Arkwright-Boston Mfrs Mut Ins Co v Aries Marine Corp, 736 F Supp 1447, 1450 (SD Tex 1990), the court held that an excess insurer had assumed the defense of its insured because, although the insured had independent counsel, the insurer had "orchestrat(ed) a settlement" with the plaintiff.

§2.11   —Absence of Conflict of Interest

Add to note 62, page 46:

See, e.g., Lone Star Indus v Liberty Mut Ins Co, 689 F Supp 329, 333-34 (SDNY 1988).

It has even been held that an insurer cannot limit its coverage to its policy limit if it does not reserve its right to do so. *See, e.g.,* Insurance Co of N Am v Kyla, Inc, 193 Ga App 555, 388 SE2d 530, 532 (1989).

Add to carryover paragraph on page 46:

E.g., State Farm Lloyds, Inc v Williams, CA No 05-89-00857-CU, slip op 14-21 (Tex Ct App 5th Cir Apr 13, 1990).

Add to note 67, page 47:

In Fire Ins Exch v Fox, 167 Mich App 710, 423 NW2d 325, 326-27 (1988), the court held that an insurer was not precluded from denying coverage because "only four months passed between the initiation of the underlying action and the date [the insurer] sent its reservation of rights letter. We feel that four months is, as a matter of law, not an unreasonable length of time."

Add to note 74, page 49:

Accord Mid-State Sav & Loan Assn v Illinois Ins Exch, 175 Ill App 3d 205, 529 NE2d 696, 700 (1988).

§2.13   Contents of Reservation of Rights Letter

Add to note 80, page 50:

See generally Shannon v Shannon, 150 Wis 2d 434, 442 NW2d 25, 32-33 (1989).
But see Federal Ins Co v Susquehanna Broadcasting Co, 727 F Supp 169, 172 (MD Pa 1989) (implying that a general reservation of rights will suffice).

Add to first paragraph of note 82, page 51:

See Battista v Western World Ins Co, 227 NJ Super 135, 545 A2d 841, 845-46 (1988) (because reservation of rights letter was not specific, it was totally ineffective; as a result, insurer was estopped from denying coverage).

Add at end of note 82, page 51:

In Richards Mfg Co v Great Am Ins Co, 773 SW2d 916, 919 (Tenn Ct App 1988), the court held that a reservation of rights was adequate even though the basis stated for the reservation was erroneous. "It is the insurer's conclusion regarding the existence or nonexistence of certain coverage that must be clearly and fairly communicated to the insured, not its legal reasons therefor."

§2.16   Consent by Insured to Defense Offered Subject to a Reservation of Rights

Add to note 108, page 57:

E.g., Battista v Western World Ins Co, 227 NJ Super 135, 545 A2d 841, 845-46 (1988).

Fla Stat Ann 627.426(2)(b)(3) (West 1983) has been interpreted to prevent a liability insurer from denying coverage unless the insurer obtained the insured's approval as to the independent counsel retained by the insurer to defend the insured. *See, e.g.,* Continental Ins Co v City of Miami Beach, 521 So 2d 232, 233 (Fla Dist Ct App 1988).

Add to first paragraph of note 109, page 58:

E.g., Jacora Sys v Central Mut Ins Co, 194 Ga App 512, 390 SE2d 876, 878 (1990).

§2.17   —Refusal to Accept Reservations When Defense Offered is Inadequate

Add to note 118, page 60:

See, e.g., United Servs Auto Assn v Morris, 154 Ariz 113, 741 P2d 246, 250 (1987).

§2.19   Notification of Preliminary Coverage Position When Insurer Does Not Provide a Defense

Add at beginning of note 127, page 63:

E.g., St Paul Fire & Marine Ins Co v Children's Hosp Natl Medical Center, 670 F Supp 393, 402 (DDC 1987).

§2.22   Declination of Coverage

Add to note 145, page 67:

In addition, Florida has a statute providing that a liability insurer shall not be permitted to deny coverage based on a particular coverage defense unless it follows specific procedures. *See generally* Country Manors Assn v Master Antenna Sys, 534 So 2d 1187, 1194 (Fla Dist Ct App 1988).

For a good discussion of what the insured must show in order to prove prejudice, *see* Evanston Ins Co v Security Assurance Co, 684 F Supp 1423, 1426-27 (ND Ill 1988); Boston Old Colony Ins Co v Lumbermens Mut Cas Co, 889 F2d 1245, 1247-48 (2d Cir 1989) (New York law); Kamyr, Inc v St Paul Surplus Lines Ins Co, 547 NYS2d 964, 967 (App Div 1989) (rejecting excess insurer's assertion that it had no duty to disclaim coverage until the primary coverage had been exhausted).

§2.23 Contents of Declination of Coverage Letter—Estoppel from Asserting Unmentioned Policy Defenses

Add to note 155, page 69:

E.g., ABCD . . . Vision, Inc v Fireman's Fund Ins Co, 304 Or 301, 744 P2d 998, 1001 (1987); Chapman v Safeco Ins Co of Am, 722 F Supp 285, 295-96 (ND Miss 1989).

Add to note 156, page 69:

See, e.g., Bleckner v General Accident Ins Co of Am, 713 F Supp 642, 651-52 (SDNY 1989) (insurer not estopped from raising coverage defense not mentioned in declination letter, because insured had not been prejudiced by insurer's action); Powell v Fireman's Fund Ins Cos, 26 Mass App Ct 508, 529 NE2d 1228, 1230 (1988) (since insurer had previously reserved its rights, its denial of coverage on one ground did not preclude it from later denying coverage on another ground); Guberman v William Penn Life Ins Co, 538 NYS2d 571, 573 (App Div 1989) ("The vast majority of jurisdictions recognize[s] that this rule of estoppel is limited in its application to those instances where the insured has suffered some degree of prejudice as a result of the insurer's attempt to shift its defense from one basis to another"); Consolidated Rail Corp v Hartford Accident & Indem Co, 676 F Supp 82, 85 (ED Pa 1987) (insurer not estopped from raising defenses not mentioned in declination of coverage letter because insured "cannot show that it reasonably relied to its detriment on [the insurer's] original denial of liability"); *see also* Gordon v Liberty Mut Ins Co, 675 F Supp 321, 323 (ED Va 1987) (court indicated that even if insured were prejudiced by fact that insurer did not mention a particular defense in its declination of coverage letter, insurer would later be able to rely on that defense if it consisted of a reason why coverage did not exist, as opposed to a reason why coverage had been forfeited); Depriest v State Farm Fire & Cas Co, 779 SW2d 347, 350 (Mo Ct App 1989); Federal Ins Co v Susquehanna Broadcasting Co, 727 F Supp 169, 171-72 (MD Pa 1989).

Add to first paragraph of note 160, page 70:

See, e.g., Hydro Sys v Continental Ins Co, 717 F Supp 700, 703 (CD Cal 1989); Judah v State Farm Fire & Cas Co, 266 Cal Rptr 455, 460 n 6 (Ct App 1990).

Add to note 164, page 71:

E.g., American States Ins Co v McGuire, 510 So 2d 1227, 1229-30 (Fla Dist Ct App 1987). *See generally* Brown v State Farm Mut Auto Ins Co, 776 SW2d 384, 389 (Mo 1989).

§2.24   —Waiver of Unmentioned Policy Defenses

Add to note 171, page 73:

Contra Intel Corp v Hartford Accident & Indem Co, 692 F Supp 1171, 1180 (ND Cal 1988) ("insurer waives its right to rely on defenses not specified in its denial which a reasonable investigation would have uncovered").

Add to note 174, page 74:

See, e.g., Consolidated Rail Corp v Hartford Accident & Indem Co, 676 F Supp 82, 85 (ED Pa 1987) (insurer not precluded from raising defenses not mentioned in declination of coverage letter because "waiver cannot operate to expand coverage under an insurance policy"); *see also* Safeco Ins Co v Marion, 676 F Supp 197, 199-200 (ED Mo 1987) (when insurer denies coverage on specified ground, it is thereafter precluded from raising a new defense to coverage for an otherwise covered risk, but not from raising a new reason as to why risk was not covered).

Add to note 175, page 74:

E.g., Intel Corp v Hartford Accident & Indem Co, 692 F Supp 1171, 1180 (ND Cal 1988); Mauer v Missouri State Employees' Retirement Sys, 762 SW2d 517, 519 (Mo Ct App 1988). *But see* Spotts v Farmers Ins Co, 762 SW2d 60, 62 (Mo Ct App 1988) (insurer, having made "general denial" of coverage, "will not be precluded from later giving a more specific reason for denying coverage").

Cf New York v Amro Realty Corp, 697 F Supp 99, 105-106 (NDNY 1988) (waiver of unmentioned policy defense if declination of coverage came after duty to defend arose, but not if it came before). *E.g.,* Zumbrun v United Servs Auto Assn, 719 F Supp 890, 895-96 (ED Cal 1989).

Add to note 177, page 75:

In Becker v State Farm Fire & Cas Co, 664 F Supp 460, 462 (ND Cal 1987), the court adopted a different intermediate position. It held that the rationale for the rule waiving unmentioned grounds for denying coverage was that it gave the insurer incentive to investigate claims before denying them. A contractual limitations clause defense (*see* §9.03) is unrelated to any investigation of whether the claimed loss is covered. Accordingly, the court held that the waiver rule did not apply to such unmentioned defenses.

§2.25 Rescinding Policy—Based on Misrepresentations in Application

Add to first paragraph of note 179, page 76:

See, e.g., Klopp v Keystone Ins Cos, 549 A2d 221, 222-23 (Pa Super Ct 1988).

Add at end of item 3 in note 180, page 77:

See generally Imperial Cas & Indem Co v Sogomonian, 243 Cal Rptr 639, 646-47 (Ct App 1988).

Add at end of note 180, page 77:

Such a holding is subject to criticism. While the public policy behind the mandatory nature of certain types of insurance, for example, insurance on automobiles, may preclude the rescission of a policy when an innocent third party has already been injured, that public policy should not apply with regard to nonmandatory types of insurance. *See, e.g.,* AG Allebach, Inc v Hurley, 540 A2d 289, 296 (Pa Super Ct 1988).

It has also been held that an insurer could not rescind a policy as against an innocent co-insured, even though the policy stated that the "entire policy shall be void if any insured has intentionally concealed or misrepresented any material fact." The court held that the policy language was not sufficiently clear. State Farm Fire & Cas Ins Co v Miceli, 164 Ill App 3d 874, 518 NE2d 357, 361 (1987).

See, e.g., Farmers State Bank v Western Natl Mut Ins Co, 454 NW2d 651, 652-53 (Minn Ct App 1990).

Add after carryover paragraph, page 76:

While not giving rise to a right to rescind, it has been held that there is no coverage for undisclosed risks that the insured was aware of at the time the policy was procured. *See, e.g., Township of Gloucester v Maryland Casualty Co,* 668 F Supp 394, 403 (DNJ 1987) ("One cannot obtain

insurance for a risk that the insured knows has already transpired");
Presley v National Flood Insurers Association, 399 F Supp 1242, 1244-45
(ED Mo 1975) (one cannot, as a matter of public policy, obtain coverage
for a loss that is in progress at time insurance is purchased).

Add at beginning of note 182, page 77:

E.g., In re Epic Mortgage Ins Litig, 701 F Supp 1192, 1243 (ED Va
1988); Howell v Colonial Penn Ins Co, 842 F2d 821, 822-23 (6th Cir
1987) (Tennessee law); Mountain Sec Savs Bank v United Guar
Residential Ins Co, 678 F Supp 610, 612 (WD Va 1987); Cummings v
Farmers Ins Exch, 249 Cal Rptr 568, 572 n 7 (App Dept Super Ct
1988). *Contra* Bloomgren v Fire Ins Exch, 162 Ill App 3d 594, 517
NE2d 290, 294 (1987); AG Allebach, Inc v Hurley, 540 A2d 289,
294-95 (Pa Super Ct 1988); Lowry v State Farm Mut Auto Ins Co, 228
Neb 171, 421 NW2d 775, 778 (1988).

*Page 77, the following cases in first paragraph of note 182 should come before
"Contra":*

Mackenzie v Prudential Ins Co of Am, 411 F2d 781, 782 (6th Cir 1969)
(Kentucky law); Fidelity & Deposit Co v Hudson United Bank, 493 F
Supp 434, 441 (DNJ 1980); State Farm Mut Auto Ins Co v Price, 396
NE2d 134, 136 (Ind Ct App 1979); Stumpf v State Farm Mut Auto Ins
Co, 252 Md 696, 251 A2d 362, 370 (1969); Formosa v Equitable Life
Assurance Socy of the United States, 166 NJ Super 8, 398 A2d 1301,
1304 (App Div 1979); Fierro v Foundation Reserve Ins Co, 81 NM 225,
465 P2d 282, 284 (1970); Massachusetts Mut Life Ins Co v Tate, 56
AD2d 173, 391 NYS2d 667, 670, *revd on other grounds*, 42 NY2d 1046,
369 NE2d 767, 399 NYS2d 211 (1977); American Gen Life Ins Co v
Gilbert, 595 SW2d 83, 87 (Tenn Ct App 1979); Fireman's Fund Ins
Co v Knutsen, 132 Vt 383, 324 A2d 223, 230 (1974).

Add to first paragraph of note 183, page 79:

See, e.g., W Va Code §§33-6-7 (b) and (c) (1957).

Add at beginning of note, 186, page 80:

E.g., Sanford v Federated Guar Ins Co, 522 So 2d 214, 216 (Miss
1988); *see generally* St Paul Fire & Marine Ins Co v Boston Hous Auth,
25 Mass App Ct 6, 514 NE2d 363, 367-68 (1987).

Add to note 187, page 81:

See, e.g., Sanford v Federated Guar Ins Co, 522 So 2d 214, 216-217
(Miss 1988) (what was referred to as a warranty in application was

referred to as a representation in policy; court therefore, finding an ambiguity, found it to be a representation).

Add to third paragraph of note 188, page 82:

See generally AG Allebach, Inc v Hurley, 540 A2d 289, 293-94 (Pa Super Ct 1988).

Add following second sentence of fourth paragraph of note 188, page 82:

E.g., In re Epic Mortgage Ins Litig, 701 F Supp 1192, 1244-45 (ED Va 1988) ("in the absence of any 'danger signals,' an insurer has no duty to investigate representations made to it by its insured and is entitled to rely upon the truth and accuracy of those representations").

Add at beginning of note 189, page 82:

See, e.g., AG Allebach, Inc v Hurley, 540 A2d 289, 294-95 (Pa Super Ct 1988); Mutual Benefit Life Ins Co v Morley, 722 F Supp 1048, 1051-53 (SDNY 1989); Powell v Time Ins Co, 382 SE2d 342, 350 (W Va 1989).

Add to note 191, page 84:

See, e.g., Singer v Nationwide Mut Fire Ins Co, 512 So 2d 1125, 1128 (Fla Dist Ct App 1987).

Add to note 192, page 84:

E.g., Golden v Northwestern Mut Life Ins Co, 229 NJ Super 405, 551 A2d 1009, 1018-19 (1988).

National Old Line Ins Co v People, 256 Ark 137, 506 SW2d 128 (1974), was overruled in Southern Farm Bureau Life Ins Co v Couger, 295 Ark 250, 748 SW2d 332, 336 (1988).

Add to first paragraph of note 195, page 84:

Cf Bauer v Grange Mut Cas Co, 33 Ohio App 3d 145, 514 NE2d 913, 916 (1986) ("where a refund is due . . . the law requires it to take place before an effective cancellation will be permitted").

Add at end of note 195, page 84:

A state statute may also prescribe the manner in which a policy can be rescinded. *See,* for example, Pa Stat Ann tit 40, §1171.5(a)(9) (Purdon 1981) (homeowner policies in effect for more than 60 days: part of the Unfair Insurance Practices Act), discussed in Metropolitan Property & Liab Ins Co v Commonwealth Ins Dept, 537 A2d 53 (Pa Commw Ct 1988).

§2.26 —Based on Concealment of Material Information Not Encompassed by Application

Add at end of first paragraph of section, page 85:

By statute in some states, the insured's misrepresentation must be in writing. *See, e.g., International Ampitheatre Co v Vanguard Underwriters Insurance Co,* 177 Ill App 3d 555, 532 NE2d 493, 499 (1988).

Add to first paragraph of note 201, page 85:

See, e.g., Royal Ins Co of Am v Cathy Daniels, Ltd, 684 F Supp 786, 791 (SDNY 1988).

Add to note 202, page 86:

Contra Insurance Co of N Am v United States Gypsum Co, 870 F2d 148, 153 (4th Cir 1989) (Virginia law).

Add to note 207, page 86:

See Mattox v Western Fidelity Ins Co, 694 F Supp 210, 216-17 (ND Miss 1988).

§2.28 Insurer Estopped from Asserting Right to Rescind

Add following first paragraph, page 89:

California Insurance Code §650 (West 1972) restricts an insurer's right to rescind after a lawsuit has been commenced on the insurance contract. The statute was discussed in *National Union Fire Insurance Co v Dixon,* 663 F Supp 1121 (ND Cal 1987).

Add at end of second paragraph, page 89:

See generally Nunley v Merrill, 513 So 2d 582, 586 (Miss 1987) ("ordinarily, a policy of insurance issued after a loss is not a valid policy"); *Township of Gloucester v Maryland Casualty Co,* 668 F Supp 394, 403 (DNJ 1987) ("One cannot obtain insurance for a risk that the insured knows has already transpired").

§2.29   Insurer Deemed to Have Waived Right to Rescind

Add to note 217, page 90:

E.g., Wis Stat Ann 631.11(4) (West) ("if after issuance of a policy the insurer acquires knowledge of sufficient facts to constitute a general defense to all claims under the policy, the defense is not available unless the insurer notifies the insured within 60 days after acquiring such knowledge"); *See* National Union Fire Ins Co v Hudson Energy Co, 780 SW2d 417, 424-25 (Tex Ct App 1989).

Add at beginning of note 220, page 91:

E.g., Dusich v Horley, 525 So 2d 507, 509 (Fla Dist Ct App 1988) (insurer can be precluded from rescinding a policy when a premium check bounces if insurer fails to notify insured within a reasonable amount of time that check bounced); Lowrey v State Farm Mut Auto Ins Co, 228 Neb 171, 421 NW2d 775, 779 (1988) (issue of fact whether time it took insurer to make rescission decision and communicate it to insured waived its right to rescind); *see also* Gurrentz v Federal Kemper Life Assurance Co, 513 So 2d 241, 242 (Fla Dist Ct App 1987) (rescission was not waived by insurer's receipt of two premium payments between time it learned of problem and time it notified insured of rescission). *Contra* Robertson v Farm Bureau Mut Ins Co, 668 F Supp 1259, 1260 (WD Ark 1987).

Add to first paragraph of note 220, page 91:

See Dayton Indep School Dist v National Gypsum Co, 682 F Supp 1403, 1414 (ED Tex 1988) (insurer waived its ability to rescind because, although knowing of facts that would permit rescission, it "remain[ed] silent and continu[ed] to sell insurance" to insured).

Add at end of note 220, page 91:

But see Mt Hawley Ins Co v Federal Sav & Loan Ins Corp, 695 F Supp 469, 477 (CD Cal 1987).

Add to first paragraph of note 224, page 93:

See Golden v Northwestern Mut Life Ins Co, 229 NJ Super 405, 551 A2d 1009 (1988).

§2.30   —Action by Insurer Inconsistent with Rescission

Add at beginning of note 227, page 94:

See Lowry v State Farm Mut Auto Ins Co,. 228 Neb 171, 421 NW2d 775, 780 (1988) (court held that sending out of premium notice could preclude insurer from rescinding even though "the notice was generated by a computer programmed to prepare and dispatch such documents at a predetermined date . . . [which] function is not part of [the insurer's] underwriting department").

Add at end of note 227, page 94:

In Dusich v Horley, 525 So 2d 507, 509 (Fla Dist Ct App 1988), the insured submitted a premium check that bounced, but before it bounced, the insurer issued the policy stating that the premium had been paid. The court held that the insurer may have "waived its right to treat the check as a conditional payment, and thereby waived the forfeiture provision in the application, by issuing a final policy which affirmatively stated that [the insured] paid the down payment." The holding is not devoid of logic. When an insurer receives a premium check that bounces, it theoretically has the option of either negating the coverage or keeping the coverage in place and suing for the unpaid premium.

§2.31   Incontestability Clauses

Add to first paragraph of note 231, page 95:

See, e.g., Batton v Connecticut Gen Life Ins Co, 847 F2d 584, 586 (9th Cir 1988) (Arizona law).

Obligations of Insured Following Notice of Claim

3

§3.02 Duty to Cooperate

Add to note 4, page 98:

E.g., Hanson v Barmore, 779 P2d 1360, 1364 (Colo Ct App 1989).

Add to first paragraph of note 11, page 101:

E.g., Holt v Utica Mut Ins Co, 157 Ariz 477, 759 P2d 623, 627 (1988); Darcy v Hartford Ins Co, 407 Mass 481, 554 NE2d 28, 33 (1990).

§3.03 Proof of Loss Clauses

Add to note 22, page 103:

In Aryeh v Westchester Fire Ins Co, 525 NYS2d 628, 629 (App Div 1988), the court ruled against the insured because, although she had submitted an unsworn statement to substantiate her loss, she had not submitted a proper proof of loss within 60 days of the insurer's request for the proof of loss.

Add to first paragraph of note 23, page 103:

E.g., Zions First Natl Bank v National Am Title Ins Co, 749 P2d 651, 655 (Utah 1988); Green v General Accident Ins Co of Am, 106 NM 523, 746 P2d 152, 154 (1987); Perry v Middle Atl Lumbermens Assn, 542 A2d 81, 89 (Pa Super Ct 1988).

Add to note 26, page 104:

See, e.g., Hall v Time Ins Co, 671 F Supp 768, 769 (MD Ga 1987) ("while it is true that normally an insurance company can require timely

proof of loss by its insured, where the insurer denies coverage abso-
lutely, . . . it can no longer rely on that contractual provision to later deny
coverage").

Add at beginning of note 27, page 104:

E.g., Smith v North Carolina Farm Bureau Mut Ins Co, 321 NC 60,
361 SE2d 571, 575 (1987); Perry v Middle Atl Lumbermens Assn, 542
A2d 81, 89 (Pa Super Ct 1988).

Add to note 31, page 106:

E.g., Moyer v Director of Fed Emergency Management Agency, 721 F
Supp 235, 237-38 (D Ariz 1989).

§3.04   Access to Books and Records, and Submission to Examinations

Add to note 33, page 107:

Only substantial compliance is required. *See, e.g.*, Piro v Pekin Ins Co,
162 Ill App 3d 225, 514 NE2d 1231, 1234-35 (1987). In Twin City Fire
Ins Co v Harvey, 662 F Supp 216, 219 (D Ariz 1987), the court held that
an insured did not breach the policy by refusing to answer questions,
because the insurer failed to explain the relevance of the questions when
asked to do so.

In examining one insured under oath, an insurer can require that
another insured that it will later examine not be present. *E.g.*, State Farm
Fire & Cas Co v Tan, 691 F Supp 1271, 1274 (SD Cal 1988).

Add at beginning of note 37, page 107:

See Piro v Pekin Ins Co, 162 Ill App 3d 225, 514 NE2d 1231, 1234
(1987) (at least if insured eventually supplies requested records, insurer
cannot complain unless it can prove that it was prejudiced by delay).

Add to note 38, page 108:

E.g., 232 Broadway Corp v Calvert Ins Co, 540 NYS2d 324, 325 (App
Div 1989); United States Fidelity & Guar Co v Conaway, 674 F Supp
1270, 1273 (ND Miss 1987); *see* McCullough v Travelers Cos, 415
NW2d 349, 351 (Minn Ct App 1987) (held against insured because he
"sued before allowing himself to be examined under oath as requested by
Travelers").

Add to first paragraph of note 40, page 108:

See Gould Investors LP v General Ins Co, 737 F Supp 812, 817 (SDNY 1990).

Add after first paragraph of note 40, page 108:

Contra Pizzirusso v Allstate Ins Co, 532 NYS2d 309, 310 (App Div 1988).

§3.06 Duty Not to Commit Fraud or Swear Falsely

Add at beginning of note 49, page 110:

See, e.g., Nipkow & Kobelt, Inc v North River Ins Co, 673 F Supp 1185, 1188 (SDNY 1987) (plaintiff swore falsely under oath concerning certain representations).

Add to first paragraph of note 49, page 110:

See, e.g., Rickert v Travelers Ins Co, 551 NYS2d 985, 986 (App Div 1990) (false answers given at examination invalidated the coverage).

Add at beginning of note 51, page 111:

See, e.g., Mutual of Enumclaw Ins Co v Cox, 110 Wash 2d 643, 757 P2d 499, 502 (1988).

Add to first paragraph of note 52, page 111:

Accord, e.g., Cummings v Farmers Ins Exch, 249 Cal Rptr 568, 572 n 7 (App Dept Super Ct 1988).

§3.07 Duty Not to Release Wrongdoer

Add to first paragraph of note 59, page 114:

See, e.g., Farmers Ins Group of Cos v Martinez, 107 NM 82, 752 P2d 797, 799 (Ct App 1988).

Add to note 60, page 115:

Of course, if the insurer had no right of subrogation, the insured's unauthorized release of the tortfeasor should not vitiate the coverage. *See* Nationwide Mut Ins Co v Starr, 575 A2d 1083 (Del 1990).

Add after carryover sentence, page 115:

It has also been held that a showing of prejudice is not necessary. *See, e.g., Paape v Northern Assurance Co of America,* 142 Wis 2d 45, 416 NW2d 665, 669 (Ct App 1987).

Add at end of note 62, page 115:

In Silvers v Horace Mann Ins Co, 378 SE2d 21, 27 (NC 1989), it was found that the insurer, by the terms of its policy, had waived any right of subrogation. Accordingly, the court held that the insurer could not deny coverage because of the insured's unauthorized release of the tortfeasor unless the insurer could somehow show that it was still prejudiced by the release.

Add at beginning of note 63, page 115:

E.g., Farmers Ins Group of Cos v Martinez, 107 NM 82, 752 P2d 797, 799 (Ct App 1988); Leader Natl Ins Co v Torres, 51 Wash App 136, 751 P2d 1252, 1255 (1988).

Add to first paragraph of note 63, page 116:

E.g., Ortega v Motors Ins Corp, 552 So 2d 1127, 1128 (Fla Dist Ct App 1989).

Add at beginning of note 64, page 116:

See, e.g., Argiro v Progressive Am Ins Co, 510 So 2d 635, 636 (Fla Dist Ct App 1987).

Add at end of note 64, page 117:

See Watherwax v Allstate Ins Co, 538 So 2d 108, 109-10 (Fla Dist Ct App 1989). *See generally* Rucker v National Gen Ins Co, 442 NW2d 113, 115 (Iowa 1989) (insurer required to show prejudice).

Add to first paragraph of note 66, page 117:

See, e.g., Bryant v Federal Kemper Ins Co, 542 A2d 347, 349 (Del Super Ct 1988).

Add to second paragraph of note 66, page 117:

See Thompson v American States Ins Co, 687 F Supp 559, 562-63 (MD Ala 1988) (in connection with uninsured motorist coverage, a no-consent-to-settlement exclusionary clause is unenforceable as to settlements with insured tortfeasors, and in general, enforceable as to settlements with uninsured tortfeasors if settlement is shown to have prejudiced insurer).

Add after second paragraph of note 66, page 117:

Some courts have refused to apply the unauthorized release rule to preclude recovery of uninsured motorist benefits on the alternate ground that an insurer does not have a right to subrogation with regard to such claims and, therefore, is not prejudiced by violation of the consent to settle clause. *See, e.g.,* Branch v Travelers Indem Co, 367 SE2d 369, 371 (NC Ct App 1988). Still other courts have held that an insurer cannot deny coverage of uninsured or underinsured motorist benefits based upon an unauthorized release of the tortfeasor unless the insurer can prove that it was prejudiced by the release; i.e., that it could otherwise actually have collected from the tortfeasor. *See, e.g.,* Kapadia v Preferred Risk Mut Ins Co, 418 NW2d 848, 852 (Iowa 1988).

Add at end of note 66, page 118:

The rule that has developed with regard to terminating underinsured motorist coverage because of an unauthorized release is that when an insured has given his or her underinsurance carrier notice of a tentative settlement prior to release, and the insurer has had a reasonable opportunity to protect its subrogation rights, the release will not preclude recovery of underinsurance benefits. *E.g.,* McDonald v Republic-Franklin Ins Co, 45 Ohio St 3d 27, 543 NE2d 456, 460 (1989); Auto-Owners Ins Co v Hudson, 547 So 2d 467, 469 (Ala 1989). Even if the insured fails to give such notice, however, the insurer may not be able to deny coverage unless it can prove that the underinsured tortfeasor had substantial other assets. *E.g.,* MacInnis v Aetna Life & Cas Co, 403 Mass 220, 526 NE2d 1255, 1259-60 (1988).

Add to note 69, page 119:

See, e.g., Puro Intl Corp v California Union Ins Co, 672 F Supp 129, 133 (SDNY 1987) (policy provisions "prohibit the insured from waiving subrogation rights, but they deal only with subrogation after a loss. Nowhere in the policy is there any stipulation that the insured may not waive subrogation rights prior to a loss").

§3.09   Duty Not to Enter into Unauthorized Settlements with Injured Party

Add at beginning of note 80, page 121:

See, e.g., Rodgers v Missouri Ins Guar Assn, 841 F2d 858, 861-62 (8th Cir 1988) (Missouri law) (since insurer had not previously breached policy, insured's settlement agreement with injured party eliminated coverage); United Servs Auto Assn v Morris, 154 Ariz 113, 741 P2d 246, 250-51 (1987).

Add to first paragraph of note 80, page 121:

See, e.g., Jones v Southern Marine & Aviation Underwriters, Inc, 888 F2d 358, 361 (5th Cir 1989) (Mississippi law); Harville v Twin City Fire Ins Co, 885 F2d 276, 279 (5th Cir 1989) (Texas law).

Add to note 81, page 121:

E.g., Gates Formed Fibre Prods v Imperial Cas & Indem Co, 702 F Supp 343, 348 (D Me 1988).

Contra Harrisburg Area Community College v Pacific Employers Ins Co, 682 F Supp 805, 810 (MD Pa 1988).

Add to first paragraph of note 82, page 122:

Contra, Harrisburg Area Community College v Pacific Employers Ins Co, 682 F Supp 805, 811 (MD Pa 1988).

E.g., Steen v Underwriters at Lloyds', 442 NW2d 158, 162-63 (Minn Ct App 1989); Buysse v Baumann-Furrie & Co, 448 NW2d 865, 874 (Minn 1989).

Add following first full paragraph, page 122:

In *United Services Auto Association v Morris,* 154 Ariz 113, 741 P2d 246, 252-54 (1987), the insured settled without the insurer's consent, and the insurer sought to deny coverage on the ground that the insured had breached the conditions of the policy. The court held (1) that an insured being defended under a reservation of rights has an absolute right to enter into a settlement, and (2) that the insurer must pay the settlement if it was one that a reasonable and prudent person in the insured's position would have settled for.

The result reached in *Morris* is correct only if the settlement accepted by the insured is one that the insurer would itself have been obligated to accept pursuant to its duty to settle. *See* §5.01. If , however, the settlement is not one that the insurer would itself have been obligated to accept, the insured necessarily breached the terms of the policy by entering into an unauthorized settlement. An insured should not be allowed to enter into an unauthorized settlement simply because it is being defended pursuant to a reservation of rights. *See generally* §§3.11 and 4.24. If it does so, and the settlement is not one that the insurer would have been duty-bound to accept, the insured should not be able to recover anything. The result under the *Morris* analysis is different because it would allow an insured that enters into an unjustifiably high unauthorized settlement to recover from the insurer the portion of the settlement that would have been reasonable. As long as the insurer complies with its contractual obligations, it should have the benefit of its contract, and should not be subjected to such disputes with its insured.

Add to note 84, page 122:

The above principles were disregarded in Stufflebeam v Canadian Indem Co, 157 Ariz 6, 754 P2d 335, 338 (1988). The insured replaced the defense counsel provided by the insurer with his own counsel, and then stipulated to the entry of a default judgment. The court held that the carrier was liable for the amount of the judgment because it allowed, without comment, the insured to substitute defense counsel, never moved to intervene in the lawsuit, and never moved to vacate the default judgment. The decision was totally unjustified. The insured breached the policy, if not by rejecting the proffered defense, then by settling without the insurer's approval. The insurer, therefore, not having any potential liability for the default judgment, had no reason to take any action to undo what the insured had done.

§3.10   Release of Insured from Obligations Under Insurance Contract—After Insurer Denies Coverage

Add following first sentence of note 87, page 123:

See, e.g., M/A Com, Inc v Perricone, 187 Ill App 3d 358, 543 NE2d 228, 231 (1989).

Add at beginning of note 89, page 123:

See, e.g., First Hays Bankshares v Kansas Bankers Sur Co, 244 Kan 576, 769 P2d 1184, 1189 (1989); Kolbe v Aegis Ins Co, 537 A2d 7, 8-9 (Pa Super Ct 1987).

Add at end of note 89, page 123:

In Amert v Continental Cas Co, 409 NW2d 660 (SD 1987), the insurers denied coverage, so the insured sued the tortfeasors that had caused his damage. He obtained a judgment against the tortfeasors, but then pursued his insurers because he claimed that he was still less than whole. The court held against the insured on the basis that he had impaired (i.e., limited) the insurers' subrogation rights. As discussed in the text, the court's analysis is clearly wrong. Once the insurers denied coverage, thereby breaching the insurance contract, the insured was free to pursue his claim against the tortfeasors on his own.
See, e.g., Berry v Nationwide Mut Fire Ins Co, 381 SE2d 367, 371 (W Va 1989). See generally Amalgamet, Inc v Underwriters at Lloyds', 724 F Supp 1132, 1141 (SDNY 1989).

Add at beginning of note 90, page 123:

See, e.g., Nu-Air Mfg Co v Frank B Hall & Co, 822 F2d 987, 993 (11th Cir 1987) (Florida law).

Add at beginning of note 91, page 124:

See, e.g., Davis v Criterion Ins Co, 754 P2d 1331, 1332 (Alaska 1988).

Add to first paragraph of note 91, page 124:

See, e.g., St Paul Fire & Marine Ins Co v Vigilant Ins Co, 724 F Supp 1173, 1181 (MDNC 1989).

§3.11   —Under Other Circumstances

Add to note 93, page 125:

See, e.g., Holt v Utica Mut Ins Co, 157 Ariz 477, 759 P2d 623, 629 (1988).

In Gates Formed Fibre Prods v Imperial Cas & Indem Co, 702 F Supp 343, 346 (D Me 1988), the court apparently rejected the argument that an insured could settle a claim made against it without the insurer's consent simply because the insurer is defending subject to a reservation of rights.

Add to note 94, page 125:

See, e.g., National Union Fire Ins Co v Continental Ill Corp, 673 F Supp 267, 273 (ND Ill 1987).

Add to note 96, page 125:

See, e.g., Nationwide Mut Ins Co v Clay, 525 So 2d 1339, 1343 (Ala 1987). *Cf* Alyas v Gillard, 180 Mich App 154, 446 NW2d 610, 613 (1989).

Add at end of section, page 126:

The court's decision in *Miller v Shugart* limited its effect in *Buysse v Baumann-Furrie & Co,* 448 NW2d 865, 874 (Minn 1989). The *Buysse* court held that:

> a liability insurer which does not deny that some part of the claim against the insured is within the coverage provided by its policy and which affords its insured a defense to a pending action for damages does not breach its contract of insurance by disputing with its

insured the amount of coverage that is available for the satisfaction of any judgment against the insured.

Accordingly, an insured that enters into an unauthorized settlement with the claimant under those circumstances loses its coverage.

Duty to Defend

4

§4.01 Existence of Duty

Add to first paragraph of note 1, page 128:

E.g., Widener Univ v Fred S James & Co, 537 A2d 829, 832 (Pa Super Ct 1988).

Contra Interstate Fire & Cas Co v Stuntman Inc, 861 F2d 203, 205-06 (9th Cir 1988) (California law) (excess insurer had duty to defend because policy referred to insurer's right to defend, provision was ambiguous, and policy did not expressly state that carrier did not have duty to defend). *E.g.,* Brown v Lumbermens Mut Cas Co, 326 NC 387, 390 SE2d 150, 152-53 (1990); Jones v Southern Marine & Aviation Underwriters, 888 F2d 358, 362 (5th Cir 1989) (Mississippi law); Board of Trustees v Continental Cas Co, 730 F Supp 1408, 1414 (WD Mich 1990).

Add at end of note 1, page 128:

The duty to defend is, technically, not ordinarily activated until a suit is instituted. *See, e.g.,* Aetna Cas & Sur Co v Gulf Resources & Chem Corp, 709 F Supp 958, 960 (D Idaho 1989); Detrex Chem Indus v Employers Ins, 681 F Supp 438, 443, 460 (ND Ohio 1987).

Add at end of first paragraph of note 2, page 129:

See, e.g., Widener Univ v Fred S James & Co, 537 A2d 829, 833 (Pa Super Ct 1988). A formal demand is not necessary. *E.g.,* Continental Cas Co v Synalloy Corp, 667 F Supp 1523, 1544 (SD Ga 1983); Jones v Southern Marine & Aviation Underwriters, 888 F2d 358, 364 (5th Cir 1989) (Mississippi law).

But see Forum Ins Co v Ranger Ins Co, 711 F Supp 909, 911-12 (ND Ill 1989) ("The duty to defend, however, is triggered only when the insured 'tenders' to its insurer the defense of an action brought against it; in other words, the insured somehow must request that its insurer assume its defense. An insurer's 'mere knowledge' that its insured has been sued is not enough").

Add to note 15, page 132:

Accord Fire Ins Exch v Abbott, 251 Cal Rptr 620, 631 (Ct App 1988) (although negligent and intentional sexual molestation was alleged in complaint, carrier had no duty to defend because intent to injure by insured was inferred).

§4.02   Resolution of Doubts and Ambiguities

Add at beginning of note 16, page 132:

E.g., United States Fidelity & Guar Co v Thomas Solvent Co, 683 F Supp 1139, 1151 (ND Mich 1988).

Add to note 19, page 134:

See Iowa Kemper Ins Co v Ryan, 172 Mich App 134, 431 NW2d 434, 436 (1988); Allstate Ins Co v Troelstrup, 789 P2d 415, 418 n 7 (Colo 1990); Auto Club Ins Assn v Williams, 179 Mich App 401, 446 NW2d 321, 323 n 1 (1989). *See generally* Fremont Mut Ins Co v Wieschowski, 182 Mich App 121, 451 NW2d 523, 524-25 (1989) ("[t]here arises no duty to defend or provide coverage where the complaint is merely an attempt to trigger insurance coverage by characterizing allegations of tortious conduct as negligent activity").

Add after first sentence of second paragraph of note 20, page 134:

E.g., United States Fidelity & Guar Co v Fireman's Fund Ins Co, 896 F2d 200, 203 (6th Cir 1990) (New York law).

Add after first paragraph of note 20, page 134:

The foregoing minority rule should not be applied, however, if it is clear that the acts complained of would not support a verdict of negligence, explaining why the plaintiff sued only for intentional wrongdoing. *See, e.g.*, Oregon Ins Guar Assn v Thompson, 93 Or App 5, 760 P2d 890, 893 (1988).

Add to second paragraph of note 20, page 134:

E.g., Mutual Serv Cas Ins Co v Country Life Ins Co, 859 F2d 548, 553 (7th Cir 1988) (Illinois law).

Add to note 26, page 136:

Accord Mutual of Enumclaw Ins Co v Gass, 100 Or App 424, 786 P2d 749, 750-51 (1990).

It has also been held that, if the factual allegations in the complaint give rise to a covered injury, the insurer's duty to defend is activated even though the actual cause of action alleged is not one encompassed by the policy. *See, e.g.*, California Mut Ins Co v Robertson, 262 Cal Rptr 173, 177 (App Dept Super Ct 1989). By contrast, in Town Crier, Inc v Hume, 721 F Supp 99, 104-05 (ED Va 1989), the court held that there was no duty to defend because, while some of the factual allegations were covered by the policy, none of the asserted causes of action were covered. *Accord* Board of Trustees v Continental Cas Co, 730 F Supp 1408, 1413 (WD Mich 1990).

§4.03   Extrinsic Evidence Giving Rise to Duty

Add at beginning of note 27, page 136:

E.g., Ogden Corp v Travelers Indem Co, 681 F Supp 169, 173 (SDNY 1988).

Add to note 27, page 137:

E.g., Boston Symphony Orchestra, Inc v Commercial Union Ins Co, 406 Mass 7, 545 NE2d 1156, 1158 (1989); Duke Univ v St Paul Fire & Marine Ins Co, 386 SE2d 762, 764 (NC App 1990); United States Fidelity & Guar Co v Executive Ins Co, 893 F2d 517, 519 (2d Cir 1990) (New York law); Westfield Ins Co v TWT, Inc, 723 F Supp 492, 495-96 (ND Cal 1989).

Add to note 33, page 138:

See United States Fidelity & Guar Corp v Advance Roofing & Supply Co, 163 Ariz 476, 788 P2d 1227, 1231-32 (Ct App 1989).

§4.04 Insurer's Refusal to Defend Based on Existence of Extrinsic Facts

Add at end of first paragraph of note 35, page 139:

Contra Iowa Kemper Ins Co v Ryan, 172 Mich App 134, 431 NW2d 434, 436 (1988); American Family Mut Ins Co v Shelter Mut Ins Co, 747 SW2d 174, 177-78 (Mo Ct App 1988).

See, e.g., Adman Prods Co v Federal Ins Co, 187 Ill App 3d 322, 543 NE2d 219, 220 (1989).

Add at end of note 35, page 140:

Accord State Farm Fire & Cas Co v Shelton, 531 NE2d 913, 919 (Ill App Ct 1988) ("at duty-to-defend stage, the court cannot assume that the insured's criminal conviction alone will preclude coverage").

A contrary result was reached in Aetna Cas & Sur Co v Sprague, 163 Mich App 650, 415 NW2d 230, 231-32 (1987) (insurer can refuse to defend based upon exclusion for intentional acts if insured has already pled guilty or been found guilty of an intentional crime by reason of his or her actions).

Add to note 37, page 140:

Burns v Underwriters Adjusting Co, 765 P2d 712, 713 (Mont 1988) (although complaint alleged solely negligence, carrier properly refused to defend because its investigation revealed that insured's conduct had been intentional).

Add at beginning of note 38, page 141:

E.g., Senger v Minnesota Lawyers Mut Ins Co, 415 NW2d 364, 369 (Minn Ct App 1987).

Add to first paragraph of note 38, page 141:

E.g., Heldor Indus v Atlantic Mut Ins Co, 229 NJ Super 390, 551 A2d 1001, 1005 (1988). *But see* Black v Fireman's Fund Am Ins Co, 115 Idaho 449, 767 P2d 824, 831 (1989); Millers Mut Ins Assn v Ainsworth Seed Co, 194 Ill App 3d 888, 552 NE2d 254, 256-57 (1989).

Contra Professional Office Bldgs v Royal Indem Co, 145 Wis 2d 573, 427 NW2d 427, 430-31 (Ct App 1988).

§4.05   Extrinsic Facts to Prove That the Person Claiming Coverage Is Not an Insured

Add to note 53, page 145:

E.g., Nateman v Hartford Cas Ins Co, 544 So 2d 1026, 1027 (Fla Dist Ct App 1989).

Add to first paragraph of note 56, page 146:

E.g., Zurich-American Ins Cos v Atlantic Mut Ins Cos, 74 NY2d 621, 541 NYS2d 970 (1989).

§4.08   Duty Following Insurer's Justified Refusal to Defend

Add to note 70, page 150:

See, e.g., Oregon Ins Guar Assn v Thompson, 93 Or App 5, 760 P2d 890, 893 (1988); Correll v Fireman's Fund Ins Cos, 529 So 2d 1006, 1008 (Ala 1988).

§4.09   Insurer's Agreement to Defend Following Unjustified Refusal to Defend

Add to first paragraph of note 76, page 151:

Cf Cologna v Farmers & Merchants Ins Co, 785 SW2d 691, 699 (Mo Ct App 1990) ("when an insurer disclaims liability . . . it may not of right exact of the insured a reservation of rights and thus become entitled to defend an action without waiver of or estoppel to assert non-liability under the policy").

§4.10   Duty When Another Insurer Is Defending

Add at beginning of note 82, page 153:

See, e.g., Zurich Ins Co v Raymark Indus, 188 Ill 2d 23, 514 NE2d 150, 165 (1987); Ceresino v Fire Ins Exchange, 264 Cal Rptr 30, 35-36 (App Dept Super Ct 1989) (carrier did not breach duty to defend because another carrier had accepted the defense).

§4.11   Excess Insurer's Duty to Defend

Add to first paragraph of note 92, page 155:

E.g., Hartford Accident & Indem Co v Continental Natl Am Ins Cos, 861 F2d 1184, 1186-87 (9th Cir 1989) (California law).

Add following first sentence of note 94, page 156:

See, e.g., Interstate Fire & Cas Co v Stuntman, Inc, 853 F2d 751, 755 (9th Cir 1988) (California law); St Paul Fire & Marine Ins Co v Children's Hosp Natl Medical Center, 670 F Supp 393, 402 n 17 (DDC 1987).

Add to note 96, page 157:

See Continental Cas Co v Synalloy Corp, 667 F Supp 1523, 1540 (SD Ga 1983); American Family Life Assur Co v United States Fire Co, 885 F2d 826, 832 (11th Cir 1989) (Georgia law).

Add after line 7 of note 98, page 157:

See Harville v Twin City Fire Ins Co, 885 F2d 276, 278-79 (5th Cir 1989) (Texas law).

Add at end of note 98, page 157:

    See generally American Re-Insurance Co v SGB Universal Builders Supply, 532 NYS2d 712, 716 (Sup Ct 1988) (absent policy language to contrary, an excess carrier is not required to drop down following primary insurer's insolvency); Morbark Indus v Western Employers Ins Co, 170 Mich App 603, 429 NW2d 213, 216 (1988) (absent policy language to contrary, an excess insurer is not required to drop down following primary insurer's insolvency).

Add to note 102, page 158:

See, e.g., United States Fire Ins Co v Aspen Bldg Corp, 367 SE2d 478, 479 (Va 1988).

§4.12   Scope of Insurer's Duty to Defend

Add at end of note 108, page 159:

    Contra Reisner v Vigilant Ins Co, 524 NYS2d 602, 604 (Sup Ct 1987) (insurer had no duty to defend in an administrative, disciplinary proceeding).

Add at beginning of note 109, page 159:

E.g., United States Fidelity & Guar Co v Thomas Solvent Co, 683 F Supp 1139, 1151 (WD Mich 1988); Washington Occupational Health Assocs v Twin City Fire Ins Co, 670 F Supp 12, 16 (DDC 1987); Overthrust Constructors, Inc v Home Ins Co, 676 F Supp 1086, 1091 (D Utah 1987); Widener Univ v Fred S James & Co, Inc, 537 A2d 829, 832 (Pa Super Ct 1988).

Add to first paragraph of note 109, page 160:

E.g., Golotrade Shipping & Chartering v Travelers Indem Co, 706 F Supp 214, 218-19 (SDNY 1989); First Newton Natl Bank v General Cas Co, 426 NW2d 618, 630 (Iowa 1988); Aetna Cas & Sur Co v Spancrete, Inc, 726 F Supp 204, 208 (ND Ill 1989).

§4.13   Provision of Partial Defense

Add at beginning of note 112, page 161:

E.g., Gon v First State Ins Co, 871 F2d 863, 868-69 (9th Cir 1989) (California law); Budd Co v Travelers Indem Co, 820 F2d 787, 790-91 (6th Cir 1987) (Michigan law).

Add to note 112, page 161:

E.g., EEOC v Southern Publishing Co, 894 F2d 785, 791 (5th Cir 1990) (Mississippi law).

§4.14   Duty to Defend Suit Seeking Injunctive Relief

Add at beginning of note 119, page 163:

E.g., Home Indem Co v Avol, 706 F Supp 728, 733 (CD Cal 1989); Jones v Farm Bureau Mut Ins Co, 172 Mich App 24, 431 NW2d 242, 245 (1988); Nationwide Ins Co v King, 673 F Supp 384, 387 (SD Cal 1987); *see* Maryland Cas Co v Armco, Inc, 822 F2d 1348, 1352 (4th Cir 1987) (Maryland law) (government's claim against insured for restitution of engineering and clean-up costs in connection with removal of hazardous waste was not covered by insurance; "the general comprehensive liability policy between the parties covers 'damages,' but not the expenditures which result from complying with the directives of regulatory agencies"); Fireman's Fund Ins Cos v Ex-Cell-O Corp, 662 F Supp 71, 74 (ED Mich 1987) ("damages include money spent to clean up environmental contamination").

A recurring issue in recent cases is whether expenses related to the closure and clean-up of waste sites constitutes damages or merely costs incident to injunctive relief. *See generally* Township of Gloucester v Maryland Cas Co, 668 F Supp 394, 398-400 (DNJ 1987) (costs of clean-up and closure do constitute damages for purpose of evaluating existence of insurance coverage).

Add at end of first paragraph of note 119, page 163:

Similarly, it has been held that an insurer has no duty to defend an insured in a juvenile proceeding. *E.g.,* United Pac Ins Co v Hall, 245 Cal Rptr 99, 101-02 (Ct App 1988).

Similarly, it has been held that a duty to defend "suits" is not activated by an EPA investigation. *See, e.g.,* Harter Corp v Home Indem Co, 713 F Supp 231, 233-34 (ND Mich 1989).

Add at end of note 119, page 163:

In Feed Store, Inc v Reliance Ins Co, 774 SW2d 73, 74-75 (Tex Ct App 1989), the insurer did not have a duty to defend because only injunctive relief was sought and the boilerplate request in the complaint for "other and further relief" did not iself constitute a demand for damages that would give rise to a duty to defend.

Add to note 120, page 164:

E.g., Hayes v Maryland Cas Co, 688 F Supp 1513, 1515 (ND Fla 1988).

Add to note 122, page 164:

See, e.g., Cincinnati Ins Co v Milliken & Co, 857 F2d 979, 981 (4th Cir 1988) (South Carolina law) (CERCLA claim not covered; policy does "not cover claims for which the insured is equitably obligated to pay"). *But see* Intel Corp v Hartford Accident & Indem Co, 692 F Supp 1171, 1189 (ND Cal 1988) (pollution cleanup and investigation costs are damages).

But see United States Fidelity & Guar Co v Thomas Solvent Co, 683 F Supp 1139, 1168 (WD Mich 1988) ("It is clear to me that once property damage is found as a result of environmental contamination, clean-up costs should be recoverable as sums that the insured was liable to pay as a result of property damage. In this context the argument concerning the historical separation of damages and equity is not convincing . . .").

If a penalty is also sought and the penalty is one that can be (*see* **§6.17**) and is covered by the policy, the duty to defend may be activated. *See generally* Detrex Chem Indus v Employers Ins, 681 F Supp 438, 451-52 (ND Ohio 1987).

Add to note 125, page 164:

See, e.g., New Castle County v Hartford Accident & Indem Co, 673 F Supp 1359, 1364-66 (D Del 1987) (suit involving claim for reimbursement of clean-up costs encompassed by policy whether the lawsuit be deemed one at law or in equity); Centennial Ins Co v Lumbermens Mut Cas Co, 677 F Supp 342, 350 (ED Pa 1987) ("even if the action is preventative or equitable in nature, the costs incurred in cleaning up property damage from toxic contamination are damages within a comprehensive general liability insurance policy").

§4.15   Duty to Appeal Adverse Judgments

Add at beginning of note 130, page 166:

See Aetna Ins Co v Borrell-Bigby Elec Co, 541 So 2d 139, 141 (Fla Dist Ct App 1989).

§4.17   Allegiance of Defense Counsel Hired for Insured by Insurer

Add to note 140, page 168:

E.g., Mitchum v Hudgens, 533 So 2d 194, 198-99 (Ala 1988).

Add after carryover sentence, page 169:

E.g., Hartford Accident & Indemnity Co v Foster, 528 So 2d 255, 268-70 (Miss 1988).

§4.18   Conflict of Interest Between Insured and Insurer

Add at end of note 146, page 170:

Accord Continental Ins Co v City of Miami Beach, 521 So 2d 232, 233 (Fla Dist Ct App 1988).

Add at beginning of note 149, page 170:

See, e.g., Foremost Ins Co v Wilks, 253 Cal Rptr 596, 601-02 (Ct App 1988); *see generally* L&S Roofing Supply Co v St Paul Fire & Marine Ins Co, 521 So 2d 1298, 1304 (Ala 1987).

Add at beginning of note 151, page 171:

See, e.g., Pennbank v St Paul Fire & Marine Ins Co, 669 F Supp 122, 126-27 (WD Pa 1987).

Add to note 159, page 174:

   See Foremost Ins Co v Wilks, 253 Cal Rptr 596, 602 (Ct App 1988). *But see* Golotrade Shipping & Chartering v Travelers Indem Co, 706 F Supp 214, 219-20 (SDNY 1989).
   Contra Ploen v Aetna Cas & Sur Co, 525 NYS2d 522, 527 (Sup Ct 1988).

Add at beginning of note 160, page 174:

E.g., Pennbank v St Paul Fire & Marine Ins Co, 669 F Supp 122, 126-27 (WD Pa 1987).

§4.20   —Satisfying Duty to Defend

Add at beginning of note 171, page 177:

E.g., Ploen v Aetna Cas & Sur Co, 525 NYS2d 522, 527 (Sup Ct 1988); Aetna Cas & Sur Co v Spancrete, Inc, 726 F Supp 204, 208 (ND Ill 1989).

Add to first paragraph of note 171, page 178:

E.g., Golotrade Shipping & Chartering v Travelers Indem Co, 706 F Supp 214, 219 (SDNY 1989).

Add at end of note 171, page 178:

   The court in Employers Ins v Albert D Seeno Constr Co, 692 F Supp 1150, 1157 (ND Cal 1988), held that the counsel selected by the insured and paid for by the insurer in a conflict-of-interest situation represents "solely the insured, and accordingly, there is no ethical requirement that prevents [such] counsel from representing the insured in coverage actions adverse to the insurer as well as in liability matters."

Add at beginning of note 172, page 178:

E.g., L&S Roofing Supply Co v St Paul Fire & Marine Ins Co, 521 So 2d 1298, 1304 (Ala 1987); *see* Pennbank v St Paul Fire & Marine Ins Co, 669 F Supp 122, 126 (WD Pa 1987).

Add to note 173, page 179:

See L&S Roofing Supply Co v St Paul Fire & Marine Ins Co, 521 So 2d 1298, 1303-04 (Ala 1987).

§4.24   —Defense Offered Subject to a Reservation of Rights

Add at beginning of note 197, page 184:

See, e.g., United Servs Auto Assn v Morris, 154 Ariz 113, 741 P2d 246, 251-52 (1987).

Add at end of note 197, page 184:

Fla Stat Ann 627.426(2)(b)(3) (West 1983) has been interpreted to prevent a liability insurer from denying coverage unless the insurer obtained the insured's approval as to the independent counsel retained by the insurer to defend the insured. *See, e.g.,* Continental Ins Co v City of Miami Beach, 521 So 2d 232, 233 (Fla Dist Ct App 1988).

Add to note 198, page 185:

E.g., United States Aviation Underwriters, Inc v Olympia Wings, Inc, 896 F2d 949 (5th Cir 1990) (Texas law).

§4.25   —Effect

Add to note 220, page 188:

See also Widener Univ v Fred S James & Co, 537 A2d 829, 833 (Pa Super Ct 1988) (insurer absolved of any further liability pursuant to its duty to defend after insured refused defense counsel that insurer provided).

§4.26   Insurer's Withdrawal of Defense of Insured

Add to note 232, page 191:

See generally Murray Ohio Mfg Co v Continental Ins Co, 705 F Supp 442, 444 (ND Ill 1989).

Add to note 233, page 191:

But see Levenfeld v Clinton, 674 F Supp 255, 259-60 (ND Ill 1987) (indicating that good faith might ordinarily require insurers to obtain "general releases for their insureds when settling claims, rather than tailoring the releases to the scope of coverage").

Add at beginning of note 235, page 191:

See Zurich Ins Co v Raymark Indus, 118 Ill 2d 23, 514 NE2d 150, 164-65 (1987) (upon exhaustion of policy limits, insurer can withdraw from cases it is defending).

Change "insured" in line 2 of note 237 on page 192 to:

injured

Add to note 239, page 193:

See Terra Nova Ins Co v 900 Bar, Inc, 887 F2d 1213, 1219 (3d Cir 1989) (Pennsylvania law).

Add to note 240, page 193:

See generally St Paul Mercury Ins Co v Medical Laboratory Network, 690 F Supp 901, 904 (CD Cal 1988) ("an insurer who assumes the defense of the insured under a reservation of rights is entitled to reimbursement of those expenses upon a determination that it had no duty to defend or indemnify the insured, provided the insured understands that such result will follow").

It has also recently been held in California that, if an insurer so reserves its rights, it can obtain reimbursement of its defense costs in the event it did not in fact have a duty to defend. *E.g.,* Walbrook Ins Co v Goshgarian & Goshgarian, 726 F Supp 777, 781-84 (CD Cal 1989).

Add following last full paragraph, page 193:

In *Omaha Indemnity Insurance Co v Cardon Oil Co,* 687 F Supp 502, 504-05 (ND Cal 1988), the insurer was allowed to recover the attorneys' fees incurred in defending the insured while the carrier successfully litigated a declaratory judgment action that it had no duty to defend. The basis for the court's decision was that the insurer's reservation of rights letter stated that it would seek such reimbursement, and the insured did not expressly refuse to consent to the reservation of rights.

§4.30   Existence of Duty to Defend After Indemnity Duty Has Been Satisfied

Add to note 263, page 201:

E.g., Zurich Ins Co v Raymark Indus, 118 Ill 2d 23, 514 NE2d 150, 162 (1987).

Add at beginning of note 264, page 201:

See Johnson v Continental Ins Cos, 248 Cal Rptr 412, 417-18 (Ct App 1988) (duty to defend terminates as to new claims brought after policy limits have been exhausted); Continental Cas Co v Synalloy Corp, 667 F Supp 1523, 1536 (SD Ga 1983).

Add at end of note 264, page 202:

Aetna Ins Co v Borrell-Bigby Elec Co, 541 So 2d 139, 141 (Fla Dist Ct App 1989); Utah Power & Light Co v Federal Ins Co, 711 F Supp 1544, 1552-54 (D Utah 1989).

In St John's Home v Continental Cas Co, 434 NW2d 112, 120-21 (Wis Ct App 1988), the court held that an insurer could not terminate its duty to defend by tendering the amount of the claim that might be covered unless such tender equals or exceeds the policy limits.

The court in Pareti v Sentry Indem Co, 536 So 2d 417, 424 (La 1988), raised the question of whether a tender of the policy limits without obtaining a release for the insured might constitute bad faith. "Any payment of the policy limits which does not release the insured from a pending claim (e.g., unilateral tender of policy limits to the court, the claimant or the insured), even if sufficient to terminate the duty to defend under the wording of the policy involved, raises serious questions as to whether the insurer has discharged its policy obligations in good faith").

In Brown v Lumbermens Mut Cas Co, 326 NC 387, 390 SE2d 150, 154-55 (1990), the insured paid its policy limit to the claimant in return for a release of the insurer. The court held that the insurer was still obligated to continue its defense of the insured.

Add to note 265, page 202:

But see Pareti v Pennsylvania Gen Ins Co, 519 So 2d 225, 227-28 (La Ct App 1988) (insurer not relieved of duty to defend, despite payment of its policy limit, because policy was ambiguous despite its provision that duty to defend ended "when our limit of liability for this coverage has been exhausted"); Brown v Lumbermens Mut Cas Co, 369 SE2d 367, 374 (NC Ct App 1988) (insurer had to continue defending despite tender of its policy limit, because policy provision stating that duty to defend ended when limit of liability was exhausted was ambiguous).

Such a policy provision is not against public policy. *E.g.,* Pareti v Sentry Indem Co, 536 So 2d 417, 422-23 (La 1988).

See, e.g., Viking Ins Co v Hill, 57 Wash App 341, 787 P2d 1385, 1389-92 (1990).

§4.33   —Attorneys' Fees

Add to first paragraph of note 276, page 205:

See, e.g., Burroughs Wellcome Co v Commercial Union Ins Co, 713 F Supp 694, 697 (SDNY 1989).

Add to note 277, page 205:

See, e.g., Duke Univ v St Paul Mercury Ins Co, 384 SE2d 36, 46 (ND Ct App 1989); Montgomery v Aetna Cas & Sur Co, 898 F2d 1537, 1541 (11th Cir 1990) (Florida law).

Add to note 280, page 206:

It has been held that if an insured sues potentially liable third parties in order to recoup the loss that the insurer wrongfully refused to cover, the insured can recover from the insurer the attorneys' fees incurred in such third-party actions. Such fees have been held to be a direct and foreseeable consequence of the insurer's breach of contract. *See, e.g.,* Ingersoll Mining Mach Co v M/V Bodena, 829 F2d 293, 309 (2d Cir 1987).

Add to note 283, page 206:

See, e.g., Johnson v Continental Cas Co, 57 Wash App 359, 788 P2d 598, 600-01 (1990); National Union Fire Ins Co v Circle, Inc, 731 F Supp 750, 755 (ED La 1990).

Add to note 288, page 207:

The mitigation rule was applied to reduce the insurer's liability for the insured's defense costs in EEOC v Southern Publishing Co, 705 F Supp 1213, 1219-20 (SD Miss 1988).

§4.34   —Damages Beyond Policy Limits

Add at beginning of note 301, page 210:

See Gray v Grain Dealers Mut Ins Co, 684 F Supp 1108, 1113 (DDC 1988).

§4.35   —Estoppel to Deny Coverage

Add to note 315, page 213:

E.g., Alabama Hosp Assn Trust v Mutual Assurance Socy, 538 So 2d 1209, 1216 (Ala 1989); Burroughs Wellcome Co v Commercial Union Ins Co, 713 F Supp 694, 697-99 (SDNY 1989).

Cf Travelers Ins Co v Waltham Indus Labs Corp, 722 F Supp 814, 830 (D Mass 1988), *affd in part, revd in part,* 883 F2d 1092 (1st Cir 1989).

Add to first paragraph of note 317, page 214:

E.g., Professional Office Bldgs v Royal Indem Co, 145 Wis 2d 573, 427 NW2d 427, 431-32 (Ct App 1988).

Add to third paragraph of note 317, page 214:

Contra Wilson v State Farm Mut Auto Ins Co, 92 NC App 320, 374 SE2d 446, 449-50 (1988) (insurer liable for settlement beyond its policy limits because it wrongfully refused to defend).

Add to end of note 317, page 214:

E.g., Aetna Cas & Sur Co v Prestige Cas Co, 553 NE2d 39, 42 (Ill App Ct 1990).

Add to note 323, page 215:

Accord, e.g., Village Management, Inc v Hartford Accident & Indem Co, 662 F Supp 1366, 1372-73 (ND Ill 1987).

§4.36   —Practical Disadvantages

Add to note 326, page 216:

See generally Holt v Utica Mut Ins Co, 157 Ariz 477, 759 P2d 623, 628 (1988).

§4.37   Insurer's Inadequate Defense—Failure to Provide Appropriate Counsel in a Conflict of Interest Situation

Add to note 331, page 217:

See, e.g., State Farm Fire & Cas Co v Neumann, 698 F Supp 195, 196 (ND Cal 1988).

§4.38   —Negligence of Insured's Defense Counsel

Add to note 342, page 220:

See, e.g., Brown v Lumbermens Mut Cas Co, 369 SE2d 367, 372 (NC Ct App 1988); Feliberty v Damon, 72 NY2d 112, 531 NYS2d 778, 780-81 (1988); Brocato v Prairie State Farmers' Assn, 166 Ill App 3d 986, 520 NE2d 1200, 1203 (1988).

Add to note 344, page 220:

In Hartford Accident & Indem Co v Foster, 528 So 2d 255, 267-68 (Miss 1988), the court rejected the argument that an insurer is not liable for defense counsel's actions because counsel is an independent contractor, but it did so in the context of an attorney who breached his fiduciary duty to the insured by favoring the carrier. Such cases are discussed in §4.40.

§4.40   Unethical Conduct by Counsel Hired by Insurer to Defend Insured

Add to note 363, page 225:

Contra Manzanita Park v Insurance Co of N Am, 857 F2d 549, 555 (9th Cir 1988) ("Arizona law holds the insurer who undertakes to defend its insured to the standard of fiduciary care assumed by the attorney whom it appoints to conduct the defense").

Duty to Settle

5

§5.01 Insurer's Duty to Settle Claims Brought Against Insured in General

Add at beginning of note 2, page 232:

See, e.g., Hartford Accident & Indem Co v Foster, 528 So 2d 255, 265 (Miss 1988).

Add to note 2, page 233:

See, e.g., Clearwater v State Farm Mut Auto Ins Co, 164 Ariz 256, 792 P2d 719, 722-24 (1990).

Add to note 4, page 233:

Cf Trotter v State Farm Mut Auto Ins Co, 377 SE2d 343, 349 (SC Ct App 1988) (duty to settle "if settlement is the reasonable thing to do"). *E.g.,* Ranger Ins Co v Home Indem Co, 714 F Supp 956, 962 (ND Ill 1989).

Add to note 5, page 233:

Cf Diblasi v Aetna Life & Cas Ins Co, 542 NYS2d 187, 191 (1989) ("A bad faith case is established where the liability is clear and the potential recovery far exceeds the insurance coverage").

§5.02   Necessity of Opportunity to Settle

Add to first paragraph of note 15, page 235:

See Heinson v Porter, 244 Kan 667, 772 P2d 778, 785 (1989). *E.g.,* Wierck v Grinnell Mut Reins Co, 456 NW2d 191, 195 (Iowa 1990).

Add to note 18, page 237:

See, e.g., Commercial Union Ins Co v Mission Ins Co, 835 F2d 587, 588 (5th Cir 1988) (insurer could not be liable for breach of its duty to settle because there was no evidence that case could have been settled within policy limits); National Union Fire Ins Co v Continental Ill Corp, 673 F Supp 267, 273 (ND Ill 1987) (insurer not liable for breach of duty to settle unless "insurer's breach also cost the insured an opportunity to settle below the policy limits"); Brocato v Prairie State Farmers' Ins Assn, 166 Ill App 3d 986, 520 NE2d 1200, 1203 (1988) ("cases dealing with a failure to settle within policy limits also include the element that the cases could actually have been settled within those limits").

Add to note 20, page 238:

See, e.g., Smith v Blackwell, 14 Kan App 2d 158, 791 P2d 1343, 1346 (1989).

§5.03   Insurer's Duty When Insured Directs It Not to Settle

Add to first paragraph of note 24, page 239:

See Mitchum v Hudgens, 533 So 2d 194, 196-97 (Ala 1988) (insurer which has not issued reservation of rights can settle without insured's consent as long as insurer does not act arbitrarily or in bad faith); Feliberty v Damon, 72 NY2d 112, 531 NYS2d 778, 780 (1988) ("Unlike bargained-for, and presumably costlier, policy provisions contemplating the insured's consent to settlement, here the parties' contract unambiguously gave the insurer the unconditional right to settle any claim or suit without plaintiff's consent").

Add to note 29, page 240:

Accord Thurston v Continental Cas Co, 567 A2d 922, 924 n 3 (Me 1989) ("evidence that (the insured) ordered its lawyers not to settle is an insufficient basis for summary judgment; there was no evidence that the lawyers had fully informed (the insured) of the risks").

§5.04   Settlement Entered into Without Insured's Consent

Add to note 35, page 241:

Note, however, that it has been held that a bad faith claim could, theoretically, be asserted against an insurance company even when settling within the policy limits. *See, e.g.,* Gardner v Aetna Cas & Sur Co, 841 F2d 82, 85 (4th Cir 1988) (Virginia law).

Add to note 38, page 241:

See also American Home Assur Co v Hermann's Warehouse Corp, 117 NJ 1, 563 A2d 444, 448 (1989) (as long as the insurer does not act in bad faith and has the right to settle claims under the policy, it can recover the deductible from the insured, despite the insured's belief that the case should not have been settled).

Add to note 39, page 241:

An insurer may settle a claim and then increase the insured's premium obligations under the terms of a retrospective rating plan. It has been held that if the insured later challenges a settlement as unreasonably high, the burden is on the insurer on the issue of reasonableness. *E.g.,* Deerfield Plastics Co v Hartford Ins Co, 404 Mass 484, 536 NE2d 322, 324 (1989).

See generally Carrodo Bros v Twin City Fire Ins Co, 562 A2d 1188, 1191-94 (Del 1989) (although the insurer settled without the insured's knowledge or consent and, although all of the funds that the insurer paid would eventually be the responsibility of the insured under the retrospective premium provision, the insurer was not liable since the settlement was one that should have been entered into).

§5.05   Insurer's Duty to Settle When It Erroneously Believes That There Is No Coverage

Add to note 44, page 243:

In Battista v Western World Ins Co, 227 NJ Super 135, 545 A2d 841, 847 (1988), the carrier was held to have breached its duty to settle because it evaluated the settlement value of the claim based upon the existence of limited coverage when, in fact, because of the carrier's failure properly to reserve its rights, it was estopped from denying coverage.

Add to note 49, page 243:

See generally Maryland Cas Co v Imperial Contracting Co, 260 Cal Rptr 797, 803-04 (Ct App 1989) (insurer entitled, under particular facts of case, to seek reimbursement from insured for amount of settlement even though insured had refused to consent to the settlement).

§5.06 Necessity of an Obligation by Insurer to Control Insured's Defense

Add at end of note 54, page 245:

For a discussion of an attorney's ethical obligations vis-à-vis settlement by reason of simultaneously representing both the insured and the insurer, *see* Hartford Accident & Indem Co v Foster, 528 So 2d 255, 273 (Miss 1988):

> [T]he attorney, after informing his clients of the settlement terms, and giving them the advice as above noted, should not be prohibited from honestly and carefully answering questions pertaining to the law and facts of the case, his impressions of the witnesses, the jury and the trial judge, such as he would normally be asked as attorney, and expected to be able to answer. At the same time he must scrupulously guard against violating his absolute, nondelegable responsibility not to urge, recommend or suggest any course of action to the carrier which violates his conflict of interest obligation.

§5.07 Insurer's Duty to Settle When Settlement Offer Is in Excess of Policy Limits

Add at end of third paragraph of note 63, page 247:

See generally Hartford Accident & Indem Co v Foster, 528 So 2d 255, 275 (Miss 1988) (although insured's defense counsel was obligated to inform insured of settlement offer, his failure to do so was not actionable because there was no evidence that it would have made any difference had insured been so advised).

§5.08 Insurer's Duty to Settle When There Are Multiple Claims Against Insured

Add to note 66, page 249:

See generally Peckham v Continental Cas Ins Co, 895 F2d 830, 835 (1st Cir 1990) (Massachusetts law).

§5.11   Necessity of Proving That Insurer Acted in Bad Faith

Add to note 89, page 255:

See, e.g., Hartford Accident & Indem Co v Foster, 528 So 2d 255, 267 (Miss 1988) (court used bad faith and negligence interchangeably).

§5.12   Determining Whether Insurer Is Guilty of Bad Faith Breach of Duty to Settle

Add at beginning of note 91, page 256:

E.g., State Farm Mut Auto Ins Co v Floyd, 366 SE2d 93, 97 (Va 1988) ("an insured, in order to recover for an excess judgment on the ground that the insurer failed to take advantage of an opportunity to settle within the policy limits, is required to show that the insurer acted in furtherance of its own interest, with intentional disregard of the financial interest of the insured").

Add at end of note 91, page 256:

E.g., Diblasi v Aetna Life & Cas Ins Co, 542 NYS2d 187, 191 (1989) ("The carrier cannot be held liable if its decision not to settle was the result of an error of judgment on its part or even by a failure to exercise reasonable care. . . . [M]ere negligence does not support an excess liability action. . . . [T]here is a cause of action only if the decision not to settle within the policy limits was made in bad faith, meaning in gross disregard of its insured's limits").

Add to first paragraph of note 96, page 258:

E.g., Certain Underwriters of Lloyd's v General Accident Ins Co of Am, 699 F Supp 732, 737 (SD Ind 1988); Gelinas v Metropolitan Property & Liab Ins Co, 551 A2d 962, 967-68 (NH 1988); State Farm Mut Auto Ins Co v Hollis, 554 So 2d 387, 391-92 (Ala 1989).

§5.16   Insurer's Liability for Settlement in Excess of Policy Limits Following Breach of Duty to Settle

Page 262, note 107 should read:

See §6.27.

Add at end of first paragraph of section, page 262:

See, e.g., National Union Fire Insurance Co v Continental Illinois Corp, 673 F Supp 267, 274 (ND Ill 1987).

§5.18 Effect of Insured's Financial Responsibility

Add to note 113, page 264:

Another question is whether an insurer can be held liable for an excess judgment if the insured has obtained a covenant not to execute. *See generally* Foremost County Mut Ins Co v Home Indem Co, 897 F2d 754, 759 n 7 (5th Cir 1990) (Texas law).

Add to note 117, page 265:

E.g., Frankenmuth Mut Ins Co v Keeley, 433 Mich 525, 447 NW2d 691, 698 (1989).

Add to note 123, page 267:

Accord Thurston v Continental Cas Co, 567 A2d 922, 924-25 (Me 1989).

§5.19 Damages for Insurer's Bad Faith Breach of Duty to Settle

Add to note 127, page 268:

See, e.g., State Farm Mut Auto Ins Co v Hollis, 554 So 2d 387, 393 (Ala 1989).

§5.22 Actions That Can Be Taken by Insurer, Insured, and Injured Party to Protect and Advance Their Interests

Add at end of first line on page 275:

See, e.g., National Union Fire Insurance Co v Continental Illinois Corp, 673 F Supp 267, 275 (ND Ill 1987).

Duty to Indemnify

6

§6.01   Existence of a Duty in General

Add to note 1, page 278:

See also §§2.29 and 2.30 for cases concerning rescission when a premium check bounces.

§6.02   Contract Interpretation

Add to note 3, page 280:

See, e.g., Kane v Royal Ins Co of Am, 768 P2d 678, 680-81 (Colo 1989).

Add to note 4, page 280:

E.g., Transcontinental Ins Co v Washington Pub Utils Dists Util Sys, 111 Wash 2d 452, 760 P2d 337, 340 (1988); Graingrowers Warehouse Co v Central Natl Ins Co, 711 F Supp 1040, 1044 (ED Wash 1989); Massachusetts Bay Ins Co v Gordon, 708 F Supp 1232, 1235 (WD Okla 1989).

See generally Murray Ohio Mfg Co v Continental Ins Co, 705 F Supp 442, 444 (ND Ill 1989) (insurance "contracts are to be construed in favor of the insured and the law does not countenance illusory coverage").

Add at beginning of note 5, page 280:

E.g., State Farm Mut Auto Ins Co v Lewis, 514 So 2d 863, 865 (Ala 1987); Town of Stoddard v Northern Sec Ins Co, 718 F Supp 1062, 1065

(DNH 1989); Boeing Co v Aetna Cas & Sur Co, 113 Wash 2d 869, 784 P2d 507, 510 (1990); Insurance Corp of Am v Dillon, Hardamon & Cohen, 725 F Supp 1461, 1465 (ND Ind 1988); Penalosa Coop Exch v Farmland Mut Ins Co, 14 Kan App 2d 321, 789 P2d 1196, 1198 (1990).

Add to first paragraph of note 5, page 280:

E.g., Pareti v Sentry Indem Co, 536 So 2d 417, 420 (La 1988).

Add after first sentence in second paragraph of note 5, page 280:

See, e.g., Dow Chem Co v Associated Indem Corp, 724 F Supp 474, 480 (ED Mich 1989).

Add to carryover paragraph of note 5, page 281:

See also Fittrov v Lincoln Natl Life Ins Co, 49 Wash App 499, 744 P2d 631, 634 (1987) (group "policy language controls in the face of a conflict when the certificate specifically states that it is subject to the terms of the master policy and directs the insured to look to the master policy"). *But see* Romano v New England Mut Life Ins Co, 362 SE2d 334, 338 (W Va 1987) ("where a certificate is provided to an insured which is at variance with the master policy, an insurer will be bound by more permissive provisions outlined in the certificate").

Add to note 6, page 282:

E.g., Imperial Cas & Indem Co v High Concrete Structures, 858 F2d 128, 131 n 4 (3d Cir 1988) (Pennsylvania law).

Add at beginning of note 8, page 283:

E.g., DiFabio v Centaur Ins Co, 531 A2d 1141, 1143 (Pa Super Ct 1987) ("only in the absence of useful extrinsic evidence will the court construe ambiguous contract language against the drafter as a matter of law"); Industrial Risk Insurers v New Orleans Pub Serv, 666 F Supp 874, 879 (ED La 1987) ("where the intent of the parties to the contract is not adequately expressed and cannot be discovered by a study of the entire contract, the court may consider preliminary negotiations leading to the contract and other parol evidence"); Ford Motor Co v Northbrook Ins Co, 838 F2d 829, 833 (6th Cir 1988) (Michigan law) (extrinsic evidence should be used to determine intent of parties); Walle Mut Ins Co v Sweeney, 419 NW2d 176, 180 (ND 1988) (if policy terms are ambiguous, court should attempt to determine parties' actual intent from extrinsic evidence).

Add to first paragraph of note 8, page 284:

E.g., Transcontinental Ins Co v Washington Pub Utils Dists Util Sys, 111 Wash 2d 452, 760 P2d 337, 340 (1988); Fiscus Motor Freight v

Universal Sec Ins Co, 53 Wash App 777, 770 P2d 679, 682-83 (1989); Cheney v Bell Natl Life Ins Co, 315 Md 761, 556 A2d 1135, 1138 (1989); Wolf Bros Oil Co v International Surplus Lines Ins Co, 718 F Supp 839, 843 (WD Wash 1989) ("even if this court were to find the contract ambiguous on its face, it must proceed to examine extrinsic evidence in an effort to resolve the ambiguity before automatically construing the policy in favor of the insured"); Carey Canada, Inc v California Union Ins Co, 720 F Supp 1018, 1026 (DDC 1989); National Union Fire Ins Co v Caesars Palace Hotel & Casino, 792 P2d 1129, 1130-31 (Nev 1990) ("extrinsic evidence of such custom and usage may help establish what the parties intended").

Add to second paragraph of note 8, page 284:

E.g., St Paul Guardian Ins Co v Canterbury School, Inc, 548 So 2d 1159, 1161 (Fla Dist Ct App 1989).

Add at end of note 8, page 284:

In Insurance Corp of Am v Dillon Hardamon & Cohen, 725 F Supp 1461, 1464-65 (ND Ind 1988), the injured parties agreed that the policy was ambiguous and should, therefore, be resolved against the insurer. The court, however, recognized that, if the insured agreed with the insurer as to the policy's meaning, any ambiguity would have to be resolved in accordance with that understanding.

Add to note 10, page 285:

E.g., Sharp v Federal Sav & Loan Ins Corp, 858 F2d 1042, 1046 (5th Cir 1988) (Louisiana law); Industrial Risk Insurers v New Orleans Pub Serv, 666 F Supp 874, 881 (ED La 1987). *Contra* Ogden Corp v Travelers Indem Co, 681 F Supp 169, 174 (SDNY 1988); Standard & Poor's Corp v Continental Cas Co, 718 F Supp 1219, 1221 (SDNY 1989); United States Elevator Corp v Associated Intl Ins Co, 263 Cal Rptr 760, 766 (Ct App 1989).

Add to first paragraph of note 12, page 286:

E.g., Allstate Ins Co v Roelfs, 698 F Supp 815, 817 (D Alaska 1987).

Add at beginning of note 14, page 286:

E.g., Moore v Metropolitan Property & Liab Ins Co, 401 Mass 1010, 519 NE2d 265, 266 (1988); Amica Mut Ins Co v Bagley, 546 NE2d 184, 186 (Mass App Ct 1989). *Contra* Zumbrun v United Servs Auto Assn, 719 F Supp 890, 898 (ED Cal 1989).

Add to first paragraph of note 17, page 288:

See, e.g., State Farm Mut Auto Ins Co v Crane, 266 Cal Rptr 422, 424 (Ct App 1990).

Add to note 18, page 288:

See, e.g., Boeing Co v Aetna Cas & Sur Co, 113 Wash 2d 869, 784 P2d 507, 514 (1990). *Contra In re* Ambassador Group, Inc Litigation, 738 F Supp 57, 63 (EDNY 1990).

Add at beginning of note 21, page 289:

E.g., Vole v Atlanta Intl Ins Co, 172 Ill App 3d 480, 526 NE2d 653, 655 (1988).

Add at end of note 21, page 289:

E.g., Morbark Indus v Western Employers Ins Co, 170 Mich App 603, 429 NW2d 213, 218 (1988); Transcontinental Ins Co v Washington Utils Dists Util Sys, 111 Wash 2d 452, 760 P2d 337, 343 (1988); Jet Line Servs v American Employers Ins Co, 404 Mass 706, 537 NE2d 107, 112 (1989); Alaska Rural Elec Coop Assn v Insco, Ltd, 785 P2d 1193, 1195 (Alaska 1990).

Add at beginning of note 22, page 289:

E.g., McCorkle v Firemen's Ins Co, 678 F Supp 562, 564 (WD Pa 1988); Engineered Prods, Inc v Aetna Cas & Sur Co, 368 SE2d 674, 675 (SC Ct App 1988).

Add at end of note 22, page 289:

E.g., St Paul Surplus Lines Ins Co v Diversified Athletic Servs, 707 F Supp 1506, 1509 (ND Ill 1989).

Add at beginning of note 24, page 290:

E.g., Silverton Enters v General Cas Co, 143 Wis 2d 661, 422 NW2d 154, 158 (1988).

Add to note 25, page 290:

E.g., United Servs Auto Assn v Baggett, 258 Cal Rptr 52, 55 (Ct App 1989).

§6.03   Reasonable Expectations Rule

Add at beginning of note 26, page 290:

E.g., Grinnell Mut Reinsurance Co v Voeltz, 431 NW2d 783, 788-89 (Iowa 1988); Gordiner v Aetna Cas & Sur Co, 154 Ariz 266, 742 P2d 277, 283-84 (1987).

Add to first paragraph of note 26, page 291:

Contra St Paul Fire & Marine Ins Co v Albany School Dist No 1, 763 P2d 1255, 1262-63 (Wyo 1988).

Add at beginning of note 30, page 292:

See, e.g., Auto Owners Ins Co v Zimmerman, 162 Mich App 459, 412 NW2d 925, 926-27 (1987) ("although [the insured] claims not to have read the insurance policy prior to the accident, he nevertheless is held to a knowledge of its terms and conditions").

Add at end of note 30, page 294:

But see §6.02.

Add at beginning of note 37, page 296:

See, e.g., Aid (Mutual) Ins v Steffen, 423 NW2d 189, 192 (Iowa 1988).

Add at end of note 37, page 296:

It has been held that representations contained in promotional materials can be looked to in construing a group policy in accordance with the insured's reasonable expectations. *See, e.g.*, Romano v New England Mut Life Ins Co, 362 SE2d 334, 339 (W Va 1987).

§6.05   Liability to Others Under Liability Insurance Policies

Add following last full sentence of note 45 on page 298:

See, e.g., Brown v Employer's Reinsurance Corp, 206 Conn 668, 539 A2d 138, 141 (1988); Conn Gen Stat §38-175 (1979).

Add at end of note 45, page 299:

See, e.g., Weeks v Beryl Shipping, Inc, 845 F2d 304, 306 (11th Cir 1988) (Florida law) (because policy at issue was an indemnity policy, insurer was liable only for "loss *actually* paid" by insured) (emphasis in original).

Add at beginning of note 49, page 299:

E.g., National Union Fire Ins Co v Continental Ill Corp, 673 F Supp 267, 275 (ND Ill 1987).

Add to first paragraph of note 53, page 300:

See, e.g., Alyas v Gillard, 180 Mich App 154, 446 NW2d 610, 613 (1989); Foremost County Mut Ins Co v Home Indem Co, 897 F2d 754, 758 (5th Cir 1990) (Texas law). *Contra* Far West Fed Bank v Transamerica Title Ins Co, 99 Or App 340, 781 P2d 1259, 1261-62 (1989); Jones v Southern Marine & Aviation Underwriters, Inc, 888 F2d 358, 361 (5th Cir 1989) (Mississippi law).

§6.06 Causation

Add to note 57, page 302:

See Auto-Owners Ins Co v Selisker, 435 NW2d 866, 868 (Minn Ct App 1989) (after failing to take medication to control epilepsy, insured drove his car, suffered a seizure, and caused an accident; there was coverage under auto policy, but not homeowner's policy, because failure to take medication was not a divisible concurring cause of accident which qualified as an independent, nonvehicle-related act of negligence). *But see* Safeco Ins Co of Am v Hirschmann, 112 Wash 2d 621, 773 P2d 413, 416 (1989) ("if the initial event, the 'efficient proximate cause,' is a covered peril, then there is coverage under the policy regardless whether subsequent events within the chain, which may be causes-in-fact of the loss, are excluded by the policy").

E.g., National Fire Ins Co v Valero Energy Corp, 777 SW2d 501, 505 (Tex Ct App 1989). *Contra* Brodkin v State Farm Fire & Cas Co, 265 Cal Rptr 710, 713 (App Dept Super Ct 1989).

Add to note 59, page 302:

In State Farm Fire & Cas Co v Estate of Evoniuk, 681 F Supp 662, 664-65 (ND Cal 1988), the plaintiff was injured by a motorcycle driven by a minor under the influence of alcohol, and she sued the driver's parents under a theory of negligent entrustment and supervision. The court held that the parents were not entitled to coverage because "the events giving rise to [the parents'] potential liability are exclusively related to the use of a motor vehicle," which was excluded from coverage. *See, e.g.*, Terra Nova Ins Co v Thee Kandy Store, Inc, 679 F Supp 476, 478 (ED Pa 1988) (although plaintiff claimed that insureds "were negligent in preventing the assault and battery, this allegation is not sufficient to avoid a properly executed assault and battery exclusion. Regardless of the language of the allegations, the original cause of the harm arose from an alleged assault and battery").

Add to note 62, page 303:

See generally Kane v Royal Ins Co of Am, 768 P2d 678, 684-85 (Colo 1989).

Add to note 64, page 303:

But see Safeco Ins Co of Am v Hirschmann, 52 Wash App 469, 760 P2d 969, 972-73 (1988) (wind and rain caused mudslide, resulting in damage; court held that there was coverage, although damage from mudslides was excluded, because "where a peril specifically insured against sets other causes in motion which, in an unbroken sequence and connection between the act and final loss, produce the result for which recovery is sought, the insured peril is regarded as the proximate cause of the entire loss").

Add to note 65, page 303:

E.g., Garvey v State Farm Fire & Cas Co, 257 Cal Rptr 292, 302-03 (1989).

Add at beginning of note 66, page 304:

E.g., Aetna Cas & Sur Co v Lumbermens Mut Cas Co, 527 NYS2d 143, 145 (App Div 1988); Campbell v Insurance Serv Agency, 424 NW2d 785, 789 (Minn Ct App 1988); Wallace v Rosenberg, 527 So 2d 1386, 1388 (Fla Dist Ct App 1988).

Add to first paragraph of note 66, page 304:

Contra Reyes-Lopez v Misener Marine Constr Co, 854 F2d 529, 533-34 (1st Cir 1988) (Puerto Rican law).

§6.07 Coverage When Excluded Risk is Not Causally Connected to Loss

Add to first paragraph of note 69, page 305:

E.g., Security Ins Co v Anderson, 158 Ariz 426, 763 P2d 246, 249 (1988).

§6.08 Change in Coverage Afforded by a Renewal Policy

Add at beginning of note 82, page 308:

E.g., Woodlawn Fraternal Lodge No 525 v Commercial Union Ins Co, 510 So 2d 162, 164 (Ala 1987); Government Employees Ins Co v Ropka, 74 Md App 249, 536 A2d 1214, 1223 (1988); Campbell v Insurance Serv Agency, 424 NW2d 785, 790 (Minn Ct App 1988); Samuelson v Farm Bureau Mut Ins Co, 446 NW2d 428, 431 (Minn Ct App 1989).

Add to note 83, page 308:

In addition, if an insured has a contractual right to renew a policy, it has been held that a change in the terms of the renewed policy is not binding upon the insured unless the insurer has provided consideration for the change. *See, e.g.,* Wold v Life Ins Co, 24 Ark App 113, 749 SW2d 346, 347 (1988) (forebearance by an insurer from cancelling a policy, after communicating its intent to cancel, constitutes adequate consideration to support a change in the terms of a renewed policy).

§6.12 —When the Other Insurance Is Uncollectible

Add at beginning of note 104, page 315:

E.g., Holland v Stanley Scrubbing Well Serv, 666 F Supp 898, 901-02 (WD La 1987).

Add to first paragraph of note 104, page 315:

E.g., Travelers Indem Co v Overseas Ace Hardware, Inc, 550 So 2d 12, 13 (Fla Dist Ct App 1989); Benton v Long Mfg NC, Inc, 550 So 2d 859, 862-63 (La Ct App 1989).

Add to note 105, page 316:

Accord Northmeadow Tennis Club v Northeastern Fire Ins Co, 26 Mass App Ct 329, 526 NE2d 1333, 1335-36 (1988).

§6.14   Breaches by Insured of Promissory Warranties

Add at beginning of note 123, page 320:

E.g., Quam v General Accident Ins Co of N Am, 411 NW2d 270, 273 (Minn Ct App 1987).

Add to first paragraph of note 123, page 320:

See generally Rehburg v Constitution States Ins Co, 555 So 2d 79, 80 (Ala 1989).

§6.16   Postjudgment Interest Taxed Against Insured

Add at beginning of note 140, page 324:

E.g., Nichols v Anderson, 837 F2d 1372, 1376-77 (5th Cir 1988) (Mississippi law).

Add to first paragraph of note 141, page 324:

See generally Steelmet, Inc v Caribe Towing Corp, 842 F2d 1237, 1245 n 10 (11th Cir 1988) (insurer is liable for postjudgment interest only on portion of judgment it was obligated to pay, unless policy provides to contrary).

Add to note 143, page 325:

See, e.g., Steelmet, Inc v Caribe Towing Corp, 842 F2d 1237, 1244-45 (11th Cir 1988).

§6.17   Punitive Damage Awards Against Insured

Add following first sentence of section, page 326:

Statutory treble damages have been treated the same as punitive damages. *E.g., Country Manors Association v Master Antenna Systems,* 534 So 2d 1187, 1195 (Fla Dist Ct App 1988). *Contra Convent of the Visitation School v Continental Casualty Co,* 707 F Supp 412, 415-16 (D Minn 1989).

Add to note 146, page 326:

E.g., Allstate Ins Co v Talbot, 690 F Supp 886, 888 (ND Cal 1988); Casey v Calhoun, 531 NE2d 1348, 1350-51 (Ohio Ct App 1987). *See*

Southern Am Ins Co v Gabbert-Jones, Inc, 769 P2d 1194, 1198 (Kan Ct App 1989) (noting that statute does allow coverage of punitive damages under certain vicarious liability situations).

In Allen v Simmons, 533 A2d 541, 543-44 (RI 1987), the court held that it was against public policy to allow insurance for punitive damages under automobile policies, because the effect of allowing such insurance was to increase the cost of automobile insurance, a necessity for most people, for the public at large.

See generally United States Fire Ins Co v Goodyear Tire & Rubber Co, 726 F Supp 740, 742 (D Minn 1989).

Add at beginning of note 147, page 326:

E.g., Baker v Armstrong, 106 NM 395, 744 P2d 170, 172-73 (1987); *cf* American Home Assurance Co v Safway Steel Prods Co, 743 SW2d 693, 704-05 (Tex Ct App 1987) (insurance for punitive damages allowed, at least when punitive damages are awarded because of grossly negligent conduct of agent); LeDoux v Centennial Ins Co, 666 F Supp 178, 180-81 (D Alaska 1987) (coverage of punitive awards for unintentional torts does not violate public policy); Home Ins Co v American Home Prods Corp, 665 F Supp 193, 196 (SDNY 1987) (coverage of punitive award for unintentionally caused injury).

Add to first paragraph of note 147, page 327:

E.g., American Protection Ins Co v McMahon, 562 A2d 462, 466-67 (Vt 1989); State Farm Mut Auto Ins Co v Wilson, 162 Ariz 251, 782 P2d 727, 731 (1989).

Add at beginning of note 150, page 327:

E.g., Pennbank v St Paul Fire & Marine Ins Co, 669 F Supp 122, 125-26 (WD Pa 1987).

§6.18   Indemnification of Attorneys' Fees

Add to note 155, page 329:

E.g., Gon v First State Ins Co, 871 F2d 863, 868-69 (9th Cir 1989) (California law); National Union Fire Ins Co v Ambassador Group, Inc, 556 NYS2d 549, 553 (App Div 1990); *cf* Board of Trustees v Continental Cas Co, 730 F Supp 1408, 1414 (WD Mich 1990).

Add following "contrary" in second sentence of second full paragraph on page 329:

(*See, e.g., American Casualty Co v Federal Deposit Insurance Corp,* 677 F Supp 600, 606 (ND Iowa 1987))

Add at beginning of note 157, page 329:

See, e.g., American Cas Co v Bank of Mont Sys, 675 F Supp 538, 543-44 (D Minn 1987) (insurer had to pay defense costs as they were incurred because policy was ambiguous on subject); Little v MGIC Indem Corp, 836 F2d 789, 793-94 (3d Cir 1987) (Pennsylvania law) (insurer obligated to pay defense costs as they become due).

Add to first paragraph of note 157, page 329:

See, e.g., Federal Sav & Loan Ins Corp v Burdette, 718 F Supp 649, 661 (ED Tenn 1989). *But see In re* Ambassador Group, Inc Litigation, 738 F Supp 57, 63 (EDNY 1990).

Add at end of note 157, page 329:

See generally Mt Hawley Ins Co v Federal Sav & Loan Ins Corp, 695 F Supp 469, 474-76 (CD Cal 1987).

§6.20   Binding Effect on Insurer of a Judgment Against Insured in the Underlying Action—Collateral Estoppel

Add at beginning of note 164, page 331:

See Senger v Minnesota Lawyers Mut Ins Co, 415 NW2d 364, 368 (Minn Ct App 1987) (insurer bound even though its duty to defend was not activated by complaint).

Add at beginning of note 166, page 333:

See, e.g., Consolidated Rail Corp v Hartford Accident & Indem Co, 676 F Supp 82, 85-86 (ED Pa 1987) (collateral estoppel applied because court found that there had not been a conflict of interest between insured and insurer in underlying action).

Add to end of note 166, page 333:

See, e.g., Insurance Co of N Am v Whatley, 558 So 2d 120, 122 (Fla Dist Ct App 1990).

Add to note 169, page 334:

In Wear v Farmers Ins Co, 49 Wash App 655, 745 P2d 526, 529 (1987), the insurer apparently controlled the insured's defense despite a conflict of interest. Nevertheless, the court refused to hold that the insurer was bound by the findings of fact in the underlying action, applying the rule that "application of the . . . principles of collateral estoppel against a liability insurer is justifiable only when the insurer's interests are in harmony with the insured's interests."

§6.22 —Collusion

Add at end of section, page 339:

Another noteworthy case is *Allstate Insurance Co v Atwood*, 319 Md 247, 572 A2d 154, 161 (1990). The court there held that an insurer is not bound by determinations made in a tort suit against its insured if such determinations were not "fairly litigated in the tort trial". The court explained that under those circumstances, "considerations of public policy and fairness militate against holding that the insurer is bound by the outcome of the tort case".

§6.24 Determining Whether Grounds for Judgment Were Outside Policy Coverage— Evidentiary Issues

Add at beginning of note 189, page 340:

E.g., Oregon Ins Guar Assn v Thompson, 93 Or App 5, 760 P2d 890, 892 (1988); Mutual of Enumclaw Ins Co v Gass, 100 Or App 424, 786 P2d 749, 751 (1990).

§6.27 Settlements Entered into by Insured with Injured Party

Add at end of note 215, page 347:

See §5.16 for a discussion of an insurer's liability for a settlement in excess of the policy limits.

Add to note 216, page 347:

E.g., Battista v Western World Ins Co, 227 NJ Super 135, 545 A2d 841, 848 (1988); St Paul Fire & Marine Ins Co v Vigilant Ins Co, 724 F Supp 1173, 1182-83 (MDNC 1989). *See generally* Amalgamet, Inc v Underwriters at Lloyds', 724 F Supp 1132, 1142 (SDNY 1989) ("once an underwriter disclaims, it may object to a subsequently negotiated settlement with third parties only if that settlement was made in bad faith").

It has been held in Texas that an insurer which wrongfully refuses to defend its insured cannot later contest the reasonableness of a consent judgment entered on a settlement between the insured and the injured party. *See, e.g.,* United States Aviation Underwriters, Inc v Olympia Wings, Inc, 896 F2d 949, 954 (5th Cir 1990) (Texas law).

Add following next-to-last sentence on page 347:

In *Hennings v State Farm Fire & Casualty Co,* 438 NW2d 680, 686 (Minn Ct App 1989), the court held that the insurer was not relieved from all liability because the settlement amount was unreasonable. Accordingly, it held that there should be a trial on the question of damages without further reference to reasonableness "of the settlement."

§6.29 Determining Whether Grounds for Settlement Were Outside Policy Coverage

Add to note 223, page 349:

See, e.g., Convent of the Visitation School v Continental Cas Co, 707 F Supp 412, 416-17 (D Minn 1989); Burroughs Wellcome Co v Commercial Union Ins Co, 713 F Supp 694, 698-99 (SDNY 1989).

Add to note 224, page 350:

In St Paul Fire & Marine Ins Co v Vigilant Ins Co, 724 F Supp 1173, 1183 (MDNC 1989), the court held that the insurer was liable for the settlement, regardless of whether there was in fact an occurrence within the policy period because: (1) the insurer had breached its duty to defend; and (2) the "settlement (should be) viewed as a cost of defending the suits".

Add to first paragraph of note 225, page 350:

See, e.g., Utah Power & Light Co v Federal Ins Co, 724 F Supp 846, 850-51 (D Utah 1989); National Union Fire Ins Co v Ambassador Group, Inc, 556 NYS2d 549, 553 (App Div 1990):

> Simply because 98% of the verdict in the first stage of the bifurcated trial was for punitive damages does not conclusively establish that 98% of the settlement was also for punitive damages, since the settlement also eliminated the need for a trial on the potentially covered alter ego claims. At the very least, therefore, there is a factual issue of the apportionment between covered and punitive damages.

§6.30 Effect of Settlement with One Insurer on Another Insurer's Liability

Add at end of note 237, page 354:

In McGuire v Davis Truck Servs, 518 So 2d 1171, 1173-74 (La Ct App 1988), the underlying insurer was insolvent. The court held that the excess insurer's policy was sufficiently ambiguous concerning the effect of such insolvency that the excess insurer became excess not over the amount of underlying insurance required by the excess policy, but excess over whatever amount could be recovered by reason of the underlying policy. *Contra* Wurth v Ideal Mut Ins Co, 34 Ohio App 3d 325, 518 NE2d 607, 610-11 (1987) (excess insurer not required to drop down by reason of primary carrier's insolvency; court gave a common-sense interpretation to language of excess policy, and held that public policy did not require a different result because excess insurer did not insure against risk of underlying carrier's insolvency).

§6.31 Coverage Through Estoppel

Add at beginning of note 241, page 354:

E.g., Shannon v Shannon, 150 Wis 2d 434, 442 NW2d 25, 33 (1989); Topeka Tent & Awning Co v Glens Falls Ins Co, 774 P2d 984, 986 (Kan Ct App 1989); Silverton Enters v General Cas Co, 143 Wis 2d 661, 422 NE2d 154, 158-59 (1988); *see* ABCD . . . Vision, Inc v Fireman's Fund Ins Cos, 304 Or 301, 744 P2d 998, 1001 (1987) (estoppel can be invoked with regard to conditions of forfeiture, but it cannot be invoked to expand scope of insurance).

Add to first paragraph of note 241, page 355:

E.g., Holland Corp v Maryland Cas Co, 775 SW2d 531, 534-35 (Mo Ct App 1989).

The doctrine has been refined by many courts to allow estoppel as to a basis for forfeiting coverage, although not as to a basis for the nonexistence of coverage in the first instance. *See, e.g.*, Gordon v Liberty Mut Ins Co, 675 F Supp 321, 323 (ED Va 1987); Fishel v American Sec Life Ins Co, 835 F2d 613, 615-16 (5th Cir 1988) (Mississippi law). *See* §6.33.

Add at end of note 241, page 355:

In Florida, the Supreme Court has interpreted a statute requiring that an insurer take certain steps when denying coverage as providing, in the event of a violation of the statute, for an estoppel only as to forfeiture type defenses. Alu Ins Co v Block Marina Inv, Inc, 544 So 2d 998, 1000 (Fla 1989).

Add at beginning of note 243, page 355:

See, e.g., Union Natl Bank v Moriarty, 746 SW2d 249, 252-53 (Tex Ct App 1987) (insurer estopped from denying coverage based upon fact that insured was not a resident of damaged house, because insurer had continued to accept premiums for coverage even though its agent had received notification of insured's change of residence); Arkwright-Boston Mfrs Mut Ins Co v Aries Marine Corp, 736 F Supp 1447, 1452 (SD Tex 1990) (quoting this text).

Add at end of note 243, page 356:

It has, however, been held that someone other than the insured cannot rely on estoppel to create coverage under the policy. *See, e.g.,* Royal Ins Co v Western Cas Ins Co, 494 NW2d 846, 848 (Minn Ct App 1989).

Add at beginning of note 244, page 356:

See, e.g., Jet Line Servs v American Employers Ins Co, 404 Mass 706, 537 NE2d 107, 113 (1989); Hartford Fire Ins Co v Spartan Realty Intl, Inc, 196 Cal App 3d 1320, 242 Cal Rptr 462, 465 (1987) (insured must demonstrate detrimental reliance on insurer's conduct in order to estop insurer from denying coverage; fact that insured refrained from hiring separate counsel did not suffice to establish such detrimental reliance); Underwriters at Lloyds' v Denali Seafoods, Inc, 729 F Supp 721, 727 (WD Wash 1990).

Add to note 246, page 358:

See Lido Co v Fireman's Fund Ins Co, 574 A2d 299, 301 (Me 1990) (no estoppel simply because insurer had previously provided coverage for a similar claim); Jacore Sys v Central Mut Ins Co, 194 Ga App 512, 390 SE2d 876, 878 (1990) (no estoppel even though insurer had previously paid a similar claim).

§6.32 —Improper Applications of Theory

Add at beginning of note 251, page 359:

E.g., Scott v Transport Indem Co, 513 So 2d 889, 894-95 (Miss 1987).

Add to first paragraph of note 251, page 359:

Contra St Paul Fire & Marine Ins Co v Albany School Dist No 1, 763 P2d 1255, 1261-62 (Wyo 1988) (agent's misrepresentations cannot expand coverage pursuant to doctrines of estoppel or waiver).

Add at end of note 251, page 359:

Similarly, in Terry v Avemco Ins Co, 663 F Supp 39, 41-42 (D Colo 1987), the court held that an insurance company could be sued for negligently failing to provide some particular coverage requested by the insured. *See also* §9.28. The court went on to hold that the fact that the insured failed to read his policy, and thereby discover the actual coverage provided, did not bar his action.

Add at beginning of note 252, page 359:

E.g., Farmers & Merchants Bank v Home Ins Co, 514 So 2d 825, 830-31 (Ala 1987) (insured bound by terms of policy even though policy did not correspond with representations made prior to issuance of policy).

Add at end of note 254, page 360:

An intentional misrepresentation as to coverage may excuse a failure to read a policy. *See, e.g.,* Appling v Home Fed Sav & Loan Assn, 185 Ga App 356, 364 SE2d 91, 94 (1987).

§6.33   Coverage Through Waiver

Add to note 256, page 362:

E.g., Lone Star Indus v Liberty Mut Ins Co, 689 F Supp 329, 333 (SDNY 1988); *Shannon v Shannon,* 150 Wis 2d 434, 442 NW2d 25, 33 (1989); Topeka Tent & Awning Co v Glens Falls Ins Co, 774 P2d 984, 986 (Kan Ct App 1989); Holland Corp v Maryland Cas Co, 775 SW2d 531, 534-35 (Mo Ct App 1989).

Add at beginning of note 260, page 362:

See, e.g., Fishel v American Sec Life Ins Co, 835 F2d 613, 615-16 (5th Cir 1988) (Mississippi law) (doctrine of waiver "cannot be used to extend the coverage of an insurance policy . . . but may only affect rights reserved in it").

§6.34   Coverage Under Insurance Binders

Add at beginning of note 268, page 366:

E.g., Pape v Mid-America Preferred Ins Co, 738 SW2d 882, 884 (Mo Ct App 1987); Howell v United States Fire Ins Co, 185 Ga App 154, 363 SE2d 560, 562 (1987).

Add at beginning of note 271, page 367:

See Pape v Mid-America Preferred Ins Co, 738 SW2d 882, 885-86 (Mo Ct App 1987) ("usual" policy conditions applied when loss occurred prior to issuance of policy).

§6.35 —Existence

Add to note 274, page 369:

See also Clements v Ohio State Life Ins Co, 33 Ohio App 3d 80, 514 NE2d 876, 882 (1986).

Add to first paragraph of note 281, page 371:

E.g., Dugan v Massachusetts Mut Life Ins Co, 736 F Supp 1072, 1075-76 (D Kan 1990).

Add to note 294, page 373:

See American Hardware Mut Ins Co v BIM, Inc, 885 F2d 132, 137-38 (4th Cir 1989) (West Virginia law).

§6.37 Damages in the Event of Breach by Insurer—Contract

Add at beginning of note 303, page 375:

E.g., Giovannitti v Nationwide Ins Co, 690 F Supp 1439, 1446-47 (WD Pa 1988); Diaz Irizarry v Ennia, 678 F Supp 957, 961-62 (DPR 1988).

Add to first paragraph of note 303, page 375:

See generally Burleson v Illinois Farmers Ins Co, 725 F Supp 1489, 1491-95 (SD Ind 1989).

§6.38 —Tort

Add at beginning of note 320, page 378:

E.g., Chitsey v National Lloyds Ins Co, 738 SW2d 641, 643-44 (Tex 1987).

Add to first paragraph of note 320, page 378:

E.g., Viles v Security Natl Ins Co, 788 SW2d 566, 567 (Tex 1990).

Add to second paragraph of note 321, page 379:

As explained in Pace v Insurance Co of N Am, 838 F2d 572, 584 (1st Cir 1988) (Rhode Island law), however, a lack of diligent investigation is not sufficient to give rise to an action in tort as long as the insurer had an objectively "fairly debatable" reason to deny coverage.

Add at beginning of note 322, page 379:

E.g., Nevada VTN v General Ins Co of Am, 834 F2d 770, 776-77 (9th Cir 1987) (Nevada law) (insurer not liable in tort unless its breach of contract was in bad faith); *see* Opperman v Nationwide Mut Fire Ins Co, 515 So 2d 263, 266 (Fla Dist Ct App 1987) (based on statute); Staff Builders, Inc v Armstrong, 37 Ohio St 3d 298, 525 NE2d 783, 788 (1988) ("an insurer has a duty to act in good faith in the processing and payment of the claims of its insured," and a "breach of this duty will give rise to a cause of action in tort").

Add to first paragraph of note 322, page 380:

E.g, State Farm Fire & Cas Co v Nicholson, 777 P2d 1152, 1157 (Alaska 1989).

Add after first paragraph of note 322, page 380:

The formulation for bad faith set forth in Justin v Guardian Ins Co, 670 F Supp 614, 617 (DVI 1987), is fair and reasonable:

> [I]n order to make out a cause of action for the tort of bad faith a plaintiff will be required to show: 1) the existence of an insurance contract between the parties and a breach by the insurer; 2) intentional refusal to pay the claim, 3) the nonexistence of any reasonably legitimate or arguable reason for the refusal (debatable reason) either in law or fact, 4) the insurer's knowledge of the absence of such a debatable reason or 5) when the plaintiff argues that the intentional failure results from the failure of the insurer to determine the existence of an arguable basis, the plaintiff must prove the insurer's intentional failure to determine the existence of such a debatable reason.

Add at end of note 322, page 380:

In addition, it has been held that whether an insurance company is justified in denying a claim must be judged by what was before it at the time the decision to deny the claim was made. *See, e.g.,* State Farm Fire & Cas Co v Balmer, 672 F Supp 1395, 1402 (MD Ala 1987).

Add at beginning of note 324, page 380:

E.g., Dickson v Selected Risks Ins Co, 666 F Supp 80, 81 (D Md 1987).

Add to first paragraph of note 324, page 381:

See generally Johnson v Federal Kemper Ins Co, 74 Md App 243, 536 A2d 1211, 1213 (1988) (tort action does not exist for failure to pay a first-party claim).

Add at end of note 324, page 381:

An issue can also arise as to whether a cause of action for an insurer's bad faith failure to pay policy benefits is preempted by statute. *See, e.g.,* National Union Fire Ins Co v Continental Ill Corp, 673 F Supp 267, 270-71 (ND Ill 1987) (statute preempted claim for bad faith refusal to pay under a first-party policy, but did not preempt breach of duty to settle claim made against an insured).

Add at beginning of note 326, page 381:

E.g., Chitsey v National Lloyds Ins Co, 738 SW2d 641, 643 (Tex 1987).

Add to note 327, page 382:

E.g., Farmers Ins Group v Trimble, 768 P2d 1243, 1246-47 (Colo Ct App 1988).

Add to note 333, page 383:

It has been held, however, that an insurer cannot recover its attorneys' fees from an insured. *See* California Fair Plan Assn v Polik, 270 Cal Rptr 243, 246-47 (Ct App 1990).

§6.39 Restitution of Payments

Add to first paragraph of note 334, page 383:

E.g., Woolsey v Nationwide Ins Co, 697 F Supp 1053, 1056-57 (WD Ark 1988).

Add at beginning of note 335, page 383:

E.g., Terra Nova Ins Co v Associates Commercial Corp, 697 F Supp 1048, 1052 (ED Wis 1988); Connecticut Gen Life Ins Co v Universal Ins Co, 838 F2d 612, 620 (1st Cir 1988) (Puerto Rican law).

Add to note 338, page 384:

Similarly, in Shotts v American Income Life Ins Co, 518 So 2d 1244, 1245-46 (Ala 1987), the insurer made a payment following a misrepresentation by the insured's counsel as to the governing law. The insurer was allowed to recoup the payment.

§6.41 Duties of Insurance Brokers

Add at beginning of note 345, page 385:

See, e.g., Clements v Ohio State Life Ins Co, 33 Ohio App 3d 80, 514 NE2d 876, 881 (1986) ("An insurance agent who advises a client that the coverage sought is in effect with the knowledge that the insurance company has not yet agreed to provide the coverage thereby incurs personal liability as an insurer. . . . In addition, if the agent is negligent in failing to acquire coverage he has undertaken to procure, he may be liable for resulting damage").

Add to note 345, page 385:

In Royal Ins Co of Am v Cathy Daniels, Ltd, 684 F Supp 786, 792-93 (SDNY 1988), the broker procured a policy that was rescinded because of the broker's failure to disclose certain facts to the insurer. The court, therefore, held that the broker had breached its duty to exercise skill, care, and diligence in procuring coverage for the insured; accordingly, it held the broker liable for the losses that the insured could have recovered if the policy had been properly obtained.

Note, however, that absent special circumstances an insurance agent does not have an affirmative duty to explain a policy to the insured. *See, e.g.,* Bruner v League Gen Ins Co, 164 Mich App 28, 416 NW2d 318, 320-21 (1987).

An agent may also have an affirmative duty to advise the insured of gaps in coverage. *See, e.g.,* Born v Medico Life Ins Co, 428 NW2d 585, 589 (Minn Ct App 1988). Moreover, if the insured expressed a desire to be fully insured and the agent advised the insured that the insurance contained all the coverage it needed, the agent can be liable for a gap in coverage. *See, e.g.,* Warehouse Foods v Corporate Risk Management Servs, 530 So 2d 422, 424 (Fla Dist Ct App 1988).

Rights and Duties as Between Insurers

7

§7.01 Conflicting "Other Insurance" Clauses

Add at beginning of note 2, page 387:

See generally Contrans, Inc v Ryder Truck Rental, Inc, 836 F2d 163 (3d Cir 1987) (Pennsylvania law) (containing lengthy discussion of what is an escape clause and what is an excess clause).

Add following carryover sentence, page 388:

When the interested insurers are both signatories to the Guiding Principles for Overlapping Insurance Coverage, it has been held that the questions raised in the text will be answered by application of the standards contained in the Guiding Principles. *See, e.g., Commercial Union Insurance Co v Bituminous Casualty Corp,* 851 F2d 98, 102-04 (3d Cir 1988).

Add at beginning of note 5, page 388:

E.g., Grinnell Mut Reinsurance Co v Globe Am Cas Co, 426 NW2d 635, 638 (Iowa 1988); Hartford Ins Co v Kentucky Farm Bureau Ins Co, 766 SW2d 75, 76 (Ky Ct App 1989); Western Cas & Sur Co v Trinity Universal Ins Co, 13 Kan App 2d 133, 764 P2d 1256, 1263 (1988); Interstate Fire & Cas Co v Auto-Owners Ins Co, 421 NW2d 355, 358-59 (1988); Equity Mut Ins Co v Spring Valley Wholesale Nursery, Inc, 747 P2d 947, 954 (Okla 1987).

Add at beginning of note 7, page 388:

E.g., Equity Mut Ins Co v Spring Valley Wholesale Nursery, Inc, 747 P2d 947, 954 (Okla 1987).

Add to note 7, page 388:

See Towne Realty v Safeco Ins Co of Am, 854 F2d 1264, 1268 (11th Cir 1988) (Florida law).

Add at beginning of note 10, page 389:

E.g., Mosca v Ford Motor Credit Co, 541 NYS2d 528, 530 (App Div 1989).

Add at end of note 10, page 389:

Contra Automobile Underwriters v Fireman's Fund Ins Cos, 874 F2d 188, 193 (3d Cir 1989) (Pennsylvania law) (escape clause with excess component still treated as invalid escape clause vis-à-vis another insurer also providing coverage).

Add at beginning of note 12, page 389:

E.g., CC Hous Corp v Ryder Truck Rental, Inc, 106 NM 577, 746 P2d 1109, 1113 (1987).

§7.02 —Recommended Approach

Add at beginning of note 24, page 393:

See, e.g., Aetna Cas & Sur Co v United Servs Auto Assn, 676 F Supp 79, 81-82 (ED Pa 1987) (as between two excess insurers, one was excess to the other because it was a "true umbrella policy"; it provided "extended coverage for a low premium; it is labelled 'excess indemnity policy'; and the named insured must maintain underlying primary insurance"); Home Ins Co v Liberty Mut Ins Co, 678 F Supp 1066, 1069-70 (SDNY 1988) ("an umbrella policy is not required to contribute to the payment of a settlement until all other applicable policies have been exhausted regardless of the wording of those policies' 'other insurance' clauses"); Carrabba v Employers Cas Co, 742 SW2d 709, 714-15 (Tex Ct App 1987) (ignoring "other insurance" clauses because policies were "not of the same character; one was a primary policy and one was an umbrella policy"); Allstate Ins Co v American Hardware Mut Ins Co, 865 F2d 592, 594 (4th Cir 1989) (West Virginia law) (umbrella policy is excess to nonumbrella policy with excess clause); Allstate Ins Co v Frank B Hall & Co, 770 P2d 1342, 1347 (Colo Ct App 1989) ("total policy insuring intent" required that umbrella policy be excess to policy designed to provide primary protection, even though latter policy had excess "other insurance" clause).

The court in Interstate Fire & Cas Co v Auto-Owners Ins Co, 433 NW2d 82, 86 (Minn 1988), applied the "intent" test in concluding that an umbrella policy with an excess clause was primary to another policy with a pro-rata clause.

Add to note 24, page 394:

See, e.g., Argonaut Ins Co v United States Fire Ins Co, 728 F Supp 298, 300-02 (SDNY 1990); Independent Fire Ins Co v Mutual Assurance, Inc, 553 So 2d 115, 117-18 (Ala 1989) (umbrella policy excess over policy with excess clause).

Add after carryover sentence on page 394:

See generally United States Fire Insurance Co v Federal Insurance Co, 858 F2d 882, 886-87 (2d Cir 1988) (New York law) (disparity between two policies in amount of premium charged was not controlling because court found "that the premium disparity reflected not different layers of coverage but rather significant differences in the number and type of risks covered").

§7.03   Resolving Conflicting Clauses

Add to note 38, page 397:

E.g., American Hardware Mut Ins Co v Darv's Motor Sports, 427 NW2d 715, 719 (Minn Ct App 1988).

See Odessa School Dist v Insurance Co of Am, 57 Wash App 893, 791 P2d 237, 242 (1990).

Add at beginning of note 45, page 398:

E.g., Allstate Ins Co v State Auto Mut Ins Co, 364 SE2d 30, 33 (W Va 1987). *Contra* Continental Cas Co v Aetna Cas & Sur Co, 823 F2d 708, 711 (2d Cir 1987) (Connecticut law).

§7.04   Proration—Between Insurers That Provide Indemnity Coverage at the Same Level

Add at beginning note 55, page 401:

E.g., Equity Mut Ins Co v Spring Valley Wholesale Nursery, Inc, 747 P2d 947, 954 (Okla 1987).

Add at beginning of note 56, page 402:

E.g., United States Fire Ins Co v Federal Ins Co, 858 F2d 882 (2d Cir 1988) (New York law); Hospital Underwriters Mut Ins Co v National Cas Co, 541 NYS2d 512, 513 (App Div 1989); Equity Mut Ins Co v Spring Valley Wholesale Nursery, Inc, 747 P2d 947, 954 (Okla 1987).

Add to first paragraph of note 56, page 402:

E.g., Cargill, Inc v Commercial Union Ins Co, 889 F2d 174, 180 (8th Cir 1989) (Missouri law).

Add at beginning of note 57, page 402:

E.g., Mission Ins Co v United States Fire Ins Co, 401 Mass 492, 517 NE2d 463, 468 (1987).

Add to note 57, page 402:

See Odessa School Dist v Insurance Co of Am, 57 Wash App 893, 791 P2d 237, 244 (1990).

Add to note 59, page 403:

E.g., Mission Ins Co v United States Fire Ins Co, 401 Mass 492, 517 NE2d 463, 468 (1987); *see generally* Continental Cas Co v Aetna Cas & Sur Co, 823 F2d 708, 711-12 (2d Cir 1987).

Add to note 61, page 403:

See generally Continental Cas Co v Aetna Cas & Sur Co, 823 F2d 708, 712 (2d Cir 1987).

Add to note 63, page 403:

See generally Continental Cas Co v Aetna Cas & Sur Co, 823 F2d 708, 712 (2d Cir 1987).

§7.05   —Between Primary Insurers When There Is Excess Insurance

Add at end of section, page 407:

E.g., Hartford Casualty Insurance Co v Argonaut-Midwest Insurance Co, 664 F Supp 373, 384 (ND Ill 1987).

§7.06   —Between Insurers of Defense Costs

Add to note 78, page 407:

E.g., Air Prods & Chems v Hartford Accident & Indem Co, 707 F Supp 762, 770 (ED Pa 1989).

Add to note 79, page 407:

E.g., Federal Ins Co v Cablevision Sys Dev Co, 662 F Supp 1537, 1541 (EDNY 1987).

§7.07 Liability of One Insurer for Another Insurer's Deductible

Add to note 83, page 408:

It has been held that under no circumstances should the allocation of defense costs among insurers result in any liability to the insured beyond the smallest applicable deductible. *See* Air Prods & Chems v Hartford Accident & Indem Co, 707 F Supp 762, 771 (ED Pa 1989).

E.g., Cargill, Inc v Commercial Union Ins Co, 889 F2d 174, 180 (8th Cir 1989) (Missouri law).

§7.08 Duty to Settle Owed to Excess Insurer

Add following first sentence of section, page 410:

Similarly, if a primary insurer pays an amount in excess of its policy limit because of its prior breach of the duty to settle, it cannot recover such excess from an excess insurer. *E.g., Occidental Fire & Casualty Co v Lumbermens Mutual Casualty Co,* 667 F Supp 679, 688 (ND Cal 1987). The excess insurer's liability can be created by either a judgment or settlement in excess of the primary carrier's limits. *See Fortman v Safeco Insurance Co of America,* 271 Cal Rptr 117, 120-21 (Ct App 1990).

Add at beginning of note 89, page 410:

E.g., National Union Fire Ins Co v Liberty Mut Ins Co, 696 F Supp 1099, 1101 (ED La 1988); Mission Ins Co v Aetna Life & Cas Co, 687 F Supp 249, 254 (ED La 1988). *See generally* Argonaut Ins Co v Hartford Accident & Indem Ins Co, 687 F Supp 911, 914 (SDNY 1988) ("primary insurer owes a fiduciary duty directly to its excess insurer to exercise good faith in handling the defense of claims and to safeguard the rights and interests of the excess insurer").

Add to note 89, page 411:

E.g., Ranger Ins Co v Home Indem Co, 714 F Supp 956, 961 (ND Ill 1989); American Centennial Ins Co v American Home Assurance Co, 729 F Supp 1228, 1232 (ND Ill 1990). *Contra* Great SW Fire Ins Co v CNA Ins Cos, 547 So 2d 1339, 1346 (La Ct App 1989); Foremost

County Ins Co v Home Indem Co, 897 F2d 754, 758-59 (5th Cir 1990) (Texas law); Twin City Fire Ins Co v Superior Court, 792 P2d 758, 759-60 (Ariz 1990).

Add to note 90, page 411:

Contra Twin City Fire Ins Co v CNA Ins Co, 711 F Supp 310, 311 (WD La 1988).

Add to note 92, page 411:

E.g., Certain Underwriters of Lloyd's v General Accident Ins Co of Am, 699 F Supp 732, 737-39 (SD Ind 1988); *cf* Turner Ins Agency v Continental Ins Co, 541 So 2d 471, 472 (Ala 1989); Home Ins Co v North River Ins Co, 385 SE2d 736, 740 (Ga Ct App 1989).

§7.09 —Effect of Settlement by Primary Insurer for Amount Less Than Its Policy Limits

Add at beginning of note 103, page 414:

See generally Kelley Co v Central Natl Ins Co, 662 F Supp 1284, 1286-87 (ED Wis 1987) (case in which such a release was used).

§7.10 Reinsurance

Add to note 108, page 415:

But see Osborn Estate v Gerling Global Life Ins Co, 529 So 2d 169, 171-72 (Miss 1988) (when reinsurance agreement "is drawn so as to indemnify against liability (as opposed to loss), an original insured may bring a direct action against the [re]insurer based on a third-party beneficiary theory").

Declaratory Judgment Actions

8

§8.04 —Resolution of Factual and Legal Issues Pertinent to Underlying Action Against Insured

Add to note 19, page 421:

In Allstate Ins Co v Atwood, 319 Md 247, 572 A2d 154, 157 (1990), the court held that when "the allegations in the tort suit against the insured obviously constitute a patent attempt to recharacterize, as negligent, an act that is clearly intentional, . . . a declaratory judgment action prior to the trial of the tort case is permissible". A few courts, however, have held that an insurer can simply deny coverage under those circumstances. *See* §4.02, note 19.

Add to note 20, page 422:

E.g., State Farm Fire & Cas Co v Shelton, 531 NE2d 913, 916-17 (Ill App Ct 1988).

§8.06   Actions by Insured Against Insurer

Add to note 31, page 424:

But see §4.09.

Add to note 36, page 426:

But see Batsakis v Federal Deposit Ins Corp, 670 F Supp 749, 759 (WD Mich 1987) ("no action" clause prohibited insured from instituting declaratory judgment action against insurer until such time as liability of insured was determined).

§8.12   —Insured as Indispensable Party

Add at end of note 77, page 434:

See, e.g., Home Ins Co v Liberty Mut Ins Co, 678 F Supp 1066, 1070 (SDNY 1988) (insured not an indispensable party because suit constituted "an inter-carrier dispute over priority of contribution").

§8.14   Attorney's Fee Awards

Add at beginning of note 84, page 436:

E.g., Economy Fire & Cas Co v Iverson, 426 NW2d 195, 201 (Minn Ct App 1988); Aetna Cas & Sur Co v Spancrete, Inc, 726 F Supp 204, 209 (ND Ill 1989).

Coverage Actions

9

§9.01 Burden of Proof

Add to first paragraph of note 1, page 442:

E.g., Allstate Ins Co v Talbot, 690 F Supp 886, 888 (ND Cal 1988); Wexler Knitting Mills v Atlantic Mut Ins Co, 555 A2d 903, 905 (Pa Super Ct 1989); Dyer v Northbrook Property & Cas Ins Co, 259 Cal Rptr 298, 302 (Ct App 1989); Merced Mut Ins Co v Mendez, 261 Cal Rptr 273, 277 (Ct App 1989).

Add to note 2, page 444:

E.g., Raprager v Allstate Ins Co, 183 Ill App 3d 847, 539 NE2d 787, 791 (1989); United States Fidelity & Guar Co v Murray Ohio Mfg Co, 693 F Supp 617, 619 (MD Tenn 1988); Merced Mut Ins Co v Mendez, 261 Cal Rptr 273, 277 (Ct App 1989).

§9.02 Statute of Limitations

Add following third sentence of section, page 444:

See, e.g., Marathon Plastics, Inc v International Insurance Co, 161 Ill App 3d 459, 514 NE2d 479, 483-84 (1987).

Add at end of section, page 446:

Finally, at least one state has a special rule requiring that insurers notify insureds of the applicable statute of limitations after the insurer has received a notice of claim under certain types of policies. A failure to notify the insured will result in the insurer being precluded from asserting a statute of limitations defense. *See, e.g.,* Del Code Ann tit 18, §3914, discussed in *Samoluk v Basco, Inc,* 528 A2d 1203, 1204 (Del Sup 1987) (casualty insurance).

§9.03   Contractual Limitations Clause

Add to note 18, page 448:

It has been held that contractual limitation clauses can also be used to defeat one insurer's claim for contribution against another. *See, e.g., Republic Ins Co v Great Pac Ins Co,* 261 Cal Rptr 863, 866 (Ct App 1989).

Add at beginning of note 21, page 449:

E.g., Green v General Accident Ins Co of Am, 106 NM 523, 746 P2d 152, 154 (1987).

Add to first paragraph of note 21, page 449:

But see Laurence v Western Mut Ins Co, 251 Cal Rptr 319, 324 (Ct App 1988). *E.g.,* Hospital Support Servs v Kemper Group, Inc, 889 F2d 1311, 1316-17 (3d Cir 1989) (Pennsylvania law).

§9.05   —Waiver and Estoppel

Add to note 31, page 451:

The fact that the insured is represented by counsel will impact on whether the reliance was reasonable. *See, e.g.,* Edmondson v Pennsylvania Natl Mut Cas Ins Co, 781 SW2d 753, 757 (Ky 1989).

Add to note 32, page 451:

E.g., Baker v Pennsylvania Natl Mut Cas Ins Co, 536 A2d 1357, 1360 (Pa Super Ct 1987).

Add to note 34, page 452:

The fact that the insurer continues to investigate the claim and requests further documentation should not in itself constitute a waiver or estoppel as to the contractual limitation period. *See, e.g.,* Issa v Reliance Ins Co, 683 F Supp 82, 83 (SDNY 1988).

Add at beginning of note 35, page 452:

E.g., Green v General Accident Ins Co of Am, 106 NM 523, 746 P2d 152, 154-55 (1987).

Add to first paragraph of note 37, page 453:

Contra Gilbert Frank Corp v Federal Ins Co, 70 NY2d 966, 520 NE2d 512, 514 (1988) ("communications or settlement negotiations between an insured and its insurer either before or after expiration of a limitations period contained in a policy is not, without more, sufficient to prove waiver or estoppel"); Edmondson v Pennsylvania Natl Mut Cas Ins Co, 781 SW2d 753, 757 (Ky 1989).

Add at end of note 37, page 453:

Note, too, that the court in Fox-Knapp, Inc v Employers Mut Cas Co, 893 F2d 14 (2d Cir 1989) (New York law) held that the insurer "did not waive its limitations defense, as a matter of law, by putting (the insured) to the expense of submitting to examination under oath and producing documents after expiration of the limitations period".

§9.07 —Applicability to Tort Actions

Add to note 56, page 457:

See Laurence v Western Mut Ins Co, 251 Cal Rptr 319, 324 (Ct App 1988).

§9.10 Direct Action Statutes

Add at beginning of note 79, page 461:

See, e.g., Commonwealth v Celli-Flynn, 540 A2d 1365, 1368-70 (Pa Commw Ct 1988).

§9.11 Actions by Injured Party Against Insurer—Policy Benefits

Add to first paragraph of note 88, page 464:

A provision in a policy prohibiting assignment does not apply to assignments of the claim after loss. *E.g.,* Hartford Cas Ins Co v Argonaut-Midwest Ins Co, 664 F Supp 373, 379-80 (WD Ill 1987).

Add to note 93, page 466:

Maine Rev Stat Ann tit 24-A, §2904, *discussed in* Amoco Oil Co v Dingwell, 690 F Supp 78, 82-83 (D Me 1988), restricts an insurer's coverage defenses when a judgment creditor of the insured attempts to collect from the insurer.

Add at beginning of note 95, page 467:

See, e.g., Brown v Employer's Reinsurance Corp, 206 Conn 668, 539 A2d 138, 141-42 (1988) (injured party could not recover from insurer because insured had breached insurance contract).

§9.12 —Payments in Excess of Policy Limits

Add at beginning of note 100, page 469:

E.g., Brocato v Prairie State Farmers' Ins Assn, 166 Ill App 3d 986, 520 NE2d 1200, 1202 (1988).

Add before "Contra" in second paragraph of note 100, page 469:

See generally Benkert v Medical Protective Co, 842 F2d 144, 149-50 (6th Cir 1988) (Michigan law) (right to sue an insurer for breach of duty to settle is assignable because it is not equivalent of a claim for fraud, which is not assignable).

Add to note 102, page 470:

E.g., OK Lumber v Providence Wash Ins Co, 759 P2d 523, 526 (Alaska 1988).

§9.19 Discovery of Insurer's Claims File—Work Product Privilege

Add following second sentence of third paragraph, page 477:

See, e.g., Bartlett v John Hancock Mutual Life Insurance Co, 538 A2d 997, 999 (RI 1988).

Add following first sentence of note 137, page 477:

See generally Escalante v Sentry Ins, 49 Wash App 375, 743 P2d 832, 843 (1987).

§9.20 —Substantial Need Doctrine

Add to note 149, page 480:

See generally Escalante v Sentry Ins, 49 Wash App 375, 743 P2d 832, 844 n 11 (1987).

In Bartlett v John Hancock Mut Life Ins Co, 538 A2d 997, 999-1000 (RI 1988), however, the court refused to compel the insurer to produce its claims file even though the insured had alleged bad faith. The court reasoned that, although the existence of a bad faith claim might support such compelled production, such production is not justified "when the underlying contract claim is still pending." The court held, therefore, that the interest of justice would best be served by bifurcating the bad faith claim from the breach of contract claim, and determining the breach of contract claim first.

§9.21 —Attorney-Client Privilege

Add at end of note 153, page 481:

See, e.g., Escalante v Sentry Ins, 49 Wash App 375, 743 P2d 832, 842-43 (1987) (foundation for utilizing civil fraud exception to attorney-client privilege can be established by in camera judicial inspection of documents).

§9.22 Prejudgment Interest Awards

Add to first paragraph of note 156, page 482:

See, e.g., Royal College Shop, Inc v Northern Ins Co, 895 F2d 670, 674-75 (10th Cir 1990) (Kansas law).

Add to note 159, page 483:

See also Republic Textile Equip Co v Aetna Ins Co, 360 SE2d 540, 545-46 (SC Ct App 1987) (although interest is allowed when judgment is obtained on policy of insurance, interest not awarded in subject case because insured prevailed on a negligence theory and damages were unliquidated).

§9.23 —Computation of Amount of Award

Add to note 164, page 484:

But see Giavannitti v Nationwide Ins Co, 690 F Supp 1439, 1447 (WD Pa 1988) (prejudgment interest runs from date of fire).

§9.24 Attorney's Fee Awards

Add to first paragraph of note 178, page 487:

The controlling Georgia statute is now Ga Code Ann §13-6-11 (1982). *See* American Family Life Assur Co v United States Fire Co, 885 F2d 826, 833 n 3 (11th Cir 1989).

Add at beginning of note 181, page 488:

See, e.g., Hendley v American Natl Fire Ins Co, 842 F2d 267, 270 (11th Cir 1988) (Georgia law) (attorneys' fees awarded against insurer because its denial of coverage was frivolous).

Add at end of note 181, page 490:

Similarly, in Zions First Natl Bank v National Am Title Ins Co, 749 P2d 651, 657 (Utah 1988), the court held that, since first-party insurance policies contain an implied obligation to perform fairly and in good faith, "[a]ttorneys fees incurred by an insured in suing its insurer because of such a breach would be recoverable consequential damages because they plainly are reasonably foreseeable by the parties at the time the contract is made".

§9.25   Recovery of Penalties

Add to first paragraph of note 194, page 493:

Many state unfair trade or insurance practices acts also contain penalty clauses. *See, e.g.*, Vail v Texas Farm Bureau Mut Ins Co, 754 SW2d 129, 137 (Tex 1988) (treble damages). Those acts are discussed in §9.34.

§9.26   Punitive Damages Awards

Add after first sentence of note 195, page 493:

E.g., Heinson v Porter, 244 Kan 667, 772 P2d 778, 785 (1989); Bettius & Sanderson, PC v National Union Fire Ins Co, 839 F2d 1009, 1016-17 (4th Cir 1988) (Virginia law).

Add at end of third paragraph of note 195, page 494:

The appellate court that decided the *Ledingham* case reversed its position in Kohlmeier v Shelter Ins Co, 170 Ill App 3d 643, 525 NE2d 94, 104 (1988), and held that punitive damages could not be awarded.

Add at end of note 195, page 495:

The Kentucky Supreme Court did an about-face and held that punitive damages were available in first-party insurance situations. *Curry v Fireman's Fund Ins Co*, 784 SW2d 176, 178 (Ky 1989).

Add at beginning of note 200, page 496:

E.g., Underwriters Life Ins Co v Cobb, 746 SW2d 810, 817 (Tex Ct App 1988) (punitive damages awarded because insurer had denied coverage based upon insured's having failed fully to disclose her medical history on application: (1) without considering fact that agent may have filled out application without including complete information provided by insured; and (2) even though insurer had ample indications of misdealings by agent to more fully investigate matter); Hughes v Blue Cross, 245 Cal Rptr 273, 280-81 (Ct App 1988) (punitive damages awarded because there was evidence that denial of insured's claim was not simply result of poor judgment but product of an inadequate investigation and analysis that was "rooted in established company practice").

Add to note 203, page 497:

See Farmers Group v Trimble, 768 P2d 1243, 1247 (Colo Ct App 1988) (statute); Staff Builders, Inc v Armstrong, 37 Ohio St 3d 298, 525 NE2d 783, 790 (1988) (proof of "actual malice, fraud or insult" required).

Add at beginning of note 204, page 498:

E.g., Aetna Cas & Sur Co v Joseph, 769 SW2d 603, 607 (Tex Ct App 1989); Underwriters Life Ins Co v Cobb, 746 SW2d 810, 817 (Tex Ct App 1988).

Add to end of note 204, page 498:

See Berry v Nationwide Mut Fire Ins Co, 381 SE2d 367, 374 (W Va 1989).

Add to note 205, page 498:

E.g., Ainsworth v Combined Ins Co of Am, 763 P2d 673, 676 (Nev 1988); State Farm Fire & Cas Co v Nicholson, 777 P2d 1152, 1158 (Alaska 1989); Sardyka v DeWitt, 784 P2d 819, 822 (Colo Ct App 1989) (statutory standard); Midamar Corp v National-Ben Franklin Ins Co, 898 F2d 1333, 1337 (8th Cir 1990) (Iowa law).

Add to note 209, page 499:

E.g., National Union Fire Ins Co v Hudson Energy Co, 780 SW2d 417, 426 (Tex Ct App 1989) (gross negligence).

Add to first paragraph of note 213, page 500:

E.g., McLaughlin v National Benefit Life Ins Co, 772 P2d 383, 389 (Okla 1988) (punitive damages improper because there was "a legitimate controversy" as to insurer's liability); Madsen v Threshermen's Mut Ins Co, 149 Wis 2d 594, 439 NW2d 607, 614 (Ct App 1989). *See* American Ins Co v Freeport Cold Storage, 703 F Supp 1475, 1478-79 (D Utah 1987); State Farm Fire & Cas Co v Balmer, 891 F2d 874, 876-77 (11th Cir 1990) (Alabama law); National Union Fire Ins Co v Hudson Energy Co, 780 SW2d 417, 426 (Tex Ct App 1989) ("delays or refusal to pay are not unreasonable where there is a legitimate question of policy construction").

Add at end of note 213, page 500:

E.g., Cossitt v Federated Guar Mut Ins Co, 541 So 2d 436, 443 (1989).

It has been held that an insurer cannot backtrack and give an arguable reason for denying coverage of which it did not have knowledge at the time of the coverage denial. *See* King v National Found Life Ins Co, 541 So 2d 502, 505 (Ala 1989); Viles v Security Natl Ins Co, 788 SW2d 566, 567 (Tex 1990).

The "arguable reason" must have existed and been considered by the insurer at the time it denied coverage. *See, e.g.,* Nationwide Mut Ins Co v Clay, 525 So 2d 1339, 1342 (Ala 1987).

Reliance on advice of counsel is not always a defense to a bad faith claim. *See generally* Gourley v State Farm Mut Auto Ins Co, 265 Cal Rptr 634, 638 (App Dept Super Ct 1990). In Industrial Indem Co v Kallevig, 114 Wash 2d 907, 792 P2d 520, 526 (1990), the court held that an insurer does not have an arguable basis for denying coverage and, therefore, acts in bad faith if it "denies coverage based upon suspicion and conjecture. . . . In other words, an insurer must make a good faith investigation of the facts before denying coverage and may not deny coverage based on a supposed defense which a reasonable investigation would have proved to be without merit."

Add at beginning of note 214, page 501:

E.g., Pace v Insurance Co of N Am, 838 F2d 572, 584 (1st Cir 1988) (Rhode Island law) (lack of a diligent investigation alone is not sufficient to support an award of punitive damages as long as insurer had an objectively "fairly debatable" reason to deny coverage).

§9.28   Reformation of Policy

Add at end of note 238, page 509:

In Koval v Liberty Mut Ins Co, 531 A2d 487, 490 (Pa Super Ct 1987), the court, although not utilizing reformation principles, recognized that if the issued coverage differs materially from the coverage for which the insured applied, and the policy provision at issue is not one that is a usual incident of the coverage applied for, the insurer must call the difference to the attention of the insured or be held to have provided the coverage applied for.

Add at end of note 241, page 510:

The insurer was allowed to reform a policy in Cincinnati Ins Co v Fred S Post, Jr, Co, 747 SW2d 777, 781-82 (Tenn 1988).

§9.30   —Waiver by Insurer of Right to Compel

Add to note 254, page 512:

E.g., Jorge v Sutton, 134 AD2d 573, 521 NYS2d 473, 474 (1987); *see* Giulietti v Connecticut Ins Placement Facility, 205 Conn 424, 534 A2d 213, 217 (1987).

§9.32   Appraisal Requirements

Add after next-to-last sentence of section, page 518:

See generally Giulietti v Connecticut Insurance Placement Facility, 205 Conn 424, 534 A2d 213, 217 (1987).

§9.33   Good Faith and Fair Dealing

Add to note 286, page 519:

See Judah v State Farm Fire & Cas Co, 266 Cal Rptr 455, 463 (Ct App 1990) (covenant of good faith and fair dealing can be breached even if policy does not provide coverage).

§9.34   Unfair Trade or Insurance Practices Act

Add to note 292, page 520:

See also Shaheen v Preferred Mut Ins Co, 668 F Supp 716, 718 (DNH 1987); Atlantic Permanent Fed Sav & Loan Assn v American Cas Co, 670 F Supp 168 (ED Va 1986); OK Lumber v Providence Wash Ins Co, 759 P2d 523, 527 (Alaska 1988). In Cardenas v Miami-Dade Yellow Cab Co, 538 So 2d 491, 494-95 (Fla Dist Ct App 1989), the court held that the injured party did not have standing to sue an insurer under Florida's statute governing the duty to settle.

In Moradi-Shalal v Fireman's Fund Ins Cos, 250 Cal Rptr 116 (Cal 1988), the California Supreme Court overruled its decision in Royal Globe Ins Co v Superior Court, 23 Cal 3d 880, 153 Cal Rptr 842 (1979), and held that a private cause of action did not exist under the Unfair Practices Act.

Mass Ann Law ch 93A, §9 (1984) expressly provides for a cause of action in favor of persons injured by acts prohibited by the Uniform Practices Act. *See generally* Jacobs v Town Clerk of Arlington, 402 Mass 824, 525 NE2d 658, 661 n 6 (1988).

Contribution, Subrogation, and Indemnity

10

§10.01 Contribution—In General

Add to first paragraph of note 1, page 522:

E.g., Great West Cas Co v Canal Ins Co, 901 F2d 1525, 1527 (10th Cir 1990) (Kansas law).

Add to second paragraph of note 1, page 522:

E.g., Indiana Ins Cos v Granite State Ins Co, 689 F Supp 1549, 1558-59 (SD Ind 1988).

Add to fourth paragraph of note 1, page 522:

Accord Mission Natl Ins Co v Hartford Fire Ins Co, 702 F Supp 543, 545 (ED Pa 1989); *contra* Farmers Ins Co v St Paul Fire & Marine Ins Co, 305 Or 488, 752 P2d 1212, 1214 (1988) (claim for contribution existed because insurers covered same risk; it did not matter that policies covered different insureds).

Add at end of note 1, page 522:

See State Farm Fire & Cas Co v Folger, 677 F Supp 844, 845 (EDNC 1988) ("the total amount of insurance payments made on a particular loss cannot exceed the value of the loss itself ").

In Wausau Ins Co v Argonaut Ins Co, 678 F Supp 1080, 1085-86 (SDNY 1988), the insurer seeking contribution was denied any recovery on the ground of laches. The court held that the plaintiff-insurer had constructive knowledge of the existence of the other insurer, but failed to notify such insurer of the lawsuit until well into the trial of the underlying action. The court required the existence of prejudice before applying laches, but it found that prejudice was present because the trial strategy had already been prepared, was in the process of implementation, and important trial testimony had already been given. What is most interesting about the opinion is that it does not analyze the liability of the nonpaying insurer from the viewpoint of whether it had a liability to the *insured* by reason of the late notice, but solely from the viewpoint of whether it had a liability to the paying *insurer* by reason of the late notice.

Prejudgment interest will normally be awarded to the insurer entitled to contribution. *See, e.g.,* United States Fire Ins Co v Federal Ins Co, 858 F2d 882, 887-88 (2d Cir 1988) (New York law).

Add to first paragraph of note 2, page 723:

See Nicholas v Anderson, 837 F2d 1372, 1377-78 (5th Cir 1988) (Mississippi law) (insurer entitled to contribution because of payment of postjudgment interest).

Add at end of note 2, page 523:

In Keystone Shipping Co v Home Ins Co, 840 F2d 181, 182-85 (3d Cir 1988), three carriers settled a claim and then sought contribution from a fourth carrier that had refused to participate in the settlement. The court properly held in favor of the fourth carrier on the ground that, although the amount of the settlement had not been unreasonable, the fourth carrier had not acted unreasonably in believing that the case should have been settled for less. Accordingly, the fourth carrier was no more bound by the settlement entered into by the other three insurers than it would have been bound had the insured itself entered into an unauthorized settlement. *See* §§3.09 & 6.27.

In Indiana Ins Cos v Granite State Ins Co, 689 F Supp 1549, 1554 n 1 (SD Ind 1988), the settlement between the paying insurer and the injured party was for $1 million, but $250,000 of it was conditioned upon a successful contribution action by the paying insurer. The court held that the insurer being sued for contribution had to make such contribution based upon the $1 million figure.

§10.02   Insurer's Right to Reimbursement for Costs Incurred in Fulfilling Duty to Defend—In General

Add to note 13, page 525:

E.g., Zurich-American Ins Cos v Atlantic Mut Ins Cos, 531 NYS2d 911, 916 (Sup Ct 1988).

§10.03 —Primary Insurer's Right to Contribution from Another Primary Insurer

Add to note 17, page 526:

In American Home Assurance Co v St Paul Fire & Marine Ins Co, 233 NJ Super 137, 558 A2d 65, 69 (1989), the court refused to allow one primary insurer contribution as to defense costs from another primary insurer because the former never requested the latter "to participate on some basis."

Add at beginning of note 20, page 526:

E.g., Indiana Ins Cos v Granite State Ins Co, 689 F Supp 1549, 1553 (SD Ind 1988); Zurich-American Ins Cos v Atlantic Mut Ins Cos, 531 NYS2d 911, 916 (Sup Ct 1988); Forum Ins Co v Ranger Ins Co, 711 F Supp 909, 914 (ND Ill 1989); United States Fidelity & Guar Co v Thomas Solvent Co, 683 F Supp 1139, 1173, 1175 (WD Mich 1988).

§10.04 —Primary Insurer's Right to Contribution from Excess Insurer

Add to note 30, page 530:

Contra Continental Cas Co v Synalloy Corp, 667 F Supp 1523, 1540-41 (SD Ga 1983).

§10.05 Subrogation—In General

Add at beginning of note 31, page 530:

E.g., Culver v Ins Co of N Am, 535 A2d 15, 19 (NJ Super Ct 1987).

Add to first paragraph of note 31, page 530:

E.g., Title Ins Co v Costain Ariz, Inc, 164 Ariz 203, 791 P2d 1086, 1089 (Ct App 1990).

Add at end of note 31, page 530:

It has been held that, in the absence of an express contractual provision providing for subrogation, an insurer is not entitled to subrogation in personal injury cases. *E.g.,* American Pioneer Life Ins Co v Rogers, 296 Ark 254, 753 SW2d 530, 532 (1988).

Add to second paragraph of note 33, page 531:

See also Pledge Tool Co v Silva, 33 Ohio App 3d 260, 515 NE2d 945, 946-47 (1986) (no equitable subrogation "where the contract of insurance is non-indemnity, such as life, automobile, or hospitalization").

Add following second paragraph of note 34, page 531:

An insurer does not lose its right to subrogation because it has breached the insurance contract. *See, e.g.,* Ingersoll Milling Mach Co v M/V Bodena, 829 F2d 293, 309 (2d Cir 1987).

Add following fifth sentence on page 533:

See generally S&B Slurry Seal Co v Mid-South Aviation, Inc, 362 SE2d 812, 819 (NC Ct App 1987) (carrier would not be able to sue wrongdoer for entire loss because carrier did not reimburse insured for entire loss, and assignment that carrier received from insured transferred only insured's claims "to the extent" carrier was entitled to subrogation).

§10.06 —Pro Tanto

Add to first paragraph of note 41, page 534:

E.g., Hill v State Farm Mut Auto Ins Co, 765 P2d 864, 868 (Utah 1988); International Underwriters/Brokers, Inc v Liao, 548 So 2d 163, 166 (Ala 1989).

Add at end of note 41, page 534:

In Culver v Ins Co of N Am, 535 A2d 15, 19-21 (NJ Super Ct 1987), the policy did not provide for pro tanto subrogation, but the insurer obtained an assignment of the insured's entire claim upon paying only a portion of the loss. The court held that the assignment was "unconscionable, violative of public policy, and in abrogation to [the insurer's] trust obligation to its insureds." Accordingly, the court held that the insurer could not retain any of the recovery from the wrongdoer until the insured had been made whole.

Add to first paragraph of note 44, page 535:

See, e.g., Hill v State Farm Mut Auto Ins Co, 765 P2d 864, 868 (Utah 1988).

§10.07   —From Wrongdoer

Add at end of note 60, page 539:

In Silvers v Horace Mann Ins Co, 387 SE2d 372, 379 (NC Ct App 1988), the court held that subrogation was not available in connection with uninsured or underinsured motorist claims because of the wording of the policy.

Add to sixth paragraph of note 61, page 540:

Accord Mission Ins Co v Hartford Fire Ins Co, 702 F Supp 543, 546 (ED Pa 1989) (insurer had no subrogation rights because insured had waived them by virtue of prior contract with wrongdoer).

Add to note 65, page 542:

Contra National Union Fire Ins Co v Engineering-Science, Inc, 884 F2d 1208, 1210 (9th Cir 1989) (California law).

Add at beginning of note 70, page 542:

E.g., Mission Natl Ins Co v Hartford Fire Ins Co, 702 F Supp 543, 546 n 6 (ED Pa 1989); United States Fidelity & Guar Co v Williams, 676 F Supp 123, 126-27 (ED La 1987); Western Motor Co v Koehn, 242 Kan 402, 748 P2d 851, 853 (1988); Aetna Cas & Sur Co v Urban Imperial Bldg & Rental Corp, 38 Ohio App 3d 99, 526 NE2d 819, 820 (1987).

Add to fifth paragraph of note 70, page 543:

See also Reich v Tharp, 167 Ill App 3d 446, 521 NE2d 530, 534-35 (1987).

Add at end of note 70, page 543:

Accord Cascade Trailer Court v Beeson, 50 Wash App 678, 749 P2d 761, 766 (1988) (a landlord's fire insurance is presumed to be held for tenant's benefit as a coinsured, absent an express agreement to contrary; landlord's insurer cannot, therefore, obtain subrogation from tenant after paying loss); McGinnis v Lashelle, 166 Ill App 3d 131, 519 NE2d 699, 701 (1988) (a landlord's fire insurance is presumed to be held for tenant's benefit as a coinsured, absent an express agreement to contrary; landlord's insurer cannot, therefore, recover from tenant under a theory of subrogation).

Sometimes, although a corporation may be an insured, its officers and directors are not. The majority rule under those circumstances is that subrogation will not be allowed against the officers or directors if they were guilty of nothing more than negligence. *See, e.g.,* Home Indem Co v Shaffer, 860 F2d 186, 187-89 (6th Cir 1988) (Ohio law).

§10.09 —Insurer as Partial Subrogee in Action Filed in Name of Insured

Add at end of note 86, page 547:

Contra S&B Slurry Seal Co v Mid-South Aviation, Inc, 362 SE2d 812, 822 (NC Ct App 1987).

Add to first paragraph of note 88, page 547:

But see S&B Slurry Seal Co v Mid-South Aviation, Inc, 362 SE2d 812, 822 (NC Ct App 1987) (insurer is a necessary party if it has received an assignment from insured of insured's claims to extent insurer was entitled to subrogation).

§10.10 —Insurer's Right as Affected by Volunteer Doctrine

Add at beginning of note 96, page 549:

E.g., Compass Ins Co v Cravens, Dargan & Co, 748 P2d 724, 730 (Wyo 1988).

Add at end of note 96, page 549:

See generally Allstate Ins Co v Quinn Constr Co, 713 F Supp 35, 38 (D Mass 1989) ("Allstate could be characterized as a volunteer only if it paid Warren when it clearly had no obligation to do so under its policy"); Sinex v Wallis, 565 A2d 1384, 1386 (Del Super Ct 1988).

Add at beginning of note 97, page 549:

E.g., Northland Ins Co v Ace Doran Hauling & Rigging Co, 415 NW2d 33, 39 (Minn Ct App 1987).

Add to note 100, page 550:

See Paktank La, Inc v Marsh & McLennan, Inc, 688 F Supp 1087, 1904 (ED La 1988).

§10.12 Right of Insurer to Indemnify or Subrogation from Another Insurer That Was Solely Liable

Add to note 121, page 554:

E.g., Canal Ins Co v First Gen Ins Co, 889 F2d 604, 611-12 (5th Cir 1989) (Mississippi law).

§10.13   Right of Excess Insurer to Indemnify or Subrogation from Primary Insurer—Costs Incurred in Fulfilling Duty to Indemnify

Add to second paragraph of note 123, page 556:

But see Travelers Indem Co v Overseas Ace Hardware, Inc, 550 So 2d 12, 13 (Fla Dist Ct App 1989).

§10.14   —Costs Incurred in Fulfilling Duty to Defend

Add at beginning of note 129, page 557:

E.g., FB Washburn Candy Corp v Fireman's Fund, 541 A2d 771, 774 (Pa Super Ct 1988).

§10.17   Use of Loan Receipt Agreement—When Recovery Sought from Another Insurer

Add to note 152, page 565:

But see Keystone Shipping Co v Home Ins Co, 840 F2d 181, 183 n 6 (3d Cir 1988) (Pennsylvania law) (allowing, without discussion, lender-insurers to sue another insurer by means of lawsuit brought in name of insured).

§10.20   Use of Assignment When Recovery Sought from Another Insurer (New)

As discussed in §10.01, when two insurers provide coverage but only one insurer agrees to make a payment on behalf of the insured, the paying insurer is entitled to contribution from the nonpaying insurer. The paying insurer, however, may attempt to obtain more than just contribution through the use of a loan receipt agreement. As discussed in §10.17, that attempt should not be successful. Another method for attempting to obtain more than just contribution is to obtain an assignment of the insured's rights against the nonpaying insurer. While such an assignment is technically valid (*see* §9.11), it should not be allowed to give the paying insurer a right to recover more than what it would be entitled to recover under general contribution principles. *E.g., Hartford Casualty Insurance Co v Argonaut-Midwest Insurance Co,* 664 F Supp 373, 382 (ND Ill 1987):

Allowing an insurer like Hartford to employ an assignment to recover the full amount of the coinsurer's insured's limits of liability may very well enable the settling carrier to obtain greater rights against the second carrier than those provided under the Illinois equitable contribution doctrine. It would encourage an insurer to negotiate with its coinsurers' insureds rather than with coinsurers. It would discourage attempts to convince the coinsurer that coverage for the insured exists. Permitting an assignment in an attempt to shift the loss disproportionately among responsible carriers promotes litigation rather than resolves it.

Cases

A

ABCD ... Vision, Inc v Fireman's Fund Ins Co, 304 Or 301, 744 P2d 998 (1987) §§2.23, 6.31

Adman Prods Co v Federal Ins Co, 187 Ill App 3d 322, 543 NE2d 219 (1989) §4.04

Aetna Cas & Sur Co v Joseph, 769 SW2d 603 (Tex Ct App 1989) §9.26

Aetna Cas & Sur Co v Lumbermens Mut Cas Co, 527 NYS2d 143 (App Div 1988) §6.06

Aetna Cas & Sur Co v Murphy, 206 Conn 409, 538 A2d 219 (1988) §1.04

Aetna Cas & Sur Co v Prestige Cas Co, 553 NE2d 39 (Ill App Ct 1990) §4.35

Aetna Cas & Sur Co v Spancrete, Inc, 726 F Supp 204 (ND Ill 1989) §§4.12, 4.20, 8.14

Aetna Cas & Sur Co v Sprague, 163 Mich App 650, 415 NW2d 230 (1987) §4.04

Aetna Cas & Sur Co v United Servs Auto Assn, 676 F Supp 79 (ED Pa 1987) §7.02

Aetna Cas & Sur Co v Urban Imperial Bldg & Rental Corp, 38 Ohio App 3d 99, 526 NE2d 819 (1987) §10.07

Aetna Ins Co v Borrell-Bigby Elec Co, 541 So 2d 139 (Fla Dist Ct App 1989) §§4.15, 4.30

AG Allebach, Inc v Hurley, 540 A2d 289 (Pa Super Ct 1988) §2.25

Aid (Mutual) Ins v Steffen, 423 NW2d 189 (Iowa 1988) §6.03

Ainsworth v Combined Ins Co, 763 P2d 673 (Nev 1988) §9.26

Air Prods & Chems v Hartford Accident & Indem Co, 707 F Supp 762 (ED Pa 1989) §§7.06, 7.07

Alabama Hosp Assn Trust v Mutual Assurance Socy, 538 So 2d 1209 (Ala 1989) §4.35

Alaska Rural Elec Coop Assn v Insco, Ltd, 785 P2d 1193 (Alaska 1990) §6.02

B

Ford Motor Co v Northbrook Ins Co, 838 F2d 829 (6th Cir 1988) §6.02

Foremost County Mut Ins Co v Home Indem Co, 897 F2d 754 (5th Cir 1990) §§5.18, 6.05, 7.08

Foremost Ins Co v Wilks, 253 Cal Rptr 596 (Ct App 1988) §4.18

Formosa v Equitable Life Assurance Socy of the United States, 166 NJ Super 8, 398 A2d 1301 (App Div 1979) §2.25

Fortman v Safeco Ins Co of Am, 271 Cal Rptr 117 (Ct App 1990) §7.08

Forum Ins Co v Ranger Ins Co, 711 F Supp 909 (ND Ill 1989) §§4.01, 10.03

Fox-Knapp, Inc v Employers Mut Cas Co, 893 F2d 14 (2d Cir 1989) §9.05

Frankenmuth Mut Ins Co v Keeley, 433 Mich 525, 447 NW2d 691 (1989) §5.18

Fremont Mut Ins Co v Wieschewski, 182 Mich App 121, 451 NW2d 523 (1989) §4.02

G

Gardner v Aetna Cas & Sur Co, 841 F2d 82 (4th Cir 1988) §5.04

Garvey v State Farm Fire & Cas Co, 237 Cal Rptr 292 (1989) §6.06

Gates Formed Fibre Prods v Imperial Cas & Indem Co, 702 F Supp 343 (D Me 1988) §§3.09, 3.11

Gelinas v Metropolitan Property & Liab Ins Co, 551 A2d 926 (NH 1988) §5.12

Gilbert Frank Corp v Federal Ins Co, 70 NY2d 966, 520 NE2d 512 (1988) §9.05

Giovannitti v Nationwide Ins Co, 690 F Supp 1439 (WD Pa 1988) §§6.37, 9.23

Giuletti v Connecticut Ins Placement Facility, 205 Conn 424, 534 A2d 213 (1987) §§9.30, 9.32

Gloucester, Township of v Maryland Cas Co, 668 F Supp 394 (DNJ 1987) §§2.25, 2.28, 4.14

Golden v Northwestern Mut Life Ins Co, 229 NJ Super 405, 551 A2d 1009 (1988) §§2.25, 2.29

Golotrade Shipping & Chartering v Travelers Indem Co, 706 F Supp 214 (SDNY 1989) §§4.12, 4.18, 4.20

Gon v First State Ins Co, 871 F2d 863 (9th Cir 1989) §§4.13, 6.18

Gordiner v Aetna Cas & Sur Co, 154 Ariz 266, 742 P2d 277 (1987) §6.03

Gordon v Liberty Mut Ins Co, 675 F Supp 321 (ED Va 1987) §§2.23, 6.31

Gould Investors LP v General Ins Co, 737 F Supp 812 (SDNY 1990) §3.04

Gourley v State Farm Mut Auto Ins Co, 265 Cal Rptr 634 (App Dept Super Ct 1990) §9.26

Government Employees Ins Co v Ropka, 74 Md App 249, 536 A2d 1214 (1988) §6.08

N

State Farm Mut Auto Ins Co v
Hollingsworth, 668 F Supp
1476 (D Wyo 1987) §1.04

State Farm Mut Auto Ins Co v
Hollis, 554 So 2d 387 (Ala
1989) §§5.12, 5.19

State Farm Mut Auto Ins Co v
Lewis, 514 So 2d 863 (Ala
1987) §6.02

State Farm Mut Auto Ins Co v
Wilson, 162 Ariz 251, 782
P2d 727 (1989) §6.17

Steelmet, Inc v Caribe Towing
Corp, 842 F2d 1237 (11th Cir
1988) §6.16

Steen v Underwriters at Lloyd's,
442 NW2d 158 (Minn Ct App
1989) §3.09

Stoddard, Town of v Northern
Sec Ins Co, 718 F Supp 1062
(DNH 1989) §6.02

Stonewall Ins Co v Hamilton, 727
F Supp 271 (WD Va 1989)
§1.02

Stufflebeam v Canadian Indem
Co, 157 Ariz 6, 754 P2d 335
(1988) §3.09

T

Terra Nova Ins Co v Associates
Commercial Corp, 697 F Supp
1048 (ED Wis 1988) §6.39

Terra Nova Ins Co v 900 Bar,
Inc, 887 F2d 1213 (3d Cir
1989) §§4.26, 6.40

Terra Nova Ins Co v Thee
Kandy Store, Inc, 679 F Supp
476 (ED Pa 1988) §6.06

Terry v Avemco Ins Co, 663 F
Supp 39 (D Colo 1987) §6.32

Thompson v American States Ins
Co, 687 F Supp 559 (MD Ala
1988) §3.07

Thurston v Continental Cas Co,
567 A2d 922 (Me 1989)
§§5.03, 5.18

Title Ins Co v Costain Ariz, Inc,
164 Ariz 203, 791 P2d 1086
(Ct App 1990) §10.05

Todd v Bankers Life & Cas Co,
523 NYS2d 206 (App Div
1987) §1.05

Topeka Tent & Awning Co v
Glens Falls Ins Co, 774 P2d
984 (Kan Ct App 1989)
§§6.21, 6.33

Town Crier, Inc v Hume, 721 F
Supp 99 (ED Va 1989) §4.01

Towne Realty v Safeco Ins Co,
854 F2d 1264 (11th Cir 1988)
§7.01

Transcontinental Ins Co v Wash-
ington Pub Utils Dists Util
Sys, 111 Wash 2d 452, 760
P2d 337 (1988) §6.02

Travelers Indem Co v Overseas
Ace Hardware, Inc, 550 So 2d
12 (Fla Dist Ct App 1989)
§§6.12, 10.13

Travelers Ins Co v Waltham
Indus Laboratories Corp, 722
F Supp 814 (D Mass) affd in
part revd in part, 883 F2d 1092
(1st Cir 1989) §4.35

Trotter v State Farm Mut Auto
Ins Co, 377 SE2d 343 (SC Ct
App 1988) §5.01

Turner Ins Agency v Continental
Ins Co, 541 So 2d 471 (Ala
1989) §7.08

Twin City Fire Ins Co v CNA
Ins Co, 711 F Supp 310 (WD
La 1988) §7.08

Twin City Fire Ins Co v Harvey,
662 F Supp 216 (D Ariz
1987) §3.04

Twin City Fire Ins Co v Superior
Court, 792 P2d 758 (Ariz
1990) §7.08

Statutes

Cal Ins Code §650 (West 1972) **§2.28**

Del Code Ann tit 18, §3914 **§9.02**

Fla Stat Ann §627.426(2)(b)(3) (West 1983) **§§2.16, 4.24**

Ga Code Ann §13-6-11 (1982) **§9.24**

Me Rev Stat Ann tit 24-A, §2904 **§9.11**

Mass Ann Laws ch 93A, §9 (Law Co-op 1984) **§9.34**

Pa Stat Ann tit 40, §1171.5(a)(9) (Purdon 1981) **§2.25**

W Va Code §33-6-7(b), (c) (1957) **§2.25**

Wis Stat Ann §631.11(4) (West 1980) **§§2.08, 2.29**

Index

A

ASSIGNMENT
Use of, when recovery sought from another insurer §10.20

L

LOAN RECEIPT
Use of assignment when recovery sought from another insurer §10.20